ISBN: 9781313346573

Published by:
HardPress Publishing
8345 NW 66TH ST #2561
MIAMI FL 33166-2626

Email: info@hardpress.net
Web: http://www.hardpress.net

LUDLOW'S MEMOIRS

C. H. FIRTH

.

London

HENRY FROWDE

OXFORD UNIVERSITY PRESS WAREHOUSE
AMEN CORNER, E.C.

New York

MACMILLAN & CO., 66 FIFTH AVENUE

Edmund Ludlow Esq.
Lieut. Genll.

THE MEMOIRS

OF

EDMUND LUDLOW

LIEUTENANT-GENERAL OF THE HORSE

IN THE

ARMY OF THE COMMONWEALTH OF ENGLAND

1625 — 1672

EDITED WITH APPENDICES OF
LETTERS AND ILLUSTRATIVE DOCUMENTS

BY

C. H. FIRTH, M.A.

IN TWO VOLUMES
VOL. I

Oxford

AT THE CLARENDON PRESS

1894

𝔒𝔵𝔣𝔬𝔯𝔡

PRINTED AT THE CLARENDON PRESS

BY HORACE HART, PRINTER TO THE UNIVERSITY

CONTENTS OF VOL. I

INTRODUCTION

LUDLOW's Memoirs were first published in 1698, six years after their author's death, in two octavo volumes, said on the title-page to be printed at Vevay. A third volume containing the post-restoration part of the Memoirs followed in 1699. Since that date they have been frequently reprinted. A second English edition appeared in 1721-2, unless it is simply the first edition with a new title-page. In 1751 an edition in three duodecimo volumes was published at Edinburgh, and during the same year also an edition in one folio volume edited by Richard Baron. These were followed in 1771 by a fifth in quarto, which Lowndes terms the best edition. A French translation of the first two volumes was published at Amsterdam in 1699, and a second edition in 1707 in three volumes. They were included in 1827 in Guizot's Collection des Mémoires relatifs à la révolution d'Angleterre. These numerous reprints are sufficient proof of the historical interest of Ludlow's work. The justification of the present edition lies in the fact that it is the first to restore a number of passages suppressed by Ludlow's editor, and the first containing critical and explanatory notes, and adding the letters of Ludlow.

The Memoirs are at once an autobiography and a history of Ludlow's own time. The aim of this Introduction is partly to complete Ludlow's account of himself, and partly to estimate the value of his contribution to the general history of the period.

As to the date at which Ludlow's Memoirs were written there is no conclusive evidence. The opening sentence shows that he began to write after the Restoration, and in all probability some time after the Restoration. Ludlow was too much a man of action and too little a man of letters, to take up his pen in the first moment of his exile, and devote himself to the task of undeceiving posterity. It is not unlikely that the idea of writing his Memoirs was first suggested to him by some incident such as that which he describes as happening in 1663. At the solemn banquet which the senators of Bern gave to Ludlow and some of his friends, one of his hosts desired to hear from the lips of their guest the causes of the fall of the English republic.

'Dinner being over, a question was started by Colonel Weiss, " How it came to pass that we, who for many years had the whole power of the three nations in our hands, were removed from the government without shedding one drop of blood?" To which I answered, that "for the right understanding of the affairs that had lately passed in England, it would be necessary to take up the matter from the beginning."'

And after a little pressing Ludlow related the story of the civil wars. and told them how the republic had been founded. and how the ambition of Cromwell and the craft of Monck had brought back the Stuarts. The scene recalls the picture of Aeneas recounting to Dido the Fall of Troy. This incident, or some other of the same nature, may well have instigated Ludlow to commit to writing his reminiscences of the events in which he had played so large a part, and his theory of the causes which had led to the overthrow of his party.

'I cannot think it,' he says. 'a misspending of part of my leisure to employ it in setting down the most remarkable counsels and actions of the parties engaged in the late Civil War; wherein I shall not strictly confine myself to a relation of such things only in which I was personally concerned, but also give the best account

I can of such other memorable occurrences of those times as I have learned from persons well informed and of unsuspected fidelity.'

What external evidence there is as to the date at which Ludlow commenced to write, consists in a story about Ludlow and the celebrated Colonel Blood. told in a pamphlet published in answer to the Memoirs in 1698 :—

'When Blood was in his prime of action, and sent over to Geneva by a party then meditating disturbance of the government, as believing Ludlow the most proper person to head and command 'em, that man of a quick and penetrating judgment, brought over but a very slender account of that great Lieutenant-General of Horse. For Blood's report, which he often upon other occasions signified to others, was, that he found him very unable for such an employment ; only that he was writing a History as he called it, which he told the Colonel would be as true as the gospel ; and which in all probability were these two volumes of Memoirs now lately printed [1].'

Blood's visit cannot be exactly fixed ; but he made his peace with Charles the Second in 1671, and spent some time in Holland after the failure of his plot to surprise Dublin Castle in 1663. His mission to Ludlow most probably took place between 1663 and 1666, and it is very likely that he was one of the emissaries employed by the exiles in Holland to persuade Ludlow to seize the opportunity offered by the war between England and the United Provinces.

The Memoirs end abruptly with the year 1672, and the latter part of them has all the air of a contemporary record, if we may judge from the greater exactness and accuracy of its details. Another argument for the comparatively early completion of the Memoirs may be derived from the manner in which Ludlow speaks of certain persons he has occasion to mention. Had he written after the execution of Algernon

[1] A Modest Vindication of Oliver Cromwell from the unjust accusa- tions of Lieut.-Gen. Ludlow, 1698, p. 2.

Sydney, which occurred in 1682, he would surely have made some reference to his fate when relating Sydney's visit to Vevay, and their subsequent communications. In the same way had he written after 1674, when Shaftesbury abandoned the Court and became one of the leaders of the popular party, he would probably somewhat have softened the extreme severity with which he always speaks of him.

From these different indications it may be inferred, in the absence of better evidence, that the Memoirs were probably written between 1663 and 1673. The original manuscript, which might have elucidated these questions, is apparently no longer in existence. A manuscript copy was some years ago in the possession of a member of the Ludlow family; but whether it was the original or simply a transcript from which the Memoirs were printed I have been unable to ascertain, for it has been appropriated by a person to whom the owner lent it.

The Memoirs were first published six years after Ludlow's death. By whom they were edited, and how they came into the editor's hands, are questions on which it is not easy to obtain satisfactory evidence. A pamphlet criticising the Memoirs, published in 1700, gives the following account of their history. Speaking of Ludlow, the author observes :

‘ 'Tis generally presumed the last of his acquaintance and confidents was S^tlings]by B[eth]el, with whom those many reams of paper, he had, whilst grumbling in Swisserland, emptied his galls into, were entrusted : and report speaks that he was tricked of them by a republican confident who best understood to make the best of them, as well for the Good Old Cause as his own advantage ; which 'tis further said the churlish Nabal was very angry at, and would have resented accordingly, had not death interposed and put an end to that dispute[1]. The usurper of the copy, having now got quiet and sole possession, consulted more than once the whole Calves-head fraternity, not without some representatives, as to the

[1] Feb. 1696.

most creditable way of publishing; where in conclusion it was resolved to cut off the superfluities of that slovenly Swiss dress 'twas left in, and notwithstanding the book's and their many prejudices against France send it forth in that allamode way of Memoirs[1].'

The name of the mysterious republican who so faithlessly obtained possession of these Memoirs is not mentioned by the pamphleteer. It is believed that he was Isaac Littlebury, author of a translation of Herodotus, published in 1709, which went through three editions in the early part of the eighteenth century, and has twice been reprinted in this. Thomas Hollis, well known for his ostentatious republicanism, and a careful collector of all the literary traditions of his party, presented a copy of Ludlow's Memoirs to the library of Bern in 1758, and inserted Littlebury's name at the conclusion of the preface[2]. Thomas Tyers, in his curious Political Conferences, makes a similar statement, and even goes so far as to call in question the genuineness of the Memoirs.

'There are well founded suspicions against the authenticity of Ludlow's Memoirs. The editor of these Conferences is not certain that doubts are not already thrown out on this point in Rawlinson's Method of Studying History[3]. But the information he has to lay before the reader he received many years ago from an oracle in history to whom it was communicated by the late Mr. Andrew Stone, who derived his intelligence from Buckley, the splendid editor of Thuanus. The purport of it is, that after Ludlow's death, which was at Vevay in Switzerland, his papers, which were numerous, were transmitted to England and placed in the hands of Littlebury, the translator of Herodotus; who fabricated or prepared the

---

[1] Regicides no Saints, nor Martyrs, 8vo. 1700, p. 1. A supplement to the 'Just Defence of the Royal Martyr' by the same author.

[2] Stern, Briefe Englischer Flüchtlinge in der Schweiz, 1874, p. xi; Life of Thomas Hollis, 1780, p. 69.

[3] 'Some have thought these Memoirs drawn up in England under the masque of Ludlow, by one who was a favourer and defender of his principles, and if not acquainted with at least an admirer of his person and practices.' Rawlinson, ii. 474.

Memoirs, from those materials, for the press. They could not have been entrusted to a better person to do Ludlow or his cause justice; for Littlebury was so immutable a republican that he did not appear at the court of King William to thank him for his appointment to be writer of the Gazette [1].'

Tyers carried his scepticism too far in expressing a doubt as to the authenticity of the Memoirs. They have every internal sign of genuineness, and stand every test which can be applied to their contents. On the other hand, his positive statement that the anonymous editor was Littlebury may be safely accepted. The political views of Littlebury agree with those expressed by the editor of Ludlow's Memoirs. The preface to vol. iii. of the Memoirs contains allusions to contemporary politics which were obviously the utterances of a disappointed Whig. The account of the Protectorate supplied him with a weapon against the government of William III, which at that moment—in March 1699—was especially effective. 'Men may learn,' he says, 'from the history of the Cromwellian tyranny that liberty and a standing mercenary army are incompatible [2].' It was the burden of this army, he argues, and the unrulinesss of these mercenaries which compelled the people to suffer the return of Charles II, hinting plainly that similar causes might

[1] Tyers, Political Conferences, 2nd ed. 1781, p. 88. The author of the preface to vol. iii of the Memoirs was extremely hostile to standing armies. So was Littlebury.

[2] The preface continues, ' For 'tis as clear as the sun at noon-day, that the Parliament by neglecting to put a period to the exorbitant greatness of Oliver Cromwell immediately after the battle of Worcester, drew destruction upon themselves and the whole Commonwealth; and gave the army such an opportunity to feel their strength as naturally led them to counsels destructive to the government. This produced that monstrous tyranny of the usurper and his bashas under the name of majors-general, and afterwards compelled the people to suffer the return of Charles II. The ingratitude of this prince to the Presbyterians, who had so well deserved from him by betraying all into his hands, may serve to admonish those who go under that, or any other denomination of religion or party, that no trust can be safely reposed, where there is found an incompatibility of manners and principles, and that a revenge taken against those who will not let us possess all, is a slender satisfaction for the hazard of utter ruin.'

lead them to recall James II. When this was written the struggle between William III and his parliament about the disbanding of the army was at its height. Now Littlebury is known to have taken part in that controversy, in one of the most famous of the many pamphlets published against the government. 'An Argument shewing that a Standing Army is inconsistent with a Free Government '—said to have been the work of a club of Whig gentlemen—was proved to have been carried to the press by Littlebury [1].

On the title-page Ludlow's Memoirs are said to have been printed at Vevay, though the type and the style of the work sufficiently show that it was issued from an English press. The contemporary critic of the Memoirs comments on this transparent fraud in the following words [2]:

'For what reason they affected so much umbrage as to date their preface from Bern, and suppose the impression at Vevay I shall not concern myself; had they said at Darby it had been nigher home, and nigher truth too; nay certainly so, by a little quibbling transition from place to person.'

This is equivalent to saying that the Memoirs were printed by John Darby of Bartholomew Close, a well-known publisher of anti-governmental literature [3]. What renders the identification still more probable is that Darby was the printer to whom Littlebury had conveyed the manuscript of the Argument against a Standing Army.

Accepting therefore the story which makes Littlebury the editor [4], and Darby the printer of the Memoirs, the next

---

[1] Published in 1697. For Littlebury's connexion with it see Luttrell's Diary, iv. 313, 315. Another of these pamphlets, 'A Short History of Standing Armies in England,' 1698, is full of reminiscences of Ludlow's Memoirs.

[2] Regicides no Saints, p. 9.

[3] 'Have no fresh batteries attacked the court lately from honest Mr. Darby's in Bartholomew Close?' asks Dick Baldwin in Tom Brown's Letters from the Dead to the Living, published in 1702. Browne's works, ed. 1730, ii. 9. 'Mr. Darby,' says Dunton, 'printed that excellent Speech of my Lord Russell and several pieces of Col. Sidney, and is a true assertor of English liberties.' Dunton's Life and Errors, ed by Nichols. i. 247; Nichols, Literary Anecdotes, i. 290 ; iii. 291.

[4] The name of John Toland has

question to be considered is the manner in which the editor handled Ludlow's manuscript. It has been shown that in his preface he seized the opportunity to use the Memoirs as a text for a Whig sermon, and he has been suspected of interpolating the text for the same purpose. But a careful examination detects no sign of any such interpolations. On the other hand it is certain that Littlebury used his position to suppress certain passages reflecting on Shaftesbury, which are now for the first time restored to their proper place in the text of the Memoirs. These passages were printed by Mr. W. D. Christie in 1871, in an Appendix to his Life of Shaftesbury [1].

He gives the following account of their origin :—

'These suppressed passages of Ludlow's Memoirs, all relating to Sir A. A. Cooper, are in Locke's handwriting among his papers in the possession of the Earl of Lovelace. There is no explanation in the manuscript as to how Locke obtained these suppressed passages. I have made many endeavours to trace the manuscript of Ludlow's Memoirs, but have entirely failed to obtain any clue. If it is in existence, it would probably be found that more has been suppressed. Ludlow's Memoirs were first printed at Vevay in Switzerland, and published in 1698 and 1699: Ludlow had died there in 1693. Locke died in 1704. There is no trace, that I am aware of, of intercourse between Locke and Ludlow. It is clear that every passage containing depreciatory mention of Shaftesbury was purposely suppressed, when Ludlow's Memoirs were published. At that time the memory of Shaftesbury was dear to Whigs; and Ludlow had possibly himself lived to wish that these passages should not see the light.'

also been coupled with the 'Memoirs,' and in the Bodleian Catalogue the editorship of the third volume is ascribed to him. The views expressed in the preface agree very well with those of Toland, but so far as I am aware there is no good evidence for this ascription. The author of 'Regicides no Saints' however certainly ascribes to Toland the selection of the papers printed at the end of volume three. He does not mention him by name, but refers to him as 'a spiteful young fellow,' whom he terms 'Amyntor,' 'Milton junior,' and the 'son of a potato.'

[1] Life of Shaftesbury, vol. i. Appendix, p. lvi.

Fortunately the history of Ludlow's own life is much clearer than the history of his writings. This is not due to his own care to inform posterity about it, for so little did he intend to write an autobiography that he omits to mention the most important event in his life. Lord Herbert of Cherbury gives a long account of his parents, but Ludlow does not even mention the names of his father or mother. Herbert even records the precise hour of his own birth (though he neglects to mention the month or the year), but Ludlow nowhere states either his age or the date of his birth. He was born at Maiden Bradley in Wiltshire, about 1617, as the matriculation register of the University of Oxford proves [1]. His father was Sir Henry Ludlow, knight, head of a family settled in Wiltshire from the fifteenth century: his mother, Elizabeth daughter of Richard Phelips of Whitchurch, Dorset, and niece of Sir Edward Phelips of Montacute. As to his own education Ludlow is equally silent. It may be surmised that he was put to school at Blandford in Dorsetshire. In 1651, when Ludlow was setting out for Ireland, his old acquaintance Payne Fisher addressed a poem to him in which he celebrated his early excellence in athletics [2]:—

O mihi post longos semper memorande sodales!
Praesidium columenque meum! quo carmine laudes
Depromam tantas? Quae prima examina sumam?
Candorem priscum pectusque ingentius annis
An memorem teneris? Puer aut quot symbola pugnae
Tunc *Blanfordiacae* dederas memoranda *palaestrae*?
Quis versare pilas, athletae aut promptior arte,
Grande vel excusso lignum vibrare lacerto?
Talibus ornata est aetatula prima trophaeis.

---

[1] Memoirs, i. 32, 66, and Appendix I. See also Hoare, Modern Wilts, Heytesbury, p. 15.

[2] 'Ad invictissimum virum Edmundum Ludloum cum versus Iernam proficisceretur soteria.' Printed at the end of Fisher's 'Irenodia Gratulatoria,' 1652. Cf. Memoirs, i. 83.

Ludlow matriculated at Trinity College, Oxford, on September 10, 1634, and took the degree of B. A. on November 14, 1636[1]. Though he gained no distinction as a scholar, he already showed signs of the qualities he was afterwards to exhibit in a larger sphere. His chief characteristic in his political career, says a hostile critic, was

' a gruff, positive humour, resolutely bent upon whatever his own will suggested, of which unmanageable disposition he gave an early specimen in that little while he was at Trinity College, where the then president kept a strict discipline, and would frequently moderate at the young students' disputations himself. It happened upon a time this positive Sir was engaged in argument about " Species Intentionales " and " Reales " or some such like topick, for he confidently affirmed something to be real which was very far from it. The good Doctor endeavoured to convince him by the following instance.

' " The fox wagging his tail and seeing its shadow upon the wall, said it was an horn ; was that an horn ? " quoth he to Ludlow ;

' " Yes, it was a horn, a real horn."

' Wherein he so pertinaciously persisted as the old man fell into a little passion, and put an end to that debate with this resolve, " Well, if it be an horn, then toot it, you fool you." How it was expressed in Latin was not related; but I had the passage from a right reverend person of great eminency who some time after was in the same presidentship, and upon a general discourse of fanatick obstinacy gave this particular instance how naturally some men's dispositions lead them thereto. For at the same contradicting rate he went on in the whole course of his life, and tho' as heavy as lead as stiff as iron would bend to none[2].'

It might fairly be added that even in his later life Ludlow did not always discover the difference between shadows and realities.

[1] Wood, Fasti, 1636; Foster, Alumni Oxonienses, 1500–1714, p. 918.

[2] Regicides no Saints, p. 49. A

similar story, without mention of Ludlow, is told by Aubrey, Letters from the Bodleian, ii. 403.

On leaving Oxford, Ludlow betook himself to London, to obtain the tincture of law which was held necessary to complete a country gentleman's education. He was admitted to the Inner Temple in 1638. There some three years later occurred the first incident in his life which he thinks worth recording—a quarrel with a fellow student in defence of the Long Parliament[1]. About the same time his fancy turned to thoughts of marriage, but in a business-like rather than sentimental way. By a curious chance the Domestic State Papers[2] contain an agreement between Edmund Ludlow, of Maiden Bradley, Wilts, of the one part, and Anthony Etherington of London, and Francis Bukley of Studley, of the other part. If Bukley and Etherington shall procure Ludlow a wife worth at the time of his marriage with her four thousand pounds, he will pay them fifty pounds apiece. And in case the wife so procured shall be worth more than four thousand pounds at the time of his marriage, out of every thousand pounds, he promises to pay a hundred pounds to the said Etherington and Bukley. Dated July 17, 1641.

The outbreak of the Civil War probably prevented this bargain from resulting in a match. When Ludlow's marriage took place he does not say, but it may be fixed with tolerable certainty in 1649. Characteristically enough, he first refers to his wife when he tells us how he invested her dowry[3]. On her name and family he is silent. She was Elizabeth Thomas, daughter of William Thomas, of Wenvoe, Glamorganshire, and Jane Stradling, daughter of Sir John Stradling, baronet, of St. Donats[4]. William Thomas died in 1636, and his widow married Michael Oldsworth, member for Salisbury in the Long

[1] Memoirs, i. 23.

[2] Cal. S. P., Dom., 1641-3, p. 54.

[3] Memoirs, i. 235, 247. The dowry seems to have been less than £4000 after all.

[4] G. T. Clark, The Genealogies of Morgan and Glamorgan, 1886. p. 558. Elizabeth Thomas was probably born about 1631.

Parliament, whom Ludlow consequently refers to as ' my father Oldsworth[1].' Edmund Thomas, Mrs. Ludlow's brother, represented Glamorganshire in the parliaments of 1654 and 1656, and is mentioned by Ludlow as one of the few gentlemen of old family who condescended to sit in Cromwell's House of Lords[2].

From the outbreak of the Civil War Ludlow's personal history becomes clearer. His father, who represented Wiltshire in the Long Parliament, belonged to the extremest section of the popular party, and having openly expressed the opinion that Charles was unworthy to be King of England, was denounced in the royal declarations as guilty of high treason. At his father's invitation, and in consideration of his age and vigorous constitution, Ludlow thought it his duty as an Englishman to take up arms for the Parliament. In his view the question at issue was perfectly simple.

' The question in dispute between the King's party and us being, as I apprehended, whether the King should govern as a god by his will, and the nation be governed by force like beasts: or whether the people should be governed by laws made by themselves, and live under a government derived from their own consent[3].'

Like Fleetwood, Harrison, and many other distinguished officers, Ludlow began his military career as a private in the Earl of Essex's life guard, which consisted of a hundred gentlemen under the command of Sir Philip Stapleton. When these gentlemen showed any capacity they usually received commissions, and were sent to raise forces in those parts of the country where their estates gave them local influence. In this way Ludlow, after eight months' service in the guards, received a captain's commission in the regiment of horse to be raised by Sir Edward Hungerford for service in Wiltshire. Next month he was appointed

---

[1] Memoirs, i. 423; ii. 15, 43.   [2] Ib. ii. 31.   [3] Ib. i. 206.

governor of Wardour Castle, and received a second commission as captain of foot. The success of the royalist
arms in the west of England during the campaign of 1643
completely isolated Wardour Castle, which by the beginning of 1644 was the only place in the county held for
the Parliament. Ludlow was obliged to surrender it on
March 18, 1644, and was conveyed a prisoner to Oxford
Castle. The courage and tenacity with which he had
maintained his post, and the boldness of his answers to the
summons of the besiegers, had gained him a wide reputation
amongst his own party. 'Amongst castle sieges,' said
a contemporary preacher, 'that of Wardour in Wilts will
be famous to posterity, both for passive and active valour
to the utmost[1].' Ludlow was accordingly exchanged as
soon as possible, and on May 10, 1644, received a commission as major of Sir Arthur Hesilrige's regiment of
cavalry in Sir William Waller's army[2].

He remained with Waller only a few weeks and then
returned to Wiltshire. In consequence of his father's death
Ludlow had succeeded to the family estates, and Parliament at the request of the local gentry had appointed him
sheriff of Wiltshire. Waller gave him a commission to raise
and command a regiment of horse and allowed him to take
his own troop of Hesilrige's regiment to form its nucleus.
Bad luck followed the regiment from the moment of
its formation. As soon as Ludlow entered Wiltshire, he
suffered a severe defeat in which his original hundred men
were reduced to about thirty (July 6, 1644). In December,
1645, he was surprised at Salisbury, and lost about eighty
more men. A dispute about the question whether he should
hold his commission from Waller, or take a new one from
Essex, resulted in his soldiers being unpaid. Finally the
major, after frequently refusing obedience to his colonel's

[1] John Bond, Occasus Occiden-
talis, or Job in the West.

[2] Memoirs, i. pp. 39, 49, 90, 91,
and Appendix III.

orders, deserted with about thirty men to the royalists. Ludlow's command came to an end April 2, 1645, when owing to some difference with the Wiltshire committee, he resigned his commission, or as he puts it 'was laid aside[1].' He had been suggested for the command of a regiment in the New Model, but it was now too late, as the list of its officers had been agreed upon. Nevertheless Hesilrige gave his late major a recommendation to Fairfax in the hope that he might find him some post in its ranks. The letter, dated May 12, 1645, was addressed to Fairfax's secretary. John Rushworth[2].

'Mr. Rushworth, I entreate you to present this gentleman, Colonel Ludlowe to Sir Thomas Fairfax. You may let him know what a good patriote his father was, and what honor this Colonel hath gayned by holding oute the siege at Warder Castle after halfe of it was blowen up. I pray you do him what good offices you can. I present my service to yourself, and so rest your loving frende and servant,

'ARTHUR HESILRIGE.'

But this letter proved fruitless, and Ludlow's military career ended for the present.

The portion of Ludlow's Memoirs relating to the first Civil War is of greater value for local than for general history. His accounts of the battle of Edgehill and the second battle of Newbury are important exceptions to this rule[3]. But even with regard to the war in Wiltshire he confines himself to a narrative of his personal adventures, and omits to mention many events of greater local importance[4]. On the other hand none of the memoirs of the period—except perhaps Mrs. Hutchinson's life of her

---

[1] Memoirs, i. 116, 482, 484.

[2] Nichols, Leicestershire, ii. 744.

[3] Memoirs, i. 42-46, 102-105. His accounts of the skirmish at Worcester, and of the affair at Brentford, also contain details deserving attention;

i. 40, 47.

[4] The sketch of this local civil war in Appendix II is meant to rectify these omissions, and to supply materials for an estimate of Ludlow's services.

husband—give so lively a picture of what may be termed
the everyday life of the war. Ludlow has been re-
proached for chronicling petty skirmishes and trivial
incidents, but it is by recording such things that he holds
up to us the very form and pressure of the times. The
chief actor himself is a typical specimen of the local leaders
of the early part of the Civil War—men without regular
military training, but of boundless courage and devotion
to their cause, owing their commands originally rather to
territorial influence than military skill, but gradually
acquiring the latter from the hard teaching of experience.
What he describes in Wiltshire was happening in every
quarter of England. While the great war which fixes the
attention of historians was slowly proceeding, every county
had its little civil war too. On every little stage the great
drama was reproduced, with its alternate tragedies and
triumphs, and alarums and incursions at every moment.
Sometimes even a family was divided against itself. Ludlow
relates that during an attempt to storm Wardour Castle
one brother killed another. In his own case, while his
brothers and his kinsmen of his own name generally took
the parliamentary side, a large number of his relatives
fought in the royalist army. His uncle Benjamin Ludlow
and his brother Robert Ludlow lost their lives in the
parliament's service ; one cousin, Gabriel Ludlow, was killed
by his side at Newbury, and another, William, was severely
wounded in one of the skirmishes in Wiltshire [1]. On the
other hand, whilst Ludlow was besieged in Wardour Castle,
first one and then another of his royalist kin appeared in
the camp of the besiegers and tried their arguments upon
him. First came 'Colonel Robert Philips, my friend and
kinsman' with a party of horse, and a demand for a private
interview, which of course led to no result. Next a ' kinsman
of mine was sent from Oxford, to offer me what terms

[1] Memoirs, i. 65, 69, 103, 131.

I would desire.' Then 'a relation of mine, one Captain
Henry Williams, who commanded a company in the
regiment which was besieging the castle,' endeavoured to
persuade me to a surrender.' Even the ferocious Sir Francis
Doddington, in summoning Ludlow for the last time, before
the intended assault, begins ' by taking notice of the relation
between our families '.' And during Ludlow's captivity,
another relation, Colonel Richard Manning, who commanded a regiment of horse in the King's service, came to
give him a friendly warning to be careful in his language.
In the ranks of the King's army Ludlow also met two old
schoolfellows. One incurred the censure of his own commander by too great anxiety for Ludlow's comfort when he
was a prisoner; the other behaved with some treachery.
Very curious is Ludlow's account of his meeting with the
latter. His troop was skirmishing with a party of royalist
horse before the walls of Winchester Castle :—

'Amongst whom observing one Mr. William Neale, who was of my
acquaintance and formerly my schoolfellow, I called to him telling
him, that I was sorry to see him there; but since it was so I offered
to exchange a shot with him.'

But Neale, whilst pretending to accept the challenge,
decoyed Ludlow under the fire of the royalist musketeers,
and he was glad to escape with only the loss of his
horse².

Guizot describes Ludlow as waging war like a gentleman,
and not like a fanatic³. His opponents certainly deserve
the same praise. Ludlow takes part in the siege of Lord
Arundel's house, and holds it against the royalists till it is
a heap of ruins. Arundel intervenes to save his life, and
Ludlow subsequently repays his kindness by endeavouring
to save Arundel's estate. Penruddock, the royalist high-
sheriff of Wiltshire, and Doddington, Ludlow's captor, both

Memoirs, i. 56, 60 61, 71, 83.   ³ 'Il fit la guerre en gentilhomme,
² Ib. i. 83, 94.   non en sectaire.'

treat him with the greatest courtesy[1]. Doubtless this treatment may be partly accounted for by the desire of the royalist leaders in Wiltshire to win over Ludlow to the King's side. The ill usage of the prisoners in Oxford Castle, and Doddington's cruelty to the garrison of Woodhouse, show the darker side of the Civil War[2]. But it is evident that in the earlier days of the contest, before the minds of the two parties became permanently embittered, political divisions did not entirely obliterate the memory of the old relations. And class feeling also helps to explain the different treatment accorded to Ludlow and his followers.

In Ludlow's own case his temper became fiercer and his views more extreme as the struggle proceeded. The difficulties with which the good cause had to contend, roused his surprise and indignation. When he first took up arms he expected a speedy triumph. 'I thought the justice of that cause I had engaged in to be so evident, that I could not suppose it to be attended with so much difficulty.' The clergy and the courtiers might adhere to the King, but the people 'would not be either such enemies to themselves, or so ungrateful to those they had trusted,' as not to support the Parliament to the utmost of their power. Before long he found that 'many of the nobility and gentry were contented to serve the King's arbitrary designs, if they might have leave to insult over such as were of a lower order.' He discovered that those of the nobility who had taken the parliamentary side 'had no further quarrel with the King, than till they could make their terms with him,' and were willing to restore him to his power without any guarantees against future misgovernment. He observed also 'the strange divisions amongst our own party, every one striving to enlarge his own power in a factious and ambitious way, not caring tho' thereby they obstructed and ruined the cause itself.' Most grievous of

---

[1] Memoirs. i. 78. 82. 455.   [2] Ib i. 86. 95.

all was 'the great corruption of the nation' at large. When the elections of 1645 took place, he feared that the people would choose 'such as were most likely to be for peace upon any terms, corruptly preferring the fruition of their estates and sensual enjoyments before the public interest[1].'

Ludlow's political career began with his election as member for Wiltshire in May 1646. From the first he associated himself with the extreme section of the popular party, whom he terms 'the Commonwealth party' or 'the Commonwealths-men[2].' In the House they were few in number, and outside it they had little influence, except in London and the army. Cromwell, as Ludlow records, once angrily described them as 'a proud sort of people, and only considerable in their own conceits.' Their friends, such as Lilburne, styled them significantly 'the honest men of the Parliament[3].' Marten was the leader of the party, and the chief article in its political creed was the necessity of turning England into a republic.

Of Ludlow's personal action in Parliament little is known beyond the facts which he relates himself. He was a poor speaker and probably took little part in its debates. When the London mob attempted to coerce the Parliament he was one of those members who urged an appeal to the protection of the army, and his name appears in the list of those who signed the engagement of August 4, 1647[4]. He disapproved of the negotiations of the army-leaders with the King, and also of the renewed negotiations between the King and the Parliament which took place in the autumn of 1647. There can be little doubt that he was one of the small minority of thirty-four members who supported, on Sept. 22, 1647, Marten's proposal that no further addresses should be made to the King. Less than four

---

[1] Memoirs, i. 38, 96, 105, 132.   [2] Ib. i. 141.
[3] Lilburne, Legal Fundamental Liberties, 1646, p. 36.
[4] Rushworth, vii. 755.

months later the majority came round to the opinion of the minority, and agreed to vote a similar resolution. It then became possible for the Commonwealth party to put forward their proposals for the future government of the nation, and they did so in the conferences recorded by Ludlow. They declared that Monarchy ' was neither good in itself, nor for us,' and demanded that the Parliament should call the King to an account for shedding the people's blood, and then proceed 'to the establishment of an equal commonwealth founded upon the consent of the people, and providing for the rights and liberties of all men[1].' But neither the leaders of the Parliament nor the chiefs of the army were at present prepared to adopt such drastic remedies, and it needed the teaching of a second civil war to produce agreement.

The second civil war was now drawing near, and a Scottish army was making ready to enter England. 'I hear of a northern vapour,' wrote one of Ludlow's constituents, 'a wind which seems to threaten a persecution. Brave Christian and Wiltshire's honoured servant, fear not, they can but kill the body[2].' Ludlow was not in much danger, for he took no active part in the second war, though he was busily employed in disarming and arresting Wiltshire royalists[3]. A proposal which he made for raising troops in the county drew upon him the abuse of the royalist newspapers. Amongst the Commissioners for levying money for these troops, Ludlow proposed 'one Read, a serving man, and such other paltry contemptible fellows, all of them sectaries.' To the objection that these persons had no estates in the county, he and his friends answered that 'they were godly men.' 'If Ludlow,' said Mercurius Pragmaticus, 'had any spark of ingenuity, he

[1] Memoirs, i. 184–6.
[2] John Long to Ludlow, March 13, 1648; Cal. S. P., Dom., 1648–9, p. 28.
[3] Cal. S. P., Dom., 1648–9, pp. 126, 134.

would never have made himself thus odious, by setting up base fellows to trample down the gentry [1].' In spite of all his aristocratic prejudices—and of these there are many signs in the Memoirs—the stress of the struggle had forced him to accept the view which Cromwell had expressed: 'men of honour and birth' were to be employed if possible, 'but seeing it was necessary the work must go on, better plain men than none.' The same necessity drew Ludlow and the Commonwealth party in general nearer to Cromwell, from whom they had been alienated by his negotiations with the King, his avowed preference for monarchy, and his suppression of the Levellers in the army. Now they felt ' obliged to strengthen his hands in that necessary work ' of resisting the invading army of Duke Hamilton, and promised him all assistance in their power. The negotiations at Newport completed the reconciliation between the Commonwealthsmen and the army. Ludlow went down to Colchester to urge Fairfax and his officers to interpose, in order to prevent the conclusion of a hollow and dangerous peace. His own view was that ' an accommodation with the King was unsafe to the people of England, and unjust and wicked in the nature of it.' That it was unsafe the King's duplicity had proved. That it was wrong he was convinced ' by the express words of God's law; That blood defileth the land, and the land cannot be cleansed of the blood that is shed therein, but by the blood of him that shed it.' The Presbyterian majority in Parliament designed 'at the most only to punish some inferior instruments, whilst the capital offender should not only go free, but his authority be still acknowledged and adored, and so the nation more enslaved than ever to a power, which though it destroys the people by thousands must be accountable to none but God for so doing [2].' Ludlow and the Commonwealthsmen held not only that the King should be punished with death, as guilty of all the blood shed in the war, but that the monarchy itself should be abolished for ever. The army leaders, taught by experience, had at last come round to their view.

On the negotiations between the officers and their allies in the Parliament, Ludlow is the most important and almost the only authority. Over one point only was there much difference between the contracting parties, but small though the difference seemed it was fraught with future division. The military republicans urged that their friends should withdraw from Westminster, and constitute themselves a provisional government under the protection of the army, until a new Parliament could be summoned. The Parliamentary republicans preferred a purgation to a dissolution, and demanded that their friends in the army should maintain them at Westminster, and expel their opponents from the house.

'Seeing there was more than a sufficient number of members in the Parliament to make a House, who were most affectionate to the public cause, it would be more proper for the army to relieve them from those who rendered them useless to the public service, thereby preserving the name and place of the Parliament, than for the members thereof to quit their stations wherein they were appointed to serve, and to leave the civil authority in the hands of those who would .... attempt to frustrate what should be agreed on by them and the army [1].'

[1] Memoirs, i. 206. Burnet comments on Ludlow's inconsistency in approving Pride's Purge and condemning Cromwell's conduct in 1653:—

'Ludlow, in his Memoirs, justifies this force put on the Parliament, as much as he condemns the force that Cromwell and the army afterwards put on the House: and he seems to lay this down for a maxim, that the military power ought always to be subject to the civil: and yet, without any sort of resentment for what he had done, he owns the share he had in the force put on the Parliament at this time. The plain reconciling of this is, that he thought when the army judged the Parliament was in the wrong, they might use violence, but not otherwise: which gives the army a superior authority, and an inspection into the proceedings of the Parliament. This shows how impossible it is to set up a Commonwealth in England: for that cannot

The army accepted the plan of its friends in Parliament. In Pride's Purge Ludlow played a leading part. He attended eleven meetings of the court which judged the King, and put his name to the death warrant. The fact that he was one of the five persons charged to select the members of the new Council of State, and was added to that body by a special vote of the House, is a further testimony to his importance. At the expiration of his first year of office he was again elected to the Council.

One of the reasons to which Ludlow owed his influential position was doubtless his connexion with the Levellers. Though he could scarcely be regarded as one of their party, and did not share many of their views, they looked upon him as their friend. ' Levelling Ludlow' is the nickname given him in a list of members of Parliament by a contemporary pamphleteer. On three occasions he intervened on behalf of Lilburne, to obtain redress for his grievances, offer bail for him, or procure his release from prison [1].

It is also evident, though the fact is proved rather by his subsequent actions and the general tone of the Memoirs, than by the little known of his Parliamentary action in the first two years of the Commonwealth, that Ludlow was in sympathy with the extremer sectaries. He continually couples together the clergy and the lawyers as the ' corrupt interests' hindering the work of reformation [2]. When he was a candidate for Wiltshire at the election of 1654, the established clergy, Presbyterians and moderate Independents alike, were his chief opponents. They branded him with the name of ' Anabaptist,' exhorted the voters to stand up for the Church, and cried with open mouth, ' No Ludlow, No Ludlow,' till they were hoarse again. What

be brought about but by a military force: and they will ever keep the Parliament in subjection to them, and so keep up their own authority.' Own Time, ed. 1833. i. 84.

[1] England's Confusion, 1659, p. 10; C. J., v. 657; Lilburne's Trial, 1649, p. 153; Picture of the Council of State, 1649, p. 15.

[2] Memoirs, i. 245.

Ludlow's view on the question of an established Church was is seen by the emphatic praise he gives to a scheme propounded by the restored Long Parliament in 1659. That body proposed ' to ease the people of the payment of tithes, and in lieu of them, to appropriate a certain sum of money for the maintenance and encouragement of the ministry . . . hoping if this could be effected, that the clergy would no longer have any other interest to promote than that of the whole Commonwealth, nor be a distinct party from the people[1].'

So long as Ireland and Scotland were still in arms against the republic, there was no possibility of the reformation in Church and State, which Ludlow desired.   In the summer of 1650 Cromwell returned from Ireland and offered Ludlow the post of second in command in that country.   With some misgivings he accepted it[2].   His friends endeavoured to persuade him that Cromwell wished to get him out of the way, lest he should prove an obstruction to his ambitious designs.   This is not probable, but it is probable that political reasons played a considerable part in the appointment.   Ludlow's military experience was small, and he had never commanded more than a regiment in the field.   However the man needed in Ireland was not simply a soldier. but a soldier who was something of a statesman. At any moment during the war the second in command might be called upon to replace the Commander-in-Chief, and to conduct important negotiations.   As soon as the war ended, and indeed even earlier, he might be required to decide questions of great political importance connected with the resettlement of the conquered country.   It was therefore desirable that the man chosen should possess some political capacity, and be assured of some parliamentary support.   Ludlow possessed the necessary qualifications

---

[1] The copy of a letter sent out of Wiltshire, Appendix i. 545 ; ii. 161, 169.
[2] Memoirs, i. 244-249.

whilst better officers did not, and the vigour and ability with which he fulfilled his task eventually justified his appointment.

In January 1651, when Ludlow landed in Ireland, the country was still far from conquered. Cromwell's first campaign had placed the coast-towns of the south, east, and part of the north under the sway of the Parliament; but as he himself reported to Lenthall, though he had gained 'a great longitude of land along the shore, yet hath it but little depth in the country.' During the spring of 1650 he had added Cashel, Kilkenny, and Clonmel to his earlier conquests, and Ireton during the rest of the year captured Carlow, Duncannon, and Waterford. At Scarriffhollis in July 1650 Sir Charles Coote had routed and destroyed the best army the Irish could bring together. But the strong cities of Limerick and Galway were still unconquered, and in the bogs and mountains of every province large bands of Irish still maintained themselves, cutting off convoys, making raids even up to the walls of Dublin, and sometimes recapturing the smaller English garrisons. The difficulty of driving the Irish out of these 'vast great bogs,' which were 'better to them in point of strength than walled towns,' is vividly pictured in a letter from Ludlow and his fellow Commissioners to the Council of State [1]. The hardships of the war were far more fatal to the invading army than the swords of the Irish. Dysentery, 'the country disease,' as Ludlow significantly terms it, slew its thousands. The plague and malignant fevers raged both amongst the Irish and the English. It was the policy of the English Commanders to reduce the Irish to submission by destroying their means of subsistence; and in consequence the army was obliged to draw most of its supplies from England. and suffered severely from the scarcity it had

[1] Memoirs, i. 497.

itself created[1]. Under such circumstances its ranks were rapidly thinned, and constant reinforcements were necessary.

' It is a sad thing to consider,' wrote the Commissioners on Feb. 5, 1652, ' what vast numbers of men have perished in Ireland by the hardships of the service, cold (through want of clothes), and diseases of the country. We are credibly informed by high officers that one third part of the recruits you sent over the last year are not now alive ; whereby your lordships may perceive what need there is of hastening over the number of recruits desired well clothed, and that aged, diseased persons, and children may not be sent over, of which sort many of the last years recruits were, which hath been a great charge to the hospitals, and of no use for your service[2].'

Ludlow's account of the reconquest of Ireland is neither a clear nor a coherent narrative of that process. The part which relates to Cromwell's two campaigns contains very serious chronological blunders. The part which deals with his own services is in the main a history of his personal adventures. But like the corresponding account of the civil war in Wiltshire it reproduces the life and the spirit of the times far better than any formally accurate record of sieges and military operations. By a hundred little touches he incidentally reveals not merely the character of the war, but the temper in which it was prosecuted by the conquerors. He relates without any disapproval the slaughter of the garrison of Drogheda, and excuses it as Cromwell did : ' this slaughter was continued all that day and the next ; which extraordinary severity I presume was used to discourage others from making opposition[3].'

Ludlow approves also of the executions which Ireton ordered after the capture of Limerick, though he seems to have voted for sparing the life of Hugh O'Neill[4]. If he praises Ireton for cashiering an officer who put some Irish to the sword after they had surrendered under the

---

[1] Memoirs, i. 235, 239, 261, 278, 286, 303.   [2] Irish Records.
[3] Memoirs, i. 234.   [4] Ib. i. 288.

belief that they would obtain mercy, it was rather the breach of faith than the cruelty which moved his censure [1]. While he describes how he stopped his soldiers from killing a party of fugitive countrymen, he relates with equal complacency how he smoked out a score of others in a cave, and put most of them to the sword [2]. Like his fellow-officers, like the English people in general, he had the massacres of 1641 always in his mind, and he was inclined to accept the principle 'that they who had shown no mercy could not deserve to receive any.' To every overture from the Irish he answered by a demand for their unconditional submission. It seemed to him unreasonable to expect

'that such who are guilty of a bloody and cruel massacre (at least engaged in withholding of them from justice who are so) should be admitted to capitulate about the settlement of this nation with the Parliament of England their lawful magistrate . . . . While you insist upon the justice of your cause and persevere in your hostility, it is not the advantage we may partake of by a settlement, nor the uncertainty of a tedious war, nor fear of having this country rendered waste and useless to us, that ought to deter us from doing our duty, or unite us to this sinful or unworthy compliance with you [3].'

Yet two months later Ludlow and his officers solemnly lamented in a letter to the Parliament their 'general aptness to lenity towards and composure with this enemy, and the several visitations upon us which ordinarily have been the consequence thereof [4].'

From the death of Ireton in November 1651 to the landing of Fleetwood in October 1652, Ludlow was acting Commander-in-chief in Ireland. By the end of 1652 the work of subjugation was practically completed, and it was possible to lay the foundations of the new order. The principles on which that settlement was based were

---

[1] Memoirs, i. 263. 274, 292.   [2] Ib. i. 270, 327.
[3] Ib. i. 263. 505, 509.   [4] Ib. i. 512.

determined by the English Parliament, but it is clear that Ludlow heartily approved of the policy he was charged to carry out. For his own share in the confiscated lands of the Irish he received the estate of Walter Cheevers at Monkstown near Dublin, which was granted to him in satisfaction for his arrears of pay[1]. According to his own account however he had expended in the public service, during his employment in Ireland, £4500 over and above his pay and allowances[2].

Whilst the transplantation of the old landowners and the establishment of the soldiers and adventurers on their lands was slowly proceeding, the news that Cromwell had expelled the Long Parliament reached Ireland. Looking back on this event when he wrote his Memoirs, Ludlow described it as an overwhelming and irremediable catastrophe. The ship of the state had foundered just as it reached the port. The victorious Parliament which had performed such great things, which had established the liberty of the people, which had subdued all its enemies at home and abroad, was overthrown by its own servant.

'The enemy by the blessing of God upon the counsels of the Parliament, and endeavours of their armies, was everywhere dispersed and conquered, and the nation likely to attain in a short time that measure of happiness which human things are capable of, when by the ambition of one man the hopes and expectations of all good men were disappointed, and the people robbed of that liberty which they had contended for at the expense of so much blood and treasure[3].'

This was Ludlow's later view. At the moment when the expulsion of the Long Parliament took place he was far from regarding it either as absolutely fatal to the happiness of the nation or as entirely unjustifiable in itself. He made no sign of opposition, and continued to act under the new government both in his civil and his military capacity.

---

[1] Memoirs, i. 381, 543.   [2] Ib. i. 361.   [3] Ib. i. 343; cf. i. 349; ii. 7, 167, 356.

This acquiescence he explains by his ignorance of Cromwell's intrigues.

'We who were in Ireland being not well informed of these clandestine practices, and no less confident that the principles of some men who joined in this attempt were directed to the good of the nation . . . though we could not but have some doubts of the ill consequences of these things, yet thought ourselves by the rules of charity obliged to hope the best, and therefore continued to act in our places and stations as before[1].'

A comparison of the proclamation issued by Ludlow and his fellow-commissioners on the expulsion of the Long Parliament, with that which they published when the Little Parliament came to an untimely end, shows that the latter event caused far more searchings of heart amongst them than the former. The failure of the Little Parliament meant the failure of the drastic schemes 'to reform the law and to reduce the clergy to a more evangelical constitution,' which Ludlow had always advocated. Rightly or wrongly he attributed the cause of this failure entirely to Cromwell. He it was who, to gratify his own 'pride and ambition,' had frustrated the intended reformation, by allying himself with 'the corrupt part of the lawyers and clergy to prevent it; and so he became their Protector, and they the humble supporters of his tyranny[2].' But even if Cromwell had not earned Ludlow's hatred, by converting an intended revolution into a conservative reaction, the quasi-monarchical form of government established by the instrument of government would not have been accepted by so consistent a republican.

Henceforth Ludlow was Cromwell's bitterest and most unyielding opponent. He obstructed for several weeks the proclamation of the Protectorate in Ireland, absented himself ostentatiously from the ceremony, and refused to

---

[1] Memoirs, i. 356.   [2] Ib. i. 365.

act any longer as one of the Commissioners for the government of Ireland, lest by so doing he should seem to acknowledge the lawfulness of Cromwell's authority. On the other hand he resolved to keep his military commission until it was forcibly taken from him, according to his enemies, because it was the more lucrative post of the two, according to his own account, because he hoped some day to make use of it against the usurper. Cromwell was reluctant to proceed to extremities against Ludlow, and Fleetwood exerted all his influence on behalf of his old comrade in arms. He was therefore allowed to continue in this anomalous position until January, 1655, when Fleetwood discovered that he was circulating pamphlets against the government[1]. The surrender of Ludlow's commission was again imperatively demanded, and to avoid giving it up he pledged himself to appear before Cromwell within a definite time, and in the interim not to act against the government. But as the Protector's advisers preferred to keep him in Ireland, the order for his coming over was countermanded, and when he landed in England, he was for six weeks imprisoned in Beaumaris Castle.

In the two interviews which Ludlow had with Cromwell and his Council, he set forth with great frankness the grounds of his opposition to the Protector's government. It was unlawful, he told Lambert, because it was 'in substance a reestablishment of that which we had all engaged against, and had with a great expense of blood and treasure abolished.' Cromwell justified his government by the substantial benefits the nation enjoyed under his rule. 'What can you desire,' he asked, 'more than you have?' 'That which we fought for,' replied Ludlow, 'that the nation might be governed by its own consent.' When Cromwell demanded, where, amid conflicting parties, that consent was to be found, Ludlow was obliged to admit

[1] Memoirs, i. 375, 377, 407.

that he meant only the consent of the limited number of persons whom he regarded as faithful to the cause. That the republic he advocated was essentially the government of a minority, and had just as little popular support as the Protectorate, Ludlow was incapable of perceiving. Nor did he succeed in disproving the argument that the Long Parliament was just as much dependent on the sword of the army as the government which had succeeded it.

On the question of submitting to the *de facto* government, Ludlow spoke out boldly, asserting that he had taken part in no plots and knew of none, but declining to engage himself not to act against it.

' If Providence open a way, and give an opportunity of appearing in behalf of the people, I cannot consent to tie my own hands beforehand, and oblige myself not to lay hold on it.'

If he could rationally hope to be supported by an authority equal or superior to the authority now in possession, and could be persuaded that the said authority would employ its power for the good of mankind, he would regard it as sufficient warrant to act.

' We ought to be very careful and circumspect in that particular, and at least be assured of very probable grounds to believe that power under which we engage to be sufficiently able to protect us in our undertaking : otherwise I should account myself not only guilty of my own blood, but also in some measure of the ruin and destruction of all those that I should induce to engage with me, though the cause were never so just[1].'

Cromwell's government contented itself with keeping Ludlow under strict surveillance, probably holding that he was not likely to move unless there were a general insurrection, and that in such an event no engagements were likely to hold good. But, as he might have been dangerous in parliament, in 1656 as in 1654 the government's influence was employed to prevent his election for Wiltshire[2].

[1] Memoirs, i. 382, 433-436; ii. 10-14.   [2] Ib. i. 388; ii. 17.

Cromwell's death reopened political life to Ludlow and his party. They were once more full of hope.

'The Commonwealthsmen were so charitable to believe that the soldiery being delivered from their servitude to the General—to which they were willing to attribute their former compliances—would now open their eyes and join with them, as the only means left to preserve themselves and the people [1].'

Ludlow was returned to Richard Cromwell's parliament for Hindon, and succeeded in taking his seat without giving the usual engagement not to act against the Protector. From the first he devoted all his efforts to effecting an alliance between the republican opposition in the parliament, and the malcontents in the army. Of the debates about the recognition of the new Protector and of the attempts of the opposition to limit his power, Ludlow gives a good summary; but his narrative of their negotiations with the officers is of far greater historical value. On that subject he is the most important and almost the sole authority [2].

When the quarrel between the Protector and the army had resulted in the fall of the house of Cromwell and the restoration of the Long Parliament, Ludlow immediately became one of the most prominent persons in the state. On the day of its return to Westminster, the Parliament appointed him one of the Committee of Safety, and a few days later he was made a member of the Council of State, and one of the seven Commissioners for the nomination of the officers of the army. He was also given the command of a regiment in the English army, in place of Col. Goffe, who was too strong a supporter of the fallen house to be allowed to keep his commission. A month later the Parliament decided to trust him with the chief command in Ireland, giving him the rank of Lieutenant-General, and making him Colonel of a regiment of horse as well as of one of foot [3].

[1] Memoirs, ii. 47.   [2] Ib. ii. 64-66, 74-78.   [3] Ib. ii. 94.

Ludlow arrived in Ireland towards the end of July, 1659, and remained there till the middle of October. During his stay he was chiefly occupied in the reorganisation of the army, displacing officers of Cromwellian sympathies, and promoting staunch republicans. For his conduct in this particular he subsequently incurred the charge of being too partial to Anabaptists and extreme Sectaries in general [1].

As soon as Ludlow returned to England he learnt that Lambert had again expelled the Long Parliament. From the beginning he had feared a breach between the officers and the parliamentary republicans, and now his fears were realised. One of the reasons that led him to accept a military command when it was first offered him, was the consideration that the 'greatest danger was like to arise from the army, the principal officers of which had been debauched from their duty by Oliver Cromwell, and had learnt their own strength when they obstructed his design to be King.'

He had observed with some dismay the 'ruffling insolence' of the great officers in their dealings with the Parliament. It was to prevent the mischiefs which he feared the ambition of the army would bring upon the state, that he had obtained leave to return so soon from Ireland, and before leaving for his post he had earnestly begged the leading officers 'not to violate the authority of the Parliament,' and the parliamentary leaders 'not to put any unnecessary hardships on those of the army [2].'

Faithful to this intention of mediating he hastened to London, and spent the next few weeks in endeavouring to restore agreement between the army and the Parliament. He refused to attach himself to either party.

'It was my judgment that if either the Parliament or the army

---

[1] Memoirs, ii. 116, 121, 468, 475.   [2] Ib. ii. 82, 90, 94, 103.

should entirely prevail one against the other in this juncture, it would hazard the ruin of both; and therefore I thought myself obliged in duty to use the utmost endeavours to bring them to a reconciliation, before I should think of declaring myself.'

He urged the leaders to lay aside their private animosities, and unite their whole strength 'to prevent the vessel of the Commonwealth from sinking.' But the army were stubbornly determined to call a new Parliament, and the parliamentary leaders equally stiff in requiring absolute submission to their authority. The proposal for a restitution of the expelled Parliament by common agreement had no prospect of success [1].

Step by step Ludlow became committed to the side of the army. Though he had refused to act on their Committee of Safety, he took part in the deliberations of the subcommittee appointed by it to consider of a form of government for the three nations, salving his conscience by the resolve that its conclusions should be submitted to the approval of Parliament. Next he agreed to the summoning of a representative council of the armies of the three nations, on the ground that it was better to be governed by the whole army than to remain in servitude to one particular section of it [2]. Finally, when he had failed to prevent the army from calling a new Parliament, he proposed a constitutional scheme of his own, interesting as his one attempt at constructive statesmanship. His aim was to impose limits on the sovereignty of either parliament or army. The essentials of the cause were to be clearly stated and declared inviolable, and twenty-one persons of known integrity, to be entitled 'Conservators of Liberty,' were to be charged to watch over the maintenance of these essentials, and in case of dispute concerning them to arbitrate between army and Parliament. A somewhat similar position had been assigned to the Protector by the

[1] Memoirs, ii. 144, 145, 155, 164.   [2] Ib. ii. 144, 149, 159, 165.

Instrument of Government. The defect of the scheme was that there was no likelihood that the Conservators would be impartial, and that they would have no power to enforce their decisions. The officers accepted the scheme, but only to frustrate it at once by electing the Conservators from their own partisans, and compromised Ludlow still further by appointing him one of them [1].

Meanwhile a conspiracy was hatching in the Irish army which was speedily to end Ludlow's authority. About December 22, 1659, he received the news that a number of officers had seized Dublin Castle, arrested his fellow Commissioners for the government of Ireland, and declared for the restitution of the Long Parliament. He hastened back, but not being allowed to land in Dublin, threw himself into Duncannon fort, and was blockaded there by the troops still nominally under his command. A few days later he heard from London that he had been accused before the now restored Long Parliament, and removed by that assembly from his posts of Commander-in-Chief and Commissioner for the civil government of Ireland. The result of all his attempts at mediation had simply been to make him suspected by the adherents of the Parliament without gaining him the confidence of the leaders of the army.

The portion of the Memoirs relating to this struggle between the Parliament and the army is of great historical value, but so far as concerns Ludlow himself, it is of the nature of an apology. It should be compared with the articles presented against him by the Irish officers, and with his contemporary vindication of his own conduct.

Ludlow hurried back to London eager to justify himself, but the hearing of his case was deferred from week to week. Monk, with whom he had refused to co-operate against Fleetwood and Lambert, was incensed against him for his refusal, and had throughout acted in conjunction with his

[1] Memoirs, ii. 172-174.

opponents in Ireland. Ludlow was therefore condemned
to be a mere spectator of public events, to witness with
impotent indignation the readmission of the members he
had helped to expel in 1648, and to see the final dissolution
of the Long Parliament. For a moment he dreamt of
rallying the malcontents of the army and the desperate
remnant of the republican party, for a last effort to prevent
the restoration of the Stuarts, but was obliged to hide
himself in the country to avoid arrest. He contrived to get
himself elected to the Convention Parliament as member
for Hindon, and was preparing to join Lambert's insurrection, when he heard of Lambert's recapture. The last
chance of maintaining the republic had vanished. 'Being
thus deprived of an opportunity of appearing in the field
for the service of my country, I resolved to go to London,
and there to wait the pleasure of God, either by acting or
suffering in his cause[1].'

In the Convention he found himself isolated and helpless.
All he could do was to protest against the Restoration by
refusing to vote for sending commissioners to Charles II,
and that done he was obliged again to conceal himself. From
the window of the house where he was hidden he could see
the troopers of the fallen Republic return from escorting
the King to Whitehall, and day after day he heard of the
arrests of his friends. For some months he succeeded
in avoiding imprisonment, by a series of artifices which
he describes with great complacency, and employed the
respite in settling his private affairs. At the end of August,
just as the government published a proclamation[2] offering
three hundred pounds for his arrest, he succeeded in
escaping to France[3].

The importance of Ludlow's escape did not lie simply in

---

[1] Memoirs, ii. 260.

[2] The proclamation is reprinted in the Life of Thomas Hollis, p. 633.

[3] Memoirs, ii. 296.

the fact that he had been one of the judges of Charles I and one of the generals of the Republic. He was dangerous to the English government because he was more than this. Many of the old leaders of the republican party were in prison, more were in their graves. Amongst the exiles there were abler heads than his, but Sydney and St. John had drawn back when the time came for shedding the King's blood. Goffe and Whalley and Hewson were soldiers as good as Ludlow—perhaps better—but they had supported the usurpation of Cromwell, and Desborough was too near akin to the Protector. But through good and evil fortune Ludlow had remained faithful to republican ideals, his devotion had never hesitated, his constancy never been seduced. Therefore the few stern fanatics, whom no reverses could teach and no odds dismay, regarded him as their destined leader. His unbending obstinacy had become a virtue. The field was lost, but 'the unconquerable will,' linked with the 'courage never to submit or yield,' might yet overthrow the triumphant and careless conqueror. Ludlow possessed these qualities, and they did not perceive how much he lacked. He had not the fertility in resources, the readiness to seize opportunities, the skill to organise conspirators, the willingness to head forlorn hopes, which make a good leader of revolts. His courage was rather active than passive in its nature, and his mind was slow to adapt itself to new situations. But as yet neither the republicans had discovered that their hopes were hollow, nor the government that their fears were unfounded. How much the government feared him the State Papers and the State Trials show. Not a plot was discovered for the next few years but he was reported to be at the head of it. Spies continually reported that he was hiding in England, and zealous officials that they hoped to arrest him. Twice during the autumn of 1660 his capture was actually announced. In October 1661 he was said to be lurking in

Cripplegate, ready to head an attack on Whitehall. Forty thousand old soldiers were to rise in arms, and in a few days, whispered his partisans, Ludlow would be the greatest man in England. In July 1662 he was expected to head a rising in the western counties. In November people said he had been seen at Canterbury, disguised as a sailor, and Kent and Sussex were scoured to find him. The conception which the government of Charles II had formed of his character is well set forth by a royalist historian :—

'But the head, and even the dictator of all conspiracies, was Ludlow; who, tho' driven into banishment, did yet govern all their counsels. Neither did they do anything, but what he commanded : and this principally increas'd the courage of the faction, that he promised to assist and support every rebellion. For he was a brave and warlike man, bold, and hot, not only a murtherer of his King, but the most inveterate enemy of the royal cause : for he had bound himself by oath, never to make his peace with his King, and that he would not accept of it, if the King would voluntarily offer him his pardon and his favour, but would wage perpetual war with all tyrants (for so they call'd the royal line) [1].'

Meanwhile the real Ludlow travelled peaceably through France, visiting, like an ordinary tourist, the sights of Paris, and noting the peculiarities of the French nation. He remarked on the dirtiness of Louis the Fourteenth's palace, and critically inspected his stables, contrasted the numbers of the clergy and the poverty of the peasants, and complained that the wines of the country did not agree with him. At last he reached Geneva, and took lodgings in the house of an Englishwoman, where, he says, ' I found good beer, which was a great refreshment to me [2].' But as he did not find himself sufficiently secure in Geneva, he removed in April 1662 to Lausanne, and thence in the following September to Vevay.

[1] Bishop Parker's History of his Own Time, trans. by Newlin, 1727, p. 10.
[2] Memoirs, ii. 298, 299.

Two other exiled regicides, William Cawley and John Lisle, had also found shelter at Geneva, and removed with Ludlow to Lausanne. To these three the government of the Canton of Bern granted on April 16, 1662, an 'Act of Protection' as Ludlow calls it, that is a formal permission given them under their own proper names to reside in the territories of that state [1]. They were described in the deliberations of the Consul as refugees for their conscience sake, but the magistrates of Vevay assured them that the principal reason for their good reception at Vevay was the consideration of their sufferings for the liberties of their country. When Ludlow and two others paid a visit of thanks to the government of Bern, they were solemnly entertained by the senators, who eagerly sought to hear from their lips the history of the revolution which had driven them to seek a refuge in Switzerland [2]. But neither the protection of the government nor the favour of the people could entirely protect the exiles from the attacks of their enemies. In the autumn of 1662, seven other refugees had added themselves to the original three, and in 1663 the wives of Ludlow and Cawley joined their husbands [3]. So large a gathering could not escape the notice of the English government, and from November 1663 a series of attempts to kill or kidnap the exiles commenced. Ludlow was especially aimed at. A friend warned him: 'You are hated and feared more than all the rest of your companions; your head is set at a great price; 'tis against you they take all this pains to find assassins [4].' But the only victim of these plots was John Lisle, shot at Lausanne on August 11, 1664.

Similar attempts either to assassinate the exiles, or by diplomatic means to procure their expulsion, continued till 1669, and possibly even later. Ludlow's account of these plots is very detailed and was evidently written whilst they were still fresh in his memory. The extracts

---

[1] Memoirs, ii. 336.   [2] Ib. ii. 345, 347-358.   [3] Ib. ii. 363.   [4] Ib. ii. 371.

from the archives of Bern and Vevay, printed by Professor Alfred Stern of Zurich in 1874, show that the account is also extremely accurate, in all that relates to the conduct of the authorities towards the exiles[1]. The question whether the plots were instigated by the government of Charles II has been much discussed, and it was vehemently denied by apologists for the Stuarts when these Memoirs were first published. But the approving notices of the murder of Lisle published in the official newspapers and the letters of the head-assassin to Lord Arlington permit no further doubt on the question[2].

In promoting these treacherous attempts against Ludlow the English government stooped to unnecessary baseness. He was not so dangerous or so energetic as their fears represented him. No doubt if an insurrection had taken place in England he would have hurried to join it. He was in correspondence with the disaffected party both in England and abroad, but he was sensible of the difficulties of overthrowing an established government, and of the instability of foreign support. His correspondence with his friends in Holland in 1665 and 1666 is very instructive. Ludlow seems to have felt no scruples about drawing his sword against his country. He was perfectly ready to accept a command from the Dutch, if the Dutch would give adequate security for the fulfilment of their promises to the republican party. Republicanism had become a religion with him, and had swallowed up national feeling. But he was resolved to be treated as an ally and not as a tool, and neither to risk his own life, nor the lives of his friends, without something more than promises to depend upon. A heavy responsibility was his. 'If he would resolve to go,' he was told, 'all the exiles would

---

[1] Briefe Englischer Flüchtlinge in der Schweiz. Aus einer Handschrift des Berner Staats-Archivs herausgegeben und erläutert von Alfred Stern. Göttingen, Peppmüller, 1874, pp. 23-32.

[2] Memoirs, vol. ii, Appendix, pp. 482, 485, 487.

accompany him; if he refused, no man would stir[1].' In holding back, and refusing to act, Ludlow did wisely, but his caution disillusioned the desperate spirits of his party. Bold Colonel Blood scornfully declared 'that he was very unable for such an employment,' and others doubtless held the same opinion. What part Ludlow took in the later conspiracies of his party there is hardly sufficient evidence to determine. When the Calendars of the Domestic State Papers for the reign of Charles II are at last completed, it will be possible to answer this question. Meanwhile it is certain that some of the persons concerned in the Rye House plot suggested Ludlow as a leader. In the winter of 1682 Col. Rumsey, Captain Walcot, who had been an officer in Ludlow's regiment, and Col. Rumbold, discussed a plan for a general insurrection, and agreed, *inter alia*, to send for Ludlow[2]. It does not appear that this proposal was actually carried into effect. In July 1683 however two of the Rye House conspirators, Wade and Nelthorpe, fugitives from England after the discovery of their design, took refuge in Switzerland, and made new efforts to persuade Ludlow to head a rising.

'We came,' says Wade, 'to Vivey in the Canton of Bern in Swisse, the latter end of July, where we were kindly received by Col. Ludlow's lady, and lived with them all the time of our abode there. About October after John Rowe came to us, who I suppose is still there. In April 1684 I received a letter from Mr. Ayloff, then at Utrecht, desiring me to try whether Col. Ludlow might be prevailed with to come into Holland, and from thence to go into the West of England to head a party as General, and informing me, that there was a design on foot to make an insurrection both in England and Scotland; he prayed me to come speedily into Holland, to give my assistance to the design. I did speak with Col. Ludlow as I was desired, but found him no wayes disposed to

[1] Memoirs, ii. 377-381, 388, 391, 395, 405.

Account of the Rye House Plot, 8vo. 1696, p. 48.

[2] The examination of Robert West.

the thing, saying he had done his work he thought in the world, and was resolved to leave it to others [1].'

Nothing is known of Ludlow's history between the year 1672 when the Memoirs close, and Wade's visit to him in 1683. The last of the letters which Professor Stern discovered in the library at Bern, is dated January 25, 1672 [2]. These letters and a few from the spies of the English government complete the picture of the life of the exiles given in the Memoirs. The little colony in Switzerland grew gradually smaller. Colonel Biscoe and John Phelps went away in 1662, hoping to make a living as traders in Holland and Germany. William Say left in 1664, frightened away by the murder of Lisle, and is next heard of in Holland [3]. Slingsby Bethel returned to England to be chosen in 1680 one of the Whig Sheriffs of London, and to be famous in Dryden's satire. Cornelius Holland probably quitted Switzerland in 1671, in hopes that the mineral springs of Germany would cure his diseases. The first to die was William Cawley, in January 1666 ; the next Nicholas Love, in November 1682. With the death of Andrew Broughton in February 1687 Ludlow must have lost his last companion, for the date of the death of John Phelps is quite uncertain, and though there is a tablet to him in St. Martin's Church, there appears to be no proof that he died at Vevay [4].

In spite of all the efforts of the English government to intercept their correspondence, the exiles seem to have maintained a pretty regular communication with their friends in England. The few letters of Ludlow which have been preserved, and the extracts contained in the Memoirs, prove this. To conceal their identity from their watchful enemies they used fictitious names. Ludlow

---

[1] The Confession of Nathaniel Wade. Harleian MS. 6845, p. 269. Cf. Macaulay, History of England.

[2] Memoirs, ii. Appendix, p. 507.

[3] Ib. ii. 344, 373.

[4] See the Epitaphs in the Appendix, ii. 512.

adopted his mother's surname, and called himself Edmund Phillips, but in his case, his real name was generally known. Cawley, whose father's Christian name was John, became William Johnson, and John Ralfeson was probably the pseudonym adopted by Cornelius, son of Ralph Holland[1].

At first at any rate the exiles must have lived a very isolated life. Their ignorance of the language prevented them from associating with the natives of the country. Ludlow mentions their inability to speak French or German, and on important occasions he always preferred to express himself in writing even to the end of his sojourn in Switzerland. Cawley was accustomed to confer with the local clergy in Latin. Under these circumstances they were fortunate in finding in the principal minister of Bern, a man who had 'a competent knowledge of the English, tongue,' was always willing to act as their interpreter with the government, and was eager to serve them by every means in his power. Mr. Humelius, as Ludlow terms him, Johann Heinrich Hummel, had lived some time in England, and was now Dean of the clergy of Bern, and both from character and position a man of great influence. The letters of Ludlow and his friends printed by Stern are all addressed to Hummel, and are derived from a volume of his MS. remains preserved in the archives of Bern[2]. His death in 1673 is the reason why no letters of later date have survived.

Another cause besides the difficulty of communication probably helped to isolate the exiles. Most of them were separatists of a rigid and uncompromising type. They held aloof from the Swiss Protestants in a manner which gave rise to reports that they were not of their religion,

---

[1] Professor Stern is inclined to identify Ralfeson with Love, p. xv.

[2] According to Professor Stern the press-mark of the volume is :—'Convents-Archiv, viii. Epit. Hist. & Epistolae virorum Clarorum. 40.'

and afforded their enemies a handle of which they were not slow to avail themselves. The government of the Canton ordered an enquiry in 1668, and the exiles were obliged to justify their attitude.

'We hold and profess the same doctrinal points of Christian faith which you do,' answered Holland, 'and do usually hear the preaching of the word by your ministers.'

He admitted that, for divers reasons, they did not receive the communion with the congregations, but added that they met together several times a week 'to pray with one another and speak to one another out of the Scriptures.' The theological motives for this abstention are set forth at length by two Swiss ministers, Mennet and Chevallier. Chevallier regarded their arguments as untenable, but reported that they held the same faith as the Swiss Protestants on fundamental points, and praised their irreproachable lives. Mennet related a dialogue on the subject. He had once told 'ce brave monsieur le général Ludlow' that every one in Vevay regarded him with favour, but many would love him still more, if he came to the communion with them.'

'Say to those good people,' replied Ludlow, 'what our Lord Jesus said to his disciples, when they told him: "We saw one casting out devils in thy name, and he followeth not us, and we forbade him because he followeth not us"; to whom the Lord answered, "Forbid him not, for he that is not against us is on our part." "We try," he continued, "to live according to the word of God, and to drive out the devil by as regenerate a life as we can attain to, and if we do not follow you with our bodies to the Lord's Supper, we are still for the Lord, and not against him," adding that this was his answer to the hardest judgment that might be passed upon them [1].'

Thanks to the tolerance of the Swiss and the good offices of Hummel and other friends this insidious attack failed,

[1] Memoirs, ii. 496-500.

and its author, as Ludlow relates with some satisfaction, came to a terrible end.

Puritanism was not incompatible with a love for field-sports, and Ludlow seems to have alleviated his exile by their aid. Whitelocke records that in 1649 when he was lieutenant of Windsor forest, Ludlow was very pressing for a day's hunting there.

'I persuaded Colonel Ludlow that it would be hard to show him any sport, the best stags being all destroyed, but he was very earnest to have some sport and I thought not fit to deny him.' Next day, he continues, 'my keepers did harbour a stag. Col. Ludlow, Mr. Oldsworth, Mr. Thomas, and other gentlemen, met me by day-break. It was a young stag, but very lusty, and in good case. The first ring which the stag had led the gallants was above twenty miles[1].'

One of the first steps Ludlow took after settling at Vevay was to procure himself 'des chiens de chasse,' and Arlington's spy reported that he had also five very fine Spanish horses[2]. What kind of sport he succeeded in getting his letters do not tell us.

Of the latter years of Ludlow's life very little is known excepting a single episode. The Revolution of 1688 seemed to open a way for his return to England, and he eagerly took advantage of it. Age and exile had not broken his constitution and he still felt fit for service. 'Though Mr. Ludlow is very old,' says a contemporary journalist, 'he is still lusty and vigorous, and may be useful both for council and action[3].'

The editor of the Memoirs states positively that he was 'sent for as a fit person to be employed' in the recovery of

---

[1] Whitelocke, Memorials, iii. 92, 93.

[2] Memoirs, ii. 487.

[3] The writer personally knew Ludlow. 'I myself,' he adds, 'have frequently heard him call Cromwell, a traitor and a perfidious person, who under the pretence of public good concealed an immeasurable ambition, and who had deceived all those who were engaged in his interests.' The State of Europe, or the Historical and Political Mercury, Nov. 1689, vol. i. p. 457 of the English translation.

Ireland [1]. According to tradition this summons came from William himself, but it is far more likely to have been an unauthorized message from some one of the extreme Whigs, such as Wildman or Hampden [2]. But whether he simply obeyed his own impulse, or accepted the invitation of others, it is clear that he hoped to be of some public service. When Ludlow bade farewell to the magistrates of Vevay, he told them that he had received a call from the Lord to return to his native country, in order to strengthen the hands of the Gideon who had been raised up to deliver the nation from the house of bondage [3]. His farewell took place on July 25, 1689, and by August he must have been again in England. About the middle of September Luttrell's Diary contains a note, probably derived from some newsletter of the period, stating that 'Col. Ludlow, an old Oliverian, and one of King Charles the First his judges, is arrived lately in this kingdom from Switzerland [4].'

Those of his old friends who were still alive doubtless flocked to see him, for a Tory pamphleteer complains that his house became the rendezvous of the detestable remains of that pernicious crew [5].

Public feeling still regarded the Regicides with horror, and only a small section, even of the Whigs, were willing to tolerate the presence of one of their leaders on English soil. On Nov. 6 an obscure Cornish member, Sir Joseph Treden-

[1] Memoirs, i. 8.

[2] A note by Thomas Hollis, in the copy of Ludlow he presented to the library at Bern, says that Ludlow was sent for by King William. Macaulay thus interprets the passage in the preface: 'Ludlow's admirers, some of whom appear to have been in high public situations, assured him that he might safely venture over, nay, that he might expect to be sent in high command to Ireland.' History of England, 1858, v. 135 Boyer in his Life of William III, 1702, says definitely that Ludlow 'upon the encouragement given him by a great courtier, came over ... to offer the King his service in the reducing of Ireland.' ii. 150.

[3] Memoirs, ii. 509.

[4] Luttrell's Diary, i. 502.

[5] A Caveat against the Whigs, 1714, part iii. p. 47. Boyer makes a similar statement.

ham, raised a debate on the subject in the House of Commons, which ended in the vote that an address should be presented to the King to issue out his proclamation for Ludlow's apprehension. No attempt was made by any one to say anything in Ludlow's defence, though doubts were expressed whether it was desirable that Parliament should interfere, and whether the fact of his presence was proved by evidence enough to warrant a parliamentary proceeding. The next day a deputation headed by Sir Edward Seymour delivered the address to William III, and the King at once promised to comply with its request[1]. Seymour, who enjoyed a grant of Ludlow's forfeited estate in Wiltshire, is generally said to have been the chief instigator of the resolution of the Commons, and from the fact that he presented the address the statement is probably correct[2]. On the other hand, it is very strange that Anchitell Grey, who records the speeches of six other members on the subject, makes no mention of Seymour as taking part in the discussion.

Ludlow made his way with very little difficulty to Holland, and thence returned to Vevay, which he never left again[3]. Hitherto he had cherished the hope of ending his days in his native country, but it was now plain that he was destined to die an exile. It was doubtless at this time that he caused to be carved over the door of his house at Vevay the well-known motto:

'Omne solum forti patria quia patris:'

words which Macaulay renders, 'To him to whom God is a father every land is a fatherland[4].'

---

[1] Memoirs, ii. pp. 510, 511.

[2] Boyer, William III, ii. 150; Grey's Debates, ix. 398 note.

[3] Luttrell, i 607. The Caveat against the Whigs says, 'He was sent over into Holland with the Dutch ambassadors, and after it was known that he was timely arrived there, out came the proclamation.'

[4] For Macaulay's comments, see History of England, chapter xvi, v. 137, ed. 1858. 'The first part,' says Addison, 'is a piece of verse in Ovid, as the last is a cant of his

The question which particular house at Vevay Ludlow lived in, has been a matter much disputed amongst local antiquarians. Where native authorities differ it would be presumptuous for a stranger to attempt to decide; but it seems to be very probable that Ludlow lived at different times in both the houses in question. The evidence collected by M. Albert de Montet appears to prove conclusively that during the earlier part of his exile, Ludlow lived in the house which M. de Montet terms the ' Maison de Sauveur.' The situation of this house agrees best with the statements made by Ludlow himself in the 'Memoirs.' On the other hand, local tradition asserts that Ludlow lived in the so-called 'Maison Grenier,' and an inscription has been put up to commemorate his residence there. The fact that the board with Ludlow's motto undoubtedly came from the ' Maison Grenier' is a strong argument in favour of the truth of the local tradition. For certainly when Ludlow left Vevay in 1689 he had no intention of returning, and doubtless permanently abandoned his old quarters in the ' Maison de Sauveur.' When he came back again there is nothing unreasonable in the supposition that he may have shifted his residence to the 'Maison Grenier [1].'

Another point on which some doubt exists is the precise date of Ludlow's death. Biographers have universally given it as 1693, basing that statement on a misunderstanding of his epitaph, where the monument which bears it is said to have been erected by his widow in 1693. In reality his death occurred towards the close of the previous

---

own.' Remarks on Italy, p. 264, ed. 1745. Ovid's lines are :—

'Omne solum forti patria est, ut piscibus aequor,
Ut volucri, vacuo quicquid in orbe patet.'
    Fasti, i. 493.

Chatham makes some interesting comments on the motto. Correspondence, i. 121.

[1] See vol. ii. Appendix ix. pp. 515-517, for M. de Montet's arguments. The accounts of the Ludlow board in the Gentleman's Magazine, 1854, i. 261, and in Hoare's Modern Wilts, say distinctly that it came from M. Grenier's house. The article in Archaeologia mentions Ludlow's change of residence.

year. Luttrell's Diary notes under November 24, 1692, that 'Major-General Ludlow is dead beyond sea, in Switzerland[1].' As the register of burials at Vevay before 1704 has been burnt it is not possible to fix the date with absolute accuracy. But the later date of the monument is explained by the fact that Ludlow's widow obtained leave to disinter her husband's remains, to remove them to another Chapel, and to put up an epitaph[2]. His final resting-place was St. Martin's Church at Vevay; the northern wall of which bears the black marble tablet erected by his widow. On the ground below is a flat stone inscribed with the epitaph of Andrew Broughton, who died five years before Ludlow. The same Church contains the recently discovered and deciphered tombstones of Cawley and Love, and the modern monument in memory of Phelps[3].

Ludlow's widow survived her husband about nine years. She returned to England very soon, and in consequence of the failure of the heirs of her brother Edmund inherited the family estates in Glamorganshire. A letter dated Nov. 10, 1694, says :—

'There is an estate of between two thousand and three thousand per annum fallen lately (besides a great personal estate) to the widow of Major-General Ludlow, who died in Switzerland; and there being one Mr. Thomas, a young man of about thirty years of age, a lieutenant in the King's army, who pretended claim to some part of the estate, she hath lately married him, she being sixty-two years of age[4].'

This young officer was probably a descendant of James Thomas, the younger brother of Mrs. Ludlow's father. She died on Feb. 8, 170½, aged seventy-two, and was buried

---

[1] Brief Relation of State Affairs, ii. 623.

[2] Gentleman's Magazine, 1854, i. 263.

[3] Memoirs, vol. ii, Appendix viii.

[4] Fifth Report of the Historical MSS. Comm. p. 385. Cf. Life of Anthony Wood, iii. 465.

at Wenvoe. Her husband, Sir John Thomas, who had been created a baronet on Dec. 24, 1694, died on Jan. 24, 170¾, at the age of thirty-nine [1].

The best portrait of Ludlow is that prefixed to the first edition of the Memoirs, which is reproduced by collotype as a frontispiece to this edition. The pencil-drawing from which it was taken was once in the possession of Thomas Hollis. Hollis describes it thus:—

'An original drawing of Lieutenant-General Ludlow, taken from the life when in England, on the Revolution, by R. White, and purchased by me, 1754, of Mr. George Vertue, engraver, in Brownlow-street, Drury-lane. T. H.' [2]

For the edition of 1751 the portrait was re-engraved by Ravenet. In the copy of that edition of the Memoirs which Hollis presented to the Library at Bern, he added under the portrait:—

'This is a very bad print from a very good drawing on vellum, by R. White, taken from the life, when the General was in England in the reign of K. William [3].'

Hollis also caused to be engraved a portrait representing Ludlow in middle age, which according to the inscription under it was 'drawn and etched 1760 by I. B. Cipriani a Florentine, from a proof impression of a seal ingraved by Thomas Simon, in the possession of Thomas Hollis [4].'

A third portrait of Ludlow engraved by Van der Gucht —a singularly bad one—appears in Ward's 'History of the Grand Rebellion digested into verse,' 8vo, 1713, and was subsequently used to illustrate Clarendon's History of the Rebellion. This was re-engraved later in Richardson's series of portraits to illustrate Granger.

---

[1] G. T. Clark, Genealogies of Morgan and Glamorgan, 1886, p. 558.

[2] Life of Thomas Hollis, p. 569.

[3] Stern, Briefe Englischer Flüchtlinge, p. xi.

[4] Life of Thomas Hollis, p. 67.

The last portrait of Ludlow which requires mention is one printed and sold by P. Stent, representing him on horseback, armed. Underneath are verses in Latin and English. The Latin verses begin

'Sic cataphractatus castris fulgebat Achilles,'

and are doubtless from the pen of Payne Fisher. The English run :—

'Thus famed Achilles in his arms did shine,
This was Gustavus picture, this is thine,
Whose piety and prowess doth outdoe
The antient heroes and the modern too.
Let England, Ireland, and remoter clymes
Chaunt forth thy atchievements, that succeeding times,
As trophies due to thy great acts, may raise
Not single garlands but whole groves of bayes.'

Originally this was a portrait of the Earl of Essex, by Hollar, done in 1643. Later, doubtless when Ludlow was appointed Lieutenant-General of the Horse in Ireland, another head was put on Essex's shoulders, and the print sold as Ludlow.

Besides the Memoirs the only work written by Ludlow was the vindication of his own conduct, published early in 1660, in the form of a letter to Sir Hardress Waller. But immediately after the Revolution several pamphlets were published in his name, and created a lively controversy :—

(1) A Letter from Major-General Ludlow to Sir E[dward] S[eymour], comparing the tyranny of the first four years of K. Charles the Martyr, with the tyranny of the four years reign of the late abdicated King James II. . . . Amsterdam, 4to, 1691.

(2) A Letter from General Ludlow to Dr. Hollingworth . . . defending his former letter to Sir E. S. . . . and vindicating the Parliament which began in November 1640. . . . Amsterdam. 4to, 1692. The preface is signed 'Edmund Ludlow,' and the tract dated Jan. 30, 169½.

(3) Ludlow no Lyar. Or a detection of Dr. Hollingworth's disingenuity in his second defence of King Charles I. . . . In a letter from General Ludlow to Dr. Hollingworth. Amsterdam. 4to, 1692. The pamphlet is signed at the end 'Edmund Ludlow,' and dated Geneva, May 29, 1692. There is a preface of twenty pages signed 'Jos. Wilson,' vindicating Dr. Anthony Walker's account of Gauden's share in the Eikon Basilike from Luke Milbourn's attack.

(4) Truth brought to Light: or the gross forgeries of Dr. Hollingworth . . . detected. In a Letter from Lieut.-General Ludlow to Dr. Hollingworth. London. 4to, 1693. Signed at the end 'Edmund Ludlow,' and dated October 1, 1692[1].

The last of these pamphlets contains an admission that the name of Ludlow was merely assumed. The preface contains an expostulation addressed to Dr. Hollingworth on his remarks about Ludlow :—

'You use General Ludlow very rudely, a person you do not know, who never meddled with you or gave you any provocation . . . you know the book you pretend to answer, though it bears his name, is none of his.'

The author of this preface evidently knew Ludlow, and was acquainted with facts concerning his residence in Switzerland which were not generally known till after the publication of the Memoirs. It was probably written by Slingsby Bethel, to whom 'Ludlow no Lyar' has also been attributed.

Ludlow's Memoirs were probably composed during the earlier part of his exile. The reasons for supposing them to have been written between 1663 and 1673 have been stated at the beginning of this Introduction. The narrow life and the bitter passions of the exile are faithfully reflected

---

[1] The first three tracts were reprinted by Baron Maseres in 1813. A volume containing the four was presented by Thomas Hollis to the library of Bern. See Stern, Briefe Englischer Flüchtlinge, p. xii; and the Life of Thomas Hollis, 68, 568, 739-743.

in their pages. It would be too much to expect from a
man in his position a calm and unprejudiced estimate of the
acts of his political opponents ; it is sufficient that his facts
are fairly accurate and that he does not intentionally mis-
represent. One of the chief motives which led Clarendon
to undertake a History of the Rebellion was a desire to
vindicate the memory of those few who out of duty and conscience had opposed it. He was resolved that virtue should
not lose its due recompense. And he also held that 'the
celebrating the memory of eminent and extraordinary
persons, and transmitting their great virtues for the
imitation of posterity' was 'one of the principal ends
and duties of history.' Ludlow's view of the duty of the
historian is very similar :—

'As the memory of those men whose lives have been remarkable
for great and generous actions, ought to be transmitted to posterity
with the praises they have deserved, that others may be excited
to the imitation of their virtues: 'tis as just that the names of
those who have rendered themselves detestable by the baseness of
their crimes, should be recorded, that men may be deterred from
treading in their steps, lest they draw upon themselves the same
infamy [1].'

Accordingly Ludlow holds up to admiration the virtues
of Bradshaw, Vane, Ireton, and others of his political
friends. When he relates the trials of the Regicides he
inserts eulogistic sketches of their lives and characters—
which induces a royalist writer amiably to term that part
of the book 'the Martyrology of Hell.' But on the whole
Ludlow's inclination is rather to gibbet the memories of the
bad men he had known, than to make famous those of the
good. Having seen his cause betrayed, he was eager to
expose the baseness of the men who had betrayed it. To
have supported the usurpation of Cromwell or to have
assisted Monk in restoring the monarchy, was a sin he could

---

[1] Memoirs, ii. 427.

not pardon. He hated a constant Cavalier much less than an apostate Republican.

The severity with which Ludlow speaks of Sir Anthony Ashley Cooper has already been pointed out. He is characterized as 'a great instrument' in the 'horrid treachery' by which Monk overthrew the republic, a man 'of all interests that agree in the greatening of himself,' a 'bitter enemy to the public and to all good men,' owing his influence to his 'smooth tongue and insinuating carriage.' If Cooper had for a time opposed the Protector, it was simply because he had been denied the hand of Mary Cromwell [1]. Monk is concisely summed up as 'a person of an ambitious and covetous temper, of loose or rather no principles, and of a vicious and scandalous conversation.' His one aim was 'to bring back the King without any conditions, in hopes thereby to procure a recompense equal to the greatness of his treachery.' While he hid his ambition under the veil of hypocrisy, he was so openly dissolute that when he was entertained by the City Companies 'it was his custom not to depart from these public meetings till he was as drunk as a beast [2].'

Cromwell's motives, like those of Monk, are represented as entirely self-seeking. He had sacrificed all the victories and deliverances of the nation, all the hopes and expectations of good men, to 'the idol of his own ambition.' Some contemporaries, like Baxter, regarded Cromwell as a man originally honest who had fallen before a great temptation. Ludlow, however, was convinced that as far back as 1646 Cromwell 'had already conceived the design of destroying the supreme authority, and setting up of himself,' and that all he did afterwards was but the execution of this design. He interprets all Cromwell's doings and sayings, by what he terms 'the comment of his after actions,' and con-

[1] Memoirs, i. 388; ii. 155, 206; see also Errata, p. lxxi.
[2] Ib. ii. 72, 244, 247.

sequently distorts and colours the facts and the conversa-
tions he records. His account of Cromwell's words is
tolerably trustworthy; but his memory of the circumstances
under which they were spoken is frequently at fault, and his
explanation of the motives which actuated them is generally
an after-thought. An examination of the evidence frequently shows that Cromwell's words are misinterpreted, or
his actions mis-stated [1]. Even in 1698, the publication of the
Memoirs was immediately followed by a modest Vindication of Oliver Cromwell from the accusations of Lieutenant-
General Ludlow [2].

' "Oliver," says the Vindicator, "was a great man let his detractors
say what they will;" and after elaborately comparing him to
Cæsar, he adds, "I do not undertake to defend all Cromwell's
actions, but only such as Ludlow's book, and disgusts against
him, assume a liberty to condemn." . . . "The question as to
Ludlow's particular is not so much whether Oliver's actions were
just and laudable, or no; but whether the Lieutenant-General,
who as it plainly appears, was a person swayed by a violent
bigotry to his own party, were a competent judge of the goodness
or badness of those actions." Politically Ludlow was as bad
as Cromwell, "as deep in the mud as Cromwell was in the mire,"
and as being a more inveterate enemy of monarchy, "he may
rather be thought the worse of the two." "So that if these Memoirs
were published to prejudice Cromwell's memory, they will miss
very much of their aim; seeing that the reputation of a bad man
can never receive much damage from the accusations of one that
is worse than himself." '

He then contrasts with some humour the services of
Ludlow to his cause with those of Cromwell, and points
out Ludlow's inconsistency in praising Ireton, whilst
condemning Cromwell.

' A clear argument that Lieutenant-General Ludlow was no other
than a thick-skulled officer of horse who might have entered into

[1] Memoirs, i. 145, 148, 344, 346, 355.
[2] Reprinted in the Somers Tracts, ed. Scott, vi. 416.

battle invulnerable in the forehead; so to extol as he does the son-in-law who was the framer and contriver of many of those very designs which he calls impious and wicked, at the same time that he expends all the small shot of his indignation against the father-in-law, for putting 'em prudently and resolutely in execution.'

Equally inconsistent is it of Ludlow to blame Cromwell for putting an end to the Long Parliament.

'To shew how partiality blinds the reason of some people, I would fain know where lay the difference between purging the House, and turning out the members that were treating with the King in the Isle of Wight, and dissolving the Republican Rump: for Oliver was as much a servant to the one as the other. Yet the Lieut.-Gen. could approve the first act, whatever exclamation he makes against the latter. Then Oliver was faithful and an assertor, now a perfidious invader of the liberties of the people.'

Towards the close of the 'Vindication' the author treats some of the charges brought against Cromwell more in detail, and appeals to the evidence of Whitelocke and Baxter to disprove them. He even goes so far as to quote Cromwell's own speeches in proof of the sincerity of his intentions, and to assert 'there is certainly much more reason to believe him, speaking as it were in the presence of God, than to give credit to an exasperated bigot jabbering to the Canton of Bern.'

So spirited a defence of his hero naturally attracted the attention of Carlyle, who summarizes the criticisms of the 'Vindication' in the introduction to his Letters and Speeches of Cromwell :—

'The anonymous critic explains to solid Ludlow that he, in that solid but somewhat wooden head of his, had not perhaps seen entirely into the centre of the universe and workshop of the destinies; that in fact Oliver was a questionable uncommon man, and he, Ludlow, a common handfast, honest, dull and indeed partly wooden man,—in whom it might be wise to form no theory at all of Cromwell.'

Of other contemporary criticisms on Ludlow's Memoirs the only one which requires mention is the 'Just Defence of the Royal Martyr K. Charles I, from the many false and malicious aspersions in Ludlow's Memoirs, and some other virulent libels of that kind,' 8vo, 1699.

On the publication of the third volume of the Memoirs the anonymous author of this 'Defence' continued it in a pamphlet entitled 'Regicides no Saints nor Martyrs,' published in 1700. With the exception of two passages already quoted these works contain little that is worth extracting, and are at once very violent and very dull. A juster appreciation of the value of the Memoirs appears in the reference made to them by another Tory writer, Roger North, the vindicator of Charles II[1] :—

'It is found that the most violent party men, being, in their way, honest, have wrote most useful histories: for however they hold fast to their dogmata with respect to Church and State, yet they relate the common proceedings with veracity, and by that means, truths come to be known, that otherwise had been buried in oblivion for ever; and of this, out of many, I shall give but one single instance, and that is of Ludlow's Memoirs.'

Of more modern criticisms of the Memoirs the most valuable is that by Guizot, admirably qualified by his studies of the Great Rebellion and the Commonwealth to estimate Ludlow's contribution to its history. In the preface[2] to his annotated edition of the 'Memoirs' he gives

[1] Examen, 1740, p. ix.

[2] In 1851 this preface revised and augmented was republished by Guizot in a volume entitled, Études sur la Révolution d'Angleterre. Portraits politiques des hommes des différents partis.' The quotations which follow are from the seventh edition, 1874, pp. 96–100. An English translation, by A. R. Scoble, was published in 1851, under the title of 'Monk's Contemporaries.'

a sketch of Ludlow's career, and passes judgment on his character as a politician and historian. His conclusion is severe but not unjust :—

'C'était un de ces esprits étroits et durs qui ne peuvent admettre qu'une seule idée, et que leur idée possède, quand ils l'ont reçue, avec l'empire d'abord de la conscience, ensuite de la fatalité. Détruire le roi et fonder la république telle fut, je le répète, l'idée fixe qui gouverna sa vie. Le despotisme du Long-Parlement, d'abord sur le parti du roi, ensuite sur la nation quand la nation voulut la paix avec le roi ; le despotisme de l'armée sur le Long-Parlement, quand celui-ci voulut la paix à son tour ; enfin, le despotisme du Rump sur l'armée et sur la nation quand, après la mort de Cromwell, toute l'Angleterre demandait un parlement complet et libre qui ne pouvait manquer de rappeler Charles II ; toutes ces violences contradictoires parurent à Ludlow justes et nécessaires, parce qu'il s'en promettait d'abord la ruine de Charles Ier, ensuite le succès du gouvernement républicain. A ce nom seul, il immola successivement les lois, les libertés, le bonheur de ses contemporains, et demeura profondément convaincu que la trahison, d'abord celle du roi, puis celle du parlement, puis celle de l'armée, puis celle de Cromwell, enfin celle de Monk, les avait seule fait échouer, lui et quelques amis fidèles, dans leurs patriotiques desseins.

'Ludlow se trompait ; c'était à lui-même, à ses fautes, à sa déraison, à ses iniquités, aux maux qu'il avait fait peser sur le pays, que le parti républicain devait s'en prendre de son mauvais sort. Il avait prétendu imposer la république à l'Angleterre comme Charles Ier voulait lui imposer le pouvoir absolu ; il n'avait tenu compte ni des intérêts réels ni des sentiments nationaux, ni des résultats immédiats de l'entreprise, ni de la justice des moyens. Il avait obstinément fermé les yeux sur les droits qu'il violait, sur les résistances qu'il rencontrait, sur les revers qu'il essuyait, sur sa propre corruption qui fut rapide et finit par attirer le mépris sur les républicains prétendus, le ridicule sur les républicains sincères. Dans son aveugle préoccupation, Ludlow, tant qu'il eût à agir, ne vit rien de tout cela ; lorsqu'au

fond de sa rétraite, il écrivit ses Mémoires, sa préoccupation fut la
même ; en revenant sur le passé, il n'y aperçut rien de ce qu'il
n'avait pas su voir en y assistant, et ses souvenirs furent aussi
étroits que l'avait été son jugement en présence des faits.'

Guizot then describes Ludlow's return to England in 1689
and his unexpectedly hostile reception. If he had understood the temper of his countrymen, if he had even understood the workings of his own mind, he might have foreseen
this, but he was wilfully blind to facts :—

'Rien ne put éclairer Ludlow sur les torts de son parti ; il ne
désapprouva dans sa conscience, et ne désavoua dans ses paroles
aucun des actes auxquels il avait concouru. Cependant il suffit
de lire ses Mémoires pour se convaincre que le souvenir de
ces actes, notamment de la condamnation de Charles Ier, lui
était fâcheux et pesant. Il a soutenu et voulu justifier sa conduite,
mais il a constamment senti le besoin de la justifier. C'est là,
dans ses Mémoires, la pensée dont tout émane, à laquelle tout se
rapporte ; on sent qu'elle le poursuit, qu'elle l'obsède ; malgré
son désintéressement patriotique, il est sous le joug d'une situation
toute spéciale, toute personnelle ; c'est lui même qu'il défend sans
cesse en racontant comment a succombé la liberté de son pays.
De là tant de faits infidèlement représentés, tant d'omissions et de
réticences qu'il est difficile de ne pas croire sémi-volontaires.
Non-seulement Ludlow n'a pas vu, dans les événements, tout
ce qu'il y fallait voir, mais il ne rapporte même pas tout ce qu'il
y a vu ; il n'ose raconter avec détail ni la mort du roi, ni la
résistance du parti presbytérien dans le parlement à la tyrannie
de l'armée, ni une foule d'actes du parti républicain que ses
propres principes condamnaient. Il a besoin de dissimuler, de
taire, de passer rapidement sur telle ou telle circonstance qui
pourtant a été grave et décisive. En un mot, son esprit est
naturellement étroit, aveugle ; et dans les bornes mêmes de son
esprit, il n'est pas libre ; dans son aveuglement il est contraint
de repousser les rayons de lumière qu'il ne peut se dispenser
d'entrevoir.'

In conclusion, after exhibiting Ludlow as a typical

example of the lamentable results of fanaticism and party spirit, this stern censor relents a little, and owns that he was at least honest and sincere :—

'Ami de la vérité et du bien, ses actions furent désintéressées et il obéit à ses croyances. Peu éclairé sur ce qui se passait autour de lui, incapable de comprendre les événements et les hommes, il avait des instincts de justice et de liberté souvent supérieurs aux lumières de son temps. Aisément abusé par ses espérances, il demeura constamment inaccessible à la crainte ; s'il eut pour son parti des complaisances coupables, Cromwell ne put jamais l'intimider ni le corrompre. Il n'apprit rien de l'expérience, mais aussi il n'en fut point vaincu ; il était entré républicain dans le parlement, il mourut républicain sur les bords du lac de Genève. Il y a peu de cas à faire de son jugement et beaucoup à blâmer dans sa vie ; mais son nom a droit à l'estime ; et parmi ceux qui, de son temps, le jugeaient avec rigueur, à coup sûr la plupart ne le valaient pas.'

In like manner Carlyle, after repeatedly insisting on Ludlow's blindness and narrowness, and his dogged, 'not to say mulish,' obstinacy, in refusing to accept Cromwell's government, confesses to a certain respect for his courage and his sincerity. 'Adieu,' he concludes, ' my solid friend, if I go to Vevay I will read thy monument there, perhaps not without emotion, after all.'

But to return from the question of Ludlow's character to the question of his trustworthiness as an historian. His memory of events of which he was an eyewitness is extremely accurate, but he is often in error in recounting affairs in which he was not personally concerned. The accuracy of his recollections of his own services in Ireland is in sharp contrast to the blunders contained in his account of Cromwell's two campaigns in that country[1]. In the early part of the Memoirs mistakes in chronology are by no means unfrequent. It is evident that in writing the

---

[1] Memoirs, i. 236-238.

pre-restoration part of the Memoirs Ludlow must have been obliged to rely almost entirely upon his memory. He speaks of having sought for assistance ' from persons well informed, and of unsuspected fidelity,' and doubtless learnt something from his companions in exile. A few anecdotes may be traced to Cawley, Bethell, or Holland [1], but they do not seem to have made any serious additions to his knowledge.

Nor can he have obtained much help either from printed or manuscript sources. His papers, which would have compromised his friends if they had fallen into the hands of the government, were doubtless destroyed before he left England. Sometimes his information seems to be derived from one or other of the pamphlets against Cromwell published during the Protectorate [2]; but in these cases he was probably drawing on his reminiscences of past reading, not summarising or quoting books which he had before him. To this rule there is one great exception, which Ludlow expressly points out. He mentions Sir John Berkeley's account of the King's negotiations with the army leaders and his flight to the Isle of Wight, ' which I have seen in a manuscript written by Sir John Berkeley himself, and left in the hands of a merchant at Geneva [3].'

From page 153 to page 182 of the first volume of the Memoirs, Ludlow follows this narrative very closely, adding very little save the account of Speaker Lenthall's flight from Westminster and some circumstances connected with the King's rejection of the Four Bills.

To this absence of any documentary aids to his memory may safely be traced some of the omissions, chronological mistakes, and confusions as to the order of events which occur from time to time in the earlier part of the Memoirs [4].

In the post-restoration part of the Memoirs the case is

[1] Memoirs, i. 134; ii. 251, 273.

[2] Ib. i. 365, 366, 370; ii. 34, 39, 45, 62.

[3] Ib. i. 153.

[4] Ib. i. 68, 147–150, 238, 337.

altered. Not only were the events related more recent, and Ludlow's recollection of them therefore much more exact, but he had the assistance of a certain number of documents. Some of these he incorporates verbatim in the Memoirs, such as the address to the Lords of Bern, the passport sent him from D'Estrades, and the letters from his friends in Holland[1]. He also received at regular intervals long accounts of the state of public affairs in England, which he summarises and occasionally extracts from in the Memoirs. Specimens of some of these letters are given in Ludlow's correspondence with Hummel, printed in the Appendix to the second volume[2]. It is evident that his friends also sent him the published accounts of the trials of the Regicides. In describing the fate of his political associates Ludlow follows these pamphlets with such closeness that he must clearly have had them before his eyes at the very time when he was writing. The titles of these three tracts are as follows :—

1. An exact and most impartial account of the Indictment, Arraignment etc. of twenty-nine Regicides, the murderers of King Charles I. 4to. 1660.

2. The Speeches and Prayers of some of the late King's Judges . . . Together with several occasional speeches and passages in their imprisonment till they came to the place of execution. Faithfully and impartially collected for further satisfaction. 4to. 1660[3].

3. The Speeches, Discourses and Prayers of Col. John Barkstead, Col. John Okey, and Mr. Miles Corbet . . . Together with an account of the occasion and manner of their taking in Holland. 4to. 1662.

[1] Memoirs, ii. 348, 354, 378-80, 391, 395, 397.

[2] Ib. ii. 337, 338, 391, 420, 482, 489, 494, 501, 502, 504, 508.

[3] This tract, which the government had vainly endeavoured to suppress, was twice reprinted in 1661, in 8vo, with additions intended to serve as an antidote to its pernicious contents. The first of these reprints bears the title of ' Rebels no Saints, or a Collection of the Speeches, &c. With observations on the same wherein their pretended sanctity is refuted,

There is also a passage in the earlier part of the Memoirs in which Ludlow makes use of the second of these three pamphlets. No part of the Memoirs is more often quoted than the description of Cromwell's expulsion of the Long Parliament, but it may be questioned whether its details have not been too implicitly accepted. As Ludlow was in Ireland at the time when that event took place, whatever he learnt about it must have been derived from others. One of his chief informants was Harrison, with whom he discussed the subject in 1656, and it seems clear that in what concerns Harrison's action towards the Speaker, Ludlow relied not simply on his recollections of his conversation with Harrison, but also on the printed record of Harrison's utterances in prison. Furthermore a comparison of Ludlow's narrative with the account given in Leicester's Diary—the earliest and the most trustworthy of all the accounts of the incident—shows that Ludlow certainly exaggerated the violence of Cromwell's behaviour[1].

In conclusion, it remains only to state the principles adopted in preparing this edition of the Memoirs, and to thank those who have assisted in the work.

The text reprinted is that of the edition of 1698–1699, with the errata noted in the third volume corrected, and two or three obvious errors of the press pointed out in subsequent editions amended. The spelling of the original has been preserved, but the punctuation occasionally altered, and superfluous capital letters removed.

and a further inspection made into the lives and practices of those unhappy and traitorous politicians. By a person of quality.' The second, entitled 'A complete collection of the Lives, Speeches, private Passages, Letters and Prayers of those persons lately executed,' contains short biographies in addition to the observations. The quotations given in the notes (vol. i. 354; ii. 6, 304-323) are from the 'Complete Collection,' which is, with the exceptions mentioned, a mere reprint of the original tract. 'Passages and Occasional Speeches,' under which name it is sometimes referred to, is simply the running title at the top of the pages.

[1] i. 352-354; ii. 6.

The names of places and persons, often strangely misspelt in the text, are corrected in the footnotes or the index. In the documents printed in the appendices the same practice has been followed, with the exception of some cases pointed out in the notes. The contractions of the originals have been extended. For the dates in the margin of the Memoirs, and for the insertions in the text of the documents marked by square brackets, the editor is responsible. His most sincere thanks are tendered to the following gentlemen for their help: to Mr. H. H. Ludlow Bruges for the pedigree of Ludlow printed in the appendix, and for information liberally supplied by him on all points of family history ; to Mr. Robert Dunlop for the loan of the transcripts of Irish State Papers which have been freely used in the notes and appendix ; to Professor Alfred Stern of Zurich for permission to reprint the letters and extracts from Swiss records published by him in 1874 in his 'Briefe Englischer Flüchtlinge in der Schweiz,' and in English and foreign periodicals; to Mr. George Parker for his help in making the index ; and to Mr. S. R. Gardiner and Mr. C. E. Doble for much advice and assistance.

OXFORD:
Feb. 26, 1894.

ERRATA

P. 116, note 2. It is uncertain whether the name of the officer referred to should be John or Francis Dowet.

p. 132, l. 34, *for* baliff *read* bailiff

p. 153, note 2, *for* 40 pages *read* 30 pages

p. 226, l. 3, insert in the margin the date 1649.

p. 277, note 1, *for* pp. 14, 16 *read* p. 1416

p. 381, note 2, *for* Appendix III *read* Appendix IV

p. 415, l. 14, *after the words* that kingdom *insert* the following suppressed passage from Locke's notes in Christie's Life of Shaftesbury, vol. i, Appendix, p. lviii: 'Sir Anthony Ashley Cooper, who was first for the King, then for the Parliament, then in Cromwell's first assembly for the reformation, and afterwards for Cromwell against that reformation, now being denied Cromwell's daughter Mary in marriage, he appears against Cromwell's design in the last assembly, and is therefore dismissed the Council, Cromwell being resolved to act there as the chief juggler himself, and one Colonel Mackworth, a lawyer about Shrewsbury, a person fit for his purpose, is chosen in his room.' These statements are refuted in Mr. Christie's notes.

p. 498, l. 3, *for* casewayes *read* causewayes

p. 513, in the signatures to this letter read for H. Walker, H. Waller: and J. Reynolds instead of S. Reynolds

MEMOIRS

OF

Edmund Ludlow *Efq;*

Lieutenant General of the Horfe, Commander in Chief of the Forces in *Ireland*,
One of the Council of State, and a Member of the Parliament which began on
November 3, 1640.

In Two Volumes.

VOL. I.

Switzerland,
Printed at *Vivay* in the Canton of *Bern.*
MDCXCVIII.

TO THEIR EXCELLENCIES

THE LORDS OF THE COUNCIL

FOR THE

CANTON OF BERN.

———◦◦———

YOUR Excellencies having been the protectors of the Author of these *Memoirs* during the many years of his exile, are justly entituled to whatever acknowledgment can be made for those noble favours, which you extended so seasonably and so constantly to him and his fellow-sufferers.

'Tis well known to your Lordships, that the Lieutenant General would have accounted himself happy to lay down that life for your service, which you had preserved by your generosity. But since he lived not to have so glorious an occasion of expressing his gratitude, (no prince, how powerful soever, being hardy enough to attack that liberty which is so well secured by the bravery and good discipline of your own people) nothing now remains to be a monument of his duty, and your bounty, but these papers ; and therefore as a just debt, they are most humbly presented to your Excellencies.

THE PREFACE

———••———

NO history can furnish us with the example of a man whose life and actions have been universally applauded : malice, or a different interest, being always ready to wound the noblest integrity. The vertues of Scipio and Cato, the best and greatest of the Romans, could not preserve them from the assaults of envy and calumny; of which, the groundless accusations of the former to the people, and the volumes of aspersions published against the latter by the usurper Julius, are a sufficient testimony. 'Tis therefore no wonder that men who endeavour to imitate those great examples, and make the service of their country the principal care of their lives, should meet with the same hard usage. What the Author of these papers did and suffered on that account, the ensuing relation will in part witness; wherein it will appear, that he contended not against persons, but things: that he was an enemy to all Arbitrary Government, tho gilded over with the most specious pretences; and that he not only disapproved the usurpation of Cromwel, but would have opposed him with as much vigour as he had done the King, if all occasions of that nature had not been cut off by the extraordinary jealousy and vigilance of the usurper.

Concerning his extraction, if that be any thing, it may be justly said, he was descended of an antient and worthy family, originally known in Shropshire, and from thence transplanted into the county of Wilts, where his ancestors possessed such an estate as placed them in the first rank of gentlemen; and their personal merits usually concurring with their fortune, gave them just pretences to stand candidates to represent the county in Parliament as Knights of the Shire, which honour they seldom failed to attain. His father Sir Henry Ludlow being chosen by his country to serve in that Parliament which began on the 3d of November, 1640, was one of those who strenuously asserted the rights and liberties of the people against the invasions made upon them by the pretended prerogatives of the Crown. The example of his father, together with a particular encouragement from him, joined to a full perswasion of the necessity of arming in defence of his country, mounted our Author, then very young, on horseback. His first essay was at the Battel of Edg-hill, where he fought as voluntier in the Life-guard of the Earl of Essex. His father dying some time after the eruption of our troubles, he went down to Wiltshire, and was unanimously chosen by that county to be one of their Knights of the Shire to represent them in Parliament; where his integrity and firmness to the true interest of his country soon became so remarkable, that he was thought worthy to be intrusted with the command of an independent regiment of horse, to defend the county for which he served from the incursions of the enemies' army. And how great a progress he made afterwards in the science of war, the military honours he received in a time when rewards were not blindly bestowed, may sufficiently manifest.

After the death of King Charles the First, he was sent into Ireland by the Parliament in the quality of Lieutenant General of the Horse. This employment he discharged with diligence and success till the death of the Lord Deputy Ireton, and then acted for some time as General, tho without that title; the growing power of Oliver Cromwel, who knew him to be true and faithful to the Commonwealth, always finding out some pretext to hinder the conferring that character upon him. The finishing part was only wanting to the compleat suppression of the Irish Rebellion, and the last stroke had been given by this gentleman, if the usurpation of Cromwel had not prevented him. Under that power he never acted: and tho the usurper employed all his arts to gain him, he remained immovable, and would not be perswaded to give the least colour or countenance to his ambition. After the death of Cromwel some endeavours were made to cause the publick affairs to revert to their former channel, in which attempts our Author was not an idle spectator. But Oliver had so choaked the springs, that the torrent took another course; and all the efforts that were made to restore the Commonwealth proving vain and fruitless, Charles the Second was permitted to act his part. Thereupon this gentleman, who had gone through innumerable hazards for the liberties of England, was stripped of his estate, and under the odious name of traitor forced to abandon his native country. That he escaped the searches made after him in England, and safely arrived in Switzerland, was almost a miracle. The preservation of his life, which was in the utmost hazard, by reason of the prejudices then reigning, obliged him to confine himself to the deepest privacy, and for a short time kept him unknown, till his exemplary life made him not only to be observed, but admired. This stranger for more than thirty years was the care of that country; and it may be justly said, that by their vigilance rather than his own, the frequent designs that were formed against his life, were defeated, and some of them exemplarily punished on the heads of their authors.

During his exile he wrote the following Memoirs, conjecturing, and I think he was not mistaken, that some of the family of Charles the Martyr might act such things as would make his country relish the relation, and regret the usage he had found.

*But it can never be expected that all men should be of the same
mind. And therefore when the whole kingdom of Ireland,
London-derry only excepted, was unhappily fallen into the hands
of the Irish Papists, and the Lieutenant General, I hope I may
say it without offence, was sent for, as a fit person to be employed
to recover it from them: when the British refugees were glad to
hear him named for that service ; and he in an extasie to serve
his country anywhere, was arrived in England ; the reception
he found there was such, as ought rather to be forgotten, than
transmitted to posterity with any remarks upon that conjuncture.
Thus being denied the honour of dying for his country, he
returned to the more hospitable place from whence he came. But
England had not one good wish the less from him on the account
of her last unkindness. For at the very article of death some of
his last words were wishes for the prosperity, peace and glory of
his country ; and that religion and liberty might be established
there on so sure and solid a foundation, that the designs of ill
men might never bring them into danger for the time to come.*

MEMOIRS

OF

EDMUND LUDLOW, Esq.

———————

HAVING seen our cause betrayed, and the most solemn promises that could be made to the asserters of it, openly violated, I departed from my native country. And hoping that my retirement may protect me from the rage and malice of my enemies, I cannot think it a misspending of some part of my leisure, to employ it in setting down the most remarkable counsels and actions of the parties engaged in the late Civil War, which spread itself through the kingdoms of England, Scotland, and Ireland; wherein I shall not strictly confine myself to a relation of such things only in which I was personally concerned, but also give the best account I can of such other memorable occurrences of those times as I have learn'd from persons well inform'd, and of unsuspected fidelity.

Those who make any enquiry into the history of K. James's reign, will find, that tho his inclinations were strongly bent to render himself absolute, yet he chose rather to carry on that design by fraud than violence. But K. Charles having taken a nearer view of despotick government in his journey to France and Spain, tempted with the glittering shew and imaginary pleasures of that empty pageantry, immediately after his ascent to the throne pulled off the masque, and openly discovered his intentions to make the Crown absolute and independent.

1625 In the beginning of his reign he marry'd a daughter of France, who was not wanting on her part to press him, upon all occasions, to pursue the design of enlarging his power, not omitting to solicite him also to mould the Church of England to a nearer compliance with the See of Rome: wherein she was but too well seconded by corrupt Ministers of State, of whom some were professed Papists; and an ambitious Clergy, whose influence upon the King was always greater than could well consist with the peace and happiness of England. 'Tis true, he called some Parliaments in the first years of his reign; but the people soon became sensible he did it rather to empty their purses than

1628 to redress their grievances. The Petition of Right, as it was called, passed in one of them; yet by the manner of passing it, and more by the way of keeping, or rather breaking it in almost every particular, they clearly saw what they were to expect from him. And tho by the votes passed in the House of Commons, (after a message from the King to require their attendance in order to a dissolution, thereby to prevent their enquiry into his father's death) complaining of the grievances of the nation, and asserting the liberties thereof, declaring it treason for any to pay custom or other

1629 taxes without the authority of Parliament, locking the door
March 2. of the House of Commons, and compelling the Speaker to continue in the chair till it pass'd, he might have observed the pulse of the nation beating high towards liberty; yet contrary to his promise to preserve the privileges of Parliament, he caused the studies of their members to be searched, their papers to be seized, and their persons to be imprisoned in the Tower, where Sir John Elliot, who was one of them, lost his life. Divers others suffered in their health and estates, being prosecuted with all severity at the common law, for discharging their duty in Parliament.
March 27. After the dissolution of which, a proclamation was published,

whereby it was made criminal in the people to speak any more of Parliaments.

The King having assumed this extraordinary power, resolved to make war against France, not upon the account of those of the reformed religion, as was pretended, but grounded upon personal discontents, and to gratify the revenge and lust of his favourite. 1627

The Rochellers, who once before, upon encouragement from England, had endeavoured to defend their just rights against the encroachments of the French King, till being deserted by the King of England, they were necessitated to accept terms from their King very disadvantageous to their affairs, were again by frequent importunities and fair promises prevailed with (tho very unwillingly) to assist the English with provisions, and such other things as they wanted, in their expedition against the Isle of Rhee: from whence our forces being repulsed, the French King sent his army against the Protestants of Rochel, whose provisions being before exhausted by the English, they applied to the King of England for succours, according to his promise: who, as if he intended to assist them effectually, caused a certain number of ships to be fitted out, under the conduct of Sir John Pennington[1]. But private differences being soon after composed, Sir John receiv'd a letter from the King, signed Charles Rex, which was afterwards found by the Parliament amongst his papers, requiring him to dispose of those ships as he should be directed by the French King; and if any should refuse to obey those orders, to sink or fire them. The King's command was put in execution accordingly, and by the help of those ships the French became masters of the sea, and thereby inabled to raise a work composed of earth, stones and piles, with which they entirely shut up the mouth of the harbour, and so prevented them from any relief that way. Being thus straitned on all sides, they were forced to yield to the pleasure of their King; and that

1625
July 15.

1627

1625

---

[1] Ludlow here confuses the loan of Pennington's ships, which took place in June-August, 1625, with the events of 1627-8. Gardiner, History of England from 1603 to 1642, v. 328-394.

1628
Oct. 18.

strong town of Rochel, wherein the security of the Protestants of France chiefly consisted, by this horrible treachery
was delivered up to the Papists, and those of the reform'd
religion in all parts of that kingdom exposed to the rage
of their bloody and cruel enemies.

About this time the most profitable preferments in the
English Church were given to those of the clergy who were
most forward to promote the imposition of new ceremonies
and superstitions: an oath was enjoined by them with an
&c. [1], several new holy days introduced, and required to be
observed by the people with all possible solemnity, at the
same time that they were encouraged to profane the Lord's

1633

Day, by a book commonly called, *The Book of Sports*,
printed and published by the King's especial command.

But this was not the only work of which the clergy were
judged capable, and therefore divers of them entered the
lists as champions of the prerogative, asserting that the
possessions and estates of the subject did of right belong to
the King, and that he might dispose of them at his pleasure ;
thereby vacating and annulling, as much as in them lay, all
the laws of England that secure a propriety to the people.
Arbitrary Courts were erected, and the power of others enlarged ; such were the High Commission Court, the Star-
Chamber, the Court of Honour, the Court of Wards, the
Court of Requests, &c.   Patents and monopolies of almost
every thing were granted to private men, to the great
damage of the publick.   Knighthood, coat and conduct-
money, and many other illegal methods were revived and
put in execution, to rob the people, in order to support the
profusion of the Court.   And that our liberties might be ex-
tirpated at once, and we become tenants at will to the King,
that rare invention of ship-money was found out by Finch,
whose solicitation and importunities prevailed with the
major part of the judges of Westminster-Hall to declare for

---

[1] Ludlow refers to the oath enjoined by Convocation in the new
Canons of 1640 : Gardiner, ix. 143.
This summary of the early part of the
reign contains many chronological
inaccuracies.   Much of it seems to
consist of vague recollections of the
Grand Remonstrance of 1641, and of
the Declaration for no further Addresses to the King, published in 1648.

law, 'That for the supply of shipping to defend the nation, the King might impose a tax upon the people : that he was to be judge of the necessity of such supply, and of the quantity to be imposed for it ; and that he might imprison as well as destrain in case of refusal.' Some there were who out of a hearty affection to the service of their country, and a true English spirit, opposed these illegal proceedings : amongst whom Mr. John Hampden of Buckingham-shire, Judge Croke, and Judge Hutton, were of the most eminent.

Prerogative being wound up to this height in England, and the affairs of the Church tending to a conjunction with the See of Rome ; before any farther progress should be made therein here, it was thought expedient, that the pulse of Scotland should be felt, and they perswaded or compelled to the like conformity. To this end a Form of Publick Prayer was sent to Scotland, more nearly approaching the Roman office than that used in England. The reading of this new service-book at Edinburgh was first interrupted by a poor woman ; but the people were so generally dis-contented with the book itself, as well as the manner of imposing it, that she was soon seconded by the generality of them ; those who officiated hardly escaping with their lives. This produced divers meetings of many of the nobility, clergy and gentry, who entred into an agreement or covenant to root out Episcopacy, heresy, and superstition.

Those of the clergy of England, who had been the chief advisers and promoters of this violence, prevailed with the King to cause all such as should persist in their opposition after a certain time, to be proclaimed traitors. But the Scots not at all afrighted with these menaces, resolved to make good their former undertaking. Which the King perceiving, and that this violent way took not effect, began to incline to more moderate counsels ; and by commission empowered the Marquiss of Hamilton to treat them into a submission, consenting to the suppression of the Liturgy, High Commission Court, and Articles of Perth. But the Scots insisting upon the abolition of Episcopacy, and the King refusing his consent to it, they did it themselves in

1638 an Assembly held at Glasco: and being informed that the King was preparing an army to compel them to obedience, agreed upon the raising of some forces to defend themselves.

1639 The clergy in England were not wanting to promote the new levies against the Scots, contributing largely thereunto; which was but reasonable, it being manifest to all that they were the principal authors and fomentors of these troubles. The nobility and gentry were likewise required to further this expedition; in which, tho divers of them did appear, yet was it rather out of compliment than affection to the design, being sensible of the oppressions they themselves lay under; and how dangerous to the people of England a thorow success against the Scots might prove.

The King perceiving an universal dislike to this war, as well in the people as in the officers and souldiers of his army, concluded an agreement with the Scots at Berwick, the 17th of June, 1639. But upon his return to London, under colour that many false copies of the said articles were published and dispersed by the Scots, to the great dishonour of the King, the said agreement was disowned, and order'd to be burnt by the hands of the hangman.

1640 Thereupon, hoping that a Parliament would espouse his quarrel, and furnish him with money for the carrying on of his design, he summoned one to meet at Westminster on the 3d of April, 1640, which, sitting but a little time, thereby obtained the name of the Short Parliament. The King by his agents earnestly pressed them to grant him present supplies for the use of his army; but they, sensible of former usage, after they had gratified him in that particular, and of the insupportable burdens and oppressions they lay under, refused to grant any subsidies till their grievances should be redressed: whereupon the King put a period to their sitting the fifth of May following; the Earl of Strafford, and others of his Council, advising him so to do, and to make use of other means for his supply; as appeared to the ensuing Parliament, by the minutes of the Secretary of State, taken at that cabal, and produced at the trial of the said Earl: the sum of whose advice 1640 was to this effect. 'Sir, you have now tried your people, and are denied by them, therefore you are clear before God and man, if you make use of other means for your supply: you have an army in Ireland, &c.' This counsel was prosecuted, and new preparations made for the carrying on of the war against the Scots; all imaginable ways used to raise supplies, privy seals sent throughout the nation for the loan of money, ship-money, coat and conduct-money pressed to the height; commodities taken up on credit, and sold for ready money; warrants also were delivered out to press men to serve in the army; brass-money was propounded, and some prepared, but that project took no effect. The clergy being permitted and encouraged by the King to sit in Convocation after the dissolution of the Parliament, took upon them not only to frame canons and oaths, but also to impose four shillings in the pound upon ecclesiastical benefices throughout the kingdom. The King, to give life to the advance of his army, marched with them in person; the Earl of Northumberland, as most popular, wearing the name of General, whilst Strafford with the title of Lieutenant General had the principal management of all.

The City of London had refused to pay some of the illegal taxes before-mentioned; whereupon divers of their chief officers were imprisoned, and an order issued forth to take away the sword from the Lord Mayor. Whereupon the people rise, and beset the house of the Arch-bishop of Canterbury, who, in conjunction with the Earl of May 11. Strafford, was supposed to put the King upon these violent and unwarrantable courses; but he made his escape by water for that time; and one of the most active of the people was seized and executed, which served only to exasperate the rest.

Upon the near approach of the English and Scots army, a considerable party of each side encountred; and the Aug. 28. English, contrary to their wonted custom, retired in disorder, not without shame and some loss. Of such force and consequence is a belief and full perswasion of the justice of an undertaking, tho managed by an enemy in other respects inconsiderable.

The King, startled at the unsuccessfulness of his first attempt, upon the petition of a considerable number of the
well-affected nobility, requesting him, that to avoid the effusion of more blood, he would call an assembly of the nobility, consented thereunto. This Council accordingly met
at York, and advised the King to a cessation of arms, and the calling of a Parliament to compose differences ; which, to the great trouble of the clergy and other incendiaries, he promised to do ; assuring the Scots of the paiment of twenty thousand pounds a month to maintain their army, till the pleasure of the Parliament should be known. In order to which, writs were issued out for the meeting of a Parliament on the 3d of November, 1640.

The time prefix'd for their assembling being come, they met accordingly : and as they were very sensible that nothing but an absolute necessity permitted their coming together, so they resolved to improve this happy opportunity to free the people from their burdens, and to punish the authors of the late disorders. To this end they declared against monopolies, and expelled the authors of them out of the House. The opinions of the judges concerning ship-money they voted unjust and illegal, fining and imprisoning those that had warranted the lawfulness thereof. And that the offenders against the publick might not escape, they ordered the sea-ports to be diligently guarded, and all passengers to be strictly examined.

This being done, they impeached the Lord Keeper Finch, the Earl of Strafford, and the Arch-bishop of Canterbury, of high treason, in endeavouring to subvert the laws, and to erect an arbitrary and tyrannical power. They declared, that they would pay the English and Scots armies to the end of May, 1641, and assist the Prince Palatine with men and money to recover his country. And now having the charge of two armies to pay, and all men suspecting they might be abruptly dissolved, as had often hapned before, and therefore refusing to credit them with such sums as were necessary, unless an act might pass to secure their sitting till they should think fit to dissolve themselves by Act of Parliament; the King gave his assent to one drawn up and passed to that purpose. Another act likewise passed to assert, that according to the antient fundamental laws of England, a Parliament ought to be held every year, and directing, that in case one was not called in three years, the Lord Chancellor or Keeper of the Great Seal should issue out writs, as is therein expressed; and if he fail in his duty, he is declared guilty of high treason, and a certain number of Lords impowered to summon the said Parliament: and if they should neglect so to do, the sheriffs and constables are vested with the same authority. But if it should happen that all the forementioned powers should be wanting in their duty, the people of England are thereby authorised to put the said act in execution, by meeting and electing members to serve in Parliament, though not summoned by any officers appointed to that end.

The Parliament then proceeded to correct the abuses that had been introduced in the preceding years: whereupon the Star-Chamber, the High Commission Court, the Court of Honour, with some others, were taken away by Act of Parliament; and the power of the council-table restrained. The commissioners of the Custom-House, who had collected customs contrary to law, were fined; and such as had been imprisoned by any of the above-mentioned arbitrary courts, were set at liberty.

A protestation was also agreed upon by the Lords and Commons, which they took, and presented to others to take; whereby all those that took it, obliged themselves to defend and maintain the power and privileges of Parliament, the rights and liberties of the people, to use their utmost endeavours to bring to condign punishment all those who should by force, or otherwise, do any thing to the contrary, and to stand by and justify all such as should do any thing in prosecution of the said protestation.

Margin notes: 1641. May 10. Feb. 16. May 3.

1641   The day prefix'd for the Earl of Strafford's trial being
March 22. come, he was brought before the House of Peers; where
the charge against him was managed by members of the
House of Commons appointed to that end. The chief
heads of the accusation were: That he had governed the
Kingdom of Ireland in an arbitrary manner: That he had
retained the revenues of the Crown without rendring a due
account of them: That he had encouraged and promoted
the Romish religion: That he had endeavoured to create
feuds and quarrels between England and Scotland: That
he had laboured to render the Parliament suspected and
odious to the King: That he was the author of that advice,
'That since the Parliament had denied to grant the King
such supplies as he demanded, he was at liberty to raise
them by such means as he thought fit; and that he had
an Irish army that would assist him to that end.' It being
the custom that a Lord High Steward should be made to
preside at the trial of a Peer, that honour was conferred
upon the Earl of Arundel. The King, the Queen, the
House of Commons, the deputies of Scotland and Ireland,
with many other persons of quality of both sexes, were
there present. I remember the Earl of Strafford in his
defence objected against the evidence of the Earl of Cork,
denying him to be a competent witness, because his enemy.
To which George Lord Digby, who was appointed one
of the managers of the charge against him, replied: that
if that objection should be of any weight with the court,
the Earl of Strafford had found out a certain way to secure
himself from any farther prosecution. Yet this man who
then spoke with so much vigour, soon altered his language,
and made a speech to the House in his favour, which he
caused to be printed; and also surreptitiously withdrew a
paper from the committee, containing the principal evidence
against the said Earl. The Parliament resenting this pre-
varication, ordered his speech to be burnt by the hands
of the common hangman.

      The House of Commons having passed a Bill for the
May 8. condemnation of the Earl, it was carried to the Lords

for their concurrence, which they gave. The King not 1641
satisfied therewith, consulted with the Privy Council, some
Judges, and four Bishops. And all of them, except one,
advise the throwing of Jonas overboard for the appeasing
of the storm. Upon which the Earl of Arundel, the Lord May 10.
Privy Seal, and two more were commissionated by the
King to sign the warrant for his execution: which they did
upon the twelfth of May following; and the 22d of the May 12.
same month the Earl of Strafford was beheaded accordingly.

At this time a treacherous design was set on foot, not
without the participation of the King, as appear'd under
his own hand, to bring up the English army, and by force
to dissolve the Parliament; the plunder of London being
promised to the officers and souldiers as a reward for that
service: this was confessed by the Lord Goring, Mr. Piercy,
and others. The Scots army was also tried, and the four
Northern Counties offered to be given to them in case they
will undertake the same design. And tho neither of these
attempts did succeed, yet the King pleased himself with
hopes, that a seasonable time for dissolving the Parliament
would come; and then all power reverting into his own
hands, he would deal with their new enacted Laws as he
had done before with the Petition of Right, and with their
members as he had done with those of the former
Parliaments. And that he might not long languish in this
expectation, he sent to the House, desiring that at once
they would make their full demands, and prepare Bills
accordingly for his assent, assuring them of his readiness
to comply with their desires. But they perceiving the
design, return'd for answer: that they could not suddenly
resolve on so weighty a work, but would do it with all
possible speed. In the meantime, to improve the present
opportunity, they prevail with the King to pass an Act for 1642
the exclusion of the Bishops out of the House of Lords; Feb. 13.
for tho he was unwilling to grant the Parliament any thing,
yet the state of his affairs was such, that he durst deny
them no reasonable thing. And now having paid to the

1641　Scots and English armies what was due to them, they dismissed them to their respective homes.

The King having laid his designs in Ireland, as will afterwards appear, was, not without great difficulty, pre-vailde with by the Parliament, to consent to the dis-banding of those eight thousand Irish papists that had been raised there by the Earl of Strafford. Soon after August. which he resolved upon a journey to Scotland ; and tho the Parliament endeavoured to disswade him from it, or at least to defer it to a fitter opportunity, he refused to hearken to them, under pretence that the affairs of that kingdom necessarily required his presence : but in truth his great business was, to leave no means unattempted to take off that nation from their adherence to the Parliament of England. Before his departure he signed a Commission to certain persons, impowering them to pass the Bills that should be tender'd in his absence.

Whilst he was about this work in Scotland, the news of the Irish Rebellion was brought to him ; that the Papists throughout that kingdom were in arms ; that their design to surprise and seize the Castle of Dublin had not succeeded, Oct. 23. being discovered by one O'Connelly, a servant of Sir John Clotworthy's ; and that the Lord Macquire and Mac-mahon, who were appointed to that end, were taken, and sent into England, where they were soon after executed for the same. The news of this rebellion (as I have heard from persons of undoubted credit) was not displeasing to the King, tho it was attended with the massacre of many thousands of the Protestants there.

Having made what progress he could in Scotland, con-firming by Act of Parliament not only what he had formerly granted them, but also what they had done in their Assembly at Glascow, and in effect whatsoever they desired of him, he returned to London ; where being received with ac-Nov. 25. clamations, and treated at the expence of the city, he became elevated to that degree, that in his first speech to the Commons he sharply reproved them, for that instead of thanking him for what he had done, they continued to multiply their demands and dissatisfactions : whereupon the Parliament were confirmed in their suspicions, that he design'd to break what he had already granted, so soon as he had opportunity and power in his hands, to plead that he was under a force, as some of his predecessors had done, and so reverse what had been enacted for the good of the people, revenge himself on those who had been instruments in compelling him thereto, and fortify himself against the like for the future.   These apprehensions made them earnestly insist upon settling the Militia of the nation in such hands as both Houses of Parliament should recommend to him, particularly representing the great dissatisfaction of the city of London that Sir William Balfour, for refusing to permit the Earl of Strafford to escape, was dismissed from Dec. 21. his charge of Lieutenant of the Tower, and the government of it put into the hands of one Lunsford, a souldier of fortune, of a profligate conversation, and fit for any wicked design.   With much difficulty this Lunsford was removed, Dec. 26. and Sir John Conyers put into his place : but the Parliament and city not satisfied with this choice, and having discovered that Sir John Suckling, under pretence of raising a regiment for Portugal, was bringing together a number of men to seize the Tower for the King, it was at last entrusted to the custody of the Lord Mayor of London [1].

About this time great numbers of English Protestants 1642 flying from the bloody hands of the Irish rebels, arrived in England, filling all places with sad complaints of their cruelties to the Protestants of that kingdom.   Whereupon the Parliament earnestly pressed the King to proclaim them rebels, but could not obtain it to be done till after many weeks ; and then but forty of those proclamations were printed, and not above half of them published : which was the more observed and resented, by reason of the different treatment that the Scots had met with, who no

---

[1] Lunsford was succeeded by Sir John Byron, who was himself superseded on Feb. 11, 1642, by Sir John Conyers. Suckling's plot was in May, 1641.   On July 17, 1643, Conyers resigned and was succeeded by Lord Mayor Pennington.   See Clarendon, iv. 284 ; vii. 202.

1642   sooner appeared in a much better cause, but they were forthwith declared rebels in every parish-church within the kingdom of England. The rebels in Ireland pretended a commission from the King for what they did, which so alarm'd the people of England, that the King thought himself necessitated to do something therein ; and there-

April 8.   fore to carry on his design, he acquainted the Parliament, that when an army was raised, he would go in person to reduce them : but they apprehending this pretended resolution to be only in order to put himself at the head of an army, that he might reduce the Parliament to his will, refused to consent ; and procured an Act to pass, for the leaving of that war to the management of the two Houses ; the King obliging himself not to give terms to any of the rebels, or to make peace with them without the Parlia-

March 19.   ment's consent.   In this Act provision was made for the satisfying of such as should advance money for the reduction of Ireland, out of the rebels' lands, in several provinces, according to the rates therein mentioned : upon which considerable sums of money were soon brought in. The Parliament neglecting no opportunity to carry on this necessary work, procured some forces to be sent from Scotland into the North of Ireland, and put into their

April.   hands the town and castle of Carrickfergus : they also dispatched several regiments of English thither, who were blessed with wonderful success against the rebels, particularly about Dublin, where the Earl of Ormond commanded. Those of the English pale by fair pretences procured arms to be delivered to them, yet basely cut off a party of five or six hundred men sent to relieve Sir Richard Titchburn, then besieged at Droghedah, who finding no hopes of relief, made his retreat to Dublin by sea. The Lord Forbes, a Scots-man, was sent with a party into Munster, where he greatly annoyed the enemy; and being furnished with some ships, sailed up the Shannon, and secured several places upon that river, particularly Bonratte, the residence of the Earl of Thomond, where he found about threescore horse fit for service. Major Adams was made governour of that house: but the enemy frequently resorting to a place called Six-Miles-Bridg, about two or three miles from thence, the English pressed the Earl to assist them to fall upon the Irish; who unwilling to oppose the English interest, and no less to make the rebels his enemies, endeavoured to excuse himself; yet upon second thoughts resolved to comply, if some care might be taken to spare his kindred: whereupon some of the English officers proposing to him that his relations should distinguish themselves by some mark, and he concluding it to be in order to secure them to the English interest, chose rather to withdraw himself into England, and to leave his house to the souldiers, where (tho he pretended he had no money to lend them to supply their wants) they found two thousand pounds buried in the walls, which they made use of for the paiment of their forces [1]. 1642

The King finding that nothing less would satisfy the Parliament than a thorow correction of what was amiss, and full security of their rights from any violation for the future, considered how to put a stop to their proceedings; and to that end encouraged a great number of loose debauch'd fellows about the town to repair to Whitehall, where a constant table was provided for their entertainment. Many gentlemen of the Inns of Court were tamper'd with to assist him in his design, and things brought to that pass, that one of them said publickly in my hearing: 'What! shall we suffer these fellows at Westminster to domineer thus? Let us go into the country, and bring up our tenants to pull them out.' Which words not being able to bear, I questioned him for them; and he either out of fear of the 1641
December.

[1] This short account of affairs in Ireland is very confused. Sir Henry Tichborne was besieged in Drogheda from Nov. 30, 1641, to the beginning of March, 1642, when the siege was raised. Some reinforcements under Major Roper and Sir Patrick Wemyss were partially cut off on Nov. 29. Lord Forbes made his expedition in 1642, but Bunratty was not garrisoned by the English till occupied by Inchiquin's forces at the close of 1645. The Irish retook it July 13, 1646. Coxe, Hibernia Anglicana, ii. 158; Bellings, Irish Catholic Confederation, vi. 402; Carte, Ormond. ed. 1851, ii. 305, 315. The story of the hidden treasure is told in the 'Aphorismical Discovery,' part i. p. 105.

publick justice, or of my resentment, came to me the next morning, and asked pardon for the same ; which by reason of his youth, and want of experience, I passed by.   By these actions of the King the suspicions of the Parliament were justly increased, and therefore they desired leave to provide a guard to secure themselves from violence ; which the King refused to grant, unless it might be of his own appointment, alledging that their fears were groundless : but they thought otherwise, being convinced that neither what had been already done was sufficiently secured, unless the Militia might be placed in such hands as they could trust ; nor themselves safe, unless attended by a guard of their own nomination.

The King's violent ways not succeeding, he fell upon other measures in appearance more moderate, yet continued his resolution to subdue the Parliament : and to colour his proceedings with a form of law, he sent Sir Edward Herbert, his Attorny General, and a member of the House of Commons, to accuse of high treason, in the name of his Majesty, Mr. William Stroud, Mr. John Pym, Mr. John Hampden, Sir Arthur Haslerig, and Mr. Denzil Hollis, members of that House ; and the Lord Kimbolton of the House of Lords : acquainting them, that he intended to proceed against them according to law, upon the following articles :

1. That they intended to change the government of the state, and to dispossess the King of his sovereign and lawful power, and to attribute to subjects an arbitrary and tyrannical power.

2. That by false reports and calumnies sown against his Majesty, they had endeavoured to alienate from him the affections of his people.

3. That they had done their utmost to debauch the troops of his Majesty, and to engage them in their perfidious designs.

4. That they had traitorously sought to overthrow the rights and true form of Parliaments.

5. That they had used force and terror to constrain the

Parliament to engage in their pernicious designs; and to that end had stirred up tumults against the King and Parliament.

6. That they had by a great treason resolved to raise arms, and had actually raised arms against the King.

7. That they had endeavoured to procure a foreign power to invade England.

Upon this the House made answer to the Attorny General, that they were the proper judges of their own members: that upon his producing the articles that he had to accuse their members with, and the consideration of them, if they found cause, they would leave them to be proceeded against according to law; but commanded him at his peril not to proceed any farther against them, or any other member, without their consent. After which they published a declaration, forbidding the seizing of any of their members without their order; authorising them to stand upon their guard; and requiring all Justices of the Peace, Constables, and other officers and people, to be assisting to them; and sent the Attorny General to prison, for his proceedings in this matter.

The King, finding his instruments thus discouraged, and being resolved to remove all obstructions in his way, went in person to the House of Commons, attended not only with his ordinary guard of pensioners, but also with those desperadoes that for some time he had entertained at Whitehall, to the number of three or four hundred, armed with partizans. sword and pistol. At the door of the House he left his guard commanded by the Lord Roxberry, entring accompanied only by the Prince Palatine; where taking possession of the Speaker's chair, and not seeing those that he looked for, he said, 'The birds are flown.' For upon notice given by a lady of the court of the King's intention, they were retired into the city. The King then demanded of the Speaker where such and such were, naming the five members: to which he answered in these words: 'I have neither eyes to see, ears to hear, nor tongue to speak in this place, save what this House gives

1642 me.' The King replied, 'I think you are in the right': and then addressing himself to the House, said; that he was sorry he had been necessitated to come thither: that no King of England had been more careful to preserve the privileges of Parliament than he desired to be; but that those five members being dangerous persons, he had been obliged to pursue them, not by force, but by the ordinary forms of justice: that he hoped the Parliament would send them to him, to justify themselves, if they could; if not, he knew how to find them: which said, he retired. The Parliament sensible of this violation of their privileges, and fearing they might be further intrenched upon, ordered a committee of the House to sit in the city of London, whither their five members were gone before for protection. The king followed them thither with a slender, or rather no guard, (so far was he from

Jan. 5. fearing either Parliament or City) designing to engage the citizens to deliver up the five members to him, and to stand by him in this horrid enterprise; but they would not be perswaded to comply with his desires in that matter. This violent attempt proving unsuccessful, the Parliament, to assert their just rights, voted it to be a breach of their privileges; and that the like might be prevented for the future, after the committee had sat a few days in the city,

Jan. 11. they returned to Westminster, accompanied with guards from the city both by land and water. Which the King being informed of, and finding that the design which he had laid had highly provoked the Parliament and people,

Jan. 10. he retired to Hampton-Court, whither those that he had formerly entertained at Whitehall soon repaired; and at Kingston upon Thames appeared in a military posture, with the Lord Digby and Colonel Lunsford at the head of them. The two Houses having notice thereof, desired the King to disperse the said troops, and to return to the Parliament. The Lord Digby was also required to attend his duty in the House: but he being conscious of his own guilt, and knowing that the King's affairs were not yet in a posture to bid open defiance to the Parliament, chose

rather to betake himself to flight; as the Queen did soon
after, upon notice that the two Houses were about to accuse
her of high treason : both of them designing not only to
withdraw themselves from the prosecution of the Parliament, but also to make what preparations they could for
the raising of an army against them : in order to which
the Queen carried with her the jewels of the crown, and
pawned them in Holland for arms and money. The
Parliament having discovered that the Lord Digby had
by a letter advised the King to retire to some place of
strength, and there to declare against them, they caused
him to be proclaimed a traitor: notwithstanding which,
the King, instead of returning to London at the earnest
desire of both Houses, in prosecution of the Lord Digby's
counsel, went farther from them. During his absence
many papers passed between him and the Parliament.
The chief aim of those of the latter was to perswade the
King to return to London, and to settle the Militia in such
hands as the Parliament should advise ; that so all jealousies
between him and his people might be removed. Those
from the King were to let them know, that he could not
part with the Militia, esteeming it to be the best jewel
of his crown ; nor return to London with safety to his
person. The declarations on both sides proving ineffectual,
and the King's designs both at home and abroad being
grown ripe, he expressed his dissatisfactions more openly,
and withdrew to York, where several lords and others
affected to his interest, resorted to him with plate, money,
men, horses and arms : amongst whom were many Papists ;
who, tho to cover the King's designs from the people,
they were forbidden to come into the court, were yet
privately encouraged, and daily listed and armed. And
as the distance of York from the Parliament was one
reason why the King went thither, so its nearness to Hull
was another. This town he endeavoured to possess himself
of, being a place of strength, where great quantities of arms
and ammunition had been laid up, upon disbanding the
army which was lately on foot in those parts, and very

1642
Feb. 23.

March 19.

convenient for the landing of men from Holland. But the Parliament suspecting the design, had sent Sir John Hotham thither to keep and defend it for their use. Notwithstanding which the King persisted in his resolution, and endeavoured, by sending divers persons of quality into the town, to surprise it ; but that way not taking effect, he appeared in person before it, demanding entrance of Sir John Hotham, which he absolutely refused to permit ; alledging, that he was entrusted with the place by the Parliament for the service of his majesty and the nation, and that he could not surrender it without their order. The King finding that he could not prevail either by promises or threatnings, caused Sir John Hotham to be proclaimed a traitor, and returned to York ; from whence he complained to the Parliament of the affront he had received at Hull ; who, to manifest their approbation of Sir John Hotham's conduct, declared that he had done his duty in denying the King admittance into the town, asserting that the command of the Militia was entrusted with the King to be employed for the good of the nation ; of which the two Houses of Parliament sitting are the proper judges.

The Parliament began now to provide for the security of all places, and sent a committee of four of their members to invite the King to return to Westminster, and to endeavour to promote their interest in the northern parts : and being informed that there was laid up in the town of Leicester a considerable quantity of arms and ammunition provided for the county ; and that Mr. Hastings, then sheriff, under pretence of bringing with him a guard to attend the judges at the assizes, resolved to secure the said magazine for the King's use ; they made choice of officers for three companies of foot, impowering them to raise the said companies for the defence of the said magazine. The captains nominated to this employment were one Major Grey, Dr. Bastwick, and one of my brothers, who having been for some time in the service of the States of Holland, was newly returned to England. These three having received their commissions

from the Parliament, went to Leicester, in order to raise
their companies; which they had not fully effected, when
the King with all his cavalry, consisting of about two
thousand horse, arrived at Leicester; against whom three
companies being no way sufficient to defend the town, they
resolved only to secure that place where the magazine lay:
but that not being large enough to receive more than one
company, the three captains cast lots whose part it should
be to defend it; which falling upon Major Grey, the other
two dispersed their men, and set forwards for London, but
had not rode many miles when they were seized by a party
of horse, which the King commanded the sheriff to send
after them, who brought them back to Leicester, from
whence they were removed to York, where they were kept
in the common gaol, and very cruelly treated. These were
the first prisoners taken on either side[1]. The magazine by
capitulation was dispersed into several parts of the county,
as properly belonging to them.

The Parliament, that they might leave no means unattempted to perswade the King to return to them, sent
down propositions, directing their commissioners at York to
deliver them to him: and because much of the intentions
of the Parliament appear in the said proposals, and for that
they were in effect the principal foundation of the ensuing
war, I conceive it will not be amiss to recite them in this
place, as they were agreed on by both Houses the second

---

[1] The King came to Leicester July 22, and Bastwick and Ludlow were seized the same day. See Susanna Bastwick's petition, Fifth Report Hist. MSS. Comm. p. 42. A letter of Sir Ed. Nicholas to Sir T. Roe says: 'Dr. Bastwick, Sir Henry Ludlow's son, and two other famous firebrands of this state, who had attended the Parliament Committee, and were stealing away secretly after them, provided of buff-coats and long pistols, were there discovered, laid fast, and ordered to be brought safe to York Castle. The magazine, awhile since conveyed from Leicester by the Earl of Stamford to his house, was delivered up to the King on Monday, and then distributed into confidential hands.' Cal. S. P. Dom. 1641-3, p. 363. Robert Ludlow referred to was the second son of Sir Henry, born 1621, matriculated at Magdalen College, Oxford, 12 July, 1636. A contemporary pamphlet entitled 'Truths from Leicester and Nottingham' says, 'Captain Ludlow is a stout man, with whom the King is much displeased.'

of June, 1642, with the title of their 'Humble Petition and Advice in nineteen Propositions sent to the King.'

'The most humble and most faithful subjects of your Majesty, the Lords and Commons assembled in Parliament, having nothing in their thoughts and desires more precious, and of higher esteem, after the honour and immediate service of God, than the just and faithful discharge of their duty towards your Majesty and this kingdom ; and being most sensible of the destruction and disorders, and of the imminent dangers and miseries which threaten your Majesty and subjects, the which have proceeded from the subtle informations, malicious practices, and wicked counsels of persons ill-affected to the true religion of God, to the peace and honour of your Majesty, and to the good of the commonwealth; after a serious consideration of the causes of these mischiefs, in all humility and sincerity they present to your Majesty this petition and advice, full of duty ; to the end that by your royal prudence, for the establishment of your honour and safety, and by a tender sense of the good and safety of your subjects, and your estates, you may please to consent and agree unto these humble desires and propositions, as the most necessary and most effectual means, by the blessing of the Lord, to remove the jealousies and differences that are unhappily begot between you and your people, and to procure to you and them a constant current of honour, peace and happiness.

'*Proposition* 1. That the Lords and all others of your Majesty's Privy Council, and such other Chief Officers of State, as well within the kingdom as on the other side of the sea, be put out of all offices and employments, except such as the two Houses of Parliament shall approve ; and that those who shall be put into their places shall be approved by Parliament ; and that those of the Council shall take an oath for the due execution of their charge in such form as the Parliament shall agree.

'2. That the great affairs of the kingdom shall not be

concluded nor passed by the advice of private persons, nor by any counsellors unknown, or that shall not have taken oath ; but that such matters as concern the publick, and are proper for the High Court of Parliament, that is your Majesty's great and supreme Council, shall be debated, resolved, and passed in Parliament, and there only ; and those who shall presume to do any thing to the contrary, shall be subject to the censure and judgment of the Parliament : and other matters of State that are proper for the Privy Council of your Majesty, shall be debated and concluded by the nobles, and others who shall be chosen for that end, from time to time, by the two Houses of Parliament ; and that every publick Act that concerns the affairs of the kingdom, and shall be agreed by the Council, shall be esteemed of no force, and as not proceeding from the royal authority, if at least the greatest part of your Council have not consented thereunto, and signed the same ; and that your Council shall be brought to a certain number that shall not exceed twenty five, nor be under fifteen ; and if it happen that any counsellor's place becomes void during the intervals of Parliament, it shall be supplied by the plurality of voices of those of your Council, which shall be either confirmed or voided at the first sessions of Parliament.

' 3. That the Lord High Steward of England, the Great Constable, the Chancellor, the Keepers of the Seals, the Great Treasurer, the Keeper of the Privy Seal, the Earl Marshal, the Admiral, the Governour of the Cinque-Ports, the Lieutenant of Ireland, the Chancellor of the Exchequer, the Master of the Court of Wards, the Secretaries of State, the two Chief Justices, and the Chief Baron, shall be chosen with the approbation of the two Houses of Parliament, and in the intervals of Parliament by the major part of the Privy Council, with the condition above mentioned in the choice of the counsellors of State.

' 4. That the Governour of the children of the King shall be chosen with the approbation of Parliament ; and in the intervals of Parliament in the manner before mentioned ;

and of the servants that are already about them, the Parliament shall change such as they think fit.

' 5. That the children of the King shall not marry without the advice of the Parliament ; and those who shall be employed therein without their knowledg, shall be punished by the Parliament.

' 6. That the laws against Popish recusants shall be put in effectual execution, and that those of them who are prisoners, shall not be set at liberty without giving good security.

' 7. That Papists shall have no vote in Councils, and that their children shall be brought up in the Protestant Religion.

' 8. That the Parliament shall reform the Liturgy and the Government of the Church, as they shall think fit, with the advice of divines : That your Majesty shall assist to put a stop to innovations, to expel suspicious and scandalous ministers, and for the countenancing of a godly and preaching ministry throughout the nation.

' 9. That it will please your Majesty to content yourself with the Order that the Parliament hath established in the Militia, until an Act be agreed on for that purpose ; and that your Majesty will recal the Declarations and Proclamations against the Orders given therein by the Parliament.

' 10. That every Member of Parliament that hath been put out of his employment or office, shall be re-established, or satisfaction given him.

' 11. That the Privy Counsellors and Judges shall take such oath as shall be agreed on by Parliament, for the doing of justice, and observing the statutes that shall be agreed on by this Parliament ; and that report be made every Session of Parliament, of the evil administration of justice.

' 12. That all officers shall enjoy their places so long, and no longer, than they behave themselves well therein.

' 13. That all persons shall be subject to the justice of the Parliament, even altho they remove themselves beyond the seas.

'14. That the amnesty accorded by your Majesty shall have such exceptions therein as the Parliament shall think fit.

'15. That the fortresses of the kingdom shall have Governours of the choice of your Majesty, yet of the approbation of the Parliament, and in the intervals of Parliament as is afore said.

'16. That the extraordinary guard that your Majesty hath at present about you, may be discharged, and that for the time to come you will raise no such extraordinary guards, but according to law, in case of actual rebellion or invasion.

'17. That it will please your Majesty to confirm your Leagues with the United Provinces, and other Princes of the Protestant religion, that you may be the more capable to defend it against Popish attempts ; which will bring much reputation to your Majesty, and encourage your subjects to endeavour in a parliamentary way to re-establish your sister and her children, and other princes, oppressed for the same cause.

'18. That it will please your Majesty to clear, by an Act of Parliament, the Lord Kimbolton, and the five Members of the House of Commons, so that future Parliaments may be secured against the consequence of such ill examples.

'19. That it will please your Majesty of your Grace to pass an Act, that the Peers created hereafter shall have no place nor voice in Parliament, at least unless they are admitted thereunto by the Parliament.

'These humble requests being granted unto us by your Majesty, we shall endeavour, as we ought, to regulate the revenue of your Majesty, and to increase it more and more, in such sort, that it shall support the dignity royal with honour and abundance, beyond whatever the subjects of this kingdom have allowed to their kings your Majesty's predecessors. We will put also the town of Hull into such hands as your Majesty shall please, with the approbation of the Parliament, and will give a good account of the

1642 munitions of war, and of the magazine. And to conclude, we shall chearfully do our endeavours to give unto your Majesty testimony of our affection, duty and faithfulness, to preserve and maintain your royal honour, the greatness and safety of your Majesty, and of your posterity.'

These propositions were delivered to the King by the commissioners of the Parliament, but without success, he being resolved to steer another course, presuming he might obtain as good terms as these, if reduced to the last extremity; and that if his arms succeeded according to his hopes, his will might pass for a law, pursuant to the opinion of those who thought no way so likely to render his authority absolute, as the making of a war upon his people. And now the fire began to break out in the west; Sir John Stawell and others drawing a party together in Somersetshire for the King, where Captain Preston and others opposed

Aug. 4. them; and about Martials Elm on Polden-Hill some of those who declared for the Parliament were killed [1]. Whereupon the Parliament ordered some horse to be raised, which they sent down under the command of the Earl of Bedford, to protect their friends in those parts. By which means the enemy being forced to quit the field, betook themselves to the Castle of Sherburn in Dorsetshire, which after a short siege was surrendred to the Parliament. Portsmouth was also secured for the Parliament by the young Lord Goring,

Aug. 2. then Governour thereof; but he afterwards declaring for

Sept. 7. the King, it was besieged and reduced by their forces, and the government of it entrusted to Sir William Lewis [2].

[1] On the first skirmishes in Somersetshire see Mr. Emanuel Green's paper on the Civil War in Somerset, in the Somersetshire Archaeological and Natural History Society's Proceedings for 1867.

[2] Sherborne siege was abandoned on account of the desertion of the Parliamentary troops, Sept. 6, 1642. Hist. MSS. Comm. X. vi. 147. Sherborne was subsequently taken by the Parliamentarians in April, 1643, and ordered to be demolished. Vicars, Jehovah Jireh, pp. 146, 302; C. J. It was again occupied for the King in Oct. 1644, and captured by Fairfax on Aug. 15, 1645. Walker, Historical Discourses, p. 99; Sprigge, Anglia Rediviva, p. 95. On the siege of Portsmouth and events in Somersetshire see Clarendon, v. 440; vi. 2, 32.

The King having set up his standard at Nottingham the 24th of August, 1642, the Parliament thought themselves obliged to make some preparations to defend themselves, having discovered that he had sent abroad to procure what assistance he could against his people, particularly applying himself to the King of Denmark, acquainting him, that the two Houses, to make their work sure against him, were endeavouring to prove Queen Ann a whore, and thereby illegitimate all her issue; earnestly pressing him in vindication of his injured sister, as well as in consideration of his own relation to him, to send him succours. This letter was intercepted and brought to the Parliament, who by a declaration protested that no such thing had ever entred into their thoughts[1]. The King also endeavoured, under pretence of law, to take away the lives of Dr. Bastwick and Captain Robert Ludlow, for acting in obedience to the commands of the Parliament; and had proceeded to their execution, had not the Parliament by a message sent to Judg Heath, and delivered to him on the bench, threatned a retaliation, by executing two for one in case they went on, which put a stop to that design[2].

---

[1] On the relations of Charles I. with the King of Denmark see Mr. Macray's report on the Danish Archives in the Forty-seventh Report of the Dep.-Keeper of Public Records. The King's instructions to Col. Cochrane contain the statement above referred to. They are printed in the 'King's Cabinet Opened,' with the letters taken at Naseby. See also Gardiner, Great Civil War, i. 45.

[2] The declaration of Parliament concerning Ludlow and Bastwick, dated Aug. 11, 1642, is printed in L. J. v. 283. Ludlow seems to confuse it with the similar declaration of Dec. 17, 1642, on behalf of Clifton, Catesby, Lilburne, and Vivers, in which Heath is threatened by name. Husbands' Collection, 802. Efforts were made to obtain their release. 'I shall do my best for the relief of Mr. Bastwick and Captain Ludlow,' writes Sir John Hotham to the Speaker, March 17, 1643, 'and shall send to-day a trumpeter to offer any two officers we have in exchange for them. They have heretofore insisted on the release of Commissary Windham for them, which I cannot agree to, as he is such a man that they have few like him.' (Report on the Portland MSS. i. 103.) Ludlow died in prison. Bastwick was exchanged in Oct. 1644, for Col. Huddleston. Vicars, Burning Bush, p. 44. Bastwick gives an account of his captivity in his 'Utter Routing of the Whole Army of the Independents and Sectaries,' 1646, p. 653.

The Parliament having passed the following votes,

1. That the King seduced by evil counsel, intends to levy war against the Parliament;

2. That when the King doth levy war against the Parliament, he breaks his trust, and doth that which tends to the dissolution of the Parliament;

3. That whosoever shall assist him in such a war, are traitors, and shall be proceeded against accordingly;

prepared for the raising of an army, and published several declarations, inviting the good people of England to assist them with their prayers, persons, and purses, to carry on this war, which they were necessitated to enter into for the defence of the religion, laws, liberties, and Parliament of England. The protestation taken by both Houses, and by them proposed to the people, to stand by each other in their just and necessary undertaking, was readily and chearfully taken by many in London and elsewhere; and divers hundreds on horseback from the counties of Buckingham, Hartford and Essex, came up with their several petitions, acknowledging the care and faithfulness of the Parliament in the discharge of their trust, and promising to stand by them in the carrying on of what they had declared for.

Declarations were also set forth by the two Houses, encouraging the people to provide horses and arms, and to bring in plate and money for their necessary defence, engaging the credit of the publick for the reimbursement of what should be so advanced. Which contributions arising to the value of a great sum, they declared their intentions of raising a certain number of horse and foot, with a July 12. proportionable train of artillery, and voted the Earl of Essex to be their general; whom the King (to take him off from the publick interest) had lately made Chamberlain of his houshold. Upon the same account he had also preferred the Lord Say to be Master of the Court of Wards, and Mr. Oliver St. Johns to be his Solicitor General. But this could not corrupt the Earl of Essex, nor hinder him from discharging vigorously that trust which the Parliament had reposed in him[1]. Divers of the Lords and Commons engaged their lives with him, and under him : of the Lords, the Earl of Bedford, who was General of the Horse, the Lord Peterborough, the Lord Willoughby of Parham, the Lord Denbigh, the Lord St. John, the Lord Rochford ; and of the Commons, Mr. Hampden and Mr. Hollis, who raised regiments ; Sir Philip Stapylton, who commanded the Earl of Essex's guard, and Mr. Oliver Cromwell, who commanded a troop of horse, and divers others. The Earl of Northumberland, who was High Admiral, staid with the Parliament. The Earl of Warwick, whom they made Vice-Admiral, kept the greatest part of the fleet in obedience to them.

Things being brought to this extremity, the nation was driven to a necessity of arming in defence of the laws, openly and frequently violated by the King ; who had made it the chief business of his reign to invade the rights and privileges of the people, raising taxes by various arts without their consent in Parliament ; encouraging and preferring a formal and superstitious clergy, discouraging the sober and vertuous amongst them ; imposing upon all the inventions of men in the room of the institutions of God : and knowing that Parliaments were the most likely means to rectify what was amiss, to give a check to his ambition, and to punish the principal instruments of that illegal power which he had assumed, had endeavoured either to prevent their meeting, or to render them fruitless to the people, and only serviceable to his corrupt ends, by granting him money to carry on his pernicious designs : a Parliament being now called, and an act passed, authorizing them to sit till they should think fit to dissolve themselves : and it being manifest to them, and to all those who had any concern for the happiness of the nation, that the King would do nothing effectually to redress the present, or to secure the people from future mischiefs ;

---

[1] Essex had been appointed Lord Chamberlain in place of the Earl of Pembroke in July, 1641. The King ordered Falkland to require his resignation, by letter dated April 9, 1642. He resigned accordingly on April 12. Clarendon, Rebellion, v. 31–35.

chusing rather to contend with them by arms, than for their satisfaction to entrust the Militia in faithful hands ; resolving to impose that by the force of his arms which he could not do by the strength of his arguments : I thought it my duty, upon consideration of my age and vigorous constitution, as an English-man, and an invitation to that purpose from my father, to enter into the service of my country, in the army commanded by the Earl of Essex under the authority of the Parliament [1]. I thought the justice of that cause I had engaged in to be so evident, that I could not imagine it to be attended with much difficulty. For tho I supposed that many of the clergy, who had been the principal authors of our miseries, together with some of the courtiers, and such as absolutely depended upon the King for their subsistence, as also some foreigners, would adhere to him ; yet I could not think that many of the people, who had been long oppressed with heavy burdens, and now with great difficulty had obtained a Parliament, composed of such persons as were willing to run all hazards to procure a lasting settlement for the nation, would be either such enemies to themselves, or so ungrateful to those they had trusted, as not to stand by them to the utmost of their power : at least (tho some might not have so much resolution and courage as to venture all with them, yet) that they would not be so treacherous and unworthy, to strengthen the hands of the enemy against those who had the laws of God, nature and reason, as well as those of the land on their side. Soon after my engagement in this cause, I met with Mr. Richard Fynes, son to the Lord Say [2], and Mr. Charles

---

[1] Ludlow was born in 1617, and was, therefore, about twenty-five when the war broke out. His father, Sir Henry Ludlow, was member for Wiltshire. On May 7, 1642, he was censured by the Speaker for saying openly in the course of a debate on one of the King's messages that the King was not fit to govern. In subsequent messages the King complains that this speech was not severely punished. Clarendon, Rebellion, v. 280. This is referred to in a Royalist satire, entitled ' The Sense of the House '—

' Who speaks of peace, quoth Ludlow,
   hath neither sense nor reason,
For I ne'er spoke i' th' House but once,
   and then I spoke high treason.'

[2] Richard Fiennes, fourth son of William first Viscount Say and Sele. Collins, Peerage, ed. Brydges, vii. 22.

Fleetwood, son to Sir Miles Fleetwood then a member of the House of Commons[1]; with whom consulting, it was resolved by us to assemble as many young gentlemen of the Inns of Court, of which we then were, and others, as should be found disposed to this service, in order to be instructed together in the use of arms, to render our selves fit and capable of acting in case there should be occasion to make use of us. To this end we procured a person experienced in military affairs to instruct us in the use of arms; and for some time we frequently met to exercise at the Artillery-Ground in London. And being informed that the Parliament had resolved to raise a life-guard for the Earl of Essex, to consist of a hundred gentlemen, under the command of Sir Philip Stapylton, a Member of Parliament[2], most of our company entred themselves therein, and made up the greatest part of the said guard; amongst whom were Mr. Richard Fynes, Mr. Charles Fleetwood, afterwards Lieutenant General, Major General Harrison[3], Colonel Nathanael Rich[4], Colonel Thomlinson, Colonel Twisleton, Colonel Bosewell, Major Whitby, and my self, with divers others. It was not long before the army under the command of the Earl of Essex was raised, and ready to march; so cheerfully did the people, hoping that the time of their deliverance was come, offer their persons and all that was necessary for the carrying on of that work. The appearance for the King was not very considerable whilst he continued at York; but when he removed to Shrewsbury, great numbers out of Wales and the adjacent parts resorted to him. The Earl of Essex having notice that the King directed his march that way, advanced with his army towards Worcester; and upon his approach to that town

Sept. 20.

---

[1] Charles Fleetwood was the third son of Miles Fleetwood, of Aldwinkle, Northamptonshire, and was admitted to Gray's Inn, Nov. 30, 1638. D. N. B. xix. 261.

[2] Member for Boroughbridge; d. 1647.

[3] Thomas Harrison, b. 1616, son of Richard Harrison, sometime mayor of Newcastle-under-Lyme, was not a member of any of the Inns of Court, but clerk to Thomas Houlker, an attorney.

[4] Nathaniel Rich, son and heir of Robert Rich, of Felstead, Essex, admitted to Gray's Inn, Aug. 13, 1639.

received advice, that a detachment commanded by Prince Rupert had possessed themselves of it for the King; and that a party of ours, impatient of delay, had engaged the enemy before our general could come up, with great disadvantage, as I afterwards observed upon view of the place. Ours consisted of about a thousand horse and dragoons, the enemy being more in number, and drawn up in a body, within musquet-shot of a bridg between Parshot and Worcester, over which our men resolved to march and attack them; but before half their number was got over, not being able to advance above eight or ten abreast by reason of a narrow lane through which they were to pass, till they came within pistol-shot of the enemy, they were engaged, and forced to retreat in disorder, tho they did as much as could well be expected from them upon so disadvantageous a ground. Some were killed upon the place; amongst whom was Major Gunter, a very gallant man, who, as I have heard, had endeavoured to disswade them from that attempt; others were drowned, and divers taken prisoners; of the last was Colonel Sands, who commanded the party, and was carried to Worcester, where, being mortally wounded, he soon died, with all possible expressions of his hearty affection to the publick cause[1]. The body of our routed party returned in great disorder to Parshot, at which place our life-guard was appointed to quarter that night; where, as we were marching into the town, we discovered horsemen riding very hard towards us with drawn swords, and many of them without hats, from whom we understood the particulars of our loss, not without improvement by reason of the fear with which they were possessed, telling us, that the enemy was hard by in pursuit of them: whereas it afterwards appeared, they came not within four miles of that place. Our life-guard being for

---

[1] On this skirmish see Gardiner, Great Civil War, i. 35; Webb, Civil War in Herefordshire, i. 144; Clarendon, Rebellion, vi. 43. Vicars and Rushworth give Sept. 22 as its date, but the letters of Lord Falkland and Nehemiah Wharton fix Sept. 23. Gunter was not killed at Worcester, but at Chalgrove, in the following year. See the Earl of Essex's letter to the Speaker, June 19, 1643.

the most part strangers to things of this nature, were much
alarm'd with this report; yet some of us, unwilling to give
credit to it till we were better informed, offered our selves
to go out upon a further discovery of the matter. But our
captain, Sir Philip Stapylton, not being then with us, his
lieutenant, one Bainham, an old souldier [1] (a generation of
men much cried up at that time), drawing us into a field,
where he pretended we might more advantageously charge
if there should be occasion, commanded us to wheel about;
but our gentlemen not yet well understanding the difference
between wheeling about, and shifting for themselves, their
backs being now towards the enemy, whom they thought
to be close in the rear, retired to the army in a very dishonourable manner, and the next morning rallied at the
head-quarters, where we received but cold welcome from
the general, as we well deserved [2]. The night following
the enemy left Worcester, and retreated to Shrewsbury,
where the King was; upon which the Earl of Essex advanced to Worcester, where he continued with the army
for some time, expecting an answer to a message sent by
him to the King from the Parliament, inviting him to
return to London. This time the King improved to compleat and arm his men; which when he had effected, he
began his march, the Earl of Essex attending him to observe
his motions: and after a day or two, on Sunday morning,
the 23d of October, 1642, our scouts brought advice that
the enemy appeared, and about nine aclock some of their
troops were discovered upon Edge-hill in Warwickshire.
Upon this our forces, who had been order'd that morning
to their quarters to refresh themselves, having had but little
rest for eight and forty hours, were immediately counter-

---

[1] Adam Baynard. Peacock, Army
Lists, 2nd ed. p. 26.

[2] Nehemiah Warton thus describes
the conduct of the life-guards: ' Even
our general's troop of gentlemen,
going to quarter themselves about
the country, were betrayed and beset
by the enemy, and, overmuch tim-
orous, immediately fled so confusedly
that some brake their horses' necks,
others their own; some were taken,
others slain, and scarce half of them
escaped; which is such a blot on
them as nothing but some desperate
exploit will wipe off.' Cal. S. P.
Dom. 1641-3, p. 393.

manded. The enemy drew down the hill, and we into the field near Keinton [1]. The best of our field-pieces were planted upon our right wing, guarded by two regiments of foot, and some horse. Our general having commanded to fire upon the enemy, it was done twice upon that part of the army wherein, as it was reported, the King was. The great shot was exchanged on both sides for the space of an hour or thereabouts. By this time the foot began to engage, and a party of the enemy being sent to line some hedges on our right wing, thereby to beat us from our ground, were repulsed by our dragoons without any loss on our side. The enemy's body of foot, wherein the King's standard was, came on within musquet-shot of us; upon which we observing no horse to encounter withal, charged them with some loss from their pikes, tho very little from their shot; but not being able to break them, we retreated to our former station, whither we were no sooner come, but we perceived that those who were appointed to guard the artillery were marched off: and Sir Philip Stapylton, our captain, wishing for a regiment of foot to secure the cannon, we promised to stand by him in defence of them, causing one of our servants to load and level one of them, which he had scarce done, when a body of horse appeared advancing towards us from that side where the enemy was. We fired at them with case-shot, but did no other mischief save only wounding one man through the hand, our gun being overloaded, and planted on high ground; which fell out very happily, this body of horse being of our own army, and commanded by Sir William Balfour, who with great resolution had charged into the enemy's quarters, where he had nailed several pieces of their cannon, and was then retreating to his own party, of which the man who was shot in the hand was giving us notice by holding it up; but we did not discern it. The Earl of Essex

---

[1] On the battle of Edgehill, and on the value of the different contemporary narratives of it, see Gardiner, Great Civil War, i. 51, and also two papers by Mr. W. T. Arnold and Col. Ross in the English Historical Review, 1887, pp. 136, 533.

order'd two regiments of foot to attack that body which
we had charged before, where the King's standard was,
which they did, but could not break them till Sir William
Balfour at the head of a party of horse charging them in
the rear, and we marching down to take them in flank,
they brake and ran away towards the hill [1]. Many of them
were killed upon the place, amongst whom was Sir Edward
Varney the King's standard-bearer, who, as I have heard
from a person of honour, engaged on that side, not out
of any good opinion of the cause, but from the sense of
a duty which he thought lay upon him, in respect of his
relation to the King. Mr. Herbert of Glamorganshire,
Lieutenant Colonel to Sir Edward Stradling's regiment,
was also killed, with many others that fell in the pursuit.
Many colours were taken, and I saw Lieutenant Colonel
Middleton, then a reformade in our army, displaying the
King's standard which he had taken : but a party of horse
coming upon us, we were obliged to retire with our
standard ; and having brought it to the Earl of Essex,
he delivered it to the custody of one Mr. Chambers, his
secretary, from whom it was taken by one Captain Smith,
who, with two more, disguising themselves with orange-
colour'd scarfs, (the Earl of Essex's colour) and pretending
it unfit that a penman should have the honour to carry the
standard, took it from him, and rode with it to the King,
for which action he was knighted [2]. Retreating towards our
army, I fell in with a body of the King's foot, as I soon
perceived ; but having passed by them undiscovered, I met
with Sir William Balfour's troop, some of whom who knew
me not would have fired upon me, supposing me to be

---

[1] This body was the royal foot-
guards, known as 'the red regiment'
commanded by the Earl of Lindsey.
Clarendon confirms Ludlow's account
of Sir *Edmund* Verney's motives.
Life, ii. 66.

[2] Sir John Smith, the saviour of
the royal standard, was killed in the
battle of Cheriton, March 29, 1644.
A life of Smith published in 1644,

'Brittannicæ Virtutis Imago,' gives
a different account of his exploit.
Smith 'had afterwards a large medal
of gold given him, with the king's
picture on the one side and the
banner on the other, which he always wore to his dying day, in a
large green watered ribband, cross
his shoulders.' Bulstrode, Memoirs,
p. 83.

an enemy, had they not been prevented, and assured of the contrary by Mr. Francis Russell, who with ten men well mounted and armed, which he maintained, rode in the life-guard, and in the heat of the pursuit had lost sight of them, as I myself had also done [1].

I now perceived no other engagement on either side, only a few great guns continued to fire upon us from the enemy : but towards the close of the day we discovered a body of horse marching from our rear on the left of us under the hedges, which the life-guard (whom I had then found) having discovered to be the enemy, and re-solving to charge them, sent to some of our troops that stood within musquet-shot of us to second them ; which though they refused to do, and we had no way to come at them but through a gap in the hedg, we advanced towards them, and falling upon their rear, killed divers of them, and brought off some arms. In which attempt being dis-mounted, I could not without great difficulty recover on horse-back again, being loaded with cuirassier's arms, as the rest of the guard also were. This was the right wing of the King's horse commanded by Prince Rupert, who, taking advantage of the disorder that our own horse had put our foot into, who had opened their ranks to secure them in their retreat, pressed upon them with such fury, that he put them to flight. And if the time which he spent in pursuing them too far, and in plundering the wagons, had been em-ployed in taking such advantages as offered themselves in the place where the fight was, it might have proved more serviceable to the carrying on of the enemy's designs. The night after the battle our army quartered upon the same ground that the enemy fought on the day before. No man nor horse got any meat that night, and I had touched none since the Saturday before, neither could I find my servant

[1] Probably Francis Russell, son of Sir William Russell, bart., of Chippenham, admitted to Gray's Inn, 15 Aug. 1633. He afterwards re-presented the county of Cambridge in the Long Parliament (1645), and was one of Cromwell's lords. Noble, House of Cromwell, ii. 407. White-lock met Russell on the march 'with twelve of his servants in scarlet cloaks, well horsed and armed.' Memorials, i. 183.

who had my cloak, so that having nothing to keep me warm but a sute of iron, I was obliged to walk about all night, which proved very cold by reason of a sharp frost.

Towards morning our army having received a reinforcement of Colonel Hampden's and several other regiments, to the number of about four thousand men [1], who had not been able to join us sooner, was drawn up ; and about daylight we saw the enemy upon the top of the hill: so that we had time to bury our dead, and theirs too if we thought fit. That day was spent in sending trumpeters to enquire whether such as were missing on both sides were killed, or prisoners. Those of ours taken by the enemy were the Lord St. Johns, who was mortally wounded, and declared at his death a full satisfaction and cheerfulness to lay down his life in so good a cause ; Colonel Walton, a member of Parliament, and Captain Austin an eminent merchant in London ; of whom the last died through the hard usage he received in the gaol at Oxford, to which he was committed [2]. It was observed that the greatest slaughter on our side was of such as ran away, and on the enemy's side of those that stood ; of whom I saw about threescore lie within the compass of threescore yards upon the ground whereon that brigade fought in which the King's standard was. We took prisoners the Earl of Lindsey, General of the King's army, who died of his wounds ; Sir Edward Stradling, and Colonel Lunsford, who were sent to Warwick-Castle. That night the country brought in some provisions ; but when I got meat I could scarce eat it, my jaws for want of use having almost lost their natural faculty.

Our army was now refreshed, and masters of the field ; and having received such a considerable addition of strength as I mentioned before, we hoped that we should have pursued the enemy, who were marching off as fast as

[1] The reinforcements were the regiments of Cols. Hampden and Grantham, with 11 troops of horse, left behind to guard the train. May, Long Parliament, ed. 1854, p. 257.

[2] For characters of Lord St. John and the Earl of Lindsey, see Clarendon, Rebellion, vi. 90, 93. On Captain George Austin, see C. J. iii. 320, 366.

1642

they could, leaving only some troops to face us upon the top of the hill : but instead of that, for what reason I know not, we marched to Warwick ; of which the enemy having notice, sent out a party of horse under Prince Rupert, who on Tuesday night fell into the town of Keinton, where our sick and wounded souldiers lay, and after they had cruelly murdered many of them, returned to their army. The King, as if master of the field, marched to Banbury, and summoned it ; and tho about a thousand of our men were in the town, yet pretending it not to be sufficiently

Oct. 27.

provided for a siege, they surrendred it to him. From

Oct. 29.

thence the King went to Oxford, and our army after some refreshment at Warwick returned to London, not like men that had obtained a victory, but as if they had been beaten. The Parliament ordered them to be recruited ;

Nov. 3.

and about the same time sent to the King, who was advanced with part of his army to Maidenhead, or thereabouts, to assure him of their earnest desire to prevent the effusion of more blood, and to procure a right understanding between his Majesty and them. The King in his answer, which was brought by Sir Peter Killegrew, professed to desire nothing more, and that he would leave no means unattempted for the effecting thereof. Upon which answer the Parliament thought themselves secure, at least against any sudden attempt : but the very next day the King taking the advantage of a very thick mist, marched his army within half a mile of Brentford before he was discovered, designing to surprize our train of artillery, (which was then at Hammersmith) the Parliament, and City ; which he had certainly done, if two regiments of foot and a small party of horse that lay at Brentford had

Nov. 12.

not with unspeakable courage opposed his passage, and stopt the march of his army most part of the afternoon [1] : during which time the army that lay quarter'd in and about London drew together ; which some of them, and particularly the life-guard, had opportunity the sooner to do, being at that very time drawn into Chelsey-fields to

[1] Gardiner, Great Civil War, i. 67 ; Clarendon, Rebellion, vi. 134.

muster, where they heard the vollies of shot that passed
between the enemy and our little party; the dispute continued for some hours, till our men were encompassed
quite round with horse and foot; and then being overpower'd with numbers on every side, many brave and
gallant men having lost their lives upon the place, the rest
chusing rather to commit themselves to the mercy of the
water, than to those who were engaged in so treacherous
a design, leap'd into the river, where many officers and
private souldiers were drowned, and some taken prisoners.
However the enemy's design was by this means defeated,
and they discouraged from any farther attempt that night.
The Parliament also were alarm'd in such a manner with
the danger and treachery of this enterprize, that they
used all possible diligence to bring their forces together,
so that by eight of the clock the next morning we had a
body of twenty thousand horse and foot drawn up upon
Turnham-green, a mile on this side Brentford: those of
ours also that lay at Kingston were marching to us by
the way of London. The enemy drew out a party of
theirs towards the hill at Acton, which we attacked,
and forced to retire in disorder to their main body. And
here again, in the opinion of many judicious persons, we
lost, as at Edge-hill before, a favourable opportunity of
engaging the enemy with great advantage, our numbers
exceeding theirs, and their reputation being utterly lost
in the last attempt. But the Earl of Holland and others,
pretending to encourage our army by their presence,
made use of their time to disswade the Earl of Essex
from fighting till the rest of our forces arrived; magni-
fying the power of the enemy to him, and thereby giving
them an opportunity to draw off their forces and artillery towards Kingston, which they did as fast as they could, leaving
only a body of horse to face us between the two Brent-
fords, the rest having secured themselves by a timely
retreat: upon this party some of our great guns, guarded
by a regiment of foot, were, towards the evening, ordered
to be fired. The life-guard was drawn up in the high-

1642

Nov. 13.

ways to secure our foot from any attempt of horse that might be made upon them; which some great men, who pretended a resolution to fight in that troop, blamed, charging the advisers thereof with rashness, in hazarding them in such a pound, where they must inevitably be cut off, if the enemy should advance upon them. But I fear this great care was only counterfeit, and that those persons well knew the enemy to be in a flying, and not in a charging condition, as it quickly appeared; for our cannon no sooner began to play upon them, but they retired to the main body of their army, the rear of which had by that time recovered Hounslow-heath. The enemy took up their head-quarters at Kingston, where, by the advantage of the bridg over the Thames, they hoped to be able, tho inferior in number, to defend themselves against a more numerous army, if they should be attacked, and to put in execution any design they might have upon the city or places adjacent. To prevent which our general caused a bridg of boats to be laid over the river between Putney and Battersey, which was no sooner finished but the enemy retired to Oxford by the way of Reading, which place they fortified, and placed a garison therein, a party of ours having quitted it upon their approach. Garisons were also placed by them in the towns of Newcastle upon Tyne, Chester, Worcester, and several others, as they had done before in York and Shrewsbury. Some of ours likewise had possessed themselves of Glocester, Bristol, Exeter, Southampton, Dover, and divers other places. The enemy being retired, our army advanced to Windsor, and made it our head-quarters for the most part of that winter : and so desirous was the Parliament to prevent any further effusion of blood, that notwithstanding the treacherous design of the late expedition, they again sent propositions of peace to the King at Oxford, being the same in effect with those delivered to him before at York; but they found no better reception than the others had done. I do not remember anything remarkable perform'd by either party this winter, save only an attempt of the enemy upon one of our quarters at Henly, where two regiments of foot, one of which was Major General Skippon's, then were, who being tired with a long march, and dispersed to their respective quarters, were fallen upon by a great body of the enemy that had advanced to the town's end undiscovered; but a small party of our men getting together, one of our gunners hastned to the artillery which was planted upon the avenue, fired once or twice upon them, and made so great a slaughter, especially of those officers who were at the head of their party, that they retreated in great disorder without any farther attempt [1].

Our General having notice that the enemy had a design upon Bristol, sent a party commanded by Colonel Nathanael Fines to reinforce that garison; by which means it was prevented, and some of their correspondents in the town thereupon executed.

About this time Sir Edward Hungerford having obtained the command of the forces in the county of Wilts for the Parliament, invited me to raise a troop of horse in his regiment : in order to which I attended him at the Devizes, and from thence went with him to Salisbury, where he seized some quantity of horse and arms from persons disaffected, and with them mounted and armed part of his men [2]. And I having done what was convenient at that time for the raising of my troop, returned to the headquarters at Windsor, where I gave them an account of the good condition of Colonel Fines and Sir Edward Hungerford, at which they were not a little surprized, having been made to believe that they and their troops were routed and cut in pieces by the enemy. Sir Ralph Hopton, Sir Bevil

See Vicars, Jehovah Jireh, p. 257.

A life of Sir Edward Hungerford is given in D. N. B. vol. xviii. He was member for Chippenham, one of the Parliamentary militia commissioners, and one of the persons excluded from pardon by the King in his declaration of Nov. 2, 1642. Hunger-

ford and his forces evacuated Devizes before 23 Feb. 1643. Waylen, History of Marlborough, pp. 185–187. This expedition to Salisbury seems to have taken place in Feb. 1643. Mercurius Aulicus, Feb. 13, 15, 23, 1643. Ludlow returned to Wiltshire about the end of April, after the capture of Reading.

1643   Greenvil, and others, were very active in raising forces for
the King in Cornwall, and the remote parts of Devonshire,
and had possessed themselves of Pendennis, Dartmouth, and
Barnstaple, as Colonel Ashburnham and others had done
of Weymouth in Dorsetshire.   And the Parliament had
ordered garisons to be put into Plymouth, Lyme, and Pool.
In the spring our army was master of the field, the King
making it his business to be only upon the defensive till the
Queen should arrive in England with an army to his
assistance, hoping to exhaust the treasure of the city of
London by delays, and thereby to cause them to abate their
zeal for the publick, omitting no opportunity by his emissaries to create and foment differences amongst them, endeavouring by all means to procure an insurrection for him,
to compel the Parliament to submit to such terms as he
pleased to impose.   The Earl of Essex marched with the
April 15.   army to besiege Reading, a frontier town of the King's,
which he had strongly fortify'd and garison'd.   The General
himself sat down on the north-west side, and the Lord Grey
of Wark on the south-east side of the town : the great
shot did some damage to the houses ; from one of which a
tile falling upon the head of Sir Arthur Ashton, a Papist,
and governour thereof, disabled him from executing that
charge during the rest of the siege, and Colonel Fielding
was made governour in his room.   The King thinking this
place to be of great importance to him, brought together
all the forces he could ; and marching on Causam-side in
April 25.   order to relieve it, was opposed by a small party of ours,
who taking the advantage of some ditches and pales to
shelter themselves, repulsed his men, and forced him to
April 26.   retreat to Oxford.   Upon this the town was surrendred upon
articles to the Earl of Essex, Colonel Fielding the governour
retiring to Oxford, where he was tried, and condemned to
die, but not executed.

At my coming into Wiltshire with three more of the life-
guard, two whereof were to be officers in my troop, and the
third in another troop of the same regiment, I found Sir
Edward Hungerford with the forces of Wilts, and Colonel

Stroud [1] with part of those of Somersetshire, besieging 1643
Warder Castle, before which they had been about a week,
battering it with two small pieces, whereby they had done
little other hurt save only to a chimney-piece, by a shot
entring at a window : but there being a vault on each side
of the castle, for the conveying away of filth, two or three
barrels of powder were put into one of them, and being fired,
blew up some part of it ; which with the grazing of a bullet
upon the face of one of the servants, and the threatning of
the besiegers to spring the other mine, and then to storm it,
if it was not surrendred before an hour-glass, which they had
turn'd up, was run out, so terrified the ladies therein, whereof there was a great number, that they agreed to surrender May 8.
it.   The government of this castle was entrusted to my
care by Sir Edward Hungerford, who left with me a company
of foot commanded by Captain Bean, and my own troop, to
defend it.   The Earl of Marlborough with some horse possessed himself of a house in our neighbourhood called Founthill, with a design to block us up ; but Sir Edward sent a
party of horse who fell upon him there, and obliged him to
quit it [2].   I levelled the works that had been raised during
the siege, sunk a well, broke down the vaults about the
castle, and furnished it with provisions, expecting to be
besieged, as I was soon after.   For within a fortnight after
I was possessed of it, the Lord Arundel [3], to whom it belonged, and whose father died soon after he had received May 19.

---

[1] Not William Strode, M.P. for
Beeralston, one of the five members,
d. 1645; but Col. William Strode of
Street, d. 1666.   See Mr. Emmanuel
Green's paper on the two Strodes,
read before the Somersetshire Archaeological Society in 1884.   The
royalist account of the siege of Wardour is printed in Appendix II.

[2] Founthill belonged to Lord Cottington, who wrote thence on Dec.
24, 1642, complaining that Sir Edward Hungerford had threatened to
quarter troops upon him unless he
paid £1000 to the service of the

Parliament.   The House of Lords
ordered Hungerford not to demand
money from Cottington, who, as a
peer of the realm, would be assessed
by the House, if for the service of the
Parliament. L. J. v. 517; Hist. MSS.
Comm. Rep. v. 62.

[3] Thomas second Lord Arundel of
Wardour, died at Oxford, 19 May,
1643. Collins, Peerage, ed. Brydges,
vii. 50.   The peerages state that he
was mortally wounded at the battle
of Lansdowne, July 5. 1643, con-
fusing him with his son Henry, third
lord. Clarendon, Rebellion, vii. 109.

news that it was taken, supposing to find me unprovided, came with a party of horse, and summoned me to deliver the place for his Majesty's use. Some who were with me advised me so to do ; yet I return'd the enemy answer, that I was entrusted to keep the castle for the service of the Parliament, and could not surrender it without their command. The enemy not being at that time ready to make any attempt upon us, retreated to their main body; of which tho the Marquiss of Hertford carried the name of General, that thereby the country might be encouraged to come in, yet Prince Maurice, as he had then the principal influence over them, so he was soon after placed in the head of them, as more likely to promote that arbitrary and boundless prerogative which the King endeavoured to set up over the people.

Having notice that some of the King's forces were at Salisbury, I went out with six of my troop to procure intelligence, and to do what service I could upon the enemy's straglers : when I came to Sutton, I was informed that six of them were gone up the town just before. Whereupon we made after them, and by their horses, which we saw tied in a yard, supposed them to be in the house to which it belonged : upon which I went in, and was no sooner within the door but two of them shut it upon me ; but my party rushing in, they ran out at another, and escaped : a third mounted one of my men's horses, and rid away ; the other three who were in a room of the house upon promise of quarter for life, surrendred themselves, with whom and six horses we returned to the castle.

Our army after they had possessed themselves of Reading, did nothing remarkable that summer, only there hapned some skirmishes, in one of which that most eminent patriot Col. Hampden lost his life by a shot in the shoulder. Sir William Waller commanded a party in the west, with which he did considerable service, tho it was so small that he marched for the most part in the night to conceal his weakness. He reduced Higham House, a place of strength, garisoned by the enemy, and protected the gentlemen of the country whilst they were raising forces for the Parlia-

ment. And being joined by Sir Arthur Haslerig's regiment
of horse, and the forces of Wilts, Somerset and Dorset, with
as many as could be spared from Bristol; he was become
so considerable, as to put a stop to the march of the
King's western army; which coming to the town where
my father's house was, wholly ruined it, and destroyed his
park. But upon their removal from thence, conceiving I
might take some straglers, or some way or other annoy the
enemy, I went thither the night after with about forty horse,
where tho I could hear of no men, yet I found much
provision, which a gentlewoman had obliged the people
of the town to bring together, and which she was preparing
to send to the King's army, with horses and carts ready
to carry it ; amongst which there was half a dozen pasties
of my father's venison ready baked, which, with as much
of the other provisions as we could, we carried away with
us. The two armies before mentioned engaged about   July 5.
Lansdown, where the success was doubtful a good while,
but at last ours obtained the victory. The Cornish-men
commanded by Sir Bevil Greenvil stood their ground till
they came to push of pike, but were then routed, and Sir
Bevil killed. The enemy retreated to the Devizes, and
ours pursued them. The news of this action being brought
to us, I marched out with my horse towards Warmister ;
and in the way searching the houses of some persons disaffected to the publick, we found two of our most active
enemies, whom we carried away prisoners. But the great
hopes we had conceived of enjoying some quiet in the west
by the means of this victory were soon blasted; for a body
of horse sent from Oxford not being attended by any from
our army, (tho as I have heard commanded so to do)
engaged our horse on Roundway Hill, where the over-   July 13.
forwardness of some of our party to charge the enemy upon
disadvantageous ground was the principal cause of their
defeat. The horse being routed, our foot also quitted their
ground, and shifted for themselves ; many of whom were
taken, and many killed, the rest retreated to Bristol, where
they made the best preparation they could to defend them-

1643
July 27

selves, expecting suddenly to be besieged, as it fell out. Sir William Waller with what horse he had left marched to London, where no means were omitted to recruit them.

Sept. 5.

Exeter was surrendred to the enemy upon terms, and Bristol besieged, which being stormed on one side, and ours not doing their duty, part of the enemy being entred,

July 26.

the Governour desired to capitulate, and delivered up the town upon articles, which were not well kept, in retaliation, as they pretended, for the like breach by ours at the taking of Reading. The Governour of Bristol was here-

Dec. 29.

upon tried and condemned by a court martial, how justly I know not; but the Parliament ordered the execution of the sentence to be suspended. About this time a gentle-man of the country, related to the Lord Cottington [1], desired a conference with me, wherein he endeavoured to perswade me to surrender the Castle of Warder, promising me any terms I would desire, and assuring me that several of the western gentlemen, finding our affairs desperate, had made their peace with the King, and that the Kentish men who were risen for him would be sufficient to accomplish his work, tho he had no other army. Also Colonel Robert Philips, my friend and kinsman, coming before the castle some time after with a party of horse, and desiring to speak with me, was earnest with me to the same effect : my answers to both were, that I had resolved to run all hazards in the discharge of that trust which I had undertaken [2].

[1] Mr. Plott; see pp. 62, 76, post.

[2] Ludlow's mother was Elizabeth, daughter of Richard Phelips, of Montacute, Somersetshire. Col. Robert Phelips was the second son of Sir Robert Phelips of Montacute, and matriculated at Wadham College, Oxford, Oct. 24, 1634, aged 15. Gardiner, Wadham Register, i. 116. In 1651 he played an important part in contriving the escape of Charles II from England. Clarendon, Rebellion, xii. 103. In 1656 he was at Bruges, holding the office of groom of the bed-chamber to the Duke of York. Memorials preserved in Bruges of

King Charles the Second's residence. Archaeologia, vol. xxxv. He was member for Stockbridge in 1661, and for Andover in 1685, groom of the bedchamber to Charles II, one of the commissioners of the Privy Seal in Dec. 1685, and chancellor of the Duchy of Lancaster, May 25, 1687. He died before March 21, 16$\frac{88}{89}$. See Chester, Westminster Abbey Registers, pp. 191, 229; Cal. S. P. Dom. 1660-1, p. 209; 1st Report Hist. MSS. Comm., p. 58; 3rd Report, p. 281. Some of his letters are printed in the Nicholas Papers, vol. ii.

The two Houses of Parliament, notwithstanding the 1613 many difficulties they met with at home, having sent over forces to subdue the rebels in Ireland, thought it also their duty to send recruits thither, and at the same time presented the Earl of Ormond with a jewel, as a testimony of their acceptance of his service at the battle of March 18. Rosse, where there was above forty of his own name and kindred killed upon the place, and the enemy totally routed, tho for a long time they had much the better of the day.

The Earl of Leicester having been voted Lieutenant of Ireland by the Parliament, and approved by the King, wanted nothing but his commission to begin his journey for that kingdom, which after several delays he received from the King; but being at Chester in order to take shipping, the carriages and draught-horses which lay there for that service, as also the clothes and other provisions designed by the Parliament for the souldiers in Ireland, were seized by the King's order, and made use of for his service here; whilst his agents there endeavoured to perswade the English souldiers in that country, that they were neglected by the Parliament : upon which false suggestion he prevailed with them to serve him in England against the Parliament ; and, contrary to his engagement to both Houses not to treat with the rebels without their concurrence, made a cessation with them, and brought over Sept. 15. many of them to serve in his army against the Parliament : who being encompassed with difficulties on all hands, and understanding that the Queen was landing with a con- Feb. 23. siderable strength at Bridlington Bay in the county of York, sent commissioners to treat with their friends in July 19. Scotland to march into England to their assistance.

In the mean time the King's army besieged the city of Aug. 10. Glocester, the King being there in person to countenance the siege. The besieged made a vigorous defence for about a month, during which the Parliament took care to recruit their army in order to relieve them. Their rendezvous was appointed on Hounslow Heath, whither some members of Aug. 22.

1643   Parliament (of which my father was one) were sent, to
inspect their condition, that their wants being known,
might be the better supplied; who found them a very
shatter'd and broken body: but the city being then very
affectionate to the publick, soon recruited them, and drew
forth so many of their trained bands and auxiliary regiments, as made them up a gallant army.   In their march

Sept. 15. towards Glocester some of ours fell upon a party of the
enemy at Cirencester, of whom they took many prisoners,
and seized a great quantity of provisions which they found
prepared for the enemy, who upon our approach raised

Sept. 7. the siege.   The Earl of Essex having relieved the town,
was marching back again, when he perceived the enemy
endeavouring to get between him and London; and to

Sept. 18. that end falling upon his rear with a strong party of horse,
they so disordered his men, and retarded the march of
his army, that he found himself obliged to engage them

Sept. 20. at Newbury.   The dispute was very hot on both sides,
and the enemy had the better at the first; but our men
resolving to carry their point, and the city-regiments
behaving themselves with great bravery, gave them before
night so little cause to boast, that the next morning they
were willing to permit the Earl of Essex to march to
London without interruption.   Few prisoners were taken
on either side : the enemy had several persons of quality
killed ; the principal of whom were the Earl of Carnarvon,
the Earl of Sunderland, the Lord Falkland, and a French
Marquiss.   We lost a Colonel of one of the city-regiments,
together with some inferiour officers.

Some of the Lords and Commons, contrary to their duty,
withdrew themselves from the Parliament at Westminster,
and went to the King at Oxford, where they met together,
but never did any thing considerable for the King's service,
and shewed themselves so little willing to assume the name
of a Parliament, that the King in a letter to the Queen (a
copy whereof was afterwards found amongst his papers)
called them his Mongrel Parliament.

Aug. 10.   In the mean time the Earl of Manchester received a

commission from the Parliament to raise forces in the
associated counties of Suffolk, Norfolk, Essex, Cambridg,
Huntington, &c., which was very necessary: for the King
was master of all places of strength from Berwick to Boston,
except Hull and two small castles in Lincolnshire; and
Ferdinando Lord Fairfax, not able to keep the field against
the Earl of Newcastle, was retired with his horse and foot
to Hull: the enemy's strength in the north no way inferiour
to what it was in the west, and none considerable enough
to oppose their march into the south.

The Earl of Newcastle, upon advice that the Lord
Willoughby of Parham had possessed himself of the town
of Gainsborough for the Parliament, sent his brother Col.
Cavendish, Lieutenant-General of his army, with a great
party of horse and dragoons to summon it, himself marching
after with the foot. Col. Oliver Cromwell having notice
thereof, and understanding by fresh experience that victory
is not always obtained by the greater number, having lately
defeated near Grantham twenty-four troops of the enemy's
horse and dragoons, with seven troops only which he had
with him, resolved to endeavour the relief of Gainsborough;
and with twelve troops of horse and dragoons marched
thither, where he found the enemy, who were drawn up
near the town, to be more than thrice his number, and no
way to attack them but through a gate, and up-hill; notwithstanding which disadvantages he adventured to fall
upon them, and after some dispute totally routed them,
killing many of their officers, and amongst them Lieutenant-
General Cavendish. Thus was Gainsborough relieved; but
the conquerors had little time to rejoice, for within two or
three hours the routed enemy rallying, and joining with the
rest of Newcastle's army, marched against them: upon
which they retreated to Lincoln that night in good order,
and without any loss, facing the enemy with three troops
at a time as they drew off the rest. Lincoln not being
defensible, Col. Cromwell marched the next day to Boston,
that he might join the Earl of Manchester, who with his
new-rais'd forces had very seasonably reduced Lynn, a town

in Norfolk not far from the sea, naturally strong, and might have proved impregnable, if time had favoured art and industry to have fortified and furnished it with provisions. But Sir Hammond Lestrange, who had before surprized it for the King, was soon surprized himself; and being suddenly summoned by the Earl of Manchester, and threatned with a storm, after he had fired a few great shot against the besiegers, thought fit to surrender it upon articles. From thence the Earl of Manchester marched to Boston, where being joined by Col. Cromwell, appointed by the Parliament to command under him, and a party of horse brought by Sir Thomas Fairfax by sea from Hull, he mustered about six thousand foot, and thirty-seven troops of horse and dragoons. To prevent any further addition to his forces, the Earl of Newcastle advanced with his army, and sent a strong detachment of horse and dragoons towards Boston, appearing by their standards to be eighty-seven troops, commanded by Sir John Henderson, an old souldier, who hearing that Col. Cromwell was drawn out towards him with the horse and dragoons, made haste to engage him before the Earl of Manchester with the foot could march up, as accordingly it fell out at a place called Winsby Field near Horncastle. In the first shock Col. Cromwell had his horse kill'd under him ; yet the encounter was but short, tho very sharp, for there being field-room enough, the fight lasted but a quarter of an hour before the Earl of Newcastle's forces were totally routed, and many of them killed : amongst them the Lord Widdrington, Sir Ingram Hopton, and other persons of quality. The enemy had no time to rally, being pursued by ours almost as far as Lincoln, which was fourteen miles off; in which pursuit divers of them were killed and made prisoners, and many horse and arms taken. Neither were they suffered to rest at Lincoln, the Earl of Manchester marching thither the day following, where the enemy's broken troops had endeavoured to fortify the higher part of the city called the Close, but had not quite finished their works when the Earl arrived, and summoned them to surrender ; which they refusing, our foot and horse fell on and took it by storm, with little loss on our side.

About this time a considerable party in Kent rose and declared for the King, which was dispersed by some forces sent from London, under the command of Col. Brown; whereby the committee of Kent were encouraged and enabled to raise a good body of horse and foot for the service of the Parliament[1].

My father apprehending that I was not likely to be relieved in three or four months, in case I were besieged; and knowing that the enemies were masters of the field in those parts, and that I was about twenty miles from any of our garisons, procured an order from the Parliament, impowering me to slight the Castle of Warder, and to draw off the garison, if I saw cause: which care of theirs quickned my zeal to their service, and put me upon endeavouring, as well as I could, to prepare for the worst. To that end being in want of ammunition, I went to Southampton, where I bought what they could spare, and returned to the castle; where being in great want of money, having always paid the country people for whatsoever I had from them, I made a seasonable discovery of money, plate and jewels, to the value of about twelve hundred pounds, walled up by the enemy: part of this sum I expended upon the garison, and gave an account thereof to the Parliament[2]. The enemy was now beginning to draw about us, yet would not actually besiege us before they had endeavoured to reduce us by treachery. To this end one Capt. White a Papist, of Dorsetshire, having found a boy at Shaftsbury fit for the purpose, gave him such instructions as he thought fit: he was not above twelve years of age, and yet, as I was afterwards informed, had already attempted to poison his grandfather. This boy he sent to the castle to desire of me to be admitted

[1] On the Kentish rising, see Browne's letter, 5th Report Hist. MSS. Comm., p. 97; Vicars, God's Ark, 11–18; Rushworth, v. 277.

[2] Amongst other ways of raising money, Ludlow obtained loans from royalists and granted protections in return. See the case of Thomas Bennet, Calendar of Committee for Compounding, p. 941.

to turn the spit, or perform any other servile employment ; to which I consented, his youth freeing him, as I thought, from any suspicion. About three or four days after a party of the enemy's horse appeared before the castle, and making a great shout, the cattle belonging to the garison, consisting of about forty cows and one bull, which they all followed, ran away at the noise : some of us endeavouring to turn them, the enemy fired so thick upon us, that one of my souldiers and myself were forced to betake our selves to a tree for shelter ; where my souldier levelling his musquet through a hole of the tree, which was about a foot in diameter, a ball from the enemy grazing upon the upper part of the hole, and thereby forced downwards, shot the young man through the hand, and me into the leg, which obliged me to keep my bed for two days. A great wall-gun called a *Harquebuz de Croq* being fired from the top of the castle, burst in the middle. At night as this boy was sitting with the guard by the fire, some of them conceived a jealousy of him ; and strictly examining him about the cause of his coming, he affirmed it to be because the master whom he served had used him cruelly for speaking some words in favour of the Parliament. With which answer they not being satisfied, threatned that unless he would confess the truth, they would hang him immediately ; and to afright him, tied a piece of match about his neck, and began to pull him up on a halbert. Upon this he promised to confess all, if they would spare his life ; and thereupon acknowledged that Capt. White had hired him to number the men and arms in the castle, to poison the arms, the well, and the beer, to blow up the ammunition, to steal away one of my best horses to carry him back to them ; for which service he was to receive half a crown : confessing that he had accordingly poisoned two cannon and the *Harquebuz* that was broken, but pretended that his conscience would not give him leave to poison the water and the beer. The great guns were made serviceable again by oiling, and making a fire in them. The poison he used was of a red colour, and made up in the shape of a candle, with part of which he had rubbed three of our guns [1].   After this deliverance we got in some cattle for our provision, but the enemy drawing into the villages about us, soon prevented us from bringing in any more: yet we ventured one morning, knowing it to be market-day, to draw out between forty and fifty pikes and firelocks, with which we went about a quarter of a mile from the castle upon the road that leads to Shaftsbury.   According to our expectation the market-people came with carts and horses loaded with corn and other provisions, which we seized and sent to the castle, paying for it the market-price, at which they were not a little surprized.   By this means we furnished our selves with three months' more provision than we had before; which we had no sooner taken in, when the enemy drew round the castle, and from that time blocked us up more closely, raising a breastwork by casting up of earth about a tree which we had cut down on the side of a hill; from whence they commanded the gate of the castle, the only way that we had to sally out upon occasion, and shot several of our men, amongst the rest my gunner, as they fetched in wood.   The person that commanded the party which lay before us was one Capt. Christopher Bowyer of Dorsetshire, who to get us out of the castle, proposed to grant us what terms we desired; to which we replied, that we designed to discharge our duty by keeping it as long as we could.   Upon this he threatned us with great numbers of horse and foot, attended with several pieces of cannon, which he said were drawing towards us, boasting of the justice of his cause, and representing to us the greatness of our danger, and the inevitable ruin that must ensue upon our obstinacy: but Capt. Bean, who at that time served as cannoneer, ours being shot, as I mentioned before, told him, that we were not at all afrighted with his menaces; but upon confidence of the justice of our cause, were resolved to

16,3

December.

---

[1] Poisoning a gun is also spoken of in an account of the siege of Lathom House.   Lancashire Civil War Tracts, Chetham Society, pp. 174, 178.

1643 , defend the place to the utmost; and warning him to look
to himself, fired a gun, with which he wounded him in the
heel ; and it being unsafe for any to carry him off by day,
his wound gangreened before night, and he died about two
days after. In the room of Capt. Bowyer one Col. Barnes
was sent by the King to command the forces that lay before
us : he was brother to an honest gentleman who was chaplain to my father, for whose sake, and because he had the
reputation of being an old souldier, a thing much valued by
the Parliament at that time, my father had procured him a
considerable employment in their service, in which he continued as long as their constant pay lasted, but that failing,
he ran away to the King [1]. Upon his coming he raised a
fort within musquet-shot of us, on the hill that surrounded
the castle, except only on the west side, where was a pond
of about six acres. The enemy possessed themselves of all
the out-houses, but used them only by night, not thinking
it safe to come at them by day; which we observing, one
evening conveyed forty men through a vault leading to
those houses, ordering them to lie private, and endeavour to
surprize them when they came; which had been effected,
if one of ours, contrary to order, upon the entrance of the
first of the enemy, had not fired his pistol, and thereby
given warning to the rest to shift for themselves. The man
who was the occasion of this disappointment was deprived
of the use of his arms till he should attempt something for
the redeeming of his reputation ; which soon after, upon a
sally we made on the enemy, he did, in which we took two
of the enemy's horses, and made some prisoners. How
many of them were killed we could not learn : on our side
some were wounded, of whom one died soon after.

A kinsman of mine, who was related to the Lord Cot-

---

[1] At the restoration Col. George
Barnes petitioned for the place of
Bailiff of Sandwich, and afterwards
for the command of a foot company
in Col. Norton's regiment, alleging
that he had sold his estates and
raised a regiment of 1200 foot for
the King; took Wardour Castle, and
made Col. Ludlow prisoner, but was
wounded and lost his only son before
Lyme. Since the disbanding of the
forces he had lived 13 years in exile
in Holland and Italy. Cal. State
Papers, Dom. 1660-1, pp. 240, 443.

tington, was sent from Oxford to offer me what terms I would desire. I permitted him to come in, that seeing our strength and provision, he might make his report to the enemy to our advantage: for things were so ordered by removing our guards from place to place, filling up our hogsheads with empty barrels, and covering them with beef and pork, and in like manner ordering our corn, that every thing appeared double, to what it was, to them. The substance of the conditions I proposed was: that if I understood from the Earl of Essex that he could not relieve us within six months, we would then deliver the castle, upon condition, that it should not be made a garison: that the Parliament should have two thousand pounds for what they had expended in the taking and keeping of it; with some other particulars, which the gentleman carried to Oxford with him: but we never had any return from him about them, neither indeed did we expect any. Our beer was now spent, our corn much diminished, and we had no other drink but the water of our well, which tho we drunk dry by day, yet it was sufficiently supplied every night. But being resolved to keep the castle as long as we could, we shortned our allowance, so that three pecks and a half of wheat one day, and a bushel of barley another, served near a hundred men, which was all our force, my troop being sent away before for want of conveniency for horse: this allowance was so short, that I caused one of the horses we had taken to be killed, which the souldiers eat up in two days, besides their ordinary.

The forces that had been sent by the Parliament to the assistance of the distressed Protestants in Ireland, being, under pretence that they were neglected, as hath been before mentioned, brought into England to serve against those who raised them; and the rebels, by the pacification made with them by the King's order, contrary to his promise to the Parliament, left in the full enjoyment of what they had gotten from the English by rapine and murder; part of those who came out of Ireland landed at Chester, and drew before Nantwich: they were commanded by one Capt.

Sandford[1], brother to Sir William Sandford, a worthy person of Gray's Inn, to whom he had solemnly promised never to engage against the Parliament : yet did he send in a very threatning summons to the town, and seconded it with a most furious assault, whilst the works were but slenderly defended, the guard consisting for the most part of townsmen, who were then gone to dinner : but it so happened, that a boy of the age of fifteen firing a musquet from the town, shot him dead in the place, which discouraged his souldiers from any farther attempt.

Col. George Monk, who had been sent by the Parliament into Ireland against the rebels, for some time scrupled to quit that service, and to engage in this, being upon that account secured on ship-board by the Earl of Ormond, whilst he sent those forces into England, lest he should have obstructed their going over ; yet having afterwards his liberty to wait on the King. was prevailed with to join with them, and soon after taken prisoner by a party from Yorkshire, commanded by Sir Thomas Fairfax, who sent him prisoner to Hull, from whence some time after he was conveyed to the Tower of London[2]. Another party of the forces from Ireland landed in the west, and marched as far as Hinden towards Warder Castle, in order to besiege it ; but being informed that the person whom they were to dispossess was a Protestant, and he into whose hands they were to put it was a Papist, they mutinied against their officers, and refused to be employed against us.

The Queen landed with an army of French, Walloons, and other foreigners, and brought with her great store of ammunition and money, procured by pawning the crown- jewels in Holland. With these and other forces the Earl of Newcastle marched to besiege Hull, of which place the

---

[1] Captain Thomas Sandford; see his letters in Rushworth, v. 300, 301. William Sanford, late of Barnard's Inn, son and heir of John Sanford of the city of Bristol. gent., was admitted to Gray's Inn, Feb. 2, 1618; matriculated at Lincoln College, Oxford, 10 Nov., 1615, aged 18.

[2] Monk's name is in the list of prisoners appended to Fairfax's letter. Rushworth, v. 302. He was released from his imprisonment in Nov., 1646.

Lord Ferdinando Fairfax was governour, who with the assistance of the seamen belonging to some ships that lay in the harbour, made so fierce a sally upon the enemy, that they were forced to quit some of their guns, and withdraw to a greater distance, leaving many of their men behind them, of whom some were killed, and others taken prisoners. Col. Overton carried himself, as I am well informed, with much honour and gallantry in this action. This bad success so dispirited the enemy, that they abandoned the siege, and retired to York; to which also the approach of winter, and the preparations of the Scots to march into England, did not a little contribute; for the Parliaments of both kingdoms had at length agreed upon terms, and removed the last and greatest difficulty, consisting in some doubtful words in the covenant, which was to be taken by both nations, concerning the preservation of the King's person, and reducing the doctrine and discipline of both churches to the pattern of the best reformed: for which Sir Henry Vane, one of the commissioners of the Parliament, found out an expedient, by adding to the first clause these or the like words, 'in preservation of the laws of the land, and liberty of the subject'; and to the second, 'according to the word of God[1].' Which being an explanation that could not be refused, prevented any farther contestation about that matter.

About this time the enemy by cruel usage put a period to the life of my brother Capt. Robert Ludlow, who was their prisoner, as I before related. The news of this, and of the danger I was in, so afflicted my father, together with his constant labours in the publick service, and possibly his dissatisfaction about the imprisonment of his good friend Mr. Henry Martin, for words spoken in the House, as he conceived in discharge of his duty, that he died, expressing himself deeply sensible of the condition of the bleeding nation, and heartily praying for the prosperity of the publick

---

[1] On the question of Vane's amendments to the draft of the Covenant, see Gardiner, Great Civil War, i. 271; Burnet, Lives of the Hamiltons, p. 307, ed. 1852.

cause [1]. The words spoken by Mr. Martin in the Parliament were to this purpose, ' That it was better one family should perish, than that the people should be destroyed ': and being required to explain himself, he ingenuously confessed that he meant the family of the King ; for which he was com-

Aug. 16. mitted to the Tower, but afterwards released, and re-admitted

1645 to his place in the Parliament. About the same time
Jan. 5. Mr. John Pym also died, who had been very instrumental

1643 in promoting the interest of the nation : his body was for
Dec. 8. several days exposed to publick view in Derby-house before it was interred, in confutation of those who reported it to be eaten with lice.

The enemy before Warder Castle kept their guards within pistol-shot of it day and night, so that we could not expect any more intelligence from abroad ; yet one of ours sent by us into the country a week before, to inform us of the state of affairs, met, at an honest man's house not far from the castle, a souldier, whom the enemy had pressed to serve them ; whose heart being with us, these two agreed, that when relief should be coming, he who was without should appear with a white cap on his head, and blow his nose with his handkerchief. In the mean time the besiegers raised a battery, and by a shot from thence cut off the chain of our portcullis, which rendering our gate unserviceable to us, we made it so to them, by barricading it up on the inside : so that now we had no way out but through a window, our other doors being walled up before. But the battery not answering their expectation, they resolved to try other experiments, either by digging a hole in the castle-wall, and putting a sufficient quantity of powder therein to blow it up, or by undermining the said wall, and supporting it with timber, and then setting it on fire : whereby they supposed

[1] Sir Henry Ludlow, Knt., born at Maiden Bradley, 1592 ; matriculated at Brasenose College, Oxford, Oct. 16, 1607, aged 15 ; graduated as B.A., Feb. 6, 1609 ; High Sheriff of Wilts, 1633 ; M.P., 1640. Died intestate ; buried at St. Andrew's, Holborn, Nov. 1, 1643. He married Elizabeth, daughter of Richard Phelips, of Montacute, Somerset. Her will is dated May 18, 1660, proved at London, Jan. 19, 166?. She was buried at St. Andrew's, Holborn, Nov. 6, 1660.

to destroy that also on which the wall rested, and so to 1643
bring down the wall. In order to this they prepared
materials to defend them whilst they were about the work,
and brought together about two dozen of oaken planks three
inches thick, which they endeavoured in a dark night to set
up against the castle-wall, half of them on one side, and half
on the other. Our sentinels discovered them on one side,
and beat them off, forcing them to leave their boards behind
them. On the other side they set them up, and in the
morning were hard at work under their shelter. We heard
a noise of digging, but for some time could not perceive
where : at length we discovered the place, and endeavoured
to remove them, by throwing down hot water and melted
lead, tho to little purpose. At last with hand-granadoes we
obliged them to quit their work, and to leave their tools behind
them, with their provisions for three or four days : and tho
we had no way out of the castle but by a narrow window,
yet we brought in their materials and provisions : for that
morning having shot the officer that commanded their
guard in the head, their trenches not being finished to
secure their approaches to the out-houses, under the shelter
of which they kept their guard ; and being admonished by
what befel Capt. Bowyer, of the danger of delaying to dress
a wound, they desired leave to carry off their wounded man,
which I granted on condition that they would commit no
act of hostility in the mean time : and when five or six of
them who carried him off were about pistol-shot from the
'wall, I appeared with forty musqueteers ready to fire on the
top of the castle, and ordered three or four men out of the
window mentioned before, who brought in their materials.

A relation of mine, one Capt. Henry Williams, who
commanded a company in Colonel Barns his regiment,
desiring to be admitted to speak with me, and I consenting,
he endeavoured to perswade me to a surrender, offering
me any conditions I would ask ; but his arguments made
no impression upon me.

In the mean time the King, to encourage his friends in
the City to rise for him, sent them a commission to that

1643   purpose by the Lady Aubogny, which she brought made up in the hair of her head; but the design being discovered, she fled for refuge to the house of the French Ambassador; who refusing to deliver her to Sir Henry Vane and Mr. John Lisle, sent by the Parliament with a guard to seize her, pretending his privilege, the House, being informed by Sir Francis Knowles, that at the time of the bloody massacre at Paris, one of the French King's secretaries who was of the reformed religion flying to the English Ambassador's house for protection, and disguizing himself amongst the grooms, was forced from thence by the King's command, ordered this Lady to be treated in the like manner, which was done accordingly. Hereupon an order was passed for the trial of those who were engaged in this conspiracy, and Mr. Thomson and Mr. Challoner were found guilty, and executed for it. Sir John Hotham and his son were also condemned to lose their heads for endeavouring to betray the garison of Hull to the enemy; which sentence was put in execution upon the son the 1st

1644/3   of January, 1644¾, and on the father the day following. Sir
Jan. 1, 2. Alexander Carew was also beheaded for endeavouring to
1644   betray Plimouth, with the government of which he was
Dec. 23. entrusted by the Parliament.

1644   About the 16th of the same January the Scots marched into England, and having Berwick secured for them, the first thing they attempted was the taking of Newcastle, which they did by storm [1]. The Lords and Commons for their encouragement having sentenced, and caused execution to be done upon William Laud, Archbishop of Canter-
1645   bury, their capital enemy, on the 10th of the same month.

   Sir William Waller being reinforced with some city-regiments, thought himself strong enough to take the field: and because the Western clothiers were often obstructed in
1643   their passage to London by the garison of Basinghouse,

---

[1] The Scots summoned Newcastle, Feb. 3, 1644, at their first coming into England, but did not take it till after their return from the capture of York and the battle of Marston Moor. The town of Newcastle was stormed Oct. 19, the castle surrendered a few days later. Vicars, Burning Bush, pp. 47, 61.

which was kept for the King, he attempted to reduce it, but was repulsed with loss[1]. After which he marched to Arundel in Sussex, where he soon beat the King's garison out of the town into the castle, which after some time, and the loss of some men, was surrendered to him, with several persons of quality therein, at mercy.

About the middle of January Sir William assured us, that if we held out a fortnight longer, he would relieve us, or lay his bones under our walls. We had also some hopes given us from Southampton and Pool, the latter of which places about this time some of the inhabitants endeavoured to betray to the Lord Crawford ; but the design being discovered, as the enemy was entring the outworks, and expecting to be admitted into the town, some great guns loaded with small shot were fired upon his men, and made a great slaughter amongst them[2]. Between these two garisons of Southampton and Pool lay my troop of horse, to do what service they could against the enemy, and to favour our relief : where my cornet, afterwards known by the name of Major William Ludlow, was shot through the body, and into the thigh and his horse in two places, by some of the enemy from an ambuscade ; being brought to Southampton, and his wounds searched, the bullet that went in at his belly was found at the chine of his back, with a piece of the wastband of his breeches, which being cut out, he wonderfully recovered to be in some measure serviceable to the publick[3].

To encourage the forces of Pool and Southampton to come to our relief, I sent them word, that they should have seven or eight hundred pounds to gratify them, which I was able to make good with what I had remaining of the

1643
Nov. 6-15.

1644
Jan. 6.

1643
Sept. 24.

---

[1] Waller came before Basing on Nov. 6, 1643, besieged it for nine days, and made three ineffectual attempts to take it by storm. G. N. Godwin, Civil War in Hampshire, 1882, pp. 68-78.

[2] Rushworth, v. 286. Pool was under the government of Col. Syden-ham. Vicars, Burning Bush, p. 72.

[3] William Ludlow of Clarendon, son of Henry Ludlow of Hill Deverill and Tadley, born 1619 ; matriculated at St. Alban's Hall, Oxford, Nov. 25, 1636, aged 17 ; M.P. for Old Sarum in Richard Cromwell's Parliament.

plate which I had found in one of the closets of the castle, as I mentioned before.

Towards the end of the winter Sir Ralph Hopton, who commanded the King's forces in the West, being informed that the battery which had fired against us for two months had done no great execution, and that Col. Barns was more employed in plundering the country than in advancing the King's service, sent Sir Francis Doddington with a further supply of men to reduce us ; and with him an engineer to undermine the castle. To this end they forced the miners of Meinshup to assist them. As soon as we heard the noise of their digging, we endeavoured to countermine them ; but the castle walls being joined with an entire wall at the foundation, the morter whereof was so well tempered that it was harder than the stones themselves, we could by no means break through it. Our medicines were now spent and our chirurgeon, who with eight of his brothers served at that time in my troop, shot through the body and disabled, tho the bullet glancing missed the vitals. One of his brothers, with another souldier, adventured out of the window in order to procure some means for his recovery, whilst some of ours by discourses, firing, and much noise, drew the enemy to the other side of the castle ; so that they safely passed their guards, and went to the honest man's house before mentioned, where they met again that friend of ours, who being pressed by the enemy to serve them, remained with them to serve us ; and received from him a letter directed to us from some of our friends encouraging us to hold out, and promising us relief within ten days : of whose approach this our friend undertook to give us notice, by the signs before agreed on. Our messengers having furnished themselves with what they went for, returned to us with this good news, this poor honest man having drawn off the sentinel by whom they were to pass.

The ten days being expired, and ten more after them, without any tidings of relief, our provisions wasting, I observed a great silence amongst the enemy ; and being

desirous to know whether our friend were upon the guard,
that we might learn of him what he knew, we took occasion from their silence to desire of them, that if they were
alive they would make some noise, tho they might not be
permitted to speak : which one of them doing by blowing
his nose, we were willing to make a further discovery; and
having told him he did it in his sleeve for want of a handkerchief, he by this time understanding our meaning,
appeared in sight, and with his handkerchief blew his nose
again, endeavouring by signs and words to inform us of
our condition, digging in the wall of the stable, and laying
the stones in order ; then discoursing with two of his
fellows, he challenged them to play at football with one
of them the next, and with the other the day after ; saying
to them aloud, that we might hear, ' If I beat the first, I fear
not the second.'   Tho we supposed that the first danger he
designed to admonish us of was the mine; yet for the
more clear discovery thereof, we laid a train of powder
upon the castle wall, which he by signs signified to us to be
what he intended.   But we were mistaken in the interpretation of his second action, by which we concluded he designed
to represent to us a speedy relief. if we could hold out against
the first ; tho it was indeed another mine prepared to spring
immediately after the first, as we afterwards found, tho we
never had the happiness to see or speak with the poor man
more.   I received a letter from Sir Francis Doddington, who
commanded in chief before us, wherein taking notice of the
relation between our families, he expressed himself ready
to do me any friendly office, and advised me to a timely
delivery of the castle, lest by refusing so to do I should
bring my blood upon my own head.   In my answer I
acknowledged his civility, assuring him, that being entrusted
with the custody of it by the authority of the Parliament
for the service of the country, I could cheerfully lay down
my life in discharge of the trust reposed in me ; for that
it would not be only in my defence, but in defence of the
laws and liberties of the nation ; and therefore cautioned
him how he proceeded any farther in assaulting us, lest he

1644   should thereby contract the guilt of more innocent blood.
His letter with my answer he sent to Oxford, as appeared
by the weekly news-paper of London, wherein they were
printed from that of Oxford, which Aulicus published to
shew my opiniatreté and Britannicus my fidelity to the
publick cause [1].

The two nights following we all continued upon the
guard ; and upon the Thursday morning, being very weary,
I lay down and slept till between ten or eleven of the clock,
at which time one of my great guns firing upon the enemy,
shook the match which they had left burning for the springing of the mine into the powder, so that the mine springing
I was lifted up with it from the floor, with much dust
suddenly about me ; which was no sooner laid, but I found
both the doors of my chamber blown open, and my window
towards the enemy blown down, so that a cart might have
entred at the breach. The party which they had prepared
to storm us lay at some distance, to secure themselves from
any hurt by the springing of the mine : but that being done,
they made haste to storm, which they might easily do at
my window, the rubbish of the castle having made them a
way almost to it. Those who stormed on my side were the
Irish yellow-coats, commanded by Capt. Leicester. My
pistols being wheel-locks, and wound up all night, I could
not get to fire, so that I was forced to trust to my sword
for the keeping down of the enemy, being alone in the
chamber, and all relief excluded from me, except such as
came in by one of my windows that looked into the court

---

[1] Ludlow's answer to Doddington
is printed in Appendix II. Doddington's own letter has not survived.
Francis Doddington, son of John
Doddington of Doddington, Somerset,
matriculated at Wadham College,
Oxford. June 17, 1621, aged 17, and
was admitted of Lincoln's Inn in
1622 ; Gardiner, Wadham Registers,
i. 55 ; Foster, Alumni Oxonienses.
He was knighted, Sept. 27, 1625.
He supported the attempts of Hopton
and Hertford to secure Somersetshire for the King and was voted
a delinquent on Aug. 5, 1642, and
for a time imprisoned by Parliament.
On account of the cruelties mentioned
later by Ludlow, he was one of the
persons excepted from pardon by
Parliament in their propositions at
Uxbridge. See Cal. of Compounders,
p. 1256 ; Collinson, Somerset, iii.
519.

of the castle, through which I called to my men there, acquainting them with my condition, and requiring them to hasten to my relief. Mr. Gabriel Ludlow my kinsman[1] not only came himself, but ordered others to my assistance, and to that end placed a ladder under the window before-mentioned, which being too short by near two yards, I was obliged to leave the breach where the enemy was ready to enter, five or six times, to take his arms and himself in; which being done, he helped in five or six more, whom I ordered to fill up the breach and the doors with the bed, chairs, table, and such things as were next at hand. This place being in some measure secured, I went to see what other breaches had been made, and to provide for their defence, and found one in the room under me well defended, but that in the ground-room on the other side not at all; there I placed a guard, and ran to the upper rooms, which had many doors and windows blown open, at every one of which I appointed a guard in some measure proportionable to the danger[2]. From thence I went to the top of the castle which was leaded, and of a sex-angular figure, with a turret upon each angle. Two of these were blown down, with part of the leads, behind which the enemy sheltered themselves, so that we could not remove them by our shot; but by throwing down some great stones, with which the mine had plentifully furnished us, we killed one of theirs, and wounded some others. Capt. Leicester was one of those who sheltered themselves behind this rubbish, and desired leave to carry off the wounded men that were with him; which I readily granted, letting them know, that we sought not their blood, but our own defence. Soon after we also had occasion to make trial of their humanity; for one of our souldiers being buried in the outward rubbish of the castle, and yet alive, sent to acquaint me with his condition, and to

---

[1] Gabriel Ludlow, son of another Gabriel Ludlow, bapt. Aug. 13, 1622. Admitted to the Inner Temple, June 13, 1638.

[2] 'My Lord last night made eleven breaches in it [Wardour Castle], dis-mounting the rebels' ordnance that lay upon the uppermost leads, with the slaughter of 12 men and of the governor, Sir Henry Ludlow's son.' Letter of Feb. 1, 1644. Cal. S. P. Dom. 1644, p. 11.

desire my help : upon which I desired of the enemy that they would dig him out, and make him prisoner ; or suffer us to do it, and we would deliver him to them : but they would consent to neither ; and when I told them that I had not used them so, but had permitted them to carry off their wounded men, they replied, that tho it was my favour to suffer that, yet their chief officer would not permit this. The poor man lived in this condition near three days, and then through most barbarous usage, being denied any relief, he died. We lost three of our men by the springing of the mine, but the rest were most wonderfully preserved. Our provision of corn, which at the rate we liv'd would have lasted three weeks longer, was blown up, with part of our ammunition ; but our provision of flesh, being for about four days, was preserved. Whilst this lasted, I thought it advisable, having repulsed the enemy, to put the best countenance we could upon our affairs, hoping by so doing we might bring the enemy to give us the better conditions. But Mr. Balsum [1] our minister, with two or three more religious men, who till that time had carried themselves without discovering any fear, pressed me very earnestly to propose a treaty to the enemy. I told them that it was a very unseasonable time to do any thing of that nature, having beat off the enemy, and three or four days' provisions left : that I did not doubt before that was spent, by a good improvement of our time, to bring the enemy to reasonable terms : whereas if we should now desire a treaty with them, they would conclude our spirits low, our condition desperate, and so hold us to harder terms, or it may be give us none at all. They replied, that if I refused to hearken to their proposal, they judged that all the blood that should be spilt in further opposition would be charged upon my account. This being a very heavy charge laid on

---

[1] Robert Balsum, born at Shipton Montague in Somersetshire and educated at New Inn Hall, Oxford. He was for some time an assistant to that celebrated puritan divine Richard Bernard of Batcombe, and afterwards minister of Stoke in the same county. Towards the end of the Civil War he settled at Berwick, and died in 1647. Brook, Lives of the Puritans, iii. 79.

me by men of age and experience, of whose integrity I had
a very good opinion, I durst not resist any longer, by balancing my youth and little experience against their years and
judgment, and therefore left it to them to do what they
should think fit ; but they assuring me they would rather
lose their lives than do any thing without me, I promised
that if they would call to the enemy for a parley, I would
answer.   Whereupon they moved it to the enemy, who took
time to acquaint their commander in chief with it.   His
answer was, that since we had refused to treat with him
whilst the castle was whole, he would not now treat with
us.   I could not forbear letting the besiegers know, that the
return was no other than I expected : that the motion did
not arise from me, but was consented to by me for the
satisfaction of some about me, who were now resolved to
expose themselves with me to the utmost hazards in
defence of the place, without demanding any terms again ;
not doubting, if we were necessitated to lay down our lives
in this service, to sell them at a good rate.   My friends
having found their advice to produce no other effect than I
had foretold, resolved for the future to be wholly disposed
of by me ; so that both officers and souldiers began to
prepare against the utmost extremity.   None of ours had
been killed by the shot during the storm, but some slightly
wounded, and their clothes shot through, a bullet from the
enemy having pierced my hat close by my head.   The
besiegers had ten killed by shot and stones in the storm,
and divers wounded : amongst the former was one Hills-
deane, who a little before he expired said, he saw his
brother fire that musquet by which he received his mortal
wound : which might probably be, his brother being one of
those who defended that breach where he, attempting to
enter, was shot : but if it were so, he might justly do it by
the laws of God and man, it being done in the discharge
of his duty, and in his own defence.   The silver plate
belonging to the house, found soon after we were close
besieged, I buried in the cellar, with the help of one of
my servants.   On Saturday the enemy began to converse

friendly with us, and a cessation of acts of hostility being agreed upon, a son of Col. Barnes, Capt. Farmer, Mr. Plott, the gentleman whom I formerly mentioned to be related to the Lord Cottington[1], and to have endeavoured to perswade me to surrender the castle before the siege, with several other officers, came up close to the breaches, where we conferred together ; and they earnestly pressing me to surrender, I told them I would not be averse to it upon fitting terms ; for had not those who owned the castle made use of it to the prejudice of the country, I presumed it had not been taken from them, and possessed by us in order to prevent the like inconveniences for the future ; against which conceiving sufficient provision made by the springing of the late mine, I was willing to quit the same, if we might have liberty to march to the next garison belonging to the Parliament, with our arms, and what else we had in the castle.   They replied, they could not answer to His Majesty the giving of such conditions to us, Sir William Waller having lately refused to receive Arundel Castle from some of the King's party upon any other terms than at mercy, who they knew to have been in a much better state of defence than we were ; and therefore pressed us to deliver ourselves upon the same condition, promising us much favour.   To this I answered, that some related to us had already experienced the favours they extended to their prisoners : that the compliance of those at Arundel ought to be no precedent to us ; and that unless we might march off, we would not surrender.   They told me, the longer I held out the worse it would be for me ; and Mr. Plott, who, as he since informed me, had prevailed with them to propose this treaty, earnestly pressed me to lay hold on the opportunity, intimating by his words and gestures, that if I refused it, I should not have another : but I resolving to defend the place as long as I could, our treaty came to nothing.   I had some thoughts of charging

[1] Clarendon speaks of 'John Plott, a lawyer of very good reputation,' as imprisoned by the Roundheads at Cirencester and released on its capture by Rupert. Rebellion, vi. 238.

through the enemy in the beginning of the night, in order to force our way to the nearest of our garisons, which I presumed might have been effected by the morning ; but the desperate condition in which we must have left our sick and wounded men, diverted me from putting that design in execution. And now the spirits of my souldiers began to flag ; my gunsmith desiring leave to go home, and several others making choice of one amongst them to speak for them, were very importunate with me to surrender ; with which expressing myself displeased, I acquainted them that I would take the best time to do it for their advantage. and thereby quieted them, so that they resolved to move me no more about it ; yet ceasing not to complain to each other of their wants and hardships, the enemy became acquainted therewith, as they afterwards told me. On the Lord's day in the afternoon the besiegers discoursed with some of our men who were upon the leads, en- deavouring to draw as many of them as they could thither, that the breaches being left unguarded, they might have an opportunity to take us by storm ; which I perceiving, made use of it to animate our men afresh, and succeeded so well therein, that the enemy by our cheerfulness began to suspect that we had some notice of relief approaching. This suspicion caused them to continue discoursing with my souldiers most part of the night, to get the truth out of them, promising them liberty to march away, if they would deliver Mr. Balsum our minister, or myself to them. The next morning many of them came up to one of the breaches, to perswade us to surrender ; which opportunity being willing to improve, having ten doors blown open by the first mine, our walls that stood being cracked in several places, and another mine ready to spring that would probably level the most part of the castle with the ground. not having provision sufficient for one day left, nor any hopes of relief, I propounded to them to yield my self their prisoner, if they would consent that those with me might march off. To which they answering, that tho my good nature led me to make that offer, yet they could not accept of it: I told them, that unless I might have four things granted I would not deliver the castle. 1st. Quarter without distinction for the lives of every one. 2dly. Civil usage for all my party. 3dly. Not to be carried to Oxford. 4thly. A speedy exchange. They promised me I should have all these made good to the full; and Col. Barns said, that if I pleased to come out to them, I should find more friends than I expected: whereupon requiring my men to be upon their guard, and not to suffer any to come near them till my return, I went out to them, and they brought me to the Lord Arundel and Sir Francis Doddington, who were without the garden-wall, where my Lord Arundel assured me, that what was agreed should be made good to me; and was pleased further to add, that tho he preferred my conversion before the enjoyment of his own children, yet if I thought fit to persist in the way I had begun, he would do his utmost to endeavour that I might be exchanged for his two sons, who were then prisoners with Sir William Waller[1]. To this I answered, that if I were convinced that the cause I had engaged in was not good, I should soon recede from it; but till then I could not but persist in the prosecution thereof. Sir Francis Doddington told me, he was glad to see me alive, but sorry to find so much resolution employed in so bad a cause. I let him know, that my apprehensions concerning the cause were very different from his, else I had not hazarded my self as I had done. He also promised the performance of the articles to the utmost of his power; and for my self, that whilst I was in his custody I should have no other prison

but his own lodgings. Thus all things being agreed upon, I returned to the castle, and ordered my souldiers to lay down their arms; which being done, the enemy directed them to draw together into a certain room in the castle, where they set a guard upon them; but gave me the liberty of the place upon my parole, offering me one or two of my own company to associate with me: whereupon

---

[1] In return for this and other kindness Ludlow interposed on be-   half of Arundel in 1653. See Appendix II.

I desired that my cousin Gabriel Ludlow, Mr. Balsum, and
a servant, might be permitted to come to me, which was
granted.   Their civility to me was such, especially that of
the Lord Arundel, that I discovered to him the plate and
other things that I had hid in the castle: but I cannot say
that they performed their articles with me in relation to
my men; for the second day after their entrance, they
threatned to take away the lives of two of them, who
having been formerly pressed by them, and their consciences
not giving them leave to serve them, chose rather to come
to us, and be besieged with us, than to have liberty to
range and oppress the country with them.   The poor men
made their condition known to me; and I went to the chief
officers of the enemy, and charged them with it as a breach
of that article by which we were to have all our lives
secured to us, in virtue of these words, 'quarter without
distinction.'   Capt. Leicester, to whom I principally applied
my self, because he pretended to most experience in things
of this nature, told me, that I only conditioned for my
souldiers, and that these who ran from them were not
mine, but theirs: I replied, that they were never theirs,
tho they had forced them to be with them, having pressed
them into their service, which they had no power to do;
but tho it should be granted that they had been theirs, yet
they were now ours, and the words of the article were,
'quarter without distinction.'   He answered, that if I had
intended to have these included, I should have particularly
named them.   I told him, that it was needless, every
particular being included in the universal; and that if
I had suspected such usage, I would have died before
I would have delivered the castle to them.   He said, that
if I disliked the conditions, they would withdraw, and leave
me as they found me.   I replied, that seeing they were
now acquainted with my necessities, that proposition was
as unworthy and disingenuous as their interpretation of the
articles; and that if they proceeded to extremities against
the two souldiers, because the power was at present in their
hands, I did not doubt that God would give me an oppor-

tunity to resent it ; and if not, I was fully assured that He would do it Himself. In the afternoon I was desired to go to Sir Francis Doddington's quarters, which were at a gentleman's house about half a mile from the castle ; to which place I was accompanied by one Lieutenant Elsing, brother to the clerk of the Parliament of that name, with whom I had a free debate concerning the justice of our cause, and the evil of their undertaking, especially of those amongst them, who, having been sent by the Parliament against the rebels in Ireland, had returned and drawn their swords against those that had raised them ; which was his case. He was so convinced of the truth of what I said, that he took the first opportunity he could find to return to us ; and to that end went to the garison of Glocester, where he was employed, and behaved himself so well, that he was advanced to the command of a Lieutenant Colonel in a regiment of foot ; in which capacity he went afterwards into Ireland, where he lost his life against the rebels [1]. Having received notice that a council of war was sitting upon the two souldiers before-mentioned, and also that they endeavoured to find some pretext to take away the life of Mr. Balsum our minister, I sent to admonish them to be careful to preserve themselves from the guilt of innocent blood ; putting them in mind, that if they proceeded to such a breach of their faith, they must expect to account for it at another time. Upon this message one Capt. Bishop observing them to persist in their bloody intentions, withdrew from the council, and soon after from the party. But Sir Francis Doddington and Capt. Leicester so ordered the matter at the council, that the two souldiers were condemned, and most perfidiously executed. They also discovered all imaginable malice against Mr. Balsum, but finding no colour to proceed against him in this publick way, they fell upon a more secret and baser method to

---

[1] Henry Elsing was clerk to the Parliament ; Christopher Elsing was ensign to the regiment of Sir Nicholas Byron in 1640. In April, 1649, Elsing was lieut.-col. in the foot regiment of Col. Robert Phaire, which formed part of the army destined for the re-conquest of Ireland.

take away his life; to that end sending three men, who broke in upon him whilst he was at prayer; but he rising up, and looking steddily upon them, observing them to stand still, demanded of them the cause of their coming, who standing some time with horror and confusion in their faces, after some conference with each other, confessed to him, that they were sent to destroy him, but that they found a superiour power restraining them, and convincing them of the wickedness of their intentions, offering to convey him out of the hands of his enemies, or to do anything else for him that he should desire. He thanked them for their kindness, and being unwilling they should hazard themselves for his sake, desired only some few necessaries, the weather being cold, and he in great want, which they readily furnished him with. Soon after he was carried away to Salisbury, and the rest of the officers and souldiers of our garison sent to Oxford, contrary to the express words of the third article of our capitulation, the enemy pretending to a positive order of the King for so doing. Sir Francis Doddington having dispatched some affairs in the country, took me with him to Winchester, and in our way thither shewed me a letter from Sir Ralph Hopton, desiring him to use all means possible to draw me to their party, which he endeavoured by making use of the best arguments he could, to prove the justice of their cause, the probability of their success, and the inconsiderableness of our strength in all parts, accompanying them with all the incouragements imaginable. The first night of our journey we lay at one Mr. Awbery's of Chalk, where we met with Dr. Earl and young Mr. Gataker, whom he desired to assist him in his design to convert me[1]. Mr. Gataker rather chid than argued with me: Dr. Earl accused the Parliament of endeavouring the destruction of learning, which I desiring

[1] Richard Aubrey, father of John Aubrey the antiquary, was at this time lessee of the manor farm of Broad Chalk, under the Earl of Pembroke. Britton, Life of Aubrey, p. 30. Dr. John Earle, rector of Bishopston, Wilts, was afterwards Bishop of Salisbury. Charles Gataker was son of Dr. Thomas Gataker. and sometime chaplain to Lord Falkland. A life of Charles Gataker is appended to that of his father in D. N. B.

him to make appear, he told me, that by abolishing episcopacy we took away all encouragement to it; for that
men would not send their sons to the University, had they
not some hopes that they might attain to that preferment.
To this I replied, that it would be much more honest for
such men to train up their children at the plow, whereby
they might be certainly provided with a livelihood, than
to spend their time and money to advance them to an
office, pretended to be spiritual, and instituted for spiritual
ends, upon such a sordid principle and consideration. Sir
Francis, as I conceived, ashamed of the doctor's discourse,
put an end to the conversation. The next day we went to
Salisbury, where, tho multitudes of people were in the
streets, and in the inn where I was lodged, no person
offered me the least incivility, tho I took the liberty in
my chamber to maintain the justice of our cause in the
presence of forty or fifty of the town. Mr. John Penruddock, High Sheriff of the county, having confined Mr.
Balsum to the county goal, and sent to him to prepare
himself to die, assuring him that he was to be executed
in a short time, came to me, and with many other expressions of kindness, desired me, that in case of any
extremity I would send to him, assuring me, that he
wished me as well as his own children, and promising
that he would ride night and day to serve me. This
poor gentleman was so unhappy, during his shrievalty,
to have two of his nephews, presuming upon their uncle's
interest, and pressing through his guards, killed by them,
he having given order that none should be permitted to
pass without a strict examination[1]. In our way to Win-

---

[1] The following account of the
death of one of Penruddock's sons is
given in a royalist paper. 'Colonel
Ludlow's officers, on St. Innocents
day last, came into Mr. Becket's
house in Lavington Parish in Wiltshire, and finding Captain Penruddock (second son to Sir John Penruddock, late High Sheriff of Wiltshire) asleep in a chair after two
nights hard duty; first pulled the
poor gentleman by the hair, then
knocked him down, and broke the
stocks of two pistols about his head,
never so much as intending him
quarter; the gentlewoman and her
three daughters fell upon their knees
and begged for his life, saying he
was a gentleman, telling whose son
he was, which the rebels no sooner

1644

chester one Mr. Fisher, an acquaintance of mine, then an officer of the King's[1], saluted me, and enquiring how I did, I answered him, 'As well as one could be in my condition'; he thereupon replying, 'Why, I hope they use you civilly, do they not?' 'Yes,' said I, 'very civilly.' Sir Francis Doddington over-hearing him, took it so ill, that he caused him to be immediately disarmed, telling him, that he was too bold, to call in question the usage of his prisoner. Being arrived at Winchester, I staid at an inn till a private lodging was provided for Sir Francis, at whose quarters, according to his promise, I lodged, whilst in his custody. Most of the officers about the town came to me at the inn, several of them pressing me to discourse, and particularly concerning the justice of our cause: I excused myself, by reason of my present circumstances; but they still persisting, I thought my self obliged to maintain the necessity of our taking up arms in defence of our religion and liberties; but some of them being wholly biassed to their interest, as they went from me, met a relation of mine, one Col. Richard Manning, who, tho a Papist, commanded a regiment of horse in the King's service[2], and told him, that they came from one of the boldest rebels that they had ever seen. The colonel coming to visit me, informed me of this discourse, advising me, whatsoever I thought, not to be so free with them, lest they should do me some mischief. The next morning,

---

heard, but a bloody villain (a collier) set a pistol to his belly, swore he would kill him for his father's sake (a gentleman of known loyalty), and so most barbarously shot him dead, though the gentlewomen all the while were on their knees begging with tears. But these rebels prospered accordingly, for these were part of those Sir Marmaduke Langdale took and killed at Salisbury on Monday was sevennight.' From 'Mercurius Aulicus,' Jan. 8, 164$\frac{3}{4}$.

[1] Payne Fisher, the poet, then a captain in the King's army. See

life in D. N. B. In 1652, Fisher appended to his 'Irenodia Gratulatoria' some Latin verses addressed to Ludlow, who was then setting out for his command in Ireland. Fisher reminded Ludlow of his school-days at Blandford, and of his exploits in their sports as well as of his feats during the war.

[2] Col. Richard Manning was killed at Alresford or Cheriton fight, March 29, 1644. Clarendon, Rebellion, XIV. 138; Godwin, Civil War in Hants, p. 133.

before our departure for Oxford, Sir Francis Doddington brought me to Sir Ralph Hopton's lodgings, which being the head-quarters, we found there most of the principal officers of that army; where the general, after he had saluted me, demanded how I, being a gentleman, could satisfy my self to bear arms against my King: I told him, that, as I conceived, the laws both of God and man did justify me in what I had done. 'Well,' said he, 'I understand you are so fixed in your principles, that I am like to do little good upon you by my perswasions; but shall desire the archbishop of Armagh to take the pains to speak with you, when you come to Oxford; and if he cannot work on you, I know not who can.' This bishop was very learned, and of great reputation for piety; yet I was assured by one who had his information from Mr. Bernard of Batcomb, that when the said Mr. Bernard earnestly pressed him to deal faithfully with the King in the controversy which was between him and the Parliament concerning episcopacy, according to his own judgment in that matter, which he knew to be against it, representing to him the great and important service he would thereby do to the church of God, the archbishop answered, that if he should do as Mr. Bernard proposed, he should ruin himself and family, having a child and many debts. For this reason those arguments which could not prevail with me, when used by others, were not likely to be of more efficacy from him, who in a business of such concernment had been diverted from the discharge of his duty by such low and sordid considerations[1].

The next day I came to Oxford, conducted by a party of horse commanded by one who was captain-lieutenant to Sir Francis Doddington, where reposing a while at a house near Christ Church till the pleasure of the King might be known concerning me, there came to me two

[1] Richard Bernard, an eminent Puritan divine, rector of Batcombe, Somersetshire, died March, 1641. Robert Balsom, before mentioned, was in later years one of Bernard's assistants. Ludlow probably got the story against Usher from Balsom.

persons very zealous to justify the King's cause, and to
condemn that of the Parliament. These men were Irish
Papists, sent over by the rebels in Ireland to treat with
the King on their part, about assisting him against the
Parliament. This I afterwards understood from one of
them, whose name was Callaghan O'Callaghan, when,
together with the brigade commanded by the Lord
Musquerry, he laid down his arms to me in Ireland. The
King looking upon such men as most fit to be confided
in, gives the Presidentship of Munster, vacant by the death
of Sir William St. Leger, to the Lord Musquerry, an Irish
rebel; which the Lord Inchequin, son-in-law to Sir William,
soliciting for, and claiming a right to it, took so ill. that
the Lord Broghill, as he since informed me, found no
great difficulty to prevail with him to declare for the
Parliament, who thereupon made him their President of
Munster[1]. In this capacity he performed many considerable
services against the Irish, taking great store of plunder
from them, and not sparing even his own kindred, but if
he found them faulty hanging them up without distinction.
Having brought together an army, he marched into the
county of Tipperary, and hearing that many priests and
gentry about Cashell had retired with their goods into the
church, he stormed it, and being entred, put three thousand
of them to the sword, taking the priests even from under
the altar: of such force is ambition when it seizes upon
the minds of men.

About this time Sir Edward Deering came from the
King's quarters at Oxford, and surrendered himself at
Westminster; where being examined in the House of
Commons, he said, that since the cessation made with the
rebels in Ireland, seeing so many Papists and Irish in the

---

[1] Sir William St. Leger died July 2,
1642. The government of Munster
was then committed to Lords Inchiquin and Barrymore jointly for
civil affairs, and to Inchiquin singly
for military affairs. After the cessation of 1643, Inchiquin came to
Oxford to ask for the presidency of
Munster, but the King had already
promised it to the Earl of Portland.
Inchiquin declared for the Parliament, July 17, 1644. Carte, Ormond,
iii. 117, 125, ed. 1851; Coxe, Hibernia
Anglicana, ii. 112.

1644

King's army, and his councils wholly governed by them, his conscience would not permit him to remain longer with the King, and therefore he was come to throw himself upon the mercy of the Parliament, and in conformity to their declaration, to compound for his delinquency. Accordingly he was admitted to composition, and an order made to proceed in like manner towards such as should come in after him. Whereupon the Earl of Westmorland, and divers others, came in to the Parliament, and desired the benefit of their declaration for composition [1].

Whilst I was attending the King's pleasure at Oxford, the captain that conveyed me thither brought me word, that he was ordered to deliver me to Mr. Thorpe, the keeper of the castle; and pretending much affection to me, told me, that the said keeper would take from me my upper garment, my money, and all that was loose about me, advising me therefore to leave such things with him, and promising to bring them to me in the morning: I not suspecting his design, delivered him my cloke, with my money, and some other things, all which he carried away with him the next day; neither could I have any redress, tho I wrote to Sir Francis Doddington, complaining of this treachery, the keeper of the castle not laying the least claim to any such thing. Our sick and wounded men, after they had been kept for some time prisoners in the hall of Warder Castle, where a Popish priest very solemnly, with his hands spread over them, cursed them three times, were carried from thence to Bristol. In the castle at Oxford I met with Mr. Balsum, and other friends, who had been with me in Warder Castle, with many more who were detained there for their affection to the Parliament, amongst whom were Col. Shilborn of Buckinghamshire, Col. Henly of Dorsetshire, Capt. Haley of Glocestershire, and Capt. Abercromy a Scotsman. I had a friend in the town who furnished me with what I wanted: those

---

[1] See 'Proceedings in Kent in connection with the Parliaments of 1640,' Camden Society, 1861, preface, p. 50; Cal. of Co. for Compounding, p. 832.

who had not any such means of relief were supplied from
London by a collection of the sum of three hundred pounds,
made for them by some citizens, and conveyed down to
them. Neither was Oxford it self destitute of some who
contributed to their relief; one Dr. Hobbs in particular,
who preached then at Carfax, an honest man of the
episcopal party, usually putting them in mind of it after
his sermon. The prisoners taken by the King's party had
been treated very cruelly, especially at Oxford, by Smith
the Marshal there[1]; but the members of Parliament that
deserted their trust at Westminster coming thither, and
sitting in Council there, having not quite lost the affections
of Englishmen, took the examination of that affair into
their hands, and suspended Smith from the execution of
his office, till he should give satisfaction concerning those
things of which he was accused. They committed the
management of the place to one Thorp, and sent some of
their number to enquire concerning our usage. In the
mean time Smith came to me by order, and offered me
the liberty of the town, and to lodg where I pleased
therein, upon my parole to be a true prisoner: but demanding of him, whether, in case I accepted his offer, I
might have the liberty to visit my friends in the castle
when I thought fit; and he answering, that it would not
be allowed, I chose rather to be confined with my friends
than at liberty with my enemies. The Lord Arundel
endeavouring to make good his promise of procuring my
exchange for his two sons, earnestly solicited the King

---

[1] On the treatment of prisoners at
Oxford, see two pamphlets: 'The
Prisoners Report: or a true relation
of the cruel usage of the prisoners
in Oxford,' by Edward Wirley, M.A.,
published March, 1643: 'The Inhumanity of the King's prison keeper
at Oxford . . . Wherunto is added
the insufferable cruelty exercised
upon the Cirencester men,' by Edmund Chillenden, 1643; the latter
is reprinted in the Somers Tracts,
ed. Scott, iv. 502. Also, 'A true
relation of the taking of Cirencester,
and the cruel dealing of the merciless
cavaliers towards the prisoners they
took,' ib. p. 510. On Captain George
Austin, see C. J. iii. 320, 366. Sir
E. Nicholas in a letter dated March
17, 1644, mentions the confinement
of Smith by the order of the Oxford
Parliament. Cal. S. P. Dom. 1644,
p. 57.

1644   to it; but tho he had been a great sufferer for his service, the King positively refused to grant his request, telling him, he had no use of children. The Lady Byron came to me, and desired me to procure her husband, who was prisoner in the Tower, to be exchanged for me, and carried a letter from me to my mother then at London, about it[1]; who soliciting the Earl of Essex our General to that effect, was desired by him not to trouble her self any more therein, assuring her that he would be as careful of me, as if I were his own son. A person from Sir Edward Stradling came also to me, in order to an exchange between us, telling me, that the King had promised that nothing of that nature should be done before Sir Edward Stradling and Col. Lunsford were exchanged[2]. The Lord Willmot sent a gentleman to acquaint me that he had procured a grant from the King, that I should be exchanged for Sir Hugh Pollard; and that if I would write a letter to the Earl of Essex with the proposal, he would send it by a trumpeter; but I judging this exchange to be very unequal, Sir Hugh being a person much esteemed for his interest and experience, proposed in my letter to the Lord-General, that he would put some other person with me into the balance against him. Whilst I was in expectation of the General's answer, we received advice that most of our foot that lay before Newark, commanded

March 21.   by Sir John Meldrum, a worthy Scotsman, were defeated and made prisoners by Prince Rupert: but this loss was in some measure recompensed by a victory obtained at

March 29.   Cherington in Hampshire, by our forces, commanded by Sir William Waller, against those of the King commanded by Sir Ralph Hopton. The numbers on each side were very near equal, and the success had been doubtful for the most part of the day, but at last the enemy was totally

---

[1] Probably Sophia, daughter of Charles Lambert and wife of Sir Nicholas Byron. He had been taken prisoner at Ellesmere in Shropshire, Jan. 11, 1644. Dugdale, Diary, p. 58; Collins, Peerage, vii, 98.

[2] Cols. Sir Edward Stradling and Sir Thomas Lunsford were both taken prisoners at Edgehill. Clarendon, Rebellion, vi. 94.

routed, and put to flight: and had good use been made of
this victory, the controversy had soon been decided in the
west; but we were not yet so happy to improve our advantages: by which negligence we got little more than the
field, and the reputation of the victory, tho the enemy lost
some of their principal officers in the fight, amongst whom
were the Lord John, brother to the Duke of Lennox, Sir
Edward Stawell, Col. Richard Manning, formerly mentioned, and that Smith who had been knighted by the
King for rescuing his standard out of the hands of Mr.
Chambers, secretary to the Earl of Essex. This fight at
Cherington happened on the 29th of March, 1644, about
a fortnight after the surrender of Warder Castle, till which
time had I been able to keep it, I should have been relieved. The enemy's officers came to the castle at Oxford
to solicit the prisoners to take arms under them; but
finding their endeavours to prove ineffectual, they soon
desisted from that attempt. After three weeks' confinement here, my exchange was agreed, the Lord-General
Essex expressing much generosity and readiness in it, as
he had promised to my mother: for lest the King should
be reminded of his promise to Sir Edward Stradling and
Col. Lunsford, or of that to my Lord Willmot in favour of
Sir Hugh Pollard, and so on either hand the design of my
liberty come to be obstructed, he consented to the exchange
of all the three for Col. Houghton, Sir John Savil, Capt.
Abercromy, and my self. Col. Henley went off also with
us, being exchanged for Lieutenant-Colonel Robert Sandys.
I was led blindfold through the city of Oxford till I had
passed their works, and the next day arrived at London,
where I found the Earl of Essex disposed to an exchange
for my officers and souldiers, which was soon after made,
and with them for Mr. Balsum, whom he entertained as his
chaplain to the time of his death. He expressed a great
desire to provide me with a command in his army: but the
Parliament, upon the instances of the gentlemen that
served for the county of Wilts, having appointed me
Sheriff thereof, upon an invitation of Sir Arthur Haslerig

to be major of his regiment of horse in Sir William Waller's army, which was designed for the service of the west, I accepted of it, and mounted the choicest of my old souldiers with me, Sir Arthur buying a hundred horse in Smithfield for that purpose: the rest of my men the Lord General took into his own company. As soon as my troop was compleated, and furnished with all things necessary, I

May. repaired to the regiment then with Sir William Waller near Abingdon, who was directed by the Parliament with his army to block up the King at Oxford on one side, whilst the Earl of Essex should do the same on the other. Which storm the Queen foreseeing, withdrew to Exeter,

June 16. where she was delivered of a daughter, which she leaving in the custody of the Lady Dalkeith, returned to France, as well to secure her self as to solicit for supplies. In the

June 3. mean time the King breaking out from Oxford, marched towards Worcestershire; upon which the Earl of Essex commanded Sir William Waller to march after him, whilst he himself with his army marched westward. This order seemed very strange to the Parliament, and to most of us, being likely to break Sir William Waller's army, which consisted for the most part of western gentlemen, who hop'd thereby to have been enabled to secure the country, and to promote the publick service. The Parliament sent to the Lord-General to observe his former orders, and to attend the King's motions; but he sending them a short answer, continued his march west, in which he took Wey-

June 17.
June 14. mouth, and relieved Lyme, that had endured a long siege, and with the assistance of the seamen, tho their works were inconsiderable, had often repulsed the enemy, and killed great numbers of them in several sallies that they made upon them. A party commanded by Sir Robert Pye was ordered to Taunton, which he reduced to the obedience of the Parliament. Upon the advance of the Earl of Essex, the army of the enemy commanded by Prince Maurice retreated farther westward. Sir William Waller, according to his orders from the general, followed the King, but could not find an opportunity to engage him; so that the

summer being almost spent, and the western gentlemen observing little done for the security of those parts to which they were related, prevailed with him to permit Col. Alexander Popham, Col. Edward Popham his brother, my self, and some others, to return into the west, in order to provide recruits for his army, and to secure the country[1]. To this end I received a commission from him to raise and command a regiment of horse, with a permission to take my own troop with me. As soon as we came into Wiltshire we were earnestly solicited to go to the relief of Major Wansey[2], who was besieged by the enemy in Woodhouse, formerly purchased of my father by Mr. Arundel, brother to the Lord Arundel of Warder[3]. Upon our approach we understanding that their forces were drawn off, staid a day or two at the Devizes; where notice being brought to us of the enemy's return before that place, we immediately advanced, and came that night to Warmister, from whence we sent a party of about forty horse, with order to bring us certain intelligence of the enemy's condition. This party meeting upon Warmister Heath with about the like number of theirs, fought them, and having

[1] Alexander and Edward Popham were sons of Sir Francis Popham of Houndstreet, Somerset, and Littlecote, Wilts, one of the Deputy-Lieutenants of Wiltshire and M.P. for Minehead, who died July 28, 1644. Alexander Popham was member for Bath. Edward succeeded his father in the representation of Minehead, became one of the admirals of the fleet of the Commonwealth, died Aug. 19, 1651, and was buried on Sept. 24 in Westminster Abbey. Cal. State Papers, Dom. 1644, p. 382; Chester, Westminster Abbey Registers, p. 144; Mercurius Politicus, Sept. 24, 1651. Essex in his letters of July 10 and 15, 1644, speaks of Alexander Popham's difficulties in raising a regiment, and of the defeat he and Ludlow experienced. Devereux, Lives of the Earls of Essex, ii. pp. 415, 417.

[2] Henry Wansey, who is described by Sir Edward Walker as 'lately a watchmaker in Warminster.' Historical Discourses, p. 39. When Penruddock and the royalists seized Salisbury in March, 1655, and made prisoner Colonel Dove, the sheriff, Major Wansey with about thirty men held the sheriff's house against them. Mercurius Politicus. On Oct. 26, 1661, he was arrested on suspicion and imprisoned in the Gate House, where he still was on Feb. 20, 1662. See his petition and narrative, Somers Tracts, ed. Scott, vii. 533.

[3] William, or Sir William, Arundel, was owner of Woodhouse, and Horningsham Castle, Wilts. See his case in the Calendar of the Committee for Compounding, p. 1794.

taken some prisoners, returned to us, with an account, that the enemy only drew off from Woodhouse to reinforce themselves for the better carrying on of their work; in order to which Sir Ralph Hopton with a thousand horse was come from Bristol. The next morning a party of the enemy's horse faced us on the heath, thereby to provoke us to charge them, and then by retreating from us, to have drawn us within their body of horse, who were marching on our left amongst the hedges, endeavouring to get into our rear; which we suspecting, forbore making any attempt upon them; and about noon finding that we were not in a condition of performing what we came about, marched off towards Salisbury[1]. We were no sooner got upon the downs, but we discovered their body of horse marching into the town; yet we continued our march, observing the enemy as well as we could, to which end I kept in the rear; and discovering them climbing the hills not far from us, I informed Col. Alexander Popham thereof, telling him, that they appearing to be at least four times our number, I thought it not at all advisable to engage them. But he saying, that since they were so near, we could not in honour avoid it, I promised him that I would not desert him. Whereupon he drew up his party into one body, which with reformed officers and others consisted of near a hundred; and I drew up my troop, consisting of the like number, into another body; but having before sent away my sumpter and led horses, upon suspicion of the event, I was obliged to ride after them to take my sute of arms which was with them, having ordered my men not to stir from their ground till I came back, in which they were very punctual. As I was returning, I met Col. Popham and all his party flying, of whom demanding the cause of this alteration of his resolution, he answered, that it was by no means advisable to fight them. I found my men standing their ground, and the enemy advancing towards them in twelve bodies, each of which seemed to be as big as ours. I thanked them for obeying my orders, and told

---

[1] For royalist accounts of this skirmish, see Appendix II.

them, that if they continued to do so, I doubted not by the blessing of God to bring them off. In order to which I sent my standard before with half a score chosen horse, and then began to march off with the rest; but finding some of my men beginning to ride for it, I put my self at the head of them, to let them see, that I could ride as fast as they; withal telling them, that if they would stand by me, I would bring up the rear. By this means I got my men to keep close together, which contributed much to their safety. The greatest part of the other company followed Col. Edward Popham to Salisbury; but his brother Col. Alexander, with about six horse, struck out of the way, and retired to Pool. After we had made about three miles of our way, one of my troopers fell from his horse, and the beast running from him, he was in great danger of being destroyed by the enemy, who was in pursuit of us; which being willing to prevent, I took him up behind me, and his horse running along with the company, was taken soon after on the top of the hill very seasonably; for my horse was by that time so far spent with the extraordinary weight, that he could not gallop any longer; but the souldier mounting his own horse, mine soon recovered his wind and strength again. Twice or thrice the enemy came up to us, demanding the word, and were as often repulsed to their body: the last time we shot one of their officers, which made them more cautious of approaching us. Many of our horses being spent, I commanded the souldiers to quit them, and to run them through, that they might not fall into the hands of the enemy, advising the men to shift for themselves, either amongst the corn, or in the villages through which we passed, whereby most of them secured themselves; but some were taken by the enemy, and killed in cold blood by one of their officers, after quarter given and their lives promised to them. At last I came to Salisbury with about thirty horse, where divers persons disaffected to the Parliament made a great shout at our coming into the town, rejoicing at our defeat, which they had heard of by some of our company, who had passed through the town about an hour before. From thence I continued my way to a place called Mutton Bridg, on one side of which there is a causway about three foot broad, where I made a halt; and ordering my party to continue their retreat towards Southampton, I kept some of those who were the best mounted with me, and made good that pass for some time against the enemy, who tho they followed us as far as White Parish, twenty miles from the place where they first began their pursuit, they took no more of our men after this halt which we put them to; so that with the rest I arrived safe at Southampton. Two days after my coming to Southampton Col. Norton received advice, that the enemy was preparing to send some forces, in order to beat off those of ours that blocked up Basing House. He being then before Winchester, and resolving to march with his troop to reinforce the besiegers, desired me with my troop to supply his place at Winchester till his return. Being unwilling to refuse any public service, tho my men were already very much harassed, I marched thither; and that those in the castle might see they were not at liberty to ravage the country, I drew out my troop and faced them: upon which they sent out what horse they had to skirmish with us; amongst whom observing one Mr. William Neale, who was of my acquaintance, and formerly my school-fellow, I called to him telling him, that I was sorry to see him there; but since it was so, I offered to exchange a shot with him, and riding up to that purpose, he re-treated towards his party, where making a stand, he called to me to come on, which I did; but he retreated again till he came within the shelter of their foot, and one with him dismounting, fired a musquet at me loaded with a brace of bullets, of which one went into the belly of my horse, the other struck upon my breast-plate, within half an inch of the bottom of it: my horse carried me off, but died that night. The necessities of my men being great, and this service not immediately belonging to me, I thought it my duty to return into Wiltshire, where I might expect to be better supplied than in Hampshire, to which county I had no relation : therefore sending to Col. Norton to make provision for the service at Winchester, I marched with fourscore horse to Salisbury; which town having triumphed upon our defeat, I thought most proper to supply us with what we wanted : and to that end having procured a list of the disaffected in the town, I required them, without delay, to collect amongst themselves five hundred pounds for the recruiting and paying of my troop, who had not received any pay since they came out. The town made many excuses, and at last prevailed with me to take two hundred pounds, with which I paid and recruited my troop; and having disposed them in the best manner I could for the service of the country, I went to London to compleat my regiment, and to furnish it with arms, and all such things as were necessary.

In the mean time Sir Francis Doddington had caused the two men that he had taken at Warder to be hanged, upon pretence that they ran away from him ; and having brought some pieces of cannon before Woodhouse, made a breach so considerable in the wall, that the besieged were necessitated to surrender at mercy, but they found very little, for they were presently stripp'd of all that was good about them: and Sir Francis Doddington being informed by one Bacon, who was parson of the parish, that one of the prisoners had threatened to stick in his skirts, as he call'd it, for reading the Common-Prayer, struck the man so many blows upon the head, and with such force, that he broke his skull, and caused him to fall into a swound ; from which he was no sooner recovered, but he was picked out to be one of the twelve which Sir Francis had granted to Sir William St. Leger to be hanged, in lieu of six Irish rebels who had been executed at Warum by Col. Sydenham, in pursuance of an order from the Parliament to give them no quarter. These twelve being most of them clothiers, were hanged upon the same tree ; but one of them breaking his halter, desired that what he had suffered might be accepted, or else that he might fight against any two for his life ; not-

1644   withstanding which they caused him to be hanged up again, and had proceeded much farther, had not Sir Ralph Hopton sent orders to put a stop to their butcheries[1].

The King having ranged about for some time, thought fit to return towards Oxford ; and being joined by some foot from thence, skirmished with Sir William Waller's June 29. army at Cropredy Bridg, wherein little hurt being done on either side, the King marched into the west, in order to a conjunction with his forces in those parts, commanded by Prince Maurice.

When I first took arms under the Parliament in defence of the rights and liberties of my country, I did not think that a work so good and so necessary would have been attended with so great difficulties : but finding by experience the strong combination of interests at home and abroad against them, the close conjunction of the popish and prelatical parties in opposition to them ; what vast numbers depended upon the King for preferments or subsistence; how many of the nobility and gentry were contented to serve his arbitrary designs, if they might have leave to insult over such as were of a lower order ; and adding to all this the great corruption of the nation, I became convinced of my former error, and began now more to wonder that they found so many friends to assist them in their just and lawful undertaking, than I had done before at the opposition they met with. In these thoughts I was every day more confirmed by observing the strange divisions amongst our own party, every one striving to enlarge his own power in a factious and ambitious way, not caring tho thereby they obstructed and ruined the cause it self. Of this I had some experience in my own particular, as well as others of a much greater figure than my self;[2] for tho my

[1] See Devereux, Lives of the Earls of Essex, ii. 418; Vicars, God's Ark, p. 286.

[2] On Sept. 7, 1644, Waller wrote to the Committee of Both Kingdoms from Farnham, his appointed rendezvous for his march westwards to relieve Essex: 'This day Col. Ludlow came to me with orders from the Committee of Wilts, to surrender to me his commission which he had from me. There are likewise orders sent from that Committee to those troops of his which were at Salis-

country-men had in my absence prevailed with the Parliament to make me sheriff of the county of Wilts, and engaged themselves to raise a regiment for me ; yet because I refused to deliver up my former commission received from Sir William Waller, and to take a new one from the earl of Essex, tho that I had from Sir William obliged me to obey the said earl as much as one given me immediately from himself, those of my country-men who were of the faction of the Earl of Essex, obstructed me in the raising of my regiment, keeping from me those arms that were bought to that end, countenancing my major, for whom I had procured that employment, against me, and detaining our pay from us ; so that I and my men had nothing to keep us faithful to the cause but our affection to it. Yet were we not wanting to improve every opportunity in the best manner we could, to the service of the country ; for having notice that a garison was put into the Lord Sturton's house, and another into that of Sir Ralph Hopton at Witham, I marched in the night first to Sturton House, which was defended against us, till each of us carrying a fagot to one of the gates, wherewith we set them on fire, together with one of the rooms of the castle, those that kept it slipped out

bury to draw away immediately to Malmesbury, and not to obey their colonel if he came with my commission to them. Last night hearing that those troops were at Salisbury. I sent directions to them not to stir from thence till they received further orders from me, and in the meantime to send out continual parties into the west to gain intelligence. How far this will now be obeyed I cannot tell. I have refused to accept Col. Ludlow's commission, and given him order to repair immediately to his troops, and to see my former orders performed, which I make no question but he will do as far as he can. My Lords, so long as I have a life I will lay it out freely in your service, but it is a very great discouragement to me to meet with nothing but opposition, and in such a time wherein we cannot admit those clashings without betraying God's cause.' The same evening Waller received the news of Essex's surrender, and an answer from Ludlow's major declining to obey his orders. Waller's commission made him general of the forces of Wilts, Gloucester, Somerset, Worcester, and Shropshire by ordinance passed Feb. 11, 1643, and he had also been appointed to command the forces sent west to relieve Essex, Aug. 23, 1644. L. J. v. 602; vi. 685. Essex, however, had made Massey commander-in-chief of the Gloucestershire forces, and the Wilts committee had also voted Massey the command of their troops. Cal. State Papers, Dom. 1644, p. 478.

at a back-door through the garden into the park, which they did undiscovered, by reason of the darkness of the night [1]. Having rendred that place untenable, we hastned to Witham, where we found in the park near a hundred cattle belonging to Sir Ralph Hopton, which served for the paiment of my souldiers : those who were within desired to treat, and demanded liberty to return home ; which was granted, upon condition to deliver up their arms, and to engage to keep no garison in that place for the time to come. Being upon my return, I took with me my hangings, pictures, best beds, and other things, which my father's servants had so well conceal'd at the first breaking out of the war in a private part of my house, that they escaped the search of the enemy, who had plundered all they could find, broken all the windows, taken away the leads, and pulled up the boards in most parts of the house. Whilst I was at London, that party which I left in the country had taken some wool and other things from the Lord Cottington, the Lord Arundel, and others, which they sold, and divided the money amongst themselves. From the Lord Cottington's they brought. amongst other things, a horse that had been taken from me before at Warder Castle.

The Lord Fairfax, the Earl of Manchester, and the Scots, besieged York, of which the Earl of Newcastle was governour, having with him a garison consisting of six or seven thousand foot, besides horse. After some time spent in the siege, Prince Rupert arrived with about eighteen thousand men, and caused the besiegers to raise the siege, who joining their forces, resolved to observe his motions, and to fight him if they found an occasion ; but that they might be a little refreshed and furnished with provisions, which they wanted, they marched towards Tadcaster. If Prince Rupert, who had acquired honour enough by the relief of York in the view of three generals, could have contented himself with it, and retreated, as he might have done, without fighting,

---

[1] Old Stourton House was destroyed in 1720. Views of it are given in Hoare's Modern Wilts, appended to the history of Frustfield, p. 7; and in the Wiltshire Archæological Magazine, i. 194.

1644

the reputation he had gained would have caused his army
to increase like the rolling of a snowball; but he thinking
this nothing unless he might have all, forced his enemies
to a battel against the advice of many of those that were
with him; in which the left wing of the enemy charging July 2.
the right wing of ours, consisting of English and Scots, so
totally routed them, that the three generals of the Parliament
quitted the field, and fled towards Cawood Castle: the left
wing of our army commanded by Col. Cromwell, knowing
nothing of this rout, engaged the right wing of the enemy
commanded by Prince Rupert, who had gained an advantageous piece of ground upon Marston Moor, and caused a
battery to be erected upon it, from which Capt. Walton,
Cromwell's sister's son, was wounded by a shot in the knee.
Whereupon Col. Cromwell commanded two field-pieces to
be brought in order to annoy the enemy, appointing two
regiments of foot to guard them; who marching to that
purpose, were attacked by the foot of the enemy's right
wing, that fired thick upon them from the ditches. Upon
this both parties seconding their foot, were wholly engaged,
who before had stood only facing each other. The horse
on both sides behaved themselves with the utmost bravery;
for having discharged their pistols, and flung them at each
other's heads, they fell to it with their swords. The King's
party were encouraged in this encounter, by seeing the
success of their left wing; and the Parliament's forces
that remained in the field were not discouraged, because
they knew it not, both sides eagerly contending for victory;
which, after an obstinate dispute, was obtained by Cromwell's brigade, the enemy's right wing being totally routed
and flying, as the Parliament's had done before, our horse
pursuing and killing many of them in their flight. And
now the enemy's left wing, who had been conquerors,
returned to their former ground, presuming upon an entire
victory, and utterly ignorant of what had befallen Prince
Rupert; but before they could put themselves into any
order, they were charged and entirely defeated by the
reserves of Cromwell's brigade. Prince Rupert, upon the

routing of the Parliament's right wing, concluding all to be his own, had sent letters to the King, to acquaint him with the victory, upon which the bells were rung, and bonfires made at Oxford. Sir Charles Lucas, Major-General Porter, Major-General Tilyard, with above a hundred officers more, were taken prisoners by the Parliament's forces: all the enemy's artillery, great numbers of arms, and a good quantity of ammunition and baggage fell also into their hands. The Prince's own standard, with the arms of the Palatinate, was likewise taken, with many others both of horse and foot. Fifteen days after this fight, being the 16th of July, 1644. the city of York was surrendred to the Parliament's forces upon articles ; and the Earl of Newcastle having had some dispute with Prince Rupert before the engagement, wherein some words had passed which the earl could not well digest, soon after left England, and the Prince retired to Bristol.

The Earl of Essex was marched with his army into Cornwall ; yet to what publick end I could never understand, for the enemy there had already dispersed themselves. Some said that he was perswaded to march thither by the Lord Roberts, to give him an opportunity to collect his rents in those parts. Upon this the King drew out what forces he could from Oxford, designing to join them with some others in the west ; by which conjunction the Parliament apprehending their army under Essex to be in danger, ordered Sir William Waller to observe the King's motions : but whether the neglect of relieving him at the Devizes, or the affront put upon him, by commanding him to follow the King after he had been ordered to attend the service of the west, or what else it was that had sower'd him, I cannot say ; yet visible it was, that so much care and expedition was not used in attending the King in his marches as was requisite. However Lieutenant-General Middleton, then under Sir William Waller, was sent with a party of horse to the assistance of the Earl of Essex ; but he kept at such a distance from him, that he afforded him little help. Neither was there that diligence as should

have been then used by the Earl of Essex himself, to
engage the King before his conjunction with the western
forces, or to fight them when they were united, they not
much, if at all, exceeding ours in number, and in courage
and affection to the cause engaged in much inferiour. But
the Earl of Essex and the Lord Roberts having led the
army into a corner of Cornwall, betook themselves to the
ships with which the Earl of Warwick attended the motion
of the army.   Being thus deserted, the horse broke through
the enemy under the conduct of Sir William Balfour, the
foot and train of artillery being left with Major-General
Skippon about Bodmin, who was forced, about the latter
end of September, 1644, to make the best terms he could
with the enemy for them, agreeing to leave their arms and
cannon behind them, and to be conducted into the Parliament's quarters, with whatsoever belonged to them ; but
before the convoy had done with them, they lost most of
their clothes, and in that condition arrived at Portsmouth,
where they found their general the Earl of Essex.

The Parliament soon caused them to be armed and
clothed again ; and the horse having forced their way, as
before mentioned, the army was speedily recruited, scarce
a man having taken arms on the other side.   The Earl of
Manchester and Sir William Waller were ordered with
their forces to draw westward of London, as well to favour
the Earl of Essex upon occasion, as to put a stop to the
enemy's approach, if he should attempt it.   The King
marched, as was expected, in great triumph out of the west,
Sir William Waller lying about Basingstoke ; from whom
I received a letter, inviting me to come to their assistance :
in order to which I began my march with some horse and
dragoons raised by Major Wansey, who had been commanded by the Earl of Essex to continue with me ; and
on the way received an order from the Committee of Both
Kingdoms, to advance towards them with what force I had[1].

---

[1] The force at Salisbury belonging to Ludlow's regiment consisted
of three troops. Waller pressed that
they should be ordered to join him,
pointing out that the new troops
belonging to Ludlow were raised by

We were very well received by them, having with us about five hundred horse, and particularly because they had been under some apprehensions that the enemy had intercepted us, who were indeed posted on our way; yet we passed by them in the night without disturbance, and came safely to our friends. Within a day or two our army advanced towards Newbury, of which place the enemies had possessed themselves. The Earl of Essex being indisposed, could not attend that service, and therefore the Committee of Both Kingdoms sent some members of their own to take care that all possible advantages might be taken against the enemy, and to prevent any contention amongst our friends concerning the command, or any other matters. The river that ran through the town defended the enemy on the south side of it, so that we could not come at them : and on the north west part of it, within cannon-shot, lay Dennington Castle, in which they had placed a garison ; so that we had no other way to the town, but on the north-east of it, where they had raised a breast-work, and furnished some houses that were without it with foot, the ground between that and the river being marshy, full of ditches, and not passable. On the north side of this high-way was a strong stone house belonging to one Mr. Doleman, having a rampart of earth about it, which was also possessed by the enemy; so that little could be done upon them the first day, save skirmishing in small parties, as they thought fit to come out to us. On our side we had the advantage

a commission granted by him, and that Ludlow's own troop belonging to Sir Arthur Haselrig's regiment, was properly part of his army. The committee at the demand of the Wiltshire gentlemen wrote to Waller, that the three troops in Wiltshire being raised upon the charge of particular men, and by them designed for Malmesbury and Gloucester, he was not to expect them to join him Their commanders, Major Duett, Capt. Bernard, and Capt. Goddard were ordered to obey what orders they should receive from Massey, but Duett turned a deaf ear to Massey's orders. Cal. S. P., Dom. 1644, pp. 479, 484, 488, 501, 524. Nor was Ludlow himself very prompt to join Waller. 'We hear not a word of Col. Ludlow's horse coming to us,' wrote Waller and Haselrig on Oct. 16. 'We hope you will not suffer 400 horse to be idle so near us when our lives and all will be at stake upon a day's labour, and that very shortly, if we mistake not.' Ib. 1644-5, p. 47.

of a hill, which served in some measure to cover our men: 1614
here we planted some of our field-pieces, and fired upon the Oct. 27
enemy, who answered us in the like manner from the town.
In the afternoon they drew two of their guns to the other
side of the river, and with them fired upon that part of ours
that lay on the side of the hill, who were much exposed to
that place where their guns were planted : my regiment being
that day on the guard, received the greatest damage ; amongst
others my cousin Gabriel Ludlow, who was a cornet therein,
and who had behaved himself so well in the defence of
Warder Castle, was killed : he died not immediately after
he was shot ; so that having caused him to be removed out
of the reach of their guns, and procured a chirurgeon to
search his wounds, he found his belly broken, and bowels
torn, his hip-bone broken all to shivers, and the bullet
lodged in it ; notwithstanding which he recovered some
sense, tho the chirurgeon refused to dress him, looking
on him as a dead man. This accident troubled me exceedingly, he being one who had expressed great affection
to me, and of whom I had great hopes that he would be
useful to the publick. In this condition he desired me to
kiss him, and I not presently doing it, thinking he had
talked lightly, he pressed me again to do him that favour ;
whereby observing him to be sensible, I kissed him ; and
soon after having recommended his mother, brothers and
sisters to my care, he died. Our enemies having secured
themselves, as I mentioned before, we were necessitated to
divide our army, in order to attack them on the north-west
side of the town by Dennington Castle ; where most of our
foot who engaged the enemy were of those who had been
lately stripp'd by them in Cornwall ; which usage being
fresh in their memory, caused them to charge with such
vigour, that some of them ran up to their cannon, and
clapped their hats upon the touch-holes of them, falling so
furiously upon the enemy, that they were not able to stand
before them, but were forced to quit their ground, and run
under the shelter of Dennington Castle, leaving behind them
several pieces of cannon, besides many of their men killed

and taken prisoners.   Those on our side commanded by the
Earl of Manchester observing the enemy to retreat in that
disorderly manner on the other side, thought it their duty
to endeavour to force their passage on this ; and to that end
our horse and foot, with some cannon, were drawn into a
bottom, between Doleman's house and the hill, where our
guns were first planted : those at the little houses, and at
the breast-work, fired thick upon us ; but our foot ran up
to the houses, and attacked the enemy so vigorously, that
they were forced to retire to their breast-work ; between
which and Doleman's house our men continued firing about
an hour and half.   But finding many to fall, and that there
was no probability of doing any good, they retreated, leaving
two drakes behind them.   Our horse had stood drawn up
within a little more than pistol-shot of the enemy's works
all the while our foot were engaged, for their encouragement
and protection against any horse that should attack them,
as also to second them in case they had made way.   I had
divers men and horse shot, and amongst the rest my own[1].
The night coming on separated us, when drawing off I
perceived that my major had secured his troop in the rear
of all, having taken care that all the regiment might not be
lost in one engagement.   In the night the enemies removed
their cannon and other carriages to Dennington Castle,
where having lodged them, they marched between our two
parties towards Oxford.   The next morning we drew
together, and followed the enemy with our horse, which
was the greatest body that I saw together during the whole
course of the war, amounting to at least seven thousand
horse and dragoons ; but they had got so much ground of
us, that we could never recover sight of them, and did not
expect to see them any more in a body that year ; neither
had we, as I suppose, if encouragement had not been given
them privately by some of our own party.   Col. Norton's
regiment of horse, with some foot, being left to block up

---

[1] 'I engaged myself to lead up
Col. Ludlow's regiment, his horse
having broken his bridle so that he
was fain to quit.'   Letter of Col.
Richard Norton, quoted in Money's
Battles of Newbury, ed. 2, p. 178.

Basing House, he desired to have more force assigned him for the more effectual carrying on that work, and particularly my regiment of horse. I was not ignorant of the hardship of that service, it not being properly my work, who was raised by and for the county of Wilts; yet having received an order to that purpose from the general, and sent my major with part of the regiment into Wiltshire for the defence of that county, I resolved to obey, especially considering that the entercourse between London and the west was much interrupted by that garison [1]. 1644

The enemy, contrary to all expectation, appeared again in a body near Newbury, where our army lay, who drew out to oppose them. Some small skirmishes happened between them, but a general engagement was opposed in a council of war by some of the greatest amongst us. Whereupon the King, in the face of our army, twice as numerous as his, had time to send his artillery from Dennington Castle towards Oxford, without any opposition, to the astonishment of all those who wished well to the publick. But by this time it was clearly manifest that the nobility had no further quarrel with the King, than till they could make their terms with him, having, for the most part, grounded their dissatisfactions upon some particular affront, or the prevalency of a faction about him. But tho it should be granted, that their intentions in taking arms were to oblige the King to consent to redress the grievances of the nation ; yet if a war of this nature must be determined by treaty, and the King left in the exercise of the royal authority after the utmost violation of the laws, and the greatest calamities brought upon the people, it doth not appear to me what security can be given them for the

Nov. 9. 10.

---

[1] The royalist narrative of the siege of Basing House. published in 1644 (reprint p. 23), speaks of the coming in of Strode's and Ludlow's horse about Nov. 5, 1644, which 'fastened their leaguer almost on a remove,' i. e. prevented the parliamentarians from raising the siege. The siege was actually raised on Nov. 13. On Nov. 6 the Committee of Both Kingdoms wrote to Ludlow saying that his regiment was to go into Wiltshire so soon as a regiment of the city foot should arrive to replace it at Basing. Cal. S. P., Dom. 1644, p. 101.

1644   future enjoyment of their rights and privileges ; nor with what prudence wise men can engage with the Parliament, who being, by practice at least, liable to be dissolved at pleasure, are thereby rendred unable to protect themselves, or such as take up arms under their authority, if after infinite hardships and hazards of their lives and estates, they must fall under the power of a provoked enemy, who being once re-established in his former authority, will never want means to revenge himself upon all those who, in defence of the rights and liberties of the nation, adventure to resist him in his illegal and arbitrary proceedings.

In the council of war before-mentioned, things were managed with such heat as created great differences between the principal officers of the army, by which this favourable conjuncture was lost ; and the season being far advanced, the army was dispersed into winter-quarters. The blockade

ov. 13. of Basing House was also ordered to be broken up, after which I returned with those under my command into the county of Wilts [1]. In the winter the Parliament caused Abingdon to be fortified, of which place Col. Brown was governour, who holding correspondence with the Lord Digby, then secretary to the King, promised him that so soon as he had finished the fortifications, and received all things necessary from the Parliament to defend it, he would deliver it to the King [2] ; by which means he kept the King's forces from interrupting him till he had perfected the work. But then, as is probable by his carriage since, observing the affairs of the Parliament in a better posture than those of the King, he altered his resolution, and in defiance of the Lord Digby, published the correspondence that had been between them about that matter. The dissatisfaction that

---

[1] Originally Waller intended Ludlow's regiment to make part of a force designed for the relief of Taunton, and on Nov. 27 orders were issued to that effect, but on Jan. 1 Ludlow was ordered to stay at Salisbury till further order ‘in regard of the danger of his marching westward till a greater army be sent.’ Cal. S. P., Dom. pp. 113, 124, 164, 194, 225, 227. The siege of Basing was abandoned Nov. 13. Walker, Historical Discourses, p. 119.

[2] Brown's correspondence is printed by Rushworth, v. 808.

arose upon the permission given the King to carry off his
artillery, rested not till the House of Commons was made
acquainted with it by Col. Cromwell, who commanded under
the Earl of Manchester, whom he charged with the breach
of his trust; but he and his friends endeavoured to lay the
blame on others, the Earl of Essex and his party adhering
to the Earl of Manchester.   Whilst I was before Basing,
some of the enemies under the conduct of Col. Coke came
to Salisbury, and were fortifying the Close for the King; of
which Major Wansey having advice, marched thither with
the forces which I had sent into Wiltshire, and falling upon
them, caused them to retire in haste: but finding the gates
fortified against him, he set fire to them, and seizing upon
all their horse, took the colonel and fourscore more
prisoners, and sent them to Southampton.

At my return into Wiltshire I received orders from the
Committee of Both Kingdoms to send what men I could
spare out of my regiment to reinforce a party commanded
by Major General Holborn, who was ordered to march into
the west to the relief of Col. Blake, besieged by the enemy
in Taunton.   I drew out two hundred horse for that service,
and was necessitated to march with them myself, my major
who had got possession of good quarters at Deane, a house
belonging to Sir John Evelyn, being not willing to remove[1].
Col. Edward Popham, Col. Starr, Col. Brewin, and Sir
Anthony Ashley, came from London with this party.   In
our march we were joined by the forces of Dorsetshire.
When we were advanced near the enemy, my troop was
ordered to a quarter of which they were in possession, but

---

[1] The manor house of West Deane, belonging to Sir John Evelyn, M.P. for Ludgershall, generally known as Sir John Evelyn of Wiltshire to distinguish him from his uncle Sir John Evelyn of Surrey. An account of West Deane and its owners is given in the Wiltshire Archæological Magazine, xxii. p. 239, by the Rev. G. S. Master. Views of the old manor house are engraved in Hoare's Modern Wilts, Alderley, p. 24, and the Gentleman's Magazine, 1826, p. 297. Evelyn died in 1685; his epitaph is printed by Mr. Master, p. 293. The Committee of Both Kingdoms wrote to Major Duett on Dec. 21, 1644, ordering him to continue to garrison West Deane till further order. Cal. S. P., Dom. 1644-5, p. 194; Portland Papers, i. 197.

quitted it upon our approach, as they did also the siege soon after, contrary to our expectation. We made use of the opportunity, and furnished the town with provisions and all things necessary; which being done, the forces of Wilts and Dorsetshire marched back to the said counties. Being returned to Salisbury, I was informed that the enemy had put a garison into Langford House, two miles from thence, whereupon I resolved to fortify the belfrey in the Close, where I might keep a small guard to secure it for a horse-quarter, and to that end had summoned workmen to perform that work. At night having drawn up my regiment in order to acquaint them with the necessity that lay upon them to be more than ordinarily diligent in their duty at that juncture, as also to divide their watches between them, and to appoint the guard for that night, I received an alarm of the enemy's approach, and that they were advanced as far as Amesbury : of which desiring to have certain information, I sent threescore horse under the command of Capt. Sadler, the only captain of my regiment then with me, some of them being absent with leave and others without, to advance towards the enemy, till by taking of prisoners, or some other way, he might get some certain intelligence concerning them, and then to come back to me. With the rest of my men I marched slowly after him, being unwilling to retire into our quarters till I had made a further discovery concerning the enemy. Capt. Sadler, according to his instructions, marched to Amesbury, and sent me word from thence, that he had advice the enemy was not far off. I sent to him to continue his march, with the same orders as before, my self with the rest of the regiment following; and being come to Nether Haven, as I think it is called, I received notice from Capt. Sadler, that he had engaged an advanced party of the enemy, and could not get off; which unexpected news, and contrary to my orders, caused me to advance with all diligence to his relief, who had approached so near their main guard, as to give them an alarm to draw together, and yet had not pursued his charge, which if he had done, he might easily have dispersed the guard, and prevented the rest from coming together; but he having only alarm'd them, stood looking upon them whilst they drew up their body, which, when I came up, I perceived to be more numerous than all ours: however thinking it unfit to shew any backwardness at such a time, I advanced with that party that was with me, which was not above one half, the rest following as fast as they could, in order to charge the enemy's body; but they, before we came within pistol-shot, faced about and ran away. Thereupon I divided my men into two parties, giving the command of one of them to one Marshall, my major's lieutenant, the chief officer then with me, except Capt. Sadler, with whose conduct the troopers were so far dissatisfied, that they refused to follow him. The other party I headed my self, and gave orders to both not to pursue farther than the town, where we agreed to rally, falling into it by several ways. My party halted according to order, after having killed and taken prisoners about thirty of the enemy, with several of their horses: but that party commanded by Lieutenant Marshall not observing his orders, having pursued the enemy at least two miles, met with other bodies of the enemy's horse drawn together upon the alarm, who killed and took some of ours prisoners, the rest retreating in a disorderly manner. At my return to Salisbury I commanded all my men to be upon the guard till the morning, without unbridling or unsadling their horses; after which I disposed my prisoners into the belfrey, and placed a guard upon them; and having set our sentinels, I received a letter from Col. Norton, desiring me to send some horse to his assistance against some of the King's forces, which as I was reading, one of my sentinels brought me word that the enemy appeared at the town's end [1]. Whereupon I immediately mounted with six more, ordering the rest to make ready; and riding up by the Three Swans, heard a great noise of horses in the street that leads into the city from Old Sarum, which caused me to return to the market-place, where finding many of

[1] The royalist account of Langdale's surprise of Ludlow is printed in Appendix II.

the enemy's horse, I went by the back-side of the town-house through a street called the Ditch, to my guard, which was drawn up in the Close, but very short of the number I expected ; for some, contrary to orders, were gone to bed, and others taking the advantage of the night had stoln away, so that those remaining were not much above thirty horse. Of these I sent ten under a cornet to charge them, my self following after with the rest, and ordering a trumpet to sound in our rear, as if more were coming on. Passing by the chief cross, where we were forced to march one by one, and entring the market-place I found the cornet pickeering with the enemy, whom I with five or six of mine charged on the left flank, so that they gave ground, and thereby pressed so hard upon their own men on the right, and they on their file-leaders, that the whole party was soon routed, and ran before us. We followed them close in the rear, and tho they made many shot at me, yet I received no wound in the whole action. About a hundred of them ran through Winchester Gate to their main body, and about twice that number fled up a street called Endless Street, whom I pursuing, my horse fell backwards with me, by a check I gave him ; but my own men being in my rear, I soon recovered on horseback, and continued the pursuit, till I found the enemy to make a stand, the street, according to its name, being walled up at the farther end, and one of them breaking back upon me, and leaping the brook, but his horse losing his feet, threw him down ; and he perceiving himself to be at my mercy, desired his life. His horse I gave to one of my men who had been dismounted ; and having examined him, I found that he was a lieutenant-colonel, his name Middleton, and a Papist. He assured me, that there were three hundred men in that party which we had routed, three hundred appointed to second them, and three hundred more attending at the town's end as a reserve, and that the whole body was commanded by Sir Marmaduke Langdale. I acquainted him that my party being not so considerable, he might probably be rescued, and therefore I could not give him quarter, unless he would engage himself to be a true prisoner, which he did, upon condition that he might be my prisoner, which I promised him. And now most of my men being dispersed, I lodged my colours at an honest man's house of the town, delivering my prisoner and wounded men to the guard in the belfrey, and with five or six made my retreat through the Close by one Mrs. Sadler's, at whose house I quartered, where I found a boy standing at the door with my sute of arms. which I put on. Upon Harnham Hill I found a cornet with about twelve of our men, with whom I resolved to return and march after the enemy; but when we came to the belfrey, and were encouraging our little guard to oppose the enemy, we discovered three of their troops marching into the Close from the North Gate, their whole body following them. Whereupon having commanded the guard to fire upon them, I charged the enemy with as many of my party as were willing to follow me, exchanging several shot with them. Their first squadron soon began to give ground ; but my guard not firing upon the enemy according to my orders, and it being now grown light, they soon perceived the smalness of our number, and refused to run as before ; so that I was forced to retire as fast as I could with my men, one of whom carried away a sword of the enemy which was run through his arm. Before they came to Harnham Bridg they overtook one of my servants whose name was Stent, who after he had long defended himself, delivered up his sword upon promise of quarter ; after which, contrary to their word, they gave him several cuts on the head, so that above threescore splinters of bones were afterwards taken out of his scull. Being come to the other side of the bridg, I turned and faced the enemy, with one of my pistols in my hand, upon which they halted a little, whereby my men had time to recover almost to the top of Harnham Hill. In this posture I stood till the enemies were come within half pistol-shot of me, and then made my retreat. Another of my servants, called Henry Coles, who entred into my father's service two days after I was born. fell also into the enemy's hands, being mortally wounded, and died two or three days after. My groom also was taken by them. Upon the descent of the hill beyond Odstock I missed the road by reason of the snow, which lying upon the ground, had covered the beaten way, so that I was obliged to cross some plow'd lands to get into it again; which while I was doing, one of the enemy came up within shot of me, and calling me by my name, asked if I would take quarter; but as he rid directly upon me, armed with back and breast, I fired a pistol at him, and shot him into the belly; by which wound he fell from his horse, and was carried to the next town, where he died two days after, as one of my troopers afterwards told me, who was taken prisoner near the same place. In Odstock Lane another of the enemies being advanced within musquet-shot of me, called me also by name, and desired me to stay and take honourable quarter. I hearing him give good words, thought he had proposed to render himself to me, and therefore stopped my horse, that I might hear him more distinctly; but he instead of that made ready his carabine to fire at me, which I perceiving, and sensible of my danger, by reason of the greatness of the enemy's number, made the best of my way towards Fording Bridg, where having rested a little, and rallied a party of my horse, I marched with them to South-ampton. At that place I endeavoured to procure some force for the relief of those poor men that were left in the belfrey at Salisbury; which as I was doing, I received advice, that after a vigorous resistance for the most part of that day, the enemies had forced a collier to drive his cart, loaden with charcoal, to the door of the belfrey, (where he lost his life) and with it burnt down the door, which in a day's time we should have secured by a breast-work; but for want thereof Lieutenant-Colonel Read was forced to yield the place to the enemy upon such terms as he could get, which were, to have their lives, and be prisoners of war. The enemy took here, and in the town, as also of those who pursued them in the night, contrary to my orders, fourscore prisoners; and had taken more if they had not received a check upon their first arrival in the town by a handful of men : for they had placed guards at the gates of most of the greatest inns in the city; but their party flying, those guards also quitted their posts, whereby many of our men had an opportunity to get off. I was slightly wounded on the breast with a sword : my horse was hurt with a shot, and died of it soon after. We had about threescore of the enemy prisoners at Southampton, taken with Col. Coke; these we exchanged for our men, having engaged to procure elsewhere the discharge of as many as we wanted of the number they had of ours, which I made good to them. The most serviceable of my horse I sent towards Portsmouth, to take advantages against the enemy as there should be occasion, remaining with the rest about Limington and Hurst Castle, resolving as soon as I could to mount my men again. The enemy hoping to surprize me in this corner marched towards me, but failed in their design. I being gone into the Isle of Wight to confer with our friends there, whom I found very well disposed to the publick service; and being informed that the enemy designed to attempt the garison of Christ-Church, we imbarked some men to reinforce them, who being ready to put to sea, news was brought that the enemies were beaten off, and so saved our men that trouble[1]. The Lord Goring having left a considerable force in the County of Wilts, marched with his army into Somersetshire, where being joined by those who had besieged Taunton, they sat down before it again : Col. Massey was sent by the Parliament to relieve the place, but finding his forces not sufficient to that purpose, he durst not attempt it.

The Committee of Both Kingdoms ordered my regiment to lie at Odium to prevent the excursions of the garison at Basing House[2]; but after we had been there a few days, my

[1] Clarendon, Rebellion, ix. 7; Godwin, Civil War in Hampshire, p. 203.

[2] The Committee of Both Kingdoms wrote to Ludlow on March 14, 1645: 'In the absence of our forces now gone towards the west we have thought fit to appoint the Lord-general's life-guard and the troops of Major Duett and Captain Saville to quarter about Blackwater and the confines of Surrey and Hants, to preserve those parts from the incursions of the enemy from Basing

major, who had more wit than courage or honesty, prevailed with the council of officers to vote our lying there unsafe and unadvisable. I being unwilling to stay contrary to their advice, without an especial order, acquainted the Committee of Both Kingdoms with the result of the council of officers, who approving their reasons, sent me orders to draw off: in obedience to which I marched into Surrey, and the first night arrived at a place called, as I think, Godliman [1] near Guilford. Sir John Evelyn endeavoured to perswade me to join Lieutenant General Cromwell, who was ordered into the west [2]; but being engaged to attend our committee about the recruiting of my regiment, I was not willing to stir till that business was effected, that I might not leave so many honest men who had lost their horses in the service, before I had procured some provision to be made for them. The disputes in the mean time continued in the two Houses concerning the conduct of the army; and tho what was objected touching the late miscarriages at the fight of Newbury, and elsewhere, amounted not to a formal charge, yet it so far prevailed with the House of Commons, as to convince them of the necessity of making an alteration in the conduct of the army, in order to bring the war to a conclusion; which resolution was

taken by the House upon a report made to them by Mr. Zouch Tate, chairman of the committee appointed for the

---

and Winchester. We have appointed you to command that party.' On the 18th, Captains Ramsey, Stevens, and Bruce were placed under his command, Major Duett ordered to join him, and the foot quartered at Farnham to assist him if needed. Ludlow himself was on both dates in London. Cal. S. P., Dom. 1644-5, pp. 345, 354, 362.

[1] i. e. Godalming.

[2] On March 3, Cromwell was instructed to join Waller and march west to relieve Melcombe Regis and the Dorsetshire parliamentarians. On March 12, Waller and Cromwell

defeated Sir James Long at Devizes, capturing 400 horses and 300 prisoners. Only about thirty of Long's regiment escaped. Long himself, the King's High Sheriff of Wiltshire, was also taken. 'Colonel Ludlow,' says a letter announcing the victory, 'is now (thanks be to God) sole High Sheriff of this county.' Vicars, Burning Bush, p. 125. Cal. S. P., Dom. 1644-5, pp. 334, 384, 399. Cromwell and Waller were at Salisbury on April 9 retreating before the advance of Goring. Carlyle's Cromwell, Letter xxiv.

reforming of the army, wherein he represented that they had been endeavouring to obey their orders, but found the condition of the army as the physician did the blood of his patient, that consulted him about the cure of a slight tumour, when the whole mass of his blood was entirely corrupted; that therefore the committee had ordered him to acquaint the House, that the whole body of their army being infected, nothing would serve for their recovery less than the entire renewing of their constitution. The House, that they might do it without giving occasion to any sinister reflections upon themselves, agreed upon a Self-Denying Ordinance, the grounds whereof were expressed to be, the clearing of the Parliament from the aspersions cast on them, of prolonging the war on purpose to gratify each other with places, and neglecting their duty in the House by holding employments in the army: they therefore enacted, that all Members of Parliament should surrender the offices they held from them, that they might the better attend their duty in Parliament. By this means the Earl of Essex, the Earl of Manchester, and Sir William Waller, were laid aside, the latter rather to shew their impartiality, than from any distrust of him, he having never discovered to that time any inclination to favour the king's cause. Upon this change Sir Thomas Fairfax was voted General, and Philip Skippon Major-General of the foot. A committee was also appointed to consider what number of horse and foot this army should consist of, and who under the General should command them. They agreed also upon the colonels, some whereof were Scots, as Middleton, Holborn, and others, who disliking the design, refused to accept of employments. Pointz was commissionated to command the forces in the north, and Massey those in the west, consisting chiefly of such as had served under Sir William Waller[1]. The committee would have named me

1615

April 1.

---

[1] Ludlow was ordered on April 10 to collect certain troops of horse in Surrey and march to join Waller. Waller was ordered at the same time to make up a regiment of 600 horse to be commanded by Col. Cooke, and to send it to the assistance of Massey. This was the regiment to which Ludlow refers. Cal. S. P., Dom. 1644-5, pp. 397, 8.

for the command of a regiment[1]; but the gentlemen who served in Parliament for the County of Wilts, pretended then that they could not spare me; yet soon after, observing me not fit to promote a faction, and solely applying my self to advance the cause of the publick, they combined against me, and procured me to be laid aside, under colour that they stood not in need of more than four troops for the service of the county, of which they offered me the command; and I should not have declined it, had I found my endeavours answered with sutable acceptance, or that they whom I served had been willing the publick cause, for which I was ready to sacrifice my life, should prosper: but the contrary being most evident; and tho some of the gentlemen continued to manifest their fidelity to the publick, and their affection to me, yet most of them having now espoused another interest, and rejoicing at any loss that fell upon ours, I chose rather to desist and wait for a better opportunity to improve my talent for the service of the publick. My major, notwithstanding his artifices, being disappointed in his expectation to command these troops, openly pulled off the mask, and with about thirty of his troop, and some strangers, under pretence of beating up a quarter of the enemy, went over to them, having sent his wife before to give them notice of his design. But his lieutenant continuing faithful to the publick, hindred most part of his troop from following him. Soon after he undertook to raise a regiment in the north parts of Wiltshire for the King; but whilst he was attempting to effect

it, an encounter happened between him and some forces of the Parliament, wherein being worsted, and endeavouring to save himself by leaping over a ditch, he fell with his horse into it, and was so bruised with his fall, that he never spoke more, thereby receiving such a recompence as was due to his treachery[2].

---

[1] Probably Haselrig's recommendation of Ludlow to Fairfax was connected with his proposed employment in the New Model. See the letter quoted in the preface.

[2] Major John Dowet, or Duett, had previously distinguished himself in the war in the west. At Lansdown according to Viears he did 'singular bravely,' and is styled 'a

About the same time that the Parliament made Sir
Thomas Fairfax General of their forces, the King made
Prince Rupert General of his, notwithstanding his late ill
success at Marston Moor, to the great dissatisfaction of
many of his council.

The committee of Wilts divided themselves, one part of
them to sit at Malmsbury, and the other to reside about
Salisbury; but wanting a place for their security, they put
a garison into Falston House[1], and Capt. Edward Doyly
contending with Major William Ludlow for the government
thereof, the committee at London gave it to the latter, who
with his troop somewhat restrained the excursions of the
King's party from their garison thereabouts. That part
of the committee which sat at Malmsbury having some
affairs to dispatch at Marlborough, went thither accompanied by Col. Devereux, governour of the place. The
first night after their arrival a party of the King's surprized them there, and took some of the committee, with
the said governour, and most of the forces they had with
them, prisoners[2].

The Parliament, tho they were not wanting to make all
fitting preparations for war, yet neglected no honest endeavours to procure peace, assuring themselves that they
should be the better enabled to bear whatsoever might be
the event of the war, if they took care to discharge their
consciences in that particular, and to manifest, that as they
had been compelled to it by mere necessity, so, if it must
be continued, it should not be through their choice or

---

man who hath given sufficient testimony of his valour, fidelity and wisdom.' Jehovah Jireh, pp. 376, 379.
He deserted in April, 1645, after
giving some trouble by his disobedience to orders. Cal. S. P., Dom.
1644-5, p. 394. He was killed in an
unsuccessful attack on Lechlade on
Nov. 24, 1645. Vicars, Burning
Bush, p. 324 ; Waylen's History of
Marlborough, pp. 227-31 ; Portland
Papers, i. 316.

[1] Falston Manor, near Wilton, was
the property of Sir George Vaughan.
Cal. Committee for Compounding,
p. 2036.

[2] Ludlow probably refers to the
surprise of Marlborough by Sir John
Cansfield in Jan. 1646, which he
appears to confuse with the capture of Rowden House near Chippenham a year earlier. See Appendix
II.

1645

obstinacy. To this end it was agreed, that commissioners should be sent from the Parliament, to treat with others to be sent from the King about conditions of peace. The

Jan. 29.

place of their meeting was at Uxbridg, where after the King had owned the two Houses as a Parliament, to which he was not without difficulty perswaded, tho he had by an act engaged that they should continue to be a Parliament till they dissolved themselves, which they had not done; and consented that his commissioners should treat in the same quality they were in before the war, the commissioners of Parliament declining to give them the titles conferred upon them since; they made some progress in the treaty, which began the 13th of January, 1645, but the proposition concerning the bishops being rejected, it came to nothing. During the treaty Mr. Love, one of the chaplains attending the commissioners of Parliament, preaching before them, averred, that the King was a man of blood, and that it was a vain thing to hope for the blessing of God upon any peace to be made with him, till satisfaction should be made for the blood that had been shed. For these words the King's commissioners demanded satisfaction; but the treaty breaking up, nothing was done in order thereunto. And now both parties renewed the war, Weymouth being

Feb. 9.

seized for the King, and some advantage obtained against

March 1.

the Parliament near Pomfret. On the other side, the forces

Feb. 22.

of the Parliament surprized the important town of Shrewsbury, whereby the King's correspondence with Wales be-

Feb. 28.

came much interrupted. They also recovered Weymouth[1] by the help of the garison of Melcolm Regis, which is separated from the said town by a small arm of the sea, with a bridg over it, and which was preserved by the industry of the governour Col. Sydenham.

Col. Cromwell, notwithstanding the Self-Denying Ordinance, was dispensed with by the Parliament; and being impower'd to command the horse under Sir Thomas Fair-

---

[1] On the loss and recapture of Weymouth, see Vicars, Burning Bush, p. 118; Longmore, Life of Sir Richard Wiseman, p. 205; W. M. Harvey, History of the Hundred of Willey, pp. 91-4.

fax, he marched with a party of horse and dragoons from Windsor, and at Islip Bridg met, fought, and defeated the Queen's Regiment of Horse, together with the regiments of the Earl of Northampton, the Lord Wilmot, and Col. Palmer, taking five hundred horse and two hundred foot prisoners, whereof many were officers and persons of quality. After which he summoned Blechington House, which was surrendred to him by Col. Windebank, son to the late Secretary of State, who coming to Oxford, was shot to death for so doing. He forced Sir William Vaughan, and Lieutenant-Colonel Littleton, with three hundred and fifty men into Bampton-bush, where he took them both, and two hundred of their men prisoners, with their arms; sending Col. Fiennes after another party, who took a hundred and fifty horse, three colonels, and forty private souldiers prisoners, with their arms: and being reinforced by about five hundred foot from Col. Brown, he attempted Faringdon House, but without success.

General Fairfax leaving Lieutenant General Cromwell to block up the King at Oxford, with the body of the army marched westward, with a design to relieve Taunton; but being ordered by the Committee of Both Kingdoms to besiege Oxford, he appointed Col. Welden to relieve that town, which he easily effected, the enemy marching off at his approach, apprehending them to be the whole army marching against them, as they before had been informed. The King sent the Prince of Wales, accompanied with Hyde and Culpeper, into the west, to raise forces; and despising the New Model, as it was called, because most of the old officers were either omitted by the Parliament, or had quitted their commands in the army, judging himself master of the field, marched towards Leicester, and by this time was grown so considerable, that the Committee of Both Kingdoms thought it high time to look after him, and to that end commanded the General with the army to march and observe his motions; but before he could overtake him, the King had made himself master of

Marginal dates: 1645. April 24. April 27. April 30. May 1. March 5.

1645   Leicester by storm, and plundered it, with the loss of
May 31.   about seven hundred men on his side, and about one
          hundred of the town. Being encouraged with this success,
          and with the consideration that he was to encounter with
          an unexperienced enemy, upon advice that our army was
          in search of him, he advanced towards them, and both
          armies met in the field of Naseby on the 14th of June, 1645.
June 8.   Some days before one Col. Vermuyden, an old souldier,
          who commanded a regiment of horse, had laid down his
          commission, whether through diffidence of success, or what
          other consideration, I know not: and in the beginning of
          the engagement Major-General Skippon, the only old
          souldier remaining amongst the chief officers of the army,
          received a shot in the body from one of our own party,
          as was supposed unwittingly, whereby he was in a great
          measure disabled to perform the duty of his place that day,
          tho extreamly desirous to do it. Under these discourage-
          ments the horse upon our left wing were attacked by
          those of the enemy's right, and beaten back to our cannon,
          which were in danger of being taken, our foot giving ground
          also. But our right wing being strengthned by those of
          our left that were rallied by their officers, fell upon the
          enemy's left wing, and having broken and repulsed them,
          resolving to improve the opportunity, charged the main
          body of the King's army, and with the assistance of two or
          three regiments of our infantry, entirely encompassed the
          enemy's body of foot, who finding themselves deserted by
          their horse, threw down their arms, and yielded themselves
          prisoners. By this means our horse were at leisure to pursue
          the King, and such as fled with him towards Leicester,
          taking many prisoners in the pursuit, who with those
          taken in the field amounted in all to about six thousand,
          and amongst them six colonels, eight lieutenant colonels,
          eighteen majors, seventy captains, eighty lieutenants,
          eighty ensigns, two hundred inferiour officers, about one
          hundred and forty standards of horse and foot, the King's
          footmen and servants, and the whole train of artillery and
          baggage. This victory was obtained with the loss of a very

few on our side, and not above three or four hundred of
the enemy.

In the pursuit the King's cabinet was taken, and in it
many letters of consequence[1], particularly one from the
Lord Digby, advising the King, before any act of hostility
on either side, to betake himself to some place of strength,
and there to declare against the Parliament; by which men
perceived that the design of making war upon the Parliament was resolved upon early, the King having followed
this counsel exactly.

The Parliament had impeached Finch of high treason,
for advising the illegal tax of ship-money, soliciting the
judges to declare it lawful, and threatning those who
refused so to do, for which good service the King had
preferred him to be Keeper of the Great Seal; but the
place being vacant upon his flight, the King would not
entrust it with Littleton before he had obliged him by an
oath to promise to send the Seal to the King whensoever he
should by any messenger require it of him; which I am
inclined to believe to have been the cause why Littleton
left the Parliament, not daring to stay, after he had, according to his oath, sent the Seal to the King by one Mr.
Elliot, dispatched to him by the King for that purpose.
The Seal being thus carried away, the Parliament finding
justice obstructed through the want of it, declared, that
the Seal ought to attend them during their sitting, and
therefore that all that was or should be done since it was
carried to the King, was null and void. Upon which a
new Seal was ordered to be made, and commissioners
nominated for the keeping of it, and putting it in execution
to all intents and purposes, the Parliament thereby exer-
cising the supreme authority in virtue of their frequent
declarations; 'That the King doth nothing in his personal
capacity as King, but in his politick capacity according to

[1] These letters are printed in 'The
King's Cabinet Opened,' 1645,—a
pamphlet published by order of the
Parliament, with a preface making
similar comments. May's observations are still more severe. Breviary
of the History of the Parliament of
England, Maseres, Select Tracts, i.
78. Cf. Gardiner, Great Civil War,
ii. 223.

law; of which the judges of Westminster Hall are judges in the intervals of Parliament; and during the sitting of Parliament the two Houses, being the great council both of King and people, are the sole judges thereof.'

In the King's cabinet were also found letters from the Queen, blaming him for owning those at Westminster to be a Parliament, and warning him not to do any thing to the prejudice of the Roman Catholicks; with a copy of his answer, wherein he promised his care of the Papists, and excused his owning the two Houses at Westminster to be a Parliament; assuring her, that if he could have found two of his mongrel Parliament at Oxford, as he called them, of his mind therein, he would never have done it; and that tho he had done it publickly, the Parliament refusing to treat with him otherwise, yet he had given order to have it entred in the journal of his council, that this, notwithstanding, should not be of any validity for the enabling them to be a Parliament. Another paper was found with them, giving some account of the troubles in Ireland, wherein the Papists who had taken arms being qualified rebels, that term was struck out, and the word Irish added by the King himself. There was likewise a letter to the French King, complaining of the unkindness and ingratitude of the Queen, and of the reasons of the removal of her servants that she brought over with her; of which it had been discretion in the King to have kept no memorials, such matters, when buried in oblivion, being next best to the not having any differences between so near relations. Many more letters there were relating to the publick, which were printed with observations, by order of the Parliament; and others of no less consequence suppressed, as I have been credibly informed, by some of those that were intrusted with them, who since the King's return have been rewarded for it. One paper I must not omit which was here found, being that very paper which contained the principal evidence against the Earl of Strafford, and had been, as before mentioned, purloined from the committee appointed by the House of Commons to

manage the charge against him, having these words written
upon it with the King's own hand, ' This paper was delivered
to me by George Digby,' tho he, as well as the rest of that
committee, had solemnly protested, that he had neither
taken that paper away, nor knew what was become of it [1].
The prisoners and standards taken in the fight were
brought through London to Westminster. The standards
were ordered to be hung up in Westminster Hall, and
the prisoners were secured in the artillery-ground near
Tuttle Fields; a committee being appointed to consider
how to dispose of them, who permitted those to return
home that would give security for their living peaceably
for the future ; but such as did not, which was much the
greater number, were shipped off to serve in foreign
parts upon conditions [2]. This success was astonishing,
being obtained by men of little experience in affairs of
this nature, and upon that account despised by their
enemies ; yet it proved the deciding battel, the King's
party after this time never making any considerable opposition. Leicester capitulated two days after, and was
surrendred; and some of our forces besieged Chester,
whilst the Scots did the like to Hereford. The General
Sir Thomas Fairfax marched with the army to relieve our
friends at Taunton, where Col. Welden was besieged, took
Highworth in his march, and dissipated the club-men,
defeated Goring's forces at Lamport, possessed himself of
the towns of Bridgwater and Bath by capitulation, and of
Sherburn Castle by storm. Bristol also was surrendred
after the outworks and fort had been taken by assault,
with divers other successes of less importance, and therefore unnecessary to be mentioned here. Lieutenant General
Cromwell being sent to reduce such garisons as were in the
way to London, began with the Castle of Winchester, which
was delivered to him upon articles ; after which he marched
to Basing House, and erected a battery on the east-side of it ;

1645

June 18.

July 10.
Aug. 5.
Sept. 11.

Oct. 5.

---

[1] Cf. Whitelocke, Memorials, i.
127, ed. 1853.
[2] On the treatment of the prisoners

taken at Naseby, see Gardiner, Great
Civil War, ii. 222; Vicars, Burning
Bush, p. 173.

1645
Oct. 14. by which having made a breach, he stormed and entered it, putting many of the garison to the sword, and taking the rest with the Marquiss of Winchester, whose house it was, prisoners. Col. Robert Hammond had been before made prisoner by the Marquiss, and was kept here by him in order to secure his own life, which he did by putting himself under the Colonel's protection, when ours entred the place. It was suspected that Col. Hammond, being related to the Earl of Essex, whose half-sister was married to the Marquiss of Winchester, had suffered himself to be taken prisoner on design to serve the said marquiss. The next place he attempted was Langford House near Salisbury, which was Oct. 17. yielded in a day or two upon articles. The works about Basing were levelled, Sherborn Castle slighted [1], as also Falston House, of which Major Ludlow was governour, who was removed to undertake the same charge at Langford House, wherein the Parliament thought fit to keep a garison by reason of its nearness to the enemy [2].

The King, as well to secure himself by getting as far from our forces as he could, as to raise a new army if possible, marched with the horse that he had left towards North Wales, hoping in his way to relieve Chester, besieged by Sir William Brereton, and by his presence in Wales to prevail with them to furnish him with a body of foot: but he found himself frustrated in both these designs: for Sept. 24. being worsted near Routen Heath by Major-General Pointz, who commanded a brigade of the Parliament's in those parts, he saw the face of affairs much altered both in North and South Wales: in the last of which, tho he was entertained civilly by some particular persons, yet the generality of the country, that during his successes had subjected themselves even slavishly to his instruments, now

---

[1] On May 4, 1646, the House of Commons resolved 'that the Castle Hill and works at the Devizes and the works about Langford House should be slighted,' and that the forces to be kept up in the county should consist of 100 horse under the command of Captain William Ludlow, then governor of Devizes, and that a garrison of 150 foot should be kept at Malmesbury. C. J. iv. 534.

[2] Accounts of the reduction of Basing House and Langford House are given by Sprigge, pp. 149, 156.

fearing he might draw the army of the Parliament after him, and make their country the seat of war, began to murmur against him, and drew together a numerous body in the nature of a club-army, whispering amongst themselves as if they intended to seize his person, and deliver him to the Parliament to make their peace. Which being reported to the King, he thought fit to retire from thence with his forces, only leaving a small garison in the Castle of Cardiff, which, together with the county, was soon after reduced to the obedience of the Parliament by Col. Pritchard, where Sir John Strangwaies was amongst others taken prisoner, who by order of the Parliament was sent up to London, and committed to the Tower[1]. The Isle of Anglesey, and such places of North Wales as had been held for the King, were surrendred to the Parliament; but Glamorganshire and the parts adjacent continued not long in their duty, but revolted at the instigation of one Mr. Kerne of Winny, who pretending great fidelity to the Parliament, was intrusted by them as their Sheriff for that county, and made use of that authority to raise the county against them, and to besiege Colonel Pritchard, and the rest of their friends in the Castle of Cardiff; who being reduced to some necessity, had been probably constrained to surrender it, had not speedy relief been procured from the Parliament under the conduct of Colonel Kirle of Glocestershire; who falling suddenly upon the enemy, routed and killed many of them.

The King's affairs being in this low condition in England and Wales, he resolved to try what might be done in Scotland ; in order to which, he commands the Lord Digby to march thither with a party of sixteen hundred horse, and to join the Marquiss of Montross then in arms for him in

Margin notes:
1645
Aug. 20.
1646
June 14.
1646
February.

[1] Cardiff, of which Sir Richard Basset was governor, was taken by Col. Herbert in Sept. 1645, and Col. Prichard was made governor Dec. 1, 1645. Edward Carne of Ewenny, High Sheriff of Glamorganshire, revolted from the Parliament, and besieged Cardiff in Feb., 1646, but the siege was raised by Major-Gen. Rowland Laugharne. Phillips, Civil War in Wales, i. 319, 357; ii. 298 ; Vicars, Burning Bush, pp. 276, 370 Report on the Portland MSS. i. 348–352.

1645

that kingdom. In obedience to the King's order, the Lord Digby marched from Newark, and in his way surprized about eight hundred of ours near Sherborn; but was after-

Oct. 15.

wards routed by Col. Copley, who recovered the men and arms taken from ours, killed forty of the enemy upon the spot, took four hundred of them prisoners, and about six hundred horses: the Lord Digby's coach and papers were also taken. This party was defeated a second time by Sir John Brown, and a third by Col. Bright, who took two hundred of them prisoners; the Lord Digby with about twenty more hardly escaping to the Isle of Man, and from thence to Ireland [1].

July.

At the approach of Sir Thomas Fairfax's army, the enemy raised the siege of Taunton; from thence the General marched to Honyton, and the next day to Colompton, from whence the enemy retired in great disorder. On October 20, the army, tho much weakned by hard duty and the rigour of the season, resolved upon the blockade of Exeter. Carmarthen Castle, Monmouth, and divers other places were surrendred to the Parliament: so that the King looking upon the rebels in Ireland as his last refuge, sends orders to the Earl of Ormond not only to continue the cessation, but to conclude a peace with them, upon condition they would oblige themselves to send over an army to his assistance against the Parliament of England. The Supreme Council of Ireland, as they called themselves, having notice of it. invited the Earl of Ormond to Kilkenny to treat about the same; who being willing to see his relations and his estate in those parts, as also to expedite that service, accepted their invitation, and

1646

marched thither with about 3000 or 4000, horse and foot,

Aug. 31.

for his guard, which by the advice of the Lord Mountgarret and the Supreme Council were dispersed into quarters in the villages thereabouts; the Earl of Ormond suspecting

[1] Digby with 1500 men left the King at Welbeck on Oct. 14, and was defeated at Sherburn on Oct. 15. On his unfortunate expedition, see Sir Edward Walker's Historical Discourses, pp. 143-5; Vicars, Burning Bush, pp. 297–301, 303, 306–310, 315; Gardiner, Great Civil War, ii. 351 4. For 'Colonel Bright' read 'Colonel Briggs.'

nothing, having sent orders to Sir Francis Willoughby, who
commanded that party under him, to that purpose : but he
being an old and experienced commander, well acquainted
with the treachery of that nation, and particularly of those
of the Popish religion, knowing how easy it would be for
the Irish to cut them off in the quarters assigned for them,
resolved not to consent to the dispersing of his men ; and
therefore desired of the Earl of Ormond, that he might
quarter with them in the field, or where his Lordship
should appoint, desiring if this would not satisfy, he might
have liberty to return home ; advising him not to trust his
person with them, notwithstanding their fair words. My
Lord hereupon leaves the care of quartering his men to
Sir Francis Willoughby ; but resolves himself to stay at
Kilkenny. Sir Francis draws the troops into Goran, a
town five miles from Kilkenny, where he kept his guards
with as much caution as if he had been in an enemy's
country. The enemy being by this means disappointed of
their design to cut off the party by surprize, resolved to
attempt it by open force ; and all the favour that the Earl
of Ormond could get amongst his relations, was to have
notice to shift for himself, which with much difficulty he
did, sending orders to his forces to march towards Dublin,
in which he was very readily obeyed by them, having had
advice that the country was rising upon them ; which they
did in such numbers, that if Col. Bagnal, governour of
Loughlyn, had not permitted them to pass the bridg there,
they had in all appearance been cut off. When they had
recovered their own quarters, they discovered a piece of
treachery, as Sir Francis Willoughby, who gave me this
account, judged it to be, tho he knew not on whom to
charge it : for they found that they had not been in a
condition to make any opposition, if the enemy had fallen
upon them, the powder with which they were furnished
having no force in it ; which came to be discovered upon
the trial of a musquet at a mark, by the small report it
gave, and the fall of the bullet half way from it : whereupon
searching further into the matter, they found all their store

1646 to be of the same sort. The Irish seized upon all the Earl of Ormond's plate, and whatsoever he had with him at Kilkenny, his haste not permitting him to save any thing[1]. By this usage his zeal for the prosecution of the treaty with the rebels became much abated. The King's commission to the Earl of Ormond was not of so large an extent as he was willing to allow, in case the treaty with the Irish came to any effect; and therefore the Earl of Glamorgan, afterwards Earl of Worcester, was impowered by private instructions from him, to promise them the liberty of the Romish religion, with divers other advantages to 1645 the Irish rebels, upon which he treated with them. Aug. 25. But because this, when it came to be publickly known in England, was highly resented by many even of the King's party, the Lord Digby, who was ordered by the King to assist in that affair, finding that the treaty was not like to take effect, to give a specious colour to the matter, as if Glamorgan had in that particular exceeded his commission, accused him of high treason, and procured him to Dec. 26. be imprison'd by the Earl of Ormond: but in letters intercepted from the Lord Glamorgan to his lady, he desired that she would not entertain any fears concerning him; for that he doubted not, if he could be admitted to be heard, that he should be able to justify his proceedings, to the confusion of those who had caused his imprisonment.

The English officers and souldiers provoked by the late treachery of the Irish, and apprehending that without assistance from England they might fall into their hands, would not be satisfied unless a message was sent to the Parliament to treat about conditions for the putting of Dublin, and the Protestant forces of Ireland, into their hands: in order to which the Parliament sent over commissioners to treat with the Earl of Ormond and the

---

[1] Cf. Carte, Ormond, ed. 1851, iii. 259-264. When these incidents occurred the articles of peace between Ormond and the Confederates had actually been agreed upon and published. Ib. p. 246. Glamorgan's negotiations and arrest took place before Ormond's peace, not after it.

council[1].   But tho the Earl was not willing that any thing
should be concluded at that time ; yet Sir Francis Willoughby was, as I have heard him say, so far convinced
of the necessity and duty that lay upon them so to
do, that he promised our commissioners to preserve the
Castle of Dublin, of which he was then governour, for
the service of the Parliament, whensoever they should
command it.

Montross having obtained a victory against those whom
the Scots had left to preserve the peace of Scotland[2], by
the means of which he was become master of a great
part of that kingdom, David Lesley was sent thither from
Hereford with most of the Scotish horse, where he defeated
the army of Montross, and reduced that nation to its
former obedience.

After the surrender of Bristol to the forces of the Parliament, Prince Rupert who had been governour thereof
returned to Oxford, where he found so cool a reception from
the King by reason of the loss of that place, that Col. Leg
then Governour of Oxford was turned out of that command
for being of his faction, and the government of that city put
into the hands of Sir Thomas Glenham.   The Prince was
for some time forbidden to wear a sword ; and tho he was
soon after restored to that liberty, yet he was never more
intrusted with any command.   The House of Commons
finding their business to increase, and their numbers to
diminish by the death of some, and desertion of others to
the King at Oxford, ordered the Commissioners of the Seal
to issue out writs to such counties, cities, and boroughs,
as the House by their particular order should direct, for
the election of members to serve in Parliament[3].   They
ordered also a jewel to be prepared of the value of about

---

[1] Carte, Ormond, iii. 278.

[2] The battle of Kilsyth, Aug. 15, 1645.

[3] 'On Aug. 21 it was resolved, though only by a narrow majority of three, that a new writ should be issued for the borough of South- wark.   During the following week a large number of constituencies received favourable answers to their petitions for permission to hold fresh elections.'   Gardiner, Great Civil War, ii. 313 ; cf. Masson, Life of Milton, iii. 400.

1645

seven hundred pounds, to be presented to Sir Thomas Fairfax; it had the House of Commons represented on one side, and the battel of Naseby on the other; three members of Parliament were deputed to carry the present to him[1];

September.

the opportunity of whose guard I took to go into the west without disturbance, which was difficult to do at that time, many of the King's party hovering about the downs, from whence they were called Col. Downs his men; who rendring the rode unsafe, I procured a guard of twenty or thirty of the county horse to accompany me during my stay in those parts. So small a number not being sufficient either to defend me, or to make any attempt, I betook my self to Col. Massey's party, commanded at that time by Col. Edward Cook[2], where I had not been long before an alarm was given, that a party of horse from Oxford had marched

1646

by, with a design to relieve Corfe Castle, besieged at that

February.

time by our forces: but before we could get our men together, they had surprized part of ours in Warham, and beaten off the guard between that place and the castle, which they relieved with what they could, and were returned

---

[1] On June 16, the House of Commons voted a jewel of the value of £500 to be made for Sir T. Fairfax. The jewel (which finally cost £800) is described in Markham's Life of Fairfax, p. 435. On Sept. 27. John Ashe and three other members were sent by the House to Sir T. Fairfax, and his letter acknowledging the gift is dated Nov. 14; C. J. iv. 175, 292. 348. See also Sprigge, p. 164.

[2] Col. Edward Cooke, a younger son of Sir Robert Cooke, of Highnam, Gloucestershire, served originally in the army of Sir William Waller, and was one of the witnesses against Nathaniel Fiennes after his surrender of Bristol. Cal. Clarendon S. P. i. 242; A true Relation of Col. Fiennes his trial, 1644, Depositions, p. 6. In April, 1645, Waller was ordered to send him and his regiment to reinforce Massey and assist in the relief

of Taunton. Whilst engaged on this service Cooke was severely wounded. Cal. S. P., Dom. 1644-5, pp. 418, 476; Sprigge, Anglia Rediviva, pp. 19, 71. He seems, from his subsequent career, to have shared Massey's political views. Cooke was at Newport on Nov. 30, 1648, when the King was seized and carried off to Hurst Castle. He drew up a narrative of the seizure which is printed in Rushworth, vii. 1344; cf. Tanner MSS. lvii. f. 437. After the restoration Cooke was in great favour with Charles II, who was wont to call him 'honest Ned Cooke.' Memoirs of Thomas, Earl of Aylesbury, pp. 27, 43, 354. He was one of the commissioners appointed to carry out the Act of Settlement and the Explanatory Act in Ireland; Carte, Ormond, iv. 123, 232.

back again [1]. In this action a brother of my father's was mortally wounded, taken prisoner by the enemy, and died the next day. Col. Cook was forced to content himself to reinforce the besiegers, and to return to his former station.

1646

The army commanded by Sir Thomas Fairfax having left a strong party to block up Exeter, advanced westward towards the enemy ; and at Bovey Tracy fought the brigade commanded by the Lord Wentworth, took four hundred horse, and about a hundred foot, prisoners, with six standards, one of which was the King's. Two regiments of ours appeared before Dartmouth, and summoned it ; but the garison being numerous, and furnished with all things necessary, refused to surrender : upon which the army advancing, possessed themselves of their outworks, and having turned their cannon upon them, two forts, distant about a mile from the town, wherein were thirty-four pieces of cannon, and two ships of war that were in the harbour, surrendred ; which the governour understanding, capitulated, and delivered the town upon articles, being permitted to march off himself ; but Sir Hugh Pollard, the Earl of Newport, Col. Seymour, four colonels, with divers others, were to remain prisoners ; and a French vessel coming into the harbour, not knowing what had passed, was seized, and letters of consequence found in her from the Queen. The Prince of Wales, who to countenance their affairs had the name of General in the Western Parts, finding their affairs desperate, shipped himself for Scilly, leaving the command of their forces to Sir Ralph Hopton, who was soon after summoned by General Fairfax to lay down his arms ; and after several messages, four commissioners on each side met at Tresilian Bridg, and came to an agreement ; the substance of which was, to deliver up all their arms, artillery, and ammunition, except what was excepted by the articles ; to be admitted to compound according to the rates fixed by the Parliament, and to have

Jan. 9.

Jan. 18.

March 2.

March 14.

---

[1] On this attempted relief of Corfe Castle, see Sprigge, pp. 189–194 ; Whitelock, i. 571, 580. The uncle mentioned was Benjamin Ludlow.

1646   liberty granted for such as desired it to go beyond sea,
which Sir Ralph Hopton and some others did. The people

March 5.   of Padstow seized a ship coming from Ireland, and perceiving a letter floating in the sea, took it up, and opening
it, found it to be from the Earl of Glamorgan, therein acquainting the King's party. that six thousand Irish were
ready to be embarked for their assistance, and that four
thousand more should follow them in a short time. Upon
the dispersion of Sir Ralph Hopton's army, most of the
forts and tenable places in the west procured the best conditions they could for themselves. Hereford was surprized

1645   on the 18th of December, by Col. Birch and Col. Morgan,
after it had been besieged for about two months ineffectually
by the Scots : in this place was taken that inveterate enemy
to the Parliament Serjeant Jenkins, with some others. In

1646   February following Byron the governour of Chester sur-
Feb. 3.   rendred that place upon terms.

The best friends of the Parliament were not without fears
what the issue of their new elections might be : for tho the
people durst not chuse such as were open enemies to them,
yet probably they would such as were most likely to be for
a peace upon any terms, corruptly preferring the fruition of
their estates and sensual enjoyments before the publick interest ; which sort of men were no less dangerous than the
other : and therefore honest men in all parts did what they
could to promote the election of such as were most hearty
for the accomplishment of our deliverance ; judging it to be
of the highest importance so to wind up things, that we
might not be over-reach'd by our enemies in a treaty, that
had not been able to contend with us in open war. To
this end I endeavoured that my uncle Mr. Edmund Ludlow
might be chosen for the borough of Hinden, where tho he

1645   was elected and returned by the principal burgesses and
Dec. 30.   baliff, yet the rabble of the town, many of whom lived
upon the alms of one Mr. George How, pretending that
they had chosen the latter, the Sheriff returned them both[1].

----

[1] Edmund Ludlow of Kingston Deverill, brother of Sir Henry Lud-   low, bapt. at Hill Deverill, June 25, 1595. Matriculated at Brasenose

By this means Mr. How got first into the House ; but they being informed of the matter of fact, commanded him to withdraw till the case should be decided by the Committee of Privileges.   Shortly after a writ being issued out for the election of two knights to serve for the County of Wilts, in the room of my father, who died in their service, and of Sir James Thynne, who contrary to his trust had deserted to the King at Oxford, the Earl of Pembroke sent to me, and acquainted me, that he understood that the county was inclined to chuse me to serve for one of their knights in Parliament, desiring me to endeavour that his second son Mr. James Herbert might be chosen for the other, promising that tho he was young, yet he would undertake he should vote honestly for the commonwealth.   I inform'd him, that I knew nothing of the intentions of the county to elect me, but hoped that if they elected his son, he would make good his promise.   His son also entred into the like engagement for himself.   At the day appointed for the election, having had several invitations so to do, I attended, according to custom and the words of the writ, which require the candidates to be present at the place of election. The Earl of Pembroke's friends desired me to consent that his son might have the first voice, which I did, tho many of the country gentlemen were unwilling to permit it : which done, the county was pleased to confer the trust upon me without any opposition.   Some who were not present, took it ill that I sent not to them to desire their company, which I excused, assuring them that I had not sent to any person, having forborn so to do, not out of any disrespect to them, or confidence in my own interest, but out of a sense of my own inability to undertake so great a charge, as well as out of a desire to have a clear and unquestionable right to an employment of such importance. When I came to the House of Commons, I met with Col. Robert Blake, attending to be admitted, being chosen for Taunton ; where having taken the usual oaths, we went

1645

1646
May 12.

College, Oxford, June 19, 1610, age   Died without issue.   See on the
14. Will proved Nov. 23, 1666.   election, C. J. v. 25, 27, 30.

1646   into the House together, which I chose to do, assuring my self, he having been faithful and active in the publick service abroad, that we should be as unanimous in the carrying it on within those doors [1].

The Parliament being sensible that the King had corrupted those forces that they had sent over to suppress the rebellion in Ireland, and that they had no great
April 9.   assurance of the Lord Inchequin, nominated the Lord Viscount Lisle, son to the Earl of Leicester, and a member of the House of Commons, to be Lieutenant for Ireland. looking upon him as the most considerable person of integrity they could think upon.   He procured the liberty of Col. Monk, then prisoner in the Tower, upon information that he had good experience in that war, and an interest in the souldiers there ; to which Mr. William Cawley gave his single negative [2].   On the 13th of April, 1646, Exeter was delivered to ours upon articles, by which all such as were in the town and garison were admitted to compound for their estates, paying two years' value for the same.
April 15.   Barnstable, Dunstar Castle, and Michael's Mount in Corn-
April 20.   wall, were also surrendred : in the last of which places the Marquiss of Hamilton was prisoner by the King's order, and restored to his liberty upon the surrender of it, which favour he acknowledged to the members of the House of Commons, attending in person at their door to that end. The most considerable body of men remaining in the field for the King was commanded by Sir Jacob Ashley, who being on his march towards Oxford, was attacked by Col. Morgan and Sir William Brereton at Stow in the
March 21.   Woald, where, after a sharp dispute on both sides, Sir

---

[1] Amongst the other ' Recruiters' elected for Wiltshire constituencies at this time, were Edmund Harvey and Henry Hungerford for Great Bedwin, Rowland Wilson, junior, for Calne, Alexander Thistlethwaite, junior, for Downton, Sir John Danvers for Malmesbury, Charles Fleetwood for Marlborough, Roger Kirkham and afterwards Sir Richard Lucy for Old

Sarum, John Dove for Salisbury, and Edward Massey for Wootton Basset ; Names of Members returned to serve in Parliament, 1878, p. 496.   Blake was member for Bridgwater, not for Taunton.

[2] Monk's appointment was approved by the Commons, Nov. 12, 1646 ; C. J. iv. 720. Cf. Gardiner, Great Civil War, iii. 352.

Jacob Ashley's forces were entirely defeated, many of them killed and wounded, and himself taken prisoner[1]. During his confinement he was heard to say, that now they had no hopes to prevail but by our divisions. Which deserves the more reflection, because he being well acquainted with the King's secrets, was not ignorant, that many amongst us, who at the beginning appeared most forward to engage themselves, and to invite others to the war against the King, finding themselves disappointed of those preferments which they expected, or out of some particular disgusts taken, had made conditions with the King not only for their indemnity, but for places and advancements under him ; endeavouring by a treaty, or rather by treachery, to betray what had cost so much blood to obtain. These men, to strengthen their interest, applied themselves to the Presbyterian party, who jealous of the increase of sectaries, of which the army was reported chiefly to consist, readily joined with them. By which conjunction most of the new elected members were either men of a neutral spirit, and willing to have peace upon any terms, or such, who tho they had engaged against the King, yet finding things tending to a composition with him, resolved to have the benefit of it, and his favour, tho with the guilt of all the blood that had been shed in the war upon their heads, in not requiring satisfaction for the same, nor endeavouring to prevent the like for the future ; designing at the most only to punish some inferiour instruments, whilst the capital offender should not only go free, but his authority be still acknowledged and adored, and so the nation more enslaved than ever to a power, which tho it destroys the people by thousands, must be accountable to none but God for so doing ; whom some persons, as it is apparent by their usage

---

[1] 'Sir Jacob Ashley being taken captive and wearyed in this fight, and being ancient (for old age's silver haires had quite covered over his head and beard), the souldiers brought him a drum to sit and rest himselfe upon ; who being sate, he said (as was most credibly enformed) unto our souldiers : " gentlemen, yee may now sit downe and play, for you have done all your worke, if you fall not out among your selves." ' Vicars, Burning Bush, p. 399.

of mankind, either think not to be, or not at all superiour to them. Another sort of men there was amongst us, who having acquired estates in the service of the Parliament, now adhered to the King's party for the preserving of what they had got; who, together with such as had been discharged from their employments by the reform of the army, or envied their success, combined together against the commonwealth. This party was encouraged and supported upon all occasions by the Scots and the City of London: the first of them, tho they began the war, and tho their assembly of ministers had declared the King guilty of the blood of thousands of his best subjects, their Covenant engaging them in the preservation of his person so far only as might consist with the laws of the land, and liberty of the subject; yet having had many good opportunities in England, and hoping for more, supposing it to be in their power to awe the King to whatsoever they should think fit, they were contented to swallow that ocean of blood that had been shed, pressing the Parliament by their commissioners to conclude upon such terms with the King, as shewed them rather advocates, than such as had been enemies to him. The latter having had their treasure much exhausted by the war, and their trade long interrupted, besides the influence the Scots had upon them by the means of their ministers, the Common Council being also debauched by Serjeant Glyn and others of that party in the House of Commons; it was not so much to be wondred at if they earnestly solicited for a speedy determination of the difference by a treaty. The King also perceiving judgment to be given against him by that power to which both parties had made their solemn appeal, thought it advisable to make use of the foxes skin, and for a time to lay aside that of the lion, sending messages to the Parliament to desire of them a safe conduct for his coming to London in honour, freedom and safety, there personally to treat with the two Houses about the means of settling a firm and lasting peace; the Scots in the mean time repeating their instances with the Parliament, to enter into the consideration of the articles of religion contained in the Covenant, to give a speedy peace to his Majesty. to pay them near two hundred thousand pounds, which they pretended to be due to them for their arrears, and to make a just estimate of the losses they had sustained by sea and land since the beginning of the war, for want of such supplies as were promised them, which they computed at more than the former sum. The Parliament, for divers reasons, thought it not convenient to comply with the King's propositions ; and in answer to the Scots, demanded of them an exact account of what was due to them, requiring them to withdraw their garisons from such places as they possessed in England. Some differences they had also with the Scots commissioners concerning the exclusion of the King from having any thing to do with the militia, and touching the Scots intermedling with the government of England, about the education of the King's children, the disbanding of armies, and an act of oblivion ; in which matters the Parliament of England would not permit the Scots to interpose; and therefore their commissioners acquainted them that they had not power to consent to any demands of that nature: whereupon the deputies of Scotland applied themselves to the two Houses, demanding that they would enlarge the powers of their commissioners to that end. But there being found in these demands of the Scots some expressions highly reflecting upon the Parliament, the two Houses declared them to be injurious April 13. and scandalous, and ordered them to be burnt by the hands of the common hangman. After which they commanded the army to besiege Oxford, who in order to that design blocked up Farringdon, Wallingford, and Woodstock ; but before they could form the siege of Oxford, the King escaped from thence on the 27th of April, 1646, of which notice being given to the Parliament by Col. Rainsborough, who lay before Woodstock ; they suspecting that he designed to come to London to raise a party against them, published an ordinance, declaring, that May 4. whosoever should harbour or conceal the King's person,

1646   should be proceeded against as a traitor to the Commonwealth. Within three or four days they received a message
from the Scots army, informing the Parliament of the
King's coming to them, and pretending to be much surprized at it ; but it appeared afterwards that this resolution
had been communicated to them before. The King was
accompanied in this expedition by one Hudson, and Mr.
Ashburnham, passing as a servant to the latter. Upon
this notice, the House of Commons sent an order to their
commissioners in the Scots army to demand the person of
the King. judging it unreasonable, that the Scots army
being in their pay, should assume the authority to dispose
of the King otherwise than by their order; resolving

May 6.   further that the King should be conducted to the Castle of
Warwick, and that those who came out of Oxford with
him should be brought to London. The next day they
commanded their army to advance, in order to hinder the
conjunction of the King's forces with the Scots. The
King, soon after his arrival at the Scots quarters, gave
order for the delivery of Newark into their hands [1]; which
having received, they surrendred to the English, and

May 7 13.   marched with the King to Newcastle ; whereof the House
of Commons being informed, and that the Earl of Leven,
General of the Scots army, had by proclamation forbidden
his forces to have any communication with the King's
party, they desisted from their resolution of advancing
their army, and of conducting the King to Warwick,
ordering the Scots to keep him for the Parliament of
England. Mr. Ashburnham was permitted by the Scots
to make his escape, but Mr. Hudson was brought to
London, and upon examination at the bar of the House of
Commons, confessed some things about the King's journey
from Oxford [2]. Commissioners being appointed by the

---

[1] The articles for the surrender of
Newark are dated May 6 ; Rushworth, vi. 269. The King's letter to
Bellasis the governor is printed in
the Portland Papers, i. 358.

[2] Hudson's examinations are

printed in the Appendix to Hearne's
Chronicle of Dunstable, and in Peck's
Desiderata Curiosa. Additional documents are in the Portland Papers, i.
368-384.

Parliament to be sent down to the Scots army in this conjuncture, they made choice of two Lords, of whom the
Earl of Pembroke was one, and four of the Commons; in
which number Col. Brown the woodmonger being nominated to that imployment, he turned about to me, who sat
behind him in the House, assuring me that he would be
ever true to us[1]. And truly I then believed him, having
met him at the beginning of the war in Smithfield buying
horses for the service of the Parliament, where he spoke
very affectionately concerning their undertaking, and served
them afterwards very successfully, especially at Abingdon,
as I mentioned before; but this wretched man soon discovered the corruption of his nature, and malignity that
lay concealed in his heart: for no sooner had the King
found out his ambitious temper, and cast some slight
favours upon him, giving him a pair of silk stockings with
his own hand, but his low and abject original and education
became so prevalent in him, as to transform him into an
agent and spy for the King, proving, as will be hereafter
related, one of the bloodiest butchers of the Parliament's
friends.

The Scots having the King in their power, pressed him
to write to the Earl of Ormond his Lieutenant in Ireland,
and to the governours and commanders of places that remained in arms for him, to lay down their arms, and to
deliver the said places to such as the Parliament of England should appoint to receive them, acquainting him that
otherwise they could not protect him. Submitting to this
necessity, he sent orders to that effect, which some obeyed,
and others refused to comply with, looking upon him to be
under a force. Amongst those who yielded obedience to
the King's orders was Montross, who disbanded the forces   July 30.
he had left, and went beyond sea. The city of Oxford

---

[1] The Earl of Pembroke with two
other Lords, and six commoners of
whom Richard Browne was one,
were appointed on Jan. 6, 1647, to
repair to Newcastle and receive the
person of the King from the Scots.
For a life of Browne, see D. N. B.
Browne was not one of the commissioners appointed on July 7,
1646, to convey the Nineteen Propositions to the King; C. J. iv. 606,
642.

1646 having been blocked up for some time, began to capitulate, lest their farther obstinacy should prove prejudicial to them, particularly in the matter of compositions for their estates, the most considerable of the King's party being there. Commissioners were appointed on both sides to treat, and came to an agreement on the 22d of June, 1646, upon such terms as the Parliament were unwilling to confirm ; but whilst they were in debate concerning the articles, they understood that Prince Rupert and others of the King's party were marched out of the town in pursuance of them ; and that the garison would be entirely evacuated before they could signify their pleasure to the army. Wherefore tho they did not approve the conditions, yet they thought not fit to do any thing in order to break them. The principal reason given by the army of their proceeding so hastily to a conclusion of the treaty, was, lest the King should make terms with the Scots, and bring their army to the relief of

June 24.
July 22.
April 26.
July 22.
Aug. 17.
Aug. 19.
Oxford. Faringdon House, Wallingford Castle, and Woodstock, were surrendred to the Parliament ; Worcester and Litchfield soon after, as also Pendennis and Ragland Castle.

Dec. 19.
The Scots by their commissioners pressed the Parliament to send propositions of peace to the King, wherein they were seconded by an insolent address from the Mayor and Common Council of the City of London [1]; in which after some acknowledgments of the care and courage of the Parliament in the reformation of the Church, and preservation of the laws, they desired of them, that such assemblies as were privately held to introduce new sects might be suppressed, lest they should breed disturbances in Church and State ; that they would hasten the establishment of peace in the three kingdoms ; that they would consider the great services of the Scots, and dismiss those who were distinguished by the name of Independents from all imployments civil and military, esteeming them to be firebrands that might endanger the publick peace, with

---

[1] Ludlow confuses the London petition of Dec. 19, 1646, with that of July 4, 1646. Both are printed in the Old Parliamentary History, xv. 5, 221.

'other particulars of the same nature. The answer of the Parliament to the said address was not much to the satisfaction of the petitioners, being a positive declaration that they resolved to preserve their authority entire to themselves. There was a party in the House of the same temper with the addressers, who earnestly endeavoured to break the army, as the principal obstacle to their designs, pretending the necessity of relieving Ireland, the loss of which they said would be infinitely prejudicial to England ; and that the way to prevent it was to send thither some part of the army, who being united in affection, and of great reputation both for courage and conduct, would strike a terror into the enemy, and undoubtedly accomplish that important work ; not forgetting to urge that the people of England were not able to bear their present burdens, and therefore must be eased. To these pretences it was replied, that it could not consist with the honour or safety of the Parliament to lessen their forces, whilst they had an army of another nation in their bowels ; who tho they were united in the same cause and interest with us, yet the best way to continue them so, was to be in such a posture as might secure us from any fear of their breaking with us ; and that the more reputation the army had, the fitter they were to be kept together for that end. After a long debate, the question was put ; ' Whether two regiments of the army July 31. should be sent to the relief of Ireland ? ' and it was carried in the negative by one voice only [1].

The Commonwealth-party taking advantage of the arguments used in the House for the relief of Ireland, and ease of the people of England, procured an order for the disbanding of Col. Massey's brigade, and money to be sent to the Devizes in the County of Wilts, where they were ordered to be drawn together for that purpose. Alderman Allen, and my self who served for that County, were commissioned to see it put in execution : in order

---

[1] The motion was that four regiments of foot and two regiments of horse from the army of Fairfax should be forthwith sent for the relief of Ireland. It was lost by 91 to 90 votes. C. J. iv. 631.

1646   to which we repaired to the Lord-General, who lay then at Cornbury, and prevailed with him and Commissary-General Ireton, with two regiments of horse, to draw to the Devizes, which we found to be very necessary : for tho many of that brigade were glad of the opportunity to return home to their several callings, having taken up arms and hazarded their lives purely to serve the publick ; yet divers idle and debauched persons, especially the foreigners amongst them, not knowing how to betake themselves to any honest employment, endeavoured to stir up the brigade to a mutiny ; but not being able to effect that, some of them listed themselves to serve against the rebels in Ireland, under Sir William Fenton and others there present to

Oct. 22.   receive them, for which we had instructions from the Parliament ; the rest dispersed themselves, and returned home [1]. The forces also that served in the North under Major-General Pointz were soon after disbanded.

July 4.   The City of London had made it their request in the petition before mentioned, that some commissioners from them might accompany those from the Parliament to the King ; but their own party in the House fearing perhaps to be outbid by them, or it may be not having quite lost

July 11.   all sense of honour, rejected that motion with contempt, alledging that they had their representatives in Parliament, and were concluded by what they acted as well as other men : upon which Mr. Martin said, 'That tho he could not but agree with what had been affirmed touching their

---

[1] On May 6, 1646, the House of Commons referred to Fairfax the disbanding of the horse late under Massey's command, empowering him to send those he did not think fit to employ in his own army to serve under Lord Lisle in Ireland, and ordering that the officers should be paid ½ of their arrears. C. J. iv. 537, cf. 577, 615, 640. Many complaints were made of the disorders of Massey's men, and Fairfax was ordered to send troops into Wilts to repress their insolencies. Ib. 581, 615, 617, 638. The disbanding finally took place in October, 1646. Gardiner, Great Civil War, ii. 530 ; Bibliotheca Gloucestrensis, cxc. ; Sprigge, p. 314 ; and Ludlow's own letter in Appendix B. About 2500 men were disbanded, and they received only six weeks' pay out of their large arrears. Alderman Francis Allen, who died in 1658, was member for Cockermouth. See Noble, Lives of the Regicides, i. 69.

being involved in what their representatives did, and their not sending commissioners as desired; yet as to the substance of what they proposed, he could not so much blame them as others had done, they therein shewing themselves in the end of the war no less prudent than they had expressed themselves honest in the beginning: for as when the Parliament invited them to stand by them in the war against the King, in defence of their religion, lives, liberties and estates, they did it heartily, and therein shewed themselves good christians and true English men; so now the war being ended, and the Parliament upon making terms with the King, and thinking fit to sue him, now their prisoner, for peace, whom they had all incensed by their resistance, the citizens having considerable estates to lose, shewed themselves prudent men, in endeavouring to procure their pardons as well as others: and tho, said he, you will not permit them to send as they desire, they have expressed their good will, which without doubt will be well accepted.' The commissioners of Parliament joining with those who were before with the King, endeavoured to perswade him to agree to the Propositions of the Parliament; but he disliking several things in them, and most of all the abolition of Episcopacy, to which interest he continued obstinately stedfast, refused his consent, upon private encouragement from some of the Scots and English, to expect more easy terms, or to be received without any at all. The Parliament willing to bring this matter to a conclusion, sent the same Propositions a second time to the King, and desired the Scots to use their utmost endeavours to procure his consent to them. The Scots commissioners, especially the Lord Loudon, pressed the King very earnestly to comply with them, telling him, that tho the Propositions were higher in some particulars than they could have wished, notwithstanding their endeavours to bring them as low as they could, according to their promises; yet if he continued to reject them, he must not expect to be received in Scotland, whither they must return, and upon his refusal of the conditions offered, deliver him up to the

1646   Parliament of England. But whatsoever they or the English could say, making no impression upon the King, the Parliament's commissioners returned with a negative from him [1].

The interposition of the Scots in this affair proving ineffectual, the war being at an end, and such considerable forces altogether unnecessary, the Parliament appointed commissioners to confer with those of Scotland concerning such things as remained to be performed by the treaty between them; that the fraternal union might continue, and the Scots depart towards their own country. In order to which the accounts of their army were adjusted, and a great sum of money agreed to be paid to them at the present, and other sums upon certain days, to their full satisfaction. Major-General Skippon, with a considerable body of men, carried down the money in specie for the paiment of the Scots army; which being received by them, they delivered the King into the hands of the Parliament's commissioners

1647
Jan. 30.   that attended him there, and began their march for Scotland, having delivered Newcastle to the English, and drawn their men out of Berwick and Carlisle, which two places were agreed not to be garisoned without the consent of both kingdoms.

1646
Sept. 14.   About this time the Earl of Essex having over-heated himself in the chace of a stag in Windsor forest, departed this life: his death was a great loss to those of his party,

Oct. 22.   who to keep up their spirits and credit procured his funeral to be celebrated with great magnificence at the charge of the publick, the Lords and Commons with a great number of officers and gentlemen accompanying him to the grave [2]. In the mean time I observed that another party was not idle; for walking one morning with Lieutenant-General Cromwell in Sir Robert Cotton's garden, he inveighed

---

[1] The propositions sent to the King at Newcastle with his three answers are printed in Gardiner's Constitutional Documents of the Puritan Revolution, pp. 208-227; Ludlow's account of the negotiations is confused and inaccurate. Loudon's speech (Rushworth, vi. 319) was delivered in July, 1646.

[2] Gardiner, Great Civil War, ii. 530.

bitterly against them, saying in a familiar way to me; 'If thy father were alive, he would let some of them hear what they deserve:' adding farther, 'that it was a miserable thing to serve a Parliament, to whom let a man be never so faithful, if one pragmatical fellow amongst them rise up and asperse him, he shall never wipe it off. Whereas,' said he, 'when one serves under a General, he may do as much service, and yet be free from all blame and envy[1].' This text, together with the comment that his after-actions put upon it, hath since perswaded me, that he had already conceived the design of destroying the civil authority, and setting up of himself; and that he took that opportunity to feel my pulse whether I were a fit instrument to be employed by him to those ends. But having replied to his discourse, that we ought to perform the duty of our stations, and trust God with our honour, power, and all that is dear to us, not permitting any such considerations to discourage us from the prosecution of our duty, I never heard any more from him upon that point.

Whilst the King was at Newcastle, the President de Bellièvre came over into England in the quality of an ambassador from the French King, with orders to endeavour a reconciliation between the King and the Parliament. He had a favourable audience from the two Houses, and their permission to apply himself to the King; but being on his way towards him, upon farther debate, they judged it not fit to subject that affair to the cognizance of any foreign prince, resolving to determine it themselves without the interposition of any, having experienced that most of the neighbouring states, especially the monarchical, were at the bottom their enemies, and their ambassadors and residents so many spies upon them, as appeared more particularly by letters taken in the King's Cabinet after the battel of Naseby, which discovered that the

1646

July 17.

July 22.

---

[1] Mr. Gardiner thinks that this conversation took place about March, 1647, on the ground that it could scarcely have taken place about the time of Essex's death, as Cromwell and his party then had a parliamentary majority. Great Civil War, iii. 35.

Emperor's resident in London held a private correspondence with the King, and there was ground to believe that the ambassador of Portugal did the like, from letters therein found from that King. These applications to the King, together with the permission granted by the Parliament to the Turky Company, to address themselves to him, for the commissionating of one whom they had nominated to be their agent with the grand Signior, under pretence that he would not otherwise be received: to which may be added the frequent overtures of peace made by the Parliament to the King, tho he had not a sword left wherewith to oppose them; and the great expectations of the people of his return to the Parliament, being informed that the heads of the Presbyterian party had promised the Scots, upon the delivery of the King, that as soon as they had disbanded the army, they would bring him to London in honour and safety: these things, I say, made the people ready to conclude, that tho his designs had been wonderfully defeated, his armies beaten out of the field, and himself delivered into the hands of the Parliament, against whom he had made a long and bloody war; yet certainly he must be in the right; and that tho he was guilty of the blood of many thousands, yet was still unaccountable, in a condition to give pardon, and not in need of receiving any: which made them flock from all parts to see him as he was brought from Newcastle to Holmby, falling down before him, bringing their sick to be touched by him, and courting him as only able to restore to them their peace and settlement [1].

The party in the House that were betraying the cause of their country, became encouragers of such petitioners as came to them from the city of London and other places to that effect; very many of whom had been always for the King's interest, but their estates lying in the Parliament's

---

[1] 'Marten this week, upon reading of letters from Holmby, desiring directions how to deal with such as flock to be touched by the King, said he knew not but the Parliament's Great Seal might do it as well, if there were an ordinance for it.' Newsletter, April 26, 1647, Clarendon S. P. ii. Appendix, xxxvii.

quarters, they secured them by their presence in the house, and at the same time promoted his designs by their votes. There was another sort of men who were contented to sacrifice all civil liberties to the ambition of the Presbyterian clergy, and to vest them with a power as great or greater than that which had been declared intolerable in the bishops before. To this end they encouraged the reduced officers of the Earl of Essex, such as Massey, Waller, Pointz, and others, to press the Parliament for their arrears in a peremptory and seditious manner, that being furnished with money they might be enabled to stand by these their patrons in whatsoever design they had to carry on. And the better to facilitate the disbanding of the army, which they so much desired, they resolved to draw off a considerable part of them for the service of Ireland; and to render the work more acceptable, voted Major-General Skippon to command them; joining the Earl of Warwick and Sir William Waller in commission with Sir Thomas Fairfax, to draw out such forces as were willing to go, to continue such as should be thought necessary for the security of this nation, and to disband the rest[1]. The army being well informed of the design, begun to consult how to prevent it; and tho many of the officers were prevailed with to engage by advancements to higher commands, yet the major part absolutely refused. The commissioners of the Parliament having done what they could in prosecution of their instructions, ordered those who had engaged in the Irish service to draw off from the army, which then lay at Saffron Walden and about Newmarket, and to be quartered in the way to Ireland; which done, they returned to London with an account of their proceedings.

The Parliament being informed of what passed, were highly displeased with the carriage of the army; but the

[1] Ludlow's account of the progress of the revolt in the army is extremely confused. He refers here to the second set of Commissioners sent by the Derby House Committee to the Army, viz. the Earl of Warwick, Lord Dacres, Sir William Waller, Sir John Clotworthy and General Massey. They arrived at Saffron Walden on April 14, and made their report to the House of Commons on April 27.

prudence and moderation of Major-General Skippon, in his report of that matter to the House, much abated the heat of their resentment. Yet some menacing expressions falling from some of them, Lieutenant-General Cromwell took the occasion to whisper me in the ear, saying, 'These men will never leave till the army pull them out by the ears': which expression I should have resented, if the state of our affairs would have permitted [1]. In this conjuncture five regiments of horse chose their Agitators, who agreed upon a petition to Parliament, to desire of them to proceed to settle the affairs of the kingdom, to provide for the arrears of the army, and to declare that they would not disband any of them till these things were done; deputing William Allen, afterwards known by the addition of Adjutant-General, Edward Sexby, afterwards Col. Sexby, and one Philips, to present it, which they did accordingly at the

April 30. bar of the House of Commons. After the reading of the petition, some of the members moved that the messengers might be committed to the Tower, and the petition declared seditious; but the House after a long debate satisfied themselves to declare, that it did not belong to the souldiery

---

[1] Skippon was at Newcastle when he was appointed to command the forces to be sent to Ireland, April 2, 1647. He arrived in London about April 27, took his seat in the Commons on April 29, and was sent down to the Army by order of April 30, and recalled by order of June 1. The report, whose moderation Ludlow praises, was probably made on June 3, and could not have been made in April. There is a similar chronological inaccuracy in the story told about Cromwell. Major Huntington tells the same story assigning it to its proper date, between Aug. 6 and Aug. 20, 1647. 'After our marching through London with the Army, his Majesty being at Hampton Court, Lieutenant-General Cromwell and Commissary-General Ireton sent the King word several times, that the reason why they made no more haste in his business was, because the party which did then sit in the House while Pelham was Speaker, did much obstruct the business, so that they would not carry it on at present; the Lieutenant-General often saying, really they should be pulled out by the ears; and to that purpose caused a regiment of horse to rendezvous at Hyde-Park to have put that in execution (as he himself expressed had it not been carried by vote in the House that day as he desired.' Major Huntington's Reasons for laying down his Commission, Maseres, p. 402. Compare Walker, History of Independency, ed. 1661, i. 49.

to meddle with civil affairs, nor to prepare or present any petition to the Parliament without the advice and consent of their General, to whom they ordered a letter to be sent to desire for the future his care therein; with which acquainting the three agents, and requiring their conformity thereunto, they dismissed them [1]. But this not satisfying, another petition was carried on throughout the army much to the same effect, only they observed the order of the Parliament in directing it to their general, desiring him to present it. The House having notice of this combina-

tion against them from Col. Edward Harley, one of their members, who had a regiment in the army, expressed themselves highly dissatisfied therewith, and some of them moved that the petitioners might be declared traitors, alledging that they were servants, who ought to obey, not capitulate. Others were not wanting, who resolved the securing of Lieutenant-General Cromwell, suspecting that he had under-hand given countenance to this design; but he being advertised of it, went that afternoon towards the

army, so that they missed of him, and were not willing to shew their teeth since they could do no more. The debate continued till late in the night, and the sense of the House was, that they should be required to forbear the prosecution of the said petition; but when the house, wearied with long sitting, was grown thin, Mr. Denzil Hollis, taking that opportunity, drew up a resolution upon his knee, declaring the petition to be seditious, and those traitors who should endeavour to promote it after such a day, and promising

---

[1] The Agitators of eight regiments drew up a letter to Fairfax, Skippon and Cromwell, which Skippon brought before the House of Commons on April 30. The three soldiers who presented the letter, Edward Sexby, William Allen, and Thomas Shepherd, were sent for and examined. Clarke Papers, i. pp. 21, 33, 82, 430. On April 27, a petition and vindication of the officers of the army was presented to the House of Commons, but its consideration was adjourned to April 30. The circumstance that letter and petition were both discussed on the same day, accounts for the manner in which Ludlow confuses them. He also confounds the petition of the soldiers, suppressed in March, with the petition and vindication of the officers, presented in April; and mis-dates Cromwell's flight.

pardon to all that were concerned therein, if they should desist by the time limited. Some of us fearing the consequence of these divisions, expressed our dissatisfaction to it, and went out; which gave them occasion, to pass two or three very sharp votes against the proceedings of the army [1]. The Agitators of the army sensible of their condition, and knowing that they must fall under the mercy of the Parliament, unless they could secure themselves from their power by prosecuting what they had begun ; and fearing that those who had shewed themselves so forward to close with the King, out of principle, upon any terms, would now for their own preservation receive him without any, or rather put themselves under his protection, that they might the better subdue the army, and reduce them to obedience by force, sent a party of horse under the command of Cornet Joyce on the 4th of June, 1647, with an order in writing to take the King out of the hands of the commissioners of Parliament. The Cornet having placed guards about Holmby House, sent to acquaint the King with the occasion of his coming, and was admitted into his bedchamber, where upon promise that the King should be used civilly, and have his servants and other conveniences continued to him, he obtained his consent to go with him. But whilst Cornet Joyce was giving orders concerning the King's removal, the Parliament's commissioners took that occasion to discourse with the King, and perswaded him to alter his resolution: which Joyce perceiving at his return put the King in mind of his promise, acquainting him that he was obliged to execute his orders ; whereupon the King told him, that since he had passed his word, he would go with him; and

---

[1] On March 29, a petition which was being circulated for signature in the army was communicated to the House of Commons by a letter from Col. Harley. The Commons passed a declaration declaring the promoters of the petition enemies to the state. This declaration was expunged on June 3, 1647, in order to conciliate the army. From the reference to Cromwell's leaving the House and going to the army it is evident that Ludlow assigns the presentation of the petition to June instead of March, and confuses the events of the two months.

to that end descending the stairs to take horse, the commissioners of the Parliament being with him, Col. Brown and Mr. Crew, who were two of them, publickly declared. that the King was forced out of their hands ; and so returned, with an account of what had been done, to the Parliament[1].

The King's officers who waited on him were continued ; and the chief officers of the army began publickly to own the design, pretending thereby to keep the private souldiers, for they would no longer be called common souldiers, from running into greater extravagancies and disorders. Col. Francis Russell and others, attending on the King, became soon converted by the splendor of his majesty; and Sir Robert Pye, a colonel in the army, supplied the place of a querry, riding bare before him when he rode abroad : so that the King began to promise to himself that his condition was altered for the better, and to look upon the Independent interest as more consisting with Episcopacy than the Presbyterian, for that it could subsist under any form, which the other could not do, and therefore largely promised liberty to the Independent party, being fully perswaded how naturally his power would revive upon his restitution to the throne, and how easy it would be for him to break through all such promises and engagements upon pretence that he was under a force. The principal officers of the army made it so much their business to get the good opinion of the King, that Whalley being sent from them with orders to use all means but constraint to cause him to return to Holmby, and the King refusing, Whalley was contented to bring him to the army[2]. Yet in the mean time a charge of High Treason June 16. was drawn up by the army against eleven members of the House of Commons, who were Mr. Denzil Hollis, Sir Philip

---

[1] Joyce's own account of his seizure of the King is printed by Rushworth, vi. 513–517; cf. Clarke Papers, i. 118. Joyce produced no written orders and pointed to his souldiers as his commission. He seized Holmby on the morning of June 3, and carried Charles away on June 4.

[2] See Whalley's letters to Fairfax, Clarke Papers, i. 122, and Fairfax's letter to Lenthall, June 7, 1647 ; L. J. ix. 248.

Stapylton, Sir John Clotworthy, Serjeant Glyn, Mr. Anthony Nichols, Mr. Walter Long, Sir William Lewis, Col. Edward Harly, Commissary Copley, Col. Massey, and Sir John Maynard, for betraying the cause of the Parliament, endeavouring to break and destroy the army, with other particulars. This charge they accompanied with a declaration, shewing the reasons of what they had done, affirming that they were obliged by their duty so to do, as they tendred the preservation of the publick cause, and securing the good people of England from being a prey to their enemies. The great end of this charge of treason being rather to keep these members from using their power with the Parliament in opposition to the proceedings of the army, than from any design to proceed capitally against them, they resolved rather to withdraw themselves voluntarily, than to put the Parliament or army to any farther trouble, or their persons to any more hazard. By these means the army, in which there were too many who had no other design but the advancement of themselves, having made the Parliament, the Scots, and the city of London their enemies, thought it convenient to enlarge their concessions to the King, giving his chaplains leave to come to him, and to officiate in their way, which had been denied before. Whilst this design was on foot, I went down to their quarters at Maidenhead, to visit the officers [1]; where Commissary-General Ireton suspecting that these things might occasion jealousies of them in me and others of their friends in Parliament, desired me to be assured of their stedfast adherence to the publick interest, and that they intended only to dispense with such things as were not material, in order to quiet the restless spirits of the Cavaliers, till they could put themselves into a condition of serving the people effectually. I could not approve of their practices; but many of the chief of them proceeding in the way they had begun, gave out, that the intentions of the officers and souldiers in the army, were to

---

[1] Ludlow's visit probably took place early in July, 1647, when the headquarters of the army were at Reading.

establish his Majesty in his just rights. The news of this being brought to the Queen and Prince of Wales, who were in France, they dispatched Sir Edward Ford[1], brother-in-law to Commissary-General Ireton, into England, to sound the designs of the army, and to promote an agreement between the King and them. Soon after which Mr. John Denham was sent over on the like errand. Sir John Barkley also upon his return to the Queen from Holland, where he had been ordered to condole the death of the Prince of Orange, came into England by the same order, and to the same purpose. It was in his instructions to endeavour to procure a pass for Mr. John Ashburnham, to come over to assist him in his negotiation ; which, with many other particulars relating to this business, I have seen in a manuscript written by Sir John Barkley himself, and left in the hands of a merchant at Geneva[2]. Being at Diepe in order to embark for England, he met with Mr. William Leg, who was of the bed-chamber to the King ; and they two came over together into England. They landed at Hastings, and being on their way towards London, were met by Sir Allen Appesley, who had been

---

[1] Edward Ford, son of Sir William Ford of Harting, Sussex, matriculated at Trinity College, Oxford, July 16, 1621, aged 16, and became a student of the Inner Temple in 1629, and was knighted at Oxford, Oct. 4, 1643. He married Sarah, daughter of Jerman Ireton. He was High Sheriff of Sussex in 1643-4 and occupied Arundel Castle for the King. Ford died in Ireland in 1670. Foster, Alumni Oxonienses ; Collections of the Sussex Archæological Society, v. 37, 45 ; Cal. of Committee for Compounding, p. 932 ; Clarendon, Rebellion, viii. 3 ; x. 134 ; Berry, Sussex Genealogies, p. 182.

[2] For the next forty pages Ludlow closely follows the Memoirs of Sir John Berkeley. These memoirs were first published in 1699, but were written much earlier. Sir Edward Nicholas writes to Lord Hatton, April 2, 1651 : 'I pray get a sight of Sir John Berkeley's relation of that unhappy business of the King's going to the Isle of Wight . . . I am now told that Sir John Berkeley intends to print that his relation.' Nicholas Papers, i. 233. Col. Bampfield writes to Thurloe in June, 1657, that Sir John Berkeley, 'upon a submissive letter written to the King, acknowledging himself to have been in an error . . . and having likewise recanted a narration, that he had written of the transactions between the late King and the Army, wherein were some undecent reflections, is restored to his attendance on the Duke of York.' Thurloe, vi. 363.

Lieutenant-Governour to Sir John Barkley at Exeter, by whom he understood that he was sent to him from Cromwell and some other officers of the army, with letters and a cypher, as also particular instructions to desire Sir John Barkley to remember his own discourse at a conference with Col. Lambert and other officers upon the surrender of Exeter, wherein he had taken notice of the bitter invectives of those of the army against the King's person; and presuming that such discourses were encouraged in order to prepare men's minds to receive an alteration of the government, had said, that it was not only a most wicked but difficult undertaking, if not impossible, for a few men, not of the greatest quality, to introduce a popular government against the King, the Presbyterians, the nobility, gentry, and the genius of the nation, accustomed for so many ages to a monarchical government; advising, that since the Presbyterians, who had begun the war upon divers specious pretences, were discovered to have sought their own advantages, by which means they had lost almost all their power and credit; the Independent party, who had no particular obligations to the Crown, as many of the Presbyterians had, would make good what the Presbytery had only pretended to, and restore the King and people to their just and antient rights; to which they were obliged both by prudence and interest, there being no means under Heaven more likely to establish themselves, and to obtain as much trust and power as subjects are capable of: whereas if they aimed at more, it would be accompanied with a general hatred, and their own destruction. He had orders also to let him know, that tho to this discourse of his they then gave only the hearing, yet they had since found by experience, that all, or the most part of it was reasonable, and that they were resolved to act accordingly, as might be perceived by what had already passed: desiring that he would present them humbly to the Queen and Prince, and be a suitor to them in their names, not to condemn them absolutely, but to suspend their opinions of them and their intentions, till their future behaviour had made full proof of their innocence, whereof they had already given some testimonies to the world; and that when he had done this office, he would return to England, and be an eye-witness of their proceedings. Thus did the army-party endeavour to fortify their interest against the Presbyterians, who tho they were very much weakned by the absence of the eleven members, yet not to be altogether wanting to themselves, passed a vote that the King should be brought to Richmond, whither he was inclined to go, having conceived a distrust of the army, grounded chiefly upon the refusal of the officers to receive any honours or advantages from him; and would not be disswaded from this resolution, till the army had obliged the Parliament to recal their vote. After which he insisted upon going to Windsor, much against the sense of the army, and could not be prevailed with to pass by the army in his way thither. This caused them to suspect that he hearkned to some secret propositions from the Presbyterians, and designed to make an absolute breach between the Parliament and the army, which Commissary-General Ireton discerning, said these words to him; 'Sir, you have an intention to be arbitrator between the Parliament and us, and we mean to be so between you and the Parliament.' But the King finding himself courted on all hands became so confident of his own interest, as to think himself able to turn the scale to what side soever he pleased. In this temper Sir John Barkley found him when he delivered the Queen's letters to him, which he did, after leave obtained from Cromwell, and a confirmation received from his own mouth of what had been communicated before to him by Sir Allen Appesley, with this addition, that he thought no man could enjoy his life and estate quietly, unless the King had his rights, which he said they had already declared to the world in general terms, and would more particularly very speedily, wherein they would comprize the several interests of the Royalists, Presbyterians, and Independents, as far as they were consistent with one another. Sir

1647   John Barkley endeavoured to perswade the King, that it was necessary for him, who was now in the power of the army, to dissemble with them, and proposed that Mr. Peters might preach before him, that he would converse freely with others of the army, and gain the good opinion of the Agitators, whose interest he perceived to be very great amongst them. But this advice made no impression upon the King. He gave him also a relation of what had formerly passed between himself and Cromwell, whom he met near Causum, when the head-quarters were at Reading, where Cromwell told him, that he had lately seen the tenderest sight that ever his eyes beheld, which July 13. was the interview between the King and his children; that he wept plentifully at the remembrance thereof, saying, that never man was so abused as he in his sinister opinion of the King, who, he thought, was the most upright and conscientious of his kingdom: that they of the Independent party had infinite obligations to him, for not consenting to the propositions sent to him at Newcastle, which would have totally ruined them, and which his Majesty's interest seemed to invite him to; concluding with this wish, 'that God would be pleased to look upon him according to the sincerity of his heart towards the King.' With this relation the King was no more moved than with the rest, firmly believing such expressions to proceed from a necessity that Cromwell and the army had of him, without whom, he said, they could do nothing. And indeed the King was not without reason of that opinion; for some of the principal Agitators with whom Sir John Barkley conversed at Reading, expressing to him their jealousy that Cromwell was not sincere for the King, desired of him, that if he found him false, to acquaint them with it, promising that they would endeavour to set him right, either with or against his will, Major Huntington, a creature of Cromwell, and therefore entrusted by him to command the guard about the King, either believing him to be in earnest in his pretensions to serve the King, or else finding the King's affairs in a rising condition, became one of his confidents, and by order of the King brought two general officers to Sir John Barkley, recommending them to him as persons upon whom he might rely: these two had frequent conferences with Sir John Barkley, and assured him, that a conjunction with the King was universally desired by the officers and agitators, and that Cromwell and Ireton were great dissemblers if they were not real in it; but that the army was so bent upon it at present, that they durst not shew themselves otherwise; protesting that however things might happen to change, and whatsoever others might do, they would for ever continue faithful to the King. They acquainted him also, that proposals were drawn up by Ireton, wherein Episcopacy was not required to be abolished, nor any of the King's party wholly ruined, nor the militia to be taken away from the Crown; advising that the King would with all expedition agree to them, there being no assurance of the army, which they had observed already to have changed more than once. To this end they brought him to Commissary-General Ireton, with whom he continued all night debating upon the Proposals before-mentioned, altering two of the articles, as he saith himself in the manuscript, in the most material points; but upon his endeavouring to alter a third, touching the exclusion of seven persons, not mentioned in the papers, from pardon, and the admission of the King's party to sit in the next Parliament, Ireton told him, that there must be a distinction made between the conquerors and those that had been beaten, and that he himself should be afraid of a Parliament where the King's party had the major vote [1]: in conclusion, conjuring Sir John Barkley, as he tendred the King's welfare, to endeavour to procure his consent to the Proposals, that they might with more confidence be offered to the Parliament, and all differences accommodated. Cromwell ap-

[1] On the modifications made in the Proposals, see Clarke Papers, i. xli; Gardiner, Great Civil War, iii. 171. The submission of the Proposals to the King probably took place on July 23.

peared in all his conferences with Sir John Barkley most zealous for a speedy agreement with the King, insomuch that he sometimes complained of his son Ireton's slowness in perfecting the Proposals, and his unwillingness to come up to his Majesty's sense: at other times he would wish that Sir John Barkley would act more frankly, and not tie himself up by narrow principles; always affirming, that he doubted the army would not persist in their good intentions towards the King.

During these transactions the army marched from about Reading to Bedford, and the King with his usual guard to Woburn, a house belonging to the Earl of Bedford, where the Proposals of the army were brought to him to peruse before they were offered to him in publick. He was much displeased with them in general, saying, that if they had any intention to come to an accommodation, they would not impose such conditions on him: to which Sir John Barkley, who brought them to him, answered, that he should rather suspect they designed to abuse him, if they had demanded less, there being no appearance that men, who had through so many dangers and difficulties acquired such advantages, would content themselves with less than was contained in the said Proposals; and that a Crown so near lost was never recovered so easily as this would be, if things were adjusted upon these terms. But the King being of another opinion, replied, that they could not subsist without him, and that therefore he did not doubt to find them shortly willing to condescend farther, making his chief objections against the three following points: 1. The exclusion of seven persons from pardon. 2. The incapacitating any of his party from being elected members of the next ensuing Parliament. 3. That there was nothing mentioned concerning Church-government. To the first it was answered, that when the King and the army were agreed, it would not be impossible to make them remit in that point; but if that could not be obtained, yet when the King was restored to his power he might easily supply seven persons living beyond the

seas in such a manner as to make their banishment sup-
portable. To the second, that the next Parliament would
be necessitated to lay great burdens upon the people, and
that it would be a happiness to the King's party to have
no hand therein. To the third, that the law was security
enough for the Church, and that it was a great point
gained, to reduce men who had fought against it, to be
wholly silent in the matter. But the King breaking
away from them, said, 'Well, I shall see them glad ere-
long to accept of more equal terms.'

About this time Mr. Ashburnham arrived, to the King's
great contentment, and his instructions referring to Sir
John Barkley's which they were to prosecute jointly, Sir
John gave him what light he could into the state of affairs :
but he soon departed from the methods proposed by Sir
John Barkley, and entirely complying with the King's
humour, declared openly, that having always used the
best company, he could not converse with such sensless
fellows as the Agitators ; that if the officers could be gained
there was no doubt but they would be able to command
their own army, and that he was resolved to apply himself
wholly to them. Upon this there grew a great familiarity
between him and Whalley, who commanded the guard
that waited on the King, and not long after a close correspondence with Cromwell and Ireton, messages daily
passing from the King to the head-quarters. With these
encouragements and others from the Presbyterian party,
the Lord Lauderdale and divers of the City of London
assuring the King that they would oppose the army to
the death, he seemed so much elevated, that when the
Proposals were sent to him, and his concurrence humbly July 28 ?
desired, he, to the great astonishment not only of Ireton
and the army, but even of his own party, entertained them
with very sharp and bitter language, saying, that no man
should suffer for his sake ; and that he repented him of
nothing so much as that he passed the bill against the
Earl of Strafford : which tho it must be confessed to have
been an unworthy act in him, all things considered, yet

was it no less imprudent in that manner, and at that time, to mention it ; and that he would have the Church established according to law by the Proposals. To which those of the army replied, that it was not their work to do it, and that they thought it sufficient for them to wave the point ; and they hoped for the King too, he having already consented to the abolition of the Episcopal government in Scotland. The King said, that he hoped God had forgiven him that sin, repeating frequently these or the like words ; 'You cannot be without me : you will fall to ruin if I do not sustain you.' This manner of carriage from the King being observed with the utmost amazement by many officers of the army who were present, and at least in appearance were promoters of the agreement, Sir John Barkley taking notice of it, looked with much wonder upon the King, and stepping to him, said in his ear, 'Sir, you speak as if you had some secret strength and power which I do not know of ; and since you have concealed it from me, I wish you had done it from these men also.' Whereupon the King began to recollect himself and to soften his former discourse ; but it was too late, for Col. Rainsborough, who of all the army seemed the least to desire an agreement, having observed these passages, went out from the conference, and hastened to the army, informing them what entertainment their commissioners and proposals had found with the King. Sir John Barkley being desirous to allay this heat, demanded of Ireton and the rest of the officers what they would do if the King should consent : by whom it was answered, that they would offer them to the Parliament for their approbation. The King having thus bid defiance to the army, thought it necessary to bend all his force against them, and especially to strengthen their enemies in the Parliament. To this end a petition was contrived to press them to a speedy agreement with the King, and presented in a most tumultuous manner by great numbers of apprentices and rabble, back'd and encouraged by many dismissed and disaffected officers who joined with them. Whilst the two Houses were in debate what answer to give to this insolent multitude, some of them getting to the windows of the House of Lords, threw stones in upon them, and threatned them with worse usage, unless they gave them an answer to their liking: others knocked at the door of the House of Commons, requiring to be admitted ; but some of us with our swords forced them to retire for the present; and the House resolved to rise without giving any answer, judging it below them to do anything by compulsion. Whereupon the Speaker went out of the House, but being in the lobby, was forced back into the chair by the violence of the insolent rabble; whereof above a thousand attended without doors, and about forty or fifty were got into the House. So that it was thought convenient to give way to their rage, and the Speaker demanding what question they desired to be put, they answered, 'That the King should be desired to come to London forthwith :' which question being put, they were asked again what further they would have; they said, 'That he should be invited to come with honour, freedom and safety:' to both which I gave a loud negative, and some of the members as loud an affirmative, rather out of a prudential compliance than any affection to the design on foot. By these votes, and the coming down of divers well-affected citizens to appease them, the tumult was somewhat allayed, and the members of Parliament with their Speaker passed through the multitude safely[1]. The next morning I advised with Sir Arthur Haslerig and others, what was fittest to be done in this conjuncture; and it was concluded, that we could not sit in Parliament without apparent hazard of our lives, till we had a guard for our defence, it being manifestly the design of the other party either to drive us away, or to destroy us. Therefore we resolved to betake ourselves to the army for protection, Sir Arthur Haslerig undertaking to perswade

[1] For accounts of the violence on the House of Commons, see Rushworth, vi. 640-644; vii. 747; Clarke Papers, i. 217; Fairfax Correspondence, iii. 381.

the Speaker to go thither, to which he consented with some difficulty[1]; and having caused a thousand pounds to be thrown into his coach, went down to the army, which lay then at Windsor, Maidenhead, Colebrook, and the adjacent places. Having acquainted as many of our friends as I could, with our resolution to repair to the army, I went down ; and the next day, being the same to which the

Parliament had adjourned themselves, the army rendezvouzed upon Hounslow Heath, where those members of Parliament, as well Lords as Commons, who could not with safety stay at Westminster, appeared in the head of them, at which the army expressed great joy, declaring themselves resolved to live and die with them. At night the Earl of Northumberland, the Lord Say, the Lord Wharton, and other Lords ; the Speaker and members of the House of Commons aforesaid, with Sir Thomas Fairfax, and many principal officers of the army, met at Sion House to consult what was most advisable to do in that juncture; which whilst they were doing, an account was brought of the proceedings of those at Westminster that day, by the serjeant of the House, who came with his

mace, to the no little satisfaction of the Speaker[2]. He acquainted them, that the remaining members being met in the House of Commons, had for some time attended the coming of their Speaker ; but being informed that he was gone to the army, they had made choice of one Mr. Pelham a lawyer, and member of the House, to be their Speaker : after which they had appointed a committee of Lords and Commons to join with the directors of the militia of London, in order to raise forces for the defence of the Parliament ; the success of which attempt they desired to see before they would declare against the army. To this end Massey, Pointz, Brown, and Sir William Waller, encouraged by the Common Council, and others, who by various artifices had been corrupted, used all possible

[1] On Lenthall's share in the business, see Clarke Papers, i. 218; and Lenthall's Declaration, Old Parliamentary History, xvi. 196.

[2] Apparently Serjeant Birkhead ; see C. J. vi. 259, 261, 263, 268; Walker, History of Independency, i. 41.

diligence to list men, and prepare a force to oppose the army; but their proceedings therein were much obstructed by divers honest citizens, who importunately solicited them to treat with the army, and also by the news of the general rendezvouz upon Hounslow Heath.

Tho the Lords had been removed from the command of the army, yet it was manifest that their influence there still continued; partly from a desire of some great officers to oblige them, and partly from the ambition of others to be of their number, who to shew their earnest desires to serve the King, being morally assured the Parliament and city were likely to be shortly in the power of the army, who might be induced to take other counsels in relation to the King, upon such success, especially considering his late carriage towards them; they sent an express to Sir John Barkley and Mr. Ashburnham, advising, that since the King would not yield to their Proposals, that he would send a kind letter to the army, before it were known that London would submit. Whereupon a letter was prepared immediately; but the King would not sign it, till after three or four debates, which lost one whole day's time [1]: at last Mr. Ashburnham and Sir John Barkley going with it, met with messengers from the officers to hasten it. But before they could come to Sion House the commissioners from London were arrived, and the letter out of season. For coming after it was known with what difficulty it had been obtained, and that matters were like to be adjusted between the Parliament and army, it lost both its grace and efficacy. Notwithstanding all which the officers being resolved to do what they could, proposed, whilst the army was in the very act of giving thanks for their success, that they should not be too much elevated therewith, but keep still to their former engagement to the King, and once more solemnly vote the Proposals, which was done accordingly.

1647
Aug. 2.

Aug. 3.

Aug. 4.

[1] See the King's letters, Clarendon State Papers, ii. 373; Rushworth, vii. 753. The first seems to be the one prepared, the second the one actually sent.

1647   The face of affairs in the city was at this time very various, according to the different advices they received; for upon the report of the advance of the army, and the taking of some of their scouts, they cried out, 'Treat, Treat:' and at another time being informed that men listed in great numbers, the word was, 'Live and die, Live and die:' but when Southwark had let in part of the army, and joined with them, they returned to the former cry of 'Treat, Treat:' to which the Lord Mayor, aldermen and Common Council consenting, were ready to admit the army as friends, being not able to oppose them as enemies, and afterwards to attend those members who had retired to the army, being in all about a hundred, to the Parliament. Having resumed

Aug. 6.   our places in the House, as many of the eleven members as had returned to act, immediately withdrew; and Pointz with other reduced officers, who had endeavoured to form a body against the army, fled. But we had other difficulties to

March 30.   encounter: for tho that vote by which the petition of the army was declared seditious, and those guilty of treason, who should prosecute the same after such a day, was razed out of the Journal; yet by reason that the bulk of the opposite party was left still in the House, the militia of London could not be changed without much difficulty, and some other votes of great consequence could not be altered at all.

Aug. 6.   However the Parliament appointed a committee to inquire into the late force that was put upon them; who having made their report, Sir John Maynard was impeached, and Recorder Glyn, with Mr. Clement Walker and others, imprisoned.

Aug. 7.   A day or two after the restitution of the Parliament, the army marched through the city without offering the least violence, promising to shew themselves faithful to the publick interest; but their actions furnished occasion to suspect them, particularly their discountenancing the Adjutators, who had endured the heat of the day: the free access of all Cavaliers to the King at Hampton Court, and the publick speeches made for the King by the great officers of the army in a council of war held at Putney, some of that

party taking the same liberty in the House of Commons,
where one of them publickly said, that he thought God
had hitherto blasted our counsels, because we had dealt so
severely with the Cavaliers.· These things caused many in
the army who thought themselves abused and cheated, to
complain to the Council of Adjutators, against the intimacy
of Sir John Barkley and Mr. Ashburnham with the chief
officers of the army, affirming, that the doors of Cromwell
and Ireton were open to them when they were shut to
those of the army. Cromwell was much offended with
these discourses, and acquainted the King's party with them,
telling Mr. Ashburnham and Sir John Barkley, that if he
were an honest man, he had said enough of the sincerity of
his intentions ; and if he were not, that nothing was enough ;
and therefore conjured them, as they tendred the King's
service, not to come so frequently to his quarters, but to
send privately to him, the suspicion of him being grown
so great, that he was afraid to lie in them himself. This
had no effect upon Mr. Ashburnham, who said, that he
must shew them the necessity of complying with the
King, from their own disorders. About three weeks after
the army entred London, the Scots prevailed with the
Parliament to address themselves again to the King, Sept. 7.
which was performed in the old Propositions of Newcastle, some particulars relating to the Scots only excepted. The King advising with some about him concerning this matter, it was concluded to be unsafe for him
to close with the enemies of the army whilst he was in it.
Whereupon the King refused the articles, and desired a Sept. 9.
personal treaty[1]. The officers of the army having seen his
answer before it was sent, seemed much satisfied with it,
and promised to use their utmost endeavours to procure a
personal treaty, Cromwell, Ireton, and many of their party
in the House pressing the King's desires with great earnest- Sept. 23.

[1] For the King's answer, see
Gardiner, Constitutional Documents,
p. 241; Clarke Papers, i. 225. The
King's answer was delivered to the
commissioners on Sept. 9, and re-
ported by them to the House of
Lords on Sept. 14. See Gardiner,
Great Civil War, iii. 189-195.

ness; wherein, contrary to their expectations, they found a vigorous opposition from such as had already conceived a jealousy of their private agreement with the King, and were now confirmed in that opinion; and the suspicions of them grew to be so strong, that they were accounted betrayers of the cause, and lost almost all their friends in the Parliament. The army that lay then about Putney were no less dissatisfied with their conduct, of which they were daily informed by those that came to them from London; so that the Adjutators began to change their discourse, and to complain openly in council, both of the King and the malignants about him, saying, that since the King had rejected their proposals, they were not engaged any further to him, and that they were now to consult their own safety and the publick good: that having the power devolved upon them by the decision of the sword, to which both parties had appealed, and being convinced that monarchy was inconsistent with the prosperity of the nation, they resolved to use their endeavours to reduce the government of England to the form of a Commonwealth. These proceedings strook so great a terror into Cromwell and Ireton, that they thought it necessary to draw the army to a general rendezvouz, pretending to engage them to adhere to their former proposals to the King; but indeed to bring the army into subjection to them and their party, that so they might make their bargain by them; designing, if they could carry this point at the rendezvouz, to dismiss the Council of Adjutators, to divide the army, and to send those to the most remote places who were most opposite to them, retaining near them such only as were fit for their purpose. This design being discovered by the Adjutators, amongst whom Col. Rainsborough had the principal interest, they used all possible industry to prevent the general muster which was appointed to be at Ware[1]; supposing the separation

---

[1] Ludlow is seriously in error in his account of the Ware rendezvous. The Agitators and the Levelling party generally in the army desired a general rendezvous of the whole army, and succeeded in obtaining a

thereupon intended to be contrary to the agreement made upon taking the King out of the hands of the Parliament, and destructive to the ends which they thought it their duty to promote.

In the mean time Cromwell having acquainted the King with his danger, protesting to him, that it was not in his power to undertake for his security in the place where he was, assuring him of his real service, and desiring the Lord to deal with him and his according to the sincerity of his heart towards the King, prepared himself to act his part at the general rendezvouz. The King being doubtful what to do in this conjuncture, was advised by some to go privately to London, and appear in the House of Lords : to which it was answered, that the army being masters of the City and Parliament, would undoubtedly seize the King there ; and if there should be any blood shed in his defence, he would be accused of beginning a new war. Others counselled him to secure his person by quitting the kingdom. Against which the King objected, that the rendezvouz being appointed for the next week, he was not willing to quit the army till that was passed ; because if the superiour officers prevailed, they would be able to make good their engagement ; if not, they must apply themselves to him for their own security. The Scots commissioners also who had been long tampering with him, took hold of this opportunity to perswade him to come to their terms, by augmenting his fears as much as they could. It was also proposed, that he should conceal himself in England ; but that was thought unsafe, if not impossible. Some there were who proposed his going to Jersey, which was then kept for him ; but the King being told by the

vote for it in the Council of the Army on Nov. 5. But on Nov. 8, Cromwell carried a vote that the Agitators and representative officers should be dismissed to their several regiments, and it was also decided that there should be three separate gatherings instead of the general rendezvous. The disturbance at Ware was caused by the attempt of the Levellers to make that gathering a general rendezvous instead of a rendezvous of seven regiments only. The first rendezvous was Nov. 15, at Ware ; the second Nov. 17, at Windsor ; the third Nov. 18, at Kingston. Rushworth, vii. 876, 878 ; Clarke Papers, i. liv.

1647   Earl of Lanerick, that the ships provided by Sir John
Barkley for that purpose had been discovered and seized,
tho Sir John affirms in his papers that none were provided,
that design was laid aside. At last the King resolved to
go to the Isle of Wight, being, as is most probable, recommended thither by Cromwell, who, as well as the King,
had a good opinion of Col. Hammond the governour there.
To this end the King sent Mr. William Leg to Sir John
Barkley and Mr. Ashburnham, requiring them to assist
him in his escape ; and horses were laid at Sutton in
Hampshire to that purpose. On the day following Sir
Nov. 11. John Barkley and Mr. Ashburnham waiting with horses,
the King with Mr. Leg came out towards the evening, and
being mounted they designed to ride through the forest,
having the King for their guide ; but they lost the way ;
so that the night proving dark and stormy, and the ways
very bad, they could not reach Sutton before break of day,
tho they hoped to have been there three hours before.
At Sutton they were informed that a committee of the
county was there sitting by order of the Parliament ;
which when the King heard, he passed by that place, and
continued his way towards Southampton, attended only by
Mr. Leg, and went to a house of the Earl of Southampton
Nov. 12. at Titchfield, having sent Sir John Barkley and Mr. Ashburnham to Col. Hammond, governour of the Isle of
Wight, with a copy of the letter left upon the table in his
chamber at Hampton Court, and two other letters which
he had lately received, one of them without a name,
expressing great fears and apprehensions of the ill intentions of the Commonwealth party against the King. The
other from Cromwell, much to the same purpose, with this
addition, that in prosecution thereof, a new guard was
designed the next day to be placed about the King, consisting of men of that party. He also sent by them a
letter to Col. Hammond, wherein after he had expressed
his distrust of the levelling part of the army, as he termed
it, and the necessity lying upon him to provide for his own
safety, he assured him, that he did not intend to desert the

interest of the army, ordering his two messengers to acquaint him, that of all the army the King had chosen to
put himself upon him, whom he knew to be a person of a
good extraction, and tho engaged against him in the war, yet
without any animosity to his person, to which he was informed he had no aversion : that he did not think it fit to surprize him, and therefore had sent the two persons before-
mentioned to advertise him of his intentions, and to desire his
promise to protect the King and his servants to the best of
his power ; and if it should happen that he was not able to
do it, then to oblige himself to leave them in as good a condition as he found them. Being ready to depart with
these instructions, Sir John Barkley said to the King, that
having no knowledge of the governour, he could not tell
whether he might not detain them in the island, and
therefore advised, if they returned not the next day, that
he would think no more of them, but secure his own escape.
Towards evening they arrived at Limmington, but could
not pass by reason of a violent storm. The next morning
they got over to the island, and went directly to Carisbrook
Castle, the residence of the governour, where they were
told that he was gone towards Newport. Upon this notice
they rode after, and having overtaken and acquainted him
with their message, he grew pale, and fell into such a
trembling, that it was thought he would have fallen from
his horse. In this consternation he continued about an hour,
breaking out sometimes into passionate and distracted
expressions, saying, ' O gentlemen, you have undone me
in bringing the King into the island, if at least you have
brought him ; and if you have not, I pray let him not
come : for what between my duty to the King, and gratitude to him upon this fresh obligation of confidence, and
the discharge of my trust to the army, I shall be confounded.'
Upon this they took occasion to tell him, that the King
intended a favour to him and his posterity, in giving him
this opportunity to lay a great obligation upon him, and
such as was very consistent with his relation to the army,
who had solemnly engaged themselves to the King ; but if

he thought otherwise, the King would be far from imposing his person upon him : but, said the governour, if the King should come to any mischance, what would the army and the King say to him that had refused to receive him ? To which they answered, that he had not refused him who was not come to him. Then beginning to speak more calmly, he desired to know where the King was, and wished that he had absolutely thrown himself upon him, which made the two gentlemen suspect that the governour was not for their turn ; but Mr. Ashburnham fearing what would become of the King if he should be discovered before he had gained this point, took the governour aside, and after some conference prevailed with him to declare, ' That he did believe the King relied on him as a person of honour and honesty, and therefore he did engage himself to perform whatsoever could be expected from a person so qualified.' Mr. Ashburnham replied, ' I will ask no more :' then said the governour, ' Let us all go to the King, and acquaint him with it.' When they came to Cowes Castle, where a boat lay to carry them over, Col. Hammond took Capt. Basket the governour of that castle with him, and gave order for a file or two of musqueteers to follow them in another boat. When they came to the Earl of Southampton's house, Mr. Ashburnham leaving Sir John Barkley below with Col. Hammond and Capt. Basket, went up to the King, and having given an account of what had passed between the governour and them, and that he was come with them to make good what he had promised ; the King striking his hand upon his breast, said, ' What have you brought Hammond with you ? O you have undone me ; for I am by this means made fast from stirring.' Mr. Ashburnham then told him that if he mistrusted Hammond, he would undertake to secure him. To which the King replied, ' I understand you well enough ; but if I should follow that counsel, it would be said and believed, that he ventured his life for me, and that I had unworthily taken it from him :' telling him further, ' That it was now too late to think upon any thing but going through the way he had forced him upon, wondering how

he could make so great an oversight:' at which expression   1647
Mr. Ashburnham having no more to say, wept bitterly.   In
the mean time Col. Hammond and Capt. Basket beginning
to be impatient of their long attendance below in the court,
Sir John Barkley sent a gentleman of the Earl of Southampton's to desire that the King and Mr. Asburnham
would remember that they were below.   About half an
hour after the King sent for them up, and before Col.
Hammond and Capt. Basket had kissed the King's hand,
he took Sir John Barkley aside, and said to him; 'Sir John,
I hope you are not so passionate as Jack Ashburnham:
do you think you have followed my directions?' He
answered, 'No indeed; but it is not my fault, as Mr.
Ashburnham can tell you, if he please.'   The King perceiving that it was now too late to take other measures,
received Col. Hammond cheerfully, who having repeated to
him what he had promised before, conducted them over
to Cowes.   The next morning the King went with the   Nov. 14.
governour to Carisbrook, and on the way thither was met
by divers gentlemen of the island, by whom he understood
that the whole island was unanimously for him, except
the governours of the castles, and Col. Hammond's captains;
that Hammond might be easily gained, if not more easily
forced, the castle being day and night full of the King's
party; and that the King might chuse his own time of
quitting the island, having liberty to ride abroad daily: so
that not only the King and those that were with him, but
also his whole party, approved of the choice which he had
made.   The King and Mr. Ashburnham applied themselves to the governour with so good success, that he and
those with him seemed to desire nothing more of the King
than to send a civil message to both Houses, signifying his   Nov. 17.
propensity to peace, which was done accordingly.

No sooner was the King's escape taken notice of by the
guards, but Col. Whalley hastened to the Parliament with   Nov. 12.
the letter which the King had left upon his table, shewing
the reasons of his withdrawing, and his resolution not to
desert the interest of the army; and tho it was visible that

1647 the King made his escape by the advice of Cromwell, and therefore in all appearance with the consent of Whalley, yet he pretended for his excuse to the Parliament, that Mr. Ashburnham had broken his engagement to him at his first coming to Woburn, whereby he had undertaken that the King should not leave the army without his knowledg and consent. Upon this advice the Parliament declared it treason for any person to conceal the King ; but the manner of his escape being soon after discovered, and that he had put himself into the hands of the governour of the Isle of Wight, they sent a messenger to the island for Mr. Ashburnham, Sir John Barkley, and Mr. Leg, but the

Nov. 19. governour refused to deliver them.

Nov. 15.   The time for the general rendezvouz of the army being now come, the Commonwealth party amongst them declared to stand to their engagement, not to be dispersed till the things they had demanded were effected, and the government of the nation established : to make good which resolution several regiments appeared in the field with distinguishing marks in their hats : but Lieutenant-General Cromwell not contenting himself with his part in an equal government, puffed up by his successes to an expectation of greater things, and having driven a bargain with the grandees in the House, either to comply with the King, or to settle things in a factious way without him, procured a party to stand by him in the seizing some of those who appeared at the rendezvouz in opposition to his designs. To this end, being accompanied with divers officers whom he had preferred, and by that means made his creatures, he rode up to one of the regiments which had the distinguishing marks, requiring them to take them out, which they not doing, he caused several of them to be seized ; and then their hearts failing, they yielded obedience to his commands [1]. He ordered one of them to be shot dead upon the place, delivering the rest of those whom he had seized,

---

[1] The best account of the rendez-vous at Ware is contained in the letters printed by Maseres in the preface to his Select Tracts, pp. xl, lvi. The mutinous regiments were those of Lilburne and Harrison.

being eleven in number, into the hands of the marshal ; and
having dispersed the army to their quarters, went to give
an account of his proceedings to the Parliament : and tho
when an agreement with the King was carried on by other
hands, he could countenance the army in opposition to the
Parliament ; yet now the bargain for the people's liberty
being driven on by himself, he opposed those who laboured
to obstruct it, pretending his so doing to be only in order
to keep the army in subjection to the Parliament ; who being
very desirous to have this spirit suppressed in the army by
any means, not only approved what he had done, but gave
him the thanks of the House for the same : whereunto, tho
singly, I gave as loud a ' No ' as I could, being fully convinced
that he had acted in this manner for no other end but to
advance his own passion and power into the room of right
and reason ; and took the first opportunity to tell him, that
the army having taken the power into their hands, as in
effect they had done, every drop of blood shed in that
extraordinary way would be required of them, unless the
rectitude of their intentions and actions did justify them, of
which they had need to be very careful.

Whilst these things were doing, the Earl of Ormond
finding that the Irish used him treacherously, and that the
inclinations of his army tended towards a submission to
the Parliament of England, invited them to send commissioners to treat about the surrender of Dublin, and
the forces commanded by him, into their hands. Which
was done, and articles agreed upon, indemnifying all
Protestants in Ireland for what they had done there,
unless they had been in the rebellion during the first
year ; and admitting them to compound for their estates
in England at two years' value. A certain sum was also
promised to be paid to the Earl of Ormond, in consideration of what he had disbursed for the army [1]. This agreement being concluded, the city of Dublin and the forces

[1] See on these negotiations Carte, £13,877 13s. 4d., of which all but
Ormond, iii. 305-310, ed. 1851. £1515 were paid to Ormond.
The sum of money in question was

1647

1648
February.

before mentioned were delivered to Col. Michael Jones, who was ordered by the Parliament to receive the same ; and the Earl of Ormond came to London, where his money was paid him, and he soon after retired into France.

1647
Dec. 14.

The chief officers of the army having subdued those of their body, who upon just suspicion had opposed their treaty with the King, thought themselves obliged by their former engagement to press for a personal treaty with him, which they procured to be offered, in case he would grant four preliminary bills : the first of which contained the revocation of all proclamations against the Parliament : the second, to make void all such titles of honour as had been granted by the King since he had left the Parliament ; and that for the future none should be conferred upon any person without the consent of Parliament : the third was a bill to except some persons from pardon : and the fourth for investing the militia in the two Houses. All which those who thought it reasonable and necessary to proceed judicially with him, were afraid he would grant ; it being visible, that had he been restored to the throne upon any terms, he might easily have gratified his friends, and revenged himself upon all his enemies. Col. Hammond and Mr. Ashburnham had frequent conferences with the King, who had made such promises to the colonel, that he declared himself extremely desirous that the army might resume their power, and clear themselves of the Adjutators, whose authority he said he had never approved. To this end he sent one Mr. Traughton his chaplain to the army, to perswade them to make use of their success against the Adjutators ; and two or three days after earnestly moved the King to send some of those about him to the army, with letters of compliment to the General, and others of greater confidence to Cromwell and Ireton, promising to write to them himself, which he did ; conjuring them by their engagements, their honour and conscience, to come to a speedy agreement with the King, and not to expose themselves to the fantastick giddiness of the Adjutators. Sir John Barkley was made choice of for this employment, who taking Mr. Henry Barkley his cousin german with him, departed from the island with a pass from the governour of Cowes; and being on his way met Mr. Traughton on his return between Bagshot and Windsor, who acquainted him that he had no good news to carry back to the King, the army having taken new resolutions touching his person. Being gone a little farther he was met by Cornet Joyce, who told him, that he was astonished at his design of going to the army, acquainting him, that it had been debated amongst the Adjutators, whether, in justification of themselves, the King should be brought to a trial; of which opinion he declared himself to be, not out of any ill will, as he said, to the King's person, but that the guilt of the war might be charged upon those that had caused it. About an hour after his arrival at Windsor, Sir John Barkley went to the General's quarters, where he found the officers of the army assembled; and being admitted, delivered his letters to the General, who having received them, ordered him to withdraw[1]. After he had attended about half an hour, he was called in again, and told by the General, with some severity on his face, that they were the Parliament's army, and therefore could say nothing to the King's motion about peace, but must refer those matters, and the King's letters, to their consideration. Then Sir John looked upon Cromwell, Ireton, and the rest of his acquaintance, who saluted him very coldly, shewing him Hammond's letter to them, and smiling with disdain upon it. Being thus disappointed, he went to his lodging, and staid there from four till six of the clock, without any company, to his great dissatisfaction. At last he sent out his servant with orders to find out if possible some of his acquaintance, who met with one that was a general officer[2], by whom he was ordered to tell his master, that he would meet him at midnight in a close behind the Garter Inn. At the time and place appointed they met, where the officer acquainted him in

---

[1] On Berkeley's mission, see Gardiner, Great Civil War, iii. 266.

[2] The general officer was probably Scout-master-general Leonard Watson.

general, that he had no good news to communicate to him ; and then descending to particulars, said, ' You know that I and my friends engaged our selves to you ; that we were zealous for an agreement, and if the rest were not so, we were abused : that since the tumults in the army, we did mistrust Cromwell and Ireton, whereof I informed you. I come now to tell you, that we mistrust neither, and that we are resolved, notwithstanding our engagement, to destroy the King and his posterity, to which end Ireton has made two propositions this afternoon : one, that you should be sent prisoner to London : the other, that none should speak with you upon pain of death, and I do now hazard my life by doing it. The way designed to ruin the King is to send eight hundred of the most disaffected in the army to secure his person, and then to bring him to a trial, and I dare think no farther. This will be done in ten days, and therefore if the King can escape, let him do it, as he loves his life.' Sir John then asking the reason of this change, seeing the King had done all things in compliance with the army, and that the officers were become superiour since the last rendezvouz : he replied, that he could not certainly tell ; but conceived the ground of it to be, that tho one of the mutineers, as he call'd him, was shot to death, eleven more made prisoners, and the rest in appearance over-aw'd, yet they were so far from being so indeed, that two thirds of the army had been since with Cromwell and Ireton, to tell them, that tho they were certain to perish in the enterprize, they would leave nothing unattempted to bring the whole army to their sense ; and that if all failed, they would make a division in the army, and join with any who would assist them in the destruction of those that should oppose them. That Cromwell and Ireton argued thus : ' If the army divide, the greatest part will join with the Presbyters, and will in all likelihood prevail, to our ruin, by forcing us to make our applications to the King, wherein we shall rather beg than offer any assistance ; which if the King shall give, and afterwards have the good fortune to prevail, if he shall then pardon us, it will be all we can pretend, and more than we can certainly promise to ourselves:' thereupon concluding, that if they could not bring the army to their sense, that it was best to comply with them, a schism being utterly destructive to both. In pursuance of this resolution Cromwell bent all his thoughts to make his peace with the party that was most opposite to the King; acknowledging, as he knew well how to do on such occasions, that the glory of this world had so dazled his eyes, that he could not discern clearly the great works that the Lord was doing. He sent also comfortable messages to the prisoners that he had seiz'd at the general rendezvouz, with assurances that nothing should be done to their prejudice; and by these and the like arts he perfected his reconciliation. For my own part, I am inclined to believe that his son Ireton never intended to close with the King, but only to lay his party asleep, whilst they were contesting with the Presbyterian interest in Parliament. And now having secured themselves of the City, and perswaded the King to deny the propositions of the Parliament, subdued the army, and freed themselves from the importunity of the King and his party, they became willing to quit their hands of him, since their transactions with him had procured them so much opposition, and to leave the breach with him upon the Parliament; where they found the Presbyterian party averse to an agreement with him upon any proposals of the army, and the Commonwealth party resolved not to treat with him upon any at all.

Sir John Barkley being return'd to his lodging, dispatch'd his cousin Henry Barkley to the Isle of Wight with two letters; one to the governour, containing a general relation, and doubtful judgment of things in the army; another in cypher, with a particular account of the foresaid conference, and a most passionate supplication to the King to meditate nothing but his immediate escape. The next morning he sent Col. Cooke to Cromwell, to let him know that he had letters and instructions to him from the King, who returned in answer by the messenger, that he durst not see him, it being very dangerous to them both; bidding him be assured, that he would serve the King as long as he could do it without his own ruin ; but desired that it might not be expected that he should perish for his sake. Having received this answer, Sir John took horse for London, resolving not to acquaint any with the inclinations of the army, or with the King's pretended escape, which he presumed would be in a few days, the Queen having sent a ship to that purpose, and pressed it earnestly in her letters. The next day after his arrival at London he received a message from the Scots Lords Lanerick and Lauderdale, desiring a meeting with him, presuming he had a commission from the King to treat ; but he acquainting them that the King had said at his parting from him, that he would make good whatsoever he should undertake to any person in his name; the Lord Lanerick replied, he would ask no other commission from him. At their second meeting they came near to an agreement, and resolved to conclude on the Monday following ; but the next day Sir John Barkley receiving a letter from Mr. Ashburnham, requiring him in the King's name to lay aside all other business, and to return immediately to the King, was constrained to go out of town that night, and to leave the treaty unfinished, to the great dissatisfaction of both parties. At his return to the island he found the King determined not to attempt his escape till he had concluded with the Scots, who, he said, being very desirous to have him out of the hands of the army, would on that account come to an accommodation upon reasonable conditions; whereas if he should leave the army before any agreement with the Scots, they would never treat with him but upon their own terms. To this end the King ordered Sir John Barkley, Mr. Ashburnham, Dr. Hammond, and Mr. Leg to review the papers relating to the treaty with the Scots, which had been managed in London chiefly by Dr. Gough a Popish Priest [1], who in the Queen's name had conjur'd the King to make his speedy escape, and in his own beseeched

---

[1] Dr. Stephen Gough or Goffe, once chaplain of Goring's regiment in the Low Countries, employed in Lord Jermyn's foreign negotiations in 1645. See life in D. N. B. vol. xxii.

him not to insist too nicely upon terms in the present exigency of his affairs: but Mr. Ashburnham hesitated much upon many expressions in the articles relating to the Covenant and Church of England, of which he was a zealous professor, making many replies and alterations; and at last insisted that the King would send for the Scots Commissioners to come to him. Accordingly Sir William Flemming was sent to that purpose; and the next day after an express came from the said Commissioners to the King, desiring that two papers might be drawn, the one to contain the least he would be contented with, and the other the utmost that he would grant to the Scots; which last they desired he would sign, promising to do the like to the first, and to deliver it to Dr. Gough upon the reception of his paper so signed. But this matter was delay'd so long, that they concluded the Scots Commissioners would be on their way before another express could be gone out of the Island. At the same time that the Scots were coming to the King, Commissioners were also sent to him by the Parliament with offers of a personal treaty, on condition that the King in testimony of his future sincerity, would grant the four preliminary bills formerly mentioned. Whilst these two sorts of Commissioners were one day attending the King as he walked about the castle, they observed him to throw a bone before two spaniels that followed him, and to take great delight in seeing them contesting for it; which some of them thought to be intended by him to represent that bone of contention he had cast between the two parties. It was proposed by some of his party that the King should give a dilatory answer to the Scots, that he might have the better opportunity to escape; and at the same time it was moved that he should offer the four following bills to the parliament, upon presumption that they could not well refuse them, nor durst grant them: the first was for the payment of the army, and for their disbanding as soon as paid: the second to put a period to the present parliament: the third to restore the King and Queen to the possession of their revenues: the fourth to

1647

Dec. 24.

settle a church-government without any coercive power;
and till such a government were agreed on, the present to
continue without any coercive authority.   This they advised
upon apprehensions, if the King should give a positive
denial, that the Commissioners might have orders to enjoin
the governour to keep a stricter guard over his person, and
thereby his designed escape be prevented.   To this advice
the King replied, that he had found out a remedy against
their fears; which was to deliver his answer to the Commissioners sealed up.   The next day after the English
Commissioners had delivered their message, and desired the
King's answer within three or four days; the Commissioners
of Scotland, Lowden, Lanerick, Lauderdale, and others,
delivered a protestation to the King, subscribed by them,
against the parliament's message, affirming it to be contrary
to the Covenant, being sent without their participation or
consent; and from this time began seriously to treat with
the King, concluding at last upon such terms as they could
obtain rather than such as they desired from him [1].   When
the time to receive the King's answer was come, he sent for
the English Commissioners, and before he delivered his
answer, demanded of the Earl of Denbigh, who was the
principal commissioner, whether they had power to alter
any of the substantial or circumstantial parts of the message;
and they replying that they had not, he delivered his
answer sealed up into the hands of the Earl of Denbigh.
Having received the King's answer, the Commissioners
withdrew for a little time, and being returned, the Earl of
Denbigh seem'd to be offended, that the King had delivered
his message sealed, alledging that they were required by
their instructions to bring his answer, which whether his
letter were or no, they could not know, unless they might
see it, saying that he had been his ambassador, and in that

---

[1] The Four Bills are printed in the
Old Parliamentary History xvi. 405,
which gives also the protests presented by the Scots to the House of
Lords, Dec. 14 and Dec. 17; ibid. pp.
429–472.   See also Gardiner, Constitutional Documents, p. 248.   The
engagement between the King and
the Scots, dated Dec. 26, 1647, is
printed for the first time by Mr.
Gardiner, ibid. p. 259.

employment would never have delivered any letter without a preceding sight of it: the King told him that he had employ'd twenty ambassadors, and that none of them had ever dared to open his letters; but having demanded whether what the Earl of Denbigh had said were the sense of them all, and finding it so to be: 'Well then,' said the King, 'I will shew it to you on condition you will promise not to acquaint any one with the substance of it, before you have delivered it to the Parliament'; which they consenting to, he desired the company might withdraw. The Commissioners proposed that the governour Col. Hammond might be permitted to stay; which the King being unwilling to allow, yet not thinking it convenient to refuse, gave way to, and by this means the governour as well as the Commissioners came to understand that the King had waved the interests both of the parliament and army, to close with the Scots, the substance of his letter being an absolute refusal of his consent to the four bills presented to him. The impression which the discovery of these things made upon the governour was so great, that before he departed from Carisbrook to accompany the Parliament's Commissioners to Newport, he gave orders for a strict guard to be kept in his absence; and at his return commanded the gates to be lock'd up, and the guards to be doubled, sitting up himself with them all night; whereby the King's intended escape was obstructed.[1] The next morning he ordered the King's servants to remove, not excepting Dr. Hammond his own kinsman[2], who taking leave of the King, acquainted him that they had left the

---

[1] Hammond writes to the Speaker of the House of Lords on Dec. 28: 'Being present this day when the King communicated to the Commissioners of Parliament his answer to the Bills and Propositions lately presented to him from both Houses of Parliament; and finding it so contrary to my expectation, I thought it my duty to take a stricter care than ordinary of the security of the person of the King, and for removing all from about him that are not there by authority of Parliament, and to take all other effectual ways and means to preserve his Majesty's person from departing hence, untill I receive the further commands of the Houses.' Old Parliamentary History, xvi. 481.

[2] Berkeley and Ashburnham now left the King.

1647 captain of the frigat and two trusty gentlemen of the
island to assist him in his escape, assuring him that they
would have all things in readiness on the other side of the
water to receive him.   At their departure the King commanded them to draw up a declaration, and send it to
him the next morning to sign, which they did, and it was
afterwards published in the King's name.   When they came
to Newport one Capt. Burleigh caused a drum to beat
to draw people together in order to rescue the King ; but
there were few besides women and children that followed
him, having but one musquet amongst them all, so that the
King's servants thought not fit to join with or encourage
them ; but went over to the other side, where they continued about three weeks expecting the King's arrival[1] ;
leaving Capt. Burleigh, who with divers of his followers
was committed to jail[2].   Upon the return of the King's
1648 negative to the four previous bills before mentioned, the
Jan. 3. Parliament voted, ' That no farther addresses should be made
to the King by themselves, or any other person, without
the leave of both houses ; and that if any presumed so to do,
Feb. 11. they should incur the guilt of high-treason.'   They also
publish'd a declaration, prepared by Colonel Nathanael
Fiennes[3], shewing the reasons of their said resolutions ;
wherein, amongst other miscarriages of the King's reign,
was represented his breaking of Parliaments, the betraying
of Rochel, his refusal to suffer any inquiry to be made into
the death of his father, his levying war against the people
of England, and his rejecting all reasonable offers of accom-
Jan. 1. modation after six several applications to him on their part.
Col. Rainsborough was appointed Admiral of the Fleet[4] ;

---

[1] Here ends Berkeley's narrative.
Ludlow considerably abridges it, but
adds little except the account of the
King's discussion with Denbigh, and
circumstances in connection with the
Speaker's flight to the army.

[2] On Captain Burley's rising and
his fate, see Hillier, King Charles in
the Isle of Wight, 1852, pp. 63–
75.

[3] ' It was brought in by Mr. N.
Fiennes, but seems penned by Sad-
ler,' says a letter to Lord Lanark,
Hamilton Papers, i. 155.

[4] On Dec. 24 the House of Commons ordered Rainsborough to proceed to sea, but the House of Lords
refused to agree.   On Jan. 1 the
Commons repeated their order in
spite of the opposition of the Lords.

and Mr. Holland, myself, and another member of the House of Commons, sent down to the head quarters at Windsor with orders to discharge from custody Capt. Reynolds, and some others called in derision Levellers, who had been imprisoned by the army for attempting to bring about that which they themselves were now doing, and to exhort the officers to contribute the best of their endeavours towards a speedy settlement.

The Scots in pursuance of their treaty with the King, made what preparations they could to raise an army, wherein the presbyterians and cavaliers join'd, tho with different designs. The same spirit began to appear also in England, many of our ships revolting to the King at the instigation of one Capt. Batten, who had been vice-admiral to the Parliament, and others, encouraged by the city and the presbyterian party. The seamen on board the ship commanded by Col. Rainsborough refused to receive him, having before-hand secured one of my brothers, with others whom they suspected to be faithful to their commander. The Earl of Warwick, as most acceptable to them, was appointed to go down to reduce them to obedience, by which means part of the fleet was preserved to the Parliament, who immediately issued out orders for the fitting out of more ships to reinforce them. With the revolted ships Prince Charles block'd up the mouth of the river ; and about the same time his brother the Duke of York, who upon the surrender of Oxford had been brought by order of the Parliament to St. James's, and provision made for him there, escaped from thence to serve the King's designs. The castles of Deal and Sandwich declar'd also for the King, and Col. Rich was sent with a party of the army to reduce them. In the mean time Lieutenant-General Cromwell not forgetting himself, procured a meeting of divers leading men amongst the Presbyterians and Independents, both members of Parliament and ministers, at a dinner in Westminster, under pretence of endeavouring a

1648

May 27

May 29.

August.

May 21.

He had been originally appointed to command the winter guard, Sept. 27, and confirmed by the Lords, Oct. 2, 1647.

1648   reconciliation between the two parties[1]: but he found it
a work too difficult for him to compose the differences
between these two ecclesiastical interests ; one of which
would endure no superior, the other no equal ; so that this
meeting produced no effect. Another conference he contrived to be held in King Street[2] between those called the
grandees of the house and army, and the Commonwealths-
men ; in which the grandees, of whom Lieutenant-General
Cromwell was the head, kept themselves in the clouds, and
would not declare their judgments either for a monarchical,
aristocratical or democratical government ; maintaining
that any of them might be good in themselves, or for us,

---

[1] On Feb. 4, 1648, 'Sir Thomas
Fairfax accompanied with some chief
officers of the army dined with the
Lord Mayor of the city of London
and some aldermen of the city.'
Rushworth, vii. 986. Walker describes Cromwell as at this time
endeavouring ' to unite all interests
in the Houses, city, and army,' and
making offers to the city of ' the
restitution of the Tower and Militia
and the enlargement of the imprisoned aldermen,' but the city,
'wiser than our first parents, rejected the serpent and his subtleties.'
History of Independency, i. 83, ed.
1661. A correspondent of the Earl
of Lanark places these overtures at
the end of March, and adds, ' This
averseness of the city puts them
upon new counsels, which the junto
of Independents have held thrice in
private since Thursday last, but have
not as I hear concluded anything ;
only 'tis reported they have amongst
themselves voted for monarchy ; and
then, the question being who should
be the monarch, Marten said, " if we
must have that government we had
better have this King and oblige
him, than to have him obtruded on
us by the Scots, and owe his restitution to them." It is said on

Thursday next it will be publicly
debated what government shall be
established.' Hamilton Papers, i.
170.

[2] During 1646 and the first part of
1647 Cromwell lived in Drury Lane.
A letter of John Lilburne's to him,
dated March 25, 1647, is addressed
to ' Lieut. Generall Cromwell at his
house in Drury Lane, near the Red
Lion.' Jonah's Cry out of the Whales
belly, p. 1. According to Lilburne,
Joyce received the order to secure
the King 'in Cromwell's own garden
in Drury-lane, Colonel Charles Fleetwood being by.' Lilburne's Im-
peachment of High Treason against
Oliver Cromwell, 1649, p. 55. It is
curious to recall Goldsmith's description of the neighbourhood :—

'Where the Red Lion, staring o'er the
          way
Invites each passing stranger that can
          pay ;
Where Calvert's butt, and Parsons'
          black champagne,
Regale the drabs and bloods of Drury-
          lane.'

In the summer of 1647 Cromwell
took up his residence in King Street,
Westminster, whilst Fairfax established himself in Queen Street.
Cromwelliana, p. 60.

according as providence should direct us. The Commonwealths-men declared that monarchy was neither good in
itself, nor for us. That it was not desirable in itself, they
urged from the 8th chapter and 8th verse of the first
Book of Samuel, where the rejecting of the Judges, and the
choice of a King, was charged upon the Israelites by God
himself as a rejection of him; and from another passage in
the same book, where Samuel declares it to be a great
wickedness; with divers more texts of scripture to the same
effect. And that it was no way conducing to the interest
of this nation, was endeavoured to be proved by the infinite
mischiefs and oppressions we had suffered under it, and
by it: that indeed our ancestors had consented to be
governed by a single person, but with this proviso, that he
should govern according to the direction of the law, which
he always bound himself by oath to perform: that the
King had broken this oath, and thereby dissolved our
allegiance; protection and obedience being reciprocal:
that having appealed to the sword for the decision of the
things in dispute, and thereby caused the effusion of a
deluge of the peoples blood, it seemed to be a duty incumbent upon the representatives of the people to call him
to an account for the same; more especially since the controversy was determined by the same means which he had
chosen; and then to proceed to the establishment of an
equal commonwealth founded upon the consent of the
people, and providing for the rights and liberties of all men,
that we might have the hearts and hands of the nation to
support it, as being most just, and in all respects most conducing to the happiness and prosperity thereof. Notwithstanding what was said, Lieutenant-General Cromwell, not
for want of conviction, but in hopes to make a better bargain with another party, professed himself unresolved, and
having learn'd what he could of the principles and inclinations of those present at the conference, took up a
cushion and flung it at my head, and then ran down the
stairs; but I overtook him with another, which made him
hasten down faster than he desired. The next day passing

by me in the house, he told me he was convinced of the desirableness of what was proposed, but not of the feasibleness of it; thereby, as I suppose, designing to encourage me to hope that he was inclined to join with us, tho unwilling to publish his opinion, lest the grandees should be informed of it, to whom I presume he professed himself to be of another judgment.

Much time being spent since the Parliament had voted no more addresses to be made to the King, nor any messages received from him, and yet nothing done towards bringing the King to a trial, or the settling of affairs without him; many of the people who had waited patiently hitherto, finding themselves as far from a settlement as ever, concluded that they should never have it, nor any ease from their burdens and taxes, without an accommodation with the King; and therefore entred into a combination through England, Scotland, and Ireland, to restore him to his authority. To this end petitions were promoted throughout all countries, the King by his agents fomenting and encouraging this spirit by all means possible, as appeared by his intercepted letters : so that Lieutenant-General Cromwell, who had made it his usual practice to gratify enemies even with the oppression of those who were by principle his friends, began again to court the Commonwealth party, inviting some of them to confer with him at his chamber [1]: with which acquainting me the next time he came to the House of Commons, I took the freedom to tell him, that he knew how to cajole and give them good words when he had occasion to make use of them : whereat breaking out into a rage, he said, they were a proud sort of people, and only considerable in their own conceits. I told him, it was no new thing to hear truth calumniated, and that tho the Commonwealths-men were fallen under his displeasure, I would take the liberty to say,

---

[1] 'I am assured by one that was a witness to it that Cromwell desired a meeting to be reconciled to Marten, but that they parted much more enemies than they met.' Letter dated Feb. 22, 1648, Hamilton Papers, i. 154.

that they had always been and ever would be considerable   1648
where there was not a total defection from honesty,
generosity, and all true vertue, which I hoped was not yet
our case.

The Earl of Warwick, with the fleet equipped for him by
the Parliament, fell down the river towards the ships commanded by Prince Charles, who presuming either that he
would not fight him, or perhaps come over to him, lay some
time in expectation ; but finding by the manner of his Aug. 29, 30.
approach that he was deceived in that particular, he thought
it convenient to make all the sail he could for the coast of
Holland.   Our fleet followed him as far as the Texel ; but
according to the defensive principle of the nobility, our
admiral thinking he had sufficiently discharged his duty
by clearing the downs, and driving the other fleet from
our coast, declined to fight tho he had an opportunity to
engage.   Deal and Sandown Castles were reduced by Col. Aug. 25.
Rich, and many of our revolted ships not finding things
according to their expectation, being constrained to serve
under Prince Rupert instead of the Lord Willoughby, who
they desired might command them, returned to the obedience of the Parliament.

The Scots making all possible preparations to raise an
army for the restitution of the King, Sir Thomas Glenham
and Sir Marmaduke Langdale went to Scotland to join
with them in that enterprize, and to draw what English
they could to promote the design.   The first of these
seized upon Carlisle by order of the Scots, tho contrary to April 29.
their articles ; whereupon the Parliament thinking it necessary to provide for the security of Berwick, placed a good April 28.
garison therein, and resolving to reinforce the militia of
each county, sent down some of their members to give life
to the preparations.   Amongst others I was appointed to
go down to the county for which I served, where we agreed
to raise two regiments of foot and one of horse [1].   In the

---

[1] On May 25, it was proposed in
the Commons that power should be
given to the Derby House Committee
to grant commissions for raising
forces in different counties to such
persons as should be recommended

mean time the enemy was not idle, and taking advantage of the discontents of Capt. Poyer Governour of Pembroke, they prevailed with him to revolt, and declare for the King. Other disaffected parts of the nation, not yet ready for open opposition, acted with more caution, preparing and encouraging petitions to the Parliament for a personal treaty with the King, of which the principal were Surrey, Essex, and Kent. In Essex they met at Chelmsford in a

tumultuous manner, and seized Sir William Masham and other members of Parliament; who being ready to use

all gentle methods to prevent farther inconveniences, sent down Mr. Charles Rich, second son to the Earl of Warwick. and Sir Harbottle Grimston, two of their members, to endeavour to quiet that tumultuous spirit, with instructions and power to promise indemnity to all that should desist from the prosecution of what they desired in this violent way [1] : which commission they managed so well, that upon their promise to present the requests of the petitioners, which were drawn up in writing, to the Parliament, and to return them an answer, the people of the country dispersed themselves to their own houses. But the sedition of the

Surrey-men was not terminated so easily, of whom many hundreds came to the doors of the Parliament; and not being satisfied with the answer the Parliament thought fit to give to their petition, after they had been heated with drink, and animated by the Cavalier party, they resolved

by the members for the said counties : but this was negatived. C. J. v. 573. However, on Sept. 6, 1648, an ordinance was passed enabling militia commissioners named for the county of Wilts, of whom Ludlow was one, to raise horse and foot for the defence of that county. On May 30 Ludlow was sent into Wiltshire with Mr. Dove and James Herbert, 'to provide for, preserve and settle the peace of that county'; ib. 579; cf. Rushworth, vii. 1108.

[1] The petition of the grand jury of the county of Essex, dated March 22, 1648, was presented to Parliament, May 4, 1648. The members for Essex were ordered down to that county on May 30, and their presence not proving enough, a letter from the House to the gentlemen of Essex was drawn up on June 3, and Mr. Rich was sent as its bearer. Sir William Masham and others of the Parliamentary commissioners were seized about June 4 by Goring's troops and remained prisoners during the siege of Colchester. C. J. v. 573, 579, 589; Gardiner, Great Civil War, iii. 395.

to force from them another answer, and with intolerable insolence pressed upon their guard, beating the sentinels to the main guard, which was drawn up at the upper end of Westminster Hall, where they wounded the officer who commanded them ; and being intreated to desist, became more violent; so that the souldiers were necessitated, in their own defence, and discharge of their duty, to fire upon them, whereby two or three of the country-men were killed : neither did this quiet them, till some horse and foot arrived to strengthen the guard, and dispersed them. Lieutenant-Colonel Cobbet who commanded the guard, being called into the house to give an account of what had passed, went to the bar bleeding from the wounds which he had received, and related the passages before mentioned : but some friends of the petitioners within doors informing the house that the matter of fact was otherwise than had been represented by the Lieutenant-Colonel, the Parliament appointed a committee to examine the truth of it [1].

Those of the secluded members who were in England being returned to the house, divers hard words passed between them and others of the Parliament ; and one day Commissary-General Ireton speaking something concerning them, Mr. Hollis thinking it to be injurious to them, passing by him in the house, whispered him in the ear, telling him it was false, and he would justify it to be so if he would follow him, and thereupon immediately went out of the house, with the other following him. Some members who had observed their passionate carriage to each other, and seen them hastily leaving the house, acquainted the Parliament with their apprehensions ; whereupon they sent their serjeant at arms to command their attendance, which he letting them understand as they were taking boat to go to the other side of the water, they returned ; and the house taking notice of what they were informed concerning

---

[1] On the Surrey petition and the riot which took place, see Rushworth, vii. 1116 ; Walker, History of Independency, Epistle prefixed to pt. i ; Portland MSS. i. 453 ; and letters under May 16, 1648, in the Clarke Papers, vol. ii. Cf. Gardiner, Great Civil War, iii. 375.

them, enjoined them to forbear all words or actions of enmity towards each other, and to carry themselves for the future as fellow-members of the same body, which they promised to do [1].

Lieutenant-General Cromwell perceiving the clouds to gather on every side, complained to me, as we were walking in the palace-yard, of the unhappiness of his condition, having made the greatest part of the nation his enemies, by adhering to a just cause : but that which he pretended to be his greatest trouble was, that many who were engaged in the same cause with him had entertained a jealousy and suspicion of him ; which he assured me was a great discouragement to him, asking my advice, what method was best for him to take. I could not but acknowledg that he had many enemies for the sake of the cause in which he stood engaged, and also that many who were friends to the cause had conceived suspicions of him : but I observed to him, that he could never oblige

---

[1] This story is a year misplaced. The votes against the eleven members were annulled on June 3, 1648, and Holles took his seat again on Aug. 14. Ireton was absent from his place all August, and probably all September also. The quarrel really took place over the vote against the army petition, on March 30, 1647, or a day or two later. A news-letter dated April 5 says. 'Mr Holles and Major Ireton going over the water to fight, were hindered by Sir William Waller and some others, who observed Mr. Holles to deride Ireton's argument in justification of the army's petition, which was the occasion of the quarrell.' Clarendon MS. 2478. On April 2. 1647, 'The House being informed that some matters of difference had happened between Mr. Holles and Commissary Ireton ; It is resolved, &c. That Mr. Holles and Commissary Ireton be injoined not to proceed, in any manner, any further upon the matter of difference informed to have happened between them. Mr. Speaker by the command of the House, laid this injunction upon them accordingly. Mr. Holles and Commissary Ireton did publicly engage themselves to submit unto, and perform, this injunction.' C. J. v. 133. Another news-letter, dated April 15, says, 'It is said that Mr. Holles went out last week to fight with Major-General Ireton, but Ireton came into the field after him without a sword, pretending it stood not with his conscience to fight, which confirms the general opinion that all the Independents are deadly cowards.' Clarendon MS. 2495. Clarendon himself, writing in 1671, improves on this story, and states that Ireton refused to fight and Holles pulled his nose, 'telling him that if his conscience would keep him from giving men satisfaction, it should keep him from provoking them.' History, x. 104.

the former, without betraying that cause wherein he was
engaged; which if he should do upon the account of an
empty title, riches, or any other advantages, how those
contracts would be kept with him, was uncertain; but
most certain it was, that his name would be abominated
by all good men, and his memory be abhorred by posterity.
On the other side, if he persisted in the prosecution of our
just intentions, it was the most probable way to subdue
his enemies, to rectify the mistakes of those that had
conceived a jealousy of him, and to convince his friends of
his integrity: that if he should fall in the attempt, yet his
loss would be lamented by all good men, and his name be
transmitted to future ages with honour. He seemed to
take well what I said, and it might have been no disservice
to him if he had acted accordingly: but his design was
rather to perswade me, for the present, of the rectitude of
his intentions, than to receive counsel from me concerning
his conduct [1].

About this time we obtained some advantages in Ireland,
where Col. Michael Jones, who had been order'd by the
Parliament to command at Dublin when the Earl of
Ormond delivered it up, with the forces he had, fought
the rebels, tho double his number, at Dungon Hill, killed
some thousands of them, and totally routed the rest [2].
Of which when the Parliament had received information,
they ordered five hundred pounds by year of the forfeited
lands in Ireland to be settled upon Col. Jones as a reward
for his good service. In England the defection began to
increase; Capt. Henry Lilburn who commanded for the
Parliament in Tinmouth Castle, which lies at the mouth
of the harbour, and is a key to Newcastle, declaring for
the King; but notice thereof being brought to Sir Arthur
Haslerig at Newcastle, of which town he was governour,
he with great expedition drew down a party before the

1648

1647
Aug. 8.

---

[1] Cromwell set out for Wales on
May 3 or May 4. Rushworth, vii.
1098. The conversation here related may have taken place any time
between September, 1647, and that
date.

[2] See Rushworth, vii. 779; Gardiner, Great Civil War, iii. 350.

place, and attacking it unexpectedly, took it by assault, before the men had been thoroughly confirmed in their revolt by the governour, whom he put to the sword, and placed another garison therein.

Many of those who had been for the Parliament in South-Wales now joining with the King's party, they grew to be a considerable body ; whereby Major-General Laughern, who upon some suspicion had been under confinement, was encouraged to get away and join himself to them ; Major-General John Stradling, Sir Henry Stradling, Col. Thomas Stradling, and several other gentlemen of those parts falling in with them. Col. Horton, with about two thousand five hundred horse, foot, and dragoons, was sent into Wales to engage them ; Lieutenant-General Cromwell following with as many more forces as could be spared from the army; who being within three or four days' march of Col. Horton, received advice that the enemy, to the number of about seven thousand, had engaged the
colonel at St. Faggons in Glamorganshire ; that upon the first attack our forces gave ground, but well considering the danger they were in, the country being full of enemies, and encouraged by their affection to the cause wherein they were engaged, they charged the enemy's van, consisting of the best of their men, with so great bravery and resolution, that they forced them to give way; which those that were in their rear, who were for the most part new-raised men, perceiving, began to shift for themselves. Upon this ours followed their charge with so much vigour and success, that the whole body of the enemy was soon routed and dispersed ; many of them were killed in the pursuit, and many taken prisoners : amongst the latter was Major-General Stradling, and divers other officers. The news of this success was very welcome to all those that wished well to the publick, and proved a great discouragement to the contrary party[1].

The petitioners of Surrey drew into a body, and in conjunction with the Kentishmen of the King's party,

---

[1] Rushworth, vii. 1110; Gardiner, Great Civil War, iii. 373.

appointed their rendezvouz upon Blackheath: but Sir Thomas Fairfax with that part of the army which he had with him disappointed that design, by possessing himself of that ground before them. However the enemy had brought together a considerable body of men, many of whom were induced to come in, upon assurances given that they should be commanded by Mr. Hales, a gentleman of a great estate in Kent; tho afterwards the Lord Goring appeared at the head of them, as had been designed from the beginning. Upon the advance of Sir Thomas Fairfax his army, the enemy, who exceeded him in number by one half at least, divided their body, sending one part to possess themselves of Maidstone and the adjacent places, and another party to block up Dover and other forts upon the coast, whilst Goring remained with the rest about Rochester. Sir Thomas Fairfax resolving first to attack those about Maidstone, fell upon them, and beat them into the town, which they had fortified before; whereupon tho the numbers within the town being at least equal to those without made it a work of great hazard and difficulty, yet considering that those with the Lord Goring exceeded either, and might march to the enemy's relief, ours resolved to storm the place, which they did the night following; the General by his own example encouraging the men to fall on, who for a good while were not able to make any considerable progress, till Col. Hewson with his regiment opened a passage into one of the streets, where the dispute growing hot, he was knocked down with a musquet; but recovering himself, he pressed the enemy so hard, that they were forced to retreat to their main guard, and falling in with them at the same time, so disordered them, that they all began to shift for themselves; wherein they were favoured by the advantage of the night: yet many of them were made prisoners, and many killed; many horses and all their artillery fell into the hands of ours. The General, as soon as he had refreshed his men, advanced towards that body commanded by the Lord Goring, which was much increased in number by the addition of those who

1648   escaped from Maidstone, but not in resolution, being so
discouraged with their relation of what had passed there,
that immediately upon our approach they began to retreat,
many of them running away to their own habitations.
Notwithstanding this, a considerable body continuing with
the Lord Goring, he sent to the city of London, desiring
leave to march through the city into Essex, designing to
recruit his men with such of that county as had lately
expressed so much affection to the King's interest.   The
City, tho much inclined to have the King received upon
terms, yet not willing absolutely to espouse the Cavalier
party, especially in a flying posture; and considering that
there was a great number still amongst them who retained
their affection to the publick cause, returned a positive
denial to Goring: so that he was necessitated to make use
of boats or other means to transport his men over the river
June 3, 4. into the county of Essex.   A party of horse was sent
from the army to keep a guard at Bow Bridg, as well to
prevent the disaffected in the City from running to the
enemy, as to hinder them from doing any thing to the
prejudice of London.

Lieutenant-General Cromwell, with that part of the
army which was with him, besieged the castle and town
of Pembroke, whither the principal of that body which fled
from St. Faggons had made their retreat[1].   In the mean
time the Presbyterian party prevailing in the House, by
reason of the absence of divers members who belonged to
the army, and were employed in all parts of the nation,
June 3. discharged from prison those who had been committed
upon the account of that force which was put upon the
House by the late tumults, and left the Parliament to the
mercy of their enemies with a very slender guard.   The
1647   Lord Lisle's commission to be Lord-Lieutenant of Ireland
April 5. expiring at the same time, they refused to renew it; by
which means the province of Munster fell into the hands
of the Lord Inchequin as President, who made use of the

---

[1] Cromwell began to besiege Pembroke about May 22; Rushworth, vii.
1118, 1121, 1128-9, 1131.

opportunity to displace those officers that had been put in
by the Lord Lisle, preferring his own creatures to their
employments, to the great prejudice of the English interest
in that country: many others who were acquainted with his
temper and principles quitted voluntarily; and tho he still
pretended fidelity to the state of England, yet he expressed
himself dissatisfied with the proceedings of the army-party
towards him. Some overtures also he had received from
the Irish touching an accommodation ; but being straitned
by them in his quarters, and therefore advancing with his
army towards them, Col. Temple and some others yet
remaining in his army being willing to improve the
occasion, pressed him so hard to resolve to fight, that he
could not well avoid it. At the beginning of the battel the
success seemed to be very doubtful, but in the end ours
obtained the victory, some thousands of the enemy being
killed, many made prisoners, and all their baggage taken[1].
Not long after this he declared against the Parliament, and
joined with the Irish rebels : some of the English officers
concurred with him in his declaration ; many left him and
came to the Parliament, who made provision for them, as
they had done for those that came away before. Tho this
conjunction of Inchequin was not concluded without the
King's consent, yet it was not a proper season for him to
condescend so far as they desired : whereby great divisions
arose amongst them ; for there was a party of Old Irish, as
they were called, headed principally by Owen Roe O'Neal,
of whom several were in the Supreme Council, who, out of an
innate hatred to the English government, joined with those
who would be satisfied with nothing less than to have the
Pope acknowledged to be their only Supreme Lord : so
that not being able to agree, their differences proved very
serviceable to the English interest. The like spirit of
division appeared amongst our enemies in Scotland, where

margin notes: 104.

Nov. 13.

1648
April 3.

---

[1] Inchiquin's despatch is printed
in Cary's Memorials of the Civil
War, i. 360. This was known as
the battle of Knockinoss, or Cnoc-
nados, which means in English
'shrub hill.' The site of the battle
is a few miles west of Mallow.
Gardiner, G. C. W. iii. 354-356.

1648   tho the number was great of those that professed their
constant adherence to their engagements contained in the
Covenant, yet when it came to a trial in their convention,
the Anti-covenanters, who were for restoring the King
without any terms, carried all before them : so that instead
of the Marquiss of Argile, the Marquiss of Hamilton was
May 10. appointed general of their army; all the inferiour officers
being of the same mold and principle ; insomuch that the
pulpits who before had proclaimed this war, now accompanied the army that was preparing to march with their
curses : for tho they could have been contented that the sectarian party, as they called it, should be ruined, provided they
could find strength enough to bring in the King themselves ; yet they feared their old enemy more than their
new one, because the latter would only restrain them from
lording it over them and others, affording them equal
liberty with themselves ; whereas the former was so far
from that, as hardly to suffer them to be hewers of wood and
drawers of water: for those who would have all power both
civil and ecclesiastical put into one hand, could not possibly
agree with such as would have it divided into many.

These affairs necessitated the Parliament to raise the
militia, in order to oppose this malevolent spirit which
threatned them from the north, and also prevailed with
Aug. 2. them to discountenance a charge of high treason, framed by
Major Huntington, an officer of the army, with the advice
of some members of both houses, against Lieutenant
General Cromwell, for endeavouring, by betraying the
King, Parliament, and army, to advance himself ; it being
manifest that the preferring this accusation at that time,
was principally designed to take him off from his command,
and thereby to weaken the army, that their enemies might
be the better enabled to prevail against them [1].

---

[1] 'Sundry Reasons inducing Major
Robert Huntington to lay down his
commission.' L. J. x. 408, Aug. 2,
1648 ; reprinted in Thurloe State
Papers, i. 94, and Maseres' Select
Tracts, i. 395. Huntington was
answered by Samuel Chidley in 'A
Back Blow to Major Huntington for
his treacherous accusation of Lieut.-
gen. Cromwell, and Comm. Gen.
Ireton,' 1648. See also ' Some Anim-
adversions on Major Huntington's

The design of the King's escape was still carried on ; but by the vigilance of the governour of the Isle of Wight and his officers it was discovered and prevented. The next morning after the discovery they found the iron bars of the King's chamber-window eaten through by something applied to them : whereupon those who were to have been instrumental in his escape, not knowing otherwise how to revenge themselves on those who had defeated their enter-prize, accused Major Rolfe, a captain in that garison very active and vigilant in his charge, of a design to kill the King, raising such a clamour about it, that the Parliament thought not fit to decline the putting him upon his trial ; but the accusation appearing to the grand jury to be grounded upon malice, they refused to find the bill. About the same time Capt. Burleigh, who had beat a drum at Newport for the rescuing of the King, was brought to his trial; and the jury having found him guilty of high treason, he was executed according to the sentence.

Those of the enemies commanded by the Lord Goring. who had fled into Essex, grew to a considerable number ; but being new-raised men, and not well acquainted one with another, upon the advance of our army retreated to Colchester, with a body so much exceeding ours which pursued and besieged them in that place, that Commissary General Ireton compared the town and those therein to a great bee-hive, and our army to a small swarm of bees sticking on one side of it ; but the number of ours was soon increased by the forces which the well-affected in the counties of Essex, Suffolk, Norfolk, and Cambridg sent to their assistance.

papers,' prefixed to the pamphlet edition of his narrative. On May 7, 1650, when Huntington applied for his arrears of pay, Parliament refused, and appointed a committee to consider charges of seditious practices against him. (C. J. vi. 408.) In 1659 he was major of the Oxfordshire militia. Cal. S. P. Dom. 1659-60, pp. 219, 241-2. After the restoration he became one of the Commissioners of the Customs, and died April 21, 1684. Major Huntington's ‛Relation of sundry particulars relating to King Charles I of blessed memory,' written for Sir William Dugdale in 1679, is printed with the 1702 edition of Sir Thomas Herbert's Memoirs (p. 151 .

1648   The Earl of Holland, who at the beginning of the Parliament had appeared active for them. and afterwards leaving them, had gone to the King at Oxford, when he supposed him to grow strong ; then again returning to the Parliament upon the declining of the King's affairs, publishing a declaration at his coming to London, that he left the King because he saw the Irish rebels so eminently favoured by him ; in this low condition of the Parliament, revolted again, and formed a party of about a thousand horse, with

July 5. which he marched from London, and declared against them, accompanied by the Duke of Buckingham, (whose sequestration, upon the account of his minority when he first engaged with the King, the Parliament had freely remitted) and the Lord Francis his brother, prevailing also with Dalbeir, formerly Quarter-Master-General to the Earl of Essex, to join with them. Their rendezvous was appointed to be upon Bansted Downs ; but the vigilance of the Parliament was such, that a party of horse and foot was soon sent after them, commanded by Sir Michael Lewesey, who without much dispute put those courtly gentlemen to the rout. The Lord Francis presuming perhaps that his beauty would have charmed the souldiers, as it had done Mrs. Kirk, for whom he made a splendid entertainment the night before he left the town, and made her a present of plate to the value of a thousand pounds, stayed behind his company, where unseasonably daring the troopers, and

July 7. refusing to take quarter, he was killed, and after his death there was found upon him some of the hair of Mrs. Kirk sew'd in a piece of ribbon that hung next his skin. The

July 10. rest fled towards St. Neots in the county of Huntington, where being fallen upon again, they were routed a second time : in which action the Parliament's souldiers, to express their detestation of Dalbeir's treachery, hewed him in pieces. The Earl of Holland was taken, and sent prisoner to Warwick Castle ; but the Duke of Buckingham escaped, and went over to France.

June 3.   Pomfret Castle being seized by some of the King's party, was besieged by the country, assisted by some of the army,

Sir Hugh Cholmely commanding at the siege; but the army finding little progress made therein, ordered Col. Rainsborough with more forces thither. appointing him to command in the room of Sir Hugh Cholmely. Whilst he was preparing for that service, being at Doncaster, ten or twelve miles from Pomfret, with a considerable force in the town, a party of horse dismounting at his quarters, and going up as friends to his chamber, under pretence of having business with him, seized him first, and upon his refusal to go silently with them, murdered him. After his death another commander being appointed in his place to carry on the siege, those in the castle were reduced to such extremities, that some of the most desperate of them resolved, together with their governour one Morris, who had been page to the Earl of Strafford, to endeavour the breaking through our forces on horseback; which they attempted, and tho most of them were beaten back to the castle by the besiegers, yet this Morris made his way through; but was afterwards taken as he passed through the country in the disguise of a beggar, and carried to York, where he was arraigned before Justice Thorpe, and being found guilty of treason, was executed for the same [1].

Lieutenant-General Cromwell, with that part of the army which was with him, besieged the town and castle of Pembroke, whither the chief of that party that fled from St. Faggons had made their retreat, as I said before; but wanting great guns, he was obliged to send for some to Glocester, which with much difficulty were brought to him. This place detained the greatest part of our army about six weeks; but it was remarkable, that about the time the Scots were entring into England, the garison for want of provisions was forced to capitulate and surrender upon

Margin notes: 1648 — Oct. 29. — 1649 — March 20. — Aug. 23. — 1648 — July 11.

[1] On the sieges of Pontefract, see Mr. Longstaffe's edition of Drake's narrative in the Miscellanea of the Surtees Society, 1860. A life of Rainborowe (as he usually spells his name), is printed in Archeologia, vol. xlvi, by Mr. Edward Peacock. Sir Henry Cholmley, not his brother Sir Hugh, was the Parliamentary commander at the beginning of the siege, and Lambert was appointed in December, 1648. Cf. Clarendon, Rebellion, xi. 116–120.

1648 articles, by which some of them were to remain prisoners, and others to be banished into Ireland for three years; amongst the latter were Col. Thomas Stradling, Sir Henry Stradling, Col. Button and Major Butler[1]; of the first were Col. Laughern, Col. Poyer, and Col. Powell.

July 8. Twenty thousand Scots being upon their march into England under the conduct of Duke Hamilton, with about five thousand English, commanded by Sir Marmaduke Langdale, some of us who had opposed the Lieutenant-General's arbitrary proceedings, when we were convinced he acted to promote a selfish and unwarrantable design, now thinking our selves obliged to strengthen his hands in that necessary work, which he was appointed to undertake, writ a letter to him to encourage him, from the consideration of the justice of the cause wherein he was engaged, and the wickedness of those with whom he was to encounter, to proceed with chearfulness, assuring him, that notwithstanding all our discouragements we would readily give him all the July 22. assistance we could[2]. The House of Commons declared

---

[1] 'My uncle Col. Thomas Stradling' is mentioned by Ludlow as one of his securities in 1660. He was probably a brother of Mrs. Ludlow's mother, who was a daughter of Sir John Stradling. Cf. Phillips, Civil War in Wales, ii. 336, 397.

[2] On Aug. 1, 1648, the House of Commons released John Lilburne from imprisonment, probably because the Presbyterian party hoped he would join Major Huntington in impeaching Cromwell. Lilburne protests that he was earnestly solicited to it again and again, but refused 'as not loving a Scotch interest then likely to swallow us up,' and supported Cromwell instead. He names Cornelius Holland, Tom Chaloner, and Col. Ludlow as well knowing the truth of this statement. He quotes also a letter which he sent Cromwell by Mr. Edward Sexby, 'whom on purpose I procured to go down to him.' 'Sir,' runs the letter, 'What my comrade hath written by our trusty bearer, might be sufficient for us both; but to demonstrate unto you that I am no staggerer from my first principles, that I engaged my life upon, nor from you, if you are what you ought to be, and what you are now strongly reported to be; although, if I prosecuted or desired revenge for an hard and almost starving imprisonment, I could have had of late the choice of twenty opportunities to have paid you to the purpose; but I scorn it, especially when you are low, and this assure yourself, that if ever my hand be upon you, it shall be when you are in your full glory, if then you shall decline from the righteous ways of truth and justice: which if you will fixedly and impartially prosecute, I am yours, to the last drop of my heart blood (for all your late severe hand towards me), John Lilburne. From Westminster

the Scots who had invaded England to be enemies, and
ordered the Lieutenant-General to advance towards them,
and fight them: but the Lords in this doubtful posture of
affairs declined to concur with them in the same : yet both
of them, with the city of London, joined in driving on a
personal treaty with the King in the Isle of Wight, and to
that end the Lords and Commons revoked the votes for
Non-Addresses; whereby the King seemed to be on sure
ground, for that if the Scots army failed, he might still make
terms with the Parliament.   The King's party in Colchester
were also much encouraged with hopes of relief from the
Scots army, who were very numerous, and well furnished
with all things but a good cause.   To fight this formidable
army the Lieutenant-General could not make up much above
seven thousand horse and foot, and those so extremely
harassed with hard service and long marches, that they
seemed rather fit for a hospital than a battel.   With this
handful of men he advanced towards the enemy, and about
Preston in Lancashire both armies met on the 17th of
August, 1648.   The English who were in the Scots army
had the honour of the van, and for a time entertained ours
with some opposition ; but being vigorously pressed by
our men, they were forced to retreat to a pass, which they
maintained against us, whilst they sent to their general
for succours ; which he not sending, on purpose, as was
said, that the English might be cut off, and his party
kept intire to enable him to set up for himself, and
give law to both nations, they began to shift for themselves : which made such an impression upon the Scots
that they soon followed their example, retreating in a
disorderly manner.   Ours followed them so close, that
most of their foot threw down their arms, and yielded
themselves prisoners.   Many of the principal officers of their
foot were taken, with all their artillery, ammunition, and

this 3 of August, 1648, being the
second day of my freedom.' Legal,
Fundamental Liberties, 1649, p. 32.
The comrade referred to was probably not Ludlow, but Wildman.
Sexby no doubt carried a similar
letter from Ludlow, and Ludlow was
certainly cognizant of this letter.

baggage : Hamilton, with four or five thousand horse in a body, left the field, and was pursued by Col. Thorney, a member of Parliament, and colonel of a regiment of horse, a worthy and a valiant man. who following them too close and unadvisedly run himself upon one of their lances, wherewith he was mortally wounded, which he perceiving by the wasting of his spirits, to express his affection to his country, and joy for the defeat of the enemy, desired his men to open to the right and left, that he might have the satisfaction to see them run before he died [1]. The enemy's body of horse kept themselves together for some days roving up and down the country about Leicestershire, which county the Lord Grey of Grooby had raised, and brought together about three thousand horse and foot to preserve the country from plunder, and to take all possible advantages against the enemy : and tho a body of horse from the army was in pursuit of the Scots, yet the Leicester-shire party came up first to them at Uttoxeter in Stafford-shire, where the body of the enemy's horse was ; and whilst the Scots were treating with the other party from the army, the Lord Grey's men observing no guards kept, entred upon them, before any conditions were made ; whereupon

Hamilton surrendred himself to Col. Wayte, an officer of the Leicestershire party, delivering to him his scarf, his George, and his sword, which last he desired him to keep carefully, because it had belonged to his ancestors. By the two parties the Scots were all made prisoners, and all their horses seized ; the Duke of Hamilton was carried prisoner to Windsor-Castle, and all their standards of horse and foot were taken and sent up to London, where the Parliament ordered them to be hung up in Westminster Hall [2]. The

[1] Col. Francis Thornhaugh, an account of whom is given in Mrs. Hutchinson's life of her husband. Cromwell terms him (letter 61) 'a man as faithful and gallant in your service as any ; and one who hath heretofore lost blood in your service and now his last ' See Life of Col. Hutchinson, i. 194 ; ii. 131.

[2] 'This day there was an appearance of all the Scots colours in Westminster Hall ; those taken from Hamilton at Preston being hang'd up on the one side, and these at Dunbarr on the other.' Mercurius Politicus, Sept. 21, 1650. See C. J. vi. 465 ; vii. 15.

House of Lords who had avoided to declare the Scots
enemies whilst their army was entire. now after their defeat
prevented the House of Commons, and moved that a day
might be appointed to give God thanks for this success.
The news of this victory being carried to the Isle of Wight,
the King said to the governour, that it was the worst news
that ever came to England ; to which he answered, that he
thought the King had no cause to be of that opinion. since if
Hamilton had beaten the English, he would certainly have
possessed himself of the thrones of England and Scotland :
the King presently replied, 'You are mistaken, I could
have commanded him back with the motion of my hand.'
Which whether he could do or no, was doubtful ; but whatever reasons he had for this opinion, it seemed very unseasonable to own it openly in that conjuncture. Lieutenant-
General Cromwell marched with part of his army to Edinburgh, where he dispossessed the Hamiltonian party of
their authority, and put the power into the hands of the
Presbyterians ; by whom he was received with great
demonstrations of joy : and tho lately they looked upon
the Independent party as the worst of their enemies, yet
now they owned and embraced them as their best friends
and deliverers ; and having notice given them that the
English army was about to return into England, they prevailed with the Lieutenant-General to leave Major-General
Lambert with a body of horse, till they could raise more
forces to provide for their own safety.

The treaty with the King being pressed with more heat
than ever, and a design visibly appearing to render all our
victories useless thereby ; by the advice of some friends I
went down to the army, which lay at that time before
Colchester ; where attending upon the General Sir Thomas
Fairfax, to acquaint him with the state of affairs at London,
I told him, that a design was driving on to betray the
cause in which so much of the people's blood had been shed :
that the King being under a restraint, would not account
himself obliged by any thing he should promise under such
circumstances ; assuring him, that most of those who pushed

on the treaty with the greatest vehemency, intended not that he should be bound to the performance of it, but designed principally to use his authority and favour in order to destroy the army; who, as they had assumed the power, ought to make the best use of it, and to prevent the ruin of themselves and the nation [1]. He acknowledged what I said to be true, and declared himself resolved to use the power he had, to maintain the cause of the publick, upon a clear and evident call, looking upon himself to be obliged to pursue the work which he was about. Perceiving by such a general answer that he was irresolute, I went to Commissary-General Ireton, who had a great influence upon him, and having found him, we discoursed together upon the same subject. wherein we both agreed that it was necessary for the army to interpose in this matter, but differed about the time; he being of opinion, that it was best to permit the King and the Parliament to make an agreement, and to wait till they had made a full discovery of their intentions, whereby the people becoming sensible of their own danger, would willingly join to oppose them [2]. My opinion was, that it would be much easier for the army to keep them from a conjunction, than to oppose them when united; it being highly probable that the first things they would fall upon after their union, would be such as were most taking with the people, in order to oblige them to assist in the disbanding of the army, under pretence of lessening their taxes: and then if the army should in any manner signify

---

[1] On the question of Ireton's share in this intervention of the army, see Gardiner, G. C. W. iii. 473, 495-500.

[2] Mr. Gardiner concludes that Ludlow's visit to the army took place in Aug. or Sept., 1647. 'I see no reason to doubt that he really went either whilst the army was before Colchester just after the surrender, or during the last two or three days of the siege, when it was quite certain that Colchester would surrender. Ludlow can never be trusted about dates, but I do not think he would have written that he went to Colchester if his visit had been at a later time when the army was at some other place. If he did go to Colchester his visit cannot have been later than about Sept. 6, as it was known in London on the 8th that Ireton was no longer there.' G. C. W. iii. 471. Ludlow was probably acting in agreement with the promoters of the London petition of Sept. 11.

a dislike of their proceedings, they would be esteemed by the majority of the people, to be disturbers of the publick peace, and accused of designing nothing save their own particular advantages.

The King's party in Colchester expecting to be included in the peace which was treating between him and the Parliament, held out to the utmost ; but being in extreme want of provisions, and destitute of all hopes of relief since the defeat of the Scots, they were forced to surrender on the 28th of August, 1648, upon articles, whereby some of the principal of them being prisoners at discretion, the court martial assembled and condemned Sir Charles Lucas, Sir George Lisle, and Sir Barnard Gascoin to die ; the last of whom being a foreigner was pardoned, and the other two were shot to death according to the sentence. The Lord Goring and the Lord Capel were sent prisoners to London, and committed to the Tower by an order of the Parliament.

The two Houses finding things in this posture, hastened the departure of the Commissioners to the Isle of Wight, with powers and instructions to treat with the King, Sept. 18. who principally insisted on that article concerning bishops, whom he accounted to be by Divine right, or rather essentially necessary to the support of arbitrary power; whereupon ministers of each side were appointed to dispute touching that subject, in order to satisfy the King's conscience. But the army having now wonderfully dispersed their enemies on every part, began to consider how to secure themselves and the common cause against those counsels that were carried on in opposition to them, under pretext of making peace with the King, and to that end drew up a declaration at St. Albans, dated the 16th of November, 1648, shewing that the grounds of their first engagement was to bring delinquents to justice; that the King was guilty of the blood shed in the first and second war, and that therefore they could not trust him with the government. This remonstrance they presented to the Parliament on the 20th of November, 1648. The King and Parliament seeing this cloud beginning to gather, endeavoured by all means possible to hasten their treaty to a conclusion. The army also were not wanting to fortify themselves against that shock, sending some of their own number to those members of Parliament, whom they esteemed most faithful to the common cause, to invite them down to the army, after they should in a publick manner have expressed their dissatisfaction to the proceedings of those who had betrayed the trust reposed in them by the good people of England, and declared, that finding it impossible to be any farther serviceable in Parliament, they had resolved to repair to the army in order to procure their assistance in settling the government of the nation upon a just foundation. At a meeting of some members of Parliament with the said officers from the army, it was resolved, that tho the way proposed by them might be taken in case all other means failed, yet seeing there was more than a sufficient number of members in the Parliament to make a House, who were most affectionate to the public cause, it would be more proper for the army to relieve them from those who rendred them useless to the publick service, thereby preserving the name and place of the Parliament, than for the members thereof to quit their stations wherein they were appointed to serve, and to leave the civil authority in the hands of those who would be ready to fall in with any power that would attempt to frustrate what should be agreed on by them and the army. In prosecution of this result the army drew to Colebrook, from whence Commissary-General Ireton sent me word, that now he hoped they should please me, which I must acknowledg they did by the way which they were taking, not from any particular advantages that I expected from it, except an equal share of security with other men ; but that the people of England might be preserved in their just rights, from the oppressions of violent men ; the question in dispute between the King's party and us being, as I apprehended, ' Whether the King should govern as a god by his will, and the nation be governed by force like beasts : or whether the people should be governed by laws made by themselves, and live under a government derived from their own consent.' Being fully perswaded that an accommodation with their King was unsafe to the people of England, and unjust and wicked in the nature of it. The former, besides that it was obvious to all men, the King himself had proved, by the duplicity of his dealing with the Parliament, which manifestly appeared in his own papers taken at the battel of Naseby, and else-where. Of the latter I was convinced by the express words of God's law; 'That blood defileth the land, and the land cannot be cleansed of the blood that is shed therein, but by the blood of him that shed it.' (Numbers, chap. 35. v. 33.) And therefore I could not consent to the counsels of those who were contented to leave the guilt of so much blood upon the nation, and thereby to draw down the just vengeance of God upon us all; when it was most evident that the war had been occasioned by the invasion of our rights, and open breach of our laws and constitution on the King's part.

The Commissioners that were appointed to manage the treaty with the King, returned with the King's answer, containing neither a positive grant, nor an absolute denial. As to the bishops, he still retained his principle of their Divine right, and therefore declared that he could not dispense with the abolition of them; but for present satisfaction, hoping by giving ground to gain a better opportunity to serve them, he consented that those who had bought their lands should have a lease of them for some years: and for satisfaction for the blood that had been shed, he was willing that six should be excepted; but withal care was taken, that they should be such as were far enough from the reach of justice. By another article, the militia was to remain in the Parliament for ten years: thereby implying, if I mistake not, that the right of granting it was in the King, and consequently that we had done him wrong in contending with him for it. By such ways and means did some men endeavour to abuse the nation.

1648   Some of our Commissioners who had been with the King pleaded in the House for a concurrence with him, as if they had been imployed by him ; tho others with more ingenuity acknowledged that they would not advise an agreement upon those terms, were it not to prevent a greater evil that was like to ensue upon the refusal of them. But Sir Henry Vane so truly stated the matter of fact relating to the treaty, and so evidently discovered the design and deceit of the King's answer, that he made it clear to us, that by it the justice of our cause was not asserted, nor our rights secured for the future [1] ; concluding, that if they should accept of these terms without the concurrence of the army, it would prove but a feather in their caps : notwithstanding which the corrupt party in the House having bargain'd for their own and the nation's liberty, resolved to break through all hazards and inconveniences to make good their contract, and after twenty four hours' debate, resolved

Dec. 5.   by the plurality of votes [2], 'That the King's concessions were ground for a future settlement.' At which some of us expressing our dissatisfaction, desired that our protestation might be entred [3] ; but that being denied, as against the

---

[1] Some account of Vane's speech and of the debate in general is given in Mercurius Pragmaticus, Dec. 5–12, 1648 ; cf. Gardiner, G. C. W. iii. 531–4.

[2] By 129 to 83 votes.

[3] Mrs. Hutchinson states that her husband and four others actually entered a protestation 'into the house-book' on Dec. 5, which is certainly erroneous. Life of Col. Hutchinson, ed. 1885, p. 146. A protest, however, was entered later. The army in their proposals of Dec. 6 demanded that members dissenting from the late vote should have leave to protest, 'that the kingdom may know who they are that have kept their trust.' Old Parliamentary History, xviii. 460. On Dec. 18 a Committee was appointed by the House ' to consider

of the manner of this dissent, and how every member should make it in Parliament, and to draw up an expedient to this purpose for the members to subscribe as dissenters from that vote, that the King's answers were a ground of peace.' Rushworth, vii. 1366.

A newspaper gives the following account of the result :—

December 20.

'The Committee formerly appointed to consider of the manner of the dissent to the vote of the House, 5th December, 1648, that the King's answer was a ground for settling the peace of the kingdom, reports the same this day, which was thus. That every member should rise up from his seat in the House and declare that he dissents to the said vote ; the House approving hereof,

orders of the House, I contented my self to declare publickly, 1468
that being convinced that they had deserted the common
cause and interest of the nation, I could no longer join
with them ; the rest of those who dissented also expressing
themselves much to the same purpose. The day following
some of the principal officers of the army came to London,
with expectation that things would be brought to this
issue ; and consulting with some members of Parliament
and others, it was concluded after a full and free debate,
that the measures taken by the Parliament were contrary
to the trust reposed in them, and tending to contract the
guilt of the blood that had been shed upon themselves, and
the nation : that it was therefore the duty of the army to
endeavour to put a stop to such proceedings [1]; having
engaged in the war, not simply as mercenaries, but out of
judgment and conscience, being convinced that the cause
in which they were engaged was just, and that the good of
the people was involved in it. Being come to this resolution, three of the members of the House and three of the

several members, to the number of
about forty, stood up one after
another, and declared their dissents,
which the Clerk entered particularly
in the Journal. The members' names
should have been inserted, if wise
men had not thought it might have
proved very inconvenient to them.
This done, the House thought it
very requisite that any member might
have liberty to express to the House
that he disapproves of the said vote
of the 5th December, 1648, and therefore past a vote to that purpose :
and because the kingdom may be
the better satisfied herein, and upon
what grounds they have retracted
and disannulled former votes, in
relation to the treaty and otherwise,
they named a Committee to draw a
Declaration concerning the same ;
upon reading whereof, they doubt
not but the kingdom will be well
satisfied.' (The Moderate, Dec. 19–
26, 1648.)

Clement Walker gives a list of the
names of those signing the protest.
History of Independency, ii. 48, ed.
1661. See also Prynne's Case of
the old secured, secluded, and now
excluded Members, 1660 ; and Cal.
S. P. Dom. 1649-50, p. 1. On Feb.
21, 1660, the House ordered the
protest and votes relating to it to
be erased from the Journals.

[1] The plan of the army embodied
in their declaration of Nov. 30,
1648, was that the existing Parliament should be immediately dissolved, and that those members who
sided with the army should withdraw from Westminster, and act as
a sort of provisional government till
the new Parliament came together.
To this the leaders of the republican
minority objected, and proposed the
purging of the Parliament instead of
its forcible dissolution. The result
was Pride's Purge. Gardiner, G.
C. W., iii. 530, 536.

1648 officers of the army withdrew into a private room, to consider of the best means to attain the ends of our said resolution, where we agreed that the army should be drawn up the next morning, and guards placed in Westminster Hall, the Court of Requests, and the Lobby ; that none might be permitted to pass into the House but such as had continued faithful to the publick interest. To this end we went over the names of all the members one by one, giving the truest characters we could of their inclinations, wherein I presume we were not mistaken in many ; for the Parliament was fallen into such factions and divisions, that any one who usually attended and observed the business of the House, could, after a debate on any question, easily number the votes that would be on each side, before the question was put. Commissary-General Ireton went to Sir Thomas Fairfax, and acquainted him with the necessity of this extraordinary way of proceeding, having taken care to have the army drawn up the next morning by seven of the

Dec. 6. clock. Col. Pride commanded the guard that attended at the Parliament-doors, having a list of those members who were to be excluded, preventing them from entring into the House, and securing some of the most suspected under a guard provided for that end ; in which he was assisted by the Lord Grey of Grooby and others who knew the members. To justify these proceedings the army sent a message to the House, representing, that whereas divers members had been expelled the House upon account of the violence done to the Parliament by the city of London and others, in 1647, yet upon the absence of many well-affected members, by reason of their employments in the army and elsewhere against the enemy, the said persons were readmitted without any trial or satisfaction in the things whereof they were accused ; whereby the Scots had been drawn to invade this kingdom, and the House prevented by the intruders and their accomplices from declaring against the invaders, who had made up the number of ninety odd votes to that purpose ; and whereas by the prevalency of the same corrupt counsels, justice had been obstructed, and a settlement of affairs hindered; and lastly, the King's concessions declared to be a ground for the settlement of peace, notwithstanding the insufficiency and defects of them; they therefore most humbly desired that all those members who are innocent in these things, would by a publick declaration acquit themselves from any guilt thereof, or concurrence therein; and that those who shall not so acquit themselves, may be excluded or suspended the House till they have given clear satisfaction therein; that those who have faithfully performed their trust, may proceed without interruption to the execution of justice, and to make speedy provision for an equal succession of representatives, wherein differences may be composed, and all men comfortably acquiesce, as they for their parts thereby engaged and assured them they would. The House, wherein there was about six score, was moved to send for those members who were thus excluded by the army; which they did, as I presume, rather upon the account of decency, than from any desire they had that their message should be obeyed; and that it might clearly appear that this interruption proceeded from the army, and not from any advice of the Parliament, to the end that what they should act separately, might be esteemed to be only in order to prevent such inconveniences as might otherwise fall upon the nation, if the whole power should be left in the hands of an army; and that their actions appearing to be founded upon this necessity, they might the better secure the respect and obedience of the people. Upon such considerations, when the serjeant returned and acquainted them that the excluded members were detained by the army, the House proceeded in the business before them [1].

Lieutenant-General Cromwell the night after the interruption of the House arrived from Scotland, and lay at Whitehall, where, and at other places, he declared that he had not been acquainted with this design; yet since

1648

Dec. 6.

[1] See on Pride's Purge the Old Parliamentary History, xviii. 447-488. Gardiner, G. C. W., iii. 537.

1648

it was done, he was glad of it, and would endeavour to maintain it.

Major-General Harrison being sent by the army with a party of horse to bring the King from the Isle of Wight, Col. Hammond, who was entrusted with the custody of him by the Parliament, disputed to deliver him ; but finding that those about him inclined to comply, he thought it not convenient to make any farther opposition [1] : so that the King was conducted from the island to Hurst Castle, and from thence to Windsor, by Major-General Harrison. Being on his way, he dined at Mr. Leviston's in Bagshot Park, who had provided a horse for him to make his escape ; but this design also was discovered, and prevented. The King being at Windsor, it was debated what should be done with him : the army were for bringing him to a trial, for levying war against the Parliament and people of England, and the Common Council of the City of London presented a petition to the Parliament by the hands of Col. Titchborn to that effect [2] ; but some of the Commonwealthsmen desired that before they consented to that method, it might be resolved what government to establish, fearing a design in the army to set up some one of themselves in his room [3] : others endeavoured to perswade them that the execution of justice ought to be their first work, in respect of their duty to God and the people ; that the failure therein had been already the occasion of a second war, which was justly to be charged on the Parliament for neglecting

Dec. 1.

Dec. 23.

1649
Jan. 15.

---

[1] The officers employed to remove the King from Carisbrook to Hurst Castle were Lieut.-Col. Cobbett and Captain Merriman. Hammond was then absent, and Major Rolph in command at Carisbrook. Rushworth, vii. 1351. Harrison was sent to bring the King to Windsor in pursuance of the vote of the House of Commons on Dec. 13, 'that the General do keep the King in safe custody and do take care that he goeth not away.'

[2] The petition was presented Jan.

15. 1649. by Col. Robert Titchborne 'in the name of the Commons of the City of London in Common Council assembled.' The Lord Mayor and Aldermen had refused to concur in it. C. J. vi. 117. The petition is printed in 'The Moderate' for Jan. 16-23, 1649. On Titchborne's earlier career, see Clarke Papers, i. 395.

[3] An account of the discussions referred to is given in Lilburne's 'Legal Fundamental Liberties of the People of England,' 1649, ed. 2, pp. 33-40.

that duty; that those who were truly Commonwealths-men ought to be of that opinion, as the most probable means to attain their desires in the establishment of an equal and just government; and that the officers of the army, who were chiefly to be suspected, could not be guilty of so much impudence and folly, to erect an arbitrary power in any one of themselves, after they had in so publick a manner declared their detestation of it in another.

In order to the accomplishment of the important work which the House of Commons had now before them, they voted, 'That by the fundamental laws of the land, it is Jan. 1. treason for the King of England, for the time being, to levy war against the Parliament and kingdom.' To which the Lords not concurring, they passed it the next day without Jan. 3. their consent; and the day after declared, 'That the people are, under God, the original of all just power: that the Jan. 4. House of Commons, being chosen by and representing the people, are the supreme power in the nation: that whatsoever is enacted or declared for law by the Commons in Parliament, hath the force of a law, and the people are concluded thereby, tho the consent of King or Peers be not had thereto.'

This obstruction being removed, several petitions were brought to the Parliament, for so the House of Commons now stiled themselves, from the city of London, borough of Southwark, and most of the counties in England, requesting that the King might be brought to justice; in Jan. 6. order to which they passed an Act, authorizing the persons therein named, or any thirty of them, to proceed to the arraignment, condemnation, or acquittal of the King; with full power, in case of condemnation, to proceed to sentence, and to cause the said sentence to be put in execution.

This High Court of Justice met on the 8th of January, 1648, in the Painted Chamber, to the number of about fourscore, consisting chiefly of members of Parliament, officers of the army, and gentlemen of the country; where they chose Serjeant Aske, Serjeant Steel, and Dr. Dorislaus to be their counsel; Mr. John Coke of Grays-Inn to be their

1649   solicitor, and Mr. Andrew Broughton their secretary; and
sent out a precept under their hands and seals for proclaiming the Court to be held in Westminster Hall on the
tenth of the said month; which was performed accordingly
by Serjeant Dendy, attended by a party of horse, in
Cheapside, before the old Exchange, and in Westminster-
Hall.   On the tenth they chose Serjeant Bradshaw to be
their president, with Mr. Lisle and Mr. Say to be his
assistants; and a charge of high treason being drawn up
Jan. 13.   against the King. the Court appointed a convenient place
to be prepared at the upper end of Westminster Hall for
his publick trial, directing it to be covered with scarlet
cloth, and ordered twenty halberdiers to attend the presi-
Jan. 17.   dent. and thirty the King [1].

All things being thus prepared for the trial, the King
was conducted from Windsor to St. James's: from whence
on the 20th of January he was brought to the bar of the
High Court of Justice, where the president acquainted the
King with the causes of his being brought to that place:
for that he contrary to the trust reposed in him by the
people, to see the laws put in execution for their good, had
made use of his power to subvert those laws, and to set up
his will and pleasure as a law over them: that in order to
effect that design, he had endeavoured the suppression of
Parliaments, the best defence of the people's liberties: that
he had levied war against the Parliament and people of
England, wherein great numbers of the good people had
been slain, of which blood the Parliament, presuming him
guilty, had appointed this High Court of Justice for the
trial of him for the same.   Then turning to Mr. Broughton,
clerk of the Court, he commanded him to read the charge
against the King; who as the clerk was reading the charge,
interrupted him, saying, ' I am not intrusted by the people,
they are mine by inheritance;' demanding by what authority they brought him thither.   The president answered,
that they derived their authority from an Act made by the
Commons of England assembled in Parliament: the King

[1] Nalson, Trial of Charles I, folio, 1684, pp. 33, 35.

said the Commons could not give an oath ; that they were   1640
no Court, and therefore could make no Act for the trial of
any man, much less of him their soveraign.   It was replied,
that the Commons assembled in Parliament could acknowledg no other soveraign but God, for that upon his
and the people's appeal to the sword for the decision of
their respective pretensions, judgment had been given for
the people ; who conceiving it to be their duty not to bear
the sword in vain, had appointed the Court to make
inquisition for the blood that had been shed in that dispute.
Whereupon the president, being moved by Mr. Solicitor
Coke, in the name and on the behalf of the good people of
England, commanded the clerk of the Court to proceed
in the reading of the charge against him : which being
done, the King was required to give his answer to it, and
to plead guilty, or not guilty.   The King demurred to the
jurisdiction of the Court, affirming that no man, nor body of
men had power to call him to an account, being not intrusted by man ; and therefore accountable only to God for
his actions ; entring upon a large discourse of his being in
treaty with the Parliament's commissioners at the Isle of
Wight, and his being taken from thence he knew not how,
when he thought he was come to a conclusion with them [1].
This discourse seeming not to the purpose, the president
told him, that as to his plea of not being accountable to
man, seeing God by His Providence had over-ruled it, the
Court had resolved to do so also ; and that if he would
give no other answer, that which he had given should be
registred, and they would proceed as if he had confessed
the charge : in order to which the president commanded
his answer to be entred, directing Serjeant Dendy, who
attended the Court, to withdraw the prisoner ; which as
he was doing, many persons cried out in the hall, ' Justice,
Justice.'   The King being withdrawn, the Court adjourned

---

[1] ' Ludlow that rogue and dog, vaunting among his friends, said that the King was nothing at all daunted at the charge, but looked with as impudent a face as if he had not been guilty of all the blood that hath been shed in this war.' Newsletter, Clarendon MS. 3003.

1649　into the Painted Chamber to consider what farther was fit to be done; and being desirous to prevent all objections tending to accuse them of haste or surprize, they resolved to convene him before them publickly twice more; after which if he persisted in his demurrer to the jurisdiction of the Court, then to give judgment against him. And that nothing might be wanting, in case he should resolve to plead, they appointed witnesses to be examined to every article of the charge. At the King's second appearance before the Court, which was on the 22nd of January, he carried himself in the same manner as before; whereupon his refusal being again entred, and he withdrawn, the Court adjourned to the Painted Chamber. On the twenty-third of January the King was brought a third time before the commissioners, where refusing to plead, as he had done before, his refusal was entered, and witnesses examined publickly to prove the charge of his levying war against the Parliament: after which Solicitor-General Coke demanded of the Court that they would proceed to the pronouncing of sentence against the prisoner at the bar: whereupon the court adjourned into the Painted Chamber, and upon serious consideration declared the King to be a tyrant, traitor, murderer, and a publick enemy to the commonwealth: that his condemnation extend unto death, by severing his head from his body, and that a sentence grounded upon those votes be prepared; which being agreed upon, the King should be ordered on the next day following to receive it [1]. The sentence being engrossed, was read on the 27th of January; and thereupon the Court resolved, that the same should be the sentence, which should be read and published in Westminster Hall the same day; that the president should not permit the King to speak after the sentence pronounced; that he should openly declare it to be the sense and judgment of the Court, and that the commissioners should signify their consent by standing up. In the afternoon the King was

[1] January 25 was spent in hearing witnesses, and on January 26 the sentence was read, agreed to, and ordered to be engrossed.

brought to the bar, and desired that he might be permitted
to make one proposition before they proceeded to sentence ;
which he earnestly pressing, as that which he thought
would tend to the reconciling of all parties, and to the
peace of the three kingdoms, they permitted him to offer
it : the effect of which was, that he might meet the two
Houses in the Painted Chamber, to whom he doubted not
to offer that which should satisfy and secure all interests ;
designing, as I have been since informed, to propose his
own resignation, and the admission of his son to the throne
upon such terms as should have been agreed upon. This
motion being new and unexpected to the Court, who were
not willing to deny or grant any thing without serious
deliberation, they withdrew to consider of it into the inner
Court of Wards ; and being satisfied upon debate, that
nothing but loss of time would be the consequence of it,
they returned into the Court with a negative to his demand,
telling him that they met there as a Court of justice commissionated by the Parliament, of whose authority they were
fully satisfied : that by their commission they were not
authorized to receive any proposals from him, but to proceed to the trial of him ; that in order thereto, his charge
had been read to him, to which if he would have pleaded,
the counsel for the Commonwealth were ready to have
proved it against him : that he had thrice demurred to the
jurisdiction of the Court, which demurrer the Court had
overruled and registred, ordering to proceed against him, as
if he had confessed the charge ; and that if he had any proposition to make, it was proper for him to address it to the
Parliament, and not to them. Then the president enlarged
upon the horrid nature of those crimes, of which he had been
accused, and was now convicted ; declaring that the only
just power of Kings was derived from the consent of the
people : that whereas the people had intrusted him to see
their laws put in execution, he had endeavoured throughout
the whole course of his reign to subvert those good laws, and
to introduce an arbitrary and tyrannical government in the
room of them : that to cut off all hopes of redress he had

1640 attempted from the beginning of his reign, either wholly to destroy Parliaments, or to render them only subservient to his own corrupt designs: that tho he had consented, the publick necessities so requiring, that this Parliament should not be dissolved but by an act of themselves, he had levied war against them, that he might not only dissolve them, but by the terrour of his power for ever discourage such assemblies from doing their duty: that in this war many thousands of the good people of England had lost their lives: that in obedience to what God commanded, and the nation expected, the Parliament had appointed this Court to make inquisition for this blood, and to try him for the same: that his charge had been read to him, and he required to give an answer to it; which he having thrice refused to do, he acquainted him that the court had resolved to pronounce sentence against him, and thereupon commanded the clerk to read it, which he did, being to this effect: that the King for the crimes contained in the charge, should be carried back to the place from whence he came, and thence to the place of execution, where his head should be severed from his body: which sentence being read, the commissioners testified their unanimous assent by their standing up. The King would have spoken something before he was withdrawn; but being accounted dead in law immediately after sentence pronounced, it was not permitted. The Court withdrew also, and agreed that the sentence should be put in execution on the Tuesday following, which would be the 30th of January, 1648. The King having refused such ministers as the Court appointed to attend him, desired that Dr. Juxton, late Bishop of London, might be permitted to come to him; which being granted, and Adjutant-General Allen sent to acquaint the doctor with the King's condition and desires, he being altogether unprepared for such a work, broke out into these expressions, 'God save me, what a trick is this, that I should have no more warning, and I have nothing ready!' but recollecting himself a little, he put on his scarf and his other furniture, and went with

him to the King, where having read the Common Prayer
and one of his old sermons, he administred the sacrament
to him ; not forgetting to use the words of the confession
set down in the liturgy, inviting all those that truly repent
to make their confession before the congregation then
gathered together: tho there was none present but the
King and himself.

The High Court of Justice appointed a committee to inspect the parts about Whitehall for a convenient place for
the execution of the King, who having made their report,
it was agreed that a scaffold should be erected to that purpose near the Banqueting House, and order given to cover
it with black. The same day, being the 29th of January,
they signed a warrant for his execution, to which about
threescore of the commissioners set their hands and seals,
directing it to Col. Hacker, Col. Hunks, and Col. Phaier,
or either of them [1]. The Duke of Glocester and the Lady
Elizabeth waited on the King the same day to take their
leave of him. An extraordinary ambassador from the
United Provinces had his audience in the Parliament; his
business was to intercede with them for the life of the King,
and to preserve a fair correspondence between England
and the States [2]. The next day about eight in the morning
the King, attended by a guard, was brought from St. James's
through the park to Whitehall, where having drunk a glass
or two of red wine, and stayed about two hours in a private
room, he was conducted to the scaffold out of a window of
the Banqueting House ; and having made a speech, and
taken off his George, he kneeled down at the block, and
the executioner performed his office. The body was
ordered to be interred at Windsor : the Duke of Lenox,
the Marquis of Hertford, the Earls of Southampton and

---

[1] Fifty-nine signed the warrant.
Ludlow's name is the fortieth on the
list. Ludlow was present at eleven
of the meetings of the King's
judges.

[2] The letters of credence and
address of the Dutch ambassadors,
together with the somewhat curt
answer of the Parliament, are printed
in Zachary Grey's Answer to Neal's
fourth volume of the History of the
Puritans, Appendix, pp. 1-12. See
also Guizot, History of the English
Revolution, Appendix.

Lindsey, with some others having leave from the Parliament. attended it to the grave.

A report of the proceedings of the High Court of Justice being made to the Parliament, they declared, that the persons imployed in that important service had discharged their trust with courage and fidelity; that the Parliament was well satisfied with the account of their proceedings, ordering them to be engrossed, and recorded amongst the Parliament-Rolls, in order to transmit the memory thereof to posterity; and resolved that the Commissioners of the Great Seal should issue a certiorari to their clerk to record those proceedings in the Chancery, and that the same should be sent to the other Courts at Westminster. and to the Custos Rotulorum of each county. Judg Jenkins, Sir John Stowel, and divers other persons, who were prisoners, and had carried themselves very insolently, now finding the Parliament to be in earnest, began to come to a better temper. Colonel Middleton, who was also a prisoner at Newcastle upon parole, ran away to Scotland ; and being required to return, answered, that his life was dearer to him than his honour. Sir Marmaduke Langdale made his escape also ; and Sir Lewis Dives through a house of office in Whitehall. The Lord Capel got out of the Tower ; but being discovered by a waterman as he crossed the Thames, he was seized in a house at Lambeth. Duke Hamilton also escaped out of Windsor Castle, and came to Southwark ; where knocking at the door of an inn, he was seized by a souldier, who knew him, and was passing by that way; whereupon he was committed to the Tower. The House of Lords becoming now the subject of the consideration and debate of the Parliament, Lieutenant-General Cromwell appeared for them, having already had a close correspondence with many of them ; and, it may be, presuming he might have farther use of them in those designs he had resolved to carry on : but they not meeting in their House at the time to which they had adjourned, much facilitated their removal ; so that the question being put, whether the House

of Commons should take advice of the House of Lords in
the exercise of the legislative power, it was carried in the
negative, and thereupon resolved, 'That the House of Peers
was useless and dangerous, and ought to be abolished;' and
an Act was soon after passed to that effect.   After this they
proceeded to declare, 'That the office of a King in this
nation is unnecessary, burdensome, and dangerous to the
liberty, safety, and publick interest of the people, and therefore ought to be abolished; and that they will settle the
government of the nation in the way of a Commonwealth.'
To this end they ordered a declaration to be published,
whereby it was declared treason for any person to endeavour to promote Charles Stuart to be King of England,
or any other single person to be chief governour thereof:
they also ordered the great seal, and other seals, which had
the image of the late King on them, to be defaced; and
appointed new ones to be made with the stamp of the
House of Commons on one side, accompanied with this
inscription, 'The Great Seal of the Parliament of the Commonwealth of England:' on the other side was engraven
the cross and the harp, being the arms of England and
Ireland, with this inscription, 'God with us:' ordering all
writs formerly running in the King's name, to be issued out
'in the name of the Keepers of the Liberty of England.'   A
High Court of Justice was constituted by Act of Parliament
for the trying of Duke Hamilton, the Earl of Holland,
the Lord Goring, the Lord Capel, and Sir John Owen[1].
Duke Hamilton pleaded that he entred into England as an
enemy, being of another nation, and born before the Act of
Union, and consequently not to be tried by the laws of this;
besides he had surrendred himself upon conditions.   The
rest of the Lords pleaded articles also, and so did Sir John
Owen: but that allegation appeared to be of no weight, by
the testimony of the general, in relation to the Lords Goring

Margin notes: 1649   Feb. 6.   March 16.   Feb. 7.   Jan. 30.   Feb. 3.

---

[1] A volume containing notes of
the proceedings of this High Court
of Justice is amongst the Clarke
Papers in Worcester College (Worcester MSS. vol. 70).   The report of
the proceedings in the State Trials
gives the legal arguments, but not
the evidence.

1649   and Capel, and by the evidence of Col. Wayte touching Duke Hamilton : the like being affirmed by other witnesses against the Earl of Holland and Sir John Owen : for if there had been any promise made to any of them, either implicitely or by word of mouth, it could only extend to protect them from the military. not the civil sword : and as to the plea for Duke Hamilton. that he was born before the two nations were united, it was answered that they tried him not as Duke Hamilton, but as earl of Cambridg, in which capacity he had sate as a peer of England, and therefore a subject thereof : so that upon full evidence they

March 6.   were all sentenced by the Court, to have their heads struck off for high treason, in levying war against the Parliament of England. Earnest solicitations and petitions were made

March 8.   for them to the Parliament ; but they thought not fit to reprieve the Duke, the Earl of Holland, or the Lord Capel. Touching the Lord Goring the House was equally divided, and the Speaker having upon such occasions the determining voice, gave it for his reprieve. Commissary-General Ireton observing no motion made for Sir John Owen, moved the House to consider that he was a commoner, and therefore more properly to have been tried in another way by a jury : whereupon the House reprieved him also[1]. The

March 9.   other three were executed a day or two after in the New Palace Yard before Westminster Hall, in pursuance of a warrant signed by the Court to that purpose, the Parliament refusing to hearken to the Earl of Denbigh, who proposed on the behalf of Duke Hamilton his brother-in-law, to give them a blank signed by the said Duke, to answer faithfully to such questions as should be there inserted. The Parliament having resolved to constitute a Council of State. the better to carry on the executive part of the government, authorized five of their members to agree upon the number and persons of such as they thought fit to be proposed to the Parliament for their approbation. The five im-

1649   powered to this end by the Parliament, were Mr. John Lisle,

---

[1] On the escape of Sir John Owen, see Life of Col. Hutchinson, ed. Firth, ii. 158 161.

Mr. Cornelius Holland, Mr. Luke Robinson, Mr. Thomas
Scot, and me, who tho sensible of my unfitness for so great
a work, and of the envy it would be attended with, yet
being required by my country to assist in this service, I resolved to use the best of my endeavours therein. The
number agreed upon was thirty-five, which we filled up with
such persons as we thought best qualified with integrity
and abilities sutable to so important a station. Four of
them were lords, and the rest commoners. The House
agreed to our report, only they were pleased to add us five Feb. 14.
to the number proposed by us. The Parliament being
desirous to exclude from their places those who were likely
to undo what they had done, and yet unwilling to lose the
assistance of many honest men, who had been in the
country during the late transactions, passed an order, that
such members as had not sate since the trial of the King,
should not be admitted to sit, till the House should be particularly satisfied concerning them ; appointing the former March 5.
five, or any three of them, to be a committee to receive
satisfaction touching the affections to the publick interest
of every member who had not sate since the time aforesaid,
and the reasons of his absence ; and to make their report
to the Parliament concerning them.

Prince Charles finding his affairs in England to be in a
desperate condition, concluded an agreement with the Irish 1649
rebels, granting them full indemnity for what they had Jan. 17.
hitherto acted, and encouraging them to carry on their
cruelties against the English by his commission. The
Lord Inchequin had already declared for him, and joined 1648
with the Irish rebels. The Earl of Ormond was dispatched Sept.
to Ireland for the same purpose ; and as a pledg that
Prince Charles would follow, his baggage and horses were
sent thither before.

The Scots fearing their clergy would not be permitted
long to insult over the people, expressed themselves highly 1649
dissatisfied with our proceedings in England, and chose Feb. 5.
rather to espouse the interest of Prince Charles, than to
enjoy the fruit of what they had contended for against his

1649 father, publickly declaring that they were obliged by the covenant to promote the government of a King, Lords, and Commons ; which government the Parliament of England had thought fit to alter. We endeavoured to satisfy their commissioners, by shewing them the reasons of our late resolutions ; but they refusing to hear them, returned home to their own country, where they found things disposed to an accommodation with Prince Charles, upon presumption that when by his assistance they had destroyed the sectarian party, as they called them, they should be able to govern him well enough : but he supposing he had an easier part to act with the Irish, whose principles were more sutable to his inclinations, refused to hearken to them at that time.

Feb. 24. Col. Edward Popham, Col. Richard Dean, and Col. Robert Blake were appointed by the Parliament to command the fleet ; the latter being designed with a squadron to cruise upon the Irish coast, in order to meet and fight the ships commanded by Prince Rupert. Col. Popham was sent towards Lisbon to intercept the Portugal fleet coming home from their islands, because they had protected some ships that had revolted from us, and sheltred them from our fleet that was in pursuit of them, and had offered some affronts to our agent Mr. Vane, who was sent thither to endeavour a right understanding between the two nations [1]. General Dean with another squadron was ordered to remain for the service of the channel. This they did, well understanding how great reputation a considerable fleet would give to their affairs, and of what importance it is to this nation always to guard the seas, and more particularly in that conjuncture.

The Parliament much inclining to preserve a good correspondence with the States General of the United Provinces,

---

[1] On Jan. 29, 1650, the Council of State determined to send Anthony Ascham as resident to Madrid, Richard Bradshaw as agent to Hamburg, and Charles Vane in the same capacity to Portugal. Cal. S. P. Dom. 1649 50, pp. 496, 498 ; cf. Masson, Life of Milton, iv, 161, 217. Popham's instructions are dated April 25, 1650. Thurloe, i. 134, 144. Ludlow confuses the events of 1649 and 1650.

sent Dr. Dorislaus into Holland to be their agent there, who, a little after his arrival at the Hague, was assaulted by about ten assassins, English and Scots, who broke into his lodgings and murdered him: and tho this action was so infamous, and contrary to the right of nations, yet the Dutch were not very forward to find out the criminals in order to bring them to justice. Mr. Ascham who was sent into Spain with a publick character also, was used in the like manner, by three persons coming to his house at Madrid, where pretending to be English merchants, they were admitted; and as he saluted the first of them, was struck into the head by him with a poniard; and his secretary endeavouring to make his escape, was killed with him[1]. The murderers took sanctuary in a church; but by an order of state they were forced from thence, and committed to prison; of which the church-men loudly complained, after their usual manner, as an injurious violation of their immunities.

The squadron commanded by Col. Blake being first ready, set sail for the Irish coast, where Prince Rupert thinking himself not in a condition to fight him, retired with his ships into the harbour of Kingsale, under the protection of the fort. Col. Popham was next dispatched with his squadron for Portugal, and was pleased to employ a brother of mine as lieutenant of that ship which was commanded by himself. The Spanish ambassador was the first that made application to us from any foreign State. But the Parliament not being satisfied with the address of his credentials, refused to receive them till it should be directed to the Parliament of the Commonwealth of England; declaring, that tho they did not affect any flattering titles, yet they resolved to have their authority owned by all those who made their addresses to them. With which the court of Spain being made acquainted, the ambassador received instructions from the

1649
May 1/11.

1650
June 6.

1649
June.

1650
April.

---

[1] An account of the death of Dorislaus is given in Cary's Memorials of the Civil War, i. 131; cf. Cal. State Papers, Dom., 1649-50, xxvii. On Ascham's death, see Thurloe, i. 148; Cal. S. P., Dom., 1649-50, xli.

King his master to that end, and framed the direction according to our desires [1].

Our affairs beginning to acquire reputation, and to carry a fair probability of success, divers Members of Parliament who had been long absent, addressed themselves to the committee before mentioned, in order to their admission to sit in Parliament, and some of them would not scruple to give any satisfaction that was desired to the questions proposed unto them ; which were, 'Whether they joined in, or approved that vote, declaring the King's concessions a ground for a future settlement? Whether they approved of the proceedings against the King? and whether they would engage to be true to a Commonwealth Government [2]?' But we apprehending such extraordinary expulsions as had been lately used, to be extremely hazardous to the publick safety, made it our endeavour to keep those from a readmission, who might necessitate another occasion of using the like remedy. And therefore, tho all possible satisfaction were given in words, we did, by weighing the former deportment of every particular member who presented himself, desire to be in some measure assured, that they would be true to what they promised, in case the Commonwealth interest should come to be disputed, before we would report their condition to the House. Some of the House of Lords having procured themselves to be chosen by the people, sat in Parliament upon the foot of their election : in which number was Philip Earl of Pembroke, who being chosen by the freeholders of the county of Berks, upon his admission
April 16. to the House, signed the engagement, as the rest of the members who sat there had done; the contents of which was, 'To be true and faithful to the Commonwealth, as it was established without a King or House of Lords.'
Sept. 18. The same engagement was taken by the Earl of Salisbury

---

[1] Cardenas was informed by the English Government in June, 1649, that they would not treat with him unless he presented new credentials, which he accordingly did on Dec. 26, 1650. See Guizot, Cromwell and the English Commonwealth, translation, ed. 1854, i. pp. 229-233, 391 ; Sydney Papers, ed. Blencowe, p. 105.

[2] Cal. S. P., Dom., 1649-50, p. 1.

and the Lord Edward Howard, when they took their places in Parliament, after they had been elected to serve there [1].

1649
May 5.

Whilst we were thus providing for our security in England, our affairs in Ireland had not the same success, the Earl of Ormond having reconciled the English in Munster to the Supreme Council of the Irish rebels, the Scots also in the north falling in with them against us : with whom some gentlemen of those parts joined, tho they had engaged themselves to the contrary. Yet one thing happened tending very much to the preservation of Dublin, and those few places that were kept for the Parliament, which was, that Owen Roe O'Neal who was general of the Old Irish, as they were termed, could by no means be brought to a conjunction with the English. Sir Charles Coote being besieged in Londonderry, agreed to supply the besiegers with powder, upon their engaging to furnish him with such provisions as he wanted, which was performed on both sides : and the Lord Inchequin who was besieging Dundalk promised to do the like for Colonel Monk, who then commanded in that place, upon the same conditions ; which was performed on Monk's part ; but as his men were carrying off the ammunition, they were fallen upon by a party of Inchequin's horse, the ammunition taken away, and many of them killed. The Scots drawing about Dundalk, most of the garison revolted to them ; whereupon Monk delivered up the place, upon condition that he should be permitted to return into England : where being arrived, he met with a cold reception from the Parliament, upon suggestion, that he had corresponded with the Irish rebels [2].

Aug. 10.

[1] The Earl of Pembroke's election for Berkshire is noted in Blencowe's Sydney Papers, pp. 68, 69, 72. He had a stiff contest with a schismatical tanner for the seat. Carte, Original Letters, i. 278. Lord Howard of Escrick represented Carlisle, and the Earl of Salisbury, King's Lynn.

'Salisbury,' notes the Earl of Leicester, ' should have done well not to have protested against it as much as he did, unnecessarily and almost in all companies.' Sydney Papers, p. 95.

[2] On the treaty between Owen O'Neill and Monk (May 8, 1649), see

1649   About this time an agent from Owen Roe O'Neal came privately to London, and found out a way to acquaint the Council of State, that if they thought fit to grant him a safe conduct, he would make some propositions to them that would be for their service. The council, to avoid any misconstruction of their actions, refused to hear him; but appointed a committee to speak with him, of which I was one, ordering us to report to them what he should propose [1]. His proposition was, that the party commanded by O'Neal should submit to, and act for the Parliament, if they might obtain indemnity for what was passed, and assurance of the enjoyment of their religion and estates for the time to come. We asked him why they made application to us, after they had refused to join with those who had been in treaty with the King? He answered, that the King had broken his word with them; for tho they had deserved well of him, and he had made them many fair promises, yet when he could make better terms with any other party, he had been always ready to sacrifice them. We asked him farther, Why they had not made their application sooner? he told us, because such men had been possessed of the power, who had sworn their extirpation; but that now it was believed to be the interest of those in authority to grant liberty of

Aphorismical Discovery, ii. 216 222, 228. On Aug. 10, 1649, the House of Commons declared its disapproval of the treaty, whilst acquitting Monk of blame.

[1] The agent mentioned was the Abbot Crelly. There is in the MS. of the Rinuccini Memoirs in the possession of Lord Leicester, a letter from Crelly giving an account of this interview, dated July $\frac{19}{9}$, 1649. For the following extract I am obliged to the kindness of Mr. Gardiner: 'Intra paucos dies confidenter praesumo me intellecturum realem eventum propositi de quo quantocyus dominationem vestram Illustrissimam certiorem reddam. Interea cum licentia humiliter rogo ut sileat dominatio sua illustrissima vel saltem suspendat determinationem rerum Iberniae. Deum maximum testor quantum in iis laboravi, et cum quibus periculis et difficultatibus, licet nondum absolverim, censeo et non absque fundamento quod intra terminum viginti dierum per me ipsum vel per alium expressum Dominationi suae Illustrissimae omnia referre voluero. Res de quibus ago sunt generales et graves et cum grandibus concilio grandium deliberate ductus in iis procedo, quandoquidem de re totius Religionis Catholicae agitur ut aliquando demonstrabitur.'

conscience; promising, that if such liberty might be extended to them, they would be as zealous for a Commonwealth as any other party, instancing in many countries
where they were so. We informed him, that it was our
opinion that the council would not promise indemnity to all
that party, they being esteemed to have been the principal
actors in the bloody massacre at the beginning of the
rebellion: neither did we think that they would grant
them the liberty of their religion, believing it might prove
dangerous to the public peace. The Council upon our
report of what had passed at the conference, concurred with
our opinion; so that having no more to do with the agent,
he was required to depart within a limited time. The Earl
of Ormond, General Preston, and the Lord Inchequin
beginning to draw their forces towards Dublin, resolved
first to reduce Tredah: in order to which they sent Col.
Worden thither with a strong detachment of horse and foot,
who attempting to take it by assault, entred with most of
his men, but was beat out again by an inconsiderable
number of ours. Notwithstanding which the garison
wanting men to defend their works, their provisions also
being almost consumed, was obliged to capitulate and
surrender, upon condition that the souldiers should have
liberty to march to Dublin, the rest to return home, and to
enjoy protection there.

Dundalk and Tredagh being surrendred to the enemy,
and Dublin threatned with a speedy siege by the forces of
the Royalists and Irish, combined together for the destruction of the English, the Parliament taking into their
serious consideration the deplorable state of their distressed
friends, resolved to send them relief with all expedition.
In the mean time the enemy marched towards Dublin,
having sent a party of horse before to invest the place, and
to prevent any relief from Meath-side; upon whose approach
Col. Jones, with the forces he had with him, was obliged to
retire to Kilcullen. A party of horse from the town made
a sally upon the enemy, and were repulsed with some loss;
but being reinforced from England by a regiment of horse

commanded by Col. Reynolds, and two regiments of foot, Col. Jones being also come into the town, they resolved upon a vigorous defence. Immediately after the landing of these supplies, Dublin was formally besieged by the enemy, who had a great army provided with all necessaries for the carrying on of the siege, and furnished by the country with provisions in great abundance, their head-quarters being at Rathmines, a mile from Dublin towards Wicklow. They took Rathfarnham by storm, and sent fifteen hundred men to fortify Baggatrath, in order to hinder our army from landing at Ringsend, being within a quarter of a mile of it, and lying triangular with it and Dublin. Baggatrath had a rampart of earth about it, and the enemy had wrought upon it, to augment its strength, a whole night before they were discovered. But the next morning Col. Jones perceiving their design, concluded it absolutely necessary to endeavour to remove them from thence before their works were finished. To that end he drew all his forces both horse and foot to the works that faced the enemy; and leaving as many as he thought necessary for the defence of the town, sallied out with the rest, being between four and five thousand, and falling upon them, beat them from their works, killing Sir William Vaughan who commanded them, and most of the men that were with him, closely pursuing the rest who fled towards their main army, where the Earl of Ormond thought fit at last to throw down his cards, which he had before refused to do, in contempt of our forces; and with his Royal army, as it was called, retreated in great disorder towards Rathmines: Col. Jones pursued him close, finding little opposition, except from a party of the Lord Inchequin's horse that had formerly served the Parliament, who defended a pass for some time, but were after some dispute broken and forced to fly. Having routed these, he marched with all diligence up to the walls of Rathmines, which were about sixteen foot high, and contained about ten acres of ground, where many of the enemy's foot had shut up themselves; but perceiving their army to be entirely routed, and their general fled, they yielded

themselves prisoners [1]. After this our men continuing their 1649
pursuit, found a party of about two thousand foot of the
Lord Inchequin's, in a grove belonging to Rathgar, who
after some defence obtained conditions for their lives, and
the next day most of them took up arms in our service.
This success was the more remarkable, because unexpected
on both sides, our handful of men being led step by step to
an absolute victory, whereas their utmost design at the
beginning of the action was only to beat the enemy from
Baggatrath : and so surprizing to our enemies, that they had
not time to carry off their money, which lay at Rathfarnham
for the paying of their army, where Col. Jones seized four
thousand pounds very seasonably for the paiment of his men.

The Parliament having an army ready to send to Ireland,
a formidable fleet to put to sea, another army to keep at
home for their own defence, and a considerable force to
guard the north against the Scots, who had declared
themselves enemies, and waited only an opportunity of
shewing it with advantage, thought themselves obliged to
expose to sale such lands as had been formerly possessed April 30.
by Deans and Chapters, that they might be enabled thereby
to defray some part of that great charge that lay upon the
nation. To this end they authorized trustees to sell the
said lands, provided they could do it at ten years' purchase,
at the least ; but such was the good opinion that the people
had conceived of the Parliament, that most of those lands
were sold at the clear income of fifteen, sixteen, and seventeen years ; one half of the sums contracted for being paid
down in ready money: besides which the woods were
valued distinctly, and to be paid for according to the
valuation. All impropriations belonging to the said Deans
and Chapters, as well as those of the Bishops, either in
possession or reversion, were reserved from sale to enlarge
the maintenance of poor ministers. Yet this was not

---

[1] Jones gives an account of his
victory in a letter printed in Cary's
Memorials of the Civil War, i. 159.
Ormond's narrative is printed in
Carte's Collection of Original Letters,
ii. 396. Cf. Grey's Examination of
Neal's Puritans, vol. iv. Appendix,
p. 13.

1649   sufficient to restrain that generation of men from inveighing against the Parliament, and conspiring with their enemies both at home and abroad, to weaken their hands, and if possible to render them unable to carry on the publick

1650   service. The fee-farm rents formerly belonging to the

March 11.   Crown were also sold; and yet such was the necessity of affairs, that notwithstanding all this the Parliament found themselves obliged to lay a tax of a hundred and

Nov. 26.   twenty thousand pounds a month upon the nation; which burden they bore for the most part without regret, being convinced that it was wholly applied to the use of the publick, and especially because those who imposed it paid

1649   an equal proportion with the rest. The Crown-lands were

July 16.   assigned to pay the arrears of those souldiers who were in arms in the year 1647, which was done by the influence of the officers of the army that was in present service, whereby they made provision for themselves, and neglected those who had appeared for the Parliament at the first, and had endured the heat and burden of the day.

In the month of September, 1649, the army embarked and set sail for Ireland; Commissary-General Ireton[1] with one part of them designing for Munster, and Lieutenant-General Cromwell, being appointed Lieutenant of Ireland, with the rest, for Dublin: but the wind blowing a strong

Aug. 14.   gale from the south, they were both put into the Bay of Dublin, where they were received with great joy: for tho the enemy's army had been beaten from the siege of that place, and Col. Jones with the small forces he had with him had made the best improvement he could of that advantage, by reducing some garisons that lay nearest to him; yet the enemies were still in possession of nine parts in ten of that nation, and had fortified the most considerable places therein. After our army had refreshed themselves, and were joined by the forces of Col. Jones, they

---

[1] On June 13, the Council of State recommended Ireton to be second in command under Cromwell, which Parliament agreed to on June 15. Jones is described as Lieut.-Gen. in the proceedings of the Council of State on Aug. 11. Cromwell was doubtless responsible for this new arrangement. Cal. S. P., Dom., 1649–50, pp. 183, 273.

mustered in all between sixteen and seventeen thousand horse and foot. Upon their arrival the enemies withdrew, and put most of their army into their garisons, having placed three or four thousand of the best of their men, being most English, in the town of Tredah, and made Sir Arthur Ashton governour thereof. A resolution being taken to besiege that place, our army sat down before it, and the Lieutenant-General caused a battery to be erected against an angle of the wall, near to a fort, which was within, called the Windmill-Fort, by which he made a breach in the wall; but the enemy having a half-moon on the outside, which was designed to flank the angle of the wall, he thought fit to endeavour to possess himself of it, which he did by storm, putting most of those that were in it to the sword. The enemy defended the breach against ours from behind an earth-work, which they had cast up within, and where they had drawn up two or three troops of horse which they had within the town, for the encouragement and support of their foot : the fort also was not unserviceable to them in the defence of the breach. The Lieutenant-General well knowing the importance of this action, resolved to put all upon it ; and having commanded some guns to be loaded with bullets of half a pound, and fired upon the enemy's horse, who were drawn up somewhat in view ; himself with a reserve of foot marched up to the breach, which giving fresh courage to our men, they made a second attack with more vigour than before : whereupon the enemy's foot being abandoned by their horse, whom our shot had forced to retire, began to break and shift for themselves ; which ours perceiving, followed them so close, that they overtook them at the bridg that lay cross the river, and separated that part where the action was from the principal part of the town ; and preventing them from drawing up the bridg, entred pell-mell with them into the place, where they put all they met with to the sword, having positive orders from the Lieutenant-General to give no quarter to any souldier. Their works and fort were also stormed and taken, and

1649   those that defended them put to the sword also, and amongst them Sir Arthur Ashton, governour of the place. A great dispute there was amongst the souldiers for his artificial leg, which was reported to be of gold, but it proved to be but of wood, his girdle being found to be the better booty, wherein two hundred pieces of gold were found quilted[1]. The slaughter was continued all that day and the next; which extraordinary severity I presume was used, to discourage others from making opposition. After that the army besieged Wexford; and having erected a battery against the castle, which stood near the wall of the town, and fired from it most part of the day, whereby a small breach was made, commissioners were sent in the evening from the enemy to treat about the surrender of it. In the mean time our guns continued firing, there being no cessation agreed, whereby the breach in the castle being made wider, the guard that was appointed to defend it quitted their post, and thereupon some of our men entred

Oct. 11.   the castle, and set up their colours at the top of it, which the enemy having observed, left their stations in all parts: so that ours getting over the walls, possessed themselves of the town without opposition, and opened the gates that the horse might enter, tho they could do but little service, all the streets being barred with cables: but our foot pressed the enemy so close, that crowding to escape over the water, they so over-loaded the boats with their numbers, that many of them were drowned. Great riches were taken in this town, it being accounted by the enemy a place of strength; and some ships were seized in the harbour, which had much interrupted the commerce of that coast[2]. Commissioners were appointed by the Lieutenant-General to take care of the goods that were found in the town belonging to the rebels, that they might be improved to the best advantage of the publick. After

---

[1] For a life of Aston, see D. N. B. He had lost his leg in 1644, in consequence of a fall from his horse whilst he was governor of Oxford.

Compare for the storming of Drogheda, Carlyle's Cromwell, Letter cv.

[2] Compare Carlyle's Cromwell, Letter cvii.

these successes the army grew sickly, many dying of the 1649
flux, which they contracted by hard service, and such
provisions as they were not accustomed to. The plague
also which had been for some time amongst the inhabitants
of the country, and the Irish army, now began to seize
upon ours. Of one or both these distempers Col. Michael
Jones, who by his courage and conduct in the service of
his country had justly deserved the applause of all, and
had been lately made Lieutenant-General of the Horse
by the Parliament, fell so desperately sick, that being no
longer able to continue in the army, he was carried, not
without reluctancy, to Wexford, where in a few days he
died, much lamented by the army, and by all that desired Dec. 10.
the prosperity of the English interest [1]. In the mean time
the Parliament was careful to send money, recruits, and all
manner of supplies necessary to Ireland ; which they were
the better enabled to do by those great sums of money
daily brought in by the purchasers of the lands of Deans
and Chapters, which they thought fit for the reasons
before-mentioned to expose to sale ; which as it was an
advantage to the nation in general, by easing them of some
part of their contributions, so was it no detriment to any
of those purchasers who were heartily engaged in the
publick service ; since if the tide should turn, and our
enemies become prevalent, such persons were likely to
have no better security for the enjoyment of their own
paternal estates. Upon this consideration I contracted
with the trustees commissionated by the Parliament, for
the mannors of Eastknoel and Upton in the county of
Wilts, wherein I employed that portion which I had
received with my wife, and a greater sum arising from
the sale of a part of my patrimonial estate [2].

---

[1] Michael Jones died at Dungarvan, and was buried in the col-
legiate church at Youghal, in the
chapel belonging to the Earls of
Cork. On his character, see Carlyle's Cromwell, Letter .cxvii, and
Whitelocke, Memorials, iii. 136.

[2] The manors of East Knoyle and
Upton were sold to Edmund Ludlow, February 22, 1650, for the sum
of £4668 12s. 7¾d. Samuel Gale,
History of Winchester, pt. ii. p. 23 ;
Hoare, Modern Wilts, Heytesbury,
p. 18.

1649   The winter approaching, and the season being very tempestuous, General Blake was obliged to enter into harbour, by which means Prince Rupert with the ships that were with him having an opportunity to escape, set sail for Lisbon, where they were received and protected; 1650 but General Popham who had waited some time for the Portugal fleet bound thither from the islands, took eighteen of them loaden with sugars and other valuable merchandizes, which he sent to England under a convoy, entrusting the conduct thereof to my brother, who, as I said before, was his lieutenant, and died in his voyage homewards[1]. With the rest he continued cruizing on the coast of Portugal, attending Prince Rupert's fleet, which being drawn up under the protection of their guns, and most of the men on shore, ours took that occasion to seize one of their frigats, by surprizing the watch, and keeping the rest of the men under deck; by which means they brought her off safe to the fleet[2].

    Our army in Ireland, tho much diminished by sickness and harassed by hard duty, continued their resolution to march into the enemy's quarters, where they reduced Oct. 16. Rosse with little opposition: Goran also was surrendred March 21. to them, together with the officers of that place, by the souldiers of the garison, upon promise of quarter for themselves; their officers being delivered at discretion, were '1650 shot to death. The next town they besieged was Kilkenny, March 28. where there was a strong castle, and the walls of the town were indifferent good. Having erected a battery on the

---

[1] Philip Ludlow, bapt. at Maiden Bradley, April 15, 1628. Died at sea, Aug. 13, 1650. His nuncupative will, proved Oct. 1, 1650, by his brother Nathaniel Ludlow, sole legatee and executor, thus commences: 'Memd. that Philip Ludlow, late of the city of Westminster, bachelor, deceased, departed this life on the high seas on board the ship Sophier, on the 13th of August last, 1650, he being commander-in-chief of the Brazeele merchant ships home-ward bound.' He was buried on Sept. 20 in Westminster Abbey, 'on the South side of the Chapel of Kings, under the long stone by Richard the Second's monument.' Chester, Westminster Abbey Registers, p. 144.

[2] On Blake's exploits off the coast of Portugal and his negotiations with the King, see Report on the Portland MSS., i. 519-523, 527, 531, 537.

east side of the wall, our artillery fired upon it for a whole   1650
day without making any considerable breach ; on the other
side our men were much annoyed by the enemy's shot
from the walls and castle. But the garison being admonished by the examples made of their friends at Tredah   March 27.
and Wexford, thought fit to surrender the town timely upon
such conditions as they could obtain, which was done accordingly[1]. Youghall, Cork and Kinsale were delivered   1649
to the forces of the Parliament by the contrivance and   Oct. 16.
diligence of some officers and well-affected persons in those
places ; and thereupon the Lieutenant-General sent a detachment under the command of the Lord Broghil to their
assistance, in case any thing should be attempted by
Inchequin, or any other, to their disturbance ; whilst he
with the rest of the army marched towards Clonmel.
Being upon his march thither, he was met by the corporation of Feather, with a tender of their submission, where-   1650
with the Lieutenant-General was so satisfied, the army   Feb. 3.
being far advanced into the enemy's quarters, and having
no place of refreshment, that he promised to maintain
them in the enjoyment of their privileges[2]. Having left
our sick men here, he marched and sat down before
Clonmel, one side of which was secured by a river, and   April 27.
the rest of the town encompassed with a wall that was well
furnished with men to defend it. Our guns having made
a breach in the wall, a detachment of our men was ordered
to storm ; but the enemy by the means of some houses
that stood near, and earth-works cast up within the wall,   May 9.
made good their breach till night parted the dispute, when
the enemy perceiving ours resolved to reduce the place,

[1] On the capture of Ross, see Carlyle's Cromwell, Letter cxii; of Gowran, Letter cxxx; of Kilkenny, Letter cxxx. On the revolt of the Munster garrisons, see Letters cxiii, cxv; and Murphy's Cromwell in Ireland, pp. 398, 193. Ludlow here confuses the campaigns of 1649 and 1650.

[2] Fethard capitulated on Feb. 3, but Ludlow is mistaken in saying that the town sent deputies to offer its surrender. It was summoned on the night of Feb. 2, and surrendered the next morning. See Murphy, Cromwell in Ireland, pp. 255-260; Carlyle's Cromwell, Letter cxix.

1650   beat a parley, and sent out commissioners to treat[1]. Articles were agreed and signed on both sides, whereby it was concluded, that the town with all the arms and ammunition therein, should be delivered up the next morning to such of our forces as should be appointed to receive the same. After this agreement was made and signed, the General was informed that Col. Hugh O'Neal governour of the place, with all the garison, had marched out at the beginning of the night towards Waterford, before the commissioners came out to treat. It something troubled the commanders to be thus over-reach'd ; but conditions being granted, they thought it their duty to keep them

1649   with the town. Dungarvan and Carrick were next reduced,
Dec. 3.   where Col. Reynolds being left with his regiment of horse, the Lieutenant-General with the army marched towards the county of Waterford. The enemy having observed ours marching on the other side of the river, took that advantage to draw together a considerable body of horse and foot, with which they marched with all diligence to

Nov. 24.   Carrick, and stormed it, not at all doubting to carry the place, wherein there was nothing but horse, armed only with swords and pistols, to defend a wall of great compass. Yet did our men manage their defence so well, making use of stones and whatsoever might be serviceable to them, that the enemy was beaten off with loss ; so that tho forces were sent from the army to relieve their friends upon the first notice of their danger, yet they found the work done at their arrival[2].

The army began now to prepare for the siege of Waterford, but by the hard service of this winter, and other accidents, being much diminished, and those that remained being but in a sickly condition, it was thought fit to send orders to Dublin, requiring the forces there who were in better health to march towards Wexford in order

[1] Ludlow entirely misplaces the siege of Clonmel, making it take place in 1649 instead of 1650. The accounts of the siege of Clonmel are collected by Mr. Gilbert, Aphorismical Discovery, ii. 408.

[2] Carlyle's Cromwell, Letter cxvi.

to reinforce the army before Waterford. The Lord Inchequin, who had notice of their march, having formed a body
of two thousand five hundred horse, and some foot, resolved
to fall upon them, which he did between Arclo and
Wexford, our forces not amounting to more than fifteen
hundred foot, and five hundred horse[1]. The enemies
charged our horse with such fury and numbers, that they
were forced to retreat to their foot; after which falling
upon our foot, they obliged them to retire to the rocks
that were on the shore in great disorder : but some of our
horse, with a part of our foot, rallying again, charged a
body of their horse with such vigour, that they broke them,
and killed many of them, amongst whom were divers
considerable persons ; which so discouraged the rest, that
tho they were the choicest of the enemy's men, and many
of ours so distempered with the flux, that they were forced
to fight with their breeches down, yet durst they not make
any farther attempt against them, but drew off and permitted ours to march to their designed rendezvouz without
any more interruption. By which it eminently appeared of
what importance it is towards the obtaining success, to
fight in the cause of our country; for these very men,
as long as they were engaged with us, performed wonders
against the rebels ; and now being engaged with them,
were almost as easily overcome as they had beaten the
Irish before : and this was so visible even to the Irish
themselves, that some time after at a consultation of the
chief officers of Leinster, where it was debated what course
to take in order to destroy our army, some advising to
draw into a body and fight us, others to betake themselves
to the woods and bogs, and from thence to break our forces
by parties; the lord of Glanmaleiro[2] assured them of a
way, which, if taken, would certainly effect it, and that was

---

[1] Carlyle's Cromwell, Letter cxv ;
Carte's Ormond, iii. 499; Murphy,
Cromwell in Ireland, p. 176. This
is known as the battle of Glas-
carrig.

[2] Lewis Dempsy, Lord Clanmaliry,
one of the seven commissioners of
Leinster who capitulated to Ludlow,
May 12, 1652. Gilbert, Aphorismical Discovery, iii. 94.

to induce us to make peace with them ; ' for,' said he, ' they are a successful army, and our men are dispirited, and not likely to get any thing by fighting with them ; and to weary them out by our surprizes and depredations is impossible, as long as the way from England is open for their supplies ; but the other way proposed will infallibly ruin them: for did not our ancestors by the same means render the conquests of Queen Elizabeth fruitless to England ? and have we not thereby ruined the Earl of Ormond and Inchequin already, who having been always successful when against us, have been famous for nothing since their conjunction with us, but the losses and repulses which they have sustained ? so that if we can perswade this army to make a truce or league with us, they will become as unfortunate as the former.'

Whilst the Lieutenant-General was making preparations for the siege of Waterford, a letter was brought to him from the Parliament, requiring his attendance in England: in order to which he left the command of the army with Commissary-General Ireton, to carry on the remaining part of the work ; going himself to visit those places in Munster which had lately submitted to the Parliament, with intention to settle the civil as well as military affairs of that province. To this end he impowered John Coke Esq. to be Chief Justice of Munster ; and having accomplished such things as he designed, embarked for England, and soon after landed at Bristol. In the mean time the treaty between Prince Charles and the Presbyterian party in Scotland hastening towards a conclusion, the forces which they had raised by the encouragement of our army, after they had rescued them from the power of the Hamiltonian party, fell upon Montrose, killed many of his men, and took him with divers other officers prisoners, and amongst them Major-General Hurry and Capt. Spotiswood, who was said to have been concerned in the assassination of Dr. Dorislaus our agent in Holland. They were all three condemned to death, and hanged ; Montrose being carried to the place of execution in an ignominious manner, with

the declarations issued out by him for the King tied about   1650
his neck, where he was executed on a gibbet of thirty foot
high.   His quarters were placed upon the gate through
which their King was to pass at his coming to Edinburgh,
which could not but move his indignation, if he had the
least sense of honour, because he had acted by his commission, and in order to vest him with that absolute and
uncontrolable power which kings think to be most for their
advantage : but the King being instructed with other
maxims, struck up the bargain with the Presbyterians, and
engaged to take the Covenant, whereupon they cried him
up for a great convert.

Some sycophants in the English Parliament, a race
of men never wanting in great councils, pressed earnestly
for settling two thousand five hundred pounds a year upon
the Lieutenant-General, according to a vote formerly
passed in the House ; or that it might at least be read once
or twice before his arrival at Westminster, he being then
upon his way from Bristol.   Upon this motion I took the
liberty to acquaint the House, that tho I would not oppose
that motion, yet it was but reasonable to make good their
promises also to persons that had served them usefully
in former occasions, desiring them to remember the past
services of those that they knew continued still to be
faithful to them, tho not then in actual employment ;
and particularly not to forget the important services of
Major-General Skippon, nor the vote they had passed to
settle one thousand pounds a year upon him, which hitherto
had been insignificant to him.   Upon this motion the   May 30.
Parliament ordered that the said sum should be paid
yearly to him out of the receipt at Goldsmiths-Hall, till
so much should be settled upon him out of the forfeited
lands in Ireland by Act of Parliament.   In consideration
of this piece of justice, the Major-General did me ever
after the honour to call me his real friend.

And now the Parliament being desirous to let the
people see that they designed not to perpetuate themselves after they should be able to make a compleat

1650

Jan. 9.

settlement of affairs, and provide for the security of the nation from enemies both abroad and at home, whom they had yet in great numbers to contend with, resolved that the House would upon every Wednesday turn themselves into a grand committee, to debate concerning the manner of assembling, and power of future successive Parliaments; the number of persons to be appointed to serve for each county, that the nation might be more equally represented than hitherto had been practised; and touching the qualifications of the electors as well as those to be elected: which order was constantly observed, and considerable progress from time to time made therein [1].

June 4.

The Lieutenant-General being arrived [2], and having resumed his place in the House, the Parliament ordered their Speaker to give him thanks in their name for the services he had done for the Commonwealth in the nation of Ireland. And now the Council of State concluding it highly necessary to make some preparations against the storm which threatned us from the North, and knowing that the satisfaction of their General was of great importance to that service, desired the Lord Fairfax to declare his resolution concerning the same, who after a day or two's consideration, at the instigation chiefly (as was thought) of his wife, upon whom the Presbyterian clergy

---

[1] The history of the discussions on this subject is given by Godwin, Commonwealth, iii. 298-306, 422, 448; Masson, Life of Milton, iv. 221, 308.

[2] Cromwell arrived at London on Saturday, June 1. 'Upon Hounslow Heath he was met by his Excellency the Lord General, with a great train of the members of Parliament and Council of State, divers companies and troops of foot and horse and many thousands of the well affected; so that the waies were thronged down to Westminster. Upon the Monday following, the Lord-Lieutenant visited the Lord General at his house in Queen Street, where there

passed many remarkable expressions of mutuall love and courtesie, sufficient to check the false tongues and wishes of the enemies of the nation. The same day, likewise, the Parliament gave his Lordship thanks in the name of the Commonwealth, as likewise did the Lord Mayor and Aldermen in the name of the City, for his most famous services in Ireland; which being added to the garland of his English victories, have crowned him in the opinion of all the world for one of the wisest and most accomplished leaders, among the present and past generations.' Mercurius Politicus, June 6, 1650.

had no small influence, seemed unwilling to march into
Scotland ; but declared, that in case the Scots should
attempt to invade England, he would be ready to lay
down his life in opposing them. We laboured to perswade
him of the reasonableness and justice of our resolution
to march into Scotland, they having already declared
themselves our enemies, and by publick protestation bound
themselves to impose that government upon us, which we
had found necessary to abolish ; and to that end had
made their terms with Prince Charles, waiting only an
opportunity, as soon as they had strengthened themselves
by foreign assistance, which they expected, to put their
design in execution, after we should be reduced to great
difficulties incident to the keeping up of an army in expectation of being invaded by them ; assuring him, that we
thought our selves indispensably obliged in duty to our
country, and as we tendred the peace and prosperity of it,
as well as to prevent the effusion of the blood of those who
had been, and we hoped upon better information would be
our friends, to march into Scotland, and either to understand
from them that they are our friends, or to endeavour to
make them so ; chusing rather to make that country the
seat of the war than our own. But the Lord Fairfax was
unwilling to alter his resolution in consideration of any
thing that could be said. Upon this Lieutenant-General
Cromwell pressed, that notwithstanding the unwillingness
of the Lord Fairfax to command upon this occasion, they
would yet continue him to be General of the army ; professing for himself, that he would rather chuse to serve
under him in his post, than to command the greatest army
in Europe. But the Council of State not approving that
advice, appointed a committee of some of themselves
to confer farther with the General in order to his satisfaction. This committee was appointed upon the motion
of the Lieutenant-General, who acted his part so to the life,
that I really thought him in earnest ; which obliged me
to step to him as he was withdrawing with the rest of
the committee out of the council-chamber, and to desire

1650

June 26.

him, that he would not in compliment and humility obstruct the service of the nation by his refusal ; but the consequence made it sufficiently evident that he had no such intention. The committee having spent some time in debate with the Lord Fairfax without any success, returned to the Council of State, whereupon they ordered the report of this affair to be made to the Parliament. Which being done, and some of the General's friends informing them, that tho he had shewed some unwillingness to be employed in this expedition himself, yet being more unwilling to hinder the undertaking of it by another, he had sent his secretary, who attended at the door, to surrender his commission, if they thought fit to receive it; the secretary was called in, and delivered the commission [1], which the Parliament having received, they proceeded to settle an annual revenue of five thousand pounds upon the Lord Fairfax, in consideration of his former services, and then voted Lieutenant-General Cromwell to be Captain-General of all their land forces, ordering a commission forthwith to be drawn up to that effect, and referred to the Council of State to hasten the preparations for the northern expedition. A little after, as I sat in the house near General Cromwell, he told me, that having observed an alteration in my looks and carriage towards him, he apprehended that I had entertained some suspicions of him ; and that being perswaded of the tendency of the designs of us both to the advancement of the public service, he desired that a

---

[1] On June 12, Parliament voted that both Fairfax and Cromwell should go on the expedition against Scotland, the latter in his old post of Lieutenant-General. Both expressed their willingness to serve, and Fairfax's new commission was passed on June 14. On June 25, Whitelocke reported from the Council of State that Fairfax wished to be excused. An account of the interview between Fairfax and the deputation from the Council is given in Whitelocke's Memorials, iii. 207. A letter of resignation from Fairfax to the Speaker was also read in the House (printed in the appendix to the Diary of Sir Henry Slingsby, ed. Parsons, p. 340). A committee was then appointed to convey to Fairfax the thanks of the House for his past services and to assure him of its continued confidence. On June 26, Rushworth returned Fairfax's commission to Parliament; C.J., vi. 423-4, 431-2.

meeting might be appointed, wherein we might with
freedom discover the grounds of our mistakes and mis-
apprehensions, and create a good understanding between
us for the future. I answered, that he had discovered
in me what I had never perceived in my self; and that if I
troubled him not so frequently as formerly, it was either
because I was conscious of that weight of business that lay
upon him, or that I had nothing to importune him withal
upon my own or any other account; yet since he was
pleased to do me the honour to desire a free conversation
with me, I assured him of my readiness therein. Whereupon we resolved to meet that afternoon in the Council of
State, and from thence to withdraw to a private room,
which we did accordingly in the Queen's guard-chamber,
where he endeavoured to perswade me of the necessity
incumbent upon him to do several things that appeared
extraordinary in the judgment of some men, who in
opposition to him took such courses as would bring ruin
upon themselves, as well as him and the publick cause,
affirming his intentions to be directed entirely to the good
of the people, and professing his readiness to sacrifice his
life in their service. I freely acknowledged my former
dissatisfaction with him and the rest of the army, when
they were in treaty with the King, whom I looked upon as
the only obstruction to the settlement of the nation; and
with their actions at the rendezvouz at Ware, where they
shot a souldier to death, and imprisoned divers others upon
the account of that treaty, which I conceived to have been
done without authority, and for sinister ends: yet since
they had manifested themselves convinced of those errors,
and declared their adherence to the Commonwealth, tho
too partial a hand was carried both by the Parliament and
themselves in the distribution of preferments and gratuities,
and too much severity exercised against some who had
formerly been their friends, and as I hoped would be so
still, with other things that I could not entirely approve, I
was contented patiently to wait for the accomplishment of
those good things which I expected, till they had overcome

the difficulties they now laboured under, and suppressed their enemies that appeared both at home and abroad against them; hoping that then their principles and interest would lead them to do what was most agreeable to the constitution of a Commonwealth, and the good of mankind. He owned my dissatisfaction with the army whilst they were in treaty with the King, to be founded upon good reasons, and excused the execution done upon the souldier at the rendezvouz, as absolutely necessary to keep things from falling into confusion; which must have ensued upon that division, if it had not been timely prevented. He professed to desire nothing more than that the government of the nation might be settled in a free and equal Commonwealth, acknowledging that there was no other probable means to keep out the old family and government from returning upon us; declaring, that he looked upon the design of the Lord in this day to be the freeing of His people from every burden, and that He was now accomplishing what was prophesied in the 110th Psalm; from the consideration of which he was often encouraged to attend the effecting those ends, spending at least an hour in the exposition of that Psalm, adding to this, that it was his intention to contribute the utmost of his endeavours to make a thorow reformation of the Clergy and Law: but, said he, 'the sons of Zeruiah are yet too strong for us'; and we cannot mention the reformation of the law, but they presently cry out, we design to destroy propriety: whereas the law, as it is now constituted, serves only to maintain the lawyers, and to encourage the rich to oppress the poor; affirming that Mr. Coke, then Justice in Ireland, by proceeding in a summary and expeditious way, determined more causes in a week, than Westminster-Hall in a year[1]; saying farther, that Ireland was as a clean paper in that

---

[1] Cromwell expresses similar views on the Law in his letter announcing the victory of Dunbar. See also Speech V. in Carlyle's Cromwell, and his letter to Sadler, Appendix 17. Cooke's projected reforms in the administration of justice in Ireland are set forth in the preface to his tract entitled 'Monarchy no Creature of God's making,' printed at Waterford in 1652.

particular, and capable of being governed by such laws as
should be found most agreeable to justice ; which may
be so impartially administred, as to be a good precedent
even to England it self ; where when they once perceive
propriety preserved at an easy and cheap rate in Ireland,
they will never permit themselves to be so cheated and
abused as now they are. At last he fell into the consideration of the military government of Ireland, complaining
that the whole weight of it lay upon Major-General Ireton ;
and that if he should by death or any other accident be
removed from that station, the conduct of that part would
probably fall into the hands of such men as either by
principle or interest were not proper for that trust, and
of whom he had no certain assurance. He therefore
proposed that some person of reputation and known
fidelity might be sent over to command the horse there,
and to assist the Major-General in the service of the
publick, that employment being next in order to his own,
desiring me to propose one whom I thought sufficiently
qualified for that station. I told him, that in my opinion a
fitter man could not be found than Col. Algernon Sidney ;
but he excepted against him by reason of his relation
to some who were in the King's interest, proposing Col.
Norton and Col. Hammond, yet making objections against
them at the same time : that against Col. Hammond I
remember was, that by his late deportment with relation to
the King, he had so disobliged the army, that he apprehended he would not be acceptable to them. After this
he entred upon a large commendation of the country, and
pressed me earnestly to think of some person capable of
that employment. By this time I perceived something of
his intentions concerning me ; but the condition of my
affairs was such, having lately married and by purchasing
some lands contracted a great debt, that I resolved not to
accept of it.

The time for the General's departure for the expedition
of Scotland drawing near, he moved the Council of State,
that since they had employed him about a work which

would require all his care, they would be pleased to ease him of the affairs of Ireland ; which they refusing to do, he then moved, that they would at least send over some commissioners for the management of the civil affairs, assuring them also that the military being more than Major-General Ireton could possibly carry on, without the assistance of some general officer to command the horse, which employment was become vacant by the death of the brave Lieutenant-General Jones, it was absolutely necessary to commissionate some person of worth to that employment, and to authorize him to be one of their commissioners for the civil government ; telling them, that he had endeavoured to find out a person proper for that service, and to that end had consulted with one there present, desiring him to recommend one fit for the same : but that neither of them had proposed any that he could approve so well as the person himself, and therefore moved that he might be appointed to that employment ; acquainting them, that tho he himself was impowered by virtue of his commission from the Parliament, to nominate the Lieutenant-General of the Horse, yet because the gentleman he proposed, upon which he named me, was a member of Parliament, and of the Council of State, he desired for the better securing the obedience of the army to me, that the Parliament might be moved to nominate and appoint me to that charge. I endeavoured as well as I could to make the Council sensible of my unfitness for an employment of so great importance, acquainting them, that upon the General's desire I had recommended one to him of such abilities, as I doubted not they would judg better qualified for it than my self, who besides my want of experience sufficient for that service, was so incumbred with debts and engagements at that time, that I could not possibly undertake it without hazarding the ruin of my family and estate. But the Council refused to allow my excuse, which indeed was real and unfeigned ; telling me, that it would be more proper to represent those things to the Parliament, when the report should be made to them from the Council : which was agreed upon to this effect ; ' That the House should be moved to appoint me Lieutenant-General of the Horse in Ireland ; and that General Cromwell, Major-General Ireton, my self, Col. John Jones, and Major Richard Salloway, or any three of us, should be authorized by Act of Parliament to be Commissioners for the administration of the civil affairs in that nation.' The news of this transaction was unwelcome to some of my nearest relations and best friends, not only for the reasons above mentioned, but upon suspicion that this opportunity was taken by the General to remove me out of the way, lest I should prove an obstruction to his designs. But I could not think my self so considerable, and therefore could not concur with them in that opinion[1]. Yet I endeavoured to clear my self of this employment, and knowing that this affair was carried on chiefly by the General's influence, I applied my self to him, acquainting him with my present circumstances, and assuring him that it was altogether inconvenient, and might prove very prejudicial to me. He replied, that men's private affairs must give place to those of the publick ; that he had seriously considered the matter, and that he could not find a person so fit for those employments as my self, desiring me therefore to acquiesce. It was not many days before the Council of State made their report of this affair to the Parliament, where I again pressed the reasons I had used before to the Council with as much earnestness as I could : but they would not hearken to me, and without any debate, presently concurred with the Council therein, with the addition only of Mr. John Weaver, a member of the House, to be one of the commissioners appointed to manage the civil government[2].

July 2.

---

[1] A correspondent writes to Sir E. Nicholas on Jan. 10, 165⅚, commenting on Ludlow's imprisonment, and adds : ‘When Cromwell, lest he should disturb him during his absence in Scotland, made him Lieutenant-General of the Irish horse, a friend called to congratulate him, when his reply was that he must needs go whom the devil drives ; so you see the jealousy between them.’ Cal. S. P., Dom., 1655 6, p. 109.

[2] Ludlow's account of the appoint-

1650

In the mean time our army proceeded successfully in Ireland, where they reduced Waterford after a siege of some weeks ; which place the enemy had considerably fortified : but their provisions failing, they were forced to

Aug. 10.

surrender it upon articles[1]. During this siege the army was supplied with all necessaries by some of our ships that came into the harbour to that end. After the reduction of Waterford a detachment was made from our army to besiege Duncannon, a place of considerable strength, having seven hundred men within to defend it, tho one third of their number had been sufficient for that purpose. This or some other cause produced the plague amongst them, which lessened their number, and made their provisions to hold out the longer : yet at last they were constrained to deliver up the place with all the arms and ammunition to

Aug. 17.

our men. The Lord of Esmond had been governour of this place for the English at the beginning of the war, and held it out for the space of six or seven months against the rebels, of whom he killed great numbers before it during

1645

the siege that he sustained ; but being driven to great

March 19.

extremities, he was obliged to surrender it to them ; which went so near the gallant old gentleman's heart, that he soon after departed this life.

July 2.

The next place our army attempted was Carlo, an inland garison, distant from Dublin about thirty miles, and lying

---

ment of the commissioners is a little confused. On June 27. the Council of State nominated Ludlow and Jones. On July 2, Parliament appointed them, naming Ludlow at the same time Lieutenant General of the Horse in Ireland. On the same day Parliament referred to the Council of State to name other fit persons as commissioners, and on Sept 13 that body nominated John Weaver and Richard Salwey. On Oct. 4, the House passed the instructions of the commissioners and added the names of Weaver and Salwey. On Nov. 20, Salwey at his own desire was dispensed from going to Ireland. Miles Corbet was appointed on Nov. 27, in place of Salwey.

[1] Ireton summoned Waterford July 1, 1650, articles were signed on Aug. 6, and the garrison marched out Aug. 10. A narrative of its capture, published by the order of Parliament, is reprinted in the Old Parliamentary History, xix. 334. An interesting correspondence between Ireton and General Preston, the governor of Waterford, is printed in Borlase's Irish Rebellion, Appendix, pp. 32-46, ed. 1743.

upon the river Barrow. The place was esteemed by the enemy to be of great importance, and therefore fortified by them with divers works; besides, it had a small castle at the foot of the bridg, and a river running under the walls of the castle. The country beyond it were also their friends, and furnished them with provisions in great abundance. To prevent which, Major-General Ireton found it necessary to employ the principal part of his forces on the other side of the river Barrow; yet by what means to secure a communication between the two parts of his army, was a great difficulty, they having neither boats nor casks sufficient for that purpose. In the end they fell upon this expedient, to bring together great quantities of the biggest reeds, and tying them up in many little bundles with small cords, they fastned them to two cables that were fixed in the ground on each side of the river, at the distance of about eight or ten yards from each other: these being covered with wattles, bore troops of horse and companies of foot as well as a bridg arched with stone.

Whilst these things were doing, most of the Earl of Ormond's forces retired into Connaught, and those of the Lord Muskerry into Kerry: the Lord Castlehaven also, after he had fired most of the small castles in Leinster and Munster, marched out of those parts[1].

But the enemy which most threatned the disturbance of the Parliament, was that of Scotland, where all interests were united in opposition to the present authority in England. They had also many who favoured their design in our nation, as well Presbyterians as Cavaliers: the former of these were most bold and active, upon presumption of more favour in case of ill success. The Parliament being sensible of these things, published a declaration, shewing that they had no design to impose upon the nation of Scotland any thing contrary to their inclinations: that they would leave them to chuse what government they thought most convenient for themselves,

---

[1] On Ireton's campaign in 1650, see Gilbert, Aphorismical Discovery, iii. 218.

provided they would suffer the English nation to live under that establishment which they had chosen : that it evidently appeared that the Scots were acted by a spirit of domination and rule ; and that nothing might be wanting to compel us to submit to their impositions, they had espoused the interests of that family, which they themselves had declared guilty of much precious blood, and resolved to force the same upon England : that these and other things there mentioned had obliged them to send an army into Scotland for their own preservation, and to keep the Scots from destroying themselves, which they were about to do ; resolving notwithstanding to extend all possible favour to such as were seduced through weakness, and misled by the malice of others [1]. After this General Cromwell hastned to the army, which consisted of about twenty thousand horse and foot, where having removed a Colonel or two, with some inferiour officers, who were unwilling to be employed in that service, and made up a regiment for Col. Monk, with six companies out of Sir Arthur Haslerig's,

and six out of Col. Fenwick's regiment, he marched into Scotland without any opposition, most of the people being fled from their habitations towards Edinburgh, whither all

the enemy's strength was drawn together [2]. The English army drew up within sight of the town, but the Scots would not hazard all by the decision of a battel, hoping to tire us out with frequent skirmishes and harassing our men, relying much upon the unsutableness of the climate to our constitutions, especially if they should detain us in the field till winter. Their counsels succeeded according to their desires, and our army through hard duty, scarcity of pro-

---

[1] A Declaration of the Parliament of England upon the marching of their Army into Scotland; Old Parliamentary History, xix. 276.

[2] Col. John Bright threw up his commission, and Col. George Gill was removed and succeeded by Col. Matthew Alured; Cal. S. P., Dom., 1650, p. 263. On Bright, see Life of Capt. John Hodgson, ed. 1882, p. 41; and D. N. B. On Gill, see Portland MSS., i. 535; Cal. of Co. for Compounding, p. 1153; C. J., vi. 450, 493, vii. 22, 97. On the formation of Monck's regiment, see Mackinnon's History of the Coldstream Guards, 1833, i. pp. 1, 21.

visions, and the rigour of the season, grew very sickly, and
diminished daily, so that they were necessitated to draw
off to receive supplies from our shipping, which could not
come nearer to them than Dunbar, distant from Edinburgh
about twenty miles. The enemy observing our army to
retire, followed them close; and falling upon our rear-
guard of horse in the night, having the advantage of a clear
moon, beat them up to our rear-guard of foot. Which
alarm coming suddenly upon our men, put them into some
disorder; but a thick cloud interposing in that very moment,
and intercepting the light of the moon for about an hour,
our army took that opportunity to secure themselves, and
arrived without any further disturbance at Dunbar, where
having shipped their heavy baggage and sick men, they
designed to return into England. But the enemy, upon
confidence of success, had possessed themselves of all the
passes, having in their army about thirty thousand horse
and foot, and ours being reduced to ten thousand at the
most. There was now no way left, but to yield themselves
prisoners, or to fight upon these unequal terms. In this
extremity a council of war was called, and after some
dispute it was agreed to fall upon the enemy the next
morning, about an hour before day, and accordingly the
several regiments were ordered to their respective posts.
Upon the first shock our forlorn of horse was somewhat
disordered by their lanciers; but two of our regiments of
foot that were in the van behaved themselves so well, that
they not only sustained the charge of the enemy's horse,
but beat them back upon their own foot, and following
them close, forced both horse and foot to retreat up the
hill from whence they had attacked us. The body of the
enemy's army finding their van-guard, which consisted of
their choicest men, thus driven back upon them, began to
shift for themselves, which they did with such precipitation
and disorder, that few of them ventured to look behind
them till they arrived at Edinburgh, taking no care of their
King, who made use of the same means to secure himself
as his new subjects had done. One party of their horse

1650

made a stand till some of ours came up to them, and then ran away after the rest of their companions. Many were killed upon the place, and many more in the pursuit: all their baggage, arms, artillery and ammunition fell into the hands of our army: many also were taken and sent prisoners into England. When the first news of this great victory was brought to London by Sir John Hipsley, it was my fortune, with others of the Parliament, to be with the Lord Fairfax at Hampton-Court, who seemed much to rejoice at it. But the victory it self was not more welcome to me than the contents of the General's letter to the Parliament; wherein amongst many other expressions savouring of a publick spirit, there was one to this effect; that seeing the Lord, upon this solemn appeal made to Him by the Scots and us, had so signally given judgment on our side, when all hopes of deliverance seemed to be cut off, it became us not to do His work negligently; and from thence took occasion to put us in mind, not to content our selves with the name of a Commonwealth, but to do real things for the common good, and not to permit any interest for their particular advantage to prevail with us to the contrary [1]. Our army in Scotland having received some recruits, advanced toward Edinburgh ; but the enemy being informed of their march, withdrew out of the town, and leaving a strong garison in the castle, retreated towards Sterling. The Parliament being very careful to supply their armies with all things necessary, caused great quantities of hay to be bought up in Norfolk and Suffolk, which they sent by sea to Scotland, where it was absolutely necessary, for the Scots army had so strongly intrenched themselves by the advantage of a wood, that ours could not possibly attack them without great hazard ; and they were furnished with provisions from Fife and the adjacent parts, which are the most fruitful in that nation, by means of the bridg at Sterling: whereas our army, which lay encamped near them, had no other country from whence they might draw provisions, but such as had been already in the possession

[1] Carlyle's Cromwell, Letter cxl.

of the enemy: besides that, hay is generally scarce in Scotland; and that a great part of our forces consisted of horse.

1650

Owen Roe O'Neal, who commanded the old Northern Irish in Ulster, that had been principally concerned in the massacre of the Protestants, being dead, the Popish Bishop of Cloghar undertook the conduct of them, and being grown considerably strong, necessitated Sir Charles Coote to draw his forces together to defend his quarters, which they designed to invade, desperately resolving to put it to the issue of a battel. Their foot was more numerous than ours, but Sir Charles exceeded them in horse. The dispute was hot for some time; but at last the Irish were beaten, tho not without loss on our side: amongst others Col. Fenwick, a brave and gallant man, was mortally wounded. The enemy's baggage and train of artillery was taken, tho not many made prisoners, being for the most part put to the sword, with the Bishop of Cloghar their general, whose head was cut off and set upon one of the gates of London-derry[1]. The news of this defeat being brought to those in Carlo, who had held out in hopes of relief from their friends in Ulster, together with a great scarcity of provisions in the place, besides the beating down of the little castle that stood at the foot of the bridg on the other side of the river, which happened about the same time, so discouraged those within, that they surrendred the place to the Lord Deputy Ireton upon articles; which he caused punctually to be executed, as his constant manner was[2].

1649
Nov. 6.

1650
July 21.

July 25.

---

[1] This battle took place at Scarriffhollis, near Letterkenny. Coote's despatch is printed in the Appendix to Borlase's History of the Irish Rebellion, p. 28. A day of thanksgiving was ordered by the Parliament for July 26. The Bishop of Clogher was Emer Macmahon, on whom, see Gilbert, Aphorismical Discovery, ii. xlviii-liii. 82-89; Old Parliamentary History, xix. 288. Col. Roger Fenwick, who was killed in this battle, had been governor of Trim in 1647. See 'A great victory against the Rebels in Ireland near Trim on May 24, 1647, by Colonel Fenwicke's forces;' and C. J., vi. 324; Coxe, Hibernia Anglicana, ii. 195.

[2] Carlow or Catherlough Castle was summoned by Ireton, July 2, 1650, and the articles of surrender are dated July 24. It was delivered up on July 25. Borlase, History of the Irish Rebellion, ed. 1743; Appendix, pp. 26-8.

1650   Pursuant to the order of Parliament, appointing me
Lieutenant-General of the Horse in Ireland, the General, as
he was directed by the said order, sent me a commission
to that end; which I received, and gave him an account
of the reception, acquainting him also how sensible I was of
my want of experience to manage so weighty an employment; but that on the other hand I would not fail to
endeavour to discharge my duty with the utmost fidelity.
He replied, that I might rely upon that God to carry me
through the work, who had called me to it; and in the close
of his letter recommended the procuring from the Parliament a settlement upon Sir Hardress Waller of the inheritance of some lands which he then held by lease from
the Earl of Ormond, and for which he paid two hundred
pounds annual rent, as a thing that might be proper for
me to do before my departure for Ireland. I was afterwards informed that Sir Hardress Waller had earnestly
solicited for this employment of Lieutenant-General of the
Horse in Ireland, and that the General not thinking it
convenient to entrust him with it, yet unwilling he should
know so much, perswaded him to believe that the Parliament had over-ruled him therein [1].

The Parliament then passed an Act, constituting Commissioners for the administration of civil affairs in Ireland,
Oct. 4. and agreed upon instructions of sufficient latitude for them
to act by [2], in particular to lay a tax on that nation not
exceeding the sum of thirty thousand pounds: to give
order for the distribution of justice, as near to the rules
of the law as the necessity of the times would permit; and

[1] On June 26, 1651, Parliament at
the suggestion of the Council of
State continued Waller in the possession of a farm for which he had
long been tenant to Ormond, relieving him from the payment of any
rent to the State till further order;
C. J., vi. 433: cf. Tanner MSS., liii.
139. On March 23, 1653, he was
voted Irish lands to the value of
£1200 a year (ib. vii. 270). There
was, however, some delay in carrying out this vote, but on April 1,
1657, Parliament passed a bill for
settling lands in Limerick on Waller
which received the Protector's assent
on June 9 (ib. vii. 492, 516, 553).

[2] The Instructions of the Commissioners are printed; C. J., vi.
479; Old Parliamentary History,
xix. 406. A Life of Miles Corbet is
given in D. N. B., vol. xii.

to consider of a method of proceeding in the courts of
justice there, to be offered to the Parliament for their
approbation. The Commissioners were those that I mentioned before, only Major Salloway desiring to be excused
from that service, Mr. Miles Corbet, a member of Parliament, was inserted in his room.

Some suspicions there were at this time that the Presbyterian party in England, especially those about London,
entertained a private correspondence with their brethren
in Scotland [1]: where tho that nation had received a great
blow at Dunbar, yet it was resolved that their King
should be crowned upon his taking the Solemn League and
Covenant, and obliging himself thereby to endeavour the
extirpation of Popery and Episcopacy. This action was
performed with all the circumstances and solemnities that
could be used in the condition of their affairs. The nobility
swore fidelity to him, and the Marquiss of Argile put the
crown upon his head with his own hands. And now
having a King like other nations, and a covenanting King
too, they doubted not of success under his conduct, presuming by this means most certainly to retrieve all their
losses and reputation. But the Parliament who had removed one King, was not frighted with the setting up of
another, and therefore proceeded in the settlement of their
affairs both military and civil ; and to that end ordered a
thousand pounds to be advanced to the Commissioners
of the civil affairs in Ireland, directing them to receive also
a thousand pounds yearly. They likewise gave orders for
the payment of a thousand pounds to me by way of advance upon my pay as Lieutenant-General of the Horse,
that I might be enabled to furnish my self with tents,
horses, and other things necessary for that service [2]. The

---

[1] See the confessions of Mr. Thomas Coke, Portland MSS., p. 576; and the depositions of the witness at Love's trial.

[2] See C. J., vi. 448. Besides this, the House on July 19 ordered the committee at Worcester House to state and certify Ludlow's accounts for arrears and advances. The committee reported on Dec. 13 that the State owed Ludlow £2091 11s. 1d., which was accordingly voted. The account is reprinted in the Appendix. C. J., vi. 444, 508.

committee of Irish affairs raised also a troop consisting of a hundred horse to accompany me, and armed them with back, breast, head-pieces, pistols, and musquetoons, with two months' pay advanced. The Lord Deputy Ireton's lady, daughter to General Cromwell, prepared to go over with us to her husband, who had removed his head-quarters to Waterford, partly because he thought that place most convenient for the service, as the enemy then lay; and partly from some disgust conceived against Dublin, where the inhabitants had extorted unreasonable rates for their provisions and other necessaries sold to our army at their arrival there for the relief of Ireland. Therefore resolving to pass through South Wales, I hastned out of town before the rest of my company, in order to take leave of my friends in the west; and from thence going to Glamorganshire, I stayed there with some relations of my wife, till the rest of the company came down [1].

Before I left the Parliament, some difference happening between the Countess of Rutland and the Lord Edward Howard of Escrick, Col. Gell, who was a great servant of the countess, informed Major-General Harrison that the Lord Edward Howard, being a member of Parliament and one of the committee at Haberdashers-Hall, had taken divers bribes for the excusing delinquents from seques-tration, and easing them in their compositions; and that in particular he had received a diamond hatband valued at eight hundred pounds, from one Mr. Compton of Sussex; concerning which he could not prevail with any to inform the Parliament. Major-General Harrison being a man of severe principles, and zealous for justice, especially against such as betrayed the publick trust reposed in them, assured him, that if he could satisfy him that the fact was as he affirmed,

---

[1] The date of Ludlow's marriage is uncertain. His seal on the death-warrant of Charles I seems to show that he was then a married man, as the arms look like those of Ludlow impaling Thomas. He married Eliza-beth Thomas, daughter of William Thomas of Wenvoe, Glamorganshire, by Jane, daughter of Sir John Strad-ling, bart., of St. Donats. She was born about 1636. G. T. Clark, The Genealogies of Morgan and Gla-morgan, 1866, p. 558.

he would not fail to inform the Parliament of it : and upon 1650 satisfaction received from the Colonel touching that matter, said in Parliament, that tho the honour of every member was dear to him, and of that gentleman in particular, naming the Lord Howard, because he had so openly owned the interest of the Commonwealth, as to decline his peerage, and to sit upon the foot of his election by the people ; yet he loved justice before all other things, looking upon it to be the honour of the Parliament, and the image of God upon them ; that therefore he durst not refuse to lay this matter before them, though he was very desirous that the said Lord might clear himself of the accusation. The Parliament having received his information, referred the consideration of the matter to a committee, where it was fully examined ; and notwithstanding all the art of counsel learned in the law, who are very skilful at putting a good appearance upon a bad cause, and all the friends the Lord Howard could make, so just and equitable a spirit then governed, that the committee having represented the matter to the Parliament as they found it to be, they dis- 1651 charged him from being a member of Parliament, sent him June 25. to the Tower, and fined him ten thousand pounds[1].

About the beginning of January the Commissioners of Parliament, the Lady Ireton, and my self, met at Milford, in order to embark for Ireland, three men of war lying ready for us in the harbour, with several ships for the transportation of my troop, with our goods and horses. We came to Milford on Saturday, and on Monday following the Lady Ireton and the Commissioners set sail with a fair wind, leaving the Guinea frigat for me, and to be convoy to those vessels that were appointed to transport the horse and other things, of which but one could be ready time enough to set sail with them, my troop being not yet mustered. The next day Mr. Lort, by order of the com-

---

[1] The charge of corruption was brought against Howard on July 30, 1650, and he was condemned on June 25, 1651. He was discharged from the Tower on Aug. 7, 1651, and his fine was remitted on April 5, 1653. C. J., vi. 448, 469, 590, 618 ; vii 274.

mittee of Parliament, mustered my troop, so that I began
to ship them on Wednesday in the afternoon; and on
Thursday morning they being all embarked, we set sail, and
tho the weather proved very calm, we arrived the next
day under the Fort of Duncannon near Waterford; where
I understood that the Lady Ireton and the Commissioners
had landed there the day before, and were gone to the
Lord Deputy at Waterford [1].

Immediately after my arrival I went to wait on the Lord
Deputy Ireton, who was much surprized at my landing so
soon after the rest of the company, and ordered good
quarters to be assigned to my troop, that they might be
refreshed before they entred upon duty: for it was observed, that the English horses were not so fit for service,
till they had been seasoned for some time with the air and
provisions of that country. Having received advice that
the enemy was marched out of Connaught and Limerick
towards our quarters in Munster, he drew a party of horse
and foot out of their winter-quarters, to which they had
been lately sent, and with them endeavoured to find out
the enemy; who upon his advance, retreated into their own
quarters. The Deputy being returned, was very careful to
prepare all things that were necessary for the army, that
they might be ready to march into the field early the next
spring; making provision of tents, arms, clothes and bread
for the souldiers; sending cannon and ammunition of all
sorts up the Shannon towards Limerick by vessels provided to that end; that being the first place which he
designed to attack the following year, having in his last
march, by putting garisons into Castle-Conel, Kilmallock,
and other places, blocked them up in some measure.

The Commissioners of Parliament, of whom the Deputy
was one, spent a considerable time in debating and resolving
in what manner justice should be administered for the
present in each precinct, till the state of affairs could be
reduced into a more exact order; and accounting it most

---

[1] The four Commissioners wrote to Lenthall announcing their arrival Jan.
25, 165$\frac{0}{1}$. See Appendix.

just, that those who had the most immediate advantage by the war, should bear the principal burden of it, they laid upon the nation of Ireland a tax proportionable to their ability; for the raising of which, together with the excise and customs that by our authority from the Parliament we were impowered to impose, we appointed commissioners for the precincts of Dublin, Waterford, Cork, Clonmel, Kilkenny and Ulster, who were to proceed according to such rules as they should receive from time to time from the Parliament's Commissioners. The governour of each precinct was appointed one of the commissioners of that precinct, Col. Hewetson being for Dublin, Sir Charles Coote and Col. Venables for Ulster, Col. Daniel Axtel for Kilkenny, Col. Zanchey for Clonmel, Col. Phaier for the county of Cork, and Col. Laurence for the county of Waterford. They appointed Col. Thomas Herbert and Col. Markham to be inspectors over the rest, and to go from place to place to see that their instructions were put in execution. Commissioners were also appointed in the several precincts for the more equal distribution of justice; and a proclamation was published [1], forbidding the killing of lambs or calves for the year next ensuing, that the country might recover a stock again, which had been so exhausted by the wars, that many of the natives who had committed all manner of waste upon the possessions of the English, were driven to such extremities that they starved with hunger; and I have been informed by persons deserving credit, that the same calamity fell upon them even in the first year of the rebellion, through the depredations of the Irish; and that they roasted men, and eat them, to supply their necessities. In conjunction with this evil they were also afflicted with the plague, which was supposed to have been brought amongst them by a ship from Spain, and bound to Galway, from whence the infection spread itself through most parts of the country, and amongst

1651

Feb. 8.

---

[1] This proclamation, to be in force till Aug. 1, 1651, signed by Ludlow, Corbet, Jones and Weaver, is printed in Several Proceedings, p. 1278. Cf. Prendergast, Cromwellian Settlement, p. 79.

others had reached Waterford, where several died of it, and particularly a kinswoman of mine, who having been driven out of Ireland with her husband and children at the breaking out of the rebellion, took the opportunity to return thither with me, and died there, with one of her children, very suddenly, having dined with me the day before. The spring approaching, we removed to Kilkenny, that place lying most convenient for the distribution of tents, clothes, and all other things necessary for the use of the army [1]: it was also near the enemy's quarters, and thereby thought most proper to favour any attempt against them from thence. Col. Reynolds, who returned from England with us, being made Commissary-General of the Horse in Ireland, was sent with a party into the King and Queen's county, and put a garison into Marriborough, appointing Major Owen to be governour of the place [2]. At his return it was agreed that a detachment from Nenagh, where Col. Abbot commanded, another from Cashil and those parts, and a third from Kilkenny, should march from their respective garisons, and contrive it so as to fall upon the quarters of Col. Fitzpatrick at the same time, which

---

[1] Two letters written by the Commissioners during their stay at Kilkenny are printed in the Appendix. From the same place they issued a number of proclamations. 1. For the preservation of houses in cities and garrison towns. March 19. 2. Against the waste of timber and wood in general. March 22. 3. For the apprehension of persons concerned in the massacres of 1641. April 22. 4. Prohibiting the export of horses, cattle and sheep, for one year. April 22. 5. For removing the families of persons in actual rebellion out of Parliamentary garrisons. April 28. 6. For the preservation of hay-meadows and the storage of hay. April 28. The Commissioners also issued proclamations: 7. Against the export of hides and leather. Cashel, May 20. 8. For the apprehension of vagrants. Clonmel, May 15. 9. On the disposal of the profits of ecclesiastical benefices. Clonmel, May 21. In addition to these, Ireton published, by his authority as general, a proclamation prohibiting officers and soldiers from marrying Irish women. Waterford, May 1. These proclamations are printed in Several Proceedings in Parliament for 1651, pp. 1278-80, 1454-61. Mr. Gilbert reprints a portion of the last in the Aphorismical Discovery, iii. 225.

[2] On this expedition, see an anonymous letter in Mercurius Politicus. p. 738, dated March 29, 1651, and also Several Proceedings, p. 1242.

were advantageously situated, encompassed with woods and bogs, and inaccessible, except by three very narrow and difficult ways, by which they were ordered to attack him separately. This enterprize was so well effected, that the place was taken, with many of the enemy's horse, besides a great number of men killed or made prisoners. At this time it happened that Col. Axtell, than whom no man was better acquainted with the country of Ireland, was accused for not performing some conditions said to have been promised to the enemy, who pretended that after they had surrendred upon assurance of mercy, they were all put to the sword, except a few who made their escape. The Colonel endeavoured to prove, that no conditions had been granted; that they were taken by force, and that they who had shewed no mercy, cöuld not deserve to receive any[1]. Tho the proof was not clear that he had promised them their lives, yet because it appeared that some of the souldiers had thrown out some expressions tending that way to the enemy, the Deputy was so great a friend to justice, even where an enemy was concerned, that tho Col. Axtell was a person extraordinarily qualified for the service of that conjuncture, he, together with the Council of War, at which the Commissioners of the Parliament were also present, suspended him from his employment.

The Lord Broghil[2], who had conceived great hopes of obtaining the command of the horse, or at least to be made a general officer, well knowing his own merit, and thereupon thinking himself neglected, made his complaint to the Deputy in a letter directed to him, and sent unsealed in

---

[1] Axtell had defeated the Marquis of Clanricarde at Meleek, Oct. 25. 1650; Old Parliamentary History, xix. 439. For his other exploits, see Mercurius Politicus for 1650, pp. 313, 411, 418. His cruelties are mentioned in 'A Collection of some of the Massacres committed on the Irish since 1641,' appended to Clarendon's Rebellion, ed. 1849, vii. 236.

[2] Roger Boyle, Lord Broghil, created Earl of Orrery in 1660. A life of him by his chaplain Thomas Morrice is prefixed to the collection of his papers published in 1743. It contains a number of fictions about the relations of Broghil with Cromwell and Ireton. Broghil had already been granted £1000 a year out of Lord Muskerry's estates; Cal. S. P., Dom., 1649–50, p. 473.

another to Adjutant-General Allen ; wherein enumerating the services he had done, the losses he had sustained, and the slender encouragements he had received, he declared his resolution not to obey the commands of any other but of General Cromwell and him. In answer to this the Deputy by another letter acquainted him, that he was sorry to find such a spirit in him ; and particularly that he should discover it at such a time when the season for action was drawing on, desiring him to come to the head-quarters, that they might confer together touching this matter. At his coming the Deputy consulted with the Commissioners what course to take in this affair. I excused my self to them from giving my advice, (his principal objection being against me) telling them, I was convinced that he had some ground for his dissatisfaction, by reason of his interest and experience in the country; I being in those respects much inferiour to him, and should not have had the confidence to have undertaken the employment I possessed, but in pure obedience to those who were in authority. The Deputy assured me, that they were abundantly satisfied with the clearness of my proceeding, and no less of my abilities to discharge the trust reposed in me, and to perform the duties of my employments, of which he was pleased to say, I had given sufficient demonstration, as well as of a constant and hearty affection to the publick interest. In conclusion, the debate concerning the Lord Broghill was brought to this question ; Whether he should be wholly laid aside, or whether something should be done in order to content him for the present, by conferring upon him some office of profit, and the title of a general officer? The latter was agreed upon, and he declared Lieutenant-General of the Ordinance in Ireland.

The Commissioners having settled affairs as well as they could, and finding the Deputy to be employed in making all necessary preparations for the ensuing service, took that opportunity to go to regulate affairs at Dublin, where after they had dispatched the publick business, in which they spent about a week, and provided houses to receive their families when they should arrive from England, they returned to Kilkenny. The enemy, who had a party of horse in those parts, had designed to surprize them in their way to Dublin, and again in their return to us; but finding them attended by a strong guard, they durst not venture to attempt it.

The enemy's forces being retreated into Connaught, which province was covered by the Shannon, and keeping strong guards upon the bridges and fords of that river, the reduction of Limerick could not well be expected till we had blocked them up on both sides. In order to which it was resolved, that Sir Charles Coote, who had with him between four and five thousand horse and foot, should march into Connaught by the way of Ballyshannon, a passage on the side of Ulster, not far distant from the sea ; and Commissary-General Reynolds was sent with his regiment of horse to his assistance.

Col. Axtell and some others about this time going for England, were taken by a pirate belonging to Scilly, whither they were all carried prisoners : the Irish who were many in the island, against whom Col. Axtell had been very active, and who had heard of the charge lately exhibited against him, pressed hard for the taking away his life. But upon consideration of the preparations making by the Parliament to send a fleet with souldiers to reduce that island, it was not thought convenient to attempt any thing against him, tho they had a strong inclination to it, for fear of an exemplary retaliation [1].

In the mean time the Parliament sent a fleet with some land-forces to reduce the Isle of Jersey, with the castle which was kept by Sir Philip Carteret for Prince Charles. Col. Haines who commanded them, met with some opposition at his landing ; but having brought his men ashore, the island generally submitted to the Parliament. The castle

---

[1] The capture of Colonels Axtell, Sadler, and Le Hunt is mentioned by Heath (p. 523), and recorded in Mercurius Politicus for March 20-27, 1651; see also Several Proceedings, March 27, April 3, 1651. They were released in June by Blake's capture of the islands.

having made some resistance, was soon after surrendred also [1].

The affairs of the Commonwealth being thus successful, and their authority acknowledged by the applications of agents and ambassadors from foreign nations to them, it was resolved to send some ministers abroad to entertain a good correspondence with our neighbours, and to preserve the interests of the subjects of this nation in those parts. To that effect the Lord Chief Justice St. Johns was dispatched with the character of ambassador extraordinary to the States of the United Netherlands, with whom Mr. Walter Strickland. our resident there, was joined in commission ; and to prevent such another attempt as had been made upon our former agent, forty gentlemen were appointed to attend him for his security and honour, ten thousand pounds being delivered to the Lord Ambassador's steward for the expence of the embassy. Yet this great equipage was not sufficient to prevent a publick affront which was offered him by Prince Edward, one of the Palatine family, as he was passing the streets. But the Prince immediately retiring to some place out of the jurisdiction of the States, secured himself from any prosecution, tho they pretended upon the complaint of our ambassadors, that they were ready to do them what right they could. The negotiation of our ministers, which was designed to procure a nearer conjunction and coalition between the two states, proved also ineffectual, the province of Holland being not so much inclined to consent to it as was expected, and Frizeland, with most of the rest of the provinces, entirely against it; presuming that such a conjunction as was demanded would be no less than rendring those countries a province to England : so that our ambassadors having used all possible means to succeed in their business, and

[1] The expedition to Jersey sailed on Oct. 17 and effected a landing on Oct. 22. Mount Orgueil Castle surrendered Oct. 28, and Elizabeth Castle on Dec. 15. Col. James Heane commanded the land forces and Blake the fleet. Castle Cornet in Guernsey was taken Dec. 19. See Mereurius Politicus, pp. 1170, 1175, 1187, 1213, 1307, 1318, 1493; Several Proceedings in Parliament, pp. 1734, 1843.

finding the Dutch unwilling to conclude with us whilst the 1651
King had an army in the field, returned to England without
effecting any thing but the expence of a great sum of
money [1].   This disappointment sat so heavy upon the
haughty spirit of the Lord Chief Justice St. Johns, that he
reported these transactions with the highest aggravations
against the States, and thereby was a principal instrument
to prevail with the Council of State to move the Parliament
to pass an Act prohibiting foreign ships from bringing any Oct. 9.
merchandizes into England, except such as should be of the
growth or manufacture of that country to which the said
ships did belong.   This law, tho just in itself, and very
advantageous to the English nation, was so highly resented
by the Dutch, who had for a long time driven the trade of
Europe by the great number of their ships, that it soon
proved to be the ball of contention between the two nations.

During these transactions, the Deputy of Ireland labouring with all diligence to carry on the publick service,
ordered the army to rendezvouz at Cashil; from whence he May 20.
marched by the way of Nenagh to that part of the river
Shannon which lies over against Killalo, where the Earl of May 23.
Castlehaven lay with about two thousand horse and foot,
disposed along the side of the river, and defended by breast-
works cast up for their security, resolving to endeavour to
obstruct our passage into Connaught.   The Deputy, as if

---

[1] On St. John's Embassy to Holland, see Geddes, John de Witt, i.
157–180; Godwin, Commonwealth
of England, iii. 375; Portland
MSS., i. 557-8, 561, 563, 564,
567, 568, 569. St. John proposed
'that the amity and good correspondence which hath anciently been
between the English nation and the
United Provinces be not only renewed and preserved inviolably, but
that a more strict and intimate
alliance and union be entered into
by them, whereby there may be a
more intrinsical and mutual interest
of each in other than hath hitherto
been, for the good of both.' This
general proposition was made more
definite a few days later: 'We pro-
pound that the two Commonwealths
may be confederated friends, joined
and allied together for the defence
and preservation of the liberty and
freedoms of the people of each,
against all whomsoever that shall
attempt the disturbance of either
State, by sea or land, or be declared
enemies to the freedom and liberty
of the people living under either of
the said governments.' Geddes, pp.
163, 171.

1651 he had intended to divert the course of the river, set the souldiers and pioneers at work to take the ground lower on our side, that the water venting it self into the passage, the river might become fordable; which so alarmed the enemy, that they drew out most of their men to oppose us. Whilst they were thus amused, the Deputy taking me with him, and a guard of horse, marched privately by the side of the Shannon, in order to find a convenient place to pass that river. The ways were almost impassable by reason of the bogs, tho Col. Reeves and others who commanded in those parts had repaired them with hurdles as well as they could. Being advanced about half way from Killalo to Castle-Conel, we found a place that answered our desires, where a bridg had formerly been, with an old castle still standing at the foot of it on the other side of the river. We took only a short view of the place, lest we should give occasion to the enemy to suspect our design. The way hither from our camp was so full of bogs, that neither horse nor man could pass without great danger. so that we were necessitated to mend them, by laying hurdles and great pieces of timber across in order to bear our carriages: which we did under pretence of making a passable way between our camp and Castle-Conel, a garison of ours, where provisions were laid up for the army. It was about ten days before all things necessary to this design could be prepared, and then Col. Reeves was commanded to bring three boats which he had to a place appointed for that purpose, by one a clock in the morning. At the beginning of the night three regiments of foot, and one of horse, with four pieces of cannon, marched silently towards the place where the boats were ordered to

June 2. lie, and arrived there an hour before day [1]. They found but two boats waiting for them, yet they served to carry over three files of musqueteers and six troopers, who having unsaddled their horses, caused them to swim by the boat,

---

[1] Accounts of the passage of the Shannon are given in the diary of one of Ireton's officers printed by Mr. Gilbert, Aphorismical Discovery, iii. 230, and in an anonymous letter printed in Mercurius Politicus, p. 887. See also Castlehaven's Memoirs.

and were safely landed on the other side. Two sentinels of the enemy were in the castle, of whom one was killed by our men, and the other made his escape. Our boats had transported about sixty foot and twenty horse before any enemy appeared ; but then some of their horse coming up skirmished with ours, wherein one Mr. How, a hopeful daring young gentleman, who had accompanied me into Ireland, distinguished himself. About a thousand of the enemy's foot advancing, our horse was commanded to retire, which they did, not without some reluctancy; but the hasty march of their foot was retarded by our guns which we had planted on a hill on our side of the river, from whence we fired so thick upon them, that they were forced to retreat under the shelter of a rising ground ; where after they had been a while, and considered what to do, finding ours coming over apace to them, instead of attacking us, they began to think it high time to provide against our falling upon them ; and having sent to all their guards upon the river to draw off, they retreated farther through the woods into their own quarters. We were no sooner got over the river, but we received advice that Sir Charles Coote and Commissary-General Reynolds were entred into Connaught, and advanced as far as Athenree. Our ships were also come up the river of Limerick with our artillery, ammunition, provisions, and all things necessary for the siege of Limerick. And now the Deputy thinking himself abundantly provided for the reduction of that important place, and not knowing what necessities the party with Sir Charles Coote might be driven to, the chief of the enemy's strength being drawn that way, he resolved to send a party of horse to him. But not being able to spare above a thousand horse for that service, he was unwilling to desire me to command them, tho he had no person with him that he could conveniently make use of therein, most of the colonels of horse being employed in their respective precincts to secure them from the incursions of the enemies. This I perceived, and offered to march with them : whereupon the Deputy furnished me with three majors, who were Major Warden of my own regiment of horse, Major Owen of the regiment of Commissary-General Reynolds, and Major Bolton of a regiment of dragoons,

a brave and diligent officer[1]. We began our march about five in the afternoon, and by twelve at night having marched between sixteen and seventeen miles, we dismounted to forage our horses, and rest ourselves. Before day we mounted and continued our march through a desolate country, the people being fled, and no provisions to be had but what we carried with us. About ten in the morning our forlorn perceived a Creaght, as the country people call it, where half a dozen families with their cattle were got together. Some of those who saw them first, presuming all the Irish in that country to be enemies, began to kill them; of which having notice, I put a stop to it, and took a share with them of a pot of sowr milk, which seemed to me the most pleasant liquor that ever I drank. In the afternoon we found the ways exceeding bad, and almost impassable, many of the hurdles which had been laid upon them being drawn away, as we supposed by the enemy: yet in a little more than twenty-four hours we had marched about forty miles, and were informed that Sir Charles Coote was besieging Portumna, a house of the Earl of Clanrickard, and that the enemies were about Athenree. Upon this notice, leaving my party advantageously posted in a place furnished with provisions for themselves and horses, I took with me sixty horse, and went to Portumna, to be informed more particularly concerning the state of affairs. At my arrival I understood that an attempt had been made upon the place, wherein our men had been repulsed; but that the enemy, having a large line to keep, and many poor people within, fearing to hazard another assault, had agreed to surrender upon articles next morning, which was done accordingly[2]. And now having found Sir Charles Coote's

---

[1] See Aphorismical Discovery, iii. 233. Ludlow's force consisted of ten troops of horse and six of dragoons.

[2] Portumna was taken before June 9. A letter of Ludlow's dated June 12, from Loughrea, is printed in the Appendix. The articles for

party in good condition, and able to deal with the enemies on that side, I returned to my body of horse, with which and five hundred more that joined me, commanded by Commissary-General Reynolds, I followed and endeavoured to find out the enemy; but they removed from one place to another with such expedition, that we could not overtake them, having left their carriages, in order to march the lighter, at a castle belonging to one Mr. Brabston, situated upon a considerable pass [1]. This place I endeavoured to reduce ; and tho it was indifferently strong, and we very ill provided for such an attempt, yet after some resistance the enemies delivered it upon articles, whereby they were permitted to carry off whatsoever belonged properly to them ; the tents and draught-oxen remaining in our possession, with several other things belonging to the Earl of Clanrickard, whom the Earl of Ormond had constituted his Deputy in those parts. Having put a garison into this place, and sent back Commissary-General Reynolds with his party to Portumna, I marched with my horse towards Limerick, and came to Gourtenshegore, a castle belonging to Sir Dermot O'Shortness, who was then gone to Galway, but had left his tenants with some souldiers, and one Foliot an Englishman to command them, in the castle [2]. At my coming before it I summoned them to submit, offering them, that in case they would dismiss their souldiers, and promise to live quietly in the obedience of the Parliament, I would leave no garison in the place, nor suffer any prejudice to be done to them. They pretending they had already submitted to Sir Charles Coote, refused to deliver the castle to any other. Tho I took this to be only a pretence, yet to leave them without excuse, and to prevent all exceptions, I

---

the surrender of Athlone are dated June 18, it was to be given up on the 22nd. Gilbert, *Aphorismical Discovery*, iii. 159. Letters of Sir Charles Coote relating to this campaign are printed in *Mercurius Politicus*, pp. 889, 905, 1246.

[1] Anthony Brabason of Ballinasloe

in county Roscommon. See a deposition concerning him printed in the Appendix to Rep. xiv. of the Deputy Keeper of the Irish Records, p. 39.

[2] Compare *Aphorismical Discovery*, iii. 239; *Mercurius Politicus*, p. 931.

sent to Sir Charles Coote to desire him to let me know how the matter stood, and to direct them to deliver the place to me. Having received an answer to my letter from Sir Charles Coote, I sent it to them, telling them, that now I expected their obedience; but instead of that they sent me a defiance, and sounded their bagpipes in contempt of us; to which they were chiefly encouraged by one of the country, whom I had sent to bring in to me some iron bars, sledges, and pickaxes, and who under colour of going to fetch them, ran away to the enemy, and acquainted them with our want of artillery and instruments to force them. I gave orders to take up all the horses from grass, to bridle and saddle them, and to tie them to the tents of their respective troops, commanding two troops to mount the guard, and to send out scouts to discover if any enemy were near. The rest of the men I drew into several parties, and assigned them their particular attacks: every souldier carried a fagot before him, as well to defend himself, as to fill up the enemy's trenches, or to fire the gates, as there should be occasion. On one side of the wall there was an earth-work about eleven foot high, with a trench of equal breadth without. The wall of the court was about twelve foot high, well flanked. On the other side the place was secured by a river. Upon our first approach the enemy shot very thick upon us, and killed two of our men, which so enraged the rest, that they ran up to the works, and helping one another to the top of them, beat off the enemy, following them so close, that by means of some ladders which those within had made use of, they got into the court, and put to the sword most of those they found there, the enemy not daring to open the gate to receive their friends. Those of ours who had entred the court, having no instruments to force the house, made use of a wooden bar which they found, and with which they wrested out the iron bars of a strong stone window about six foot from the ground, and forced the enemy by their shot out of that room, where being entred, they put to the sword those that were there. Lieutenant Foliot finding his case desperate, resolved to sell his life at as dear a rate as he could, and charged our men, who were nine or ten in number, with a tuck in one hand, and a stilletto in the other, defending himself so well with the one, and pressing them so hard with the other, that they all gave ground ; but he closing with one of them whom he had wounded, and probably might have killed, gave an opportunity to another to run him through the body, by which wound he fell, and the house was quickly cleared of the rest. Most of the principal of the enemies being got into the castle, our men fired a great number of fagots at the gates, which burned so furiously, that the flame took hold of the floors and other timber within through the iron grate, which being perceived by those in the castle, they hung out a white flag, begging earnestly for mercy, and that we would take away the fire. I commanded my men to leave shooting, and acquainted the besieged, that if they expected any favour from us, they must throw down their arms, which they presently did : whereupon I ordered the fire to be taken away, and gave a souldier twenty shillings to fetch out two barrels of powder that was near the fire, which continued to burn so fiercely that we could not put it out, but were obliged to throw up skains of match into the chambers, by which those in the castle descended to us, being about fourscore in number, besides many women and children. We secured the men till the next morning, when I called a council of war ; and being pressed by the officers, that some of the principal of them might be punished with death for their obstinacy, I consented to their demand, provided it might not extend to such as had been drawn in by the malice of others. Those who were tenants to Sir Dermot O'Shortness, and country-men, I dismissed to their habitations, upon promise to behave themselves peaceably, and to engage against us no more : the rest of them we carried away with us. Whilst we were spending our time in sending to Sir Charles Coote, and expecting his answer, I had sent a party of horse to find out some of the enemies that were marched towards the barony of Burren ; and tho they could not overtake them,

1651

June 17.

yet they met with four or five hundred head of cattle, and seized them, which proved a great refreshment to our party, and to the army that was besieging Limerick, whither we returned, and gave an account of our proceedings to the Deputy, who expressed himself well satisfied with the same [1].

At my return I found that our army had possessed themselves of one of the enemy's forts that stood in the midst of the Shannon upon the fishing ware, in this manner. A small battery of two guns being erected against it, one of them was fired into a room, and breaking the leg of a souldier there, so frighted the rest, that betaking themselves to their boats, they abandoned the place; which ours perceiving, fired so thick upon them with their

June 16.

shot, that all those who were in one of the boats, whether moved by fear or promise of life I know not, surrendred to our men; yet some of them were put to the sword, at which the Deputy was much troubled, judging that they would not have quitted the means they had in their hands for their preservation, but upon terms of advantage, and therefore referred the matter to be examined by a court martial [2].

Those in the town having considered of the summons sent to them by the Deputy for the surrender of the place,

June 18.

agreed to treat concerning articles, supposing that they might obtain more favourable conditions than when they should be driven to extremities. Accordingly six commissioners were appointed on each side. Those for the enemy were Major-General Purcel, Mr. Stockdale, Recorder of the town. Col. Butler, Jeffrey Barrow, who had been one of their Supreme Council, Mr. Baggot, and one more whose name I do not remember. The commissioners

---

[1] Ireton gives an account of Ludlow's expedition in a letter to the Speaker dated June 27, 1651, printed in Mercurius Politicus, p. 931.

[2] See Mercurius Politicus, pp. 931, 975. 985, and Ireton's fine letter of July 15, 1651; Several Proceedings, p. 1486. Ireton cashiered Col. Tothill and his ensign for this breach of faith. This took place on June 16. Aphorismical Discovery, iii. 239.

nominated by the Deputy were Major-General Waller, Col.
Cromwell, Major Smith, Adjutant-General Allen, my self,
and one more whom I have also forgot. We met them in
a tent placed between the town and our camp, where we
dined together, and treated of conditions for several days;
but they having great expectations of relief, either by the
King's success against us in Scotland, or by the drawing
together of their own parties in Ireland, who were able to
form an army more numerous than ours, insisted upon such
excessive terms, that the treaty was broken up without
coming to any conclusion[1]. The fort which we were preparing in order to block them up on one side of the town
being almost finished, and materials ready for building a
bridg to be laid over the Shannon to preserve a communication between our forces on each side, we resolved to
endeavour the reduction of a castle possessed by the
enemy, and standing beyond their bridg. To that end a
battery was erected, and a breach being made, the Deputy
remembring the vigour of the troopers in the action at
Gourtenshegore, desired that one might be drawn out of
each troop to be an example to the foot that were to storm :
which being done, they were armed with back, breast, and
head-piece, and furnished with hand-granadoes. One Mr.
Hacket, a stout gentleman of the guard, was made choice of
to lead them on, who were in all not above twenty. This June 21.
design succeeded beyond expectation; for our men having
thrown in their grenadoes, marched up to the breach, and
entred with Mr. Hacket at the head of them, being followed
by those who were ordered to sustain them. The enemy
not being able to stand before them, quitted the place, and
retired by the bridg into the town. The castle was immediately searched, and four or five barrels of powder were
found in a vault ready to take fire by a lighted match left
there by the enemy on purpose to blow up our men. The
Deputy gave Mr. Hacket and the rest of the troopers a
gratuity for their good service, and upon the encouragement

[1] The conditions offered and demanded are given by Mr. Gilbert, Aphorismical Discovery, iii. 241-4.

1651 of this success, formed a design to possess himself of an island that lay near the town, containing about forty or fifty acres of ground and encompassed by the river: in order to which boats were prepared, and floats sufficient to transport three hundred men at once, and orders given to fall down the river about midnight. Three regiments of foot and one of horse were appointed to be wafted over.

June 23. The first three hundred, being all foot, were commanded by Lieutenant-Colonel Walker, who being landed on the island with his men, marched up to the enemy's breastwork, which they had cast up quite round the place; but they having discovered our men before their landing, had drawn most of their forces together to oppose them; so that being oppressed by the enemy's numbers, they were most of them forced into the water, and all either killed or drowned. except two or three only who came back to the camp. Our bridg being finished, and a small fort to defend it erected at the foot of it, the Deputy, with most part of the army, marched over to the other side of the river, where he marked out ground for three bodies of men to encamp separately, each to consist of about two thousand, giving orders for the fortifying of those places, assigning to each regiment their proportion, and quartering them by brigades in the most convenient manner he could, either to defend themselves, to relieve each other, or to annoy the enemy: and as soon as the great fort on which our men had been long working was rendred defensible, he drew off all our forces from this side of the river, except a thousand foot, and about three hundred horse.

In the mean time the enemy was endeavouring to draw their forces together to relieve the place, well knowing of what importance it was to their affairs. To that end the Lord Muskerry had brought together about five thousand horse and foot in the counties of Cork and Kerry, and David Rock between two or three thousand more in the county of Clare. The Lord Broghil and Major Wallis

July 19. were sent to oppose Lord Muskerry, whilst I with another detachment was ordered to look after the other. The

Lord Broghil soon met with the Lord Muskerry, and after some dispute entirely defeated him, killing many of the Irish, and taking others prisoners, with little loss on our side[1]. I passed the river at Inchecroghnan, of which the enemy having advice, drew off their forces from Caricgoholt, a garison of ours, which they were besieging, whereby Capt. Lucas, who was governour of the place, wanting provisions, took that opportunity to quit it; and being joined by Capt. Taff's dragoons, came safe to us. Whilst I was endeavouring to find out the enemy, advice was brought to me, that they, to the number of three thousand horse and foot, were marching with all diligence to possess themselves of the pass at Inchecroghnan, thereby designing to obstruct our return to the army before Limerick : which being confirmed by a letter we intercepted, I drew out two hundred and fifty horse with sixty dragoons, and sent them before, with orders to take possession of the pass, marching after them with the rest of my party. When I was almost come to the pass, I was informed by those sent before, that they had found a small number of the enemy's horse there, who immediately retreated upon the advance of our men, some of whom were in pursuit of them. Presently after advice was brought, that the enemy made good a pass leading to some woods and bogs which they used for a retreat; whereupon I went to take a view of their posture, that if it were necessary I might order a greater force to succour our men. Being come up to the place where the dispute was, I found that Connor O'Brian, deputed by the Lord Inchequin to command in the county of Clare, had been shot from his horse, and carried away by his party[2]. The enemy retreated to a pass, and fired thick upon us; but we advancing within pistol-shot of them, they quitted their ground, and betook themselves to their woods and bogs.

[1] An account of this victory is given in The Aphorismical Discovery, iii. 247. On Broghil's other exploits see his letter, Several Proceedings, pp. 14, 16; Mercurius Politicus, pp. 896, 995; Tanner MSS., liv. 76.

[2] See the case of the widow of Connor O'Brien; Prendergast, Cromwellian Settlement, p. 68.

1651

July 25.

Divers of them were killed in the pursuit; yet the ground was so advantagious to them, and their heels so good, that tho we pursued them with all possible diligence, and sent out parties several ways, yet we could not take above two or three of them prisoners. Having dispersed this party, and relieved the garison of Caricgoholt, I returned to the army before Limerick, where I found a considerable progress made in our works on the other side of the town, and a reinforcement from England of between three and four thousand foot, whose arrival was very seasonable and welcome to us, having lost many men by hard service, change of food, and alteration of the climate [1]. The Deputy fearing that the plague, which raged fiercely in Limerick, might reach our army, and to the end that care might be taken of our sick and wounded men, caused an hospital to be prepared, and furnished with all things necessary; and whilst the works were finishing against the town, he went to visit the garison of Killalo, and to order a bridg to be made over the river at that place, for the better communication of the counties of Tipperary and Clare. I accompanied him in this journey, and having passed all places of danger, he left his guard to refresh themselves, and rode so hard that he spoiled many horses, and hazarded some of the men; but he was so diligent in the publick service, and so careless of every

---

[1] 'Above 3000 recruits,' says a letter written in June, 1651, 'are landed since May 19, and 2000 before; and indeed choicer men by press I mean for bodies) than the volunteers, which were so full of children, that the officers have abused their trust; in bringing such who are fitter for school than manlike exercises.' The same paper under Wednesday, June 25, states, 'It appears by letters from Chester, that they have shipped lately for Ireland of impressed soldiers from Chester-water, 315, and from Liverpool 855, from Bristol 1700, from Minehead and Appledore 750, from Bideford 600, from Milford-Haven 900, from Beaumoris 275, in all 4795, and more are daily going. Besides these impressed men there have since March last been transported into Ireland of volunteers and soldiers drawn out of garrisons in England, 4350 and odd, so that the whole number of recruits already sent into Ireland this summer, is 9145.' Mercurius Politicus, pp. 890. 891. By an Act passed April 18, 1651, Parliament had ordered 10,000 pressed men to be levied in England and Wales. Waller with 2500 recruits joined Ireton on June 27. Aphorismical Discovery, iii. 241.

thing that belonged to himself, that he never regarded 1651
what clothes or food he used, what hour he went to rest,
or what horse he mounted.

In the mean time our army in Scotland, lying near
the enemy's camp at Torwood, who were plentifully furnished with provisions from the county of Fife, it was
resolved that a party of ours, commanded by Colonel
Overton, should be sent in boats from Leith and Edinburgh into that county, to contrive some way to prevent
the enemy's supplies from thence. This party was followed by four regiments of horse and foot commanded
by Major-General Lambert. Of which the enemy having
notice, sent Sir John Brown, who was esteemed to be
a person of courage and conduct, with part of their army
to oppose them. It was not long before the two parties
came to an engagement, wherein the enemy was totally
routed; Sir John Brown who commanded them, with about July 20.
two thousand of his men killed, many made prisoners, and
all their baggage taken [1]. The Scots being deprived of
their usual supplies from Fife, and not expecting any from
foreign parts, by reason of the number of our ships cruizing
on their coast, resolved to march into England, having
received encouragement so to do from their old and new
friends there. They passed the river Tweed near Carlisle,
there being a strong garison in Berwick for the Parliament,
and were considerably advanced on their march before
our army in Scotland were acquainted with their design.
Major-General Harrison, with about four thousand horse
and foot, somewhat obstructed their march, tho he was not
considerable enough to fight them; and being joined by
Major-General Lambert with a party of horse from the army,
they observed the enemy so closely as to keep them from
excursions, and to prevent others from joining with them [2].
The Scots who were in great expectation of assistance from
Wales, and relied much upon Col. Massey's interest in
Glocestershire, advanced that way. Few of the country

---

[1] See Carlyle's Cromwell, Letter clxxv, &c.

[2] See Carlyle's Cromwell, Letter clxxx.

1651 came in to them; but on the other side, so affectionate were the people to the Commonwealth, that they brought in horse and foot from all parts to assist the Parliament: insomuch that their number was by many thought sufficient to have beaten the enemy without the assistance of the army; some even of the excluded members appearing in arms, and leading regiments against the common enemy.

At the same time, upon notice that the Earl of Derby was at the head of fifteen hundred horse and foot in Lancashire, Col. Lilburn was sent that way with about eight hundred men, who meeting with the Earl's forces near Wigan, after a sharp dispute for about an hour, totally routed them. The number of the slain was considerable on the enemy's side: the Lord Widdrington with other persons of quality were killed. All their baggage was taken, and three or four hundred made prisoners, with the loss only of one officer, and about ten private souldiers of Col. Lilburn's [1]. The Earl of Derby himself was wounded,

Aug. 25. and escaped to Worcester; but bringing not above thirty tired horse with him, the townsmen began to repent their revolt from the Parliament.

The Scots having possessed themselves of the city of

Aug. 22. Worcester [2], and fortified it as well as they could in so short a time, resolved to attack our army, which was now advanced to that place, and posted on each side of the Severn, ready to receive them, with General Cromwell at their head. Their first attack was made upon Lieutenant-General Fleetwood's quarters that were on the other side of the river, who with some forces of the army, and a reinforcement of the militia, made a vigorous resistance. The General fearing he might be overpower'd, dispatch'd some troops to his assistance by a bridg laid over the river, commanding Major-General Lambert to send another

[1] Lilburn's letters to Cromwell and Lenthall are printed in Cary's Memorials of the Civil War, ii. 338.

[2] An account of the loss of Worcester drawn up by the Parliamentary committee is printed by Cary, ii. 335.

detachment to the same purpose; but he desired to be excused, alledging, that if the enemy should alter their course, and fall upon those on this side, they might probably cut off all that remained; which was not unlikely, for soon after most of the enemy's strength fell upon that part of the army where the General and Major-General Lambert were. The battel was fought with various success for a considerable time; but at length the Scots army was broken, and quitting their ground, retreated in great disorder to the town, where they endeavoured to defend themselves. Major-General Harrison, Col. Croxton, and the forces of Cheshire, entred the place at their heels; and being followed by the rest of the army, soon finished the dispute, and totally defeated the enemy. Three English Earls, seven Scots Lords, and above six hundred officers, besides ten thousand private souldiers, were made prisoners. The King's standard, and a hundred [and] fifty-eight colours, with all their artillery, ammunition and baggage, was also taken. On our side, Quarter-master General Mosely, and Capt. Jones, with about a hundred private souldiers, were killed, and Capt. Howard, with one Captain more, and about three hundred souldiers wounded. This victory was obtained by the Parliament's forces on the 3d of September, being the same day of the same month that the Scots had been defeated at Dunbar the preceding year[1]. Col. Massey escaped into Leicestershire, but being dangerously wounded, found himself not able to continue his way, and fearing to be knock'd on the head by the country, delivered himself to the Countess of Stamford, mother to the Lord Grey of Grooby, who caused his wounds to be carefully dressed, and sent notice of his surrender to the army. Whereupon a party was dispatched with orders to conduct him from thence to London, as soon as he should be fit to travel, which was done, and he committed prisoner to the Tower. The Scots King with the Lord Wilmot were concealed by three countrymen, till they could furnish him

[1] For accounts of Worcester, see Carlyle's Cromwell, Letters clxxxii, clxxxiii; Cary, ii. 353–363.

1651   with a horse, with which he crossed the country to one
Mr. Gunter's near Shoreham in Sussex, carrying one Mrs.
Lane behind him, from whence in a small bark he escaped
Oct. 15.   to France.

The General after this action, which he called the
crowning victory, took upon him a more stately behaviour,
and chose new friends; neither must it be omitted, that
instead of acknowledging the services of those who came
from all parts to assist against the common enemy, tho he
knew they had deserved as much honour as himself and the
standing army, he frowned upon them, and the very next day
after the fight dismissed and sent them home, well knowing,
that a useful and experienced militia was more likely to
obstruct than to second him in his ambitious designs.
Being on his way to London, many members of the Parliament, attended by the City, and great numbers of persons
of all orders and conditions, went some miles out of the
town to meet him, which tended not a little to heighten the
spirit of this haughty gentleman.

Lieutenant-General Monk, whom the General had raised
to that employment, and ordered to command in Scotland
Aug. 15.   during his absence, took Sterling Castle; and then marched
with about four thousand horse and foot before Dundee [1].
But being advised that General Lesley, the Earl of Crawford, and others, were met at Elliot to consult of means to
relieve that town, he sent a party of horse and dragoons
commanded by Col. Alured and Col. Morgan, to surprize
Aug. 28.   them, which they did; and the principal of them being
taken, were sent prisoners to London, where they were
committed to the Tower. After this he summoned the
Sept. 1.   town of Dundee; but the place being well fortified, and
provided with a numerous garison, refused to surrender;
whereupon he storm'd it, and being entred, put five or six

---

[1] An account of the siege and
capture of Stirling written by William
Clarke, Monk's secretary, is printed
by Cary, ii. 327. On the capture of
Dundee, see Cary, ii. 345, 351, 367.

Monk's account of the capture of the
Committee of Estates is in Cary, ii.
346; Alured's own letter in Mercurius Politicus, p. 1054.

hundred to the sword, and commanded the governour, with divers others, to be killed in cold blood.

Tho the news of these successes much discouraged our enemies in Ireland, yet those in Limerick were not without some hopes, that either the plague, or scarcity of provisions, together with the badness of the weather, might constrain us to raise the siege ; and therefore refused to accept such conditions as we were willing to grant. The line which we had made about the town and the forts being in a condition of defence, the Deputy resolved to look after the enemy in the county of Clare, and if possible to get some provisions from thence for the relief of the army. He took July 19. me with him, knowing I had been in those parts before, and between three and four thousand horse and foot. At our approach to the places where the enemies usually were, we divided our body, the Deputy being at the head of one, and I at the head of the other party ; hoping by this means so to encompass the enemy, that they should not escape us : but tho we sometimes came within sight of them, and used our utmost endeavours to engage them, yet by reason of the advantages they made of the woods, rocks, hills, and bogs, for their retreat, we could do them little hurt, save by seizing their horses and cattel. In the absence of this party from the army, the enemy with two thousand foot made a sally out of Limerick so unexpectedly upon our men, that they had almost surprized our guard of horse ; but ours immediately mounting, and being not accustomed to be beaten, charged them, and notwithstanding the inequality of the forces, they being much superiour to us in number, put them to a stand, till a party of horse and foot came to their relief, and forced the enemies to retreat under the walls of the town, from whence their men fired so thick upon ours, that their own men had time to get into the town.

When this account was brought from Sir Hardress Waller to the Deputy, he was upon his return to the army before Limerick, having left me with about two thousand horse and foot, as well to ease our quarters about the town, not

knowing how long we might lie before it, as to endeavour
to perswade the garison of Clare Castle, a strong place,
and situated upon the river, to surrender. To that end
being arrived in the army, he sent one Lieutenant-Colonel
White, who had served the enemy, and now had a commission to raise forces for the King of Spain, with an
order to me, to permit him to go to the said garison, that
he might inform them of the impossibility of their receiving
any relief, and of the necessities to which Limerick was
already reduced, and thereby prevail with them to make
speedy provision for themselves, and to list under him:
but his design proving ineffectual, I found myself obliged
to return to the camp before Limerick, where we made
provision for a winter-siege.

Great numbers of people endeavoured to get out of the
town, sent out by the garison either as useless persons, or to
spread the contagion amongst us. The Deputy commanded
them to return, and threatned to shoot any that should
attempt to come out for the future : but this not being
sufficient to make them desist, he caused two or three to be
taken out in order to be executed, and the rest to be whipped
back into the town. One of those that were to be hanged was
the daughter of an old man, who was in that number which
was to be sent back : he desired that he might be hanged in
the room of his daughter, but that was refused, and he with
the rest driven back into the town. After which a gibbet
was erected in the sight of the town walls, and one or two
persons hanged up, who had been condemned for other
crimes, that those within might suppose that execution to
be for coming out ; and by this means they were so terrified,
that we were no farther disturbed on that account.

The Deputy, upon information received that some in the
town were desirous to surrender, and that others did
violently oppose them, endeavoured by letters and messages
to foment the division, declaring against several persons by
name that were most active and obstinate for holding out,
that they should have no benefit by the articles to be
agreed upon, severely inveighing against a generation of men

whom he called souldiers of fortune, that made a trade of 1651
the war, and valued not the lives or happiness of the people.
This wrought the desired effect, and so encouraged the
complying party, that it was carried for a treaty, and commissioners again appointed on each side. We insisted that
about seventeen of the principal persons in the place should
be excepted out of the articles, of which number were Col.
Hugh O'Neal the governour, the Mayor of the city, the
Bishops of Limerick and Emmene, Major-General Purcel,
Sir Geoffrey Galloway, Sir Jeffrey Barrow, one Wolf a
priest, Sir Richard Everard and others. But these made so
strong a party that the treaty was broke up without any
agreement, and no other way left to reduce them but by
force. In order to which the Deputy caused the great
guns to be landed from the ships, and others to be brought
from the adjacent garisons. With these he erected a battery
against the town in the most convenient place that could
possibly have been found, being against a part of the wall,
which tho it was of the same height and thickness with the
rest of it, and also as well flanked ; yet it proved not to be
lined with earth within, as all the other parts were, nor had
any counterscarp without.

In the mean time the Parliament seeing a period put to
the war in England and Scotland, and that of Ireland drawing towards a conclusion, resolved to gratify such officers as
the General recommended to their favour ; and thereupon
settled a thousand pounds yearly on Major-General Lambert, Sept. 9.
three hundred on Major-General Overton, the same on Col.
Pride and Col. Whalley; five hundred pounds annually on 1652
Commissary-General Reynolds, a thousand pounds per March 12
annum on the Lord Broghil. They also settled four thousand pounds a year on the Lord-General himself, out of 1651
the estates of the Duke of Buckingham and Marquis of Sept. 11.
Worcester, besides the two thousand five hundred pounds a
year formerly granted. This they did to oblige him by all
means possible to the performance of his duty, or to leave
him without excuse if he should depart from it. They Sept. 11.
ordered also an Act to be brought in for settling two

1651

thousand pounds per annum on the Lord-Deputy Ireton ; the news of which being brought over, was so unacceptable to him, that he said, 'They had many just debts, which he desired they would pay before they made any such presents ; that he had no need of their land, and therefore would not have it ; and that he should be more contented to see them doing the service of the nation, than so liberal in disposing of the publick treasure.' And truly I believe he was in earnest ; for as he was always careful to husband those things that belonged to the State to the best advantage, so was he most liberal in employing his own purse and person in the publick service.

Our battery being now in order, and the regiments that were appointed to storm disposed to their several posts, we began to fire ; directing all our shot to one particular part of the wall, wherein we made such a breach, that the enemy not daring to run any farther hazard, beat a parley, and

Oct. 27.

soon came to a resolution to surrender upon the articles we had offered before, delivering up the east-gate of the out-town, which was separated by a river having a draw-bridg over it from the other town [1]. The Deputy ordered all the arms and ammunition to be carefully preserved, and the souldiers who were not of the town to be drawn up between the place and our army, that such as desired it might have convoys to conduct them to their respective parties ; and that those who would return to their habitations, might have passes granted to that effect. The governour Col. Hugh O'Neal met the Deputy at the gate ; where he presented him with the keys of the city, and gave order for the marching out of the souldiers who were not townsmen, according to

Oct. 29.

the articles. They were in number about two thousand five hundred men. As they were marching out, two or three of them fell down dead of the plague. Several of them also lay unburied in the church-yard. The governour waited on the Deputy to shew him the stores of arms, ammunition

---

[1] On the siege and capture of Limerick, see Aphorismical Discovery, iii. 19-22, 263, where the surrender is attributed to the treachery of Major Fennell and others.

and provisions, which were sufficient to have lasted near three months longer. He shewed him also the fortifications, and whatsoever else he desired of him, withal acquainting him, that nine or ten of those who were excepted from the benefit of the articles had surrendred themselves to his mercy, and were waiting his orders in a certain house which he named : upon which the Deputy commanded a guard to be set upon them, and committed the governour also to their custody. The Bishop of Emmene and Major-General Purcel, with Wolf the priest, were taken in the pest-house, where they had hid themselves, Jeffery Barrow and Sir Geoffrey Galloway surrendred themselves. Two days after the delivery of the town the Mayor came to the place of worship, where our court of guard was met ; and whether by his words or actions he gave cause of suspicion I cannot tell, but they seized him, and upon examination found who he was; whereupon they committed him to prison [1]. The Bishop of Limerick was the only person excepted that was yet undiscovered ; but we afterwards understood him to be one of a more peaceable spirit than the rest. A court martial was assembled, and the Bishop of Emmene, with Major-General Purcel, required to acquaint them, if they had any thing to say why they should not die according to the sentence passed upon them. The Bishop said, that having many sins to confess, he desired time to prepare himself to that purpose, which was granted. Major-General Purcel fell upon his knees, and begged earnestly for his life, but that was denied. This poor man was of so low a spirit, that wanting courage at the time of his execution, he stood in need of two musqueteers to support him. The Bishop died with more resolution, and Wolf the priest was also executed. The governour and Jeffrey Barrow were also condemned to die ; but the Deputy resolving to hear them, demanded of the governour what he had to say for himself : who answered, that the war had been long on foot before he came over ; that he

---

[1] Dominic Fanning. An account of his arrest and death is given in Aphorismical Discovery, iii. 21, 258, 267.

came upon the invitation of his country-men ; that he had always demeaned himself as a fair enemy ; and that the ground of his exception from the articles, being his encouraging to hold out, tho there was no hope of relief, was not applicable to him, who had always moved them to a timely surrender, as indeed he made it appear ; and therefore hoped, that he should enjoy the benefit of the articles, in confidence of which he had faithfully delivered up the keys of the town, with all the arms, ammunition and provisions, without embezlement, and his own person also to the Deputy [1].   But the blood formerly shed at Clonmel, where this Col. O'Neal was governour, had made such an impression on the Deputy, that his judgment, which was of great weight with the court, moved them a second time to vote him to die, tho some of us earnestly opposed it, for the reasons before mentioned by himself ; and because whatsoever he had been guilty of before, had no relation to these articles, which did not at all exempt him from being called to an account by the civil magistrate for the same. The court having passed sentence of death a second time against him, the Deputy, who was now entirely freed from his former manner of adhering to his own opinion, which had been observed to be his greatest infirmity, observing some of the officers to be unsatisfied with this judgment, referred

it again to the consideration of the court, who by their third vote consented to save his life.   Jeffrey Barrow having the same question put to him with the rest, answered, that it was not just to exclude him from mercy, because he had been engaged in the same cause as we pretended to fight for, which was for the liberty and religion of his country. The Deputy replied, that Ireland being a conquered country,

---

[1] The author of the Aphorismical Discovery praises Ireton's 'noble care' of Hugh O'Neill, iii. 21. For Jeffrey Barrow read Barron.   A spirited letter from O'Neill to Ireton is printed in Aphorismical Discovery, iii. 258. Ireton in his letter to the Parliament ib. p. 267 , says that he is ' not yet well resolved' how to deal with the excepted persons.   Three, viz. Dominick Fanning, the Bishop of Emley, and Major-General Purcell, were promptly hanged.   On Nov. 1, the vote condemning O'Neill was rescinded.

the English nation might with justice assert their right of 1651
conquest : that they had been treated by the late government far beyond their merits, or the rules of reason ;
notwithstanding which they had barbarously murdered all
the English that fell into their hands, robbed them of their
goods which they had gained by their industry, and taken
away the lands which they had purchased with their money:
that touching the point of religion, there was a wide
difference also between us, we only contending to preserve our natural right therein, without imposing our
opinions upon other men ; whereas they would not be
contented unless they might have power to compel all
others to submit to their impositions upon pain of death.
The Council of War looking upon what he had said for himself to be hereby fully refuted, adjudged him to die, as
they did the Mayor also ; and the sentence was executed
accordingly.

Limerick being taken, it was debated in a Council of War,
whether we should march to Galway in order to reduce that
place, which had been besieged for some time by Sir
Charles Coote and Commissary-General Reynolds [1]. I concurred with the Deputy, that the garison being under a
great consternation by the loss of Limerick, would probably
be soon brought to reason ; but most of the officers complaining of the ill condition of their men through sickness
and hard service, representing also the near approach of
winter, we being already entred into the month of
November, the Deputy contented himself to send only
a summons to General Preston governour of Galway, with Nov.
offers of such conditions as were first tendred to those of
Limerick, assuring him at the same time, that if he refused
them, he should have no better than they had been lately

---

[1] On Nov. 19, the Commissioners
wrote to the Council of State : 'The
Lord Deputy intends to make Athlone his headquarters, and hath given
order for the building of some houses
in the town, and fortifying of the
same, as being conceived the most
advantageous place for a strong inland garrison of any in Ireland,
being seated on the Shannon in the
centre of the nation.' Irish Records,
$\frac{A}{89}$ 49, p. 211.

obliged to submit to [1]. This proposition he rejected ; but being unwilling to hazard the event, took shipping soon after, and went beyond sea.

Whilst the Deputy was settling affairs at Limerick, he ordered me with a party to march into the county of Clare

to reduce some places in those parts. Accordingly I marched with about two thousand foot and fifteen hundred horse to Inchecroghnan, fifteen miles from Limerick ; but it being late before we began our march, and night over-taking us before we could reach that place, as we were passing the bridg, one of my horses that carried my waters and medicines fell into the river, which proved a great loss to me, as things fell out afterwards. The next day I came before Clare Castle, and summoned it, whereupon they sent out commissioners to treat, tho the place was of very great strength ; and after three or four hours' debate, we

came to an agreement, by which the Castle was to be de-livered to me the next morning [2], the enemy leaving hostages with us for the performance of their part. That night I lay in my tent upon a hill, where the weather being very tempestuous, and the season far advanced, I took

a very dangerous cold. The next morning the enemy marched out of the Castle, and received passes from me to return home, according to the articles. After which having appointed Col. Foulk and a garison to defend it, I marched towards Carickgoholt. That night my cold increased, and the next morning I found myself so much discomposed, that Adjutant-General Allen, who was then with us, earnestly pressed me to go aboard one of the vessels that attended our party with ammunition, artillery and pro-visions, and to appoint a person to command them in my absence. But being unwilling to quit the charge committed to my care, I clothed myself as warm as I could, putting

---

[1] Ireton's letters to Preston and to the city of Galway with their answers, which are dated Nov. 12, are printed in Mercurius Politicus, pp. 1400-4.

[2] The articles for the surrender of Clare are printed in Several Proceedings in Parliament, p. 1778, Dec. 4-11, 1651. Col. Stephen White was to have the benefit of the articles if he agreed to them within a fort-night.

on a fur coat over my buff, and an oiled one over that ; by
which means I prevented the farther increase of my distemper, and so ordered our quarters that night, that I lay
in my own bed set up in an Irish cabin, where about break
of day I fell into so violent a sweat, that I was obliged to
keep with me two troops of horse for my guard, after I had
given orders for the rest of the men to march.   In this condition I continued about two hours, and tho my sweating
had not ceased, I mounted in order to overtake my party,
who had a bitter day to march in, the wind and the hail
beating so violently in our faces, that the horses being not
able to endure it, often turned about.   Yet in this extremity
of weather the poor foot were necessitated to wade through
a branch of the sea, near a quarter of a mile over, up to the
waste in water.   At night we arrived within view of Carickgoholt, my distemper being but little abated, and my body
in a continual sweat.   The next day I summoned the
garison to surrender the Castle : in answer to which they
sent out commissioners to treat, who at first insisted upon
very high terms; but finding us resolved not to grant their
propositions, they complied with ours, and the next day
surrendred the place.   Liberty was given by the articles to
such as desired it, to go and join the Lord Muskerry's
party in the county of Kerry: the rest to return home, with
promise of protection as long as they behaved themselves
peaceably, excepting only such who should appear to have
been guilty of murder in the first year of the war, or afterwards.   Having placed a garison in Carickgoholt, I returned
towards Limerick, and being on my march thither, I was
met by an officer of the guard, with orders from the Deputy
for my return ; who thinking it impossible to reduce this
garison by force in such a season, was unwilling that the
souldiers should remain longer in the field, exposed to such
cruel and sharp weather.   The messenger also acquainted
me, that the Deputy was coming towards us, which he did,
as well to view the country, in order to the more equal
distribution of winter-quarters and garisons, as to let us
see that he would not command any service, but such as he

was willing to take a share of himself. Upon this advice I hastned with a party to meet him, giving orders for the rest to follow as fast as they could conveniently. At our meeting I gave him an account of what I had done, with which he was very well satisfied. After two days' march, without anything remarkable but bad quarters, we entred into the Barony of Burren, of which it is said, that it is a country where there is not water enough to drown a man, wood enough to hang one, nor earth enough to bury him ; which last is so scarce, that the inhabitants steal it from one another, and yet their cattle are very fat ; for the grass growing in turfs of earth, of two or three foot square, that lie between the rocks, which are of limestone, is very sweet and nourishing[1]. Being in these parts we went to Lemmene, a house of that Connor O'Bryan whom we had killed near Inchecroghnan ; and finding it indifferent strong, being built with stone, and having a good wall about it, we put a garison into it, and furnished it with all things necessary. The next day the Deputy with a party of horse went to view some other places where he designed to appoint garisons, in order to prevent the sending of provisions into Galway, to which this country lies contiguous. I was very desirous to attend him according to my duty, but he having observed my distemper to continue upon me, would not permit it ; and when I pressed it more earnestly, he positively commanded me to stay. That day there fell abundance of rain and snow, which was accompanied with a very high wind, whereby the Deputy took a very great cold that discovered itself immediately upon his return ; but we could not perswade him to go to bed, till he had determined a cause that was before him and the court martial, touching an officer of the army, who was accused of some violence done to the Irish ; and as in all cases he carried himself with the utmost impartiality, so he did in this, dismissing the officer, tho otherwise an useful man, from his command for the same. The next day we marched

---

[1] On the Barony of Burren, see Prendergast, Cromwellian Settlement, pp. 121, 122.

towards Clare Castle, and found the way so rocky, that we
rode near three miles together upon one of them, whereby
most of our horses cast their shoes ; so that though every
troop came provided with horse-shoes, which were delivered
to them out of the stores, yet before that day's march was
over, a horse-shoe was sold for five shillings.

The next morning the Lady Honoria O'Bryan, daughter
to the late Earl of Thomond [1], being accused of protecting
the goods and cattle of the enemy, under pretence that
they belonged to her, and thereby abusing the favour
of the Deputy's safeguard, which he had granted to her,
came to him; and being charged by him with it, and told,
that he expected a more ingenuous carriage from her ; she
burst out into tears, and assured him, if he would forgive
her, that she would never do the like again, desiring me,
after the Deputy was withdrawn, to intercede with him for
the continuance of his favour to her : which when I acquainted him with, he said, ' As much a cynick as I am,
the tears of this woman moved me ;' and thereupon gave
order that his protection should be continued to her.   From
hence I would have attended him to Limerick ; but so
much more care did he take of me than of himself, that he
would not suffer it ; desiring me to go that day, being
Saturday, and quarter at Bonratto, a house of the Earl of
Thomond's, in order to recover my health, and to come
to him on Monday morning at Limerick.   Accordingly I
came, and found the Deputy grown worse, having been let
blood, and sweating exceedingly, with a burning fever at
the same time.   Yet for all this he ceased not to apply himself to the publick business, settling garisons and distributing
winter-quarters, which was all that remained to be done
of the military service for that year.   I endeavoured to
perswade him, as I had often done before, that his immoderate labours for his country would much impair, if

---

[1] Honoria, or Honora, 5th daughter
of Henry, 5th Earl of Thomond (d.
1639`.   She married (1) Sir Francis
Englefield of Wotton-Basset in Wiltshire, (2) Sir Robert Howard,
Auditor of the Exchequer, 6th son
of Thomas, first Earl of Berkshire.
Lodge, Peerage of Ireland, i. 261.

1652 not utterly destroy him; but he had so totally neglected himself during the siege of Limerick, not putting off his clothes all that time, except to change his linen, that the malignant humours which he had contracted, wanting room to perspire, became confined to his body, and rendred him more liable to be infected by the contagion. I was unwilling to leave him till I saw the event of his distemper; but he supposing my family was by this time come to Dublin[1], would not permit me to stay, and I finding I could in no way be serviceable to him, submitted to his desires. I found the Commissioners of Parliament at Dublin, and acquainted them with the state of affairs in those parts from whence I came, and with the resolutions taken by the Deputy at Limerick; but soon after my

Nov. 26. arrival, the sad news of his death was brought to us, which was universally lamented by all good men, more especially because the publick was thereby deprived of a most faithful, able and useful servant[2].

The Commissioners of Parliament taking into their consideration what method to observe in that conjuncture, and presuming that my command in the army was next to that

Dec. 2. of the Deputy, resolved by a letter to acquaint the officers of our forces in Ireland with their judgment, and to require them to yield obedience to me accordingly. I earnestly desired them to forbear sending any such letter, which I did, not out of a feigned modesty, but from a real sense of the weight of such an undertaking, and my own inability to perform the duty of that important station[3]. For tho the

---

[1] The Commissioners wrote to Ludlow from Dublin on Nov. 25, saying: 'The cross winds and tempestuous weather of late we do believe doth keep your Lady from coming over to this place, but we do hear that Captain Sherwin, Commander of a very good frigate, lies at Beaumaris, who is and will be ready to convoy your Lady by the first opportunity.' Irish Records, A 49, P. 234.

[2] For comments on Ireton's death, see the letters of Col. Thomas Herbert (Cary, Memorials of the Civil War, ii. 391), Col. Hewson (Several Proceedings, p. 1780), and Lord Broghil (Mercurius Politicus, p. 1301).

[3] Documents relating to Ludlow's appointment as Commander-in-Chief are printed in the Appendix.

work seemed to be almost finished, yet there remained great difficulties behind, the enemy possessing some strong places and islands, and having many thousands yet in the field ; there being also in the Parliament's pay between seven and eight thousand horse and dragoons, with above two and twenty thousand foot. For these and other reasons I desired them that they would reserve the power to themselves, till the Parliament should send over some person to undertake that employment ; which they might do soon enough, the season of action being already past, the troops dispersed into their winter-quarters, and nothing of importance likely to be done before the next spring ; acquainting them, that being one of their number, I could be as serviceable in their deliberations and resolutions, as if I were entrusted with the sole power. But all that I could say was not sufficient to disswade them from sending the letter before mentioned ; and tho it met with a general submission, yet I resolved not to undertake any thing without their advice and consent, which they readily promised to afford me.

Some of General Cromwell's relations, who were not ignorant of his vast designs now on foot, caused the body of the Lord Deputy Ireton to be transported into England, and solemnly interred at Westminster in a magnificent monument at the publick charge [1] ; who if he could have foreseen what was done by them, would certainly have made it his desire that his body might have found a grave where his soul left it, so much did he despise those pompous and expensive vanities ; having erected for himself a more glorious monument in the hearts of good men, by his affection to his country, his abilities of mind, his impartial justice, his diligence in the publick service, and his other vertues, which were a far greater honour to his memory, than a dormitory amongst the ashes of kings, who, for the most part, as they had governed others by their

---

[1] On Ireton's funeral, see Life of Col. Hutchinson, ii. 186, ed. 1885 ; Mercurius Politicus, p. 1299. Its pomp was very offensive to the Fifth-monarchy men and advanced Republicans; Cal. S. P. Dom., 1652-3, p. 425.

1651   passions, so were they themselves as much governed by them.

June 2.

Oct. 31.

The Isles of Scilly and Man were reduced to the obedience of the Commonwealth; but nothing extraordinary happening at their reduction, at least not coming to my knowledge, I purposely omit the relation of those actions [1].

About this time we were informed that Sir George Ayscue, who had been sent by the Parliament to the Western Islands, which still continued in arms against them, arrived

Oct. 16.

at the Barbadoes on the 26th of October, 1651, and having opened a passage into the harbour by firing some great

Oct. 17.

shot, seized upon twelve of their ships without opposition [2]. The next morning he sent a summons to the Lord Willoughby to submit to the authority of the Parliament of England; but he not acknowledging any such power, declared his resolution to keep the island for the King's service. But the news of the defeat of the Scots and their King at Worcester being brought to Sir George Ayscue, together with an intercepted letter from the Lady Wil-

Nov. 12.

loughby, containing the same account; he summoned him a second time, and accompanied his summons with his Lady's letter to assure him of the truth of that report. But the Lord Willoughby relying upon his numbers, and the fewness of those that were sent to reduce him, being in all but fifteen sail, returned an answer of the like substance

---

[1] On the capture of Scilly, see Mercurius Politicus, 1651, pp. 766, 788, 793, 807. 855, 865; Several Proceedings, pp. 1237, 1268, 1271, 1276, 1291; Nicholas Papers, i. 250, 255. The fleet sailed from Plymouth April 12, 1651, and effected a landing on Tresco Island, April 18. An account of the surrender of the Isle of Man is printed in Mercurius Politicus, Nov. 6-13, 1651, p. 1197. It was surrendered to Col. Robert Duckinfield by articles dated Oct. 31, 1651.

[2] Ayscue arrived at Barbadoes Oct. 16, according to his own despatch. On the history of the reduction of the island, see Cal. S. P., Colonial, 1574-1660, pp. 342-60, 362-74; Several Proceedings in Parliament, pp. 1943, 2097; Mercurius Politicus, pp. 1422, 1429, 1472, 1563. Ludlow closely follows Ayscue's letter of Feb. 26, 1652, printed in Mercurius Politicus, p. 1563, April 22-29, 1652. A pamphlet entitled 'A brief relation of the beginning and ending of the troubles of the Barbadoes, set forth by A. B.,' 1653, attributes the revolt chiefly to the intrigues of Col. Humphrey Walrond and his brother Edward.

with the former. Whereupon Sir George Ayscue sent two
hundred men on shore, commanded by Captain Morrice,
to attack a quarter of the enemy's that lay by the harbour,
which they executed successfully by taking the fort and
about forty prisoners, with four pieces of cannon, which
they nailed up, and returned on board again. At this
time the Virginia fleet arriving at the Barbadoes, it was
thought fit to send a third summons to the Lord
Willoughby; but finding that neither this, nor the declaration sent to them by the commissioners of Parliament
to the same purpose, produced any effect, Sir George
Ayscue landed seven hundred men from his own and
the Virginia fleet, giving the command of them to the
same Captain Morrice, who fell upon thirteen hundred
of the enemy's foot and three troops of their horse, and
beat them from their works, killing many of their men, and
taking about a hundred prisoners, with all their guns. The
loss on our side was inconsiderable, few of ours being killed
upon the place, and not above thirty wounded. Yet these
successes were not sufficient to accomplish the work, there
being above five thousand horse and foot in the island, and
our Virginia fleet preparing to depart for want of provisions.
In this conjuncture Colonel Muddiford, who commanded
a regiment in the island, by the means of a friend that
he had in our fleet, made his terms, and declared for the
Parliament. Many of his friends following his example,
did the like, and in conjunction with him encamped under
the protection of our fleet. Upon this the most part of
the island were inclined to join us ; but the Lord Willoughby
prevented them by placing guards on all the avenues to our
camp, and designed to charge our men with his body of
horse, wherein he was much superior to them, had not
a cannon-ball that was fired at random, beat open the door
of a room, where he and his council of war were sitting ;
which taking off the head of the sentinel who was placed
at the door, so alarmed them all, that he changed his
design, and retreated to a place two miles distant from the
harbour. Our party, consisting of two thousand foot and

1652
Nov. 22.

Dec. 1.

Dec. 7.

1652   one hundred horse, advancing towards him, he desired to treat; which being accepted, Colonel Muddiford, Colonel Collyton, Mr. Searl and Captain Pack, were appointed commissioners by Sir George Ayscue; and by the Lord Willoughby, Sir Richard Pierce, Mr. Charles Pym, Colonel

Jan. 11.   Ellis and Major Byham. By these it was concluded, that the islands of Barbadoes, Mevis, Antego and St. Christophers should be surrendered to the Parliament of England : that the Lord Willoughby, Colonel Walrond, and some others, should be restored to their estates ; and that the inhabitants of the said isles should be maintained in the quiet enjoyment of what they possessed, on condition to do nothing to the

March 12   prejudice of the Commonwealth. This news being brought to Virginia, they submitted also, where one Mr. George Ludlow, a relation of mine[1], served the Parliament in the like manner as Colonel Muddiford had done at the Barbadoes.

1651   The Parliament of England being desirous after all these successes, to convince even their enemies, that their principal design was to procure the happiness and prosperity of all that were under their government, sent commissioners to Scotland to treat concerning an union of that nation with England in one Commonwealth ; directing them to take care, till that could be effected, that obedience should be given to the authority of the Parliament of the Common-

Oct. 23.   wealth of England. The commissioners appointed to this end on the part of the Parliament, were Sir Henry Vane, the Chief Justice St. Johns, Mr. Fenwick, Major Salloway, Major-General Lambert, Colonel Titchborn, Major-General Dean and Colonel Monk. This proposition of union was cheerfully accepted by the most judicious amongst the Scots, who well understood how great a condescension it was in the Parliament of England, to permit a people

---

[1] George Ludlow, son of Thomas Ludlow of Dinton, bapt. Sept. 15, 1596 ; will proved Aug. 1, 1656. He was appointed a member of the council of Virginia, by commission from Charles II at Breda, June 3,

1650. Cal. S. P., Colonial, 1574–1660, p. 340. On the surrender of Virginia, see Mercurius Politicus, p. 1605 ; the articles are printed p. 1615 ; cf. Thurloe, i. 197.

they had conquered, to have a part in the legislative power [1].

The States-General being highly displeased with the late Act of Navigation passed by the Parliament, which they accounted to be a great obstruction to their trade, resolved to leave no means unattempted to procure it to be repealed. To this end they sent three ambassadors to England, who pretending a desire to finish the treaty begun formerly between the two States, requested that things might be as they were at the time of our ambassador's departure from Holland, designing thereby that the Act lately passed for the encouragement of our seamen should be suspended, and all such merchandizes restored as had been seized from the Dutch by virtue of the said Act. The Parliament refusing to consent to this proposal, the States-General gave orders for the equipping a considerable fleet, consisting of about a hundred ships of war, giving notice to the Parliament by their ambassadors of these preparations, and assuring them that they were not design'd to offend the English nation, with whom they desired to maintain a friendly correspondence, and that they were provided to no other end, than to protect their own subjects in their trade and navigation. But the Parliament being unwilling to rely upon the promises of those, who by their past and present actions had manifested little friendship to us, resolved to make what preparations they could to defend themselves [2].

This alarm awakened us to a diligent performance of our duty in Ireland, fearing that the Hollanders might transport some foreign forces by their fleet, to the assistance of the Irish, who were not only still numerous in the field, but had also divers places of strength to retreat to. Our suspicions were farther increased by the advices we received of a treaty on foot between the Duke of Lorain and Theobald Viscount Taff, with other Irish, to bring the forces of that

---

[1] On the union with Scotland, see Godwin, Commonwealth, iii. 310; Masson, Life of Milton, iv. 302, 360.

[2] See Geddes, John De Witt, i. 193.

Duke into Ireland against us, in order to extirpate all hereticks out of that nation, to re-establish the Romish religion in all parts of it, and to restore the Irish to their possessions; all which being performed, he should deliver up the authority to the King of Great Britain, and assist him against his rebellious subjects in England: that all Ireland should be ingaged for his re-imbursement: that Galway, Limerick, Athenree, Athlone, Waterford, and the fort of Duncannon, should be put into his hands as cautionary places, with other things of the same nature[1]. The report of this agreement being spread amongst the Irish, encouraged them to make all possible opposition against us, in expectation of the promised succours. The Commissioners of the Parliament on the other hand, laboured with all diligence to dispose their affairs in the best manner they could for the publick service; in order to which they sent to the several commanders of our army to excite them to the discharge of their duty, making provision of arms, ammunition, clothes, tents, and all things necessary to the carrying on the war in the ensuing spring. A general meeting of officers was also appointed to be held at Kilkenny to consult about the best method of employing our arms against the enemy[2]: and because the propositions offered by the late Lord Deputy to those of Galway had been no farther prosecuted by reason of his death, orders

Dec. 3. were dispatched to Sir Charles Coote, authorizing him to conclude with them, in case they should accept the conditions at or before the ninth of the next January[3]. According to

---

[1] On the negotiations with the Duke of Lorraine, see Memoirs of Ulick, Marquis of Clanricarde, folio, 1757, Appendix: 'The Proceedings of the treaty between the Duke of Lorraine's Ambassador and me.' A treaty was signed between Clanricarde and Stephen de Henin, Lorraine's ambassador on April 4, 1651 (ib. p. 19), and another July 2, 1651, between Lord Taaffe, Sir Nicholas Plunkett, and Geoffrey Browne, 'deputies authorised on the behalf of the kingdom and people of Ireland' (ib. p. 35).

[2] The Commissioners came to Kilkenny on Dec. 20, 1651. Their policy is set forth at length in the letters and declarations printed in the Appendix.

[3] The Commissioners wrote to Coote on Dec. 3: 'We have upon debate thought it convenient to advise your Lordship to proceed in

their orders the officers met at Kilkenny, by whom being 1652 informed of what they thought necessary for the ensuing service, we acquainted the Parliament and Council of State with the particulars of such things as were requisite, desiring them to send them over with all convenient speed, that no time might be lost when the season of the year should permit us to take the field. We published two proclamations to prevent the country from supplying the enemy with arms and other necessaries ; wherein drawing a line as it were about the Irish quarters, we required all persons to withdraw Feb. 13. themselves and their goods from the places of their resort within a limited time ; which if they refused to do, we declared them enemies, and ordered all officers and souldiers to treat them accordingly: commanding also all smiths, Jan. 13. armourers and sadlers that lived in the country to retire in twenty days with all their families, forges and instruments, into some garison of the Parliament, on pain of forfeiture of their goods and tools, besides six months' imprisonment for the first offence, and of death for the second. We ordered also that all those who had withdrawn themselves out of our protection, and joined with the enemy, since the coming over of General Cromwell, should be deprived of the benefit of quarter. Having published

the treaty with Galway according to the articles proposed by the late Lord Deputy to them, being the same formerly offered to the city of Limerick. If they shall make such exceptions to the proposals as the Commissioners of Limerick did, you may make to them the like explanation as his Lordship made to as many of their exceptions as you conceive to be of public advantage to grant. And for your clearer understanding of our intention in this particular, we have sent you inclosed a copy of our resolution upon the debate together with copies of the said articles and of the exceptions thereunto, and the concessions and explanations thereupon. The articles you may (if you find it necessary) communicate to the governor and inhabitants of the town. But the exceptions and answers to them you are to keep to yourself to make use of as you shall find occasion.' Irish Records, $\frac{A}{89}$ 49, p. 260. These articles and the answers to the exceptions of the Limerick commissioners are reprinted by Mr. Gilbert, Aphorismical Discovery, iii. 241. The limitation of time mentioned by Ludlow is not stated in this letter, but is mentioned in the remarks on the Galway negotiations in Mercurius Politicus, p. 1559.

these and other orders of the like tenour, we appointed the Lord Broghil, Commissary-General Reynolds, Sir Hardress Waller, Colonel Axtel, and the rest of the officers, to cause them to be put in execution, as occasion should require.

Having finished our affairs at Kilkenny, and dismissed the officers to their respective quarters, I resolved to go Feb. to Portumna to make all things ready for the siege of Galway. Being on my march on the other side of Nenagh, an advanced party found two of the rebels, one of whom was killed by the guard before I came up to them, the other was saved ; and being brought before me at Portumna, and I asking him if he had a mind to be hanged ? he only answered, ' If you please '; so insensibly stupid were many of these poor creatures. The Commissioners having done their business in this place, and given directions for the carrying on the siege of Galway, with power to treat, as before mentioned, to Sir Charles Coote, we returned to Dublin, and at our arrival were informed, that the barony of 1651 Burren relying upon the security of their places of retreat, Dec. had refused to pay the contributions which they had promised; upon which Sir Hardress Waller had been obliged to lay the country waste, and to seize what he could find, that it might be no longer useful to the enemy[1]. We had advice also from Ulster, that some of our troops had killed and drowned about a hundred and forty Tories who infested that province with their robberies.

1652 The time limited by the proclamation, requiring the Feb. 28. Irish to withdraw from the places mentioned therein, being expired, I marched with a party of horse and foot into the fastnesses of Wicklo, as well to make examples of such as had not obeyed the proclamation, as to place a garison there, to prevent the excursions of the enemy. Talbots-town was the place I thought fittest for that end ; which having rendred defensible against any sudden attempt, and furnished with all things necessary, I marched farther into

---

[1] An account of this foray is given in Several Proceedings, p. 1933, and Mercurius Politicus, p. 1375.

the country. The next morning I divided my men into
three parties, sending away Colonel Pretty with one of
them to his own quarters, lest the enemy should fall upon
them in his absence ; with the other two we scoured by
different ways the passes and retreats of the Irish, but met
not with many of them; our parties being so big, that the
Irish, who had sentinels placed upon every hill, gave notice
of our march to their friends : so that upon our approach,
they still fled to their bogs and woods. When I came to
Dundrum, a place lying in the heart of the enemy's quarters,
I perceived the walls and roof of an old church standing,
wherein I placed captain Jacob with his company; who
was afterwards very serviceable against the enemy. The
like methods being taken by the Lord Broghil, Colonel
Zanchey, Colonel Abbot and other officers, the Irish were
reduced to great extremities[1].

About fourscore of the inhabitants of Galway went
privately out of the town, and seizing a hundred head of
cattel, designed to drive them thither ; but being upon
their return, they were met by a party of ours, who killed
threescore of them, and recovered all the cattel. This
disappointment was attended with another much greater ;
for two vessels loaden with corn endeavouring to get into
the harbour of Galway, being pursued by two of our frigats,
one of them was taken, and the other forced upon the rocks
near the Isle of Arran, where she was lost.

The Parliament having received an account of the

---

[1] A letter from Col. George Cooke
to the Commissioners (March 17,
1652) explains the nature of these
forays : ' In searching the woods and
bogs we found great store of corn,
which we burnt ; also all the houses
and cabins we could finde ; in all of
which we found great plenty of corn;
we continued burning and destroying for four daies, in which time we
wanted no provision for horse or
man, finding also houses enough for
our men to lye in, though we burnt
our quarters every morning and continued burning all day after. He
was an idle soldier that had not
either a fat lamb, veale, pig, poultry,
or all of them, every night to his
supper. The enemy of these parts
chiefly depended upon this country
for provisions : I believe we have
destroyed as much as would have
served some thousands of them untill next harvest.' Cooke was killed
on April 1 by Captain Nash. Several
Proceedings, pp. 2055, 2063.

1652

hopeful condition of their affairs in Ireland, and of the great appearance there was of a speedy determination of that war, appointed a committee to summon before them

Jan. 30.

those adventurers, who in the year 1641 had advanced monies upon the lands in Ireland. The said persons being met at Grocers-Hall, chose twenty-eight deputies to manage the business with the committee in the names of all the rest. In conformity to this proceeding the Commissioners of Parliament in Ireland began to consider of qualifications and heads under which the Irish should be brought, that the innocent might be freed from their fears and apprehensions ; that justice might be done, and the guilty punished according to the different nature of their crimes : of which the Irish having notice, and considering the declining condition of their affairs in all parts, sent a letter directed to the Commissioners of the Parliament of England from the principal, as they called themselves, of the king-

Feb. 20.

dom of Ireland, and subscribed by Gerald Fitz-Gerald, on the behalf of their assembly held at Glanmaliero in the province of Leinster [1]; representing, that being advised that the Commonwealth of England is in a condition to give honourable and sure terms to them, they are in an entire disposition to receive them ; and to that effect desire in the name of that and the rest of the provinces, a safe conduct for every one of them, with blanks subscribed to that end, that they may impower and send some of their members to present propositions to the commissioners that are or should

March 12.

be authorized to that purpose. To this the Commissioners answered in substance, that tho the letter was subscribed by one, under the pretext of an authority which they could not own without prejudice to that of the Parliament ; yet for the satisfaction of those concerned, they thought fit to declare, that the establishment of this nation doth of right belong only to the Parliament of England, who will dis-

---

[1] The two Declarations of the Commissioners in answer to these overtures are printed in the Appendix. For Gerald Fitzgerald's letter, and the further propositions made by the Leinster envoys, see Aphorismical Discovery, iii. 60-64 ; Several Proceedings in Parliament, pp. 2045-9.

tinguish those who have always lived peaceably, or have already submitted to their authority, and put themselves under their protection, from such as have committed and countenanced the murders and massacres of the Protestants during the first year of the rebellion, as well as from those who continue still in arms to oppose their authority : that they cannot in justice consent to an act so prejudicial to the peace of the country, as would involve quiet and peaceable people in the same prosecution with those who are in open hostility : that they cannot grant safe conducts to such as persist in their opposition to the Parliament, to assemble from all provinces, and to communicate their designs to each other : but that all those who will lay down their arms, and submit to the Commonwealth, shall have as favourable conditions as they can justly expect [1].

This resolution of the Commissioners being made publick. the Irish fell upon another expedient : in pursuance of which the Earl of Clanrickard, who had been left deputy by the Earl of Ormond, sent a letter directed to me, then Commander-in-Chief of the forces of the Parliament in Ireland, in the words following.

'SIR;

' Many of the nobility, clergy, and other persons of quality, subjects of this kingdom, with the corporation of Galway, having considered the present state of affairs, and the ruinous effects which this long war hath produced, have solicited me to desire of you a conference for the establishment of the repose of this nation, and to obtain a safe conduct for the commissioners, whom by their advice I shall

---

[1] Ludlow's account of his correspondence with Clanricarde is inaccurate. Clanricarde's letter should be dated Feb. 14, Ludlow's answer Feb. 24, as the copies in the Irish Records show. See also Aphorismical Discovery, iii. 57. The wording of the letters is also different. Ludlow announced Clanricarde's overtures to Parliament in a letter dated March 2, reprinted in the Appendix. Clanricarde's letter was sent first to Coote, and forwarded by him to Ludlow. Several Proceedings, p. 1998; Mercurius Politicus, p. 1466. The dates assigned in the newspapers vary. Ludlow's answer to another overture, from Sir Richard Blake, is given in the Appendix.

judg capable to be sent to you for that end. It is this which hath obliged me to send you an express, with this protestation, that I shall not abandon them, till I see such conditions granted them, as they may with honour accept : for want of which I am resolved to continue the authority and protection of his Majesty over them, even to extremity, not doubting but by Divine assistance, with the forces we have already, and the succours which shall be sent us by his Majesty and allies, we shall be found in a condition to change the present state of affairs, or at least to render your former conquests of little advantage, and in the end to sell our lives at a dear rate if we shall be forced thereto : the which leaving to your consideration, and expecting your certain answer and resolution, I remain,

Sir, your Servant,

24 March, 1652.   CLANRICKARD.

'POSTSCRIPT.

· If you please to send a safe conduct, I desire it may be addressed to Sir Charles Coote, or whom you shall think fit near to this place, with a pass for the number of five commissioners, and their retinue of about twenty persons, to the end that having notice thereof, I may send a list of the names of the said commissioners.'

To this I returned the following answer.

' My Lord ;

' In answer to yours of the 24th of March, by which you propose a treaty for the settlement of this country, and desire a safe conduct for the commissioners you shall judg fit to employ in the management of that affair, I think fit, in pursuance of the advice of the Commissioners of the Parliament of England, and of many officers of the English army, to advertise you, as hath been already answered to those who have sent propositions of the like nature, that the settlement of this nation doth of right belong to the Parliament of the Commonwealth of England, to whom we

are obliged in duty to leave it; being assured, that they
will not capitulate with those who ought to submit to them,
and yet oppose themselves to their authority, and upon
vain and frivolous hopes have refused such offers of favour
as they would gladly accept at present: so that I fear they
will be constrained to proceed against them with the highest
severity; which that you may prevent by your timely submission, is the desire of,

My Lord,

Your humble Servant,

Edmund Ludlow.'

That passage in my answer touching their readiness to
accept such terms as they had formerly rejected, was
grounded upon notice sent by Sir Charles Coote[1]; that
the town of Galway, since the time limited by the commissioners for their submission was expired, desired a
treaty: whereupon I had acquainted him, that seeing the
besieged had refused the conditions formerly offered, they
ought not now to expect the like, after such an addition of
trouble and charge as they had lately put us upon; yet for
all this caution Sir Charles Coote concluded a treaty with
them, immediately after the return of my answer to the
Earl of Clanrickard; upon conditions much more advantageous to them than those formerly proposed, and very
prejudicial to the publick, undertaking to get them ratified

1652 (margin)

March 10. (margin)

Jan. 10. (margin)

---

[1] On March 10, Coote wrote to
Ludlow: 'There have been very
high contests in the town of Galway,
betwixt the soldiery and the town,
the Lord Clanriekard joyning with
the souldiery, pressing the towne
not to submit without capitulating for
the nation; which the town hath
refused to concur with him in, but
onely to capitulate for themselves,
and leave the country to themselves.
And though Clanriekard intends
another addresse unto the Lieut.-
Gen. concerning the nation, yet the
towne will goe forward in a treaty
for themselves.

'I expect some publick proposures
from them on Tuesday next, and
have had good ground to conceive
that they will suddenly submit to
the first Articles sent them by the
late Lord Deputy, and your Honour's
order. The only thing which they
scruple at is, a parting with a third
part of their personall estates in
town.' Several Proceedings in
Parliament, p. 2057.

1652

by the Commissioners of Parliament within twenty days, and in the mean time promising that they should be inviolably observed [1]. The Commissioners of Parliament having received the articles, and conceiving it to be unjust as well as imprudent to give the best terms to those who made the longest opposition. and of what dangerous consequence it might be, if that place were not fully secured

April 10.

to the English interest, spent the whole night in consultation with the officers of the army, and in the end resolved, that they could not consent that any should receive the benefit of those articles who had been any way concerned in the murdering of the English in the first year of the war : that they would not oblige themselves to permit any to live in Galway whom they should hereafter think fit to remove from thence for the security of the place : that they cannot consent that the burgesses shall enjoy any more than two thirds of their estates lying near the town : that they will not suffer the habitations of such as have been forced to quit the place upon the account of their affection to the Parliament, to be detained from them. With these and some other alterations they declared their consent to the rest of the articles before-mentioned ; which if those of the town refused, they ordered that our men should not enter ; and if entred, that they should restore the possession of it to the garison [2] : but notwithstanding this expedition,

---

[1] Mercurius Politicus, p. 1550, notes : 'From Dublin, April 12. On Saturday last (April 10) we were informed by letter from Sir Charles Coote to the Commissioners of Parliament signifying that Galloway was to be surrendered upon articles by 12 of the clock this day, and how that he had received hostages for delivery thereof.'

[2] The Commissioners wrote to Coote on April 10 : 'Your Lordship's letter from Terrilan the 6th instant was delivered us by Col. Cole at 7 this evening, and we finding it to be a matter of very great concernment

we have imparted the same to sundry officers of the army now present with us, and after consultation and debate had thereupon, could not satisfy ourselves to concur to the confirmation thereof as now they stand, and therefore by the advice of the said officers have made such resolutions and alterations therein as are mentioned in the inclosed, which we commend unto your Lordship's care to communicate to the inhabitants of Galway, and to let them know that in duty and honour to the Parliament, we cannot consent to the articles made with them and

the messenger that was dispatched with the resolutions of   1652
the Commissioners, came too late, and all that could be
obtained was a promise from Sir Charles Coote, to endeavour to perswade those of Galway to accept of the
articles with the amendments made by the Commissioners.

The Parliament having resolved upon the incorporation
of Scotland with the nation of England into one free state
or Commonwealth, and to reimburse themselves some part
of that treasure they had expended in their own defence
against the invasions of the Scots, declared the goods and   February.
lands formerly belonging to the Crown of Scotland to be
confiscated, and also those that were possessed by such
persons as had assisted in the invasion of England by
Duke Hamilton in the year 1648, or had appeared in arms
since, under the King of Scots, in order to subvert the
present government ; excepting those who since the battel
of Dunbar had abandoned the said King of Scots, and by
their merits and services had rendred themselves worthy of
favour : that all such who are not comprehended under the
said qualifications, and shall concur with them in their just
enterprize, shall receive the benefit of their protection, and
enjoy their liberties and goods equally with the free people
of England.   In pursuance of this declaration of the Par-   February.
liament, their commissioners in Scotland published another,
wherein they discharge from confiscation all merchants and
tradesmen, who possess not in lands or goods above the
value of five hundred pounds, and are not prisoners of war,
souldiers of fortune, moss-troopers, or such as have killed
or committed outrages against the English souldiers, contrary to the laws and customs of war.   They also emitted a
proclamation, abolishing in the name of the Parliament all   Jan. 31.
manner of authority and jurisdiction derived from any other
power but that of the Commonwealth of England, as well in

the soldiers, otherwise than with
the said alterations.' Irish Records,
$\frac{A}{90}$ 50, p. 46. See also the letters of
the Commissioners to the Speaker
and Council of State printed in the
Appendix, and for the articles and
exceptions, Mercurius Politicus, pp.
1559. 1636, 1647.

1652   Scotland as in all the isles belonging to it. After this they summoned the counties, cities and boroughs, to agree to the incorporation before mentioned ; of which eighteen of one and thirty counties, and twenty-four of fifty-six cities and boroughs consented to send their deputies to the Parliament of England, most of the rest excusing themselves for want of money to defray the expences of their representatives [1].

This business being accomplished, and an Act passed for the incorporation of England and Scotland into one Commonwealth, the Parliament were prevailed with by the importunities of some of their own members, and in particular of General Cromwell, that so he might fortify himself by the addition of new friends for the carrying on

Feb. 24. his designs, to pass an Act of general pardon and amnesty : whereby tho it had thirty-eight several exceptions, many persons who deserved to pay towards the reimbursement of the publick no less than those who had been already fined, escaped the punishment due to their misdemeanours, and the Commonwealth was defrauded of great sums of money, by which means they were rendred unable to discharge many just debts owing to such as had served them with diligence and fidelity.

In Ireland the rebels were so pressed by our forces in all parts, that they began to think it necessary to treat about conditions of submission, and many of them obtained liberty to be transported into foreign service ; wherein the Commissioners of Parliament assisted them with ships : so that the Irish officers were in many places deserted by

March 7. their own souldiers. Col. Fitzpatrick was the first who submitted, on condition to be transported with his regiment into the service of the King of Spain, which was a great blow to the Irish Confederacy, who were very desirous to treat in conjunction, hoping to obtain more favourable

---

[1] See Mercurius Politicus, pp. 1407, 1431 ; Several Proceedings in Parliament, Feb. 19-26, 165½ ; and Sir Henry Vane's report to Parliament, March 16, 165½, C. J., vii. 105. For the answers of the shires and burghs of Scotland, see Portland Papers, i. 626-45.

terms, in consideration of their numbers; insomuch that 1652
they published declarations against him, and the Irish
clergy excommunicated him, and all those who joined with
him [1]. Notwithstanding which Col. Odowyer, Commander- March 23.
in-Chief of the Irish in the counties of Waterford and
Tipperary, followed his example, and proposed a treaty to
Col. Zanchey, who having received instructions from the
Commissioners, concluded an agreement with him; the
principal articles whereof were to this effect : that the arms
and horses belonging to the brigade of Col. Edmund
Odowyer shall be delivered up at a certain price : that he
and his party shall enjoy their personal estates, and such a
proportion of their real estates as others under their quali-
fication shall be permitted to do : that the benefit of the
articles shall not extend to such as had murdered any of
the English, or had been engaged in the rebellion during
the first year ; or to any Romish priests, or to those who
had been of the first general assembly; those also who had
taken away the life of any of ours after quarter given, and
those who had deserted us and joined themselves to the
enemy, were excepted out of the treaty: all others to have
liberty to live in our quarters, or to transport themselves
into the service of any foreign State in friendship with the
Commonwealth of England [2].

Whilst the ambassadors from Holland were in treaty
with the Commissioners appointed by the Parliament to
that end, the Dutch fleet consisting of forty-three ships of
war, commanded by the Heer Van Tromp, came into the
Downs. Major Bourn [3] having with him a squadron of eight May 18.

[1] The articles with Col. John Fitz-
patrick are printed in the Aphorismical Discovery, iii. 293; and the
declaration against him on p. 389.
See also the letter of the Commissioners, March 23, 1652, Appendix. His forces amounted to
5284 men. At the Restoration, Fitz-
patrick was lucky enough to recover
some portion of his estate; 9th
Report, Hist. MSS. Comm., pp. 160,

163, 165, 168; 8th Report, p. 543.

[2] The articles with O'Dwyer are
printed in Mercurius Politicus, p.
1529; and the Aphorismical Discovery, iii. 294. Col. Sankey's
letter gives a good account of the
treaty (ib. p. 296).

[3] A life of Bourne is given in the
D. N. B., vol. vi. A few details may
be added. Bourne lived for some
time at Boston, and was admitted a

1652

men of war, perceiving two of the Dutch ships making sail towards him. sent to them to demand the reason of their approach ; and an answer being returned, that they had a message to deliver from Admiral Van Tromp to the English commander of that squadron, they were permitted to come up to that purpose.   The captains of the two Dutch ships, after they had saluted Major Bourn by striking the flag, went on board him, and acquainted him, that they were sent by their Admiral to let him know, that riding with his fleet near Dunkirk, he had lost many cables and anchors by bad weather, and was now brought by a north wind more southward than he designed, of which he thought himself obliged to give him notice to prevent any misunderstanding.   Major Bourn told them he was willing to believe what was said, and that the truth of it would best appear by their speedy retreat.   With this answer the two captains returned to their fleet ; which coming within cannon-shot of Dover-Castle with their sails up, and flag at the top-mast, not saluting the fort according to custom, the garison was constrained to fire three guns at the Hollanders, to put them in mind of their duty : but their Admiral made no answer, and still keeping up his flag, lay in the road till the next day about noon, at which time he weighed anchor, and set sail towards Calais.   The rest of the English fleet consisting only of thirteen men of war commanded by General Blake, who had been upon the coast of Sussex, returning into the Downs soon after the departure of the Dutch, was joined by Major Bourn, and those eight ships he had with him.   But Admiral Van Tromp being obliged to take care of some rich merchant

freeman of Massachusetts, June 2, 1641. According to Winthrop he was by trade a carpenter, entered the Parliament's service during the Civil War, and became major to Col. Rainborow's regiment. Winthrop. History of New England, ii. 245. 265, 452, ed. 1853. Hannah, the wife of Nehemiah Bourne, was buried in Bunhill Fields cemetery on June 21, 1684, and from the language of her epitaph her husband seems to have been still alive at that date. Proceedings in Reference to the Preservation of the Bunhill Fields Burial Ground, 1867, p. 61. Was not Nehemiah Bourne father of the Zachary Bourne who was implicated in the Rye-House plot ?

ships bound home to Holland from the Straits, returned
towards the Downs ; and being come within cannon-shot
of our fleet without striking their flag, General Blake commanded three several guns one after the other to be fired
at him. Whereupon he answered with one gun, which shot
through the English flag, and followed it with a whole
broad-side, setting up a red standard on his topmast, as a
signal to the whole fleet to prepare to fight. The engagement began about four in the afternoon, and lasted till nine
at night, with great loss to the enemy, and little damage on
our side, tho their fleet was double our number. We took
two of their men of war in the fight, one of which was
brought away, and the other being very much shatter'd,
sunk down as our men were carrying her off[1]. The
Council of State having received an account of this action,
made their report of it to the Parliament, who passed a
vote for the justification of General Blake ; and resolving
to have satisfaction for this assault, placed a guard upon
the Dutch ambassadors, at their lodgings in Chelsey, and
sent General Cromwell and Mr. Denis Bond, a member of
Parliament, down to the fleet, with assurances that nothing
should be wanting for their encouragement.

The event of this undertaking not answering the expectations of the Hollanders, serving only to provoke the
English nation, and to publish their own dishonour, they
endeavoured to make the world as well as the Parliament
believe, that the quarrel was begun by General Blake, or at
least that what had been done was not by their orders ; and
therefore desired that the treaty might go on, and that the
prisoners taken in the late fight might be restored. To
this end they sent over the Heer Paw of Heemsted to
carry on the treaty in conjunction with the ambassadors

---

[1] See 'A brief relation of the
occasion and manner of the late
fight in the Downs, May 19, 1652,'
Mercurius Politicus, p. 1620. 'The
Answer of the Parliament of the
Commonwealth of England to three
papers delivered to the Council of
State . . . as also a narrative of the
late engagement . . . and likewise
several letters, examinations and
testimonies,' 1652. Cf. Heath's Chronicle, p. 585; Geddes, John de Witt,
p. 208.

they had sent before into England[1]. This minister was
received with all the usual demonstrations of honour, and
being admitted to audience, pressed for an accommodation
of all differences, and a cessation of all acts of hostility
between the two nations ; assuring the Parliament that his
masters had given orders to their ships to strike to the
English flag, in the same manner as had been practised in
former times : but being demanded to shew his powers, he
produced nothing save letters of credence and passports,
referring himself to the other ambassadors in that point,
with whom he made some general propositions to the Parliament, and desired them to declare their demands.   By
these proceedings of the Dutch the Parliament perceiving
that this difference was not like to be decided by a treaty,
contented themselves to require satisfaction for the injuries
received, and assurance that nothing of that nature should
be attempted for the future ; which if the ambassadors
would consent to, they declared themselves ready to proceed in the treaty, and to grant a cessation of arms.   But
so little were they disposed to give the satisfaction demanded, that they made no farther mention of the cessation
which they had so earnestly pressed ; and having taken
their audience of leave, they broke off the treaty abruptly,
and returned home.

In Ireland, tho the number of those that submitted on
condition to be transported into foreign service, was so
great, that they became a great burden to us before we
could procure shipping for their transportation, and tho the
enemy had received several defeats by our forces during
the winter, wherein many of them had been killed and
taken ; yet they continued to make incursions into our
quarters, carrying away cattel and other booty : and having

---

[1] The Dutch ambassadors in Eng-
land were three, Jacobus Cats, Gerard
Schaep, Paulus Vanderperre.   To
these were added as extraordinary
ambassador, Adrian Pauw, Lord of
Heemstede ; his credentials are dated
June 14 (new style).   See for Pauw's
proceedings, 'A Declaration of the
Parliament of the Commonwealth of
England, &c., July 9, 1652 ;' Geddes,
John De Witt, p. 193.

lately seized upon the horses belonging to two troops of dragoons, they were so encouraged, that Sir Walter Dungan, Commissary-General of the enemy's horse, and Capt. Scurlock, a forward officer and one who had done us much mischief, with five hundred foot and two hundred and fifty horse, marched into Wexford, with a design to plunder that county. Lieutenant-Colonel Throgmorton, who commanded in those parts, having informed us of their march, we sent two troops of horse to his assistance, who with them and about four hundred foot charged the enemy upon their return, and after some dispute routed them [1], killing two hundred of them upon the place, and many more, with divers officers, in the pursuit; besides several of the Irish taken prisoners, with the loss of about twenty killed, and a hundred wounded on our side. The booty which the enemy had gotten consisting chiefly in five hundred cows, was all recovered.

The season of action advancing, the Commissioners of Parliament went to Kilkenny, as well to confer with the officers from all parts of Ireland, as to make the necessary preparations for the ensuing service; of which the Earl of Westmeath, who commanded the enemy's forces in Leinster, having notice, sent to desire a safe conduct for commissioners to be named by them to treat with us at Kilkenny on their behalf; which being granted, they appointed Commissary-General Dungan, Lewis Viscount of Glanmaliere, Sir Robert Talbot, Sir Richard Barnwel, Col. Walter Bagnol, Col. Lewis Moor, and Col. Thomas Tyrrell, to be their commissioners. And on our part, Commissary-General Reynolds, Col. Hewetson, Col. Lawrence, Col. Axtel, Adjutant-General Allen, Major Henry Owen, and Mr. James Standish, Deputy-treasurer of the army, were commissionated to treat and conclude with them, in conformity to such instructions as they received from a general council; and after several days' conference the commissioners on each part came to an agreement

Marginal notes: 1652 — May 2. — April 17. — May 12.

---

[1] Several Proceedings in Parliament, pp. 2184, 2187; Mercurius Politicus, p. 1607; Aphorismical Discovery, iii. 390.

1652   upon terms that were the same in substance with those
formerly granted to Col. Edmund Odowyer and his party,
with liberty left for the Lord Muskerry, Major-General
Taaf, and other commanders of the Irish in the provinces
of Munster, Connaught, and Ulster, yet in arms, to come
in and accept of the same conditions within a limited time.
The articles were approved by the Earl of Westmeath on
the behalf of the Irish, and on the part of the Commonwealth of England by me, as Commander-in-Chief of their
forces in Ireland [1].

Jan. 17.   In the mean time the committee appointed by the
Parliament for the Reformation of the Law in England,
made a considerable progress in that matter : judges were
also sent into Scotland for the administration of justice
there, which they performed to the great satisfaction of
April 27. that people.   The Parliament also appointed a committee
to consider of means to set at work all the poor throughout the nation, and to make provision for such as were not
able to work, that there might be no beggar in England.

May 26.   In Scotland our forces having reduced the castle of
Dunotter, which was the last garison of that nation that
held out against the Parliament of England, it was resolved
to make four considerable forts, one at Inverness, another
at Leith, a third at Ayre, and a fourth at St. Johnstoun [2]:
and because the enemy being entirely beaten out of the
field, was retired to the mountainous parts, which to that
time had been accounted inaccessible by the English ; it
was agreed to endeavour to clear those places of them
also, being perswaded that where any went before, others
June.   might follow after.   To this end our men were divided
into three parties : the first consisted of Colonel Overton's
regiment of foot, and a regiment of horse commanded by
Major Blackmore : the second of Colonel Hacker's regi-

---

[1] These articles, known as the
Kilkenny Articles, are printed in the
Aphorismical Discovery, iii. 94, and
Several Proceedings, p. 2171.

[2] On the surrender of Dunotter,
taken by Col. Thomas Morgan, see

Several Proceedings in Parliament,
1652, p. 2208, where Morgan's letter
and the articles of capitulation are
printed.   On the forts, see Heath's
Chronicle, p. 582.

ment of horse, and one of foot commanded by Colonel Lilburn; and the third was composed of the regiment of horse of Major-General Dean, and of a regiment of foot belonging to Lieutenant-General Monk. Each of these having a party of dragoons to attend them, rendezvouzed at Loughaber, and from thence fell separately into the enemy's quarters, where they killed many of them, and burned their provisions, pursuing them so close, that as they fled from one party, they fell into the hands of another; by which means they were in a short time entirely dispersed.

The Irish that submitted according to the articles, and delivered up their arms and horses to the commissioners appointed by me to receive them, were in all about three thousand. But many of them finding themselves within that exception concerning the murders of the English, or hoping to obtain better conditions, or, it may be, taking pleasure in their predatory life, continued still in arms. Of this number was the Lord Muskerry, who commanded the Irish in Munster, and at the time of our treaty with those of Leinster, had sent one Colonel Poor to Kilkenny, to acquaint us that he designed to come in upon the same conditions; but we suspecting his sincerity, by the means of some letters which we intercepted, were not wanting to prepare what was necessary in order to reduce him and his party by force; and having finished our affairs at Kilkenny, I removed with the Commissioners to Clonmel, and from thence to Youghal, and so to Cork.

The rebels in Connaught and Ulster, instead of submitting, as was expected, got together a body of about five thousand men under the conduct of the Earl of Clanrickard and Sir Phelim O'Neal, with which they besieged and took the fort of Ballishannon. Whereupon Sir Charles Coot and Colonel Venables drew out what forces they could, and advanced towards them with such expedition, that they were near the place before the enemy had notice of their march; who finding themselves surprized, retreated to the bogs, leaving a small garison in Ballishannon: but

1652 being pursued by our men, who killed and wounded about three hundred of them, in which number were thirty officers, and took from them seven or eight thousand cows, upon whose milk they chiefly subsisted, twelve hundred of them came in and laid down their arms: upon which the

May 26. garison they had placed in Ballishannon, surrendred upon articles [1].

Major-General Lambert making great preparations to come over to us in the quality of Deputy to General Cromwell [2], the commission of the said General to be Lieutenant of Ireland expired. Whereupon the Parliament took that affair into their consideration; and tho there were not wanting many amongst them, who affirmed the title and office of Lieutenant to be more sutable to a monarchy than a free Commonwealth, yet it was likely to have been carried for the renewing his commission under the same title. But he, having at that time another part to act, stood up, and declared his satisfaction with what had been said against constituting a Lieutenant in Ireland, desiring that they would not continue him with that character.

May 19. Upon which the question being put, the Parliament willing to believe him in earnest, ordered it according to his motion. He farther moved, that tho they had not thought fit to continue a Lieutenant of Ireland, they would be pleased, in consideration of the worthy person whom they had formerly approved to go over with the title of Deputy, to continue that character to him. But the Parliament having suppressed the title and office of a Lieutenant in Ireland, thought it altogether improper to constitute a Deputy, who

[1] Aphorismical Discovery, iii. 320; Mercurius Politicus, p. 1666; Several Proceedings, p. 2245.

[2] Lambert's appointment was approved by Parliament on Jan. 30, 1652. He was then in Scotland, but arrived in London on Feb. 24 to prepare for his journey. According to Mrs. Hutchinson he 'too soon put on the prince, immediately laying out five thousand pounds for his own particular equipage, and looking upon all the Parliament-men who had conferred this honour on him as underlings, and scarcely worth the great man's nod.' This 'untimely declaration of his pride' led, in her opinion, to the abolition of the Lord Lieutenancy. Life of Col. Hutchinson, ii. 188.

was no more than the substitute of a Lieutenant ; and therefore refused to consent to that proposal, ordering that he should be inserted one of the Commissioners for civil affairs, and constituted Commander-in-Chief of their forces in Ireland [1]. In the management of this affair, Mr. Weaver, who was one of the Commissioners of Ireland, but then at London, and sitting in Parliament [2], was very active, to the great discontent of General Cromwell, who endeavouring to perswade the Parliament that the army in Ireland would not be satisfied, unless their Commander-in-Chief came over qualified as Deputy, Mr. Weaver assured them that upon his knowledg, all the sober people of Ireland, and the whole army there, except a few factious persons, were not only well satisfied with the present Government both civil and military of that nation, but also with the governours who managed the same ; and therefore moved that they would make no alteration in either, and renew their commissions for a longer time. This discourse of Mr. Weaver tending to perswade the Parliament to continue me in the military command, increased the jealousie which General Cromwell had conceived of me, that I might prove an obstruction to the design he was carrying on to advance himself by the ruin of the Commonwealth. And therefore, since Major-General Lambert refused to go over with any character less than that of Deputy, he resolved by any means to place Lieutenant-General Fleetwood at the head

[1] The office of Lord Lieutenant was abolished May 19, by 39 to 37 votes, Hesilrige and Marten being tellers for the majority, Whitelock and Harrison for the minority. On June 15, Vane reported to the House that Cromwell's appointment as Lord Lieutenant, being limited for three years, expired on June 23. On July 9, Fleetwood was appointed Commander-in-Chief and Commissioner. C. J., vii. 133, 142, 152, 167. On Aug. 24, new instructions were passed for the Commissioners (ib. p. 167). Old Parliamentary History, xx. 92. They were to remain in office till Sept. 1, 1654.

[2] Weaver was sent over to England to hasten the resolutions of Parliament and obtain their answer for the guidance of the Commissioners. See 'Considerations to be offered to Parliament by Mr. Weaver.' On Feb. 18, 1653, the officers of the army in Ireland presented a complaint against him to Parliament begging for his removal. He was dismissed on Feb. 22. C. J., vii. 127, 260, 261 ; Portland Papers, i. 644, 673.

of affairs in Ireland[1]. By which conduct he procured two great advantages to himself, thereby putting the army in Ireland into the hands of a person secured to his interest by the marriage of his daughter; and drawing Major-General Lambert into an enmity towards the Parliament, prepared him to join with him in opposition to them, when he should find it convenient to put his design in execution.

In the mean time I was not wanting in my endeavours to reduce the enemy in Ireland, and to that end marched with about 4000 foot and 2000 horse towards Ross in Kerry; where the Lord Muskerry made his principal rendezvouz, and which was the only place of strength the Irish had left, except the woods, bogs and mountains; being a kind of an island, encompassed on every part by water, except on one side, upon which there was a bog not passable but by a causway which the enemy had fortified. In this expedition I was accompanied by the Lord Broghil, and Sir Hardress Waller, Major-General of the foot. Being arrived at this place, I was informed that the enemy received continual supplies from those parts that lay on the other side and were covered with woods and mountains; whereupon I sent a party of two thousand foot to clear those woods, and to find out some convenient place for the erecting a fort, if there should be occasion. These forces met with some

June 13. opposition; but at last they routed the enemy, killing some, and taking others prisoners; the rest saved themselves by their good footmanship. Whilst this was doing, I employed that part of the army which was with me in fortifying a neck of land, where I designed to leave a party to keep in the Irish on this side, that I might be at liberty with the greatest part of the horse and foot to look after the enemy abroad, and to receive and convoy such boats and

---

[1] Corbet and Jones wrote to Fleetwood on hearing of his appointment: 'This morning we received notice of your being appointed by the Parliament to be Commander-in-Chief here in Ireland, and of your present resolution of coming hither, which as it is no small enjoying to us, so we do believe that such here as do truly love the Lord and his cause, will and do bless the Lord for this mercy to us and them.' July 29, 1652

Irish Records, $\frac{A}{90}$ 50, p. 201.

other things necessary as the Commissioners sent to us by sea [1]. When we had received our boats, each of which was capable of containing a hundred and twenty men, I ordered one of them to be rowed about the water in order to find out the most convenient place for landing upon the enemy: which they perceiving, thought fit, by a timely submission, to prevent the danger that threatned them ; and having expressed their desires to that purpose, commissioners were appointed on both parts to treat. The articles were the same in effect with those granted to the Irish in Leinster and other places. But much time was spent in the discussion of some particulars, especially that concerning the murder of the English, which was an exception we never failed to make ; so that the Irish commissioners seeming doubtful whether by the wording that article they were not all included, desired that it might be explained ; to which we consented, and it was accordingly done. They also made it their request, that instead of that article relating to their real estates, whereby they were to enjoy such a part as should be allotted to them by the qualifications to be agreed upon, it might be expressed, that they wholly submitted to the mercy of the Parliament therein. The exercise also of their religion was earnestly insisted upon by them ; but we refused to oblige our selves to any thing in that particular, declaring only, that it was neither the principle or practice of the authority which we served, to

---

[1] 'We were fain to provide in this town and at Kinsale materials for two pinnaces to carry guns in them, and two boats more for transportation of men, each boat to carry about 60 men together with oars, rowers, and about 50 sawyers, &c., and to send them by sea to the Bay of Dingle, where they arrived about Friday last the 13th instant.' Commissioners to Council of State, Cork, June 24. Notifying Ludlow of the sending of the workmen and materials, the Commissioners add : 'We have gotten Mr. Chudleigh to go along with them, who is employed now by the State for the naval business being formerly a ship-carpenter, but is one of good estate and good repute amongst the workmen who are the more willing to go because he goeth. We think you will not have the like in giving direction and ordering the making of boats or bridges.' June 15, 1652. Irish Records, $\frac{A}{90}$ 50, pp. 151, 169.

impose their way of worship upon any by violent means. With these explanations the commissioners, after a fortnight's debate. concluded the agreement, the Lord Muskerry and my self confirming it ; his son with Sir Daniel Obryan were delivered to me as hostages for the performance of the articles [1] : in consequence of which about five thousand horse and foot laid down their arms, and surrendred their horses [2].

Whilst this was doing in Munster, Col. Grace with some forces that had not submitted. passed the Shannon, and being joined by many of the Irish of Connaught and Galway, began to grow considerable, being about three thousand, most of them foot. Col. Ingoldsby having notice of them, drew together a party about Limerick, and march-
ing with them to find out the enemy, attacked them at a pass. which they disputed for some time ; but our horse breaking in upon some of their foot, and encouraging the rest to fall on, the Irish quitted their post, and shifted for themselves [3]. In this action many of them were killed and taken prisoners, the rest escaping to the bogs and woods. After this defeat Col. Grace and his party was forced to submit. and to that end treated with Col. Zanchey, but found that his obstinate resistance so long had done him no
service ; for Col. Zanchey upon the surrender of Inch to him. and the submission of Col. Grace's forces, caused a captain, a lieutenant, and a serjeant, with other officers,

---

[1] 'The Lord Muskerry hath been very effectual in the performance of his articles; upon the surrender of the garison of Rosse, 960 able men marched out and laid down arms, and since that 2000 foot. 700 horsemen mounted and 300 unmounted laid down arms, being his entire whole party except Murtogh O'Brien who lately went to Kerry from Thomond and about 200 men with him, who keep in the mountains and fastnesses.' Corbet and Jones to the Council of State from Waterford,
July 22, 1652. Irish Records, $\frac{A}{90}$ 50, p. 198.

[2] See for the articles of surrender, Gilbert, Aphorismical Discovery, iii. 324. Muskerry had liberty given him to transport 5000 men to serve any foreign State in amity with England. The Appendix contains two letters of Ludlow's relating to this campaign, and others from the Commissioners to the Parliament.

[3] See the letter of the Commissioners, June 24, 1652 (Appendix), and Several Proceedings, p. 2275.

to be shot to death, for revolting at Carrick to the enemy, 1652
according to the liberty he had reserved to himself in that
case by the capitulation[1]. In the north of Ireland Col. June 17.
Theophilus Jones being sent out with seven troops of horse,
one of dragoons, and three hundred foot, to get provisions
for the relief of those parts, met with a party of the enemy,
consisting of sixteen hundred foot and three hundred horse,
whom he charged, and after a sharp dispute routed, and put
to flight, killing many of their officers, and three hundred
souldiers upon the place. All the arms of their foot were
taken, and a hundred and fifty horse, with the loss only of
six of our men killed, and about twenty wounded[2]. The
Earl of Clanrickard finding the Irish affairs in a desperate
condition, with what forces he had left retired into the
isle of Carrick, where being encompassed by our men on
all sides, he submitted, and obtained liberty to transport June 28.
himself with three thousand men to any foreign country in
friendship with the Commonwealth, within the space of three
months[3].

The Parliament having already sent over to us five
companies of foot under the command of Lieutenant-Colonel
Finch[4], who had done very good service at the battel of
Worcester, resolved to send eight hundred more out of the
regiment of Major-Gen. Lambert, and an intire regiment

---

[1] On Grace's surrender, see the Articles, Aphorismical Discovery, iii. 130, where his portrait is also reproduced. Sankey's letter announcing his success is reprinted in Several Proceedings, p. 2413; the original is Tanner MS. 53, f. 108.

[2] This fight is described in two letters printed in Mercurius Politicus, July 1-8, 1652, pp. 1710, 1714.

[3] The articles between Clanricarde and the commissioners of Sir Charles Coote are printed in Aphorismical Discovery, iii. 331. See also the letter of the Commissioners, July 22,

Appendix. A letter from them to Clanricarde is in the Tanner MSS. vol. 53, f. 65.

[4] When Col. Duckenfield's regiment was disbanded, five companies of it were designed for Ireland, for the completing of Sir Hardress Waller's regiment, and the command of them given to Lieut.-Col. Simon Finch. Cal. S. P., Dom., 1651-2, pp. 79, 110, 117, 152, 179, 184. Finch finally obtained lands in Limerick and Tipperary which he succeeded in retaining at the Restoration. Seventeenth Report of Dep. Keeper of Irish Records, p. 19.

commanded by Col. Clark [1]; which forces were procured rather to promote the designs of General Cromwel, than from any need we had of them; our military service in Ireland, by the blessing of God, drawing towards a conclusion, most of the Irish forces having submitted and laid down their arms, no garison of any strength holding out against us, and many thousands of the enemy sent into foreign service [2]. The souldiers of Lambert's regiment were countermanded upon his refusal to go to Ireland without the character of Deputy; but the regiment of Col. Clark being thoroughly principled for Cromwel's design, continued their march by order of the Parliament, who were perswaded to constitute Lieutenant-General Fleetwood Commander-in-Chief of their forces in Ireland, and one of their Commissioners for the civil affairs in that nation.

The States General, upon the return of their ambassadors from England, dispatched orders to their Admiral to take all advantages against the English, and solicited the King of Denmark to break with us also, encouraging him to detain twenty-two English merchant ships which he had formerly seized coming through the Sound [3]. The Parliament, to prevent the dangers that might ensue by farther delay, gave orders to General Blake to fall upon the subjects of Holland wheresoever he should meet them, and particularly

---

[1] On Nov. 18 the Council of State decided that the five companies of Sir Hardress Waller's regiment left in England should be made up to a full regiment, to be under the command of Col. John Clarke. The regiment was originally to consist of 1200 men, but on April 19 it was ordered to be recruited up to 2000. It sailed from Bristol and landed at Waterford in June, 1652, about 1500 strong. Cal. S. P., Dom., 1651-2, pp. 22, 220; letter of Irish Commissioners to Ludlow, June 21, 1652.

[2] On Jan. 15, 1653, the Commissioner wrote: 'There are gone from Ireland to the service of the King of Spain since April last about 13,000 men.' On July 22 they stated that 20,000 were lately transported and about 7000 now transporting into foreign parts. Between 1651 and 1654, calculates Mr. Prendergast, 34,000 were transported into foreign parts. 'Forty thousand of the most active-spirited men' is Sir William Petty's estimate. Prendergast, Cromwellian Settlement, pp. 86-8; Irish Records, $\frac{A}{90}$ 50.

[3] On the attitude of Denmark during the war, see Geddes, John de Witt, i. 169, 192, 275, 377.

to interrupt their fishery upon the northern coast, sending
the regiments of Col. Ingoldsby and Col. Goff on board the
fleet. General Blake having received these instructions, set
sail for the north [1], where meeting with about six hundred
herring-busses, under a convoy of twelve men of war, he
took and sunk the whole convoy; and having seized the
fish that the busses had taken, he released all the vessels
with the seamen belonging to them. Which action was
blamed by some, who thought that by the help of those
ships we might have been enabled to erect a fishery, and
thereby have made some reparation to the English nation
for the damages which they had sustained from the Dutch ;
and that by detaining their mariners we might have weakned
and distressed them considerably, they wanting men for the
management of their shipping. In the mean time Sir George
Ayscue, who was lately returned from the reduction of
Barbadoes, and had convoyed into the river five merchant
ships richly laden from the East Indies, fell upon a fleet of
Hollanders consisting of forty merchant-men under the convoy of four men of war [2]. Of this fleet he took seven, forced
divers on shore, and the rest narrowly escaped. About
the same time a ship from Guiny, valued at forty thousand
pounds, was by some of ours taken from the Dutch, with
many other rich ships, to the great prejudice and interruption of their trade. To apply some remedy to this, the Dutch
Admiral with his fleet came into the Downs, and anchored
by Sir George Ayscue, who was retired under Dover-Castle,
being much inferiour in number to the enemy; but the
Hollanders after a short stay left our fleet, and set sail,
without attempting any thing against us [3]. At Leghorn
some of their men of war preparing to seize such English
merchant ships as lay in that port, the Grand Duke sent a

[1] Mercurius Politicus, pp. 1688,
1704, 1785, 1790, 1800; Heath, p.
598.

[2] Ayscue's letter, July 3, Mercurius
Politicus, p. 1720; Several Proceedings, p. 2277; Heath, p. 597; Geddes,
i. 227–233. Ludlow omits all mention of Ayscue's battle with Tromp
on Aug. 16. Several Proceedings,
p. 2384; Heath, p. 599; Mercurius
Politicus, p. 1887.

[3] Mercurius Politicus, p. 1735;
Heath, p. 598; Several Proceedings,
pp. 2376, 2384.

1652 message to the Dutch, to let them know, that if they
committed any acts of hostility against the English nation in
that harbour, their goods in the town should be responsible
for it. Admiral Blake returned to the Downs, and being
informed that a French fleet was going to relieve Dunkirk,
then besieged by the Spaniards, called a council of war, and
by their advice sent a squadron after them, which coming up
Sept. 4. with the French, took divers of their ships, and dispersed the
rest ; by which means chiefly the town was soon after
Sept. 6. surrendred [1].

The Irish being reduced to extremity, and most of the
country in the hands of the English, the Parliament resolved
to give the adventurers possession of lands proportionable
to the several sums they had advanced, and also to satisfy
the arrears of the army out of the same, as they had formerly promised : which that they might be enabled to per-
Aug. 12. form, they passed an Act, confiscating so much of the
estates of those who had acted against the English, as they
judged the quality of their crimes to require, and extending
their clemency to those who had carried themselves peaceably [2]. In the mean time that I might bring such as remained yet in arms against us to a necessity of submitting,
July. I marched with a party of about four thousand horse and
foot ; and having scoured the counties of Wexford and
Wicklo [3], placing garisons where I thought convenient, I

[1] Heath, p. 603; Mercurius Politicus, pp. 1837, 1862, 1892 ; Several
Proceedings, p. 2421 ; Guizot, Cromwell, i. 268, trans. 1854.

[2] The Act for the Settlement of
Ireland passed Aug. 12, 1652. On
Oct. 11, 1652, Ludlow and the Commissioners ordered the Act to be
published and proclaimed in every
precinct 'by beat of drum and sound
of trumpet.' Prendergast, p. 97.
The Commissioners in forwarding
the Act to Ludlow on Aug. 30, recommended him to take special care
by the disposition of his forces and
garrisons to prevent ' disturbance in

the country upon the publishing the
Act, which may probably be endeavoured by those that are made
incapable of pardon, they being very
numerous and of great interest.' The
same expectation of a new outbreak
is shown by a letter of the Commissioners to the commanders in the
several precincts, Sept. 6, 1652.

[3] A letter from Jones and Corbet
to the Council of State, July 22,
1652, says : 'The parties that yet
stand out are that of O'Brien's, who
skulks in the mountains of Kerry,
Cork and Tipperary. The party
commanded by Grace, being com-

went to Tredagh, where I met the rest of the Parliament's Commissioners[1]; and having staid eight days in that place to settle affairs, I continued my march into the county of Meath, and coming to Carrick Mac Ross, a house belonging to the Earl of Essex, where the rebels had barbarously murdered one Mr. Blany a justice of peace in that country[2]. I caused it to be fortified, and put a garison in it, being advantageously situated to restrain the enemy's excursions[3]. From hence I went to visit the garison of Dundalk, and being upon my return, I found a party of the enemy retired within a hollow rock, which was discovered by one of ours, who saw five or six of them standing before a narrow passage at the mouth of the cave. The rock was so thick, that we thought it impossible to dig it down upon them, and therefore resolved to try to reduce them by smoak. After some of our men had spent most part of the day in endeavouring to smother those within by fire placed at the mouth of the cave, they withdrew the fire, and the next morning supposing the Irish to be made uncapable of resistance by the smoak, some of them with a candle before them crawled into the rock. One of the enemy who lay in the middle of the entrance fired his pistol, and shot the first of our men into the head, by whose loss we found that the smoak had not taken the designed effect. But seeing no other way to reduce them, I caused the trial to be repeated,

---

puted about 1000 foot and some few horse, who keep in the fastnesses in King's and Queen's counties, and are attended by Col. Sankey with the forces of Tipperary, and by Col. Axtell with the forces of Kilkenny. The party commanded by Phelim McHugh McBirne and the Cavanaghs in the fastnesses of Wicklow and Wexford, towards whom Lieut.-Gen. Ludlow is now marching with about 2000 horse and foot to plant garrisons in those fastnesses to dislodge or break the enemy (who can and will avoid engagement be the forces never so many that come against

them).' Irish Records, $\frac{A}{90}$ 50, p. 198.

[1] Corbet and Jones wrote from Drogheda on Aug. 9. Ludlow signs a joint letter from thence on Aug. 11.

[2] Richard Blaney, M.P. for Monaghan, whose death is described in the 'Depositions' printed by Miss Hickson; 'Ireland in the Seventeenth Century, Or the Massacres of 1641.' 1884, pp. 189, 209, 213.

[3] Carrickmacross is in Monaghan. Major Moore of Col. Ingoldsby's regiment was made governor by Ludlow.

and upon examination found that tho a great smoak went into the cavity of the rock, yet it came out again at other crevices: upon which I ordered those places to be closely stopped, and another smother made. About an hour and half after this, one of them was heard to groan very strongly, and afterwards more weakly, whereby we presumed that the work was done; yet the fire was continued till about midnight, and then taken away, that the place might be cool enough for ours to enter the next morning. At which time some went in armed with back, breast, and head-piece, to prevent such another accident as fell out at their first attempt; but they had not gone above six yards before they found the man that had been heard to groan, who was the same that had killed one of our men with his pistol, and who resolving not to quit his post, had been, upon stopping the holes of the rock, choaked by the smoak. Our souldiers put a rope about his neck, and drew him out. The passage being cleared, they entred, and having put about fifteen to the sword, brought four or five out alive, with the priest's robes, a crucifix, chalice, and other furniture of that kind. Those within preserved themselves by laying their heads close to a water that ran through the rock. We found two rooms in the place, one of which was large enough to turn a pike; and having filled the mouth of it with large stones, we quitted it, and marched to Castle-Blany, where I left a party of foot, and some horse, as I had done before at Carrick and Newry, whereby that part of the county of Monaghan was pretty well secured[1]. We continued our march to Monaghan, and so to Aghur, where we cast up some works, and left a garison to defend it. Near this place lay the creaght of Lieutenant-General O'Neal, son to that O'Neal who after several years' imprisonment in the Tower of London died there[2]: he came over

---

[1] Captain Baker of Ludlow's own regiment was made governor of Castle Blaney. A few days later 46 of his horse were surprised by the Irish while they were grazing.

[2] On May 1, 1652, Col. Venables concluded articles of agreement with Colonels Therlogh O'Neill and Art O'Neill, at Dundalk. One of these two may be referred to here.

from the service of the King of Spain to be Lieutenant-
General to the army of Owen Roe O'Neal ; but upon some
jealousy or particular discontent was laid aside. This man
with his wife, who he said was niece to the Dutchess of
Artois, and some children, removed, as the Irish do generally in those parts, with their tenants and cattel, from one
place to another, where there is conveniency of grass, water
and wood ; and there having built a house, which they do
compleatly in an hour or two, they stay till they want grass,
and then dislodg to another station. This way of living
is accompanied with many inconveniences to the publick
service ; for they not only give shelter to the enemy, but
take all advantages themselves both to plunder and kill,
none knowing whence they come, or whither they go, and
so can neither easily be prevented nor found out[1]. From
hence I marched to Inniskillin in the county of Fermagnah,
that I might take a view of the place, and likewise provide
materials to fortify Lesneskey, otherwise Bally Balfoar,
and to reduce an island kept by the Irish in Loughern, with
another fort they possessed near Bulturbet. Being at Lesneskey, I was met by Commissary-General Reynolds, who
with a party of horse and foot had dispersed the enemy in

---

[1] 'The "keraghts," "creaghts," or
"kerriaghts," frequently mentioned
in connection with the Irish army
of Ulster, consisted of several home-
less families, who wandered from
place to place with their herds and
flocks, maintaining themselves and
contributing to the victualling of their
army.' Gilbert, Aphorismical Discovery, i. xxxiv. On Jan. 25, 1653,
the Commissioners wrote to the commanders of the 'Precincts': ' Upon
serious consideration of the inconvenience of permitting the Irish to
live in creaghts after a loose disorderly manner, whereby the enemy
comes to be relieved and sustained,
and the contribution oft damaged,
we issued out an order of Oct. the
11th, for the fixing such persons
upon lands proportionable to their
respective stock, and enjoining them
to betake themselves to tillage and
husbandrys, and in case of refusal
to seize upon the cattle and stock of
such persons, and appraising them
upon oath to expose them to sale
for the best advantage of the Commonwealth.' The Commissioners
wish to know how far their orders
have been carried out, and add,
' that in the fixing of all such creaghts
you be very careful that the persons
be disposed of in such places as may
be at most distance from their relations and friends, to the end all relief
may the better be debarred from the
enemy.' $\frac{A}{90}$ 50, p. 414.

1652

Letrim. Having fortified this place, and made some preparations for the reduction of the island before mentioned,

September. I received advice from the Commissioners of Parliament at Dublin, that Lieutenant-General Fleetwood had landed at Waterford, and was gone to Kilkenny, where they designed to attend him [1]. The news of his arrival was very welcome to me, having found my care and fatigues recompensed only with envy and hatred; and therefore having given orders where I was for the carrying on the publick service,

October. I hastned after the Commissioners; and being come to Kilkenny, I saluted the Commander-in-Chief, and congratulated his safe arrival [2]; after which I gave him an account of the affairs of the army, with assurances of my resolution to obey his orders. In this place Col. Walter Bagnal, who had been one of the hostages delivered to us for the performance of the treaty concluded with those of the province of Leinster, was by the Marshal detained prisoner upon an accusation brought against him for the murder of an English-man; which crime being excepted out of those articles and all others at any time granted to the Irish, the Commissioners thought themselves obliged in duty to put him upon his trial, and to that end caused him

---

[1] The Commissioners wrote to Fleetwood from Drogheda on Sept. 14, congratulating him on his arrival. 'This morning your letter of the 11th instant brought us the welcome news of your safe arrival, for which we desire to bow our knees and lift up our hearts in all thankfulness to the Father of all mercies, that in the midst of these storms in this tempestuous season hath vouchsafed his sweet and great mercy to you and our dear friends with you. As to our coming to Kilkenny, we shall hasten the same as soon as this distance can with any conveniency afford opportunity, and do hope on Saturday night we shall by the help of God be ready there to meet with you, or to receive your further com-

mands. The Lieut.-Gen. of the Horse is now in Ulster where he hath been this month last past, and we hope that work he designed by his going thither is near accomplished, and his last letter signified to us that he did purpose to return hither the ending of this week . . . his lady doth tomorrow remove with us to Dublin, and there to stay till his return thither.' $\frac{A}{90}$ 50, p. 290.

[2] See letter of Ludlow and other Commissioners from Kilkenny, Oct. 14, 1652, reprinted in the Appendix. Fleetwood signed in conjunction with them, on Oct. 22, a letter on behalf of Sir Hardress Waller which is amongst the Tanner MSS. vol. 53, p. 139.

to be brought before them, where upon full proof they con- 1652
demned him to be shot to death; which sentence was
executed accordingly [1]. The Lieutenant-General remained
some time at Kilkenny; but the Commissioners having
dispatched their affairs in those parts, returned to Dublin,
and I accompanied them thither.

The Holland fleet appearing off the Goodwin Sands,
Admiral Blake hastned the foot souldiers aboard, and set
sail after them; but they tacked about, and made away
towards the French coast; where being joined by the ships
commanded by Vice-Admiral De Ruyter, they returned
towards our fleet, and came within six leagues of the North
Foreland. Capt. Mildmay in the Nonpareille, about four Sept. 28.
in the afternoon, exchanged some shot with them; and
soon after the English Admiral, with a few more, came
up also, the rest of the fleet by reason of bad weather
being yet far behind. The Dutch kept themselves close
together, firing several single shot at ours, which our
Admiral thought not fit to answer, till the rest of his fleet
was come up to him, and then he began to fire on the
Admiral of Holland. The fight lasted from five till seven,
when night parted them, the Reer-Admiral of the enemy
having lost all his masts, and two more of their ships most
part of their rigging. Capt. Mildmay followed them close,
and being come up with them, commanded his small shot
to be fired into that ship that made most sail, immediately
after which he boarded and took her. This done, he

---

[1] Walter Bagenal's name appears
at the head of the list of persons
condemned by the High Court of
Justice at Kilkenny. Mercurius
Politicus, p. 2151; cf. Aphorismical
Discovery, iii. 134; Hickson, i. 161;
ii. 52-60. He was Ormond's cousin,
and Carte describes him as condemned upon slight pretences and
false evidence. On April 16, 1656,
the Irish Council wrote to Mr.
Hampden: 'There is a youth now
in Dublin whose father Col. Bagenal
suffered about 4 years since at Kilkenny by sentence of the High Court
of Justice, whereby his estate which
was considerable became forfeited to
the Commonwealth. He left divers
young children. The Council here
are desirous that this young man
should be bound an apprentice to
some person in London, where he
may be virtuously trained up and
by benefit of good education and
distance hence be wholly estranged
from his Popish relations.' $\frac{A}{30}$ 28, p.
146.

pursued another, and in half an hour overtook her, and forced her to yield also. In one of these ships was the Dutch Rear-Admiral, whom Capt. Mildmay took out, with the rest of the men, and then let her sink, she being so disabled, that he despaired of bringing her off[1]. The next morning our fleet pursued the Dutch, who made away with all possible speed, and about four in the afternoon bore up with them ; but none of our great ships except the admiral being able to reach them, the night separated them again. The next day the Dutch recovered Goree and others of their harbours, so that our fleet thought fit to desist any farther pursuit of them. On our side we had but three of our men and Capt. Jarvis killed, with about twenty wounded. The enemy's loss was considerable, many of their men being killed and wounded, besides several taken prisoners ; and three of their ships sunk and taken. Fourteen more were also brought into their ports much damaged in the engagement, with great numbers of wounded men on board. Their fleet coming to Goree, the captains were forbidden to come a shore till enquiry should be made touching those who had refused to fight in the first encounter with the English. Hereupon the enmity of the Dutch against the English nation grew to such a height, that to render them odious, and to encourage their own subjects to come in to serve against them, they caused the execution of the late King to be represented on the stage in a most tragical manner : insomuch that those of the Prince of Orange's party were not without hopes that the States of Holland would rather surrender their liberties to the Prince, than quietly suffer England to live under the government of a Commonwealth. Some prejudice we received in two encounters with the Dutch in the Mediterranean Sea ; but those slight successes were wholly owing to their number, and not at all to their courage or conduct[2].

---

[1] Relations of this engagement are printed in Mercurius Politicus, p. 1926 ; Several Proceedings, p. 2475 ; Heath, p. 605 ; Life of Sir William Penn, i. 440 ; Geddes, John de Witt, i. 252-8.

[2] Captain Richard Badiley was defeated by Admiral Van Galen off

The Parliament gave audience to ambassadors from Venice and Portugal, referring the consideration of their instructions to the Council of State, who were required to report their opinions touching them to the Parliament. They also ordered a letter to be drawn up and dispatched to the Grand Duke of Tuscany, to give him thanks for the good usage received from him by the English merchants at Leghorn. About the same time thirty frigats were appointed to be built, as well to increase the fleet, as to secure the trade of the nation by cruising. Eighteen men of war were likewise sent into the Sound under the conduct of Capt. Hall, who at his arrival before Elsenore, delivered a letter to the governour of that place for the King of Denmark, with assurances that he was come thither for no other end than to convoy home two and twenty English merchant ships formerly seized by the said King at Copenhagen. The King of Denmark seemed much offended that Capt. Hall had entred the Sound without his leave, and sent four thousand men to Cronenburg and Elsenore, to reinforce those places, giving orders to his fleet to join with the Hollanders, who were not far off, and to fight the English in case they attacked the Dutch. These great preparations obliged Capt. Hall to retire from thence, and to return to Newcastle. Hereupon the Danish ambassador at London had his audience of leave from the Parliament, and his master began to prepare twenty ships of war for the assistance of the Dutch, alledging himself bound so to do by a treaty with them : in order to which he caused the goods belonging to the English to be taken out of the two and twenty ships before-mentioned, and to be sold, declaring openly for the Hollanders.

In the mean time the reformation of the Law went on but slowly, it being the interest of the lawyers to preserve the

Marginal dates:

1652
June 15.
Sept. 30.
Sept. 30.
Sept. 28.
Sept. 9.
Sept. 30.
Sept. 27.
Oct. 29.

Corsica, Aug. 27, 28, 1651. The Phœnix, taken in this engagement, was recaptured Nov. 20, but on March 4, 1652, Captain Henry Appleton and six ships, blockaded by the Dutch in Leghorn harbour, were defeated and all but one taken. Mercurius Politicus, pp. 1920, 1996, 2140, 2166, 2323, 2339, 2349; Heath, pp. 608, 613 619, 622.

1652 lives, liberties and estates of the whole nation in their own hands. So that upon the debate of registring deeds in each country, for want of which, within a certain time fixed after the sale, such sales should be void, and being so registred, that land should not be subject to any incumbrance : this word 'incumbrance' was so managed by the lawyers, that it took up three months time before it could be ascertained by the committee [1].

The Act for putting a period to the Parliament was still before a committee of the whole House, who had made a considerable progress therein, having agreed upon a more equal distribution of the power of election throughout England : and whereas formerly some boroughs that had scarce a house upon them chose two members to be their representatives in Parliament, (just as many as the greatest cities in England, London only excepted) and the single county of Cornwall elected forty-four, when Essex and other counties bearing as great a share in the payment of taxes, sent no more than six or eight ; this unequal representation of the people the Parliament resolved to correct, and to permit only some of the principal cities and boroughs to chuse, and that for the most part but one representative, the city of London only excepted, which on account of the great proportion of their contributions and taxes were allowed to elect six. The rest of the four hundred, whereof the Parliament was to consist, (besides those that served for Ireland and Scotland) were appointed to be chosen by the several counties, in as near a proportion as was possible to the sums charged upon them for the service of the State, and all men admitted to be electors who were worth two hundred pounds in lands, leases or goods [2].

---

[1] On Dec. 26, 1651, Parliament referred the subject of law reform to a committee, appointing a committee to select fit persons, whose nominations were approved on Jan. 17, 1652. C. J.: see also Masson, Life of Milton, iv. 385 ; Inderwick, The Interregnum, p. 201. 'I remember well,' said Cromwell in 1657, 'at the old Parliament we were three months, and could not get over the word "Incumbrances."' Carlyle's Cromwell, Speech xiii.

[2] On the history of the ' Bill for a New Representative,' see Masson, Life of Milton, iv. 308, 404. The

Divers informations were brought against the Irish for murders committed at the beginning of the rebellion and since upon the English. The principal of the accused were Col. Maccarty Reagh, who was seized in the county of Cork; the Lord Mayo in the county of Galway; the mother of Col. Fitz-Patrick in the province of Leinster, with many others [1]. And for the encouragement of the plantations in Ireland, the Parliament permitted the people of England to transport thither all sorts of cattel and grain free of all custom, and ordered that their Commissioners in Ireland should raise a revenue there for all such as had been wounded and disabled, and for the widows and children of those that had been killed in the publick service [2].

The vice-admiral of Prince Rupert's fleet carrying forty pieces of cannon, was brought into Plymouth by the English seamen she had on board, who finding a favourable occasion, near Cape de Verd seized the captain and the rest of the company, being all French and Dutch: upon which the Council of State received orders from the Parliament to reward the said seamen, and to prepare an Act to encourage others to follow their example [3].

The Dutch Admiral Van Trump, with one hundred and ten ships of war, and some fire-ships, being joined by seventeen men of war from Zealand, sailed from Goree with orders to convoy safe out of the Channel a fleet of near five hundred merchant ships, designed for France, Spain, Portugal, Italy, Barbary, and the Levant, and to take all the advantages he could against the English. Hereupon the

Instrument of Government carried into effect the scheme passed by the Long Parliament, and originally suggested in the Agreement of the People.

[1] The task of bringing these informations was specially assigned to Dr. Henry Jones, the Scoutmaster General. See the letter of the Commissioners to Jones, Aug. 9, 1652. Already in the debates of the officers at Kilkenny in the pre-ceding April, Jones had brought forward the depositions collected in 1642.

[2] See C. J., vii. 166.

[3] See the narrative of William Coxon of the recapture of the ship Marmaduke of London, ' which was late Vice-admiral to Prince Rupert and called by him the Revenge of Whitehall.' Cal. S. P., Dom., 1651-2, p. 308; Several Proceedings in Parliament, p. 2206.

Parliament passed an act for the sale of the estates of some, who having been adjudged delinquents, had refused to lay hold of the favour extended to them of compounding; which they did to ease the people of some part of the charge of this war against the Dutch; yet their occasions

were so pressing, that they were constrained to lay a tax for some months of one hundred and twenty thousand pounds a month, which the people willingly paid, because they knew that it was wholly employed in their service.

Most of the Dutch merchant ships were by bad weather and contrary winds driven back into their harbours, but their men of war kept out at sea; and Van Trump having received advice that Admiral Blake had sent away twenty of his ships to convoy a fleet of laden colliers from Newcastle, twelve towards Plymouth, and fifteen up the river, which had suffered some damage by storm, and that he had left with him but thirty-seven ships of war, came into the Downs with fourscore men of war, and thirty of the ablest merchant-men of the fleet he was appointed to convoy. Notwithstanding which inequality of number it was unani-

mously resolved in a council of war to fight the Dutch fleet. Accordingly a day or two after ours engaged them about noon, and the fight continued till night separated them [1]. In this fight we lost two ships, the Garland of 40, and the Bonaventure of 36 guns; and tho in recompence we burnt one of their admirals, and killed many of their men, particularly two secretaries who were on board their admiral, yet the Dutch were exceedingly elevated with this little success; and being informed that the English fleet was in great want of all sorts of naval stores, they published a placaet to prohibit the exportation of them hither under severe penalties. They also threatned to drive us out of the islands which we possessed in America, and to that end sent some ships to join Prince Rupert, which with those revolted English made up in all twenty-five sail. The King of Denmark likewise promised to assist them by

[1] See the relation of this battle in Mercurius Politicus, Dec. 2-9, pp. 2064, 2097, 2103, 2124.

the next spring with thirty ships of war, for the sum of one million of guilders which they agreed to pay to him [1].

In the mean time the Parliament having received information of the misbehaviour of some officers in the late engagement, appointed a committee, whereof Sir Henry Vane, Mr. John Carew, and Major Salloway, were the principal, impowering them to place and displace officers, and to regulate all matters relating to the sea, in such a manner as might be most conducing to the service of the state. These commissioners used such care and diligence in the discharge of this trust, that the face of affairs soon became much alter'd for the better; the ships that were unserviceable repaired, a considerable fleet put to sea well officer'd and well mann'd, the store-houses replenish'd with all manner of necessary provisions, and thirty frigats preparing to be built. Lieutenant-General Monk was also added to the Generals Blake and Dean, in the room of Col. Edward Popham lately deceased, to take care of the equipping and commanding the fleet. And that nothing might be wanting on our part to preserve a good correspondence with such foreign states as were in amity with us, the Parliament sent the Lord Commissioner Whitlock on an extraordinary embassy to the Crown of Sweden, where he was received with all the honours due to his character [2].

The Commissioners for the Irish affairs being at Dublin, Lieutenant-General Fleetwood came thither with his family; after whose arrival a commission was issued out for the trials of such as were accused of having murdered the English, which was directed to persons of known ability and integrity in each province [3]. To those formerly ac-

Right margin dates:
1652
Dec. 10.
Nov. 26.
1653
November.
1652
November.

---

[1] Ludlow makes no mention of the three days' battle off Portland, Feb. 18, 19, 20, 1653. Geddes, i. 486; Mercurius Politicus, pp. 2250–76.

[2] On Dec. 23, 1652, Parliament determined to send an ambassador to Sweden, and on Dec. 31, Viscount Lisle was selected. His instructions were not ready till March 22, 1653. After the expulsion of the Rump,

Whitelocke was chosen by the Council of State to serve instead of Lisle, Aug. 1653, and embarked on Nov. 6, and arrived at Upsala in December. See Whitelocke's Journal of the Swedish Embassy, ed. Reeve, 1855.

[3] Extracts from the records of the High Court of Justice are printed in Miss Hickson's 'Ireland in the Seventeenth Century, or the Massacres of

1652   cused was added the Lord Muskerry, who was charged to
have put many Englishmen to death in the way between
his house of Mackroom and the city of Cork. Upon this
accusation the said lord was seized, and ordered to be
prosecuted by the Court of Justice at Dublin for the same.
The Commissioners also by order of the Parliament published a declaration to inform the publick, and particularly the adventurers, who had advanced money upon the
Irish lands, that the war in Ireland was concluded. This
they did as well that the said adventurers might have what
was justly due to them, as that the poor wasted country
of Ireland might have the assistance of their own purses
and labour, to recover the stock and growth of the land ;
the Irish having all along eaten out the heart and vigour of
the ground, and of late much more than ever, being in
daily apprehensions of being removed.

All arrears due to the English army in Ireland were
satisfied by the Parliament out of the estates forfeited by
the rebels, which were delivered to them at the same rates
with the first adventurers [1]. In this transaction those of
the army shewed great partiality, by confining the satisfaction of arrears only to such as were in arms in August
1649, which was the time when the English army commanded by Lieutenant-General Cromwel arrived in Ireland ;
and tho the hardships endured by those who were in arms
before had been much greater, yet nothing could be obtained but such a proportion of lands in the county of
Wicklo, and elsewhere, as was not sufficient to clear the
fourth part of what was due to them [2]. Those who

1641, 1884, vol. ii. p. 172-235. The
first of the courts set up opened its
proceedings at Kilkenny, Oct. 4, 1652.
The commission to the Galway court
is dated Dec. 17, 1652. Other courts
sat at Waterford, Cork, Dundalk
and Dublin. Coxe, Hibernia Anglicana, Reign of Charles II, p. 70.

[1] Ludlow refers to the Act for the
Satisfaction of the Adventurers for
lands in Ireland, and of the arrears

due to the soldiery there, and of
other public debts, passed Sept. 27,
1653. Possibly he confuses it in
point of time with the Act for stating
the accounts of officers and soldiers
employed in Ireland, passed Aug.
25, 1652. The process by which the
confiscated lands were divided is
described in Prendergast's Cromwellian Settlement of Ireland, 1875.

[2] See Prendergast, pp. 187-195.

solicited the affairs of the army in Ireland with the Parliament, having perswaded the adventurers that there were
forfeited lands enough in one moiety of nine principal
counties, they accepted of them for their satisfaction, and
the other moiety was assigned by the Act for the satisfaction of the souldiers; the rest of Ireland was also
disposed of, only the province of Connaught was reserved
for the Irish under the qualifications agreed upon by the
Parliament: according to which they were to be put
into possession of the several proportions of land which
had been promised them in the said province; that so the
adventurers, souldiers, and others to whom the Parliament
should assign their lands, might plant without disturbance,
or danger of being corrupted by intermixing with the
natives in marriages or otherwise, which by the experience
of former times the English had been found to be, rather
than to have bettered the Irish either in religion or good
manners: and that the natives being divided by the River
Shannon from the other provinces, and having garisons
placed round and amongst them in the most proper and
convenient stations, they might not have those opportunities to prejudice the English as formerly they had.
An Act being drawn up to this purpose, the Parliament   Sept. 2'
passed it, reserving the counties of Dublin, Kildare, Carlo
and Cork, (together with the remaining part of the lands
formerly belonging to the Bishops, Deans and Chapters of
Ireland, whereof some had been already applied, to augment the revenues of the College of Dublin) to be disposed
of as the Parliament should think fit.

The forfeited lands were divided between the adventurers and souldiers by lot, according to an estimate taken
of the number of acres in the respective counties, in conformity to an order from the Commissioners of Parliament;
by whom were appointed sub-commissioners to judg of the
qualifications of each person, and others, who upon certificate from the sub-commissioners for determining qualifications, were required to set out so much land in the
province of Connaught as belonged to every one by virtue

1653 of the said Act. They also established a committee to sit at Dublin to receive and adjudg all claims of English and others to any lands, limiting a time within which they were obliged to bring in and make appear their respective claims to be legal ; to the end that the adventurers, souldiers, and others, might be at a certainty. and after such a time free from any molestation in the possession of their lands ; and that none through ignorance or absence might be surprized, they prorogued the said time twice or thrice to a longer day.

The Courts of Justice erected at Dublin and in other parts, proceeded vigorously in making inquisition after the murders that had been committed [1]. Maccarty Reagh, after much search into the matter whereof he stood accused, was acquitted by the court sitting at Cork ; and so was the Lord Clanmaliere by that of Kilkenny; but the mother of Col. Fitz-Patrick was found guilty of the murder of the English, with this aggravation, that she said she would make candles of their fat. She was condemned to be burnt, and the sentence was executed accordingly. Col. Lewis Moor and Lewis Demley were also found guilty of murder, for which they were hanged [2]. Sir Charles Coote, with the rest of the Court of Justice in the province of Connaught, proceeded against the Lord Mayo [3], and de-

Jan. 15. clared him guilty of the same crime, for which he was executed according to the sentence pronounced against him [4].

[1] A list of sentences passed by the court is given by Miss Hickson, ii. 232. Other lists are printed in Mercurius Politicus, pp. 1969, 2151, 2371, 2590, 2823. Most of the persons condemned were executed without any delay.

[2] Charles MacCarthy Reagh was acquitted in Dec. 1652. On his subsequent history, see Prendergast, Ireland from the Restoration to the Revolution, p. 51. On Lord Lewis Dempsey, Lord Clanmalier, ib. p. 52; Mercurius Politicus, pp. 2026,

2153. Bridget Darcy, wife of Florence Fitzpatrick, and mother of Col. John Fitzpatrick before mentioned. See Mercurius Politicus, p. 2009.

[3] Depositions against Lord Mayo are printed by Miss Hickson, i. 375–399; ii. 1–4, 255. This was Theobald Bourke, 3rd Viscount Mayo. Lodge, Irish Peerage, ii. 334. The court at Galway was established by commission dated Dec. 17, 1652.

[4] The Commissioners (including presumably Ludlow) wrote to Col.

The trial of the Lord Muskerry was long. by reason of a
clause which he urged in his defence from a printed copy
of the articles made with him; which tho it had been
unjust for me to grant in the terms there mentioned, yet
would have cleared him, and thrown the blame and guilt
upon me; for articles given ought to be made good. But
this clause upon search into the original, which I kept,
appeared to have been inserted by themselves in the print
which they produced for evidence, under pretence of having
lost the original articles signed by me. Notwithstanding
which, it appearing that tho divers of the English were
murdered by the convoy appointed to conduct them safe
to Cork, the Lord Muskerry had taken what care he could
for their security, and had done what in him lay to bring
the person who was guilty of that blood to justice, the
court acquitted him, and he was permitted according to his
articles to pass into Spain. I have heard that upon his
arrival in that kingdom a faction appeared against him,
upon account of his former opposition to the Pope's Nuntio
in Ireland; so that he finding but cold entertainment there,
entred into a treaty to put himself and his men into the
service of the Venetians [1].

Phaire on Dec. 28, 1652, ordering
him immediately to carry out the
sentences passed. 'Taking into consideration how in those inquiries we
have made into the innocent blood
of the English and other Protestants
that hath been shed in this land,
the Lord hath evidently appeared
in discovering and finding out the
authors of those murders, that so they
may be brought to condign punishment, we dare not draw upon our
heads the guilt of delaying the exact-
ing that justice; and therefore lest
you might be inclinable to respite
(beyond the time limited the sentences of the High Court of Justice,
by which those persons committed
to your custody stand condemned to
die, we hold it our duty to declare
our sense herein, which is that you
do forthwith perform that duty which
lies on you.' Irish Records, $\frac{A}{90}$ 50,
p. 383.

[1] Muskerry was allowed to embark for Spain after his capitulation
to Ludlow, and tried after his return
to Ireland in 1653. 'The Lord
Muskerry,' writes Col. John Jones
on March 1, 1653, 'is lately landed
at Cork, and says he will cast himself upon the Parliament's mercy,
pretending the clergy in Spain had
determined to murder him, and that
Portugal would not entertain him, of
all of which I believe but my share.'
Gilbert, *Aphorismical Discovery*, iii.
371. Muskerry's trial is printed by
Miss Hickson, ii. 192; cf. Carte,
Ormond, iii. 629; Thurloe, ii. 94.

1653   Luke Took, the head of a sept in the county of Wicklo,
being conscious of his guilt, had formerly desired my pass
to come and treat with me about conditions for laying
down the arms of himself and party; and to induce me to
give him more favourable terms, said, he had a horse and
saddle worth a hundred pounds, which he desired I would
accept of. I refusing his present, he took it as an ill omen
to him ; for they are so accustomed to bribe their magistrates in that country, that if any one refuse their presents,
they presently conclude him to be their enemy, and give
their cause for lost ; and therefore he submitted not at
that time. But now supposing he could by no means
avoid falling into our hands, by reason of the number of
our garisons placed in all parts amongst them, who by
this time were as well acquainted with their retreats and
fastnesses as themselves, and it may be thinking there
would not appear sufficient evidence to prove him guilty,
he submitted upon the same condition I had formerly
offered to him, which was, that he should be liable to
be questioned for murder, whereof being accused before
Jan. 27. the court at Dublin, he was convicted, sentenced, and
executed [1].

Sir Phelim O'Neal, head also of a sept, and one who
had as great a share as any in the contriving and carrying
on the massacre and rebellion, fell into the hands of the
Lord Cawfield, whose brother he had caused to be murdered at the beginning of the rebellion in this manner.
O'Neal being a neighbour of the Lord Cawfield, came to
him under the pretence of friendship, with about half a
dozen friends, to his castle of Charlemont, where being
received, he and those that were with him were carried to
drink in the cellar by the Lord Cawfield, (both of them
being too much addicted to that which the world calls
good fellowship). After some time Sir Phelim O'Neal
fires a pistol, which was a signal agreed on, and im-

---

[1] Should be Luke Toole; see Mercurius Politicus, pp. 2241, 2371, Feb.
17-24, 1653; Hickson, ii. 33, 34.   Ludlow's Irish names are frequently
inaccurate.

mediately thirty Irish entred and surprized the castle,
taking the lord, his mother, lady, and children, with the
rest of the family prisoners; and after three or four days
murdered the Lord Cawfield, the rest hardly escaping with
their lives. But now the Commissioners of Parliament
having by their prescribed lines, within which all were obliged to inhabit, withdrawn provisions from the enemy, who
could not be supplied without hazard of their lives, thought
fit as a further means to reduce them, to set a sum of
money upon the heads of the principal of those who yet
persisted in their rebellion, upon some twenty, others forty,
and upon Sir Phelim O'Neal a hundred pounds, to bring
him dead or alive[1]. This was such an incouragement to
look after him, that one of the country people having
notice that he was in an island in the north, gave intelligence thereof to the Lord Cawfield, who having brought
together a party of horse and foot, entred the island in
boats, and seized him there. From thence he carried him
to Dublin, where divers of his cruelties to the English
being proved against him, he was sentenced by the Court
of Justice to be put to death, and his head to be set upon
the gate that stands at the foot of the bridg, which was put
in execution accordingly[2].

Thus the enemy by the blessing of God upon the
counsels of the Parliament, and endeavours of their armies,
was everywhere dispersed and conquered, and the nation
likely to attain in a short time that measure of happiness
which humane things are capable of, when by the ambition
of one man the hopes and expectations of all good men
were disappointed, and the people robbed of that liberty

---

[1] A Declaration, May 22, 1652, recites that certain persons, know-ing they cannot obtain pardon, re-fuse to submit, and orders that any one bringing in the heads of any of the persons named shall be duly paid a given sum. For the person or head of Lord Muskerry, £500, for Col. Maccarty Reagh, £200, &c. A second proclamation on Aug. 23, offered £300 for Sir Phelim O'Neill. Irish Records, $\frac{A}{82}$ 42, pp. 238, 313.

[2] Sir Phelim O'Neill's trial is printed by Miss Hickson, ii. 181; for depositions against him, ib. i. 203, 223, 326; on his supposed com-mission from Charles I, ib. i. 113–119; ii. 373.

which they had contended for at the expence of so much blood and treasure.

General Cromwel had long been suspected by wise and good men ; but he had taken such care to form and mould the army to his humour and interests, that he had filled all places either with his own creatures, or with such as hoped to share with him in the sovereignty, and removed those who foreseeing his design, had either the courage or honesty to oppose him in it. His pernicious intentions did not discover themselves openly till after the battel at Worcester, which in one of his letters to the Parliament he called The Crowning Victory [1]. At the same time when he dismissed the militia, who had most readily offered themselves to serve the Commonwealth against the Scots, he did it with anger and contempt, which was all the acknowledgment they could obtain from him for their service and affection to the publick cause. In a word, so much was he elevated with that success, that Mr. Hugh Peters, as he since told me, took so much notice of it, as to say in confidence to a friend upon the road in his return from Worcester, that Cromwel would make himself king [2]. He now began to despise divers members of the House whom he had formerly courted, and grew most familiar with those whom he used to shew most aversion to ; endeavouring to oblige the royal party, by procuring for them more favourable conditions than consisted with the justice of the Parliament to grant, under colour of quieting the spirits of many people, and keeping them from engaging in new disturb-

---

[1] 'The dimensions of this mercy are above my thoughts. It is, for aught I know, a crowning mercy.' Carlyle's Cromwell, Letter clxxxiii. In the same letter Cromwell praises the newly raised militia 'for their singular good service, for which they deserve a very high estimation and acknowledgment,' adding, 'they are all despatched home again, which I hope will be much for the ease and satisfaction of the country.'

[2] Compare Peters' statement to Ludlow in 1656. Whitelocke says that Cromwell 'carried himself with great affability and seeming humility, and in all his discourses about Worcester would seldom mention anything of himself, but of the gallantry of the officers and soldiers, and gave (as was due), all the glory of the action to God.' Memorials, iii. 352, ed. 1853.

ances to rescue themselves out of those fears, which many who had acted for the king yet lay under; tho at the same time he designed nothing, as by the success was most manifest, but to advance himself by all manner of means, and to betray the great trust which the Parliament and good people of England had reposed in him. To this end he pressed the Act of Oblivion with so much importunity, that tho some members earnestly opposed its bearing date till after some months, as well in justice to those of that party who had already fined for their delinquency, that others as guilty as themselves might be upon an equal foot with them, as that the state might by that means be supplied with money, which they wanted, and that such who had been plundered by the enemy might receive some satisfaction from those who had ruined them, yet nothing could prevail upon the General; and so the Act was passed: the Parliament being unwilling to deny him any thing for which there was the least colour of reason.

But tho he had gained this point, and eagerly coveted his own advancement, he thought it not convenient yet to unmask himself; but rather to make higher pretences to honesty than ever he had done before, thereby to engage Major-General Harrison, Col. Rich, and their party, to himself. To this end he took all occasions in their presence to asperse the Parliament, as not designing to do those good things they pretended to; but rather intending to support the corrupt interests of the clergy and lawyers. And tho he was convinced that they were hastning with all expedition to put a period to their sitting, having passed a vote that they would do it within the space of a year, and that they were making all possible preparations in order to it [1]; yet did he industriously publish, that they were so in love with their seats, that they would use all means to perpetuate themselves. These and other calumnies he had

---

[1] Ludlow probably is thinking of the vote of Parliament on Nov. 18, 1651: 'Resolved that the time for the continuance of this Parliament, beyond which they resolve not to sit, shall be the 3rd of November, 1654.'

with so much art insinuated into the belief of many honest and well-meaning people, that they began to wish him prosperity in his undertaking. Divers of the clergy from their pulpits began to prophesy the destruction of the Parliament, and to propose it openly as a thing desirable. Insomuch that the General, who had all along concurred with this spirit in them, hypocritically complained to Quarter-master-General Vernon, 'that he was pushed on by two parties to do that, the consideration of the issue whereof made his hair to stand an end.' 'One of these,' said he, 'is headed by Major-General Lambert, who in revenge of that injury the Parliament did him, in not permitting him to go into Ireland with a character and conditions sutable to his merit, will be contented with nothing less than their dissolution [1]. Of the other Major-General Harrison is the chief, who is an honest man, and aims at good things, yet from the impatience of his spirit will not wait the Lord's leisure, but hurries me on to that which he and all honest men will have cause to repent [2].' Thus did he craftily feel

---

[1] The statement that Harrison was eager to dissolve the Parliament and that Cromwell opposed it is confirmed by a letter from Daniel O'Neill to Hyde written in March, 1653. 'The council of the army,' writes O'Neill, 'is divided into two parties, (1 the faction of Cromwell, (2) the faction of Harrison. The heads of Cromwell's faction in the army are Whalley, Barkstead, Goffe, &c., whose design is to maintain and continue the government in the hands of these men that are of the house at present, they knowing that if Harrison's party prevails Cromwell and his party must down. This party of Cromwell consist chiefly of the mere Independants. The head of Harrison's party in the army are Lambert, Rich, Pride, &c., whose design is to put the government into other hands and to rout the present members of Parliament, supposing them to be very corrupt and that it is fit that others should rule as well as they, the continuance of men in government tempting of them to corruption ... The common opinion of people is that Harrison's party prevails ; this is also very evident. I have heard some that are of Harrison's private council say that they doubted not but to bring their design about before Midsummer next.' Cf. Nicholas Papers, ii. 13. This document, and others relating to the expulsion of the Rump, are printed in full in the English Historical Review.

[2] 'My Lord Lambert, they say, endeavours to heighten the Commonwealth party against the present government; vindicates himself touching his past actings for the late Lord Protector, by his being animated against divers of the principal persons of the Long Parliament, by the instigation of his late highness, whoe,

the pulse of men towards this work, endeavouring to cast the infamy of it on others, reserving to himself the appearance of tenderness to civil and religious liberty, and of skreening the nation from the fury of the parties beforementioned.

This mine of his was not wrought with so much privacy but it was observed by some discerning men of the Parliament, especially by those who had the direction and management of the war with Holland. These men endeavoured to countermine him two ways : first by balancing his interest in the army with that of the fleet, procuring an order from the Parliament, whose ear they had upon all occasions, by reason of the importance of the war with the Dutch, to send some regiments of the army to strengthen the fleet ; and secondly by recommending, as an easy way to raise money in that exigency, the sale of Hampton-Court, and other places, that were esteemed as baits to tempt some ambitious man to ascend the throne[1]. The Parliament having ordered these things to be done, the General, sensible of the design, and of the consequences of suffering the army to be new-moulded, and put under another conduct, made haste to execute his former resolutions, railing to Col. Okey and other officers of the army against divers members of the Parliament, affirming that little good could be expected from that body where such men had so great an influence. At the same time he made the most solemn professions of fidelity to the Parliament, assuring them, that if they would command the army to

he says, privately perswaded Sir Henry Vane and Sir Arthur Haslerig against his being sent into Ireland with convenient powers for the charge of Lord Deputy, both upon religious and prudent pretences ; and that as soon as he had underhand crossed him in that employment, he was the first whoe exasperated him agaynst those persons, telling him, that not anything troubled him more than to see honest John Lambert soe ungratefully treated ; with many other expressions to this purpose.' Col. Bamfylde to Thurloe, April, 1659, Thurloe, vii. 660.

[1] On Dec. 31, 1652, it was resolved by the Parliament to rescind the former vote exempting Hampton Court from sale, and to proceed to sell it. C. J., vii. 239 The Little Parliament on Sept. 26, 1653, ordered the sale to be stayed till further order. Ib. vii. 324.

break their swords over their heads, and to throw them into the sea, he would undertake they should do it. Yet did he privately engage the officers of the army to draw up a petition to the Parliament, that for the satisfaction of the nation they would put that vote which they had made for fixing a period to their sitting, into an Act: which whilst the officers were forming and debating, the General having, it seems, for that time altered his counsels, sent Col. Desborough, one of his instruments, to the council of officers, who told them, that they were a sort of men whom nothing could satisfy; that the Parliament were more ready to do any good than they to desire it; that they ought to rely upon their word and promise to dissolve themselves by the time prefixed; and that to petition them to put their vote into an Act, would manifest a diffidence of them, and lessen their authority, which was so necessary to the army. The General coming into the council whilst Desborough was speaking, seconded him; to which some of the officers took the liberty to reply, that they had the same opinion of the Parliament and petition with them, and that the chief argument that moved them to take this matter into consideration, was the intimation they had received, that it was according to the desires of those who had now spoken against it, and whose latter motion they were much more ready to comply with than their former [1]. Thus was this business stifled for the

---

[1] Ludlow's account is very confused. He apparently refers to the army petition of Aug. 12, 1652, presented on Aug. 13, by Whalley, Okey, and four other officers. The 12th clause of that petition requests 'that for publique satisfaction of the good people of this nation, speedy consideration may be had of such qualifications for future and successive Parliaments, as tend to the election only of such as are pious and faithful to the interest of the Commonwealth to sit and serve as members in the said Parliament.' Mercurius Politicus, p. 1803; Old Parliamentary History. Probably, as Ludlow says, the officers wished to add a clause demanding that Parliament should put a period to their sitting, but were dissuaded by Cromwell. The council of officers held several long meetings to discuss this petition. A news-letter amongst the Clarke Papers, dated Aug. 3, 1652, says, ' His Excellency and the council of officers sat yesterday from nine in the morning till six at night,

present, none being so well able to lay the evil spirit as those that had raised it. But either the General's ambition was so great, that he could not forbear ascending the throne till the time limited by the Parliament for their sitting was expired, or his fears hastned him to the accomplishment of his design, lest the disinterested proceeding of the Parliament, who were about to leave the nation under a form of government that provided sufficiently for the good of the community, might work the people into a greater aversion to his selfish design. Certain it is that he vehemently desired to be rid of this Parliament that had performed such great things, having subdued their enemies in England, Scotland, and Ireland ; established the liberty of the people, reduced the kingdom of Portugal to such terms as they thought fit to grant ; maintained a war against the Dutch with that conduct and success, that it seemed now drawing to a happy conclusion ; recovered our reputation at sea, secured our trade, and provided a powerful fleet for the service of the nation. And however the malice of their enemies may endeavour to deprive them of the glory which they justly merited, yet it will appear to unprejudiced posterity, that they were a disinterested and impartial Parliament, who tho they had the sovereign power of the three nations in their hands for the space of ten or twelve years, did not in all that time give away

---

they keep all private.' A pamphlet entitled, 'A Declaration of the Army to his Excellency the Lord General Cromwell for the dissolving of the present Parliament and the choosing a new representative,' published Aug. 10, 1652, says : ' The officers of the army having had several consultations and conferences touching the dissolving of this present Parliament and electing a new representative, but after much time spent in debate thereof presented a model of their proposals to his Excellency the Lord General Cromwell ; with the subscriptions of most of the officers of the army. And by a general condescension it was drawn up in a declaratory way to the Parliament; but exceeding high they are in their proposals.' Whitelocke says: 'in discourse of it with Cromwell I advised him to stop this way of petitioning by the officers of the army with their swords in their hands, lest in time it might come too home to himself; but he seemed to slight, or rather to have some design by it, in order to which he put them to prepare a way for him.' Memorials, iii. 446.

amongst themselves so much as their forces spent in three months; no, not so much as they spent in one, from the time that the Parliament consisted but of one House, and the Government was formed into a Commonwealth. To which ought to be added, that after so many toils and hazards, so much trouble and loss for the publick good, they were not unwilling to put an end to their power, and to content themselves with an equal share with others, for the whole reward of their labours. Of this Cromwel was very sensible, as well as of their great skill and experience in the management of publick affairs, and of the good esteem they had acquired amongst the most discerning part of the nation, and therefore was very desirous to lay them aside with as little noise as might be. To this end, after he had resolved not to suffer the Act for their dissolution to be finished, he would needs perswade them to be the instruments of their own destruction, by putting a period to themselves, and at the same time investing a certain number with the supreme authority, not doubting when they had so done, to find pretences enough to disperse any such, well knowing that when the face of civil authority was once taken away, the power would naturally fall into the hands of that person who had the greatest interest in the army, which he supposed to be himself. This made him join with Major-General Harrison, being confident that when he had used him and his party to dissolve the present Government, he could crush both him and them at his pleasure. And tho it was no difficult matter to discover this, yet those poor, deluded, however well-meaning men, would not believe it. But all were not so blind, for divers members of the Parliament whom he endeavoured to cajole into a good opinion of his design, being very sensible of the great mischiefs that must necessarily ensue from such courses, resolved either to disswade him from them, or endeavour to countermine him therein. To this end they had several meetings with Cromwel [1], at one of which, when he and his party laboured

---

[1] Cromwell states that these meetings began in Oct., 1652, and that ten or twelve of them took place. Carlyle's Cromwell, Speech i. Whitelocke

to shew that it was impossible for the Parliament, con- 1653
sisting, as they said, for the most part of men interested in
the corruptions of the law and the clergy, to effect those
things that good men expected from them, Major Saloway
desired of them, that before they took away the present
authority, they would declare what they would have established in its room ; to which it was replied by one of the
General's party, that it was necessary to pull down this
Government, and it would be time enough then to consider what should be placed in the room of it. So both
parties understanding one another, prepared to secure
themselves.

The Parliament now perceiving to what kind of excesses
the madness of the army was like to carry them, resolved to
leave as a legacy to the people the Government of a Commonwealth by their representatives, when assembled in
Parliament, and in the intervals thereof by a Council of
State, chosen by them, and to continue till the meeting
of the next succeeding Parliament, to whom they were to
give an account of their conduct and management. To
this end they resolved, without any further delay, to pass
the Act for their own dissolution[1] ; of which Cromwel
having notice, makes haste to the House, where he sat April 20.

gives an account of some of them ;
see also the Army's Declaration of
April 22, 1653.

[1] On the nature of the Bill, see
Masson, iv. 405. The objection of
the army to it is plainly stated in
their Declaration. The corrupt party
in Parliament it affirms, 'long opposed and frequently declared themselves against having a new representative ; and when they saw
themselves necessitated to take that
bill into consideration, they resolved
to make use of it to recruit the House
with persons of the same spirit and
temper, thereby to perpetuate their
own sitting.' This is still more
plainly stated in the official account

of their expulsion in 'Several Proceedings in Parliament.' 'By the
said Act these present members were
to sit, and to be made up by others
chosen, and by themselves approved.'
Old Parliamentary History, xx. 130,
139. The second objection was that
the qualifications of electors and
persons eligible as members were
not sufficiently clearly defined to exclude neuters, malignants, and other
unfit persons. See Carlyle's Cromwell, Speeches i and xiii. It was
not the provision for the dissolution
of the present Parliament Cromwell
and the soldiers objected to, but the
provisions relative to the constitution
of the new Parliament.

down and heard the debate for some time. Then calling to Major-General Harrison [1], who was on the other side of the House, to come to him, he told him, that he judged the Parliament ripe for a dissolution, and this to be the time of doing it. The Major-General answered, as he since told me ; ' Sir, the work is very great and dangerous, therefore I desire you seriously to consider of it before you engage in it.' ' You say well,' replied the General, and thereupon sat still for about a quarter of an hour ; and then the question for passing the Bill being to be put, he said again to Major-General Harrison, ' this is the time I must do it ;' and suddenly standing up, made a speech, wherein he loaded the Parliament with the vilest reproaches, charging them not to have a heart to do any thing for the publick good, to have espoused the corrupt interest of Presbytery and the lawyers, who were the supporters of tyranny and oppression, accusing them of an intention to perpetuate themselves in power, had they not been forced to the passing of this Act, which he affirmed they designed never to observe, and thereupon told them, that the Lord had done with them, and had chosen other instruments for the carrying on his work that were more worthy. This he spoke with so much passion and discomposure of mind, as if he had been distracted [2]. Sir Peter Wentworth stood up

---

[1] Ludlow discussed the expulsion of the Rump with Harrison in 1656 (see vol. ii. of these Memoirs), and must have learnt these details from him then.

[2] Leicester's account of Cromwell's speech makes him much less violent in his demeanour and language : ' After a while he rose up, put off his hat, and spake ; at the first and for a good while, he spake to the commendation of the Parlement, for theyr paines and care of the publick good ; but afterwards he changed his style, told them of theyr injustice, delays of justice, self-interest and other faults ; then he sayd, per-

haps you thinke this is not Parliamentary language, I confesse it is not, neither are you to expect any such from me ; then he putt on his hat, went out of his place, and walked up and down the stage or floore in the middest of the House, with his hat on his head, and chid them soundly, looking sometimes, and pointing particularly upon some persons, as Sir B. Whitlock, one of the commissioners for the greate scale, Sir Henry Vane, to whom he gave very sharpe language, though he named them not, but by his gestures it was well known he meant them.' Blencowe, Sydney Papers,

to answer him, and said, that this was the first time that ever he had heard such unbecoming language given to the Parliament, and that it was the more horrid in that it came from their servant, and their servant whom they had so highly trusted and obliged : but as he was going on, the General stept into the midst of the House, where continuing his distracted language, he said, ' Come, come, I will put an end to your prating ; ' then walking up and down the House like a mad-man, and kicking the ground with his feet, he cried out, ' You are no Parliament, I say you are no Parliament ; I will put an end to your sitting ; call them in, call them in : ' whereupon the serjeant attending the Parliament opened the doors, and Lieutenant-Colonel Worsley with two files of musqueteers entred the House ; which Sir Henry Vane observing from his place, said aloud, ' This is not honest, yea it is against morality and common honesty.' Then Cromwel fell a railing at him, crying out with a loud voice, ' O Sir Henry Vane, Sir Henry Vane, the Lord deliver me from Sir Henry Vane [1].' Then looking upon one of the members, he said, ' There sits a drunkard ; ' and giving much reviling language to others, he commanded the mace to be taken away, saying, ' What shall we do with this bauble ? here, take it away [2].' Having brought all into this disorder,

p. 139. Whitelocke is briefer and less detailed : ' Entering the House he in a furious manner bid the Speaker leave his chair, told the House that they had sat long enough. unless they had done more good : that some of them were whore-masters, looking then towards Henry Marten and Sir Peter Wentworth : that others of them were drunkards, and some corrupt and unjust men and scandalous to the profession of the gospel, and that it was not fit they should sit as a Parliament any longer, and desired them to go away . . . Some of the members rose up to answer Cromwell's speech, but he would suffer none to speak but ihmself, which he did with so

much arrogance in himself and re-proach to his fellow members that some of his privados were ashamed of it.' Memorials, iv. 5.

[1] ' At the going out they say the Generall sayd to young Sir Henry Vane, calling him by his name, that he might have prevented this ex-traordinary course but he was a juggler, and had not so much as common honesty.' Leicester's Jour-nal, Blencowe's Sydney Papers, p. 141.

[2] ' He bid one of his soldiers to take away that fool's bauble the mace.' Whitelocke. ' Then the Generall went to the table where the mace lay which used to be carryed before the Speaker, and

1653 Major-General Harrison went to the Speaker as he sat in the chair, and told him, that seeing things were reduced to this pass, it would not be convenient for him to remain there. The Speaker answered, that he would not come down unless he were forced. 'Sir,' said Harrison, 'I will lend you my hand;' and thereupon putting his hand within his, the Speaker came down[1]. Then Cromwel applied himself to the members of the House, who were in number between 80 and 100, and said to them, 'It's you that have forced me to this, for I have sought the Lord night and day, that he would rather slay me than put me upon the doing of this work[2].' Hereupon Alderman Allen, a member of Parliament, told him, that it was not yet gone so far, but all things might be restored again; and that if the souldiers were commanded out of the House, and the mace returned, the publick affairs might go on in their former course: but Cromwell having now passed the Rubicon, not only rejected his advice, but charged him with an account of some hundred thousand pounds, for which he threatned to question him, he having been long treasurer for the army, and in a rage committed him to the custody of one of the musqueteers. Alderman Allen told him, that it was well known that it had not been his fault

---

sayd, "Take away these baubles."' Leicester. The subsequent history of the mace is related by Mr. St. John Hope in the Antiquary for Jan., 1891.

[1] Harrison, in 1660, gave the following account of his own share to his friends: 'The breaking of the Parliament was the act and design of General Cromwell, for I did know nothing of it; that morning before it was done he called me to go along with him to the House, *and after he had brought all into disorder, I went to the Speaker and told him, Sir, seeing things are brought to this pass it is not requisite for you to stay there: he answered, he would not come down unless he was pulled out; Sir, said I,*

I will lend you my hand, and he putting his hand into mine, came down without any pulling.' A compleat collection of the lives, speeches, &c., of those persons lately executed, with observations by a person of quality. 8vo., 1661.

[2] 'I speak in the presence of some that were at the closure of our consultations, and as before the Lord— the thinking of an act of violence was to us worse than any battle that ever we were in or that could be to the utmost hazard of our lives; so willing were we, even tender and desirous if possible that these men might quit their places with honour.' Carlyle's Cromwell, Speech i.

that his account was not made up long since ; that he had often tendred it to the House, and that he asked no favour from any man in that matter [1]. Cromwel having acted this treacherous and impious part, ordered the guard to see the House clear'd of all the members, and then seized upon the records that were there, and at Mr. Scobell's house. After which he went to the clerk, and snatching the Act of Dissolution, which was ready to pass, out of his hand, he put it under his cloak, and having commanded the doors to be locked up, went away to Whitehall.

This villanous attempt was much encouraged by Nieuport and the other ambassadors lately arrived from Holland, with instructions to conclude a peace; who finding the Parliament supported by the affections of the people, because acting for their interest, and therefore not to be forced, much less cheated into an unjust and disadvantageous agreement, instigated Cromwel to take the power into his hands, well understanding that he would soon be necessitated to make peace with them upon what terms they should think fit [2]; in the mean time resolving to interrupt our trade, and to put the nation to a great expence to maintain a fleet for the guard of the seas, which they knew the people would be unwilling to keep when they should perceive that it served only to uphold and strengthen a tyranny. They also had made preparations to send over money, arms, and men, with Lieut.-Gen. Middleton, to enable the mountaniers of Scotland to give disturbance to the English interest there.

Cromwel being returned to Whitehall, found the council

---

[1] Alderman Francis Allen, member for Cockermouth, died Sept. 6, 1658. Smyth's Obituary, p. 48. A ballad describing Cromwell's expulsion of the Parliament refers to him—

'Allen the Coppersmith was in great fear,
  He did us much harm since the wars
    began;
  A broken citizen many a year,
  And now he's a broken Parliament
    man.' The Rump, p. 306.

[2] The four Dutch ambassadors did not arrive till the end of June, 1653. Cal. S. P., Dom., 1652-3, pp. 426, 435; Thurloe, i. 316. Ludlow's story is impossible. On the dealings of Cromwell with the ambassadors, see Thurloe, i. 386, 395, 416, 418, 438; Geddes, John De Witt, i. 333.

of war in debate concerning this weighty affair, and informed them, that he had done it, and that they needed not
to trouble themselves any further about it[1].   Some of the
officers of the army well affected to the publick cause, and
not of his juncto, of whom were Col. Okey and others,
repaired to the General, to desire satisfaction in that proceeding, conceiving that the way they were now going
tended to ruin and confusion.   To these, having not yet
taken off his mask, but pretending to more honesty and
self-denial than ever, he professed himself resolved to do
much more good, and with more expedition than could be
expected from the Parliament : which professions from him
put most of them to silence, and moved them to a resolution
of waiting for a further discovery of his design, before they
would proceed to a breach and division from him.   But
Col. Okey being jealous that the end would be bad, because
the means were such as made them justly suspected of
hypocrisy, enquired of Col. Desborough what his meaning
was to give such high commendations to the Parliament
when he endeavoured to perswade the officers of the army
from petitioning them for a dissolution, and so short a time
after to eject them with so much scorn and contempt;
who had no other answer to make, but that if ever he
drolled in his life, he had drolled then.

We who were in Ireland being not so well informed of
these clandestine practices, and no less confident that the
principles of some men who joined in this attempt were
directed to the good of the nation ; and that tho some
might be such arrant knaves as to have other designs, yet

---

[1] 'Upon his return from the dissolution of Parliament back again to
the Council of Officers he acquainted
them of his exploit, and then told
them, that now they must go hand
in hand with him and justifie what
was done to the hazard of all their
lives and fortunes, as having advised
and concurred in it. Adding, that
when he went into the House, he
intended not to do it ; but the spirit
was so upon him, that he was over-
ruled by it, and did not therefore
consult with flesh and blood at all,
nor did he premeditate the doing
thereof, though he plainly saw the
Parliament designed to spin an ever-
lasting thread.' Heath, Flagellum,
1663, p. 135.

trusting that an impossibility of accomplishing the same would oblige them to fall in with the publick interest, and not to be so very foolish to attempt the setting up for themselves, tho we could not but have some doubts of the ill consequences of these things, yet thought our selves by the rules of charity obliged to hope the best, and therefore continued to act in our places and stations as before[1].

Cromwel having interrupted the Parliament in the morning of the 20th of April, 1653, came in the afternoon to the Council of State, (who were assembled to do their duty at the usual place) accompanied with Major-General Lambert and Col. Harrison, and told them at his entrance; 'Gentlemen, if you are met here as private persons, you shall not be disturbed; but if as a Council of State, this is no place for you; and since you can't but know what was done at the House in the morning, so take notice, that the Parliament is dissolved.' To this Serjeant Bradshaw answered; 'Sir, we have heard what you did at the House in the morning, and before many hours all England will hear it: but, Sir, you are mistaken to think that the Parliament is dissolved; for no power under heaven can dissolve them but themselves; therefore take you notice of that.' Something more was said to the same purpose by Sir Arthur Haslerig, Mr. Love, and Mr. Scot; and then the Council of State perceiving themselves to be under the same violence, departed[2].

Soon after Cromwell had thus barbarously treated the

[1] The Commissioners of the Parliament in Ireland took no public notice of the change except by publishing a declaration for a general fast. The declaration is reprinted in the Appendix.

[2] The order books of the Council of State end abruptly with April 15, so that they afford no evidence as to the events of April 20. Bordeaux mentions Cromwell's visit to the Council: 'Hier, après dîner, on devait choisir un nouveau Président au Conseil d'Etat; mais le dit Général Cromwell y étant venu leur déclara qu'ils ne se missent plus en peine de s'assembler en ce lieu, et que leur pouvoir était expiré.' Guizot, Cromwell and the English Commonwealth, i. 492. The story is also confirmed by a letter to Hyde which says: 'When Bradshaw began to dispute that they sat by authority of Parliament, he was told that if he and his company would not depart by fair means they should be forced.' Nicholas Papers, ii. 12.

Parliament, and effaced the civil authority, he sent for Major Saloway and Mr. John Carew, to whom he complained of the great weight of affairs that by this undertaking was fallen upon him ; affirming, that the thoughts of the consequences thereof made him to tremble, and therefore desired them to free him from the temptations that might be laid before him ; and to that end to go immediately to the Chief Justice St. Johns, Mr. Selden, and some others, and endeavour to perswade them to draw up some instrument of government that might put the power out of his hands. To this it was answered by Major Saloway; 'The way, Sir, to free you from this temptation is for you not to look upon your self to be under it, but to rest perswaded that the power of the nation is in the good people of England, as formerly it was.' Cromwel perceiving by this answer that he was better understood than he could have wished, fell upon another expedient before he would openly discover himself, appointing a meeting of the chief officers of the army to be at Whitehall, in order to consider what was fit to be done in this exigency.

Major-Gen. Lambert, Col. Harrison, and divers other officers, were at this assembly, where Major Saloway, tho he had then no command, was desired to be present. Major-General Lambert moved that a few persons, not exceeding the number of 10 or 12, might be intrusted with the supreme power : Major-Gen. Harrison was for a greater number, inclining most to that of 70, being the number of which the Jewish Sanhedrim consisted ; but after some debate it was resolved that out of each county and city in England, Ireland, and Scotland, a certain number of persons [1], as near as might be proportionable

[1] 'A true State of the Case of the Commonwealth,' 4to, 1654, gives the following account of their deliberations : 'Untill they (the Parliament) were actually dissolved, no resolutions were taken in what model to cast the government; but it was after that dissolution debated and discussed by the officers of the army as res integra; the question being then put, whether the power should be reserved in the hands of a few, or of a greater number of persons in order to an establishment. It was

to their payments toward the publick charge, should be
nominated by the council of officers to be sent for to meet
at Westminster, on a certain day, where all the authority
of the nation should be delivered into their hands by
an instrument signed and sealed by the General and the
officers, obliging themselves to yield obedience to their
orders. The gentlemen who were summoned met at the
time and place appointed, where after they had heard the
General's harangue, in which he seemed to acknowledg
the goodness of the Lord in that he saw that day wherein
the Saints began their rule in the earth, &c. they went
into the House wherein the Parliament used to sit, where
they voted themselves to be the Parliament of the Commonwealth of England, Scotland, and Ireland. Many of the
members of this assembly had manifested a good affection
to the publick cause ; but some there were among them
who were brought in as spies and trapanners ; and tho they
had been always of the contrary party, made the highest
pretensions to honesty, and the service of the nation.
This assembly therefore being composed for the most part
of honest and well-meaning persons, (who having good intentions, were less ready to suspect the evil designs of
others) thought themselves in full possession of the power
and authority of the nation, and therefore proceeded to the
making of laws relating to the publick ; amongst others
one concerning the plantation of Ireland, settling the

conceived by some that the former
would prove the more effectual
means; but by others, that the
latter would be every jot as effectual, and besides bring this advantage along with it, that it would
be much more satisfactory to the
generality of the army and to the
good people of the nation . . .
whereupon . . . it was at length resolved to fall upon the latter. And
in order hereunto, it was agreed
likewise that such persons should
be called together out of the several
counties, as were reputed men fearing God and of approved fidelity;
in the choice of which persons such
indifference was used, and so equal
liberty allowed to all then present
with the Generall, that every officer
enjoyed the same freedom of nomination, and the majority of suffrages
carried for the election of each single
member.' As a rule the Independent
congregations in each county recommended a certain number of
persons from whom the Council of
Officers made a selection. Milton
State Papers, pp. 92, 123.

lands there upon the adventurers and souldiers, together with an Act for mariners, one for payment of some publick debts, with divers others. They also made some progress in the reformation of the Law, having appointed a committee to that end.

In Ireland we disbanded some of our forces to the number of about 5000 horse and foot [1], and summoned a council of officers to adjust the arrears of the souldiers, and to put them into possession of the land assigned for their satisfaction ; who judging that it would not hold out to satisfy the whole, rated the best land of each county according to its intrinsick value, reserving the worst to be equally distributed amongst them, when the arrears should appear to be satisfied on the foot of the new valuation. The county of Dublin was in this estimate rated at 1500*l.* for 1000 acres ; the county of Wexford at 800*l.*, the county of Kilkenny at 1000*l.* All which counties being within the province of Lempster, were rated by the Act at 600*l.* for 1000 acres. Instructions were also given to the committee for stating the accounts of the arrears of the souldiers, by which those who were disbanded in Connaught had their arrears assigned in lands about Sligo, those in Munster in the county of Cork, &c. [2] Those who had been for some time with the Lord Inchequin, and therefore thought fit to be disbanded, had their arrears assigned (upon my desire) together, about Collen, in the county of Kilkenny, that they might be the better able to defend themselves, and assist their friends upon occasion. Col. Theophilus Jones's regiment was reduced, his own troop and some others appointed to compleat mine, and Col.

---

[1] Musters taken in July, 1652, showed that the total number of soldiers and officers to be provided for in Ireland for the year ending Sept., 1653, amounted to 34,128 men ; of whom 7365 were horse, 1447 dragoons, and the rest infantry.

[2] See the votes of the council of officers held at Dublin Castle, June 9, 1653. Mercurius Politicus, June 30 - July 7, p. 2557. Compare Prendergast, pp. 195, 213. The troops disbanded were those who had served under Coote, Monk, and Inchequin. The council of officers proposed to disband 5000 foot and 3000 horse and dragoons, and that the standing army should be made up to 18,000 foot, 5000 horse and 1000 dragoons.

Jones to be Major of my regiment in the room of Col.
Warden, who was disbanded.

The pay of some of the officers of the army was also reduced, but yet they now received the pay of seven days per week, whereas before they had but four; but the general officers who had been paid seven days for a week, had some ten shillings, others five shillings per day abated of their pay; amongst whom it fell heavier on me than any other, for as my work was double both as a Commissioner of Parliament, and Lieutenant-General of the Horse, so were my expences also, being oblig'd to keep a more plentiful table than any other of the Commissioners, and more than twenty horses continually in my stable ready for service: but indeed could I have seen our victories employed to the good of the Commonwealth, I should have been satisfied without any other encouragement: and I can clearly make it appear, that during the four years I served in Ireland, I expended 4500*l.* of my own estate more than all the pay that I received.

The commissioners for the management of affairs by sea having not finished the time limited by the Parliament for their acting, nor clearly seeing to what extremities things would be driven, continued to act in their station; which they did with that diligence and vigour, that since the late engagement in the Downs they had equipped a very considerable fleet, and furnished it with all sorts of provisions, ammunition and men. This fleet was commanded by Dean and Monk as Admirals, by Penn as Vice-Admiral, and by Lawson as Reer-Admiral. On the 2d of June, 1653, early in the morning they attacked the Dutch fleet commanded by Van Tromp, Evertson, De Witt and De Ruyter, on the coast of Flanders. Lawson who commanded the Blew Squadron charged through the Dutch fleet with forty ships, which storm falling principally on De Ruyter's squadron, Van Tromp bore up to his assistance; which when our Admirals, who were both on the same ship, perceived, they engaged Tromp with the body of the fleet, and the fight continued till three in the afternoon, at which time the wind coming up contrary to the English, the Dutch fled, and were pursued by the lightest of our frigats.   The next morning the two fleets found themselves again near each other, but for want of wind could not come to engage till about noon, at which time the dispute began, and continued very hot on both sides till ten at night.   Our fleet charged the Dutch with so much resolution, and put them into so great disorder, that tho their Admiral fired on them to rally them, he could not procure more than twenty ships of his whole fleet to stand by him, the rest making all the sail they could away to the eastward.   But the wind blowing a fresh gale from the westward, ours pursued them so effectually, that they sunk six of their best ships, and blew up two others that were in the body of their fleet, taking eleven of their biggest ships, and two others, with thirteen hundred prisoners, among whom were six of their principal captains ; and had not the rest of their fleet sheltered themselves between Dunkirk and Calais, where it was unsafe to expose our great ships by reason of the sands, we had probably taken or destroyed most of the rest [1].   The Hollanders were much superiour to the English in number of ships ; but such was the courage and conduct of our men, that we lost but one ship in the fight, had but one captain killed, except Admiral Dean, which indeed was a great loss, and about one hundred and sixty private men killed and wounded. Our fleet having put their prisoners on shoar, and left some of their ships to be refitted, returned to the coast of Holland, where they took many prizes.   The people in Holland seeing themselves as it were besieged by the English fleet, constrained the magistrates by their clamours to send their fleet again to sea, which they reinforced with divers great ships, and some fireships, so that they made up in all one hundred and forty sail.   The English fleet

[1] See Thurloe, i. 269-79 ; Mercurius Politicus, June 2 9, 1653; the latter prints the letters of Blake and Monk.   A day of thanksgiving was appointed by the General and Council of State for June 23.   Mercurius Politicus, p. 2501 ; Geddes, John de Witt, i. 311.

were little more in number than ninety, yet resolved to
fight the enemy; and accordingly detaching the lightest
of their frigats, assisted by some greater ships, they engaged the Dutch, and maintained the fight till they were
separated by the night. The next day little was done,
but on the day after they fought again ; and tho many of
our men were sick of the scurvy, and that the Dutch had
fireships, of which we had none, the wind also entirely
favouring them, yet did the fight continue in equal balance
till two or three in the afternoon, about which time their
Admiral Van Tromp was killed with a musket-ball, as he
walked upon the deck with his sword drawn. This so
discouraged the enemy, that they made all the haste they
could away towards the Texel, and were pursued with that
diligence by ours, that the ship of Cornelius Evertzen was
sunk, with about thirty more, as we were informed by the
prisoners taken or saved from perishing. The victory was
great, but cost us dear, for we lost eight of our brave captains, whose names were, Graves, Peacock, Taylor, Crisp,
Newman, Cox, Owen and Chapman, with about four hundred
men[1]. We had also about seven hundred wounded, and
amongst them five commanders, yet we lost but one ship
in this fight. Our Admiral having put his prisoners with
the wounded men on shoar, and taken in provisions, returned with the fleet to the coast of Holland, where many
of the officers of the enemy's fleet and others ingenuously
acknowledged that the hand of God was against them, and
that they ought not to contend any longer with us.

The English fleet being now absolute masters of the sea,
no ship could stir out of the Texel without their permission.
The Dutch were willing to impute their ill success to the
treachery and cowardice of their officers ; but so it was, by
the blessing of God upon the endeavours of the Parliament
and their fleet, that since the beginning of the war we had
taken, sunk and destroyed, between fourteen and fifteen

[1] See Monk's letters, Old Parliamentary History, xx. 193; Mercurius
Politicus, p. 2638; Thurloe, i. 392,
401, 415; Geddes, John de Witt, i.
344. A public thanksgiving was
ordered for Aug. 25.

hundred of their ships, of which many were considerable men of war. Their seamen generally declined the service, neither had they a sufficient number of ships to put to sea, tho they had been furnished with all other accomodations. In short, matters were brought to that pass, that Myn Heer Nicuport, one of the ambassadors from Holland, demanded of some of the Parliament-party what they intended to do with them, endeavouring by all means possible to perswade them that the ruin of the Dutch would be prejudicial to themselves. Our friends plainly told him, that they desired nothing but a coalescence with them, and then would be as ready to promote the good of Holland as their own. To this the ambassador replied, that he would engage his masters should send us a blank, and that what conditions soever we should think fit to write on it, they would subscribe. Soon after they sent ambassadors to treat in good earnest concerning a peace, which they were the more necessitated to do, by reason of some divisions amongst themselves on account of the Prince of Orange's interest. But this attempt proved ineffectual, and they not able to prevail, as long as the face of authority remained in England, without consenting to the coalescence. For many of the present assembly acting with sincerity for the publick, and therefore little suspecting the treachery of others, resolved whilst they had opportunity to be doing their duty, and to discharge the trust committed to their care, according to the best of their judgment, for the good of the Commonwealth. They issued forth orders for regulating the excise and customs, and enlarged the powers of the committee established for trade. They made all necessary preparations for carrying on the war by sea, and declared General Robert Blake, General

Dec. 3. George Monk, Major-General Desborough, and Vice-Admiral Penn, to be the four Generals of the fleet of the Commonwealth, impowering them with some others to manage the affairs of the Admiralty for six months.

Aug. 10. They also gave order to prepare an Act to erect a High Court of Justice for proceeding against such as should surprize or betray any of the fortresses, magazines, or ships of the Commonwealth into the hands of the enemy; and also against those who should, contrary to the laws already made, proclaim any to be King of England or Ireland, whereby it is manifest they suspected the design on foot, tho their jealousy did not at all defer, but rather hasten the execution of it.

The perfidious Cromwel having forgot his most solemn professions and former vows, as well as the blood and treasure that had been spent in this contest, thought it high time to take off the masque, and resolved to sacrifice all our victories and deliverances to his pride and ambition, under colour of taking upon him the office as it were of a High Constable, in order to keep the peace of the nation, and to restrain men from cutting one another's throats[1]. One difficulty yet remained to obstruct his design, and that was the Convention, which he had assembled and invested with power, as well as earnestly solicited to reform the law, and reduce the clergy to a more evangelical constitution. And having sufficiently alarmed those interests, and shewn them their danger from the Convention, he informs them farther, that they cannot be ignorant of the confusion that all things are brought into by the immoderate zeal of those in authority, and to what extremities matters might be reduced, if permitted to go on ; possibly, said he, to the utter extirpation of law and gospel from amongst us ; and therefore advised that they would join their interests to his, in order to prevent this inundation. His proposition was readily embraced by the corrupt part of the lawyers and clergy, and so he became their Protector, and they the humble supporters of his tyranny[2]. But that his usurpation

---

[1] 'Truly I have, as before God, often thought I could not tell what my business was, nor what I was in the place I stood in, save comparing myself to a good constable set to keep the peace of the parish.' Carlyle, Speech xi. Cf. 'The Protector (so-called) in part unveiled,' 1655, p. 72.

[2] The allegations made against the Little Parliament are set forth at length in the 'True State of the Case of the Commonwealth,' 1654, pp. 13-22, and more briefly in Cromwell's 3rd and 13th speech in Carlyle's Cromwell. It is defended in 'An Exact Relation of the Transac-

might seem less horrid, he so contrived it by his instruments, that some of the Convention must openly manifest their disapprobation of their own proceedings, and under divers specious pretences put a period to their sitting. To this end it was agreed by Mr. Rouse, Chairman to that assembly, and the rest of Cromwel's junto, to meet earlier in the House than was usual, which was done accordingly on the 12th of December, 1653, hoping by surprize to obtain a vote for their dissolution. Being met, Col. Sydenham, Sir Charles Wolseley and others, according to their instructions, bitterly inveighed against the transactions of the Convention, and particularly charged them with a design to destroy the army, by not making a sufficient and timely provision for their pay. They alledged, that tho they had voted them a sum of money, yet having resolved to raise it by way of a pound-rate, it would take up so much time to bring it in, that the army must either starve by want, or oppress the country by free quarter. A second ground of their invectives was taken from a motion made that the great officers of the army should serve without pay for one year. They accused them also of endeavouring to destroy the clergy, the law, and the propriety of the subject, instancing in their denying a right of presentation to the patrons of ecclesiastical benefices : in general, that they had not a frame of spirit to do justice, which they would have made out by their not relieving Sir John Stawell, when he made his application to them. Thus they endeavoured to cajole the clergy, lawyers, Cavaliers, and all interests, except that which they should have had most regard to.

They thought to have prevented any debate about their design, by meeting so early in the morning : but they were deceived, and enough found in the House to answer their objections. To that concerning the army it was said, that the pound-rate was found to be the most equal way of raising money, and therefore resolved upon by them ; not

tions of the late Parliament, their beginning and ending, by L. D.,' 1654, which was written by Praisegod Barbone himself. It is reprinted in the Somers Tracts, ed. Scott, vi. 266.

at all doubting that it would come in soon enough for the soldiers' supply : that they thought it reasonable and just, that the great officers of the army who were possessed of plentiful estates, and had received all their arrears, should abate somewhat of their superfluities, and serve for a little time freely, as well as those who were employed in civil affairs, whose labour and hazard was as great, and both equally concerned in the publick good : especially considering how much this conduct would contribute to the ease and satisfaction of the people, who could not be ignorant that there were now no pressing occasions of charge or danger, the enemy being every where entirely subdued. To what had been done in order to a reformation of the law and clergy, it was answered, that as they conceived there was great need of it, so they had been told that they were called together principally for that end ; and that if they had done any thing too much therein, the gentlemen who blamed them for it were very unfit so to do, having themselves been the men that pressed them continually to go much farther than they had done. To the objection concerning presentations they said, that the method used therein seemed to them too unreasonable to be continued, it being in effect to give a power to the greatest of the parish, who were not always the best, to prescribe what religion they pleased to the parishioners, by presenting a person, howsoever unfit for that office, to be their minister. Lastly, in answer to the charge of denying relief to Sir John Stawel, it was answered, that the consideration of that matter was before them, and that they would not fail to act as his case deserved. The debate thus spun out, the House began to fill, so that Cromwel's party despairing to carry their design by vote, broke off in an abrupt manner, saying, that it was not a time to debate, but to do something that might prevent those inconveniences which they pretended did threaten them. Then Mr. Rouse, who was of the plot, descending from his chair, went out of the House, and with the rest of the cabal repaired to Whitehall, where they subscribed a writing, taking notice of the power with which the army had intrusted them, and of the sense they had of their own inability to bring any thing to perfection for the good and settlement of the nation : and that therefore they resigned that power into the hands of Cromwel, from whom they had received it.

The other part of that assembly, who came with honest minds and sincere intentions to perform their duty and to serve their country, kept their places in the House, and would not quit them till they were removed by a guard of souldiers sent by Cromwel to that end[1]. And it seems remarkable, that tho this body of men had not a clear authority according to the national constitution, and were called together with a design of rendring them odious, as well as to scare the lawyers and clergy into a compliance with Cromwel ; yet many being convinced of the rectitude of their intentions, were brought over daily to approve their actions. And as this treacherous and unworthy resignation of the power to Cromwel could not be carried by a vote in the House, so I have been informed that the major part of those who were members of that assembly could never be perswaded to sign the paper for that resignation, tho importuned to it by all politick and devilish arguments imaginable.

This Convention, who derived all the authority they had from Cromwel, being dissolved, after they had driven the clergy and corrupt part of the lawyers into his net, as had

---

[1] According to a letter from Bussy Mansell, 'about forty' members and the Speaker went to resign their powers to Cromwell. 'Twenty-seven stayed in the House a little time speaking to one another, and going to speake to the Lord in prayer. Col. Goffe and Lieut.-Col. White came into the House, and desired them that were there to come out. Some answered they were there by a call from the Generall, and would not come out by their desire unless they had a command from him. They returned no answer, but went out and fetched two files of musketeers, and did as good as force them out; amongst whom I was an unworthy one.' Thurloe, i. 637, cf. p. 630. For other accounts, see Ellis, Original Letters, Series II. 3. 372, and the pamphlet entitled, 'A true Narrative of the Cause and Manner of the Dissolution of the late Parliament, by a member of the House then present at that transaction,' 1653, and Carlyle's Cromwell, Speeches iii, xiii.

been designed, all men were full of expectation what step he would take next to advance himself. And because all honest men who stood near the centre of his actions had lost all hopes of good from him, he began to court and cajole those that were at a distance, whom he hoped the more easily to surprize, as less acquainted with his treacherous designs. Amongst others I received a message from him by one of my relations, to assure me of his friendship and intentions to do as much for me as for any man.

After a few days a council of field-officers was summoned, where Major-General Lambert having rehearsed the several steps and degrees by which things had been brought to the present state wherein they were, and pressed the necessity incumbent upon the army to provide something in the room of what was lately taken away, presented to them a paper intituled, ‘ An Instrument of Government,’ which he read in his place. Some of the officers being convinced that the contents of this Instrument tended to the sacrificing all our labours to the lust and ambition of a single person, began to declare their unwillingness to concur in it. But they were interrupted by the Major-General, and informed that it was not now to be disputed, whether this should be the form of government or not, for that was already resolved, it having been under consideration for two months past: neither was it brought before them with any other intention than to give them permission to offer any amendments they might think fit, with a promise that they should be taken into consideration [1]. The council of officers perceiving to

[1] Unfortunately very little is known about the consultations of the officers in which the Instrument of Government was drawn up. Some account is given in an intercepted letter: ‘ Thursday last being the next day after our late Parliament was broken up . . . Lambert with many officers of the army came into the councill chamber at Whytehall, where many were expecting the event. All, except those who belonged to the army, were ordered to withdraw; which done Lambert produced a paper signed by the most part of the late Parliament, wherein they acknowledged their disability to manage the weighty affaires of the land, and therefore did desire the General to assume the power by him given to them. This being read, then he told them it was fit for them to thinke of some way to put things in a way in order to the government of

what terms they were restrained, proposed, that it might be declared in this Instrument, that the General of the army should after this first time be held uncapable of being Protector; (for that was the title given by this Instrument to the chief magistrate, tho some were said to have moved that it might be King [1]); that none of the relations of the last Protector should be chosen at the next succeeding election; and that a general council of all the commission officers who were about the town should be summoned to consider thereof.   To these propositions they could obtain no other answer, than that they should be offered to the General, which was the title they yet gave to Cromwel.   At the next meeting of officers it was not thought fit to consult with them at all; but they were openly told by Major-General Lambert, that the General would take care of managing the civil government; and then having required them to repair to their respective charges, where their troops and companies lay, that they might preserve the publick peace, he dismissed them.

the land.   It was by them resolved that a lord governor of the three nations should be chosen,' &c. Thurloe, i. 632.

On Lambert's share in drawing up the Instrument, a pamphlet says: 'The sudden coming forth of which Instrument declares plainly that it was not a new thing, but that which was thought of, contrived, and appointed some time before those friends were turned out of the House; and all this was done by five or six, or very few more, as is confidently reported and believed: there being several officers of the army that will not stick to say as much; and which is also evident by this; for though they were all sent for upon a pretence of being taken into consultation; yet when they came thither, they did little else but walk to and fro in the rooms without, whilst the business was carried on by a few within; and staying several times very late at night, still expecting to be sent for in, Major-General Lambert comes out to them, and tells them they might go home, for there was no occasion at that time to make use of them; so that to me it clearly appears their being sent for, was only to this end the better to colour over and cloak their design.'   The Protector Unveiled, 1655, p. 12.

[1] Cromwell in his speech to the hundred officers in 1657, said: 'Time was when they boggled not at the word (King), for the Instrument by which the government now stands was presented to his Highness with the title (King) in it, as some there present could witness, pointing at a principal officer then in his eye, and he refused to accept of the title.' Burton's Diary, i. 382.

Thus was this important business that so highly concerned the nation, and in some measure all Europe, in a clandestine manner carried on and huddled up by two or three persons; for more they were not who were let into the secret of it, so that it may justly be called a work of darkness. This Instrument appointed the legislative power to be in the Representative of the people and the Protector; that a Parliament should be chosen every three years, which should sit five months, if they thought fit, without any interruption: that their first meeting should be on the thirteenth of September next ensuing: that the members of whom the Parliament was to consist, should be chosen by the people: that whatsoever they would have enacted, should be presented to the Protector for his consent; and that if he did not confirm it within twenty days after it was first tendred to him, it should have the force and obligation of a law; provided that it extended not to lessen the number or pay of the army, to punish any man on account of his conscience, or to make any alteration in the Instrument of Government; in all which a negative was reserved to the single person. It provided also that all writs should issue out in the Protector's name: that most of the magistrates should be appointed, and all honours conferred by him: that he should have the power of the militia by sea and land: that in the intervals of Parliament the nation should be governed by the Protector and his council, who were not to exceed the number of one and twenty, nor to be under thirteen. The first persons nominated to be of his council were Major-General Lambert, Col. Desborough, Mr. Henry Lawrence, Sir Charles Wolsely, Col. William Sydenham, Mr. Francis Rouse, Philip Viscount Lisle, Col. Philip Jones, Col. Montague, Mr. Richard Major, Walter Strickland, Esq., Sir Gilbert Pickering, Major-General Skippon, and Sir Anthony Ashley Cooper, in all fourteen. It was observed, that in the choice of this council, such were put in for the most part who had been principal instruments in the interruption of the late assembly, and leading men in the resignation of that power into the hands of Cromwel; and

1653

because nothing of honour or conscience could be presumed to oblige them to be faithful to Cromwell and his government, tho they took an oath to that purpose, he as a publick robber having possessed himself of the purse of the nation, distributed a thousand pounds a year to each of his council.

1654
Aug. 1.

He also established a commission for the viewing and taking care of all forests, fees and lands belonging to the late King, Queen, and Prince, under pretence of improving them to the advantage of the Commonwealth, but indeed in order to convert them to his own profit. The management of the treasury was put into the hands of Cols. Desborough, Montague, and Sydenham, who were his creatures; to whom was added Mr. William Masham, a worthy gentleman and a member of Parliament, placed there by Cromwel, upon information that he had divers relations of considerable interest in the clergy-party, together with a numerous family and small estate during his father's life, which considerations prevailed with the said gentleman to accept of that employment [1].

Things being thus prepared, the Mayor and Aldermen of London were required to attend at Whitehall in their scarlet gowns, whither when they came the design was imparted to them, and they being under the power of an army, were forced to contribute to this pageantry, by

1653
Dec. 16.

accompanying Cromwel to Westminster-hall. The Commissioners of the Seal, the Judges, and Barons of the Exchequer, marched first, the Council of the Commonwealth following them, and then the Mayor, Sheriffs, and the Aldermen of London in their robes. After them came the General with a great number of the officers of the army, Major-General Lambert carrying the sword before him, into the Court of Chancery; where after the General had heard the Instrument of Government read, and taken the oath as

---

[1] Cols. Montague and Sydenham, Mr. William Masham, and five others, were approved by the Council of State on Aug. 2, 1654, as Commissioners of the Treasury. Cal. S. P., Dom., 1654, p. 284. Ludlow possibly confuses this appointment with the ordinance of Dec. 31, 1653, appointing commissioners for inspecting the treasuries; ib. 1653-4, p. 317.

directed in the close of the said Instrument, Major-General 1653
Lambert kneeling presented him with a sword in the
scabbard, representing the civil sword ; which Cromwel
accepting, put off his own, intimating thereby that he
would no longer rule by the military sword, tho like a
false hypocrite he designed nothing more. The Commissioners delivered the Seals to him, and the Mayor of
London the sword, all which he restored again, with an
exhortation to use them well; and having assured them
that he would not have undertaken this charge, but to
make use of it for the good of the publick, he returned
to Whitehal in the same manner and order as he came.
His council having taken their places, issued out orders to
all counties and considerable corporations for the proclaiming Oliver Cromwel Protector of the Commonwealth of
England, Scotland, and Ireland ; and care was taken to
alter all legal writs and process from the title of the
Keepers of the Liberties of England, to that of Protector.
A declaration also was published impowering all those who
stood lawfully invested with any office of judicature or
with the power of the Admiralty on the 20th of the
present December, to continue in their imployments till
farther order.

The news of this great alteration of affairs was very
unwelcome to us in Ireland [1], because contrary to the oaths
which had been taken, and especially to the engagement,
whereby all that took it, promised fidelity to the Commonwealth of England, as it was established without a King
or House of Lords : which engagement having subscribed
both with hand and heart, I was resolved to use my best

---

[1] The state of feeling in Ireland at
the commencement of the Protectorate is described in a letter to
Thurloe. Thurloe, ii. 162. The
Anabaptists were extremely hostile,
though a letter from Kyffin and other
leaders of their sect in England somewhat mollified their hostility. Sir
Hardress Waller and the Limerick
Anabaptists sent an address to Cromwell, and their example was followed
by Mr. Patient's congregation at
Dublin. An address from the army
(undated) was possibly presented
about this time. Thurloe, ii. 117 ;
Milton State Papers, pp. 145, 148,
159.

1653   endeavours, either to oppose this usurpation, or at least not
to do any thing that might contribute to the strengthning
of it. To this end, when it was pressed by some court-
parasites amongst us, that seeing things were brought
to this pass, and that there was now no other face of
authority in being ; therefore to prevent the designs of our
enemies, the Commissioners of Parliament should proclaim
Cromwel Protector in Dublin and other parts of Ireland :
I objected against it as a thing evil in itself, tending to the
betraying of our cause, and contrary to an Act of Parliament ; that if it were but dubious whether it were evil or no,
we ought at least to expect an order from those who had
the power in their hands, which as yet we had not received.
By this means I hindred the proclaiming of him in Ireland
for more than a fortnight, tho continually earnestly pressed
to a compliance. But a day being appointed for the consideration of that affair, the Commissioners with three or
four chief officers, of whose integrity and abilities we had
the best opinion, met in Lieut.-General Fleetwood's chamber
in the castle, where after near five' hours debate, and the
question put, the votes were found to be equal on both
sides. In that instant of time Mr. Roberts the Auditor-
General [1], coming thither upon some particular business of
the army, Lieut.-General Fleetwood being well acquainted
with his flattering spirit, and earnestly desiring to have the
thing done, gave him liberty to declare his opinion ; which,
when he had done in the affirmative, the Lieut.-General
took his concurrence (he being a general officer) to be a
decision of the controversy. So it was resolved to be done,
and an order directed to be drawn up for that purpose,
which the Commissioners endeavoured to perswade me to
sign ; but I positively refusing so to do, they ordered it
to be signed by their secretary in the name of the commission ; which way was taken, that it might not appear

---

[1] The Lord Deputy and Council,
by instructions dated Nov. 17, 1654,
appointed Henry Markham, Edward
Roberts, and Richard Kingdon to be
Commissioners General of the assessments and all other public revenues of
Ireland. Irish Records, $\frac{A}{26}$ 24, p. 1.

that any of the Commissioners' hands were wanting to the proclamation [1]. At this ceremony there was but a thin appearance, some captains and inferior officers; but no colonel nor general officer, except Sir Hardress Waller and one Col. Moore were present. The Herald-at-Arms, who made proclamation, was clothed in black ; but the artillery, which was at the command of Lieut.-General Fleetwood, wasted some of the powder belonging to the publick, the report of which was very unwelcome musick to me, who desiring to be as far from this pageantry as I could, rode out of town that afternoon.

Having done what I could to obstruct the proclamation of that, which was called an Instrument of Government, imposed upon the people by the military sword, contrary to many oaths and solemn ingagements, as well as to the interest and expectations of the people, I thought my self obliged in duty to act no further in my civil capacity as Commissioner of Parliament, lest I should seem by acting with them, to acknowledg this as a lawful authority: to that end I forbore to go to Cork-House, which was the usual place where the Commissioners of Parliament met ; but Lieut.-General Fleetwood by great importunity did once prevail with me to be present there, and to give my advice in some things that absolutely concerned the peace of Ireland ; after which time I never gave any vote amongst them, or set my hand to any of their orders, tho pressed to

---

[1] Ludlow's story is confirmed by a letter to Thurloe from Jenkyn Lloyd : ' The order for proclaiming his Highness was signed only by their secretary, whereas others are usually signed by themselves. The reason whereof I understand to be, that three Commissioners having signed it, it was tendered to the Lieut.-Gen. also, who refusing used this expression, that he would rather cut off his hand ; and then the three others blotted out their names. His objections against his Highness and government are founded upon several Acts of Parliament, viz. that of the 30th of January, 1648; March 17, 1648; May 14, 1649; May 10, 1649; July 14, 1649. The Mayor and Aldermen of this city [Dublin] sent three several times to the Commissioners for leave to proclaim his Highness, and were always denied with this reason, that there was not any direction from England for soe doing.' Thurloe, ii. 163. The proclamation is given in the Appendix.

do it by divers honest and well-meaning men. But because I was always ready to call in question my own judgment, when different from knowing and conscientious persons, I consented that a day might be appointed to consult with them touching my duty in this conjuncture. The most weighty arguments which were then used to perswade me to continue in my imployments were, that supposing Cromwel to be a tyrant, to have no just call to his present imployment, and a wicked man, as most of them were so ingenuous to acknowledg him to be; yet they declared themselves to be of opinion, that a good man might act under him; and for proof of this they urged the example of Cornelius, who was a centurion under Nero. To this I answered, that tho in an evil government already established. an honest man may take an imployment, and bless God for such an opportunity of doing good, yet our case seemed to me to be very different, the dispute lying now between tyranny and liberty; and that I durst not in any measure contribute to the support of tyranny against the liberty of my country. Another argument much pressed was, that by declining my station I should neglect an occasion of doing some good, and lay a necessity upon those in power to imploy others, who might do mischief. To this I replied, that it was not lawful to do the least evil for the attaining the greatest good; and that I apprehended it to be an evil thing to fortify Cromwel in his usurpation; that I hoped I should do more good by my open protestation against his injustice, and declining to act under him, than by the contrary means: for should all men who continued well affected to the interest of the Commonwealth, refuse to act in the present state of affairs, there could be no way thought of, in my opinion, more probable to reduce the usurper to his right senses; who not daring to trust such as had acted against him, must of necessity by this means be left destitute of instruments to carry on his unjust designs. A third argument was, that I should wait to see how he would use his power, which if he improved to evil ends, I should then find many others to join with, who would be as ready to oppose him as my self. To this also I answered, that I was fully convinced of the injustice of his undertaking; that he had betrayed his masters, under colour that they would not reform the law and the clergy; and that having called an assembly in order, as he pretended, to accomplish that work, he had now broken them also for endeavouring to do it; that as soon as he had made the corrupt interests of the nation sensible of their danger, he had contracted an alliance with them, and was become their Protector; that it could not be reasonably expected that he should do any thing towards their reformation, because every step he should take towards the lessening of their credit, would tend to the weakening of his own authority; and that he was no less necessitated to be a vassal to them, than he designed the rest of the nation to be slaves to him. Tho for these and other reasons I durst not act in my civil capacity, yet I was unwilling to decline the exercise of my military authority as Lieutenant-General of the Horse [1], having received my commission from the Parliament, which I resolved to keep, till it should be forced from me, and to act by it in order to attain those ends for which I received it, the principal whereof were, to bring those to justice who had been guilty of the blood of many thousands of English Protestants, and to restore the English who remained alive to the lands which had been taken from them by the Irish. And tho much of this work was already effected; yet it was no less a duty to bring it to perfection than to begin it, and to defend our country-men in a just possession, than to gain it for them. Neither was it impossible that as one had made use of the military sword

---

[1] 'The Lieutenant-General hath behaved himselfe most childishly, not refrayning very poysenous and bitter expressions in publique meetings; for which I conceive it is that he is soe much cryed up by the A[nabaptists] of late, and ever since admitted to the private weekely meetings, which before was denyed him. He refuses to act as C[ommissioner], and acts only as Lieutenant-General. The riddle can be resolved noe otherwise then by this distinction, that the one is more beneficial than the other.' Jenkyn Lloyd to Thurloe, March 13, 1654; Thurloe, ii. 163.

to destroy the civil authority, so others might have an opportunity to restore it by the same means.

One of the first important affairs of Cromwel's new government, was to make peace with the Dutch, which the low condition they had been brought into by the good conduct of the Parliament made them earnestly to desire. In the articles some seeming provision was made for bringing those to justice, who had been guilty of the blood of the English at Amboyna, if they could be found. The Dutch also undertook to reimburse to our merchants the losses they sustained by the seizure of twenty-two ships in Denmark; the duty of striking the flag to the English in the narrow seas was acknowledged, and compliance promised with the Act of Parliament, whereby all foreign commodities were forbidden to be brought into England save in English bottoms, except by such vessels as properly belonged to that country where those commodities should grow. By another article it was agreed that the enemies of the respective nations should not be protected by either of them; but there was no provision made by this treaty for the coalescence so much insisted upon during the administration of affairs by the Parliament[1].

The Lord Whitlock, who had been sent ambassador to the Crown of Sweden by the Parliament, acquainted the Queen with the late change of government, producing letters of credence from Cromwel, and owning him as his master; upon which he was received as kindly as formerly by the

---

[1] It was the theory of the extreme Republicans that perseverance in the war would have reduced the Dutch to accept the 'coalescence' demanded, and that Cromwell threw away the fruits of the Long Parliament's victories. 'We might have brought them to oneness with us,' said Mr. Bulkeley in 1659. 'Their ambassadors did desire a coalition. This we might have done in four or five months. We never bid fairer for being the masters of the world.' Burton's Diary, iii. 111, cf. pp. 164, 389, 440, 458, 490. Cromwell wisely abandoned the proposal for the coalescence of the two Republics, and sought simply for a close alliance for the common interests of European Protestantism. Geddes, John de Witt, i. 334, 363. The Fifth Monarchy men were even more hostile to the peace with Holland than the Republicans. Thurloe, i. 442, 501, 519, 534.

Queen, who signed the articles agreed upon by the two
nations, to the great satisfaction of both [1].

Cromwel having thus all clear before him, and no enemy
in the field, except only in the Highlands of Scotland,
a considerable army by land, and a powerful fleet at sea, all
the souldiers fully paid, with a month's advance; the stores
sufficiently supplied with all provisions for sea and land;
three hundred thousand pounds of ready money in England,
and one hundred and fifty thousand pounds in the treasury
of Ireland; he removed from the Cockpit, which house the
Parliament had assigned him, to take possession of Whitehal,
which he assigned to himself [2]. His wife seemed at first
unwilling to remove thither, tho afterwards she became
better satisfied with her grandeur; but his mother, who by
reason of her great age was not so easily flattered with
these temptations, very much mistrusted the issue of affairs,
and would be often afraid, when she heard the noise of a
musquet, that her son was shot, being exceedingly dissatisfied unless she might see him once a day at least; but she
shortly after dying [3], left him the possession of what she
held in jointure, which was reported not to exceed sixty
pounds by year, tho he out of the publick purse expended
much more at her interment, and amongst other needless
ceremonies, caused many hundred torches to be carried
with the hearse, tho she was buried by day-light.

This usurper endeavouring to fix himself in his throne by

---

[1] The treaty, though dated April
11, was not finally ratified and sealed
till April 28. Whitelocke, Journal
of the Swedish Embassy, ed. by H.
Reeve, 1855, ii. 165.

[2] 'It is supposed the Lord Protector will remove with his family to
Whitehall at the latter end of this
week.' Mercurius Politicus, March
9–16, 1654.

[3] 'My Lord Protector's mother of
ninety-four years old died the last
night, and a little before her death,
gave my lord her blessing in these
words: "The Lord cause his face to

shine upon you, and comfort you in
all your adversities, and enable you
to do great things for the glory of
your most high God, and to be a
relief unto his people; my dear son,
I leave my heart with thee; a good
night."' Thurloe to Pell, Nov. 17,
1654; Vaughan, i. 81. See Marvell's
Poem on the first anniversary of the
Protectorate, ll. 161–64. Mercurius
Politicus notes under Nov. 18, 1654,
'The mother of his Highness the
Lord Protector, dying full of days,
was this night very solemnly interred at Westminster.'

1654 all ways imaginable, gave direction to the judges, who were ready to go their several circuits, to take especial care to extend all favour and kindness to the cavalier party. He himself restored Col. Grace, a notorious Irish rebel, to his estate[1]; and sent a letter in favour of the Lord Fitz-Williams, who had been Lieutenant-General in Preston's army in Ireland[2]: but he dealt otherways with those whom formerly he had most courted, summoning Major-General Harrison, Col. Rich, Mr. Carew, and others, before the council; requiring such of them as had commissions from him to surrender them, upbraiding Major-General Harrison with his carriage to him, and charging him with coveting his imployment when he was sick in Scotland: and because they refused to engage not to act against him and his government, he sent them to several prisons. Major-

1655 General Harrison was ordered to be carried to Carisbrooke

February. Castle in the Isle of Wight, Mr. Carew was sent to Pendennis in Cornwal, and Col. Rich confined to the custody of the Serjeant at Arms. Soon after Mr. Rogers, Mr. Feak, and Mr. Sympson, ministers, having publickly declared against his usurpation both by printing and preaching, were also imprisoned[3]. So having changed his interest, and taken off his masque, he sent his second son Col. Henry Cromwel into Ireland, to feel the pulse of the officers there touching his coming over to command in that nation, where he arrived attended only by one servant; and landing near my

---

[1] Cromwell wrote to Fleetwood on behalf of Col. John Grace, whose case had previously been recommended by the English Council. Cal. S. P., Dom., 1654, pp. 276, 337.

[2] Oliver, second Viscount Fitzwilliam of Meryon, d. 1667. Lodge, Peerage of Ireland, iii. 9. On Cromwell's intervention on his behalf, see the Protector's letter of Feb. 16, 1654, and the answer of the Commissioners, April 18, 1654. Irish Records, $\frac{A}{90}$ 50, pp. 646, 669; $\frac{A}{30}$ 28, pp. 328-9; cf. Thurloe, iii. 548.

[3] On the opposition of these three ministers, see 'Some Account of the Life and Opinions of a Fifth-Monarchy Man (John Rogers), by Edward Rogers,' 1867, p. 106. Rogers was not imprisoned till July, 1654, first at Lambeth House, and then removed in Sept., 1655, to Windsor, and finally in Nov., 1655, to Carisbrooke. Feake was released in Dec., 1656, and Rogers in Jan., 1657. On the hostility of the Welsh Anabaptists, see Thurloe, ii. 93, 116, 128, 129, 174; v. 755.; Cal. S. P., Dom., 1653-4, p. 304.

country-house, I sent my coach to receive him, and to bring him thither, where he stayed till Lieut.-General Fleetwood with several officers came with coaches to conduct him to Dublin [1]. Having made what observations he could of persons and things in Ireland, he resolved upon his return ; of which having given me advice, I desired him to take my house in his way, and to that end dined with him on the day of his departure at the Lieutenant-General's in the castle. After dinner we went together to my house at Moncktown [2], where after a short collation walking in the garden, I acquainted him with the grounds of my dissatisfaction with the present state of affairs in England, which I assured him was in no sort personal, but would be the same were my own father alive, and in the place of his. He told me that his father looked upon me to be dissatisfied upon a distinct account from most men in the three nations; and thereupon affirmed that he knew it to be his resolution to carry himself with all tenderness towards me. I told him that I ought to have so much charity for his father, to believe that he apprehended his late undertaking to have been absolutely necessary, being well assured that he was not so weak a man to decline his former station, wherein his power was as great, and his wealth as much as any rational man could wish, to procure to himself nothing but envy and trouble. I supposed he would have agreed with me in these sentiments ; but he instead of that acknowledged the ambition of his father in these words ; 'You that are here may think

---

[1] An account of Henry Cromwell's arrival is given in Thurloe, ii. 163: 'The Lieutenant-General being at his country-house halfe a mile distant from the place of his landing, sent his coach immediately to meet his lordship, himselfe soon after following on horsebacke, and with much expression of courtesy and civility invited him to his house.'

[2] Ludlow's house and estate had been once the property of Mr. Walter Cheevers of Moncktown. The es-tate, forfeited by the alleged com-plicity of Cheevers in the rebellion, had been granted by Cromwell to Ludlow, and Cheevers ordered to transplant to Connaught. On his case, see Prendergast, Cromwellian Settlement, pp. 176-9, 186, ed. 1875. Two papers from the Irish Records, relating to his case, are printed in Appendix III. Cf. Prendergast, Ire-land from the Restoration to the Revolution, pp. 23, 60, 81.

he had power, but they made a very kickshaw of him at London.' I replied that if it were so, they did ill; for he had deserved much from them. Then I proceeded to acquaint him with my resolution not to act in my civil employment, and my expectation not to be permitted to continue in my military command ; to which he answered, that he was confident I should receive no interruption therein. I told him I could not foresee what his father would do ; but inclined to think that no other man in his case would permit it. To this I added, that the reason of my drawing a sword in this war, was to remove those obstructions that the civil magistrate met with in the discharge of his duty; which being now accomplished, I could not but think that all things ought for the future to run in their proper and genuine channel : for as the extraordinary remedy is not to be used till the ordinary fail to work its proper effect, so ought it to be continued no longer than the necessity of using it subsists ; whereas this that they called a government had no other means to preserve it self, but such as were violent; which not being natural, could not be lasting. 'Would you then,' said he, ' have the sword laid down ? I cannot but think you believe it to be as much your interest to have it kept up as any man.' I confessed I had been of that opinion whilst I was perswaded there was a necessity of it, which seeming to me to be now over, I accounted it to be much more my interest to see it well laid down, there being a vast difference between using the sword to restore the people to their rights and privileges, and the keeping it up for the robbing and despoiling them of the same [1]. But company coming

---

[1] 'Ludlow and Jones are very highly dissatisfied, though Jones more cunning and close in it ; but Ludlow hath not spared any company or opportunitie to vent his venomous discontents, and that in reproachful and reflectinge language, verry much to the amazement of all sober men, amongst whom he hathe rather lost than gained acceptation by it. He hath refused to act in his civill capacitie since the change; but will not leave his military, because profittable, unlesse it be taken from him.' Henry Cromwell to Thurloe, March 8, 165¾: Thurloe, ii. 149. In a second letter he adds, ' I would take advantage by Ludlowe's frowardness to put him out of the army, and put Gen. Desborow in his place.'

in, and the time for his going on board approaching, we
could not be permitted to continue our discourse : so after
we had taken leave of each other, he departed from Ireland,
and upon his arrival at Chester was attended by many of
the late King's party ; and amongst others by Col. Molson,
who inquiring of him how he left affairs in Ireland, he
answered very well, only that some who were in love with
their power must be removed [1].

In the mean time Cromwel so ordered matters at London,
that he procured himself, his officers, and council to be
invited by the city to dinner, which was managed with all
possible state. He and the rest of his company rode on
horseback through the city ; the Mayor and Aldermen met
him at Temple-Bar, where the Mayor, as an acknowledgment of his authority, delivered the sword to him, and he
(as Kings use to do) restored it to him again. He was
harangu'd by the Recorder, and the Mayor riding bareheaded
carried the sword before him, the several Liveries in their
gowns standing on each side of the streets, where he passed.
Commissary-General Reynolds and Col. Whalley led a
troop of three hundred officers to Grocers' Hall, being the
place appointed for the entertainment ; which being ended, he
bestowed a badg of his usurpation in conferring a knighthood
upon Alderman Thomas Viner, then Mayor of London [2].
This was principally contrived, to let the world understand
how good a correspondence there was between him and the
city of London ; yet amongst discerning men it had a
contrary effect, who knew it to be rather an act of force than
of choice in the city, as appeared in the great silence and
little respect that was given him in his passage through the
streets : and tho he, to invite them to it, rode bare-headed
the greatest part of the way ; and tho some of his creatures

1654

Feb. 8.

[1] At the Restoration, Col. Roger
Mostyn was made one of the gentlemen of the King's privy chamber.
When he was arrested on suspicion
in 1658, Henry Cromwell wrote on
his behalf to Thurloe, describing
Mostyn as a person 'from whom I
have received many civilities in my
voyages for and from Ireland.' Thurloe, vii. 129.

[2] An account of this entertainment
is given in Mercurius Politicus, pp.
3262, 3265, 3270.

1654   had placed themselves at the entrance of Cheapside, and began to shout, yet it took not at all with the people [1].

About this time Cromwel having resolved upon a foreign expedition, drew out five or six thousand men, by which artifice he not only alarm'd foreign states, but also engaged all the reformade officers to his party, who otherwise would have been ready to join with any party against

Dec. 9.   him.   Col. Venables was chosen to command this army; and tho the particular design of these preparations was not certainly known, yet it was soon suspected to be against some of the King of Spain's territories.   Vice-Admiral Pen commanded the fleet that was to transport them, which consisted of sixteen or seventeen men of war, besides the vessels

1655   of transportation.   When they arrived at the Barbadoes,

Jan. 29.   they made proclamation there, that whosoever would engage in the undertaking should have his freedom, whereupon about two thousand servants listed themselves to the great damage of the planters [2].   The Spanish ambassador being informed that the fleet was gone towards the West-Indies, and that the storm was likely to fall upon some of his master's territories, made application to Cromwel to know whether he had any just ground of complaint against the King his master, and if so, that he was ready to give him all possible satisfaction.   Cromwel demanded a liberty to trade to the Spanish West-Indies, and the repeal of the laws of the Inquisition.   To which the ambassador replied, that his master had but two eyes, and that he would have him to put them both out at once [3].   The goods of our

[1] 'Oliver at his return had the second course of a brickbat from the top of a house in the Strand by St. Clements, which light upon his coach, and almost spoiled his digestion with the daringness of the affront; search was made but in vain, the person could not be found, and vengeance was not yet from heaven to rain upon him.' Heath's Chronicle, p. 662. In Gregorio Leti's Life of Cromwell this develops into the story of Lucretia Grenville's attempt to shoot Cromwell from a window.   Cf. The Travels of Edward Brown, 1739, p. 20.

[2] On the enlistment of servants, see Modyford's letter; Thurloe, iii. 620.

[3] Cromwell quotes this reply; Carlyle's Cromwell, Speech V. On his Spanish policy, see Thurloe, i. 705, 759.

merchants trading in Spain were seized for want of timely
notice to withdraw their effects from thence. And one
Major Walters with others concerned with him in the
transportation of Irish souldiers into the Spanish service,
lost thirty thousand pounds, which remained due to them
from the King of Spain.

1655

The fleet being arrived at Hispaniola, whether thro any
difference between Col. Venables, who commanded the army,
and Vice-Admiral Pen, who commanded the fleet, or for
what other reason is not easy to determine, they neglected
to land their army near the town, as was advised by
many of the officers, and as they might easily have done,
with great probability of taking the town, which most of
the inhabitants had deserted : but the army having landed
far from the town, were upon their march towards it, when
the forlorn was attacked at the entrance of a wood by
forty or fifty fellows, who were imployed to kill the wild
cows of that country. This inconsiderable number of men
put the forlorn to flight; and they retreating in great
disorder struck the whole army with such a panick fear,
that they began to shift for themselves, and could not be
prevailed with either by promises or threatnings to keep
their ground. Which being observed by Major-General
Haines, and five or six officers more, they resolved either
to put a stop to the pursuit of the enemy, or not to outlive
the disgrace ; thereupon they made a stand and fought
them, till the Major-General and most of the rest were
killed [1]. During this time our forces rallied, yet could not
recover courage enough to charge that inconsiderable
enemy; and those very men, who when they fought for
the liberties of their country, had performed wonders, having

April 13.

April 26.

---

[1] For an account of this disaster,
see Thurloe, iv. 504, 509, 514.
646, 650, 689, 754. With Major-
General James Heane fell Lieut.-
Col. Clarke, Major Forgison or Fer-
guson (?), Captains Butler, Powlet,
Hinde, Hancocke and others. See
also 'A brief and perfect journal of
the late proceedings and successes
of the English army in the West
Indies,' 1655. Harleian Miscellany,
ed. Park, iii. 510. An excellent
account of the expedition is given in
Granville Penn's Memorials of Sir
William Penn, 1823, vol. ii.

1655

now engaged to support the late erected tyranny, disgracefully fled when there was none to pursue them. The expedition against Hispaniola proving unsuccessful, they shipped themselves, and soon after arrived at the Island

May 10.

of Jamaica, belonging also to the Spaniards : which being but meanly fortified, the inhabitants, who lived for the most part together in the principal town, ran away, and betook themselves to the woods, leaving what they could not carry away to be plundered by the army. Col. Venables being disabled by sickness to perform the functions of his office, was permitted by the council of officers to return into England ; and Vice-Admiral Pen suspecting he would lay the whole blame of that affair on him, obtained leave also : and being both arrived, they were heard at White-

Sept. 20.

hall one against the other; where the accusations of both seemed to be of more weight than the defences of either of them. So Pen was committed to the Tower, and Col. Venables confined to his lodging, the distemper that was upon him excusing him from a stricter imprisonment [1].

1654

According to the promise contained in the Instrument of Government, it was resolved to issue out writs for the election of members to serve in an assembly at Westminster, who were to be chosen, not by small boroughs, and two for each county, as formerly, but in such manner as had been agreed upon by the Parliament in the bill [2] for chusing successive representatives, which indeed was much more equal and just. And because it was provided by the same Instrument, that thirty members should be sent by Ireland, and the same number by Scotland, to sit in the

May 9.

House, letters were sent by Cromwel and his council to the Commissioners there, acquainting them with that clause in

[1] Penn left Jamaica on June 25, and reached England Aug. 31. Venables arrived Sept. 7. Penn was heard before the Council on Sept. 12, Venables on Sept. 20. Both were committed to the Tower on Sept. 20; Penn's release was ordered Oct. 25, that of Venables Oct. 30. Cal. S. P., Dom., 1655, pp. 343, 396, 403. A good life of Venables is given in the notes to Robinson's 'Discourse of the War in Lancashire,' p. 97.

[2] The first edition reads 'rule,' which makes nonsense.

the Instrument of Government, and desiring their advice touching the ensuing election [1]. Some of the Commissioners in Ireland were of opinion, that if the proprietors should chuse, they would return such as were enemies to the English interest, and therefore proposed that for this time Cromwel and his council should nominate the thirty who were to be chosen for that nation. This question coming before the Commissioners before the arrival of the new set nominated by Cromwel, tho I resolved to intermeddle as little as might be, yet this advice seemed so strange to me, that I could not forbear to desire of them, that seeing we had no more of liberty left but the name, they would at least retain the form, in hopes that in time men might become so sensible of their own interest as to be enabled thereby to recover the efficacy and substance of it, especially since it was most probable that by the influence of those in power the same persons would be chosen that they desired. To this they agreed; and having proportioned the cities and counties for the election before the issuing out the writs, a private junto was held by Lieutenant-General Fleetwood, who agreed upon the persons that they would have chosen for each place, which they had

[1] 'For the Lieutenant-General Fleetwood in Ireland. Sir, by the Instrument whereby the government of this Commonwealth is settled, thirty persons are to be chosen and sent from Ireland to serve in the Parliament of the Commonwealth. But the distribution of these persons in reference to the several places for which they are to serve, to wit what places are fit to send members to Parliament, and how to be proportioned, with the manner of electing them, is not determined by the said Instrument, but left to me by advice of the Council. And we being now upon consideration thereof, do think it necessary that we should have the advice of yourself and the other Commissioners there upon the place in this business. To which end I desire you to consider with the said Commissioners, to what places and in what manner the thirty persons may be distributed with most equality; and with respect to the present affairs, whether you conceive any places or parts in Ireland to be capable of electing members themselves, and if [so] under what qualifications, or whether the present condition of affairs be not such as that particular persons be called by writ for the next Parliament. I desire your advice and judgment upon the whole with all the expedition that may be because the writs of summons are to issue out by the first of the next month. Your loving friend, Oliver, P., May 9, 1654.

Irish Records, $\frac{A}{28}$ 26, p. 35.

a great advantage to effect, having nominated and fitted the sheriffs and other officers for that purpose [1]. The court-party endeavoured to promote the election of such as would center in adoring the idol lately set up, however different in opinions about other matters. The clergy in some parts proved so strong, that they carried it against those agreed on by the court; but both parties concurred in the decrying all such who would not sacrifice the cause of the publick to the ambition of men. In England they better understood the design that was carrying on, insomuch that many persons of known vertue and integrity were chosen to sit in this assembly, in particular the Lord President Bradshaw, Sir Arthur Haslerig, Mr. Thomas Scott, Mr. Robert Wallup, and divers others. And though I was in Ireland and under a cloud, and that there was the like packing of the cards for the election in the county of Wilts as in other places, the Cavaliers and the imposing clergy, the lawyers and court interest, all joining against that of the Commonwealth, and having preferred a list of ten men (the number which was to be chosen by that county) as those whom they would have to be chosen, they cite the parishes and every particular person therein to appear, who when they came upon the hill were headed by Sir Anthony Ashley Cooper, a man of a healing and reconciling spirit, of all interests that agree in the greatening of himself, being now one of Cromwell's council. The well wishers to the public interest, according to the practice of their antagonists, prepared a list of such as they judged faithful to the public cause, but the other party not contented with

---

[1] Fleetwood, Jones and Corbet answered on May 19: 'In obedience to your commands . . . concerning the elections of persons in this nation to serve in the next ensuing Parliament, we have considered of the present condition of this desolate country, wherein several counties be totally waste and uninhabited, and in others the inhabitants not yet in any settled condition . . . in which respect we cannot satisfy ourselves as the present state of affairs here do stand to present any particular way and course for such election at this time.' Irish Records, $\frac{A}{90}$ 50, p. 691. In spite of their remonstrance the writs were sent over and elections took place. A list of persons elected is printed in Thurloe, ii. 445, 530, 558.

their policy make use of force, threatening those who oppose them as such who designed disturbance in the state by promoting the election of such as were dissatisfied with the present Government ; but notwithstanding all they could say or do, and though the under-sheriff was made for their turn, the high-sheriff being absent, the Commonwealth party appeared so equal, that it could not be decided without a poll, and both parties were so numerous that the usual place for election was too strait, so that they consented to adjourn the meeting unto Stonnage[1], where there was room enough. The great work is to keep me from being elected who knew not of one person's intention to appear for me, being at that time in Ireland, neither had I been free to have sat had I been elected as a member to serve in that assembly (a Parliament I could not own it to be, the Long Parliament being only interrupted by the sword), knowing well that if they should beyond expectation do anything for the good of the people, they should receive an interruption by the power of the sword, under which they then were. Yet did Sir Anthony Cooper and Mr. Adoniram Byfield, a busy clergyman, not contented with their share in that tyrannical Government, or hoping that it would conduce to that which was more so, make harangues to the people, labouring to convince them that it was desirable to choose such as were of healing spirits, and not such as were for the putting of all things into confusion and disorder ; but the people well knowing their persons, designs, and interests, and that yet nothing could prevent tyranny and confusion but the settling of such a Government as would provide for common good, and needed not the military sword to uphold it, but would be supported by the affection of the people, stick close to the former resolution, and pleased in the first place to cry up me as one they would entrust in that assembly. The other party, finding mine greater than any of theirs when divided, unite in their first vote for Sir Anthony Cooper, whom the under-sheriff on the view adjudgeth to be first chosen,

---

[1] i. e. Stonehenge.

1654

though the party that appeared for me conceived themselves much injured therein ; but the other party had all the power in their hands, and knew they should be protected by him, who called himself the Protector, do they what they would[1]. When the time appointed for the meeting of this assembly was come, Cromwel went in a coach to Westminster, accompanied by his horse and foot guard. with many officers of the army on foot; where being arrived, his first business was to appear in his kingly garb at the Abby, there to hear a sermon with the members of that assembly before they went about their other affairs.

Sept. 4.

Which done, he went into the Painted Chamber, where he entertained the members with a tedious speech, wherein he endeavoured to make it appear, that things were brought to this pass, not by his contrivance, but by the over-ruling hand of God ; assuring them, that he was much rejoiced to see so free an assembly of the people met together, and that he resolved to submit himself to their judgment. But notwithstanding these specious pretences, he caused the Lord Grey of Grooby, Mr. John Wildman, Mr. Highland, and others, who had always manifested a constant affection to the Commonwealth, to be excluded from the House. And tho many undue methods had been used at the elections to procure those to be chosen who were enemies, and to keep out many who were known friends to the common cause[2]; and tho they saw themselves under the power of one who they knew would force his way to the throne, yet they appeared in a few days not to be for his purpose, but resolved, at the least, to lay a claim to their liberties. For whereas the court-party would have obliged

---

[1] This account of the Wiltshire election is one of the passages of Ludlow's Memoirs suppressed by the editor in 1698. Transcripts of it and of the other suppressed passages were found amongst Locke's papers in the possession of the Earl of Lovelace. See Christie's Life of Shaftesbury, vol. i. Appendix, p. lvi. A pamphlet relating to this election,

entitled 'The copy of a letter sent out of Wiltshire,' is reprinted in the Appendix to this edition of Ludlow.

[2] On the election of Mr. Samuel Highland for Southwark and the reasons for setting it aside, see Cal S. P., Dom., 1654, p. 305. On other elections, ib., preface, pp. x–xiv, and pp. 271, 277, 279, 280, 299, 311, 314, 316, 319, 327, 331, 334.

them to approve at once the whole Instrument of Govern- 1654
ment which they had framed, the assembly took it in
pieces, and referred the consideration of it to a committee,
where the first question fallen upon was, 'Whether the
Supreme Legislative power of the Nation shall be in a
single person and the Parliament?' In this debate Sir
Arthur Haslerig, Mr. Scott, and many others, especially
the Lord President Bradshaw, were very instrumental in
opening the eyes of many young members who had never
before heard their interest so clearly stated and asserted ;
so that the Commonwealth-party increased daily, and that
of the sword lost ground[1]. Cromwel being informed of
these transactions by his creatures, and fearing to have
that great question put ; lest he should be deposed, by a
vote of this assembly, from the throne which he had
usurped, caused a guard to be set upon the door of the
House early in the morning, and sent to the Mayor of Sept. 12
London to acquaint him with the reasons of what he was
about to do, to the end that he might prevent any disorders
in the city. The members coming at the usual hour, were
refused the door, and required to attend him in the Painted
Chamber ; where he taking notice of what was under
debate in the House, contrary to the privilege of a Parliament, (as he would have this thought to be) told them, that
being called by virtue of the Instrument of Government to
that assembly, they were bound up by the indentures
themselves, upon which they were returned, from altering
the government by a single person and a Parliament ; and
that the country having owned him by electing a Parliament called by his writ, and that the Judges with the
Justices of the Peace having acted by virtue of his authority, he was resolved not to permit that point to be called
in question, acquainting them, that no person should be
admitted, for the time to come, to sit as a member in that

---

[1] These debates lasted from Sept. 6 to Sept. 11. The substance of the arguments is reported by Mr. God-dard, member for King's Lynn. A compromise proposed by Matthew Hale had been practically agreed upon. Burton's Diary, vol. i. pp. xxii, xxxiii ; vol. iii. p. 142.

1654   assembly, till he had subscribed an acknowledgment of the government by a single person and a Parliament[1]. Some of those who had been chosen members of this Convention, had already declined the House, upon account that Cromwel and his council had excluded from their places divers persons who had been constantly faithful to the publick interest ; but so soon as this visible hand of violence appeared to be upon them, most of the eminent assertors of the liberty of their country withdrew themselves, being perswaded they should better discharge their duty to the nation by this way of expressing their abhorrence of his tyrannical proceedings, than by surrendring their liberties under their own hands, and then treating with him who was possessed of the sword, to recover some part of them again. However this engagement was signed by about one hundred and thirty members within a day or two, and some days after several others subscribed it, and took their

Sept. 14. places in the House, where a debate arising touching the said recognition, they passed a declaration, that it should not be intended to comprehend the whole government contained in the forty-two articles of the Instrument, but that only which required the government of the Commonwealth to be by a single person and successive Parliaments. And to this the major part consented, hoping that by their compliance with him, in making provision for his safety, and the government of the nation during his life, he would have been satisfied therewith, and in gratitude would have judged the people after his death to be of age and wisdom sufficient to chuse a government for themselves. This great point touching the single person being thus overruled, they applied themselves to the consideration and debate of the remaining clauses of the Instrument of Government. They declared that he should be Protector

Sept. 20. during his life[2], and limited the number of forces to be

---

[1] Carlyle's Cromwell, Speech III.
[2] The chief debate was on the 32nd article, on the question whether the Protectorate should be hereditary or elective. Lambert spoke strongly to make it hereditary. Burton, vol. i. p. li.

1651

kept up in England, Scotland, and Ireland, with provision for the paiment of them. They agreed upon the number of ships that they thought necessary for the guard of the seas, and ordered two hundred thousand pounds a year for his own expence. the salaries of his council, the judges, foreign intelligence, and the reception of ambassadors. They also voted a clause to be inserted, to declare the rights of the people of England, and particularly that no money should be raised upon the nation but by authority of Parliament. And whereas by the Instrument of Government it was provided, that if the Parliament were not sitting at the death of the present Protector, the Council of Officers should chuse a successor; they resolved, that nothing should be determined by the Council after his death, but the calling of a Parliament, who were then to consider what they would have done. Besides these things, I can remember no remarkable variation from what was formerly set down in the paper called the Instrument of Government, except this additional vote, that no one clause of this should be looked upon as binding, unless the whole were consented unto [1]. Which they did, lest Cromwel should interrupt them, and taking what made for his own advancement, reject what was advantageous to the Commonwealth. Much time was spent, and pains taken, to effect this within the time limited, so that hardly any private business was done all that time, except an order given to the excise-office for satisfying an old debt pretended by Col. John Birch, one of their members, a nimble gentleman, and one who used to neglect no opportunity of providing for himself.

Nov. 3.

The usurper, that he might make way for his posterity to succeed him in his greatness, changed the title of Lieutenant-General Fleetwood from that of Commander-in-Chief to that of Deputy of Ireland, to continue till such

---

[1] The alterations made by this Parliament in the Instrument of Government are best shown by the draft bill printed in Mr. Gardiner's 'Constitutional Documents,' and by his comparison of it with the Instrument, pp. lx, 353.

1654

Aug. 27.

time as it should be thought fit to recal him from thence, and to establish his son Harry in his place. In order to this a commission was sent to Fleetwood from Cromwel, wherein those who were before called commissioners are now stiled only his counsellors [1]. Having thus modelled the government of Ireland, he began to apply his care to

1655
August.

that of Scotland ; and knowing Monk to be a souldier, and faithful enough to him, as long as he would gratify his vicious, covetous. and ambitious inclinations, he entrusted him with the command of the forces, and made him one of the commissioners for civil affairs in that nation [2]. But that he might balance him with some of another temper, who might be a guard upon his actions, he sent Col. Adrian Scroop to be one of the commissioners there also, having first caused the castle of Bristol, whereof he was governour, to be slighted, not daring to trust a person of so much honour and worth with a place of that importance [3]. He likewise sent thither Col. Whetham with the same character, who having been one of the late assembly, as well as governour of Portsmouth. and understanding that a design was on foot to make Cromwel king, had in the House applied to him the saying of the prophet to Ahab, ' Hast thou killed, and also taken possession ? ' By which words it appearing that this gentleman was not for Oliver's

[1] Aug. 27, 1654, is the date of instructions from the Lord Protector 'with the advice of our council to our right trusty. &c., Charles Fleetwood, and to those hereby nominated of our council with our Deputy.' The Councillors were commissioned for three years. They were Col. Robert Hammond. Richard Pepys, William Steele, Miles Corbet, Robert Goodwin and Matthew Tomlinson. Henry Cromwell was added Dec. 25, 1654, and William Bury. Aug. 4, 1656. Fourteenth Report of the Keeper of the Irish Records.

[2] The Council of Scotland, the establishment of which was publicly announced at the beginning of August,

1655, consisted of Lord Broghil, General Monk, Col. Charles Howard, Col. Adrian Scroope, Col. Nathaniel Whetham, Col. Thomas Cooper, Col. William Lockhart, Mr. John Swinton and Mr. Samuel Desborough. Emmanuel Downing (father of Sir George) was clerk of the Council. See Thurloe, iii. 423, 711, 727; Cal. S. P., Dom., 1655, pp. 108, 152, 255, 260 ; Masson, Life of Milton, v. 86.

[3] The demolition of Bristol Castle was ordered Feb., 1655. The Royal Fort at Bristol was ordered to be slighted on June 24, 1655. Cal. S. P., Dom., 1655, p. 257; cf. Thurloe, iii. 172, 182, 184.

turn, he removed him from Portsmouth, and sent him to Scotland to be one of the commissioners there also. The Lord Broghil was made President of the Council in Scotland, with an allowance of two thousand pounds a year, with a promise from him, who never kept any but such as suted with his corrupt ends, that his service should be dispensed with after one year, and yet his salary to continue.

In Holland the party of the Prince of Orange having long obstructed the signing of the articles agreed upon between that State and Cromwel, the States General sent Myn Heer Beverning ambassador into England, to assure Cromwel, that if the Provinces did not agree to the articles within eight days, he had power from the States General to sign them in their names[1]. But before this peace was concluded, the King of Scots party had obtained succours to be sent to their friends in Scotland, who were augmented to the number of about five thousand horse and foot, having received fifteen hundred foot, two hundred horse, and great numbers of arms brought to them by seventeen Holland ships[2]; so that it was thought fit to take Lieutenant-General Monk from the fleet, the war at sea being now over, and to send him to take care of affairs in Scotland; but chiefly to keep the officers there from drawing to a head against Cromwel's usurpation. Lieutenant-General Middleton, with about one hundred men more, for the most part officers, five hundred arms, and one hundred and fifty barrels of powder, landed also in the north of Scotland. To oppose these

---

[1] On the concluding negotiations, see Geddes, John de Witt, i. 381–410. The treaty was completed by the passing of the Act of Exclusion by the States of Holland, May 4. The States of Holland bound themselves not to elect the Prince of Orange or any of his line, Stadholder or Admiral of their province, and to resist the election of the same as Captain-General of the army of the seven confederated Provinces. Geddes, pp. 381–419.

[2] The best account of this rising, which was headed by William Cunningham, Earl of Glencairn, is in the 'Account of the Earl of Glencairn's expedition,' published in 1822 with the Memoirs of John Gwynne, and with an appendix of extracts from Mercurius Politicus. The rising began in August, 1653; Middleton landed about the end of February, 1654.

1654

forces we sent fifteen hundred men from Ireland under Lieutenant-Col. Braine, into the mountains of Scotland, who contributed very much to the suppression of them.

May.

Monk being arrived in Scotland, divided his army into several bodies, the two principal of which were commanded by himself and Col. Morgan[1]. With these they pursued the enemy so closely, that at a council of war held by them in the county of Murray, they made a resolution to disperse themselves upon every alarm, and to meet again at a rendezvouz to be agreed upon. This being resolved, they advanced towards the quarters of Col. Braine, where they were warmly received, and forced to retire. Middleton, to avoid the pursuit of ours, dispersed his foot into inaccessible quarters, and drew together about six hundred horse at Kennagh; whereby Monk perceiving that his design was to tire out our forces, declined following him so close, endeavouring to drive him upon Col. Morgan, whom Monk had informed of the enemy's march. Middleton seeing himself no farther pursued, stayed at Kennagh; whereupon Monk having received advice of the approach of Col. Morgan's party, advanced with his forces towards the enemy, who retiring towards Badenorth, and being

July 19.

about to take their quarters that night at Loughary, found themselves engaged at a narrow pass by Col. Morgan, who designed to quarter at the same place. Middleton endeavouring to retire, was obstructed by a morass; and being hotly pursued by Col. Morgan's forces, and much harassed by difficult marches, was soon routed, many of his men were killed, and many taken prisoners; four hundred of their horse were taken, together with the charging and sumpter horses of Middleton himself, who being wounded in the action, saved himself with much difficulty on foot[2]. His commission, instructions, and divers letters written to him

---

[1] Monk arrived in Scotland in May, 1654. Thurloe, ii. 261. For his instructions, see Cal. S. P., Dom., 1654, p. 83.

[2] See the letters of Monk and Morgan printed in Mercurius Politicus, July 27–Aug. 3, 1654, p. 3661, and the narrative of Gen. Monk's march, p. 3695.

and his friends, by their King, were taken also ; and had
not such as fled been favoured by the bad ways and the
night, very few had escaped. The news of this defeat
coming to the enemy's foot, who were in number about
twelve hundred, they immediately disbanded themselves,
and divers of the enemy's principal officers came in and
submitted, and amongst them the Earl of Glencarne,
Lieutenant-Col. Maxwell, Lieutenant-Col. Herriott. the
Lord Forester, and Sir George Monroe. Yet notwithstanding this low condition of that party in Scotland, the clergy
refused to observe such fasts as were appointed by the
Government in England, and instead of them appointed
others by their own authority, wherein they exhorted the
people, amongst other things, to seek the Lord, to preserve
the ministry among them, to forget the offences of the
House of the Stewarts, and to turn from his people the
sad effects of a late eclipse.

A fleet commanded by General Blake was sent into the
Mediterranean, to require satisfaction from the Grand Duke
of Tuscany, for injuries done to our merchants, and for
entertaining and harbouring Prince Rupert's fleet ; in which
expedition he not only procured the satisfaction demanded,
but rendred the power of England so formidable not only
to all Italy, but even to the Grand Seignior himself, that
they expressed a greater readiness to preserve the friendship of the English than ever they had done before [1].

In the mean time Cromwel having assumed the whole
power of the nation to himself, and sent ambassadors and
agents to foreign states, was courted again by them, and
presented with the rarities of several countries ; amongst the
rest the Duke of Holstein made him a present of a set of
gray Frizeland coach-horses, with which taking the air
in the Park, attended only with his secretary Thurlow,

(margin: 1651)

(margin: October.)

(margin: Sept. 29.)

---

[1] The fleet sailed Sept. 29. Blake's
earlier letters have not been preserved. Professor Laughton states
that Ludlow's assertion about the
reparation obtained from the Duke
of Tuscany 'is entirely unsupported
by exact evidence, and is virtually
contradicted by Blake's silence in
his extant letters from Leghorn.'
D. N. B. v. 177. Blake bombarded
Tunis on April 4, 1655. Cf. Heath's
Chronicle, p. 676.

and guard of Janizaries, he would needs take the place of the coachman, not doubting but the three pair of horses he was about to drive would prove as tame as the three nations which were ridden by him : and therefore not contented with their ordinary pace, he lashed them very furiously. But they unaccustomed to such a rough driver, ran away in a rage, and stop'd not till they had thrown him out of the box, with which fall his pistol fired in his pocket, tho without any hurt to himself; by which he might have been instructed how dangerous it was to intermeddle with those things wherein he had no experience [1].

The Representative sitting at Westminster, tho garbled as he thought fit, proving not sufficiently inclined to serve his designs, but rather in prudence yielding to the strength of the present stream, in hopes the people might in time recover their oars, and make use of them for the publick good ; he grew impatient till the five months allowed for their sitting should be expired ; during which time he was restrained by that which he called the Instrument of Government, from giving them interruption. And tho they differed not in any material point from that form of government which he himself had set up, unless it were in reserving the nomination of his successor to the Parliament ; yet did the omission of this one thing so inrage him, that he resolved upon their dissolution. They had prepared all things to offer to him, and had been very cautious of giving him any just occasion of offence, well knowing that in case they had given him the least pretence of dissatisfaction, he would have laid all the blame at their door ; and therefore they prudently left the settling of the Church government, and the liberty that was to be extended to tender consciences (an engine by which Cromwel did most

---

[1] Accounts of this incident are given in Thurloe, ii. 552, 674; Vaughan, Protectorate of Oliver Cromwell, i. 69. See also Marvell's poem on the first anniversary of the Protectorate, ll. 175-224, and Wither's 'Vaticinium Casuale, A Rapture occasioned by the late miraculous deliverance of his Highness the Lord Protector from a desperate danger.' See also Heath's Chronicle, p. 671 ; Report on the Portland MSS., i. 678.

of his work) to the consideration of the next assembly [1]:
whereupon he wanting wherewith justly to accuse them,
unless it were for too much complying with him to the
prejudice of the Commonwealth, after he had perused the
form of government which the assembly had agreed upon,
and tendred to him for his consideration : the five months
of their sessions, according to the souldiers' account of
twenty-eight days to the month, being expired, they were
ordered to attend him on the 23rd of January 1654 [2], in
the Painted Chamber, where he made up with words and
passion what he wanted of matter to charge them with,
accusing them of endeavouring to bring all things into
disorder and confusion, by raking into the particulars of
the Instrument of Government, which he extolled very
highly. He charged them with neglecting to make provision for the army, and necessitating them thereby to take
free quarter, to the great dissatisfaction of the country, if it
had not been prevented by the care, and at the expence
of the officers. In this and in many other particulars he
very much preferred the wisdom and prudence of the Long
Parliament, which was the part he proposed now to act,
having determined to cry down this. And because he
could not accuse them of any practices against liberty of
conscience, he charged them with their principles, and
imputed to them all those discontents and designs, which
were on foot by several parties against the present government, affirming that if they had not their rise from some
that sat amongst them (which he thought he should make
appear) yet they grew like shrubs under their shadow.
And that he might obviate that objection, which his own
conscience told him was the true reason of his dissatisfaction
with what had been agreed on in this assembly, he told
them that their not settling the government on him and
his heirs was not the reason why he refused to consent
to what they presented to him. 'For,' said he, 'so fully am
I convinced (in the judgment I now am) of the injustice of

---

[1] See Burton's Diary, vol. i. pp.
lix, lx, lxxix, cxii–cxix.

[2] January 22. Speech IV. in Carlyle's Cromwell.

hereditary government, that if you had offered me the whole Instrument of Government with that one alteration in favour of my family, I should have refused the whole for the sake of that ; and I do not know tho you have begun with an unworthy person, but hereafter the same method may be observed in the choice of magistrates, as was amongst the children of Israel, who appointed those that had been most eminent in delivering them from their enemies abroad to govern them at home.' In which excuse three things seem remarkable ; first, that tho in the judgment he then was hereditary government was unjust, yet he reserved a liberty to alter his opinion, if he should find persons and things inclining that way. Secondly, in declaring this to be his present opinion, he flattered the ambition of Major-General Lambert, and kept him in expectation of succeeding him, and so secured his assistance in carrying on his wicked design. In the third place, by designing that the General should be always chosen Protector, it appears that he would have had the nation to be perpetually governed by the military sword. Thus did this wise man (as he would be thought) weaken his own interest, and lose the affections of the people : for as by his interruption of the Long Parliament, he disobliged the most sober part of the nation, so by the dissolution of this assembly he opened the eyes of the rest, who had been hitherto made to believe that he was necessitated to that extraordinary action, because they would not do those good things for the nation which were expected from them ; and by this reproachful dismission of the Convention, which consisted for the most part of men of moderate spirits, and who had gone in the judgment of the most discerning men, but too far in compliance with him for the purchase of their present peace, he made a considerable part of those who had been friends to him, irreconcilable enemies, and sent the members into their respective countries to relate to their neighbours and those that sent them what an unreasonable creature they had found him.

Having dissolved the pretended Representative called by

his own authority, he began by bribes to corrupt others to his interest; and to this end ordered the arrears of Col. Hewetson for his English service to be paid in ready money, and his Irish arrears to be satisfied out of forfeited lands in the county of Dublin, at the rate of the adventurers, in such places as he should choose [1]. He ordered two thousand pounds to be paid out of the treasury to Mr. Weaver in lieu of what the Parliament had settled upon him out of the forfeited lands in Scotland [2], and ten thousand pounds in ready money to Major-General Lambert in consideration of one thousand pounds by year out of the said forfeited lands given to him by the Parliament, not regarding how he lavished away the public treasure, so as he might procure such instruments as he thought would be subservient to his unjust designs.

By this time many began openly to discover their discontents, and particularly the friends of the Scots King, who tho he saw clearly his game playing by this usurper, through the divisions he made amongst those whose interest it was to be united in opposition to him; yet being impatient of delay, and not caring how many he sacrificed, so as he might with more expedition recover the exercise of his power, he sent over divers commissions for the raising of horse and foot, and prevailed with some young gentlemen of little consideration and less experience to accept them, and to engage against a victorious army commanded by one, who spared not the purse of the Commonwealth to procure intelligence. By which means he caused a great number of arms that were provided for the execution of this design to be seized, and imprisoned divers persons concerned in it; wherein he made use of one Baily a Jesuit, who discovered his kinsman one Mr. Bagnal,

---

[1] Col. Hewson was granted, July 18, 1654, Luttrellstown for his arrears. Prendergast, Cromwellian Settlement, p. 197; 14th Report of Dep. Keeper of Irish Records, p. 43; Thurloe, ii. 357.

[2] On the grant to Weaver, see Cal. S. P., Dom., 1654, pp. 260, 276. On April 14, 1653, Parliament had voted him Scottish lands to the value of £250 a year. C. J., vi. 278. The evidence for Ludlow's statements about Cromwell's payments to Weaver and Lambert does not appear.

son to the Lady Terringham, together with his own brother Capt. Nicholas Baily[1], accusing them both of accepting commissions for raising a regiment, which Mr. Bagnal upon his examination did not deny. But notwithstanding this discovery, so confident were these young men of success, that they still carried on their plot, and appointed a day for the execution of it. Cromwel suspecting that they might have some grounds for their confidence, dispatched Commissary-General Reynolds to Ireland with orders to cause some forces to be imbarked for England, and accordingly about two thousand foot and three hundred horse were ordered to be sent over to his assistance[2], the foot to be commanded by Col. Sadler, and the horse by Major Bolton. This party being drawn to the water-side, some of the private soldiers, whether from any scruple of conscience, or from an unwillingness to leave their wives, children, and plantations in Ireland, I cannot say, refused to imbark, tho Lieut.-General Fleetwood with several field-officers of the army were present; alledging that they had listed themselves to fight against the rebels of Ireland, and in prosecution of that obligation were ready to obey all commands; that they knew not against whom they should be drawn to engage in England, possibly against some of their best friends, and therefore desired to be excused from that service. The officers resolving to compel them by force to go aboard, called a court-martial upon the place, where they condemned one of the most active to death, and ordered one entire company to be cashiered; both which orders were immediately put in execution, by breaking the company, and hanging the man upon the mast of one of the ships: at this execution Col. Hewetson, who had been

---

[1] Thomas Bayly, son of Lewis Bayly, Bishop of Bangor. Major Nicholas Bayly was knighted for his services at the Restoration and made governor of the island of Arran. Nicholas Bagenal was son of Arthur Bagenal, and grandson of Sir Henry Bagenal, knight marshal of Ireland. His mother married, as her second husband, Sir Arthur Tyringham.

[2] Fleetwood was originally ordered to send over 3000 foot, but kept back four companies. They landed at Liverpool about Jan. 21, 1655. Thurloe, iii. 75, 136, 311; Mercurius Politicus, pp. 5079, 5084.

lately obliged in the matter of his arrears, as a mark of his 1655 gratitude gave order that the poor man should be hanged higher than was at first designed.

The Cavalier plot was still on foot in England; and tho divers of them were imprisoned, and many arms seized, yet it was still resolved to attempt something. To this end a cartload of arms was conveyed to the place of rendezvouz agreed upon for the northern parts, where it was reported the contrivers of this design were to be headed by the Lord Wilmot. But receiving some alarm upon their first meeting, March 8. and fearing lest the regular forces should fall upon them before they were sufficiently prepared for their defence, they dispersed themselves, and left their arms behind them. The only considerable party that appeared were those at Salisbury, which they had an opportunity of doing under March 11. colour of going to the assizes[1]. They consisted of about one hundred and fifty horse, and drew together in the night, and were ordered to seize the judges there in circuit, the sheriff of the county, and such other persons as they should suspect to be enemies to the design. Col. Wagstaff was said to be their commander; but Col. Penruddock, a gentleman of that country, appeared most forward in giving out the necessary orders and directions. Capt. Hugh Grove, and Mr. Jones of Newton, with several other gentlemen of those parts, were amongst them. They proclaimed Charles the Second to be King of England, &c., seized the judges, and having taken away their commissions, set them at liberty. They carried the sheriff Mr. Dove away with them to Dogtown, to which place they thought fit to retire, apprehending more danger at Salisbury, their forces not at all answering their first expectations. From thence they marched as far as Blandford in Dorsetshire, but so few joined them in their way, that at their arrival there they exceeded not the number of two hundred horse. Most

---

[1] On this insurrection, see 'Cromwell and the Insurrection of 1655,' *English Historical Review*, 1888, p. 323; 1889, p. 313. See also, Mr. W. W. Ravenhill's papers entitled 'Records of the Rising in the West, 1655,' in the Wiltshire Archæological Magazine, vols. xiii, xiv.

men looked upon them as flying, divers of their own party stealing from them as fast as others came to them ; and those that staid with them, did so rather to secure themselves, and obtain better conditions, than from any hopes of succeeding. What they did served only to alarm the army, some troops of which pursued them into Devonshire, where they were fallen upon by Major Unton Crook, and defeated. Divers of them were taken prisoners, and amongst them Col. Penruddock. Mr. Jones, and Capt. Grove. Major-General Wagstaff, Mr. Mompesson, and several others escaped. and went privately to their own habitations; but upon information given that they were concerned in this plot, they were seized and secured in order to trial. The prisoners taken in the fight pretended articles for life from Major Crook, alledging that otherwise they would not have delivered themselves on so easy terms ; but the Major absolutely denied any such thing : so that a commission of Oyer and Terminer was issued for their trial, and Mr. Attorney General Prideaux was sent from London to prosecute them. The Chief Justice Rolls was nominated in the commission to be one of their judges, but he refused to act therein, on account that the prisoners had done a particular injury to him in seizing his person at their first rising, and therefore he thought himself unfit to give his judgment in their case. wherein he might be thought a party concerned. Some of them were condemned at Salisbury, and some at Exeter, of which number were Col. Penruddock and Capt. Grove ; and in aggravation of their crimes it was urged. that this was their second offence of this kind, and that it was committed against much favour and kindness, not only in that they had been permitted to compound for their estates at a reasonable rate, when they had forfeited all, but also that an Act of Oblivion had been granted to them and their whole party, whereby they were put into a condition of enjoying the advantages of all the victories of those to whom they had been enemies. To this they answered, that they did not rise against those who had extended that favour to them, but against a person who had dissipated those men, and established himself in their place. And I cannot tell by what laws of God or man they could have been justly condemned, had they been upon as sure a foundation in what they declared for, as they were in what they declared against. But certainly it can never be esteemed by a wise man to be worth the scratch of a finger to remove a single person acting by an arbitrary power, in order to set up another with the same unlimited authority. Col. Penruddock and Capt. Grove were executed by behead- ing, according to the sentence pronounced against them; but Mr. Jones of Newton Tony being allied to Cromwel, was pardoned after he had been found guilty by the jury, and Major Crook was ordered to have two hundred pounds by year out of Mr. Mompesson's estate for his good service in the suppression of this party.

The usurper was not a little startled at this insurrection, suspecting that so small a number would not have appeared without more considerable encouragement; and therefore tho he had lately so meanly stooped to court the Cavalier party, and thereby highly provoked his antient friends to a just jealousy and indignation, he resolved now to fall upon them, and to break through all their compositions, even the Act of Oblivion it self, in the obtaining and passing of which he had so great a hand. To this end he commanded a tenth part of their estates to be levied, in order as he pretended to maintain those extraordinary forces which their turbulent and seditious practices obliged him to keep up. In defence of which oppression I could never yet hear one argument offered that carried any weight, either with respect to justice or policy: for having by his treachery and usurpation disobliged those with whom he first engaged, he seemed to have no other way left to support himself, but by balancing his new with his old enemies, whom by this fresh act of injustice he rendred desperate and irreconcilable, they being not able to call any thing their own, whilst by the same rule that he seized one tenth, he might also take away the other nine parts at his pleasure. And to put this detestable project in execution, he divided England into cantons, over each of which he placed a Bashaw under the title of Major-General, who was to have the inspection and government of inferiour commissioners in every county, with orders to seize the persons, and distrain the estates of such as should be refractory, and to put in execution such further directions as they should receive from him[1].

In the army there were not wanting some that still retained an affection to the cause of their country, which appeared more particularly in a petition to Cromwel, signed by many of them, containing things so sutable to the desires of honest men, that it proved on that account very unwelcome to the usurper. Amongst others Col. Okey endeavoured to perswade the officers of his regiment to stand by him in the prosecution of the ends of it, but was interrupted in that design by his major, for whom he had not without difficulty obtained that employment[2]. It was also pretended, that Major-General Overton, with some officers of the army in Scotland, designed to seize upon Monk, and to march with that army to London for the restitution of the Parliament: upon suspicion of which he was seized and sent prisoner to London, where he was committed to the Tower[3].

About three hundred of the petition aforesaid, together with another writing called the Memento, were sent into Ireland in a box directed to me, and accompanied with

---

[1] The districts were marked out and the Major-Generals chosen in Aug. 1655, but the new organisation was not officially announced till Oct. 31. See Masson, Life of Milton, v. 49; Cal. S. P., Dom., 1655, pp. 275, 296. For the powers of the Major-Generals, see Old Parliamentary History, xx. 461.

[2] In the autumn of 1654, a petition was circulated signed by Cols. Okey, Alured and Saunders. The petition, which criticises the too great power attributed to the Protector by the Instrument of Government, and demands the summoning of a free Parliament, is calendared by Mrs. Green under Dec. 20, 1653. Cal. S. P., Dom., 1653-4, p. 302. In the 'Case of Col. Matthew Alured,' 1659, containing an account of his sufferings, it seems to be dated 1654, and it was certainly circulated in the winter of 1654-5. Alured, Okey and Saunders were tried by court-martial in Dec. 1654. Saunders submitted and retained his command till 1656, Alured and Okey were cashiered, and the former for a time imprisoned.

[3] On Overton's case, see English Historical Review, 1888, p. 330.

a short letter without any subscription [1]. Which papers, when I had perused, and found them to contain such truths as were very proper to prepare the minds of men to imbrace the first opportunity of rescuing themselves from the present oppression, I thought it my duty to procure them to be dispersed as much to the advantage of the publick as I could. Wherein I was particularly assisted by Capt. Walcot, one of the faithful officers of my regiment, and divers others of my friends [2]. I acquainted Lieutenant-Col. Brayfield with my design, and sent some of the papers to Major Davis, who was then at Dublin, but resided usually in Connaught, thinking him to be a proper person to be imployed to disperse them in that province. The said Major Davis having received the papers, came to me, and desired to know if they came from me. I answered him, that tho I wished my name might have been concealed, yet that question being put to me, I durst not deny it; and having further informed him of the reasons which moved me so to do, he declared himself to be fully satisfied with them. But it afterwards appeared, that upon the first receipt of those papers, he had acquainted Mr. Roberts, the Auditor-General, therewith, presuming him to be well affected to the common cause; which proving otherwise, the said Roberts informed Lieutenant-General Fleetwood of what he knew. The Lieutenant-General having also had advice that I had discoursed with Lieutenant-Col. Brayfield in the castle-yard, and suspecting it might be upon the same business, sent for Major Davis and the said

---

[1] 'Heare hath ben some papers called "Mementoes," and other papers spread up and downe the army by that gentleman, who, I had hoped, my friendshipe would have prevented any such attempt. Through mercy I cam to the discovery of it in time, and hope any danger is prevented.' Fleetwood to Thurloe, Jan 3, 165⅘; Thurloe, iii. 70; cf. Burton's Diary, i. cxliv.

[2] Lieutenant-Col. Alexander Bray-

field was cashiered as 'a busy and turbulent person,' and 'a promoter of seditious papers,' by Henry Cromwell in 1657. Thurloe, vi. 505, 527, 540, 552, 563, 599; cf. Clarke Papers, i. 437. Fleetwood praises Brayfield highly. Thurloe, iii. 567. Captain Thomas Walcot is mentioned again by Ludlow in 1660. He was executed July 20, 1683, for complicity in the Rye House Plot.

Lieutenant-Colonel to examine them, who confessed so much of the matter as was a ground for him to dispatch a messenger to me in order to enquire concerning the truth of it. The person imployed was one Major Wallis, who coming to my house at Moncktown, informed me, that Lieutenant-General Fleetwood had received information, that I had dispersed some of the late petitions and Memento's. To which I answered, that seeing the thing which I desired to carry on privately was not concealed, I should not decline to affirm, that my conscience obliged me not to smother so much truth as those papers seemed to me to contain. He then told me, that the Lieutenant-General desired to speak with me about that matter, and I promised to attend him the next morning. Accordingly I went to him, and after some conference concerning the papers, he produced an order from Cromwel and his council to this effect ; ' That whereas I had declared my self dissatisfied with the present government, he the said Lieutenant-General Fleetwood was required to take care, that my charge in the army might be managed some other way.' He added, that he had received the said order some months since, but would not communicate it to me till now, when upon the distribution of these papers he durst not conceal it any longer, lest he should be accounted a confederate with me. I replied, that if my life as well as my employment had been at stake, I durst not have omitted what I thought to be my duty in this particular : that having no power to dispute their pleasure, I should at present look upon it as a law to which I must submit. Some time after Mr. Benjamin Worseley was sent to acquaint me, that Lieutenant-General Fleetwood had been in expectation of hearing from me touching my submission to the order he shewed me, either by letter, or the surrender of my commission. I answered, that I thought neither of them necessary ; and hoped that my retirement into my own country, which I suddenly designed, might be sufficient. But it was determined that I should not so easily quit the publick stage. For the next morning I was desired to

attend the Lieutenant-General, which accordingly I did, 1655
and found eight or ten of his advisers with him. The
design of their meeting was to perswade me either to
deliver up my commission, or to engage under my hand,
not to act by virtue of it, till I should first receive commission so to do from Cromwel, or Lieutenant-General
Fleetwood. To the first I answered, that I durst not
deliver my commission to any other power save that of
the Parliament, who had entrusted me with it ; and that
it was all I had to justify me for doing many things
wherein the lives of men had been concerned. To the
second I could by no means consent, because I durst not
tie my own hands from acting by virtue of it, when I should
be justly called upon so to do. Being returned to my
house, doubtful what the event of this contest might be,
and desirous to have good advice before I proceeded any
farther, I sent to four or five officers, of whose integrity
I had a good opinion, to ask their judgment in this case.
The result of our conference was, that I should in a letter
to Lieutenant-General Fleetwood state the justice of my
call to the employment whereof I was possest, and the
conditions on which I received my commission, being
particularly solicited to it by Cromwel himself, when he
appeared in the shape of a Commonwealths-man : the
authority that gave me my commission ; the present defection from that authority and common cause, which
Cromwel as well as I had engaged to maintain ; the duty
incumbent upon me to disperse the said books, because the
substance of my dissatisfactions was contained in them ;
withal to declare what I would be satisfied with, if it might
be attained ; and if that could not be, how far I thought
my self obliged to submit. A letter to this effect being
drawn up by me, with the advice of the officers above-
mentioned I sent it to the Lieutenant-General, and some
time after received a message from him to acquaint me,
that according to a late order brought to him from England,
I must either deliver my commission, or be sent prisoner
thither. I told the messenger, that I could not comply

1655 with his demand, tho I should be sent prisoner to Rome ; but that the commission lay in a cabinet in my closet, where he might find it if he thought fit to break open the door and take it away. But he having no other orders than to demand the delivery of my commission, departed without it[1]. A day or two after Mr. Miles Corbet came to my house by order of the Lieutenant-General, and shewed me the letter that Cromwel had sent to require him to demand the surrender of my commission, and in case of refusal to secure my person in Ireland, or to send me prisoner to England. He used what arguments he could to induce me to a compliance, which when I had heard, I set down in writing my answer, to be delivered to Lieutenant-General Fleetwood, which was in substance to let him know, that I looked upon my commission to be of no more danger to them than if it was actually taken from me, and cancelled at the head of the army ; but that I was not willing by a voluntary submission to own the justice of the present order, because I had received the said commission from the Parliament to serve as an officer in their army, in order to the execution of justice upon those who had murdered and oppressed the English Protestants ; and that I durst not consent to be withdrawn from that duty by any save that authority alone which had placed me in that station : that if I had received my commission immediately from the General, I should not willingly return it at his pleasure in this conjuncture, as well in regard to the duty I owed to the publick, as to the army : that it could be

---

[1] 'I know you understand what late commands his Highness sent me concerning Lieut.-Gen. Ludlow. I shall intreate that you will acquaint his Highness, that upon the Councell's former letter I did desire to have his commission delivered to me. His answer upon the whole is to this purpose, that he conceives it to be much against his principles, by which he hath acted, to deliver it up without a legal conviction ; but saith, if I command it from him he will give it under hand (but not deliver it up), that he will not act by it without my order. I intend to put him out of the muster rolls ; and if his Highness please, I could wish (by reason of our ancient acquaintance), he would give me liberty to dispense with his last commands.' Fleetwood to Thurloe, Jan. 17, 165⅞ ; Thurloe, iii. 113.

esteemed nothing less than a wilful betraying of that cause
for which I had contended in conjunction with the army, if
I, who had been honoured with an employment in a war
raised for the defence of liberty against the arbitrary power
of a single person, should voluntarily submit to what was
proposed.   For since the whole authority in the three
nations was assumed by the army, if I should acknowledg
the intire disposal of all things relating to that army to
reside in the General, what would this be but to declare my
consent to give up the power of the Parliament, army, and
nation into his hands ?   However, to avoid extremities, as
far as I was able, I proposed that if a council of the officers
who were about Dublin might be called, and that upon
a full hearing and debate of the matter they should declare
it to be my duty, I would submit, as to the higher powers,
having none at present to appeal to from them but God.
This expedient being not approved, the Lieutenant-General
sent Mr. Miles Corbet again to me, with a proposition, that
I would chuse either to go to London, or to be confined in
Ireland.   In answer to which, and upon consideration of
the discomposure of my affairs in England, by reason of
a great debt left upon my estate at my departure thence,
not likely to be lessened by my absence ; and being very
desirous to come to a speedy trial for my refusal to deliver
my commission, I made choice of the former.   Mr. Corbet
then told me, that a man of war should be prepared for my
transportation, provided that I would give my word to
appear before Cromwel, and not to act any thing against
him in the mean time, to which I consented.   For tho
I durst not engage to disable my self from acting whilst
nothing was objected against me, lest I should thereby not
only have given away my own liberty, but also make an ill
precedent for other men ; yet being now accused of a
pretended crime, I was contented to pass my parole to
appear as desired, and in the mean time not to act against
him [1].   When the Lieutenant-General perceived that I was

[1] ' Lieutenant-General Ludlow's
engagement. "Whereas Mr. Justice
Cook, Colonell Herbert, and Captain
Shaw (by virtue of an order of the

1655 resolved on my journey, he desired me to put off my departure for two months, pretending that things being in some disorder in England, he feared Cromwel might apprehend a necessity of using me with more severity than he wished ; and to soften this delay, gave a warrant for the paiment of a sum of money to me for defraying my expences whilst I staid, together with those of my journey to London. And indeed what he said concerning the disorders of England was not without ground, things running every day more and more into confusion, the Cavaliers being enraged to see the throne usurped, and those who had hazarded all for their country finding themselves cheated, custom and excise raised without authority of Parliament, and taxes imposed to no other end than to support the pride and insolence of a single person. Some there were that openly opposed these oppressions, and amongst others Mr. George Cony a merchant, who having refused to pay custom, it was violently taken from him, and he thereupon sued the collector at the common law. But Cromwel resolving to put a stop to such dangerous precedents, caused the counsel for Mr. Cony, who were Serjeant Maynard, Serjeant Twysden, and Mr. Wadham Windham,

May, 8. to be sent to the Tower, where they had not been above three or four days, when they unworthily petitioned to

lord Deputy and Council, dated the 29th of this instant January), are authorised to demand and to receive my two military commissions, as Lieutenant-General of the horse and colonell of horse in Ireland; or to take my parole in writing, that by or before the 10th day of March next (wind and weather favouring) I should present myself unto the lord Protector; I do hereby engage my parole unto the above said gentlemen, that I will accordingly (the Lord permitting) tender myself unto the lord Protector at Whitehall by that time ; and that in the mean time I shall act nothing directly or in-directly to the disturbance of the peace, or the prejudice of the present government. Witness my hand at Moncktowne, near Dublin, the 30 January, 1654.

"EDMUND LUDLOW."'

On Feb. 2, 165$\frac{3}{4}$, Fleetwood writes: 'I have taken Lieut.-Gen. Ludlow's parole in pursuance of his Highness' order by Cornet Bradley, whereby he hath engaged to attend his Highness by the 10 of March, and saith, he intends to live in Somersetshire with a sister-in-law, to avoid jealousies and temptations.' Thurloe, iii. 136, 142.

be set at liberty, acknowledging their fault, and promising   165:
to do so no more, chusing rather to sacrifice the cause of
their client, wherein that of their country was also eminently
concerned, than to endure a little restraint with the loss
of the fees of a few days [1].   By this means when the cause
came to the next hearing, Mr. Cony was necessitated to
plead for himself, which he did in as short a manner as
he could, referring it wholly to the judg, whether that tax
being not authorized by Parliament, ought to be paid by
the law of the land; and declaring that he would abide by
his judgment therein.   Serjeant Rolls, then Chief Justice
of the Upper Bench, tho a conscientious man, and a lover
of civil liberty, yet not daring to determine it for him, said,
that something must be allowed to cases of necessity.   To
which Mr. Cony replied, that it was never wont to be a
good plea in law, for a man to make necessities, and then
to plead them.   But the judg wanting courage, would not
give judgment against the usurper; and being too much
an honest man to give it for him, he took time till the next
ensuing term, to consider what rule he should give in the
case.   In the mean time, upon consideration that his continuance in that station was likely to ensnare him more
and more, he desired by a letter to Cromwel to have his   June
quietus; and Serjeant Glyn was appointed to succeed him
in his employment, as a fitter instrument to carry on the
designs on foot.   The new Chief Justice, before he came
to sit on the bench, took care to have this business accommodated with Cony, who lost his reputation by withdrawing himself from a cause wherein the publick was
so much concerned.   Sir Peter Wentworth, a member of
the Long Parliament, caused also a collector in the country
to be arrested and prosecuted at his suit, tho he could

---

[1] See 'Narrative of the Proceedings of the Committee for preservation of the Customs in the case of
Mr. George Cony, by Samuel Sel-
wood,' 4to, 1655. Godwin, History
of the Commonwealth, iv. 174, treats
Cony's case and the legal opposition
in detail. Twisden, Maynard and
Windham were summoned before
the Council on May 18, and committed to the Tower; they petitioned
for their release May 25, and were
released early in June. Cal. S. P.,
Dom., 1655, pp. 167, 179, 196.

hardly procure an attorney to appear, or counsel to plead for him. Cromwel having received notice of this prosecution, sent a messenger with an order to bring him before the Council; where being examined concerning the

ground of his proceeding, he told them, that he was moved to it by his constant principle, 'That by the law of England no money ought to be levied upon the people without their consent in Parliament.' Cromwel then asked him, whether he would withdraw his action or no? To which he replied, 'If you will command me, I must submit'; and thereupon Cromwel having commanded it, he withdrew his action [1]. Some time after taking the liberty in a discourse with him to reprove him for that retractation, he made me this answer, that no man could have done more than he did to the time of his appearing at the Council, and that if he had then failed in any thing, it must be attributed to his age of threescore and three years, when, said he, 'the blood does not run with the same vigour as in younger men.' It having been discovered that the Lord Grey of Grooby had given to a person a copy of the Memento which I had before dispersed in Ireland, he was sent for to London, and committed prisoner to Windsor Castle for the same. The next term he sued for a Habeas Corpus, which the Chief Justice, according to law, granted him, but the Governour of Windsor Castle refused to give obedience to the order of court, and so rendred it ineffectual to him; insomuch that he could not obtain his liberty till he had given a pecuniary security not to act against the government, which he chose to do rather than to engage his parole, thereby hazarding only the loss of so much money, and preserving his honour and integrity. Col. Sexby was also suspected to have had a hand in the dispersion of the petitions and Memento's before-mentioned; and thereupon was sent for in order to be secured, which he having notice of, fled, but was pursued

---

[1] A warrant to arrest Sir Peter Wentworth and bring him before the Council was issued on Aug. 24, 1655, he was discharged and heard on Aug. 28. Cal. S. P., Dom., 1655, pp. 300, 596. For Wentworth's case, ib. p. 296.

so close, that his man was taken with his portmanteau.
Cromwel being disappointed of taking him, pretended on
the account of antient friendship to pass by what he had
done, and proposed to imploy him as his agent to those
of Bourdeaux, who had applied themselves for succour
against the oppressing ministry of France.   The Colonel
being under necessity, accepted of the imployment, and
Cromwel ordered him a sum of money to supply his present
occasions, with letters of exchange for more at Bourdeaux.
Being thus furnished, he went over to France, where his
business being betrayed to the magistrates of Bourdeaux,
they gave order to seize his person ; but he having received
advice of their intentions, made his escape by night over the
wall of the town, and departed from that kingdom [1].

In Ireland it was thought fit to disband some part of the
army, yet rather to free themselves of some of the dis-
contented party than that nation of the charge.   In order
to this, a list was produced lately sent from England,
appointing what regiments of horse and foot should be
broken [2].   Of these mine was to be one, tho care was
taken that those of my regiment, or any other, that would
sail with any wind, should be provided for ; and it must
be acknowledged, that they were so just to allow both

[1] Sexby had been the chief leader
of the Agitators in 1647.   For his
early career, see Clarke Papers, vol.
i. pp. 82, 431.   In 1650 he obtained a
commission as Lieut.-Col., but was
cashiered in June, 1651.   From the
summer of 1651 to about Aug. 1653,
he was employed on a secret mission
in France.   On August 23, 1654,
he was ordered £1000 for his ex-
penses during his mission.   From
the autumn of 1654, he was actively
engaged in the republican plots
against Cromwell, fled from England
in 1655, and began at once to in-
trigue with the royalists and the
Spanish government.   Cal. S. P.,
Dom., 1654, p. 160; Akerman, Letters
from Roundhead officers, p. 27;

Thurloe, ii. 657: vi. 809.
[2] The Irish council wrote to the
Protector on Nov. 14, 1654, that the
Irish army could not at present be
safely reduced below 15,000 foot and
4,000 horse.   After the transplantation of the Irish rebels to Connaught
had been effected, it might be further
reduced to 12,000 foot, 3000 horse,
and 600 dragoons.   Irish Records,
$\frac{A}{30}$ 28, p. 14.   The disbanding mentioned by Ludlow took place in
August, 1655.   For a list of the
regiments disbanded, and the lands
assigned to them, see Thurloe, iii.
710, 715; Mercurius Politicus, pp.
5580-4, 5620; Prendergast, Cromwellian Settlement, pp. 216-220.

officers and souldiers their full arrears out of the forfeited lands in each county, according to the rates that had been set upon them by the general council of officers, wherein the goodness and conveniency of every county was estimated and equally balanced. The arrears of my regiment fell by lot to be satisfied in the county of Wexford, where I ordered Capt. Walcot, my Captain-Lieutenant, with my Coronet and Quarter-master, to act for me, which they did ; and my proportion in the said land yielded me about one hundred pounds the first year, and afterwards near two hundred. It was reported to be farther improveable ; but I never saw it, and know not whether I ever shall. My Lieutenant-Colonel having had his arrears with the rest of the regiment, was accused of saying that this distribution would prove invalid without an Act of Parliament, and the crime aggravated by one, who informed at the head-quarters as if he designed to excite the souldiers to a mutiny ; whereupon he was sent for, and committed to custody till he gave assurance of his quiet and peaceable behaviour [1].

The design of seizing the riches of the Spaniards in the West Indies having proved unsuccessful, and instead of bringing gold or silver home, much was transported from hence thither, where many of our men daily perished through want and the excessive heats of that climate ; yet it was resolved to keep Jamaica, of which place Col. Fortescue was made Governour, and Commander-in-Chief

[1] Henry Cromwell, in a letter to his father concerning the disbanding and settlement of the soldiers, says : 'At our returning home by Wexford, wee were informed of some persons, whoe had been liberall in seditions revileinge expressions against the gouvernment and your highness; and wee had just grounde to believe, that they would have showed themselves further if they had hade power. They putt it to the question, whether the present gouvernment were according to the worde of God and their former engagements and declarationes, which as wee weer informed was carried in the negative. These officers moste of them weer of late Lieutenant-General Ludlowe's regiment, and I doubte too much of his spiritt and principle. Wee have brought Lieut. Coll. Scott, whoe was the ringleader, prisoner with us, and hope to let them see that gouvernment is not to be played withall.' Thurloe, iv. 74.

of the forces there, after the return of Col. Venables[1]. Amongst others that died, there was one Mr. Winslow, who had been designed to be governour of some place, when they could get it[2]. In this expedition one Mr. Gage a priest died also, who was reported to have been a principal adviser of this undertaking[3]. Col. Fortescue continued not long in his imployment before he died also : after whose death Col. Edward Doily was made Commander-in-Chief, and he falling to plant, made a shift to get a subsistence, which was but a poor return for the expence and loss sustained in this attempt. And as Cromwel was thus prodigal of the lives of Englishmen abroad, so was he no less of our liberties at home ; for not contenting himself with the death of many of those who had raised arms against him, and seizure of the goods of that party, he transported whole droves of them at a time into foreign parts, without any legal trial[4]. In the number of those that were sent away was Mr. William Ashburnham, Sir Tho. Armstrong and others, to whom may be added Lieut.-Col. John Lilburn, who contrary to all law, and after an

---

[1] Richard Fortescue succeeded Venables in command and died Oct., 1655. Edward Doyley was then made Commander-in-Chief and President of the Council for three months, by the officers of the Jamaica army, until the Protector should appoint. The Protector appointed Robert Sedgwick, who died in June, 1656. Doyley was again acting Commander-in-Chief, but in spite of his requests for the post, Col. William Brayne was appointed. Brayne died Sept. 2, 1657, and Doyley succeeded at last to the command and held it till the Restoration. Thurloe, iii. 581, 650; iv. 153; v. 138, 668; vi. 110, 391, 453, 512.

[2] Edward Winslow, one of the three commissioners for the management of civil affairs sent out with the expedition. For his letters during the early part of it, see Thurloe, iii. 249, 325. He died on May 7, 1655. Memorials of Sir W. Penn, ii. 98. Winslow is famous as one of the founders of the colony of Plymouth, and its governor in 1633, 1636, and 1644.

[3] Thomas Gage, sometime a Dominican friar who recanted, married, and became in 1642 rector of Acrise, Kent. He was the author of ' The English American, his Travail by Sea and Land,' published in 1648, a book describing the Spanish colonies in America. Burnet confirms Ludlow's statement about his influence in originating the undertaking. Own Time, ed. 1833, i. 137.

[4] On this transportation of royalist prisoners, see English Historical Review, 1889, p. 335.

1655

acquittal by a jury, had been formerly banished. And now to prevent Major-General Overton from the benefit of a Habeas Corpus, for which Cromwel was informed he intended to move, tho he had no reason to alledg why it should be denied him ; yet he sent him in custody to Jersey, with the hazard of his life and to the great prejudice

Feb. 10. of his estate. Major John Wildman was also seized upon, and it was pretended that he was taken dictating to his servant a declaration for levying war against Oliver Cromwel. The citizens of London were made acquainted with it, and the said major brought to London by a guard of horse, and committed prisoner to the Tower[1].

Oliver having felt the pulse of the army in Ireland, as was observed before, resolv'd to send his son Harry thither, that being on the place, he might be the more able to fix the soldiery to his interest. In his journy to Ireland with his wife and family he was everywhere caressed by the Cavalier party, and particularly entertained by Col. Mosson in North Wales, where the health of his father was drunk by the said Colonel. After some time spent

July 9. in those parts he put to sea, and upon his arrival in the bay of Dublin the men of war that accompanied him, and other ships in the harbour, rung such a peal with their cannon, as if some great good news had been coming to us ; and tho the usual place of landing for those who come in ships of war was near my house, yet he and his company went up in boats to the Rings-end, where they went ashore, and were met there by most of the officers civil and military about the town[2] : the end of his coming over was not at first discovered, and conjectured to be only to command in the army as Major-General under Lieut.-General Fleetwood. The two months agreed on at the desire of the Lieutenant-General for my stay in Ireland being expired, he renewed his request that I would again defer my

[1] Wildman's Declaration is printed by Whitelocke, Memorials, ed. 1853, iv. 183; cf. Thurloe, iii. 147.

[2] On Henry Cromwell's coming to Ireland, see Mercurius Politicus, July 19-26. pp. 5485, 5501 ; Thurloe, iii. 614, 632.

journey to England for two months longer, to which I consented, not doubting that it proceeded from his friendship to me[1]. But the last two months drawing near to an end I began to prepare for my journey; which being observed, an order pursuant to instructions from England was brought to me by Col. Thomas Herbert, secretary of the Council, requiring me to remain in Ireland[2]. The secretary told me that he had it in commission from Lieut.-General Fleetwood to acquaint me that upon his own account, and notwithstanding this order, he would take upon him to give me permission to go into England for setling my affairs there, if I would engage to return within six months, and not act against the present Government during that time.

Tho I thought my self very ill used, not only by being denied the opportunity of coming to a speedy trial for not delivering my commission at the command of the General, but also by being prevented to take care of my private affairs without these fetters; yet I let him know that I would attend the Lieutenant-General the next morning concerning this matter: which having done according to my promise, he pressed me to comply with his request,

---

[1] 'In my last I did acquaint you that Lieut.-Gen. Ludlow was suddenly to come for England; and though I had no orders to the contrary, yet feareing that his highness might judge it inconvenient for his present comeing into England, he hath renewed his former parole to the 10th of September next, but he hath some concernments of his own by reason of his being out of pay and the breaking up of his family. I desire to know his highness' pleasure, whether I may not dispense with him for some months to goe into England; but whilst he doth remaine here, I thinke I can doe no less than give him halfe pay during his detainment, haveing nothing in this nation but his custodium:

I should be glad to receive directions heerein.' Fleetwood to Thurloe, April 25, 1655; Thurloe, iii. 407.

[2] 'To the Commissioners for Ireland.
'My Lords,
'His Highness the Lord Protector and Council have (upon consideration), thought fit that Lieut.-General Ludlowe forbear his coming to England till they shall give further order, which they have commanded me to signify to you, and desire your care that he be not permitted to come from Ireland to England till his Highness and the Council of State shall give other order accordingly. Signed in the name and by the order of the Council. Whitehall, 24th April, 1655.'

Irish Records, $\frac{A}{28}$ 26, p. 54.

with the general argument of the duty that lay upon me to submit to the higher powers. I answered, that as I conceived it was yet in dispute who were these higher powers, whether the government of a Common-wealth or that of a single person ; that I knew not whether within the time prefixed by him for me to engage not to act, I might have an opportunity so to do, and therefore durst not engage to the contrary. He demanded of me what I judged an opportunity to justify me in such an under-taking ? To which I replied, such an appearance of good men, as might probably balance the power of the single person : I took the liberty also to tell him, that he him-self had already justified that principle by his own practice in acting against the King ; but, said he, 'we had the authority of the Parliament for our justification': 'but what,' said I, 'have you to countenance you in your actions now for a single person against the Parliament, which I may not have to justify me in acting with another power against this single person? and for any thing I know, the same Parliamentary authority that commissionated us all to act against the King, may within that time authorize me to act against the present single person.' Two or three con-ferences and messages passed between us upon this business, the result of all which was, that I promised to render myself a prisoner to Cromwel, who might farther dispose of me as God should permit him : but this offer not proving satis-factory. the Council seconded their former order, and re-quired me not to go out of Ireland without their farther directions. Finding my self thus surrounded, and well knowing that this hardship was imposed upon me by order from Whitehal, and that what the Lieutenant-General had proposed was out of affection to my person, I thought my self obliged to use my utmost endeavours to secure him from suffering for his civility and friendship to me : to that end I proposed that tho I could not engage positively not to act during six months, as was desired, because, whatever opportunity might be offered, I should then have my hands tied during the said time ; yet I would promise not to act within that time against the present Government, unless I had first surrendred my self to the General, or Lieut.-General Fleetwood, and desired of them to be freed from this engagement[1]. Lieut.-General Fleetwood consented to this proposition, professing his readiness to comply with my desires in what he could ; and accordingly this agreement being drawn up to our mutual satisfaction, together with his permission for my departure to England, was signed by him at the Phenix, in the presence of Mr. Corbet, then Chief Baron in that nation. The next day Col. Lawrence came to me, and after some discourse, told me that by reason of some opposition which the Lieutenant-General had met with in my affair, he had sent him to desire of me, that notwithstanding what had passed between us, I would respite my journey for a fortnight or three weeks longer, in which time he doubted not to clear my way for me. I presently suspected from what corner the wind blew, but knew not how to help myself for the

1655
Aug. 28.

---

[1] 'Whereas I have lately received a command for my restraint from going into England, yett nevertheles, the Lord Deputie of Ireland taking into his consideration the pressing necessities, which lyeth upon me for the settleing of my affaires in England ; and he permitting my repair thither, I doe hereby engage, that I will not advise, contrive, consent, abett, or act, directly or indirectly, any thing to the prejudice or disturbance of the present government under his Highness the Lord Protector, unles before I shall advise, contrive, consent, abett or act as above said, directly or indirectly any thing to the disturbance of the said government, I shall render myself personally unto his highnes, or to the said Lord Deputie, and desire to be [free] from this engagement. Dated at the Phoenix, August 29, 1655.

'EDMUND LUDLOW.'

Fleetwood apologised for accepting this engagement on the ground that he had received no recent instructions concerning Ludlow, and that 'his restraint here if he had not come, would have bin more disservice to my lord Protector than it can be in England.' Henry Cromwell, however, wrote to Thurloe, saying that if Ludlow were given leave to come to England 'you would find him very troublesome, and that you would be necessitated to deale with him as you have done with Harrison, which would make him considerable. He declares it, that he will not be under any obligation, because he does not knowe, but that God may give ane opportunity for him to appear for the libertie of the people. He is verry high and much dissatisfyed, and therefore there ought to be further care what is done as to him.' Thurloe, iii. 744.

present. The next morning Mr. Corbet sent me a message, to desire that I would meet him on the road betwixt my house and Dublin; which having done according to his appointment, he acquainted me more particularly with what had happened, telling me that Col. Cromwel was so enraged at the form of our agreement, that he had written to his father concerning it, in so much that if I should venture to go, he doubted I might be obstructed by the way, which would not only be troublesome to me, but dishonourable to the Lieutenant-General. He assured me also that Lieut.-General Fleetwood would take such care to represent the matter in England, that all obstacles to my passage might be removed in a short time, and desired of me that I would not have the worse opinion of him for not performing at present what he had promised. In answer to Mr. Corbet, I let him know that I found my self so much disposed to the contrary, that whereas once I thought the Lieutenant-General could have done more for me if he would, now I clearly perceived he had done more on my account than he could well answer.

It now began to be publick that Lieut.-Gen. Fleetwood was suddenly to depart for England, tho it was given out that his business there was only to advise in some particular affairs, and that he should speedily return to Ireland. Sept. 6. At his departure he was accompanied by Col. Cromwel and his lady, the Council, the mayor and aldermen of Dublin, with most of the considerable persons then about the city. They brought him as far as my house, which stood near the place of embarking, where after a short stay he went on board, and departed for England, leaving with me a permission to transport my self into England, which was to take effect about a month after, requiring all persons to permit me to pass without interruption. He promised me likewise that in the mean time he would take care to remove all difficulties that might hinder me, and that it should be the first business he would do after his arrival at London.

Some time after I understood by a letter from my father

Oldsworth[1], that Lieut.-General Fleetwood had assured him that I would suddenly be in England, and that he had left me a passport as sufficient to that purpose as he could give, or I needed ; which being spoken by him after he had been with his father Cromwel, made me presume he had cleared the way for me. Having received this advice, I prepared for my journey, and waiting on Mr. Corbet to take my leave of him, I shewed him the Lieut.-General's pass, and that clause in my father Oldsworth's letter which related to it. He told me that Col. Cromwel, who was then in his progress, had sent a message to him that he should acquaint me with a second order lately brought from England to require positively my stay in Ireland[2]; but withal added, that being unwilling to be imployed in such unwelcome messages to his friends, he had made his excuse to the Colonel by letter, which he presumed was accepted by him, because he had heard nothing of it since that time, and therefore declared that he mentioned it not to me as a person commissioned so to do, but only as a friend. I told him that I should take no notice of it, but proceed on my voyage, as I had before designed, having already hired a vessel to that end. He then desired that I would stay till the return of Col. Cromwel, which would certainly be

---

[1] Michael Oldsworth represented Old Sarum in the last of James the First's Parliaments, and in the first two of Charles the First's. He is vaguely described as 'of London.' In the Parliaments of 1628 and 1640. and in the Long Parliament, he sat for the city of Salisbury. On July 18, 1649, Parliament voted that Oldsworth should be granted a patent as one of the registers of the Prerogative Court (C. J., vi. 263). Jane Thomas, Ludlow's mother-in-law, after the death of William Thomas (d. 1636), married Michael Oldsworth, whom Ludlow therefore terms his 'father Oldsworth.' He was secretary and general factotum to Philip, Earl of Pembroke, and is often mentioned in the satires and libels against the latter. Walker describes him as 'governor of Pembroke and Montgomery, and hath a share with his lord out of Sir Henry Compton's office worth £3000 a year, and is a keeper of Windsor Park' (History of Independency, p. 173).

[2] Aug. 28, 1655. 'To reply to a letter to Thurloe from Mr. Herbert, Clerk of the Council in Ireland, praying Council's pleasure concerning Lieut.-Gen. Ludlow's return to England, that observance of Council's former order is expected, till further order be given.' Council Order-book, Cal. S. P., Dom., 1655, p. 300.

within two or three days, lest it should be suspected that he had advised with me about my departure. I being unwilling to bring any prejudice upon him, consented to defer my journey till the return of Col. Cromwel, and endeavoured to attend him on the day of his coming to town; but he arriving late in the night, I found my self obliged to go home without speaking to him, by reason of a humour fallen upon one of my legs, which had been hurt by a horse; so that I was constrained to put my wife to the trouble of making my excuse; who acquainting him with my condition, and shewing him the Lieutenant-General's pass, with the clause in that letter before mentioned, assured him that the composure and settlement of my estate in England necessarily required my presence there. He told her that he knew nothing to hinder my passage, and that a man of war was ready in the harbour for our transportation; and desiring her to dine, promised that after dinner they should go together to Cork House, to speak with Mr. Corbet her husband's old friend, as he favoured me to call him, and that the work should be done. My wife accordingly went with him full of expectation that the business she came about would be effected; but after he had consulted with Mr. Corbet, he told her, that tho I had the Lieutenant-General's pass, yet because he had since received a command for my stay, he could not give order for my departure: that if she would go, she should have a ship of war to transport her, which she excused, unless I might have permission to go also. ' Then,' said she, ' tho you will not grant a warrant for my husband's going, I hope you will not order his stay.' ' No indeed,' said Col. Cromwel, ' I shall not, tho I think it would be much better for him to stay: tho what I speak is as a friend, and not as one in authority.'

Upon consideration of these particulars: 1st. That I had the Lieutenant-General's order, who was then the chief officer in Ireland, together with Mr. Corbet's advice for my going, who was one of the Council, in case I were not ordered to stay, and also Col. Cromwel's promise, who was principal in command upon the place, that he would not detain me, I resolved to go aboard. And having written a letter to Col. Cromwel to assure him that the end of my going to England was to settle my discomposed family and estate, I ordered it not to be delivered to him till the next day about noon, and endeavoured to get on board with my wife and servants on that day, but the wind blowing hard. and the weather being very bad, no boat could be procured that would adventure to sea. At last I prevailed not without difficulty with the master of one of the largest herring-vessels that was in the bay to carry me and my family to the ship which was to transport me, and lay about a league and half from the shoar. We departed between two and three in the afternoon, and were accompanied to the ship by about two hundred people of the place, so that it could not be justly said, as it was afterwards, that I stole away privately, the road by which the vessel must necessarily pass being also within sight of Dublin. Being arrived on board the man of war, which lay ready for us, we weighed anchor about eleven a clock that night, and recovered the harbour of Beaumaris by next day at noon, about which time my letter to Col. Cromwel was according to my order delivered to him by my servant. The weather was so tempestuous, that we durst not adventure to land till the second day after our arrival, when the wind somewhat abating, we went a shore, where the governour of Beaumaris met us, and furnished us with horses to carry us to the town. We observed him to look a little melancholy, yet suspected not the reason of it. But after dinner the governour as civilly as he could acquainted me, that one Capt. Shaw who was then in town, had brought him an order from Col. Henry Cromwel, and the rest of the Council in Ireland, to detain me there till the pleasure of his father should be known concerning me[1]. I desired a sight of the order, and

---

[1] On Oct. 16, 1655, Thurloe wrote to Henry Cromwell: 'The messenger brought us news, that Lieut.-Gen. Ludlow and his familye came over with him, which was very much unexpected here. The messenger alsoe tells us, that he met (at Beaumaris where he landed before the Lieut.-General) Capt. Shawe, who stayed there to apprehend hym, which was well liked of, and an expresse is sent hence to confirme these orders,

found it to be directed to the governour of Beaumaris, Chester, or any other garison, or commander of any of the forces, &c., and signed by Henry Cromwel, [Richard] Pepis, Matt. Thomlinson, and Miles Corbet. Capt. Shaw excused himself for being employed in this message, and told me, that the day after I left Ireland, he being just then arrived from England, and very weary of his journey, went to bed, where he had not been above an hour before he was sent for by Col. Cromwel, and told, that being inform'd of my departure for England, which was expressly against an order receiv'd from his father, he had immediately summoned a Council, where it had been agreed to send after me, and to secure me wheresoever I should be overtaken, and that he had pitched upon him as a fit person to be imployed in this business, and to attend his father and the Lieutenant-General with an account of it. He said he had endeavoured to get himself excused, but neither his weariness by reason of his great journey, nor any other arguments would prevail with Col. Cromwel. I told him, that those who resolved to worship the rising sun, must not refuse to run upon more ungrateful errands than this, even towards the best of their friends, and therefore could not suppose that any respect which he expressed to have for me should prevail to excuse him from this imployment : however, that I thought Lieutenant-General Fleetwood, whom I knew to be the person he hoped to advance himself by, would not take it well that he should be instrumental in offering this affront to his authority, he being chief governour of Ireland, and I on my journey by his passport and permission, who I hoped understood his own power[1]. The Lord Fitz-Williams, a

and to secure him, in case those given in Ireland should not be executed.' Thurloe, iv. 88.

[1] Fleetwood was naturally indignant at the disregard of his authority, and the Council thus explained their conduct. ' Your letter of the 23rd of Oct. last came safely to us, and as to that business about Lieut.-Gen. Ludlow, we shall only add to what was formerly mentioned, that we are very sensible of that trouble your Lordship mentioned to be upon you, for that he did go into England under your Lordship's protection, so as some reflection might seem to be on your reputation, which we hold ourselves to be always obliged to be much more sensible of than of our own, or of any con-

civil person, tho a papist, and one who had been Lieutenant-
General to Preston when he commanded an army of Irish
rebels, came over with us from Ireland, and being ready to
take horse for London, was pleased to give me a visit before
he went, wherein he not only expressed himself very sorry
to see me under restraint, but assured me of his readiness
to use his utmost endeavours with his Highness the Lord
Protector, as he thought fit to call him, in my behalf.   I
gave him my thanks for his civility, but thought it a strange
revolution of affairs, that the interest of a gentleman who
had been Lieutenant-General in the army of the Irish rebels,
should be so much greater than mine in the General of the
army of the Commonwealth.   Capt. Shaw being ready to
depart for London, and desiring to know if he could do any
service for me there, I gave him a letter for Lieutenant-
General Fleetwood, which was to let him know what had
hapned since his departure, wherein I thought him to be
much more concerned than my self; and that being his
prisoner, and coming upon his permission, the affront was
wholly done to him, tho the suffering part fell to my share.

cernment of our own. But my Lord, though that license and protection of your Lordship's was under consideration before us when we ordered his restraint, yet that that did satisfy us was that after that license and protection there came also another command from his Highness and Council prohibiting his going into England, whereof the Lieut.-Gen. had notice, and thereupon he was with all civility and tenderness to him desired not to go over until your pleasure were further known; and in consideration of his civility then unto us, we laid no further restriction upon him; and we for our parts were very confident that he would not have gone away, though more free that his lady and family might go, and did proffer any ship in the harbour to attend his passage, and so we rested in that considera-tion until we had notice (it being the day after his departure) that he was gone. And not knowing how affairs might stand in England, but finding he was suddenly gone with-out our notice, we did hold it our duty to make stay of him where he could be found, until his Highness' pleasure were known therein; which we may truly say was done out of sense of our duty and to answer the trust reposed in us, and not out of any intention to put any the least prejudice to the said Lieut.-Gen., otherwise than by stay of him until his Highness was acquainted there-with, and much less do the least act that might seem to reflect upon your honour.' Signed by H. Cromwell, Pepys, Corbet, and Tomlinson, Nov. 28, 1655. Irish Records, $\frac{A}{30}$ 28, p. 107.

In the evening I was conveyed to a widow's house in the town, where I had the conveniency of a chamber and dining-room, with a sentinel placed at the stairs-head. With great impatience I expected the return of the post from London, hoping that the matter would be so represented by Lieutenant-General Fleetwood and Capt. Shaw, that I might have my liberty [1]. But the usurper, whose jealousies increased with his guilt, being informed of my landing, dispatched an order to the governour of Beaumaris, to this effect, ' That whereas Lieutenant-General Ludlow was stoln out of Ireland, he should take care to keep him in strict and safe custody, and not to permit any to speak with him.' Upon the receipt of this order, the governour, resolving to make his fortune by any means, proposed to imprison me in the castle, the air of which place is so unhealthy, that the souldiers dare not lodg there ; and it is observed, that few prisoners who have been confined there have ever recovered from the distempers which they contracted. I told him, that being in his power, I could not resist ; but the warrant requiring no such thing, a time might come wherein he might be called to account for what he now did. Where-upon he thought fit to let me remain at my lodgings, but permitted no man to come to me save my own servants, and of those not above two. One cause of this severity toward me, as I conjecture, was, that I might not have an opportunity of speaking with the officers of the Irish brigade. lest I should have put them in mind of their duty, who having served Cromwel's turn in assisting to suppress the late attempts against him, were now returning for Ireland, and lay at Beaumaris in expectation of a wind. Neither did their cruelty extend only to me; but Col. Cromwel having notice that Col. Kempstone, who married

[1] 'Captain Shaw hath been with his Highness to give an account of his securinge Ludlowe in Beaumaris Castle. It gives very little satisfaction to a person here, that he is secured haveinge my Lord Deputie's passe, and his Highness is as little satisfied on the other hand, and therefore keepes him in prison, and soe is like to doe.' Thurloe to Henry Cromwell, Oct. 23, 1655 (iv. 108).

my sister[1], had assisted me in my going away, and had not given advice to him of it, committed him to prison, where he was used with equal severity as my self, tho he alledged in his justification that he knew not that I was guilty of any crime, nor that I was forbidden to depart from Ireland ; and tho he did not know of any necessity I had of a pass for my going, yet he well knew that I had one from Lieutenant-General Fleetwood, the chief officer of Ireland, and that he only accompanied me to the water-side, as a hundred more had done.

To prevent any false representation of the state of my business, I gave an account of it to my friends in Ireland, as well as to those in England. Some of my letters were intercepted, and in one of them was found an expression to this effect : 'Tho I know not of any crime whereof I am guilty, yet I am worse used by those with whom I have engaged, than by those against whom I fought ; for when I was made prisoner by the latter, no person was denied the liberty of coming to me, and I was permitted in publick to give my reasons in justification of the proceedings of the Parliament ; but the present powers being as it seems more conscious of their own guilt, will not permit me either to see or speak with any of my friends.' After I had been six weeks a prisoner, Capt. Shaw returned to Beaumaris with an order for my discharge, on condition that I would sign an engagement which he brought ready drawn, to oblige my self never to act against the present Government. He told me, that Lieutenant-General Fleetwood suspecting my unwillingness to sign any such paper, had desired Col. John Jones to accompany him to me, and either to perswade me to subscribe it, or to accommodate the business as well as he could. Accordingly Col. Jones came to me with Col. Sadler, who commanded the Irish Brigade before-mentioned, and who had been long in the town, tho he durst not come to me before this time. Upon the perusal of this engagement,

---

[1] Col. Nicholas Kempson married Ludlow's sister Elizabeth. A letter from her to Ludlow is printed in the Appendix to vol. ii.

which was proposed as the condition of my discharge, I soon came to a resolution, that I would not sign it, if my life as well as my liberty had lain at stake ; acquainting them with the reasons of my refusal, and with the engagement given to Lieutenant-General Fleetwood, by which I stood obliged to render my self a prisoner either to Cromwel or himself, which I was ready to perform. Col. Sadler said, that it was highly reasonable, and as much as could be expected from me ; and added, that he was confident the difference between Cromwel and me was grounded upon mistakes, he having heard him express great affection to me, with protestations that he wished me as well as any man in the three nations. I thought it not convenient to take much pains to undeceive him, but was rather willing he should believe that he spoke in earnest, tho indeed he loved no person living any farther than he served to promote his ambition ; for how could it be expected that one who had sacrificed his conscience and honour, as well as the cause of his country, to the idol of his pride, should scruple to trample under foot any man that stood in his way ? One of the company endeavoured to perswade me to sign the paper as it was drawn, reserving to my self those explanations which I had before proposed, or else to look upon my self as free from any obligation, being under a force. To which I answered, that I thought it below a man to be compelled to any act against his conscience, with an intention to violate the same ; and that to reserve any explanations to my self, as it had been against my practice, so was it contrary to my principles, unless the governour would consent to accept my subscription to the engagement with such an explanation as I was willing to make. Thus despairing to obtain the liberty of pursuing my journey at that time, I prepared to send my wife to settle my affairs as well as she could ; and the company being gone to dinner, I wrote letters to my friends and relations ; when on a sudden Col. Jones and Col. Sadler came up to tell me that the governour was willing to discharge me if I would sign the engagement with such an explanation as I had proposed. Hereupon I desired the governour not to do any thing out of respect to me, that might not consist with the duty of his place, or prove to be to his prejudice, my explanation being in my opinion an absolute repeal of the engagement as soon as I had rendred my self. He replied, he had considered of it, and was willing to accept of it, if I would sign it. Whereupon the company desired me to draw my own explanation, which I did to this effect, viz.—' I look upon this engagement now tendred to me for my subscription by the governour of Beaumaris, by order from, &c. to be no longer of any force than till I have rendred my self a prisoner at Whitehall, and in that sense only I subscribe it.' Having drawn and signed two copies of this explanation, and procured them to be attested by Colonel John Jones, Colonel Sadler, and Capt. Shaw, I delivered one of them to the governour, and kept the other my self, and then signed the engagement. Capt. Shaw informed me that Lieutenant-General Fleetwood had been much concerned for my restraint, and had expressed himself highly displeased with him for undertaking that imployment ; that he had used all possible diligence for my liberty, in which he had met with great opposition ; in particular, that Major-General Lambert had endeavoured to perswade him that I was of such principles, and such a spirit, as not to deserve my liberty, tho I cannot remember that our familiarity had ever been so great as to enable him to give a character of me.

Having thus cleared my way, I departed from Beaumaris, and passing over Penman-Maur I arrived at Conway the first night[1]. From thence in two days I reached Wrexham, where after we had been treated two or three days by Col. Jones, my coach which I had sent before from Ireland being brought to us, we set forward on our journey for London ; but the ways being extremely bad, by reason of a frost which yet was not able to bear the coach, it was

---

[1] The crossing of Penmaenmawr was one of the great perils of the journey to Ireland. Ray's Itinerary, ed. 1844, p. 128. By Defoe's time it had lost its terrors. Tour, ed. 1724, II. iii. 97.

near three a clock before we came to Whitchurch, tho it was not above twelve miles. But being desirous to reach London if possible that week, fearing if Cromwel should hear of my being on the road he would send to stop me, we travelled till nine a clock that night, and the next after till twelve. The next day we came to Coventry about four in the afternoon, where Col. Whalley commanded as Bashaw, or Major-General. After some refreshment we continued our journey, and by the help of the moon-light and the snow that lay on the ground we reached Dunchurch a little after twelve ; there we rested till about three, and then set forward toward Tocester, where we arrived by six that night, and between one and two the next morning we began our journey for London : but at Stony-Stratford the coach breaking, my wife and I, with two or three servants, took horse, and about six of the clock in the evening of the 10th of December, one of the shortest days of the year, we came to Westminster, having travelled fifty miles that day. The same night I waited on Lieutenant-General Fleetwood, to acknowledg his care of me, and to acquaint him with the condition on which I had my liberty to come up, and with the explanation upon which only I had signed the engagement proposed to me, and desired of him that the whole matter of fact might be plainly stated to his father-in-law, and that I might be now accounted free from that engagement, according to the explanation. He told me, he was glad to see me there, and would take care to acquaint his Highness, as he called him, with what I had said, and to represent it as much as might be to my advantage. The next Wednesday after my arrival, about

eight in the evening, Cromwel sent a gentleman, one Mr. Fenwick, to let me know that he would speak with me. I found him in his bed-chamber at Whitehall, and with him Major-General Lambert, Col. Sydenham, Mr. Walter Strickland, Col. Montague, and soon after came in Lieutenant-General Fleetwood [1]. The first salute I re-

---

[1] On Dec. 13, 'the Council ordered the Lord Deputy of Ireland, Lam- bert, Sydenham, Montague, and Strickland to speak with Lieut.·Gen.

1655

ceived from him was to tell me, that I had not dealt fairly with him in making him to believe I had signed an engagement not to act against him, and yet reserving an explanation whereby I made void that engagement; which, if it had not been made known to him, he might have relied upon my promise, and so have been engaged in blood before he was aware. I told him, I knew not why he should look upon me to be so considerable; neither could I apprehend how it had been possible for me to deal more fairly and openly with him than I had done: for I had told his governour at Beaumaris, that if my life as well as my liberty had been at stake, I could not sign the engagement simply, and therefore had resolved to continue there, had not the governour himself expressed a desire to accept of my subscription with that explanation. And because I accounted it to be in effect a repeal of the engagement, I had told him so, and desired him to do nothing out of respect to me that consisted not with his duty; notwithstanding which the governour told me, he was free to accept my subscription, so that I knew not but he might have received instructions so to do. 'No,' said Cromwel, 'he had none from me.' 'That was more,' said I, 'than I knew; and if you had not notice as well of the one as the other, it was not my fault, for I had acquainted you with neither; and those who informed you of the one, I presumed had made you acquainted with the other also.' He then objected to me, that I was stolen from Ireland without leave: to which I made answer, that tho I knew no cause why I should either be detained in Ireland, or obliged to ask leave to depart, yet to avoid all pretence of exception against me, I had taken care to procure even that too, as far as it was possible, having a passport for England from Lieutenant-General Fleetwood, the chief officer of Ireland, with the advice of Mr. Corbet, one of his Council, for my coming, and his son Harry's promise not to obstruct

Ludlow on to-day's debate, and report.' Cal. S. P., Dom., 1655-6, p. 56. The interview which Ludlow dates on Dec. 12, probably took place on Dec. 13; cf. p. 109.

me in my journey. He next asked me, wherefore I would not engage not to act against the present Government, telling me, that if Nero were in power, it would be my duty to submit. To which I replied, that I was ready to submit, and could truly say, that I knew not of any design against him. 'But,' said I, 'if Providence open a way, and give an opportunity of appearing in behalf of the people, I cannot consent to tie my own hands before-hand, and oblige my self not to lay hold on it.' 'However,' said he, 'it is not reasonable to suffer one that I distrust to come within my house, till he assure me he will do me no mischief': I told him, I was not accustomed to go to any house unless I expected to be welcome; neither had I come hither but upon a message from him, and that I desired nothing but a little liberty to breathe in the air, to which I conceived I had an equal right with other men. He then fell to inveigh bitterly against Major Wildman, as the author of the petition from the army before-mentioned, reviling him with unhandsom language, and saying he deserved to be hanged; and that he must secure me also, if I would not oblige my self never to act against him. I told him I had gone as far as I could in that engagement which I had given to Lieutenant-General Fleetwood; and if that were not thought sufficient, I resolved with God's assistance to suffer any extremities that might be imposed upon me. 'Yes,' said he, 'we know your resolution well enough, and we have cause to be as stout as you; but I pray who spoke of your suffering?' 'Sir,' said I, 'if I am not deceived, you mentioned the securing my person.' 'Yea,' said he, 'and great reason there is why we should do so; for I am ashamed to see that engagement which you have given to the Lieutenant-General, which would be more fit for a General who should be taken prisoner, and that hath yet an army of thirty thousand men in the field, than for one in your condition.' I answered, that it was as much as I could consent to give, and what Lieutenant-General Fleetwood thought fit to accept. Then beginning to carry himself more calmly, he said that he had been always ready to do me what good offices he could, and that he wished me as well as he did any one of his Council, desiring me to make choice of some place to be in, where I might have good air. I assured him, that my dissatisfactions were not grounded upon any animosity against his person ; and that if my own father were alive, and in his place, they would, I doubted not, be altogether as great. He acknowledged that I had always carried my self fairly and openly to him, and protested that he had never given me just cause to act otherwise.

When Cromwel had finished his discourse, some of those who were present began to make their observations, and in particular Col. Montague thought it worthy his notice, that I had intimated, if providence should offer an occasion, I was ready to act against the present Government; but the rest of the company seemed ashamed of what he said. Major-General Lambert then desired to know from me why I could not own this as a lawful Government : 'because,' said I, 'it seems to me to be in substance a re-establishment of that which we all engaged against, and had with a great expence of blood and treasure abolished.' 'What then,' said he, 'would you account to be a sufficient warrant for you to act against the present authority?' I answered, when I might rationally hope to be supported by an authority equal or superiour to this, and could be perswaded that the said authority would employ its power for the good of mankind. 'But who shall be judg of that?' said he ; 'for all are ready to say they do so, and we our selves think we use the best of our endeavours to that end.' I replied, that if they did so, their crime was the less, because every man stands obliged to govern himself by the light of his own reason, which rule, with the assistance of God, I was determined to observe. Col. Sydenham said, we might be mistaken in judging that to be a power giving us a just and rational call to act, which may not be so. I told him, that we ought to be very careful and circumspect in that particular, and at least be assured of very probable grounds to believe the power under which we engage to be sufficiently able to protect us in our undertaking ; otherwise I should account my self not only guilty of my own blood, but also in some measure of the ruin and destruction of all those that I should induce to engage with me, tho the cause were never so just.

This discourse being ended, I was desired to withdraw into the next room, where Lieutenant-General Fleetwood came to me, and laboured to perswade me to engage, as was desired, tho but for a week. I made answer, that I was not willing to do it for an hour : 'then,' said he, 'you shall engage to me.' I told him I looked upon my self already obliged by the conditions of my late engagement, further than which I could not go ; and thereupon returned to my lodging, in order to imploy my leisure about my private affairs during that time.

APPENDICES.

———••———

D

om

n t

v, o
Di

—————
UD.
Ma

<table>
<tr><td>|</td><td>|</td></tr>
<tr><td>:hoh
pt.</td><td>URSULA, married
— Scrope.</td><td>PHILIPPA, married Thomas,
son of Sir John Zouch,
Knt., Dorset.</td></tr>
</table>

<table>
<tr><td>DLC LUDLOW, bapt. ⚮ JANE BENNETT, dau. of
tle erstock, 3 March,   John Bennett, of Steeple
Married at War-   Ashton and Smallbrook.
r, 15 Feb. 1624.   Died 19 Dec. 1683.
.OW 646.
). M
36,
Mar
)'A</td><td>GEORGE LUDLOW,
bapt. at Dinton, 15
Sept. 1596. Will
proved 1 August,
1656. Member of
Virginian Council.
Vide Memoirs, i.
298.</td></tr>
</table>

ow.

—————
LU married John
h Ef Cossington.
J. Vent dated 21
)1.)56.

<table>
<tr><td>|</td><td>|</td><td>|</td></tr>
<tr><td>RAN Frome, bapt.
Aug. 1634.
of the Ameri-</td><td>WILLIAM LUDLOW, of
Sarum, bapt. at
Warminster, 11
April, 1637.</td><td>JOHN LUDLOW, bapt.
at Warminster, 9
Jan. 1640.</td></tr>
</table>

<table>
<tr><td>|</td><td>|</td><td>|</td></tr>
<tr><td>UDI DLOW.
atec
for</td><td>JANE LUDLOW.</td><td>JOHN LUDLOW.</td></tr>
</table>

PEDIGREE OF LUDLOW OF HILL DEVERILL, CO. WILTS.

ARMS. Argent, a chevron between three martlets' heads erased, sable. CREST. A demi-martlet couped, sable. MOTTO.

APPENDIX II.

SKETCH OF THE CIVIL WAR IN WILTSHIRE.

LUDLOW's account of the Civil War in Wiltshire is confined to At. J. those events in which he took part himself. An outline of the general history of the struggle in that county is necessary to understand the bearing of the particular incidents he records, and to estimate the value of his personal services.

At the beginning of the Civil War the adherents of the Parliament had the upper hand in Wiltshire. The Royalist nobility and gentry were for the moment powerless. A petition from the city of Salisbury in support of the policy of the Parliament had been presented on Feb. 24, 1642 (L. J. iv. 611). The Earl of Pembroke was appointed Lord-Lieutenant of Wilts and Hampshire and Governor of the Isle of Wight, and despatched to Wiltshire on Aug. 12, 1642, to execute the militia ordinance (L. J. v. 281, 284, 299, 544). He returned to London in October, having settled the militia in Wiltshire and secured the Isle of Wight, and brought with him numerous prisoners seized by the Parliamentary forces in the west (Vicars, Jehovah Jireh, p. 182). In the absence of Pembroke the Deputy-Lieutenants appointed by him exercised the powers with which Parliament had entrusted him. On Nov. 2, King Charles published a proclamation of 'grace, favour, and pardon' to the inhabitants of Wilts, excepting only four persons, who were to be proceeded against as traitors and stirrers of sedition. These four persons, the leaders of the Parliamentary party in the county, were Sir Edward Hungerford, Sir Henry Ludlow, Sir John Evelyn, and Walter Long, Esq. (Husbands, Ordinances, 4to, p. 732). The ordinance for levying money for the support of Essex's army assesses Wilts at the rate of £725 per week, and appoints to collect the money Sir Edward Hungerford, Sir Edward Baynton, Sir Nevill

App. II. Poole, and Sir John Evelyn, Knights; Edward Baynton, Edward Tucker, Edward Goddard, Alexander Thistlethwait, junior, Edward Poole, Thomas Moore, John Ashe, and Robert Jennour, Esquires (ibid. pp. 934, 942). The ordinance for sequestering the estates of Royalist delinquents in the county (April 1, 1643) gives the additional names of Denzill Holles, William Wheeler, and John White (Husbands, Ordinances, folio, p. 20).

But before the year 1642 was ended the prosperity of the Parliamentary cause in Wiltshire received a great check. The town of Marlborough, which had from the first distinguished itself by its zeal for the Parliament, was captured by a detachment from the King's army at Oxford commanded by General Wilmot (Clarendon, Rebellion, vi. 156, 157; Waylen, History of Marlborough, pp. 154–168; Rushworth, v. 82). Clarendon describes the town as 'the most notoriously disaffected of all that county; otherwise, saving the obstinacy and malice of the inhabitants, in the situation of it very unfit for a garrison.' On Feb. 2, 1643, another detachment from Oxford, under the command of Prince Rupert, captured Cirencester in Gloucestershire, and the Wiltshire Roundheads promptly evacuated the neighbouring post of Malmesbury (Clarendon, vi. 237–8; Bibliotheca Gloucestrensis, pp. 159–185). Malmesbury was at once occupied by a Royalist garrison under Lieut.-Col. Herbert Lunsford (ib. p. 173; Mercurius Aulicus, Feb. 4 and Feb. 6, 1643). Thus on two sides the Royalist outposts were pushed forward into Wiltshire, and the way was opened for further conquests.

But even more fatal than these victories were the quarrels of the Parliamentary leaders themselves. A feud between Sir Edward Hungerford and Sir Edward Baynton, which Ludlow does not mention, produced most pernicious consequences to the common cause. Each accused the other of treachery. Each in turn was arrested by the other, and succeeded in effecting his escape. The following account of this incident is given in the newspapers of the two parties, and in a published letter from Baynton to the Earl of Pembroke.

Mercurius Aulicus, Jan. 11, 1643, says:—

'News was brought from Wiltshire how that a difference falling out betwixt Sir Edward Hungerford and Sir Edward Baynton (both which his Majesty had excepted amongst others out of his general pardon for that county) the business grew into that heat that Baynton had seized on Hungerford's person, and held him prisoner in the town of Malmesbury. But Hungerford escaping by a flight to Cirencester, he obtained some of the forces of that place to pursue his quarrell, and came so suddenly to Malmesbury that he surprised Baynton, carried him prisoner to Cirencester, and still keeps him there ; though Baynton, as a pledge of fidelity unto the two houses of Parliament, had sent a great part of his goods to the Isle of Wight as a place wholly in their hands.'

The same paper on Feb. 3, after mentioning the capture of Cirencester, and giving a list of prisoners, says, ' Sir Edward Baynton, who was brought prisoner hither from Malmesbury, had the good luck to be conveyed before to some gaol in London.'

The Parliamentary papers give the following story :—

' When Prince Rupert was coming with his forces against Cirencester, an alarm was given to Gloucestershire, Somersetshire and Wiltshire, who according to their mutual association to defend each other, raised forces to send speedy aid to Cirencester. . . . It so fell out that Sir Edward Baynton (who hitherto hath been very zealous for the Parliament, and no doubt is so still but that some passion overcame him) disbanded all his forces at the Devizes and Malmesbury, both which towns sent to Sir Edw. Hungerford for protection, who immediately sent them aid, and that night Lieut. Eyre with 140 dragoons came to Malmesbury, where Sir Edw. Hungerford was, under pretence of assisting him ; and in the night time, this Sir Edward Baynton's Lieutenant suddenly and in an uncivil manner (threatening to kill him if he spoke a word of it to his soldiers) carried him away prisoner, but notice of this was given to the forces of Cirencester, who (though Prince Rupert was nigh the town) sent 3 troops of horse, and rescued Sir Edw. Hungerford, and brought away Sir Edward Baynton, and Lieutenant Eyre prisoners to Cirencester, and were back time enough to affront Prince Rupert, who with 7000 men came up the hill and so went down again, and now that country is peaceably settled.' (The Kingdoms Weekly Intelligencer, Jan. 10–17, 1643.)

' It is confirmed that Sir Edw. Baynton had a design of carrying Sir Edw. Hungerford to Oxford. You may by this see what confidence is to be put in roaring boys.' (Spec. Passages, Jan. 17–24, 1643.)

Baynton's own narrative enters into more detail, and gives his charges against Hungerford.

' TO THE RIGHT HONOURABLE THE EARL OF PEMBROKE.
   ' My noble good Lord,
   ' On Monday night last being at Malmesbury, which is a town under my command, within 8 miles of Cisseter, where I had drawn up

500 men of my regiment for their aid, and two companies more upon their march; about nine of the clock at night there came about 500 horse, and dragoneers of the Earl of Stamford's forces, out of Glocestershire, commanded by Lieutenant Colonel Furbush and Lieutenant Colonel Carr, his Lordship being then at Exeter, and desired lodging of me for that night, whereupon as soon as I was certainly informed who they were I took order for the billeting of them, and let them in, which as soon as I had done, they came to me pretending a great deal of friendship, but on the sudden seized upon me in my lodging, plundered me and my soldiers of all that we had, and the next morning carried me and Captain Edward Eyre to Cisseter, with as much ignominy as was possible, upon two poore dragoneeres, although they took from me as many horses for my own saddle as were worth 300 pound; within two days they carried me to this towne where they keep me in the same manner at this time; but I thank God, they dare accuse me of nothing, but say, that I would not bring up my forces to Cisseter, which I conceive I was no way bound to do, especially Prince Maurice his quarter being at Farringdon and Wantage, having there 1000 horse, within two miles of Wilts; they say likewise that I had seized upon Sir Edward Hungerford, which I had just cause to do; for besides the correspondence between him and my Lord Seymour, which I can bring pregnant proof of, he sent twice to my Serjeant Major, to command him to draw up my forces to such places as he should appoint, pretending that he had an order from the Parliament for it, and sent to my soldiers to leave me, and come to him, which I could make no other interpretation of, but that he intended to betray me: whereupon I resolved to send him in safe custody to the Parliament, but he fled to Cisseter, and there I do very believe, did bribe the two Scotch lieutenant colonels to perform this exploit: for he fled out of Wilts about six weeks agone, and carried all his family and goods into Somersetshire, where he doth now reside, and only comes skulking now and then into Wilts to put tricks upon me. I have served my country under your Lordship's and your brother's command these 20 years, wherefore I beseech your Lordship to undertake for me, for I am resolved never to desert the cause, but desire to appear at the Parliament with as much speed as may be, which I hope your Lordship will further, for his sake, who will ever be

'Your most humble Servant,

'E. BAYNTON.

'GLOUCESTER,
'*Jan.* 15, 164⅔.'

Parliament decided the dispute in Hungerford's favour. On Jan. 10, 1643, an ordinance had been passed for raising in Wiltshire two regiments of horse of four troops each, and one regiment of 1000 dragoons, to be under the command of the Earl of Essex. The task of raising them was entrusted to Sir Edward Baynton, as the Commander-in-chief of the county forces, with the assistance of other members of the Parliamentary committee. On Jan. 31, the Commons voted that Hungerford should supersede Baynton as Commander-in-chief, and a new ordinance was passed in which his name replaced Baynton's (C. J. ii. 954; L. J. v. 543, 587).

It was at this time that Hungerford invited Ludlow to leave Essex's body-guard and raise a troop of horse (Memoirs, p. 49). Ludlow accordingly joined Hungerford at Devizes, his head-quarters, and accompanied him in his expedition to Salisbury. Of this expedition Mercurius Aulicus gives the following account :—

Feb. 13, 1643. 'It was further certified this day, that Sir Edw. Hungerford, one that his Majesty had excepted out of his general pardon for the County of Wilts, having since his departure from Malmesbury gotten together a body of rebels under his command, marched with them towards Salisbury, which he easily entered ; and having seized on all such money, plate, and arms as he could find, or otherwise was betrayed unto him, he put the town to the ransom of £500 to save the residue of their goods from spoil and plundering.'

Feb. 15. 'This day it was advertised also, that Sir Ed. Hungerford having missed the prey he chiefly sought for in the city of Salisbury (which was Sir George Vaughan, High Sheriff of the County of Wilts), returned back to the Devises as his surest fortress, which had before been fortified by Sir Ed. Baynton. From whence he writ letters to the House of Commons, signifying that the works there were so great and large that he had not men enough to make them good, if any of the King's forces should be sent that way : complaining also that for want of such necessary supplies he was not able to relieve the town of Cirencester, which misfortune might otherwise have been prevented.'

Feb. 23. 'It was confirmed this day for certain, having been doubt-fully reported two days before, that Sir Edward Hungerford despairing to make good the Devises by his own forces, and having little hope to be supplied from the two houses of Parliament, had utterly forsook the place : and that Lieutenant Colonel Lunsford, who was left Governor in Malmesbury with a garrison of 400 foot and a troop of horse, had took possession of the town and Castle for his Majesty, by means whereof the whole county of Wilts is very likely to be freed of the Rebels forces, and become wholly at the King's devotion.' (On Hungerford's abandonment of Devizes see also Waylen's Marl-borough, p. 187.)

Ludlow, after accompanying Hungerford to Salisbury, returned to Essex's head-quarters, and stayed in his army till after the capture of Reading (April 26, 1643). During his absence Sir William Waller, marching westward after his recent capture of Chichester, levied contributions at Winchester and Salisbury, and on March 23 recaptured Malmesbury. Waller sent this account of his exploit to the Earl of Essex :—

' I sate down before the place yesterday a little after noon. At my first comming their horse shewed themselves in a bravado under the side of a wood, about a quarter of a mile from the town, but upon the first proffer of a charge they retired hastily towards Cicester-way before we could come up to them ; whereupon we fell to worke with the towne, which is the strongest in land-scituation that ever I saw : in the skirts of the town there were gardens walled in with dry stone wall, from whence the enemy played upon us as we came on, but within halfe an houre we beat them out of those strengths, and entered the outer or lower town with our horse and foot, and kept possession of it, the enemy withdrawing into the upper, where they had bin at cost to fortifie. We fell on the west port, in which they had cast up a breast work, and planted a peece of ordnance : the street so narrow at the upper end next the work, that not above four could march in breast ; this businesse cost hot water. As we fell on we advanced two drakes, and under that favour our musqueteers possessed themselves of some houses ne'er the port, from whence we galled the enemy very much. If our men had come out roundly we had then carryed it, but the falling of some cooled the rest ; and so the first assault failed after a fight of neer halfe an hour. Whilst we were preparing to renew the assault, the enemy shewed himself neer the town, with seaven, or (as some say) ten troops of horse ; whereupon Sir Arthur Hazelrig fell out upon them with eight troops, but upon his approach they retired speedily. In the mean time before his return that night,we gave on again upon the town, and had a very hot fight, which after an hours continuance at the least, we were fain to give over for want of ammunition, the main part whereof was unluckily stayed behind by a mischance of the carriage, and could not come up till the next morning. I was in such want of powder, and especialy ball, that if the enemy had falen out upon me, I could have maintained a very small fight, and I had no notice hereof from the officer, untill I was reduced to this straight ; whereupon I thought fit to draw off the drakes that night, or rather morning, for it was neer two of the clock. The better to effect this, and to prevent the hazard of the enemies sally, I caused all the drums to beat, and trumpets to sound, drawing both horse and foot out into the streets : as in preparation to an assault, with all the strength I had ;

which gave the enemy such apprehension, that immediately they sent out a drum, and craved a parly. They yeelded upon quarter, and gave me entrance about seven or eight of the clock that morning. They were about three hundred foot, and a troop of horse, but the horse [as] I related formerly, shifted for themselves upon our first coming. We have prisoners, Colonell Harbert Lunceford, Colonell Cook, Lieutenant Colonell Dabridgecourt, Sergeant Major Finch, six Captains, six Lieutenants, six Ensignes, one Cornet, and four quarter-masters, besides ordinary souldiers, part wherof we mean to send to Gloucester, the rest to Bristoll.' (A letter from Sir William Waller to the right honourable Robert Earl of Essex, of a great victory he obtained at Malmesbury in the county of Wilts, 4to, 1643. See also Godwin, Civil War in Hants, 1882, pp. 54-56; Vicars, Jehovah Jireh, p. 292; Mercurius Aulicus, March 22, 25, April 2, 1643.)

Waller committed the care of Malmesbury to Sir Edward Hungerford.

'We left him not without commanders,' wrote Waller to the Parliament; 'he had two Serjeant-Majors, able men, and the companies of his own regiment, and a company of dragoons, with ammunition and two hundred muskets to put into the countrymen's hands that offered themselves very freely. We conceived that Sir Edward Hungerford's power in the country, with that strength, would easily have defended that place; but for reasons best known to himselfe, he quitted it.' (Bibliotheca Gloucestrensis, p. 195; cf. Mercurius Aulicus, March 20, 22, 25, April 2, 1643.)

Hungerford retorted by publishing a remarkably badly written vindication, which explained rather than justified his conduct. It is dated 'Bath, April 28, 1643,' and signed by Thomas Hungerford.

'I was appointed,' he says, 'to take charge of that towne and accordingly expected to have it left with all things for defence, but much business happening, and Sir William Waller hastening out of towne upon his designe towards Gloucester, before any consultation could be had concerning the settlement thereof, upon Thursday I went out of Malmesbury towards Tedbury, with Sir William Waller, at what time the town was left with more prisoners than souldiers, without ammunition and money; and by the way mentioning to Sir William Waller, the dangerous condition of that towne if he left not there a very considerable party, especially in case he removed to any remote place, without forceing the enemy first from Cirencester, who was there at that time very stronge both in horse and foot, whereupon Sir William Waller did that evening at Tedbury order 3 barrells of powder to be presently sent unto Malmesbury, and appointed Major Clyfton to repair thither to joyne with Major Trayle in the ordering of the forces there, that Captain Talbot with his troop should presently go thither to guard the prisoners from thence the next day to Bath, and Captain Walden with his parcell of dragoons, near upon 20, to remain at Malmesbury. I conceiving that the said Serjeant Major Clifton, sent thither by Sir William Waller, was a commander able and fit to give direction and secure the towne, I left all my forces with him at Malmesbury, and went myselfe to Bath attended onely with my owne servants speedily to send more ammunition, men and horse, whereof there was not at Malmesbury a sufficient number for scouts, as also to get money for the payment of the garrison at Malmesbury. Whilst I was about this worke, had gotten my horses together, made up two companies ready on their march towards Malmesbury, with ammunition (which was wanting there) for ordnance, and a supply of other ammunition, newes was brought that Malmesbury was abandoned, (and for ought I could understand) rather upon the conceipt then sight of an enemy. The cause of this conceived to be, from an apprehension of the power of an enemy neare them ; the small force they had then in the towne (not exceeding 120 souldiers) to make resistance ; the backwardness of the country to come in to beare armes or to assist with money (who seemed very forward whilest Sir William Waller was present, but altered their mindes so soone as they did see him with his army to be departed from them) ; my souldiers generally discontented that they had not pillage as others who tooke lesse paines (as they thought) and lost no blood, overburthened with duties, being but a few in number, and howerly raised with allarumes ; the captaines at oddes amongst themselves, Major Trayle that should have reconciled all, not so carefull as he ought, Major Clifton that was sent to joyne with him, gone away from thence to Bath, these two being the able commanders especially trusted for the defence of the towne. One of the officers also amongst them did much increase their feares, and seeing false alarumes, and after as their number decreased, did helpe to disarme the remainder ; also two of the captaines that should have encouraged them, told them they were all but dead men, if they did not flie presently, they being the first that showed them the way by their example ; after this the souldiers could not be stayed, but in spite of their captain and officers which were left, who sought to keepe them in, they ran away, so that in an houre or two there were scarce tenne souldiers left in the towne. Thus was Malmesbury left at 11 of the clock upon Saturday at night, no enemy entring until seven of the clock next morning being Sunday.'

Mercurius Aulicus for March 25, 1643, relating the re-occupation of Malmesbury, claims that 11 colours, 8 guns, and a great deal of ammunition were found in the town, 'their new governor of the town, his Lieutenant-Colonel with 400 or 500 souldiers being all taken prisoners.' ' At present,' concludes Hungerford's letter, ' the enemie hath in garrison there 400 foot and Curston his troope of horse. Collonell Bamfeild is appointed governor.'

In April, however, when the King was obliged to collect his scattered forces to make up an army for the relief of Reading, the garrison at Malmesbury was drawn off (Mercurius Aulicus, April 22, 1643).

Now that the King's forces in Wiltshire were diminished, Hungerford, returned from Somersetshire, began to plunder the Royalist gentlemen, and laid siege to Wardour.

' Out of Wiltshire they write that Sir Edward Hungerford hath been a long time in Sommersetshire, whereby their country hath been left in a naked condition, but that of late he is returned with Colonell Stroud, to Mear, whither they have brought along with them 700 horse and foot, and also that they were there joyfully entertained, and had free quarter given them ; and that during their abode at Mear, their souldiers seized upon Master Arundel's cattell, and killed almost all his goates on Horningsham Common, and they also got into the parke at Longleat, and killed some of Sir James Thinne's fallow deer, and afterward they marched to Warder Castle.' (Joyful Newes from Plimouth, 1643.)

A detailed account of the siege of Wardour, of the devastation wrought by the besiegers, and of the barbarity of Sir Edward Hungerford to his prisoners, is given in Mercurius Rusticus, No. 5. It forms a proper companion picture to Ludlow's account of the siege he sustained.

' On Tuesday the second of May 1643, Sir Edward Hungerford, a chief commander of the rebels in Wiltshire, came with his forces before Wardour Castle in the same county, being the mansion-house of the Lord Arundell of Wardour : but finding the castle strong, and those that were in it resolute not to yield it up unless by force, called Colonel Strode to his help. Both these joined in one made a body of 1300, or thereabout. Being come before it, by a trumpet they summon the castle to surrender : the reason pretended was, because the castle being a receptacle of cavaliers and malignants, both Houses of Parliament had ordered it to be searched for men and arms ; and withal by the same trumpeter declared, that if they found either money or plate, they would seize on it for the use of the Parliament. The Lady Arundell (her husband being then at Oxford, and since that dead there) refused to deliver up the castle ; and bravely replied, that she had a command from her Lord to keep it, and she would obey his command.

'Being denied entrance, the next day, being Wednesday the third of May, they bring up the cannon within musquet shot and begin the battery, and continue from the Wednesday to the Monday following, never giving any intermission to the besieged, who were but twenty-five fighting men to make good the place against an army of 1300. In this time they spring two mines ; the first in a vault, through which beer and wood and other necessaries were brought into the castle : this did not much hurt, it being without the foundation of the castle. The second was conveyed into the small vaults ; which, by reason of the intercourse between the several passages to every office, and almost every room in the castle, did much shake and endanger the whole fabrick.

'The rebels had often tendered some unreasonable conditions to the besieged to surrender ; as to give the ladies, both the mother and the daughter-in-law, and the women and children, quarter, but not the men. The ladies both infinitely scorning to sacrifice the lives of their friends and servants to redeem their own from the cruelty of the rebels, who had no other crime of which they could count them guilty but their fidelity and earnest endeavours to preserve them from violence and robbery, chose bravely (according to the nobleness of their honourable families from which they were both extracted) rather to die together than live on so dishonourable terms. But now, the castle brought to this distress, the defendants few, oppressed with number, tired out with continual watching and labour from Tuesday to Monday, so distracted between hunger and want of rest, that when the hand endeavoured to administer food, surprized with sleep it forgat its employment, the morsels falling from their hands while they were about to eat, deluding their appetite : now, when it might have been a doubt which they would first have laded their musquets withal, either powder before bullet, or bullet before powder, had not the maid servants (valiant beyond their sex) assisted them, and done that service for them : lastly, now, when the rebels had brought petarrs, and applied them to the garden-doors (which, if forced, open a free passage to the castle), and balls of wild-fire to throw in at their broken windows, and all hopes of keeping the castle was taken away ; now, and not till now, did the besieged sound a parley. And though in their Diurnals at London they have told the world that they offered threescore thousand pounds to redeem themselves and the castle, and that it was refused, yet few men take themselves to be bound anything the more to believe it because they report it. I would Master Case would leave preaching treason, and instruct his disciples to put away lying, and speak every man truth of his neighbour. Certainly the world would not be so abused with untruths as now they are ; amongst which App. II. number this report was one: for if they in the castle offered so liberally how came the rebels to agree upon articles of surrender so far beneath that overture ? For the Articles of Surrender were these :

'First, That the ladies and all others in the castle should have quarter.

'Secondly, That the ladies and servants should carry away all their wearing apparel; and that six of the serving men, whom the ladies should nominate, should attend upon their persons wheresoever the rebels should dispose of them.

'Thirdly, That all the furniture and goods in the house should be safe from plunder ; and to this purpose one of the six nominated to attend the ladies was to stay in the castle, and take an inventory of all in the house ; of which the commanders were to have one copy and the ladies another.

'But being on these terms masters of the castle and all within it, 'tis true they observed the first article, and spared the lives of all the besieged, though they had slain in the defence at least sixty of the rebels. But for the other two they observed them not in any part. As soon as they entered the castle, they first seized upon the several trunks and packs which they of the castle was making up, and left neither the ladies nor servants any other wearing-clothes but what was on their backs.

'There was in the castle, amongst many rich ones, one extraordinary chimney piece, valued at two thousand pounds; this they utterly defaced, and beat down all the carved works thereof with their pole-axes. There were likewise rare pictures, the work of the most curious pencils that were known to these latter times of the world, and such that Apelles himself (had he been alive) need not blush to own for his. These in a wild fury they break and tear to pieces ; a loss that neither cost nor art can repair.

'Having thus given them a taste what performance of articles they were to expect from them, they barbarously lead the ladies, and the young lady's children, two sons and a daughter, prisoners to Shaftes-bury, some four or five miles from Wardour.

'While they were prisoners, to mitigate their sorrows, in triumph they bring five cart-loads of their richest hangings and other furniture through Shaftesbury towards Dorchester : and since that, contrary to their promise and faith, given both by Sir Edward Hungerford and Strode, they plundered the whole castle : so little use was there of the inventory we told you of, unless to let the world know what Lord Arundell lost, and what the rebels gained. This havock they made within the castle. Without they burnt all the out-houses ; they pulled up the pales of two parks, the one of red deer the other of fallow ; what they did not kill they let loose to the world for the next taker.

In the parks they burn three tenements and two lodges; they cut down all the trees about the house and grounds. Oaks and elms, such as but few places could boast of the like, whose goodly bushy advanced heads drew the eyes of travellers on the plains to gaze on them; these they sold for four-pence, sixpence, or twelve-pence a-piece, that were worth three, four, or five pound a tree. The fruit-trees they pluck up by the roots, extending their malice to commit spoil on that which God by a special law protected from destruction even in the land of his curse, the land of Canaan; for so we read: "When thou shalt besiege a city, thou shalt not destroy the trees thereof by forcing an ax against them, for thou mayest eat of them, and thou shalt not cut them down and employ them in the siege; only the trees which thou knowest that they be not trees for meat thou shalt destroy." *Deut.* xx. 19, 20. Nay that which escaped destruction in the Deluge cannot escape the hands of these children of the Apollyon the destroyer. They dig up the heads of twelve great ponds, some of five or six acres a-piece, and destroy all the fish. They sell carps of two foot long for two-pence and three-pence a-piece: they sent out the fish by cart-loads, so that the country could not spend them. Nay, as if the present generation were too narrow an object for their rage, they plunder posterity, and destroy the nurseries of the great ponds. They drive away and sell their horses, kine, and other cattle, and having left nothing either in air or water, they dig under the earth. The castle was served with water brought two miles by a conduit of lead; and, intending rather mischief to the king's friends than profit to themselves, they cut up the pipe and sold it (as these men's wives in North Wiltshire do bonelace) at six-pence a yard; making that waste for a poor inconsiderable sum which two thousand pounds will not make good. They that have the unhappy occasion to sum up these losses, value them at no less than one hundred thousand pounds. And though this loss were very great, not to be paralleled by any except that of the Countess of Rivers, yet there was something in these sufferings which did aggravate them beyond all example of barbarity which unnatural war till now did produce, and that was Rachel's tears, "lamentation and weeping and great mourning, a mother weeping for her children, and would not be comforted, because they were taken from her." For the rebels, as you hear, having carried the two ladies prisoners to Shaftesbury, thinking them not safe enough, their intent is to remove them to Bath, a place then much infected both with the plague and the small-pox. The old lady was sick under a double confinement, that of the rebels and her own indisposition. All were unwilling to be exposed to the danger of the infection, especially the young lady, having three children with her; they were too dear, too rich a treasure to be snatched away to such probable loss without reluctancy: therefore they resolve not to yield themselves prisoners unless they will take the old lady out of her bed, and the rest by violence, and so carry them away. But the Rebels fearing lest so great inhumanity might incense the people against them, and render them odious to the country, decline this; and, since they dare not carry all to Bath, they resolve to carry some to Dorchester, a place no less dangerous for the infection of schism and rebellion than Bath for the plague and the small-pox. To this purpose they take the young lady's two sons (the eldest but nine, the younger but seven years of age), and carried them captives to Dorchester.

'In vain doth the mother with tears intreat that these pretty pledges of her lord's affections may not be snatched from her. In vain do the children embrace and hang about the neck of their mother, and implore help from her, that neither knows how to keep them, nor yet how to part with them : but the Rebels, having lost all bowels of compassion, remain inexorable. The complaints of the mother, the pitiful cry of the children, prevail not with them ; like ravenous wolves they seize on the prey, and though they do not crop, yet they transplant those "olive branches that stood about their parents' table."'

Lord Arundel, naturally seeing no reason why two young children should be treated as prisoners of war, wrote to Sir William Waller, begging him to restore his sons. Waller's answer which follows is taken from a paper amongst Clarendon's MSS. (No. 1719) containing a rough draught of several letters of Waller's concerning the exchange of prisoners and similar subjects.

'I shall readily apprehend any occasion that may enable me to serve you, but in this particular concerning the restitution of your children itt is my unhappiness that I am not capable of performing your command, they being by an order from the Parliament (directed to Sir Edward Hungerford) removed to London. I was a meer stranger both to their taking and removall, and therefore I presume your nobleness will impute nothing to me in either. If there be anything within the narrow sphere of my power, wherein I may be serviceable, your Lordship shall find me most ready to give demonstration that I am,' &c., &c.

Parliament refused to surrender Lord Arundel's children. On June 17, 1643, the Commons resolved that Martin Holbech of Felsted in Essex, a celebrated Puritan divine and schoolmaster, should 'be desired to receive into his house and to take the care and tuition of the two sons of Lord Arundel of Wardour.' On May 10, 1644, it was voted that they should be exchanged for the children of Lord Robartes, 'now prisoners with the king.' At this Sir Edward Hungerford claimed, that before they were released he should be satisfied for the cost of keeping them (C. J. iii. 131, 488, 553, 573). Parliament resolved that Wardour Castle should be maintained as a garrison and Ludlow was appointed its governor (C. J. iii. 79 ; vi. 508). At the time when he accepted this post the Parliamentary cause in Wiltshire was in a very critical condition. Owing to the quarrels of Baynton and Hungerford, to Hungerford's incapacity, and to the loss of Marlborough, the original enthusiasm shown by the people in general had greatly declined. The temporary success just gained was due entirely to the drawing off of the King's forces. The Parliamentary forces in Wiltshire were ill disciplined, and weak in numbers. The general ill success of the Parliamentary arms during the summer of 1643 rendered Ludlow's position still more precarious. On July 5, 1643, Waller practically defeated Hopton at Lansdowne, and on July 9 besieged him at Devizes as he strove to make his way to Oxford. On July 13, however, the siege was raised and Waller's army destroyed at Roundway Down by Prince Maurice and General Wilmot (Clarendon, vii. 110–120 ; Bibliotheca Gloucestrensis, p. 201 ; Gardiner, Great Civil War, i. 202–4). All the west (excepting Plymouth and Lyme, and one or two other ports) now fell into the hands of the Royalists. Bristol was captured on July 27, Exeter on Sept. 7, and Gloucester besieged in August.

During the summer of 1643, a Parliamentarian garrison had again occupied Malmesbury ; but about July 21 that town was again captured by the Royalists. Mercurius Aulicus for July 23 thus relates its recapture :—

'It was advertised this day that certain of his Majestie's forces, being in their march towards Bristol, had taken Malmesbury from the Rebels. The towne had been abandoned by his Majestie, and all the garrison and ordnance removed thence by his especiall command, at such time as the Earl of Essex had beleaguered Reading ; and not possessed by the Rebels, till that of late it was thought fit by some of their principall leaders to put a garrison of 80 horse and 400 foot into it, with some 9 peeces of cannon, for the better bridling of the country, and awing of the parts adjoyning whome they plagued sufficiently. But notice being given to some of his Majesties commanders quartered thereabouts, where the guards were weakest, and the towne most fit for an assault, they fell upon it in the night (about two nights since), and having forced an easie passage through the carelesse guards, made themselves masters of the place; as also of the cannon, armes, and ammunition; some of the souldiers being killed and the most parte taken; the rest providing for themselves, by some close conveyances, under the covert of the night.'

In consequence of this capture Ludlow's position at Wardour became still more exposed and isolated. The nearest garrisons from which he could expect succour were Gloucester, itself hard pressed, and Portsmouth, both of which remained in the Parliament's hands throughout the war. Smaller posts like Southampton and Poole could send little assistance. Seeing the danger of his position, his friends on the Royalist side endeavoured to induce him to surrender. His father, solicitous for his safety, apprehending that he could not be relieved in three or four months if he were besieged, and knowing that the enemy were masters of the field in those parts, and that he was twenty miles from any other Parliamentary garrison, procured an order from the Parliament empowering his son to destroy the fortifications of the Castle and draw off his troops. But Ludlow repulsed these overtures, rejected this chance of safety, and prepared quietly for the worst. The position he held was of little military value. The value of the defence of Wardour lay in the example which, in a time of discouragements and defeats, it gave to all those who were fighting for the Parliament, in the indomitable courage and tenacity with which he maintained his trust. It was the display of these qualities which founded Ludlow's reputation amongst Puritan soldiers, and drew the attention of the leaders of his party. What made his conduct still more prominent was the absence or removal of the local leaders who had originally championed the Parliamentary cause in Wiltshire. His father died in October 1643. Sir Edward Hungerford, after the capture of Wardour, disappears from the history of the local war. His later exploits had Somersetshire for their scene. Sir Edward Baynton, arrested in August 1643, for making false and scandalous charges against Lord Say and Mr. Pym, was under restraint in London till August 1644 (C. J. iii. 228, 235, 606). At the time of his arrest, Baynton, as the following letter to Sir Edward Hyde shows, was secretly endeavouring to make his peace with the King.

'HONOURED SIR,

'I should have trobled you before nowe but that I could not have any oppertunity of writing. In the first place, lett me entreat you toe present my humble service toe my Lord Marques of Hertford, with this request toe you both, that his Lordship with your assistance would procure my pardon from the King, which if you cann obtayne I will presently cume home toe my howse in Wilts, and if I am never able toe requite soe great a favor, yet I desire you both to be confident that your greatest enemies shall never justly reproatch you for procuring my pardon. I have written toe Sir Lewis Dives and Mr. Robert Longe, whoe if you please toe speake with [them] will be able toe assist you with some reasons for this shute of

'Your assured friend to serve you,

'NEWPORT,   'ED. BAYNTON.
this 26th of August, 1643.

'My sonne Rogers is heare with me, and if he may have his pardon, which Sir John Heale hath undertaken toe procure, we entend toe runn one fortune.'

Sir John Evelyn of Godstone, suspected of disaffection and accused of spreading scandalous reports against his leaders, was arrested about the same time, and kept in custody till September 1644 (C. J. iii. 217, 220, 640). Ludlow was thus the only representative of these original leaders who was still fighting for the cause in Wiltshire.

The siege of Wardour began in earnest about December 1643, and lasted about three months. Before the besiegers sprang their mine, and when they were preparing to storm, Sir Francis Doddington sent Ludlow a final summons, reminding him of the relation between their families, and urging him to spare further bloodshed by a timely surrender. Ludlow returned the following answer, printed at the time in the newspapers of both parties, and here from the Tanner MSS. in the Bodleian Library (lxii. p. 627).

'For the Right Worshipfull Sir Francis Doddington, the gentlemen and souldiers lying before Wardour Castle.

'SIR,

'As I may not ommitt my thankefull acknowledgment for the expression of your respects unto our family, soe may I not passe by the cleareing of mine innocency touching any offence committed against my leidge Soveraigne. I shall never seeke by-paths (by deserting my Saviour, who is the way, the truth, and the life) to attaine the haven of peace, and happynesse. Yet shall I not bee soe presumptuous upon the mercys of the Almighty, to draw downe his justice upon my head, for the guilt of so many men's blood, as are now with me, by an obstinate resolution to withstand all opposers without hopes of releife. If you shall thinke fitt therefore (according to the scope of my late discourse) to permitt that a messenger have free egresse and regresse unto our armies, by whome if I understand our condition to [be] soe helpelesse, as by you I am informed it is, I shall then ease you of a chardgeable and dangerous summer seidge, by proposeing suche tearmes, as to any indifferent man, shall seeme most reasonable. If soe be you shall continue to lend a deafe eare to this motion, I have heerein laboured to dischardge a good conscience, and doe assure my selfe (knoweing in whome I have trusted) that for all the blood that hath or shall bee spilt, either on your part in assaulting, or on ours in defending our lawfull rights, there shall bee a strict account requiered from you at the dreadfull day of judgement, without your serious and timely repentance.

'EDMUND LUDLOWE.

'WARDOUR CASTLE,
 this 13th of March, 1643.'

On March 18, 1644, Ludlow was forced to surrender, as the Castle had become utterly untenable. Mercurius Aulicus, after quoting the letter, thus comments on the surrender:—

' Master Ludlow left off preaching within four or five days, for when he saw the mine deprive him of his fortifications, he delivered up himselfe and all the garrison (75 persons) without so much as promise of quarter, with all the canon, arms, ammunition, baggage, and the Lord Arundel's plate, which it seems had not yet found the way from home. At the springing of the mine Captain Lister attempted to enter and lost 5 common soldiers, Col. Barnes lost 5 more by occasional shots ; which ten were all that were lost from the beginning of the siege. Captain Ludlow had more blown up at once, and the rest with himself are since brought prisoners to Oxford Castle.' (Aulicus, March 19, 1644.)

Ludlow was very civilly treated by Doddington after his surrender, though the conditions promised to his men were not fairly kept. Lord Arundel himself showed Ludlow much kindness, which the latter endeavoured to requite eight years later, by intervening on behalf of Arundel with the Parliament. This letter also is amongst the Tanner MSS. (liii. 192).

'MR. SPEAKER,
 ' When I had the honour of sitting with you in Parliament, a motion being made for the insertion of the Lord Arrundell of Wardour's estate

APP. II. into the Bill of Sale, I tooke the bouldnes to informe you of his timely
submission, of his fairer deportment ever since, and of his constant
endeavours to compound, which I was the rather induced to doe, from
the sence I had of the favour he intended mee upon the rendition of
Wardor Castle, when finding Sir Francis Dodington, who comanded
before that place, resolved to give me noe quarter, he procured a power
from Sir Ralph Hopton, who then comanded in cheife in the West, to
give me my life, in case Sir Francis Dodington should have persisted.
Att that time you were pleased not to expose his estate to sale, but by
a later addiccion you have ordered it to be sold, I dare not suppose,
but upon full consideracion of all circumstances, neither am I unacquainted with your pressing necessities for money, and of my duty
to acquiesce in your pleasure herein, yett upon the importunity of a
gentleman who is sent of purpose to Ireland by the Lord Arrundell to
desire [me to][1] lay thus much before you, I have presumed soe to doe,
for which I humbly begg your pardon, and desire the God of wisdome
to direct you in all your weighty affaires, subscribing myselfe,

'Mr. Speaker,

'Your most humble

'and faithfull Servant,

'DUBLIN,   'EDM. LUDLOWE.
3° *Januarii*, 1652.'

[*Endorsed*:—Lt.-Gen. Ludloe's lettre for the Lord Arundell, Jan. 3,
1652.]

Wardour Castle was the last fortress held by the Parliamentarians
in Wiltshire, which now passed entirely under the control of the
Royalists. Two months later however they once more gained a
footing there. Col. Edward Massey, after his successful defence of
Gloucester in Sept. 1643, had adopted a vigorous offensive policy
against the adjacent Royalist garrisons. During the winter of 1643-4
he captured a number of fortified houses in the neighbourhood of
Gloucester, and in May, 1644, succeeded by a sudden attack in re-
capturing Malmesbury. ('Ebenezer, a full and exact relation of the
severall remarkable and victorious proceedings of the ever renowned
Colonell Massey from May 7 to May 25, 1644,' reprinted in
Bibliotheca Gloucestrensis, pp. 325-337.) The following account
of this exploit is given by John Corbet, Massey's chaplain, in his
'Historicall Relation of the Military Government of Gloucester'
(ib. p. 98). Massey, after capturing Beverston Castle in Gloucester-

---

[1] [A hole in the MS. here.]

shire on the night of May 23, 1644, marched to Malmesbury and summoned it on the 24th.

'Whilst the horse faced the towne Colonell Massie sent in the summons, but the enemy put on the appearance of bravery, fired upon the horse, and Colonell Henry Howard governor of the garrison sent back a resolute answer. Thereupon our foot and artillery were brought up from Tedbury, and within two houres drawne into the suburbs and lower part of the towne. The foot broke their way through the houses till they came almost up to the workes, and the only place of entrance into the towne, which is built upon the levell of a rocke. Colonell Massie caused a blinde to be made crosse the street to bring up the ordnance, within carbine shot : when on the sudden the fancie of an alarm seized upon our men in the heate of the businesse, that the enemy were sallying out upon them, which was nothing so. This un-expected accident strucke those men that at other times would brave it in the face of an enemy, with such distraction and feare, that they all fled, and left their cannon in the open street. This meere conceite was like to overturne all : but they within observed not. After a while the souldiers recovered themselves, regained and kept their ground, and the governour resolved to storme the towne in three places at once. The severall parties were drawne out to the places of assault, but this designe miscarried through the mis-understanding of the signall. The parties returne unto the governour, who resolved to make the assault at breake of day in one place where himselfe kept the only passage into the town, having no draw-bridge at the entrance, but only a turn-pike, whereas the other parts were almost inaccessible, guarded by a steepe descent, and double channell round about. The houses within pistol shot of the workes were our maine advantage, by which meanes our men were brought safe under the shelter of their workes. And the gover-nour observing the late effects of a panick feare amongst his owne men, gave the charge that they should fall on all together with a sudden and confused noise, to amaze the enemy and disturbe the command of the officers. The forlorne hope advanced, seconded with a good reserve ; all put on together, came up to the turne-pike, and threw in granadoes, the enemy made many shots at randome, in the disadvantage of a rainy night, and their muskets lying wet on the workes. So that our men came all in a croude to the narrow passage, and thronged in, and not a man slaine or wounded in the storme. One only was killed the night before in helping to make the blinde. Colonell Howard was taken at the workes after three shots received in severall parts of his garment, each of which missed his body. An hundred musketiers were taken prisoners, many having escaped ; besides those of Beverston-Castle, who came hither for refuge the day before. This service was performed gallantly by our men, after three daies' continuall march.

Upon the first entrance Colonell Massie preserved the town from plunder, nor at any time did he suffer his souldiers to ransacke any place that he took by storme, giving this reason, that he could judge no part of England an enemie's countrey, nor an English town capable of devastation by English souldiers.'

On the receipt of the news of the capture, the House of Commons voted (May 31, 1644) ' that the town of Malmsbury and the Castle of Beverston, as to the government of them, shall be left wholly to the disposal of Colonel Massey' (C. J. iii. 511). Massey accordingly sent Col. Nicholas Devereux and his regiment to garrison Malmesbury, and appointed Col. Thomas Stephens governor of Beverston Castle.

During July Parliament passed two important ordinances concerning Wiltshire. The first passed on July 1, 1644, established what was known as ' The Western Association,' consisting of the counties of Wilts, Dorset, Somerset, Devon, and Cornwall, and the towns of Bristol, Exeter, and Poole, appointing committees in each to put in force the sequestration ordinances, and levy taxes. The second ordinance, passed on July 15, referred to Wiltshire alone, and appointed a local Committee with power to raise troops and money to maintain them. The preamble states :—

' Whereas the said County of Wilts and the inhabitants thereof, for the space of almost two years now last past, have lain under the intolerable pressures, taxes, impositions, and plunderings, of the enemy's forces by means whereof they are now in a very sad condition ; for remedy whereof there is great and urgent necessity that such a competent number of horse, foot, and arms should be forthwith raised, as may defend and preserve the said county, and maintain the garrison of Malmesbury,' &c. (L. J. vi. 612, 637 ; Husbands, Ordinances, folio, 1646, pp. 514, 526.)

Malmesbury was still maintained under the jurisdiction of Massey. Essex, on his march into the West in the summer of 1644, had made Massey Commander-in-chief of the Gloucestershire forces, and the Committee of Wilts also voted him the command of their troops (Cal. S. P., Dom., 1644, p. 478). Hence the conflict of jurisdictions between Massey and Waller to which Ludlow refers in his Memoirs (pp. 95, 101). On May 24, 1645, Massey was by another ordinance made Commander-in-chief of the forces of the Western Association, with the stipulation however that if Fairfax marched into the Western counties, Massey should be under his orders (ib. p. 652).

Personally none was more closely affected by this conflict than Ludlow himself. On his release from imprisonment he had accepted a commission as major and captain in Sir Arthur Haselrig's regiment of horse in Sir William Waller's army (May 10, 1644). Then on July 30, 1644, he had received a new commission as colonel of a regiment of horse in the pay of the Wiltshire Committee, and to form the nucleus of this regiment carried with him the troop he had raised for Haselrig's regiment. This commission was apparently from Waller, and the Committee of Wilts wished Ludlow to surrender it, and to take instead a commission from Essex which would have placed him under the orders of Massey. The situation was further complicated when Waller in August, 1644, was sent into the West with a body of cavalry to relieve Essex, and expected the Wiltshire horse to march with him (Cal. S. P., Dom., 1644, pp. 239, 343, 475, 478, 490, 501, 511). Moreover, while Ludlow seems to have been anxious to serve under Waller, his major, Francis Dowett or Duett, would only receive orders from the Wiltshire Committee.

Ludlow seems to have parted from Waller's army at the end of June, 1644. Immediately he arrived in Wiltshire he was summoned to relieve Major Wansey at Woodhouse, and was, as his own account in the Memoirs shows, completely routed by Sir Ralph Hopton's forces. The two Royalist accounts of this defeat which follow may be compared with Ludlow's narrative. Describing the march of the King's army into the West in July, 1644, Sir Edward Walker says :—

'At Bath . . . we refreshed our army a day and gave assistance to a party drawn out of Bristol under the command of Sir Francis Doddington, to regain a house of Mr. Arundel's called Woodhouse, near Frome, possessed by one Wansey, a person of equal quality with many of the rebels officers though lately a watchmaker in Warminster. And here it will be very pertinent to let you know that a little before this time, Ludlow the mock sheriff of Wilts, the two Pophams, Stroud, and others settled themselves as a committee at the Devizes, endeavouring to draw his Majesty's subjects from their due obedience ; and then placed this Wansey in Mr. Arundel's house. For regaining of which and prevention of their further growth, the Lord Hopton sent Sir Francis Doddington with some troops of horse and dragoons to quarter thereabouts. But the rebels grew so strong as they threatened his quarters ; upon intelligence whereof the Lord Hopton drew a greater strength from Bristol and joined with him ; resolving if the rebels failed to attempt his quarters, to be with them the next night at their head-quarters. But the rebels confident of their strength came to Warminster, and the next day being the 7th of July the scouts of both parties met and fought, which gave the alarm. The Lord Hopton presently advanced and charged the rebels ; whereupon they presently brake and ran so fast, as the Lord Hopton's horse, having marched all night, could not follow them ; yet Sir Francis Doddington's horse pursued them close, and had execution of them to Salisbury (full 16 miles) and through and beyond it 6 miles more. In this long pursuit he slew about 100, took as many more prisoners, besides 100 new pair of pistols, and about 40 musquets, and released divers countrymen the rebels had taken ; and so dispersed this growing body, as that of 300, not 40 got in to Southampton. Sir Francis having fought almost a summer's day, and chased them 22 miles, returned with his prisoners and arms. And now he had more leisure to prosecute his design of getting Woodhouse, which he had brought to good perfection by the time we came to Bath ; from whence his Majesty sent a party of foot, with two pieces of cannon to his assistance. Who, the besieged being obstinate, took it the next day by assault ; in which they slew about 20, and took their governor Wansey, and about 80 more prisoners. Sir Francis did not compliment, but used them as rebels and presently hung up about 14 of them, and could hardly be induced to spare the rest, who were at length sent prisoners to Bristol.' (See Edward Walker's Historical Discourses, 1705, p. 39.)

Mercurius Aulicus for Saturday, July 6, gives the following story :—

'To-day we must tell you of a better scouring yet, bestowed upon the Rebels by the noble Lord Hopton, who perceiving an inconvenience growing upon Wiltshire, through a New Committee which was then in rearing up, consisting of Captaine Ludlow the Mock Sheriffe of that County, the Two Popphams, Stroud, and one Bennet. These worthy Commissioners sat downe about the Devizes, and enticed the Country in, began (as the manner of that Faction is) to draw into an Assembly, and had put an obstinate fellow with some foot into Master Arundels house at Hornesham. For prevention whereof the Lord Hopton sent Sir Francis Doddington with a partee of horse and Dragoons to quarter about that house, and take what advantage he could upon the enemy on either hand. But the Rebels Committee grew so strong as they began to threaten Sir Francis his troops, who sending intelligence yesterday to Bristol, that the same night the Rebels resolved to advance upon him, the Lord Hopton thereupon marched instantly from Bristol, and by two of the clocke next morning came to his owne house at Wittham neare the Rebels Quarters; with intention if they came, to joyne both parties to repell them; but if they fail'd, not to faile to visit them next night at the Devizes. But the Rebels kept their word, and came yester night to Warminster, and this morning early both Scouts met and fought, which giving the Alarme, the Lord Hopton advanced towards them three miles east of Warminster, where he charged the Rebels with such skill and courage that they presently brake, and ranne so fast away, that his Lordships Horse (having marched all night) were too weary to follow them. Yet Sir Francis Doddington with his fresh Horse pursued them close, and had full execution on them from place to place till they came to Salisbury (16 long miles), followed them through Salisbury, and six miles farther, to the borders of Hampshire, all the way having slaughter upon them, killed betwixt 100 and sixescore, tooke above fourescore, released many Country-men whom these Rebels had seized on, and so dispersed all their body that there were but 37 left (of 350) which crept into Southampton. The Souldiers took above 100 paire of the Rebels new Pistols, 40 Muskets, 50 backe and brests, and pillage to a good value. Alexander Poppham, being hardly pressed, his horse fell with him in the street at Salisbury; and had he not worne a better head-peece than his owne, his braines had been dashed out: but his man so ready to horse him again, for his paines was taken with the horse that fell, and Pistols. Sir Francis Doddington having followed them 22 miles (farre enough for one day) returned backe to Stockton with the Armes and Prisoners.'

The defeat of Ludlow and Popham was necessarily followed by the capture of Woodhouse, which was taken by assault by Hopton's forces on July 17. According to Mercurius Aulicus, 14 of the garrison were killed and 87 taken prisoners (Mercurius Aulicus, July 25). The Parliamentary newspapers charged Sir Francis Doddington with cruelty to his prisoners, and the charge is repeated by Ludlow (Memoirs, p. 95; Diary of Nehemiah Wallington, ii. 224; Whitelocke, i. 284). The Royalist answer is given in Mercurius Aulicus for Aug. 11:—

'We must answer one particular wherein the Rebels have slaundered us three weekes together: for because the Lord Hopton lately tooke

Woodhouse (a rebellious garrison neare Hornesham in Wiltshire) they all cry out in print, that the bloudy Cavaliers cruelly murthered men, women, and children at Wood-house in Wiltshire, and hanged up some Clothiers, whom they found in that garrison, which is so pure a slaunder, that there was not one woman or child in that House ; and though the garrison was taken by assault, yet they all had quarter allowed them, except some Renegadoes, who formerly tooke pay for His Majesty at Bristol, and were now found in Armes rebelling against him.'

Of military movements in Wiltshire during the three months which followed Ludlow's flight to Southampton and the capture of Woodhouse there are few notices. Whitelock gives only a confused story (i. 277). Ludlow's re-entry and levying of contributions in Salisbury probably took place in August or September, 1644, as Waller reported to the Committee of Both Kingdoms on Sept. 7, 1644, that Ludlow was at Salisbury with three troops of horse. The capture of Lord Stourton's house and of Sir Ralph Hopton's house at Witham (mentioned in the Memoirs, p. 97) probably took place about this time. Massey reported also, on Sept. 5, that Royalist forces from Bath and Bristol had forced Col. Devereux to withdraw his garrison from the house of Lady Ayres at Chalfield in Wiltshire. When Waller arrived at Salisbury, on Sept. 10, on his march westwards to relieve Essex, Ludlow's three troops were absent (Cal. S. P., Dom., 1644, pp. 475, 479, 489).

In the autumn of 1644 the King, after forcing Essex's foot to surrender at Lostwithiel, slowly made his way back to Oxford. A map at p. 485 of Mr Gardiner's Great Civil War, vol. i, shews the route which he followed. Waller and Sir Arthur Haslerig with a small body of horse were charged by the Parliament to check his march. They were to be joined by Essex's horse under Sir William Balfour (which had escaped when the foot surrendered), and by the horse of Manchester's army. Manchester's whole army was to march west to give battle to the King before he could 'regain his circle of fortresses round Oxford' (ib. 495). Manchester however showed no zeal to advance westwards, and though he sent his horse as far forward as Salisbury, recalled them immediately to Marlborough (Cal. S. P., Dom., 1644–5, pp. 26, 29). Waller was obliged to fall back before the advance of the King's superior forces, and retreated from Shaftesbury where he had been at the beginning of

October into Wiltshire. On Oct. 10 he was at Winterbourne Stoke, where he halted four or five days. On Oct. 15 he retreated to Andover. His forces were weak in numbers, not more than 3,000 horse and dragoons, though twelve troops of Manchester's horse had then joined him. They were badly armed and badly clothed, and without foot unable to engage. 'You must not expect,' he wrote to the Committee, 'to hear we have done any service; the best we can hope for is to trouble and retard the enemy's march and make them keep close together. Should we engage the horse before your foot come up, and they miscarry, your foot would be all lost, and the King could go which way he pleased.' He complained bitterly that Ludlow and the Wiltshire regiment had not joined him (ib. pp. 31, 41, 47; cf. Ludlow's Memoirs, i. 101).

King Charles and his army arrived at Salisbury on Oct. 15. Whilst there he placed a garrison of 100 men under Col. Griffin in Longford House, and also established a temporary garrison at Wilton. By Goring's advice he resolved to fall upon Waller at Andover, and endeavour to destroy his forces before they joined Essex or Manchester. The attack took place on Oct. 18. Goring who commanded took eighty prisoners and drove Waller out of Andover, but the delay of Prince Maurice's foot prevented any completer success (Cal. S. P., Dom., 1644-5, pp. 46, 52, 57, 60; Diary of Richard Symonds, pp. 128-141; Sir Edward Walker's Historical Discourses, p. 106). Mercurius Aulicus for Oct. 12, 1644. gives the following account :—

'His Majesty leaving Somersetshire in so good condition advanced into Wiltshire (Sir William Waller, Balfoure, and the rest still retreating before him) and came into Salisbury on Tuesday last, whence the rebels made such haste that they left good store of their friends behind them in the towne which His Majesties forces seized on. . . .

'His Majesty stayed at Salisbury Tuesday night, Wednesday and Thursday, and on Friday advanced towards Andover in Hampshire where the rebels lay, with intention to stoppe his Majesties motion; somewhat short of Andover a forlorne hope being sent out, met with another of the rebells very neare their maine body; both charged and kept their ground, till two bodies of his Majesties horse came up and marched into the field where the rebels stood; at sight whereof the rebells forces began to fly out at the other end of Andover towne; yet made not so good speed but that his Majesties horse overtook them, and slashed them soundly, especially in a lane entring into the towne, where that body of rebells was routed and very good execution done upon them, persuing them through Andover a good way beyond, till the darke night stopped further persuit. Which done his Majesty marched into Andover and lay there all night.'

Ludlow and his Wiltshire horse joined the main body of the Parliamentary army just before the second battle of Newbury (Oct. 27), and after taking part in that battle were sent into Hampshire to take part in the siege of Basing House, where they remained from Nov. 5 to Nov. 13. They were then ordered back into Wiltshire (Memoirs, pp. 101–5). Towards the middle of November, Sir William Waller was ordered to send a party of horse to the relief of Taunton. This detachment, under the command of Major-General Holborne and Commissary-General Vandruske, marched about the end of November, and Ludlow with 200 of his regiment formed part of their force (ib. p. 107 ; Cal. S. P., Dom., 1644–5, pp. 102, 113–4, 124, 194, 196, 204, 227 ; Christy, Life of Shaftesbury, i. 72 ; English Historical Review, 1889, p. 521 ; Vicars, Burning Bush, pp. 77, 81). This service was successfully performed about the middle of December, and Ludlow then, contrary to the orders of the Committee of Both Kingdoms, left Holborne's forces, and returned to Salisbury.

During his absence on this expedition—and not during his absence at the siege of Basing as the Memoirs state (p. 107)—Major Wansey and Major Duett surprised Col. Cook at Salisbury. An account of this incident is given by Vicars, Burning Bush, p. 74. The following extract is from 'The Scottish Dove,' Dec. 6–13, 1644 :—

' We had Intelligence come on Saturday night from Salisbury, that Col. Norton, Major Duet, Major Wansey, etc. fell upon two Regiments of the Enemies Horse that were quartered in Salisbury, and put them to great disorder, so that some fled away, some got into the Close near the Cathedral, and barricado'd the gate ; but our souldiers fired the gate, and forced in upon the Enemy, and took Sir Francis Cook, Lieutenant-Col. Hook, and a Captain, two Cornets, with divers other Officers ; divers were slain of the Enemy, and not above 4 men on our side ; there was of the Enemy many prisoners taken, and eight score horse, and odde, besides there was taken divers arms and other ammunition.'

Immediately after Ludlow's return from the West, his regiment was surprised in its quarters at Salisbury, and routed with great loss. A Parliamentary paper, the 'Perfect Diurnal' for Jan. 6–13, 1645, states that this surprise happened 'on Friday last,' i. e. Jan. 3, and that 'neere two hundred' of the regiment were lost. 'Mercurius Aulicus' represents the surprise as occurring on Monday, Dec. 31, and gives an account of the incident under Jan. 4, 1645. A Parliamentary garrison near Chippenham had just been taken by the Royalists.

'Now because this house was taken in Wiltshire M. Ludlow thinks himself concerned in honour, and therefore he would needs revenge himself on His Majesties horse-quarters at Uphaven in this County, to which place M. Ludlow came with his Regiment of horse (out of which he spared forescore on Saturday was seavenight, for so many were then taken from him at Wilsford near Amesbury by Col. Long, High Sheriff of Wiltshire) and now he hoped to recruit himself on this quarter of Colonel Anderson's, where M. Ludlow beat in the outguards, but found the Colonel in such readines drawne up on the other side of the towne, that his worship was beaten back, and persued by Colonel Anderson, who took one Captain, one Coronet with other Prisoners. Sir Marmaduke Langdaile having the Alarum in his Quarters, and being in great readinesse drew out after the Rebells, whom as soon as he understood to be return'd to Salisbury he resolved to fall into their Quarters, and performed it so gallantly, that he beat them all up, took almost all their Horses, and there being some Foot retyred into the belfrey in Salisbury Close, he sent for Foot from Longford house and forced them thence, where they purposed to make a garrison. He took in all five Captains, besides diverse other Officers, fourscore Prisoners, 150 Horses and Armes, some Powder and Match, and three Colours. M. Ludlow himself escaped very narrowly, though very much hurt, his whole Regiment absolutely Routed. Those few which escaped fled into Deane house (a garrison of the Rebels) but the Lord Goring sending some Horse after them found the fugitives gone thence, and the garrison also quitted, the Rebels labouring to reach Southampton, to which place M. Ludlow was chased once this yeare before.' (Mercurius Aulicus, Jan. 4, 164⅘; see also Jan. 8.)

A new commander now appears on the scene. Langdale's cavalry seems to have been part of a force under General Goring, who was advancing from the West with the intention of penetrating into Sussex. On Dec. 29 Goring was at Calne, on Jan. 9 at Farnham, on Jan. 22 at Salisbury. He had been granted a commission,

Dec. 21, 1644, as Lieutenant-General of Hampshire, Sussex, Surrey, and Kent, and hoped to renew with better fortune Hopton's attack in the winter of 1644, but could penetrate no further than Farnham.

'Some attempts he made in the beginning upon Christ Church in Hampshire, a little unfortified fisher town, yet was beaten off with loss ; so that he was forced to retire to Salisbury, where his horse committed such horrid outrages and barbarities as they had done in Hampshire, without distinction of friends or foes, that those parts (which before were well devoted to the King), worried by oppression, wished for the access of any forces to redeem them.' (Clarendon, Rebellion, ix. 8.)

Goring returned shortly to besiege Taunton, leaving Wiltshire to the local Royalist commanders.

The winter of 1644–5 was marked by a great increase in the number of garrisons in Wiltshire. Longford House, it has been noted, was garrisoned in October by the Royalists. On Nov. 2, the Committee of Both Kingdoms writes 'that the enemy is fortifying two houses near Salisbury, viz. at Wilton and Goldborne, which if they be perfected will be of great prejudice to those parts' (Cal. S. P., Dom., 1644–5, p. 92). Highworth was made a garrison about December, and the castle of Devizes strengthened and permanently occupied. 'We see,' writes the Parliament Scout for Dec. 20, 'they intend to reduce the West into the state of the Netherlands, and have a garrison at every five miles, and not to fight so often' (quoted by Waylen, History of Marlborough, p. 213).

The King sent an able engineer, Sir Charles Lloyd, to take command of the garrison established at Devizes, to superintend and fortify the minor local posts, and to decide which were to be abandoned and which maintained. Lloyd's military experience was to supplement the zeal of the nominal Sheriff, Sir James Long. On the Parliamentary side Malmesbury was the chief garrison, and its governor, Col. Nicholas Devereux, was the most experienced leader. Ludlow, like Long, was nominally Sheriff, and commanded a regiment of cavalry.

Like the Royalists, the Parliamentarians adopted the plan of establishing numerous small garrisons. Major Duett about December garrisoned Sir John Evelyn's house at West Deane (Cal. S. P., Dom., 1644–5, p. 194). A little later Mr. Blake's house at

Pinnel near Calne was garrisoned by a detachment of Parliamentarians from Malmesbury. Lacock House was occupied about the same time. Finally, the governor of Malmesbury erected a garrison at Rowden House between Malmesbury and Devizes.

But the Parliamentary forces were far too weak to hold so many posts, and the attempt to do so caused serious loss. The first to fall was Pinnel House, taken on Dec. 28, of whose capture Mercurius Aulicus gives this account :—

Friday, January 3. 'Besides this, M. Massie hath more affliction on the other side of his Dominions ; for his Deputies at Malmsbury lately made a garrison at Mr. Blake's House at Pinnel neare Calne in Wiltshire, betwixt Chippenham and the Devizes ; the House is pretty strong and Moated about, whereof the Lord Goring having intelligence, sent some force against it on Saturday last (Decemb. 28) ; at first Summons the Rebels denied to surrender, till they saw His Majesties Forces begin to fall on, and then they presently submitted themselves prisoners at mercy, and accordingly had their lives given them ; in this House were taken 59 prisoners, more Armes than Men, whereof 60 good Firelocks, 6 Horses, the other were fled that morning. When the Scoutmaster Generall (who was sent to take possession) entred the House, the Rebels begged they might not be stripped naked, he bid them look out and they might see His Majesties Souldiers all new cloath'd, so as they would not take the Rebels cloaths if offered to them ; nor was there so much as one Rebell suffered to be plundred, though they were not promised anything but their lives ; who upon their comming forth, said, "they never meant to keep it against the King's Forces"; that is, they would keep it no longer than they were able.'

On Jan. 4, Sir Charles Lloyd, who seems to have been instructed by Prince Rupert to garrison Mr. Blake's house if possible, wrote to the Prince :—

'The howse I am not able to maintaine by reason I have not wherewithall ; therefore this night next after your letter I shall give order. for the demolishing of it, which I believe will be rendred unserviceable by tomorrowe at night.'

In a second letter, dated Jan. 8, he added :—

'Blagg's house I have made unhabitable, and have drayned the moate. I could not burne it because it would have incensed the country against me.'

In both letters he complains of want of ammunition :—

'The Sheriff is come whose only regiment I have, and that patched from many runaways from the discontented troops. The Sheriff's expect noe command from me by his privilidge, and the officers unwillinge to command them lest they should disband, as they have done.'

He begged Prince Rupert to allow him the disposal of Colonel Howard's regiment which Lord Goring had offered him, and hoped also to be able to raise two or three troops :—

' The High Sheriff hath been out with me about Malmesbury, which I find inconsiderable in horse. Indeed I shall humbly desire your Highness to thanke him for his care, for hee takes infinite paines in shewinge himselfe obedient to your commands, and his willingness points at a good omen to my imployment here.' (Transcripts of Prince Rupert's correspondence in the possession of the editor.)

A month later Lacock House and Rowdon House were also captured by the Royalists. Aulicus for Feb. 15, 1645, thus relates the manner of their taking :—

' This morning Sir Charles Lloyd sent an Expresse of the taking it, the manner and occasion whereof was thus. About tenne daies since, the Lord Hopton sent his Regiment from Bath (with his Lieutenant Colonell Bovell) to enquarter and make a garrison of the Lady Stapylton's house at Lacocke, three miles from Chippenham in Wiltshire. Upon their approach they found the House prepossessed by the Rebells, which made them march to His Majesties garrison at the Devizes, where Sir Charles Lloyd governour of the Towne, and Colonell James Long High Sheriffe of that County, were ready to assist them by forcing the Rebels from Lacocke. Before they came to Chippenham they understood the Rebels had removed from Lacocke to a more convenient House at Rowdon, (belonging to Sir Edward Hungerford) within halfe a mile of Chippenham, some of the Rebels being then in Chippenham. They sent Captain Web with a forlorn hope into Chippenham, who tooke Ludford (the governour of Rowdon House) with 8 more prisoners in the Towne. This done Sir Charles Lloyd and Colonell Long drew before Rowdon House, (Sir Charles had a good strength of foote there, and Colonell Long had his owne Regiment, 300 good horse), and by a Trumpet summoned it for his Majesty. The Rebels refused to submit, being 'twixt 2 and 300 foote ; therefore they sent to the Lord Hopton for some Cannon which were presently brought to them by Sir Francis Dodington. But after the House had beene two daies beseiged, Colonell Stephens the Mock Sheriffe of Gloucestershire came from Malmesbury with 120 horse to their releise, and having made his way through the Out-guards got into the House with ammunition and some provision ; but before he and his Rebels could get off againe, Colonell Long's horse, and L.-Col. Tirwhit with foot charged them so gallantly, that they beate the Rebels backe into

the House, killed some of them, and hurt more, after which they fell APP. II.
upon 40 musquettiers, which came out to secure the horse's passage,
seventeene whereof they killed. Sir Bernard Asteley was now come
with 100 horse and 300 foote from Cirencester, and Sir Francis
Dodington with the Cannon from Bristoll, whereupon they summoned
it againe, but the Rebels still stood out, till this day about nine of
clocke in the morning, and then they submitted themselves prisoners,
being betwixt 3 and 400 horse and foot, whereof 40 Officers, viz.
Colonell Stephens, 6 Captaines, Captaine Ludford, Capt. Clifford,
Capt. Seaman, Capt. Scarborough, Capt. Laurence, and Capt. Stamford,
who is both Marshall and Scoutmaster to their Garrison at Malmesbury;
7 Lieutenants of horse and foote, Lieutenant Goodwin, Lieutenant
Smith, Lieutenant Davies, (of horse), Lieutenant Pudsey, Lieutenant
White, Lieutenant Brotman, Lieutenant Davies (of foote); 5 Co-
ronets, Coronet Eden, Coronet Miller, Coronet Crowder, Coronet
Shot, Coronet Downes; 6 Ensignes, Ensigne Thornbury, Ensigne
Cary, Ensigne Symons, Ensigne Massinger, Ensigne Palmer; besides
5 Quartermasters, 8 Corporals, 2 Gentlemen Reformadoes, (Master
Hine and Master Thwait) with 317 common souldiers, 120 horses,
and almost 400 armes. Not any one Rebell was plundered to
the value of a penny, (though Prisoners at mercy), and when it was
pressed to them, that some of His Majesties souldiers (there present)
had beene stript naked when by them taken prisoners; an impudent-
ingratefull Rebell answered, That the Cavaliers often had no power
to plunder them, for God would not suffer it. Nay, we can assure
you, that His Majesties Forces found in this House many bullets beaten
into slugs, with horse haires drawne through them, (we need not tell
the mischeivous reason) one of which presently cost gallant Captaine
Sanders his life, though shot in the foot onely. Colonell Lloyd hath
made this House unfit for another garrison, but Lacocke is now possessed
by Lieutenant Colonell Bovell with the Lord Hopton's Regiment.
Colonell Stephens was asked why he rebelled against his King, since
the hand of God appeared evidently for His Majesty, which had brought
him through so many difficulties from a handfull of men at first, to have
so many Townes and Armies? Master Stephens answered, that 'twas
not so, " For (said he) almost all the Gentry were ever for the King." '

It is sufficiently evident that the local forces alone would never
have won Wiltshire for the Parliament. Its conquest was due to
the aid of the Parliament's main armies, and the general success of
the cause elsewhere.

At the end of January, 1645, it was resolved to send Waller to the
West to relieve Taunton and other garrisons; the difficulty however
was to find sufficient troops for the purpose. Those men whom

Waller had at Farnham wanted shoes, arms, and other necessaries, before they could take the field. About Feb. 12 came the news of the capture of the outworks of Weymouth, and orders were immediately sent to Waller to march at once ' to countenance and encourage the garrisons in the west,' with all his forces if possible, but if necessary with the horse alone (Feb. 13, C. J. iv. 46; cf. Portland MSS. i. 208). On Feb. 18, the Commons angrily demanded why he had not yet marched. The reason for this delay was the mutinous conduct of Waller's soldiers (Whitelock, Memorials, ed. 1853, i. 389 ; Cal. S. P., Dom., 1644–5, pp. 303, 307). Waller however started and got as far as Petersfield (Feb. 17), but as Goring was advancing to meet Waller, the Committee of Both Kingdoms ordered him to advance no further. On Feb. 27, Cromwell and his regiment were ordered to join Waller, ' to go with him upon this expedition into the West for relief of Melcombe and the garrisons and places adjacent, and for preventing and breaking the enemy's levies and recruits.' (C. J. iv. 63 ; Cal. S. P., Dom., 1644–5, p. 334.)

According to Whitelock, Waller's force was raised by this to about 5,000 horse and dragoons (Memorials, i. 401).

At the outset this expedition was very successful. An attempt of the governor of Winchester to beat up Waller's quarters was defeated with loss. Lord Percy and thirty prisoners were taken at Andover a few days later (Whitelock, i. 402, 406). A greater success was the capture of Col. Sir James Long's regiment.

' SIR,

' These lines are to certify you that, upon intelligence that Colonel Long lay with his regiment about the Lavingtons, I marched from Andover, on Monday last, to Amesbury, and there refreshing my troops till midnight, I advanced from thence in three parties : the first, commanded by General Cromwell, fell in between those quarters and the Devizes ; the second, commanded by Sir Hardress Waller, fell in at Trowbridge, to cut off their retreat between Bath and those parts ; with the third I fell in at Lavington. It was my fortune to find an empty form, the enemy being drawn off to Westbury and Steeple Ashton ; but the rest had better fortune, and in the end I had my share too. Cromwell lighted upon two troops at Poterne, Sir Hardress Waller upon the rest of regiment at Westbury and Steeple Ashton ; who beat the enemy in upon my quarter, where my regiment lighted upon them. Of 400 horse there escaped not 30. The Colonel and most of the officers, with 300 soldiers taken prisoners, with about 340 horses and good store of arms. Blessed be the Lord for this success, which I hope will be the earnest of a further mercy. I was inforced to refresh our horse here, after this toilsome march and service in the worst ways and basest weather that ever I saw. I am this day marching towards Holborne to join with them, so soon as possibly I can. I have no more to add but that I am etc.,

'WILLIAM WALLER [1].

'WEST LAVINGTON,
  13 *March* 164⅘.'

Waller and Cromwell joined Col. Holborne, and other local Parliamentary forces in Dorsetshire, but they were not strong enough to effect anything considerable against Goring's superior strength. The details of the expedition are vague (Whitelock, i. 411, 412; Cal. S. P., Dom., 1644-5, pp. 376, 384, 393; Cal. Clarendon MSS. i. 259-263; Mercurius Aulicus, April 11, 12, 19; Gardiner, Great Civil War, ii. 137; Sanford, Studies and Illustrations, pp. 618-622). Goring's troops were successful in several skirmishes, though as usual the Royalist newspapers greatly exaggerated these small successes. One of these was the surprise of a part of Col. Popham's regiment, on the borders of Wiltshire (Mercurius Aulicus, April 12, 1645).

By the 9th of April, Waller and Cromwell were back at Salisbury, expecting to be attacked by the combined forces of Goring, Sir Richard Greenville, and possibly Prince Rupert. Cromwell wrote to Fairfax on the night of the 9th of April, pressing for reinforcements :—

'Send us with all speed such assistance to Salisbury as may enable us to keep the field and repel the enemy, if God assist us : at least to secure and countenance us so, that we be not put to the shame and hazard of a retreat; which will lose the Parliament many friends in these parts, who will think themselves abandoned on our departure from them. Sir, I beseech you send what horse and foot you can spare towards Salisbury, by way of Kingscleere, with what convenient expedition may be.' (Carlyle's Cromwell, Letter xxiv.)

The same night Cromwell wrote to Col. Whalley :—

SIR,
    I desire you to be with all my troops and Colonel Fiennes his

[1] Sanford, Studies and Illustrations of the Great Rebellion, p. 616.

troops also at Wilton at a rendezvous by break of day tomorrow morning, for we hear the enemy hath a design upon our quarters tomorrow morning.

> 'Sir, I am your cousin and servant,
>
> 'OLIVER CROMWELL [1].
>
> 'SARUM,
> *Wednesday night at* 12 *o'clock.*'

Goring was anxious enough to bring Waller to a battle, but he was summoned back to besiege Taunton by the council of Prince Charles, and when the Committee of Both Kingdoms discovered Goring's retreat, Waller's little army was broken up, the best part of it being ordered to Reading to be incorporated in the New Model (Cal. S. P., Dom., 1644–5, pp. 399, 415).

Fairfax, after defeating the King at Naseby on June 14, and re-capturing Leicester four days later, turned to the south-west to relieve Taunton and fight Goring and the King's western army, marching through part of Wiltshire on his way.

'On Friday, June 27,' records Sprigge, 'the army marched to Wanburrow, and on the way made an halt, and drew up before High-worth garrison, (being a church fortified by a line and bulwarks) summoned the place, Major Hen the governor refused to yield : they planted their ordnance, men were designed to storm, who being ready to fall on, he took down his bloody colours, and sounded a parley and yielded upon quarter. The soldiers had good booty in the church, took seventy prisoners and eighty arms. The place standing convenient in a line for the garrison of Malmesbury, the general appointed the governor of Malmesbury to continue the place a garrison, for the better enlarging the Parliament's quarters.' (Anglia Rediviva, ed. 1854, p. 60.)

Vicars adds that the Royalists lost Col. Sir Thomas Nott, who was killed in attempting to defend the bridge at the end of the town (Burning Bush, p. 180). Fairfax then marched south, by Marl-borough, Almsbury, and Burchalk, to Blandford in Dorsetshire, leaving the Wiltshire Parliamentarians to make head as best as they could against the Royalists and the Clubmen. Both were very active. Major Duet with a party from Devizes surprised and captured some stragglers who stayed behind the army in Marlborough.

During his passage through Wiltshire and Dorsetshire, Fairfax

---

[1] Sanford, p. 623.

came into collision with the 'Clubmen' who were very numerous in those two counties.

'They pretend only,' wrote Fairfax to the Parliament on July 3, 'the defence of themselves from plunder, but not to side either with the King's forces or the Parliament's but to give free quarter to both. The heads of them all are so far as I can learn such as have been in actual service in the King's army, or those that are known favourers of that party ; nay, some having commands at the present with the King.'

He proceeded to give an account of their organisation. They had appointed treasurers, and issued warrants for raising money :—

'They enlist themselves under several officers, and meet daily in great bodies at the rendezvous, and boast they can have 20,000 men at 24 hours' warning. For assembling them together, their heads send out to several towns, and by ringing of bells and sending of posts from one rendezvous to another in the several towns and hundreds they draw into great bodies; and for distinction of themselves from other men, they wear white ribbons, to show, as they say, they are desirous of peace. They meet with drums, flying colours ; and for arms they have muskets . . . fowling pieces, pikes, halberts, great clubs, and such like.'

Their profession of neutrality was accompanied by attempts to mediate between the two parties :—

'They take upon them to interpose between the garrisons on either side ; and when any of their forces meet in places where they have sufficient power, as Salisbury and the like, they will not suffer them to fight, but make them drink together, and so make them depart to their several garrisons.'

On June 13, 1645, the heads of the Clubmen had met at Salisbury the commanders of the two adjacent garrisons, and had arranged a treaty for the peace of the county and the maintenance of those garrisons till the petitions of the Clubmen had been answered by King and Parliament; their leaders undertook to pay £50 a week to the Parliamentary garrison at Fallersdown (or Falston) House, and a similar sum to the Royalist garrison at Langford House. In spite of this ostensible neutrality Fairfax regarded them as inclined to the Royalists :—

'They have come into our horse-quarters, and steal horses where they find them at grass, and carry them into the woods. They will obey no warrants, no further than they are compelled, for sending in of provisions for the army, or draughts for the carriages, in these two counties. They are abundantly more affected to the enemy than the Parliament, and publicly declare whatsoever party falls on them they will join with the other; and those of the inhabitants of these counties who are really affected to the Parliament, that do not join with them, are daily threatened by them and suspect the issue of it will be very mischievous.'

'For the present,' he concludes, 'I shall offer to your Lordships the commanding of Colonel Fiennes's and Colonel Norton's regiments of horse into these parts; who with the assistance of Colonel Ludlow, Sheriff of Wilts, and the garrisons in these parts may be able, at least, to prevent them from drawing into any great bodies to the disturbance of the country.' (Sprigge, p. 61; L. J. vii. 484; Old Parliamentary History, xiv. 10-20.)

Fairfax's subsequent dealings with the Clubmen of Dorsetshire and Somersetshire are recorded at length by Sprigge. Those of Wiltshire, who were in close alliance with the Clubmen of the other two counties, gave less trouble, and were reduced to order in the same way and at the same time (Sprigge, pp. 62-66, 74, 83, 86-91).

Save for a few skirmishes, duly recorded in the newspapers of the two parties, the next few weeks were barren of events in Wiltshire. The most important incident was the capture of Chippenham by Sir James Long, which is thus recorded in Mercurius Aulicus :—

'Tuesday, August 12. Colonell James Long (Sheriffe of Wiltshire) having borrowed of Sir Charles Lloyd (Governour of Devizes) 50 Foote and a Troope of Horse, marched with Major Dowet to Lacock to consult with the Governour Lieutenant Colonell Bovel (Lieutenant Colonell to the Lord Hopton) about the surprizall of Chippenham. They resolved to give Chippenham a sound alarme, and as that was answered to proceed farther. For which purpose Lieutenant Colonell Bovel drew out 20 horse under Major Cooke, and 40 bold musketteers, before whom he himselfe marched on foot, protesting not to ride till he had horsed his men on the Rebels. With this Party (the retreat being secured) they advanced neare Chippenham, where taking a prisoner they understood the workes were but slenderly manned, and the Rebels' Horse being newly gone forth, they resolved to fall on, which Major Dowet did with great courage, and Captain Williams of the Devises with 20 foot; after which Col. Long and Major Cook joyning with Lieutenant Col. Bovell (with his foote) fell on where there were two brest workes, the uttermost of which had a narrow Advenue, the inner had no entrance at all; the first worke was soone passed, and whiles Lieut. Colon. Bovell most gallantly possessed himselfe of the houses next the worke, Colonell Long with the Horse fired pistols over the worke, some horse found meanes to get up a banke, whence they rode on top of the workes, and leapt into the Towne, charging into the market place. There was very sharp service at the turne-pike, where Major Dowet with his horse showed much courage, charging up so stoutly that at last he forced the Rebels thence and got the Turn-pike. The Rebels now hearing strange Trumpets in the Town, shewed more courage then before, for they rallied foure times, and made a street good almost an houre : in attempting whereof Coronet Dowet (Major Dowet's Brother) received two shots and his horse three, the Coronet (a couragious young man) is since dead with three common souldiers, but (which is strange) not any Officer or Souldier besides either shot or wounded, onely Major Dowet shot in the collar of his dublet, and the cheeke of his Caske shot off. In fine (without further losse or hurt) those Rebels in the streete were killed, taken, or drowned, and the Towne wholly masterd ; wherein they tooke Lieutenant Colonell William Eyres, 2 Captaines in charge, 2 Lieutenants, 2 Ensignes, divers inferior Officers, and 80 prisoners besides, the rest escaped away in the darke (there were 240 of Massey's old foot in the Towne, as his 8 drummers now prisoners confesse) who left behind all their Armes which were betwixt 2 and 300 very good muskets and firelockes, a great quantity of Ammunition, many granadoes and firepikes, with 30 horse ; all which these gallant Gentlemen brought safe along with them, having killed the Rebels' Marshall, 1 Sergeant and 10 common Souldiers, besides many drowned ; the Inhabitants of the Towne not loosing the value of sixpence, though taken by assault.

' Since this taking Chippenham, Sir Charles Lloyd, Colonell Long, and Major Dowet marcht from the Devizes with 100 Horse and 20 Dragoones, and hearing that 300 of the Rebels' Horse and 60 Dragoones (commanded by one Martin) were refreshing themselves in Auburne, they resolved to fall upon them. For which purpose they disposed themselves into 4 parties, Major Dowet commanded the forlorne hope (the Officers were Reformadoes except 4 of Sir Charles Lloyd's Captaines) who without any alarme fell in among the Rebels, and cleered the Towne ; the Major and all other Officers did their parts gallantly, and had taken 60 prisoners : but some Common Souldiers in the Reserve dispersing themselves to plunder among the Rebels, gave the Rebels time to rally, and fall on with much advantage while the Souldiers were thus scattered. Yet after some skirmishing (with losse of 4 men whom they tooke prisoners) the Rebels were all beaten quite out of the Towne, flying severall wayes ; but execution was not persued, for the prisoners confessed that Fincher (the Rebels' Quartermaster Generall) was at hand with 500 fresh Horse to releive them ; so as they timely retreated, having 18 long miles home to the Devizes, where they came safe with 17 prisoners, whereof 2 were Lieutenants, divers good horses taken, but especially the Dragoones exchanged their tyred jades for the Rebels' best horses.'

On September 13, 1645, after the storming of Bristol, Fairfax called a council of war to advise as to the next movements of his army. It was there decided that instead of marching further west in order to relieve Plymouth detachments should be sent eastwards,

'to clear those garrisons that did interpose between the West and London; which latter was very necessary, for that if those garrisons were not reduced they would hinder correspondency between London and the army, except at high rates of very excessive trouble and charge to the army by convoys upon every occasion.'

Accordingly Col. Rainsborough with three regiments was detached to reduce Berkeley Castle, whilst Cromwell and four regiments marched against Devizes. The castle of Devizes was strongly fortified, and governed by one of the King's best engineers, Sir Charles Lloyd. Nevertheless, it only held out for a week, and surrendered on Sept. 23. According to Sprigge's view the cause of the collapse of the defence was the accuracy of the artillery fire of the besiegers. A second authority asserts that the governor surrendered before it was necessary, in order to retain the plunder he had accumulated (Sprigge, pp. 132–135; Vicars, Burning Bush, p. 276; Walker, Historical Discourses, p. 142; Cal. S. P., Dom., 1645–7, p. 180; 'A letter concerning the Storming of Devizes,' 4to, 1645, by Sam. Bedford, British Museum E. 303 (2); Waylen, History of Devizes, 1839, pp. 140–147; Military Memoir of John Gwynne, 1822, pp. 38, 64).

Immediately after the surrender of Devizes, Cromwell sent Col. Pickering and two regiments to invest Laycock House. The governor, Col. Bovell, seeing no prospect of successful resistance, at once yielded and received good terms (Sept. 24; Sprigge, p. 135). On Oct. 8, Winchester after six days' siege surrendered to Cromwell, and on Oct. 14 he took Basing House by storm. From Basing Cromwell marched to Langford House.

'I hope,' he wrote to Fairfax, 'the work will not be long. If it should, I will rather leave a small part of the foot (if horse will not be sufficient to take it in) than be deterred from obeying such commands as I shall receive.'

But the governor, Sir Bartholomew Pell, surrendered at once, and on Oct. 18 the last Royalist garrison in Wiltshire was evacuated. Cromwell was now able to rejoin Fairfax, which he effected on Oct. 24. APP. II.

· 'There was now,' says Sprigge, 'no garrison in the way between Exeter and London to intercept the passage, so that a single man might travel without any fear of the enemy.'

The only Royalist garrisons which could still disturb the peace of Wiltshire, or levy contributions there, were those on the borders of Berkshire, such as Farringdon, Donnington Castle, Radcote, and Oxford, where the bulk of the King's forces were quartered (Sprigge, pp. 156–7 ; Carlyle's Cromwell, Letters xxxiv, xxxv). In a skirmish with a party from one of these garrisons, Major Duett was killed, he having deserted from Ludlow's regiment in the spring of this year. The governor of Malmesbury's account of his death follows.

COLONEL NICHOLAS DEVEREUX TO WILLIAM LENTHALL.

[1645, November 25.]—'The County of Wilts being late freed of the enemies' garrisons, I conceived it most advantageous to the State's service to place such forces as I have under command in the securest holds next adjacent unto the enemy who are powerful at Farrington and Radcourt, to prevent their incursions on these parts of Wilts. On Thursday last I sent a party of foot to Lechlade, which is near both their garrisons, whereunto were near quartered some Gloucester horse by agreement between Colonel Morgan and myself. Yesterday morning there came out a party of 30 horse from Radcourt to Lechlade to prevent us from fortifying there. Captain William Moore, whom I sent thither to command that party, and some horse of Gloucester received them, and in the dispute which was but short, only Captain Aytwood on the enemies' side was shot through the thigh, whereupon they retreated calling our party damned rogues, &c., promising also to return soon with a greater party. The same night at 7 of the clock Major Duett with 120 horse and 100 foot went thither from Farrington to surprise—if he could—our party of foot ; but our sentries firing at them gave the alarm to our foot. Whereupon Captain Moore drew out to a wall 60 musqueteers, who flanked the enemy as they came into Lechlade, and after an hour and a half's hot dispute betwixt them and the enemy, they repelled them out of the town, killing on the place six of them. Within half an hour after, the Gloucester horse taking the alarm came into Lechlade, whence both horse and foot pursued the enemy, and close under Radcourt wall they encountered each other, where our forces killed of the enemy Major Duett . . . and twenty more upon the place, took 30 prisoners, whereof five of the King's life guard, one cornet, 26 horse, and about 60 fire-arms. In this accident we lost not one man, only two hurt, not mortally, I hope. Shall send up by Wednesday a most malevolent man, one Lieutenant-Colonel Nott, who hath been as mischievous in his actions as Duett. . . . He, as I am persuaded, drew the King's forces into our quarters at Cricklade, where we lately lost 40 horse. . . . We have concluded to place another garrison betwixt Farrington and Marlborough, where most of the remainder of the horse and foot of Wilts shall quarter this winter to wait on the Far-rington forces, as they come abroad.' (Report on the MSS. of the Duke of Portland, i. 316.)

In spite of all these successes it was still some time before Wiltshire was freed from the burdens of war. A certain number of posts were still garrisoned by the Parliament. Such were Malmesbury, Langford House, Highworth, and probably some others. On Nov. 6, 1645, the Committee of Both Kingdoms re-quired the Wiltshire Committee to certify the number of garrisons still maintained in that county, but their answer is not preserved (Cal. S. P., Dom., 1645-7, p. 219). Through the winter of 1645-6 Fairfax's army lay between Wiltshire and the King's forces in the West, whilst Col. Whalley and a force of cavalry lay near Oxford with orders to prevent the King's horse from falling on Fairfax's rear or making forays into neighbouring counties (ibid. pp. 247, 251, 260, 262, 316, 317, 325; Sprigge, pp. 174, 209, 189). Whalley's protection was not altogether effective. Under Dec. 24, 1645, Whitelock notes that 'a party from Farringdon surprised some countrymen as they were choosing a new burgess for Calne in Wilts' (Memorials, i. 550). In January a more serious inroad was made by a body of horse under Sir John Camsfield. Their exploits are recorded in Mercurius Academicus for Jan. 22, 1646:—

'Our Oxford Horse marched hence on Monday, and in their journey met with a very convenient Party of the Rebels in Wiltshire, where after a short dispute, they took Men, Horse, Armes, and Am-munition; and to assure you it is true, here follow the words of the Expresse which brought it.

'Sir, Yesterday morning Sir John Camsfield came hither with a gallant Party of Horse, unto whom I joyned neer 200 of this Garrison, and about one of the clock in the after-noone of the same day, he marched to Ogborne in Wiltshire, where intending to quarter that night, App. II. the Quartermaster of my Regiment of Horse pursued a horseman of the Enemies, and taking him, brought him to Sir John Camsfield, who discovered that the enemy had drawn into Marleborough an houre or two before, with three Troopes of Horse, and 150 Foot, intending to Garrison there, upon which intelligence, Sir John Camsfield marched thither about eight of the clock that night, and with his Forlorne fell into the Towne, and after with the whole body of Horse, kill'd seven of their Foot-Souldiers that gave fire from the Maine-guard, beat the rest of the Foot into the Church, took most of their Horse, and thirty Prisoners, whereof Colonell Ayres Governor of the Devizes, Goddard a Committee man, and Captain Whyte Commissary Generall, with three or foure Officers more are the Principall. Which done, having summon'd them in the Church, they denied to render themselves ; but about two or three houres afterwards desired Parlee, and presently yielded themselves with condition for their lives and to March away without Ammunition or Armes to Malmesbury, which was granted, they being in number about 50 common men, a Captain and a Sergeant, the rest are all dissipated and taken. Colonell Devereux was likewise in the towne, and very hardly escaped on foot out of a back-dore. The Prisoners are all with mee, besides others taken the night before at Pidlington, who were to have met these Horse and Foot at Marleborough, and were beaten up by Colonell Philips and Major Foil, who drew from hence, and took 31 Horses and eight Prisoners, and came in within an houre after Sir John Camsfield was upon his March, so that I hope we have put them by for a while for making a Garrison there, which fell out very happily for the preservation of the Country. No losse on our party but only an Officer or two of my Regiment slaine, and some few hurte. I desire to know his Maiesties pleasure concerning the prisoners. The Ammunition taken was three barrels of powder, three hundred of Match, and fifty Musquets, all of which is safely brought hither : I take leave and rest, Sir,

" Your most humble servant,

" FARINGDON,
21 January, 1645."

' By this it may appeare, that Colonell Whaley, of whom the London Mercuries have made so much noyse, is not so strong or so vigilant to observe the motion of our Oxford Horse, as they have reported of him and undertaken for him.'

On Jan. 27, the Committee of Both Kingdoms wrote to Fairfax :—

' We are informed by the gentlemen of Wilts of the loss of all their horse lately at Marlborough, there taken by the enemy, whereby their county is at present under the power of that party, and rendered altogether unable to furnish those recruits which are now ordered to be there levied for your army. They conceive a regiment of horse will be sufficient to defend them until they can raise more of their own, which they intend to do speedily. We recommend this to your consideration, and desire you to do therein what you conceive to be best for the public service.' (Cal. S. P., Dom., 1645–7, p. 325.)

The alarm of the Wiltshire Committee was exaggerated. Camsfield returned to Oxford Jan. 31, after releasing forty Royalist prisoners at Salisbury, and no more raids took place. The Committee of Both Kingdoms, on Feb. 3, ordered the governor of Langford House to send 100 men to take part in the siege of Corfe Castle, 'there being no enemy near that can offend and endanger you.' On April 10, the governor of Malmesbury was ordered to send 300 foot to blockade Farringdon, and the governor of Highworth was similarly ordered to detach whatever foot he could spare for the same purpose (ibid. pp. 333, 406). Fairfax on his return from the West passed through Wiltshire, and halted from 20 to 23 April at Salisbury on his way to Oxford (Sprigge, p. 252). With the surrender of Oxford and Farringdon, June 20, the Wiltshire forces were set free to return home, and the war ended.

The disbandment of the local levies was the only thing which remained to be done. Making out the accounts of the soldiers was a task of some difficulty. Robert Nicholas, one of the Subcommittee of Accounts for Wiltshire, wrote to the General Committee of Accounts in Nov. 1646, complaining of the slowness of the process:—

'Whereas you directed a commission for Wilts, enabling a subcommittee to take the accounts in this county, the noble knight of our shire, Col. Ludlow, has very faithfully prosecuted the same, yet he found a great fainting amongst us, so that he could only swear five of us, and since then this business has slept; but it is a great pity that it should do so for it is one of the most important employments at this time.' (Cal. S. P., Dom., 1645–7, p. 491.)

A more serious business than the disbanding the forces raised by the county committee was the disbanding of the little army raised by Massey, as major-general of the associated counties. It took place at Devizes in Nov. 1646, under the superintendence of

Fairfax himself (Sprigge, p. 314). Ludlow, as the Memoirs tell us APP. II. (p. 141), took part in the work, by special order from Parliament, and sent the following account of his mission to the Speaker.

[EDMUND LUDLOW AND FRANCIS ALLEIN
TO WILLIAM LENTHALL, SPEAKER.]

' HONORED SIR,

'We are nowe by the blessing of God waded through the depths and difficulties of that busines wherin we were appointed to be assisting to the Generall, in order to the paying, reducement, and disbanding of the brygade, late under the comand of Colonel General Massie, there having beene nothing wanting in his Excellency in the faire and faithfull management of this whole worke, and we having mutually used according to instructions all possible endeavours to engage both officers and souldiers for the service of Irland, upon the conditions exprest in the said instructions, and finding a generall dislike of the said conditions and noe possibility of reducing them to that imployment, we proceeded to the other part of our instructions, which relate to paying and disbanding, according to which the whole brygade have received their six weekes pay, the officers being engag'd to bring them to a second rendezvous in their course, as before, when and where at the head of each regiment, a proclaymation is to be published and a pass to be delivered to each souldier, a copie of bothe is here inclosed. All which was accordingly done at the head of the Plymouth regiment yesterday, and they presently therupon dispersed themselves. The like is to be done to-day with another regiment, and soe with the rest till wee have finished the whole, not doubting but that we shall find the like civilitys in the officers and quiet behaviour in the souldiers to the perfecting of the worke, as we have hitherto found from them both in the progress of it. And as we conceive the leaving the souldier free to dispose of his horse hath much conduced to the one, soe an expectation in the officer to continue in your favour and to partake of your justice hath invited him to the other. We hope shortly to attend you with more full accompt of our proceedings, in the meanewhile we are

' Your most humble servants,

' EDMUND LUDLOWE. FRANCIS ALLEIN [1].

' DEVISES,
· 22 *October*, 1646.'

[1] Tanner MSS. lix. 566.

APPENDIX III.

——— ✦ ———

THE ACCOUNT OF LIEUT.-GEN. LUDLOW.

'In obedience to an order of this Honourable House, of the nineteenth of July last, 1650, we have examined the account of Edmund Ludlow, Lieutenant-General of the Parliament's forces in Ireland, for the pay he demands as due for his service done to the Parliament, in the several qualities hereafter mentioned; and also for and concerning all such monies as he hath paid and disbursed for the service of the State; and also of all such monies and goods as he acknowledgeth to have received for and towards the same; as followeth; viz.

	£ s. d.	£ s. d.
The said Lieutenant-General Ludlow craves allowance, as Captain of a troop of horse under the command of Sir Edward Hungerford in the county of Wiltes, from the tenth of April 1643, to the fifth of April 1644, being three hundred and sixty days, at four-and-twenty shillings per diem	432 0 0	
He craves allowance as Captain of foot, from the third of May 1643, to the third of April 1644, being three hundred and thirty-five days, at fifteen shillings per diem	251 5 0	
He craves allowance, as Captain of a troop of horse, in Sir Arthur Haselrig's regiment, in Sir William Waller's late army, and as Major of the same regiment, from the tenth of May 1644, to the two-and-twentieth of July 1644, being seventy-three days; viz. as a Captain of a troop, at four-and-twenty shillings per diem, eighty-seven pounds, twelve shillings;		
(Carried forward)	683 5 0	

	£	s.	d.	£	s.	d.
(*Brought over*)	683	5	0			

as Major to the regiment at twelve shillings per diem, forty-three pounds, sixteen shillings; in all . . . 131 8 0

He craves allowance, as Colonel of a regiment of horse, and as Captain of a troop in the same regiment, from the thirtieth of July 1644, to the second of April 1645, being two hundred and forty-six days; viz. as Colonel, at thirty shillings per diem, three hundred and sixty-nine Pounds; as Captain, at four-and-twenty shillings per diem, two hundred and ninety-five pounds, four shillings; in all 664 4 0

—————— 1478 17 0

'The said Lieutenant-General hath not produced to us any Commission, Certificate, or Muster-Rolls, whereby his actual service in the said several qualities might appear, the said Lieutenant-General affirming to this Committee that all the said Vouchers were taken by the enemy when Wardour-Castle was surrendered, and when his quarters were fallen upon at Sarum.

'Also the said Lieutenant-General craves allowance of monies by him disbursed, at several times, to officers and soldiers, for their pay, and otherwise for the service of the forces under his command; viz.

	£	s.	d.	£	s.	d.
For the pay of officers and soldiers . .	1671	9	4			
For furniture for his troop. . . .	30	0	0			
For ammunition	25	0	0			
For workmen employed in and about the reparations of the said castle, and houses thereto belonging	150	0	0			
For furnishing the castle with victuals for horse and man, with twenty pounds for payment of quarter	920	0	0			
In all				2796	9	4

'The said Lieutenant-General hath not produced to us any Acquittances, or other Vouchers, whereby the payment of the said sum of two thousand seven hundred and ninety-six pounds, nine shillings and four-pence might appear, as in his accompt is expressed; he affirming the same were taken by the enemy at the rendition of the said castle.

	£	s.	d.	£	s.	d.
Sum total, whereof he craves allowance, as aforesaid				4275	6	4
Against which, the said Lieutenant-General acknowledgeth to have received, at sundry times, of several persons, in money and goods belonging to the State, for and towards his pay and disbursements, as aforesaid, as by the accompt of the particulars thereof, delivered in under his hand, appears . . .	2221	0	0			
Deducted for free quarter, according to the instructions of the eight-and-twentieth of May 1647, out of the said several pays, the sum of	472	0	3			
				2693	0	3
And then resteth				£1582	6	1

'Memorandum, we have not cast up the pay which the said Lieutenant-General demands for six horses, as he was Captain of a troop of horse, amounting to five hundred and nine pounds, five shillings; because it hath not appeared to us, by any Muster-Rolls, that he kept the said horses.

'Besides what is above acknowledged to have been received, the said Lieutenant-General acknowledgeth, that, of the money, plate, jewels, etc., which were found by some of his soldiers buried in the walls of Wardour-Castle, there came into his hands to the value of about twelve hundred pounds.

'Sir John Danvers Knight, John Dove, and Edward Ash, Esquires, certify under their hands, 31° Julii last past, that the said Lieutenant-General Edmund Ludlow was Governor of Wardor-Castle, from the third day of May 1643, to the five-and-twentieth day of March following; for which we have not cast up any pay in this accompt, there being no establishment for allowing thereof: all which we humbly submit to the consideration of this Honourable House.

'THOMAS RICHARDSON. HENRY BROAD.

RI. WILCOX. WM. JESSOP.

NIC. BOND.

'Resolved, by the Parliament, that the sum of one thousand five hundred eighty-two pounds six shillings and a peny be and is hereby allowed of as due from the State to Lieutenant-General Edmund Ludlowe, upon this account.

'Resolved, that the sum of five hundred and nine pounds five shillings be allowed unto the said Lieutenant-General Ludlow for six horses, as captain of a troop of horse.

' Resolved, that the said Lieutenant-General Ludlow be, and is hereby, discharged of and from the money, plate, jewels, etc., that were found buried in the walls of Wardour-Castle, which came to his hands, to the value of about twelve hundred pounds ; and of and from any further account for the same.

' Resolved, that the said several sums of one thousand five hundred eighty-two pounds six shillings and a peny, and five hundred and nine pounds and five shillings, amounting to two thousand ninety-one pounds eleven shillings and a peny, be hereby allowed to the said Lieutenant-General Ludlow, out of such estates of delinquents as shall be exposed to sale : and that the trustees, contractors, and all other officers for sale of the said lands, be authorized and required to allow unto the said Lieutenant-General Ludlow, or his assigns, in any purchase of any of the said lands, the said sum of two thousand ninety-one pounds eleven shillings and a peny, as money doubled upon those lands, accordingly [1].

[1] From the Journals of the House of Commons, vol. vi. p. 508. Dec. 13, 1650.

APPENDIX IV.

---·---

LETTERS ILLUSTRATING LUDLOW'S SERVICES IN IRELAND, 1651-1654.

I.

[The Irish Commissioners to the Speaker.]

'SIR,

'It has pleased God to give us and all our company a safe and expeditious passage over the seas, for whiche mercye wee blesse His Holy Name. Att our arrivall wee found the armye in worse condition, and the enemie uppon more daringe termes then wee expected ; and this obliges us strictly to be the more instant with you to take the affaire of this nation to hart, and as seasonably as is possible to speed away the designed recruits and supplies. The Lord Dep. Generall was in the feild before our comeinge hither, and wee have not yet spoaken with him, but wee daily expect to see him or heare from him ; and in all thinges wherein our activity may bee serviceable to the publicke, wee shall remitt nothing of our utmost endeavours, but shall strive to our powers to bee answerable to the charge intrusted to us. Wee hope God will still continue to declare against your enemies, as hee hath hitherto done marveilously in this lande, and ere longe make us relators of better tidinges. We shall omitt noe opportunity to render our selfs

'Your humble servants,

'EDM. LUDLOWE.   MILES CORBETT.

JO. JONES.   JOHN WEAVER [1].

'WATERFORD,
'*Jan.* 25, 1650.'

II.

[The Irish Commissioners to the President of the Council of State.]

'MY LORD,

'We have since we came to this towne received severall petitions from the inhabitants of diverse countyes, now under your protection, wherein (manifesting their affection to live under the protection and government of the Parliament) they desire to knowe what assurance

---

[1] From Grey's Examination of Neal's History of the Puritans, vol. iii. Appendix, p. 82.

they shall have for the enjoyment of their religion, lives, libertyes and
estates, wh[en] they may to the utmost of their power, cheerfully
contribute to the maintenance of the army, and improve their lands,
which wilbe a meanes to settle the distracted condition of the country,
and reduce those in hostility against the State. To which petitions
(conceiving upon probable conjectures that the enemy have it in
designe to stirre the natives to a general insurrection this next summer,
by possessing them with an opinion of an utter extirpation of them,
when those that are nowe in arms are subdued) we thought necessary
to return them this answer: that we would represent theire desires
in those particulars to the Parliament, and as soon as the Parliament's
resolutions thereupon came to our hands we would communicate the
same unto them. We doe humbly conceive that (as the State and
condition of affaires at present stand here), if the inhabitants now
under protection, should (upon an apprehension that the Parliament
will extend noe favour or mercy towards them) give over tillage and
husbandry and join with those forces which keepe in the bogs and
woods almost in every county, the war will be much lengthened and
made very burthensome to England, by necessitating constant and considerable supplyes of recruits of men (which hitherto have bene very
much wasted by sickness and want of clothes and wholesome dyett)
and likewise supplyes of corne and other victuals for all the forces,
until the land can be competently planted with English to till the
ground. And the hopes and designes of forraigne enemyes to work
disturbance, as well in England as here, wilbe strengthened. And
therefore (upon serious consideration of the present state of affaires
here, and that the justice and mercy of the Parliament might be extended to all the people here, in some measure proportionable to theire
respective demerits) we have framed the inclosed qualifications to be
tendered (if thought fit) to the consideration of the Parliament wherein
nothing is inserted which relates to their religion (humbly conceiving
it more seasonable for the Parliament to declare their pleasure in that
particular, when the country is more thoroughly settled). But we
humbly conceive that if the Parliament shall please to hold forth
some termes of favour and mercy to them in these other things it
will probably quiett the mindes of many, and justify the severity and
justice of the Parliament against such as embrace not their clemency.
All which we leave to your Lordship's further consideration, and
remayne 'Your Lordship's humble servants,

'H. IRETON. MILES CORBETT. EDM. LUDLOWE.
JO. JONES. JOHN WEAVER[1].

' KILKENNY,
' *24th March,* 1650.

[1] Reported and read April 22, 1651.

' Some of us this day are with my Lord Deputy's approbation going towards Dublin, to take an accompt of affaires, and settle customs and excise there, and (with God's leave) intend sometime the next weeke to returne to this place [1].'

III.

[From the Irish Commissioners to the Speaker.]

' SIR,

' Little hath happened here of late worthy your knowledge. The Lord Deputy within these five days at a councell of his principal officers, resolved to take the field forthwith in order to the reducing of Connaught, which is yet intirely in the power of the enemy. And orders are already gone forth to Sir Charles Coot, and others to that end, and of this wee hope to give you a further account ere long.

' There is also order given for part of the forces to take the advantage of this dry season, to foard over the Shannon, and to secure a passage for the army, and this designe is at this present to be put in execution. As soon as this was resolved, the 11 instant wee heard of the safe comming of some cloathes and ammunition in the Diligence of Yarmouth, whereof there was very great want.

' Also since that, the Jonas and some other vessels comming in, have brought us further both ammunition, cloaths and other supplies, with some few soldiers, and we hope also some money, we beseech you to hasten away our officers with their recruits ; and also to hasten the timely providing and sending of money, without which your affaires here, which are now very hopeful, may receive great prejudice.

' Our action of late hath been only to send several parties abroad in severall places, to meet with the Tories that doe now much infest our quarters, and whose incursions and insolencies will be increased in these parts, as the army draw into the field, but the Lord Deputy hath taken the best course he can to prevent the same, by leaving moving bodies behind to prevent their designes. The enemies are much heightened with hopes of relief from the Duke of Lorraine.

' Your Honour's most humble servants,

—— —— ——[2]

' KILKENNY,
'*April* 19, 1651.'

---

[1] From the Tanner MSS. vol. lvi. f. 253.

[2] Probably signed by Ludlow, Corbet, Jones and Weaver. An earlier letter from Kilkenny, undated but read in Parliament on April 22, signed by Ludlow, Corbet, Jones and Weaver, is printed in Cary's Memorials of the Civil War, ii. 253. Cary also prints a letter, dated July 1, from Corbet, Jones and Weaver; ib. p. 280. It was thought unnecessary to reprint these again. This letter is from ' Severall Proceedings in Parliament,' p. 1277.

IV.

[Lieut.-Gen. Ludlow to the Commissioners of the Parliament.]

'MY NOBLE FREINDS,

'I should oftner give you an accompt of proceedings here but that the conveniency of messengers is wanting. I presume you heare long beefore this of my L. Deputies being beefore Limmerick; my Lord hearing of S^r. Ch. Coote's being at Portumna and the enemy like to engage him, resolved to advance with his armye towards him, but was overvoted by his counsell of warre to send a party of horse and dragoones which hee did to the number of about 1000. These hee intrusted with mee with which I marcht up to Portumna to my Lo. President before Portumna, where I founde him in a much better condition than I expected, that place having then conditioned to surrender the next morninge, which it did accordingly; the enemy lying encamped at Ballinsloo having the conjunction of Castlehaven and of the Ulster forces resolved (as wee heare) to ingage our armye: but upon notice given them of the advance of this 1000 horse from my L. Dep^t. their counsayls were presently alterd. Clanriccard and Castlehaven went for Gallway with diverse others of their cheife gentry, the remaynder beeing (as neere as wee can learne) about 600 horse and 2000 foote under the command of Lieut. Generall Ferrall and Sir Walter Dungan, upon the advance of Commissary Generall Reynolds from Sir Cha. Coote with about 700 horse and 500 foote, and myselfe with the like number of select horse, wee forced retreat from Ballinsloo, which place wee have taken in, and placed a guerrison therein of about 40 foote and 20 horse. The place is considerable in that it lyeth upon a passe of the river Suke. I was engaged by my conditions with the gentleman one Capt. Brabson who was both governour and owner of the house to sollicit you for the favour of one of his ploughes and a stock of cattle from contribution, which I hope when you charge that countrye you will take into consideration. From thence hearing that the enemy encamped at Moylag wee advanced thither, but founde them fled rather then marched to Tuum, when wee understood that they had notice of our pursuite of them and were gon to Erconnaught, wherupon wee resolved to follow this wildgoose chase no longer: but to retire to our severall quarters. Com. Generall Renolds with Col. Coote and Col. Cole are marched to my Lo. President, and I with my party am marching to my Lo. Dep^t. who had ordred mee to leave Com. G. Reynolds his troope and Major Owen's with my Lo. President and had commanded mee to write to yourselfs and Col. Hewson to see them satisfied out of his treasury the last fortnight's pay, which is beehinde unto them, but now having by his Lordship's order in the roome of them sent 2 troopes of dragoones,

I know not how hee would have them payed, but shall acquaint you if my Lo. thinke fit to trouble you therin. So craving pardon for this trouble and begging the presence of the Lord may continually goe alonge with us I subscribe

'Your, &c.,

'EDMUND LUDLOW[1].

'LORREAY,
'*June* 12, 1651.'

V.

[The Irish Commissioners to the Speaker.]

'RIGHT HONOURARLE,

'We have not of late troubled you with our letters, not having anything worth your knowledge to impart unto you, and shall now let you know the present posture of your affairs here. Limbrick is close besieged with strong forts round about it, and Sir Hardress Waller with the greatest part of the foot of the marching army, and 9 troops of horse, to man the works and make good the siege. The Lord Deputy and Lieut. General with 12 troops of horse, the lifeguard, and 3 troops of dragoons and about 2000 foot (whereof some are sick) in a marching body attend all motion of the enemy, who as they gather and make any attempts, he is ready to meet with them. The enemy consists of 2000 old foot, and about 500 or 600 horse under Marlock [Murtogh] O'Bryan and David Roch, who have been a troublesome growing enemy, and have put my Lord and his party to many hard marches in bogs and mountains to find them out. Yet through the helpe of God, your forces have been enabled to disperse them, and have frustrated their attempts, and have lodged strong garrisons where their principal hauntes are, and what forces are not placed in the said garrisons, being 10 troops of horse and 1500 foot, are so placed as to prevent the field enemy of that side the Shannon, from attempting anything on Limerick, and to countenance the garrisons, and to receive provisions from the Shannon, and to justify the siege of Limerick as occasion serves. The Lord Broghill with the Munster horse, 2 troops of horse and one of dragoons out of the marching army, and the party designed for Kerry, and the old foot of 2 regiments in the county of Cork doth attend the motion of Muskerry, who since his rout is growing strong again, and in that rout (whereof you have heard) the heate of that service was not a little on the troops sent from the marching army. Col. Zanchy with 6 troops of horse and 5 or 6 of dragoons is gon towards Bur to relieve, and countenance the garrisons in those parts, and to prosecute Fitz-Patrick, who hath reigned, and done much mischiefe in those parts, and about Kilkenny, and Tiperary, and Col. Cook is ordered to joyne with him, and as we hope (and

---

[1] Tanner MSS. liv. 81. Written apparently at Loughrea.

gather out of his own letters) he is marching according to those orders :
the number of horse and foot with Col. Cook in this march is not yet
come to our knowledge. This account we had of the forces in those
parts as they were the 23 of August last : Sir Charles Coote with his
party lies before Gallaway on one side thereof, but he wants forces to
make a close siege to the other side : Commissary General Reynolds,
Col. Hewson, Sir Theophilus Jones, and Col. Venables had orders to
conjoin, and make a body about Athlone, to watch and follow Clanrickard, and that body he was gathering about Jamestown out of Ulster,
and Leinster, to disturb the siege at Limerick, or Galloway, and by the
blessing of God that body is dispersed, and by report (but the
certainty thereof we cannot affirm) Clanrickard, Castle-haven, and
some others of that rank are gone towards Slego, in order to transport
themselves beyond the seas.

'But of the dispersed forces some of them are gone towards Cavan
to joyne with the Tories there, and others in Ulster, who before were
kept from doing further mischief by Col. Venables, but upon his
motion towards Athlone did take that advantage, and have preyed
and taken away the cows and cattle about Omagh the fronteer of your
Ulster forces in the county of Tyrone, and also another party did face
Dundalk attempting a castle within a mile of it, burning some corne,
but was repulsed. Col. Venables with about 1500 old foot, and 500
horse, and 3 troops added of Col. Hewson's is now in Cavan to ingage
that party of the enemy if he can that came out of Connaught with
O'Riley, and are joined in Cavan with the Ulster forces far more
numerous than himself, but if they do not engage with him, he is
ordered to reduce Ballynecargy, O'Riley's house, the strongest fort of
the enemy in Cavan, where he is to place a good party both of horse
and foot after the same is reduced.

'And a new troop is lately raised out of Antrim and Down, to
secure the passes into the counties, during the absence of Venables.
Com. General Reynolds with the addition of the Lemster forces
attends the motion of Dungan, (the Com. General of the enemy) with
the residue of Clanrickard's forces in Lemster, whom he has pursued
into the King's County, through a great fastness called Glanmalere,
and driven over the Barrow, now in a flying posture, and retired into
Wicklow, to join with Shurlock, Byrne, Nash, and other Lemster forces.
The Com. General Reynolds and the Lemster forces consist of 800
horse and dragoons, and 600 foot, and this is the present posture as
we doe understand of your marching army, and other the forces here in
Ireland.

'By all this above mentioned, it will appear that the work is not yet
done in Ireland, and as you may well perceive, your forces have not
been idle or unactive all this summer, so there is much to be yet done,
for which God will have us to wait, and look up to him and to him

APP. IV. alone, and not to the arm of flesh ; and therefore as we desire that all due acknowledgment of praise may be given to him for what he hath done, so his grace and help and blessing is to be blessed, that it may be vouchsafed to his unworthy servants here. And wee beseech you to consider, that this summer's action hath been a great wasting of your horse and foot, and though many recruites in number have come over for foot, yet there is just cause of complaint, that a great party of the same were lame, blind, children, aged, and fitter for an hospital than an army, and all of them without cloathes ; and for the army and forces, they are now engaged in services, or in chase of the enemy, but the contribution and assessments to be raised for their pay are much decreased, and made impossible to be raised in many places by the great wasting the enemy hath made in all quarters of late. So we hope you will see there is a necessity that supplyes for money, and additions of forces, especially of horse be continued, and sent over, and so we shall take our leave and rest

'Your most humble servants,

'Jo. Jones. John Weaver. Miles Corbet.

'Dublin,
'*Sept.* 18, 1651 [1].'

VI.

[*The Irish Commissioners to the Speaker.*]

'Mr. Speaker,

'By our last of the 18th of September wee gave an accompt how your military affayrs then stood, and as to Munster and Connaught wee cannot add anything to what wee then informed, not having since heard anything of moment from those parts, so as wee doe believe the sieges and affaires there are much what in the same posture as they then stoode. As to the forces in the north under Col. Venables, hee had lately besiedged Ballynecargy, a place very considerable within the County of Cavan : but not finding such other helpe comming to his assistance as was intended and expected, and wanting ammunition and provisions, his men began to fall sick, and finding the enemye had 400 in that fort, and within 2 miles another great bodie of 2300 foote, and about 6 or 700 horse, and finding the enemye to retreate to a bogge that did befriend them when your forces marched towards them ; and not being able to send any party considerable for any supplyes without too much weakening of their partye, that had so powerful an enemy so near to them, and their forces in other parts were all so imployed that none could be spared to carry the provisions

---

[1] Read in Parliament, Oct. 1, 1651, and printed in 'Severall Proceedings' for that date, p. 1627.

The copy amongst the Irish State Papers is dated Sept. 18. A few corrections have been made from it.

that were in readines for them, they were constrayned to rise from
that siedge, and drew near their own quarters at Dundalke ; and after
their supplyes from Belfast, Carlingford, and other parts are come to
them, they are resolved to return to the County of Cavan, and if the
enemye will not fight with them, yet they hope to hinder the enemye
from any other designe either towards Connought or elsewhere, and to
take the best quarter they can to place a good part of their forces this
winter, that may bee in readines to attend the motions of the enemy in
those parts upon all occasions. In Leynster the enemy is very active,
and hath severall bodies that are in motion in several partyes, and
having preyed and wasted about Wexford hath stormed Rosse, kild
20 of your souldiers, taken 16 barrels of powder, with match and ball
proportionable ; but your souldiers helde the church and a house lately
fortified, and the enemye having stayd a night and a day did retreat
with some loss, but tooke £700 of the inhabitants to save the towne from
burninge. Comiss.-Gen. Reynolds, Col. Zanchy, and Col. Axtell are con-
joined before Ballyban, Fitz-Patrick's strongholde in the King's County,
and, as we hear, Fitz-Patrick Westmeath and Grace's forces are
gathering together to remoove that siedge if they can. Another bodye
of the enemye, sayd to be 2000, were the 30th of September at Mollingar
attempting the castles there, and burnt part of the town, but were
beaten off with the loss of 40 men on their part, and severall [of] their
officers wounded, and Sir The. Jones, having 2 troopes with him, came
very seasonably to our friends' assistance, and the enemye left the place,
and in a bog left 6 of their horses. This morning wee heard that
Skurlock, and his party that had been at Wexford and Ross, are now
in a body in Wicklo, within 8 miles of this place ; they are reported
to be about 2000 horse and foot, but here is no force to remoove them.
Col. Cooke and Col. Pritty are to attend their motions, but where
they are at present wee doe not understand. As to your sea affayrs in
these parts wee have not heard of nor seene any one Parliament ship
betwixt Carrickfergus and Waterford since July, so as the enemy at
sea hath done much mischeife. One Bartlet about Carrickfergus hath
taken vessels out of the harbour, landed men on shore, and taken men
out of their houses : and at Wexford one ship of late with 3 guns hath
taken 11 English barques at the port, and none dare go out or come
in till the seas be cleared, which is a greate hindrance to the fishing and
all other trading, at this season, so as the customs, and excise and
trading must needs sinke, if not prevented. It is no small trouble to us
to see that that litle part of this wasted country that pays contribution
is so preyed and burnt by the enemy, that wee know not how the poor
souldier can be payd out of the assessments, unles supplyes bee sent
to your forces in the severall parts of this nation, which wee doe and
must most humbly pray for. These things wee humbly present to your
consideration, and beseech the Lord to teach us to submit to his holy

will, and to believe and wayt that he may be gratious to us. Wee shall only ad that wee are

'Your most humble servants,

'MILES CORBETT. JO. JONES. JOHN WEAVER [1].

'DUBLIN,

' *Octr.* 8, 1651.'

Read Oct. 17, 1651.

VII.

[The Irish Commissioners to the Speaker.]

' MR. SPEAKER,

' Wee have this day received intelligence from Col. Sankey under his own hand of the newes of the rendring of Limerick to my Lord Deputy, a copy whereof wee send you inclosed. Wee doubt not but his Excellency will give you a full accompt of this great and seasonable mercy, as soone as the difficulty of passage, from the place where now his Lordship is, will permitt. Wee shall only add that the enemy hath considerable parties, in severall parts of this nation, whereof wee have given lately particular accompt (so far as hath come to our notice) to the Councell of State ; and the forces before Limerick, and those that have been in continual marches in attending the motion of the enemy, all this summer have bene much wasted, especially the new recruits, soe as there will be a necessity of more forces to bee sent over, which wee doe beseech you to consider of, soe as this worke may bee vigorously carried on and your servants here enabled to reduce those enemies, that we hope are gathered together that in the Lord's due time they may be destroyed. Wee are now preparing to goe to Athlone, 50 miles from this city upon the Shannon, my Lord Deputy holdinge that to bee the most fit place for the head quarters this winter, where wee shall meet his Lordship, in order to settle those parts and put in execution such orders as we have, or shall receive from the Parliament. Wee shall only add that wee are,

' Your most humble servants,

'MILES CORBETT. JO. JONES. JOHN WEAVER [2].

'DUBLIN,

' *October* 31, 1651.'

Read Nov. 1, 1651.

VIII.

[The Irish Commissioners to the Council of State.]

' MY LORDS,

' Wee have troubled your Lordships with many dispatches expressing the condition of your affaires heere ; and because the last of

---

[1] Tanner MSS. lv. 73.   [2] Tanner MSS. lv. 67.

the nineteenth of November[1] might miscarry (the packet boat having sett out hence in a very stormy night), wee have heere sent inclosed a duplicate of the same, since which tyme there is noe alteration in affaires heere, save that our necessities growe more and more upon us, which wee humbly desire may be taken into your serious consideration, and that a speedy signification of your Lordships' pleasure in those particulars represented to your Lordships in the said papers may bee sent us. Colonel Abbott, who came from Limbricke and was there on Friday, 21st November last, informs us that the Lord-Deputy was then very ill of a feaver, and that the disease was not then come to the height. Wee hope the Lord will spare his life to carry on the worke committed to his trust, God having qualifyed, and much enabled him for so great a trust. Since the surrender of Limbricke, Clare Castle in Toomond, Carrick-Colta, a strong castle of Sir Dan. O'Bryan, upon the furthest point in Toomond on the mouth of the Shannon, were rendred to Lt. Gen. Ludlow; a copie of the Articles wee have here inclosed. The Castle of the Neale in the County of Mayo (being reported to be a place of good strength, and of greate use to streighten the enemy in Eri-Connaught and stop relief to Gallway) is delivered to Sir Charles Coote.

' Having neither money in the Treasury, nor corne in the stores heere to furnish the soldiers with bread, wee have taken up of one William Burleton three hundred pounds, which wee intend to imploy to buy corne for the present use of the forces, without which they cannot subsist, and have ordered Mr. Daniel Hutchinson to charge the same upon the Treasurers at Warr; wee humbly desire your Lordships to order the same to be paid accordingly. If wee could have procured a more considerable summe, we had not troubled your Lordships to order so small a parcell.

' Of the 22 men exceptted from the benefitt of the Articles for the surrender of Lymbricke seaven were executed, viz. Major-Gen. Purcell, the Bishopp of Emelee, Mr. Stretch, the late Mayor of Limerick, Sir Jeffrey Galloway, Jeffrey Baron, a lawyer, Dr. Higgins, and Dominicke Fanning, an Alderman. Hugh O'Neale, the Governour, is pardoned for life, and some others, about 8 of them, are not taken.

' Wee have noe more at present to add, but that wee are

' Your Lordships' most humble Servants,

' MILES CORBETT. JO. JONES. JOHN WEAVER [2].

' DUBLIN,
' *December* 1, 1651.'

Read December 9, 1651.

---

[1] A long letter mainly on the surrender of Limerick, the fortification of Athlone, and the financial ne- cessities of the government. A copy is amongst the Irish State Papers.

[2] Tanner MSS. lv. 97.

IX.

[The Irish Commissioners to the Speaker.]

'MR. SPEAKER,

'This morning came unto us the sad newes of the death of the Lord-Deputy, his gain (we are assured) is very great, he doth now rest from his sore great labours, and is with the Lord. But our losse and (we may well say) your losse also of such a servant is very great. Upon consideration of your present posture of your army, that is not yet settled in their winter quarters, and when they are they must be in readyness to attend all motions of a restless, desperate enemy, and to prevent (as we humbly conceive) some disorders that might otherwise arise, upon the whole matter, (having consulted with some of your servants that are nowe here with us,) did take these resolutions enclosed. We shall only adde our most humble request, that your pleasure therein may be with all convenient speede declared, and in the meanetime we shall not be wanting to attend your service to the uttmost of our power, and in order thereunto, we doe purpose forthwith to repaire to Kilkenny, where we shall have oportunity to consult with many officers of your army for the better carrying on of your affaires ; and (we hope) shall meete with the treasure last sent for Ireland at Waterford, of which there is need enough. And (we believe) we shall goe from thence into Conaught to settle your affairs there, and then dispose of ourselves as may most conduce to your service. Thus (having hearts full of greife, and hands full of your service,) we can adde noe more at present, but assure you we are,

'Sir,

'Your most humble servants,

'MILES CORBETT. JO. JONES. JOHN WEAVER [1].

'DUBLIN,
'*Decemb.* 2, 1651.'

Read Decemb. 9, 1651.

X.

[The Irish Commissioners to Cromwell.]

'TO THE LORD LIEUTENANT OF IRELAND,

'May it please your Excellency,—Since the writing of the enclosed, we have received the sad news of the death of that incomparable man the late Lord Deputy who expired of a fever at Limerick the 26th of the last month by which we have been put upon the enclosed resolutions which we offer to your Lordship's consideration. We have this testi-

---

[1] Tanner MSS. lv. 99.

mony within us that we had no other aim than the promotion of the App. IV public service, and we are sure the Lieutenant-General is so self-denying a gentleman that he will with more cheerfulness lay it down than he now takes it up, when it shall seem so good to the wisdom of the Parliament or your Excellency. Upon discourse with the Lord-Deputy in his life-time, we found his opinion was that Presidents of Provinces were an unnecessary burthen to the state and country, and we are so much of the same judgment that we humbly offer it may be well considered of before any more be named. We desire not to add to your Lordship's just cause of sorrow by any repetition of the loss the Commonwealth hath by the death of the Lord-Deputy, or how much we are like to suffer by it in our own particular, but rather to beseech the Lord to support you under it for the public good of the nation, and the private comfort of my Lord.

'Your [most humble servants],

'MICHAEL CORBET. JOHN JONES. JOHN WEAVER [1].

'*Dec.* 2, 1651.'

XI.

[*The Irish Commissioners to the Council of State.*]

'The Parliament have in Ireland above 350 guarrisons which at present must bee continued, being placed in port towns, walled citties and towns, and in castles upon passes, and in the other places of advantage for the keeping of this country in subjection, annoying the enemy and preventing—as much as may be—their conjunction there. Although the Parliament have now in pay in Ireland and in view as ordered already to come over upwards of 30,000 foot, yet in respect of the numerousness of the guarrisons now maintained, and of the number of about 100 guarrisons more that must bee placed in the counties of Wicklow, Longford, King's and Queen's Counties in Leinster, Kerry in Munster, Galway, Roscommon, Mayo, Sleigo and Leitrim in Connaught, Tyrone, Cavan, Fermanagh, Monaghan and Armagh in Ulster, as these places shalbe reduced, the said number of forces must for some time be held up and the charge continued. The enemy now in armes are conceived to be noe lesse in number then thirty thousand men, all which—except those in the guarrisons of Galway, Sleigo, Roscomon, James Towne, and some other few small guarrisons—live in woods, boggs, and other fastnesses, yeilding them many advantages in order to their security and livelyhood, wherof they cannot easily be deprived, viz. :—

'1. First, The countrey being allmost every where in the counties

---

[1] From the Irish State Papers, Commonwealth Series, $\frac{A}{89}$ 49, p. 243. The spelling modernised by the transcriber.

above mencioned interlaced with vaste great boggs in the middest of which there are firme woody grounds like islandes, into which they have passes or casewayes through the boggs where noe more then one horse can goe a breast, which passes they can easily mainteine, or suddainely break up soe as noe horse can approach them, and being inured to live in cabbins and to wade through those boggs they can fetch prey from any part of the countrey to releive themselves and prosecute their designes which are to robb and burne those places that yeild our forces subsistance.

' 2. Secondly, Those fastnesses being unpassable for horse, and into which foote cannot goe without some experience and hardship to wade in water and tread the bogg ; such of our forces as attempt to goe are subject by cold to get the countrey disease which wastes and destroyes many of them and being gott into those places their unacquaintedness with the passes through the woods etc., renders them incapeable to pursue and subject to surprises.

' 3. Their fastnesses are better to them in point of strength then walled towns. 1. Because they cannot be [bes]eiged in them ; 2. Because they can draw all their strength out of them to act their designes without hazarding the losse of the place.

' 4. Fowerthly, They have exact and constant intelligence from the natives of the motions of any of our forces, and of opportunities to act their designes upon us. But our forces have seldome or never any intelligence of their motions from the natives, who are possessed with an opinion that the Parliament intend them noe tearmes of mercy, and therfore endeavour to preserve them as those that stand betwene them and danger.

' For the speedier breaking of their strength it is humbly proposed :—

' 1. First, That such of the contrymen now in proteccion as shall goe out into armes against the Parliament be declared to be excepted from pardon for life or estate.

' 2. Secondly, That such persons of the enemie's party as are now in armes—except preistes, Jesuites, and other persons excepted from pardon by any rules or qualificacions held forth by the Parliament— and shall, by a set day, lay downe armes, disband their men, and deliver up their armes in some of our guarrisons, and ingage themselves to live peaceably and submit to the authority of the Parliament, shall have liberty to make sale of their horses, and to live under the proteccion of the Parliament, and shall have the benefit of such termes as the Parliament shall hold forth to persons in their condicion. And if the Parliament shall hold forth any termes to their prejudice, which they shall not be willing to submitt unto, or if they desire to serve any forreigne prince or state, they shall have . . . . . moneths time for to transport themselves into any of the partes beyond the seas, and shall have liberty in the meane time to transport—and to that end to treate with the agentes of any forraigne prince or state in amity with the Parliament and Commonwealth of England for the transporting of—such regimentes and companies as they can raise to carry over with them for the service of such prince or state, and for their continuance in the command of them being transported.

'It is conceived that such termes as these would move most of their leading men to lay downe armes and carry away most of their fighting men, which would add much to the security and peace of the inhabitantes here.

'3. Thirdly, That guarr[isons] . . . . [m]ay be to . . . . their fastnesses to disturbe . . . . take away their preyes, ... and that the said fastnesses and [the parts n]ext adjacent to them be layd waste and none to inha[bit them] upon paine of death, to the end that releef and intelligence may be taken from them.

'4. Fowerthly, That some thing may be held forth to such of the inhabitantes—as desire to live peaceably and are not guilty of bloud and murther—in order to the security of their lifes and encouragement to follow husbandry if it be thought fitt.

'For the more speedy lessening of the charge in maynteining the present forces.

'1. First, That the Adventurers upon lands in Ireland doe cast lotts where their lands shalbe assigned them according to the proposalles in the annexed paper, to the end they may presently beginne to plant notwithstanding the warr is not ended, and may plant together, and thereby be strengthened, which the Act doth not provide for them, and to the end the Parliament may more freely dispose of the rest of their land to publique advantage.

'2. Secondly, That a Pale be made by secureing all the passes upon the Boyne, and the Barrow, and the space of ground betweene them, making those two rivers one intire line for the better securing the inhabitantes to plant and follow husbandry within the said line—the same being once cleered of the enemy—which wilbe effected by planting a strong guarrison in the fastnes of Wicklowe, and the like for the county of Waterford lying betweene the Sewer which falles to Waterford. and the Nore which goes to Youghall and many other places — which may be done without much charge and kept without increasing the number of the forces, inland guarrisons being lesse usefull when these lines are made. Such lines being made, the countrey within them will in a short time be inhabited, and yeild more security to the people then now they have within a mile of the best guarrison wee possesse. and probably more profit to the Commonwealth then all the landes in Ireland now doth; whereas now while the countrey is open, the enemy have libertie upon the approach of our forces to fly out of one fastnes into another, and soe avoid engaging, and weare out our men and destroy those places that yeild our forces subsistance.

K k 2

'Thirdly, that all the forces may be fixed to their respective guarrisons and quarters, and may have landes assigned them as well for their arreares [as part] of their present pay to the end they may be [encouraged to follow hu]sbandry and to mainteine their owne intearest as [well as that of] the Commonwealth. Provided that such of them as marry with Irish [women] shall loose th[eir] commands, forfeit their arreares and be made incapable to inhabit landes in Ireland.

'EDMUND LUDLOW. JOHN JONES.
MILES CORBET. JOHN WEAVER.

' KILKENNY,
'*January* 8, 165½.'

Enclosed :

' For the ascertaining the Adventurers allotments.

' It is propounded that some Counties in each province be set apart and divided into four allotments, each of such allotments to contain a sufficient proportion of lands to satisfy the Adventurers, to the end that the lots may be cast presently by the Adventurers in which of those allotments their proportion shall be fixed.

' 1. The first allotment to consist of the Counties of Limerick and Kerry in Munster and the Counties of Clare and Galloway in Connaught.

' 2. The second allotment to consist of the Counties of Kilkenny, Wexford, Wicklow, and Catherlogh in Leinster.

' 3. The third allotment to consist of the Counties of Westmeath and Longford in the province of Leinster, and the Counties of Cavan and Monaghan in the province of Ulster.

' 4. The fourth allotment to consist of the Counties of Fermanagh and Donegal in the province of Ulster and the Counties of Leitrim and Sligo in Connaught.

'And although it be conceived that there is in any one of these allotments more forfeited lands than will upon admeasurement satisfy the Adventurers according to the Act, yet that it may appear that not only full satisfaction is intended them but also an advantage of strength and security in having their several proportions assigned unto them together, which the Act did not provide for ; it is further proposed that, if the first allotment chance to fall short upon admeasurement of giving the satisfaction intended, that then in such case the one moiety of such defect be supplied out of the forfeited lands in the County of Mayo, next adjacent to the Counties of Clare and Galway.

' 2. That the second allotment proving defective be supplied out of the forfeited lands in the Queen's County and King's County in Leinster next adjacent to the said second allotment.

'3. That the defect of the third allotment be supplied out of the forfeited lands in the County of Fermanagh in Ulster next adjacent to the said third allotment.

'4. That the defect of the fourth allotment be supplied out of the forfeited lands in the County of Mayo in Connaught and of Cavan in Ulster next adjacent to the said fourth allotment[1].'

App. IV

XII.

[*The Irish Commissioners to the Speaker.*]

[' MR. SPEAKER],

'Haveing nowe bene in these partes three weekes where we have mett with all the Generall Officers and most of the Feild Officers of your army, and consulted with them about the disposeing of your forces in theire winter quarters, soe as may be of most advantage to your service, and what wilbe necessary to be provided for this next summer's service, we have given accompt to the Councell of State thereof. We have resolved the next weeke (by the helpe of God) to be at Portumney in Connaught, where we doe expect to meet with Sir Charles Coote and other your servants in those partes, of which we doe hope to give accompt by our next. We shall onely nowe acquaint you that att this meeting with your officers and servants here, we have observed in them great diligence and affection, with much unanimity to obey your commands and to carry on your service in this nation. And we could not but take notice of the good hand of God that soe disposed of the windes that have bene soe tempestuous and contrary for many weekes together, yet the day before our comeing hither the last treasure sent from you did safely arrive att Waterford, which had bene long expected and for want whereof your forces would soone have bene reduced to many straights. Nowe by this seasonable relief they are much refreshed ; the same being disposed of and equally distributed according to the course used by the Lord-Deputy in his life tyme. But how little doth remayne thereof, and what further supplyes and necessaryes are requisite to be sent hither in order to your service, we have given full accompt to the Councell of State. There is not any considerable action done of late worthy your notice, but your forces are at present in such a posture, as they are ready to meet with all attempts of the enemy, and (by the blessing of God) are in a hopefull way to doe good service against them whose motions they doe dayly attend. Your pleasure touching a Commander-in-Chiefe in this

---

[1] From the Report on the Portland MSS. i. 622, with corrections and additions from another copy.

Nation, and what qualifications the Parliament shall please to hold forth to the Irish, hath bene longe expected and much desired by

'Your most humble servants,

'MILES CORBETT.   JO. JONES.
    EDM. LUDLOWE.   JOHN WEAVER [1].

'KILKENNY CASTLE,
    '9th Jan., 1651.'

XIII.

[*The Irish Commissioners to the Speaker.*]

'MR. SPEAKER,

'Our last by Major Morgan, gave you an accompt of our then being at Kilkenny, and of our purpose to go to Portumney in Connaught, where wee have bene accordingly, and as at Kilkenny wee had a meeting with most of the officers of the army, and of the severall forces in Munster and Leinster, and received a full accompt of your affairs at present in those parts, soe (at our being at Portumney) Sir Charles Coot, and the officers in that Precinct under his command, and under Commissary-General Reynolds, did repayre unto us, and give us alsoe a full accompt of your forces and affaires in those partes. And as wee have done our endeavour to settle the assesments, excise, customes, and other revenues in those provinces to the utmost as can be raised, soe by advise of the officers of the army, several things have been taken into consideration and resolved upon, in order to the carrying on of the next summer's service, and what is neccessary to be provided in order there unto, and what were necessary to be sent from England hither, in the mean time to make your forces now in their winter quarters as useful and active against the enemy as may be ; and of all these wee have given a particular accompt to the Councell of State, who wee doubt not will present the same to you, as your occasions will permit, and may bee for your service.

'Wee shall now onely add, that in those meetings wee have seen much of God, in disposing the hearts of your officers, and servants heere, in such a manner as it doth appear unto us, there is a general concurrence, and unity of spirit in them all to carry on the worke of the Lord to bee done in this land : and since they parted from us, most of them in their severall quarters have made attempts upon the enemy, and in particular Colonel Zankey, Colonel Axtel, and Col. Abbot, drew severall parties at one time to Ballibrane, in Munster, which was Fitz-Patrick's stronghold, and comming at three severall passes at one time upon that place, they took the castle there, which they slighted, and burnt great quantities of corne and provisions, and all their houses, and put 500 to the sword, and drive away what cattle they found there.

[1] Tanner MSS. lv. 112.

The like attempt Col. Hewson, Col. Pretty, and other parties have begun to make at Glanmellur, the great fastnesses in Wickloe, and have there destroied and burnt their corne and houses, and all provisions of the enemy they could meete with. At Gallway the enemy made a sally out to fetch in a prey of cattle, but your forces lying in the forts neere, upon notice thereof fell upon them, and rescued the prey, and killed 60 of the enemy upon the place, most of them were citizens.

'And at a gentleman's castle neere Tecroghan, there came two companies of the enemy to surprise the same, but the commander of the garrison at Tecroghan, upon notice thereof, sent timely to prevent that designe, and killed 40 on the place, and took 100 armes.

'And very many other attempts have been made in other partes by your forces, so as the enemy of late have been straightened, and many of them of late put to the sword.

'Our humble suite unto you is, that care may be taken to send over supplies of money for the payment of your forces, without which they wilbee put to miserable exigencies, and alsoe that the recruites, tents, clothes, corne, and ammunition and other necessaries wee have mentioned in our letter to the Councell of State, may have money provided for the buying of them, soe as they may be timely sent over, it much conducing to your service, and for the ending of the warre, that your forces may be in the feild in the beginning of May next, or sooner if the horse can live abroad.

'Severall of the enemies party have made some overtures to come in, and submitt, and at our being at Kilkenny and Portumney, with advise of your officers there, some rules have been given to those commaunding in cheife in severall quarters to receive such whose coming in may be for your service, but the not knowing your pleasure, concerning the quallifications or termes to be held out to the Irish, doth render us not soe serviceable in those particulars, as otherwise wee conceive wee might bee ; wherefore wee humbly desire your pleasure, therein may be speedily declared. We have no more at present, but to assure you, that we are,

'Sir, Your most humble servants,

'EDM. LUDLOWE. JO. JONES.
MILES CORBETT. JOHN WEAVER [1].

'DUBLIN,
'*Feb.* 13, 1651.'

Read Feb. 13, 1651.

---

[1] Tanner MSS. lv. 121. Printed in 'Severall Proceedings in Parliament,' p. 1938. In a long letter of Feb. 5 to the Council of State, the Commissioners discuss the financial needs of the army and government, especially with regard to the province of Connaught. The portion of the

XIV.

[*The Earl of Clanricard's Letter to the Commander-in-Chief of the Parliament's Forces in Ireland, Feb.* 14, 1651.]

'SIR,

'Several of the Nobility, Cleargy, and other persons of quality and interest in the Kingdom, together with the Corporation of Gallway, being met in this town, and having taken into their consideration the present state and condition of affairs, and the destructive effects of a long-continued War, have made it their sute and request unto me, to propose unto you the entertaining of a treaty, in order to a settlement in this Kingdom, and for your safe conduct to such Commissioners, as I by their advice shall think fit to imploy unto you, for the carrying on of that matter; which request of theirs I have consented unto by this express directed to you to that effect, with this further intimation, that I shall not quit or decline them or their interest, until I see them settled in a good condition, fit for the Nation to accept: or if that will be denied them, resolved to continue his Majesties authority and protection over them to the uttermost trial; and do not doubt, by God's assistance, with the Forces and Arms we have already, and such aids and supply as probably may come from his Majesty and his allies abroad, but that we may be so enabled as to alter the present state of affairs, or if that should fail, at least make the conquest you have hitherto gained, for a long time of little use or advantage to you; and sell our lives at a dear rate if compelled thereunto. And so leaving it to your consideration, and expecting your timely answer and certain resolution,

'I remain your servant,

'CLANRICARD [1].

'GALLWAY,
'*Feb.* 14, 1651.

'If you please to send the safe conduct desired, I desire it to be sent to Sir C. Coot, or any other you shall think fit near this place, with a blank for the number of five Commissioners and their retinue,

army in Connaught, under the immediate command of Sir Charles Coote, consisted of 34 companies of foot, being 2291 private soldiers besides officers, and 14 troops of horse containing 982 troopers. The total pay of these forces, including the allowance to Coote, is computed at £4975 per mensem.

[1] In a letter to the Council of State, dated March 1, the Commissioners say: 'The enemy themselves confess their condition to be very low and desperate. The last week there came to this town a trumpeter from the Earl of Clanricard with a letter to the Commander-in-Chief of your forces, a copy whereof and of the answer returned thereunto we herewith present your Lordships.'

not exceeding in the whole the number of twenty; whereby, upon .\l'l'. I\ intimation from him, I may send him a list of the names of the Commissioners.

' To the Commander in chief of the Parliament Forces in Ireland.'

XV.

[Lieutenant-Generall Ludlowe's Answer to the Earle of Clanricard's Letter, Feb. 20, 1652.]

' MY LORD,

'By your Lordships of the 14. instant, you propose unto me the entertainment of a treaty, in order to the settlement of this kingdome; and doe desire my safe conduct for such Commissioners as you shall think fit to imploy unto me, for the carrying on of that matter. Whereunto, upon advice with the Commissioners of the Parliament of England, and divers Generall and Field-Officers of their Army, I have thought fit to give you this return : That the settlement of this Nation doth of right belong to the Parliament of the Commonwealth of England, to whom we leave the same, being assured they will not therein capitulate with those who ought to be in submission, yet stand in opposition to their authority : but if the Lord have that mercy in store for any who are at present in armes against them, as to incline their hearts to a submission to that government, which he by his providence hath placed over them, upon timely application to the ministers here, on the behalfe of particular persons, or places, such moderate terms will yet be consented unto, as men in their condition can rationally expect. As to the intimation of your future hopes and resolutions, I shall onely say this much, that it hath been the practice of those who have served the Parliament in this Cause, to act according to their duties, and to leave the successe to him who disposes the issues of all things ; and as the Lord hath hitherto enabled them exemplarily to proceed against those whose hearts have been hardened upon vain and groundlesse expectations, to withstand offers of such favour as have been made unto them, so I assure my selfe hee will still own them in his own way and work. Wherein that we may be continually found, is the desire of

' Your Lordships humble servant,

' EDM. LUDLOW [1].

' DUBLIN,

' 29 *Feb.*, 1651.

' For the Lord of Clanricard.'

---

[1] These letters are from ' Mercurius Politicus,' April 1–8, 1652, pp. 1514, 1515. On the date of this correspondence, see ' Ludlow's Memoirs,' p. 305 note. The right date is probably Feb. 20, as given in ' Severall Proceedings,' p. 2047.

XVI.

[*Edmund Ludlow to the Lord Deputy.*]

'MAY IT PLEASE YOUR EXCELLENCYE,

'Since my last to your Lordship, a trumpeter of the enemyes brought hither letters from the Earle of Clanricard desiering a safe conduct for five commissioners from him to treate with the like number of ours about the settlement of this kingdome, as he calls it, which transaction according to our duty wee thought not fit to intermeddle withall, and muche lesse would wee consent that their enemyes should be consulted withall therein, and therefore returned them a negative to their desiers, as will appeare by the coppy, and the answere which the Commissioners of Parliament have presented to the Counsaile of State. Though the letter speaks much resolution in case of our refusall yet Sir Charles Coote gives intimation in his, that in case this generall tender bee rejected, hee is assured that Galloway and severall considerable persons of them will make application for themselves but [there] is noe confidence to bee put in them . . . it v . . . Fitzpatricke now in treaty with Commissary-Gen¹. Raynolds and the Lord Muskery, with my Lord Broghill. The issues of all things are in the hand of our Father, and that's the ground of our rejoyceing. Its generally acknowledged by them all that their condition is very low, and indeed your forces are every where very active upon them. Coll. Axtell writes word that they have lately in his precinct killed an hundred of the enemy and taken many of their horse, Capt. Gilbert at Trecroghan lately tooke Leift. Coll. Terrell and two or three officers more, Major Meredith lately drove thirty of them into a bogg and put them all to the sword. Capt. Colthrop lately killed one Capt. Hicks, one of the activest captaines the enemy had in Wicklo, and three more. Major Bolton lately killed and tooke five and twenty of the enemy, with their horse, and endangered Scurlock. I heare even now by Leift. Coll. Huetson that Capt. Prestons hath met with Nashe and his troop, whome they have sore wounded and taken prisoner, and killed sixteene of his men. It hath pleased the Lord to take away Capt. Staffe from among us, who was a very active instrument and was slain in falling upon the enemy in the county of Thomond and in the barrony of Ibreckan in that county. The Lord was mercyfull unto us in this bitter dispensation, for though Captaine Staffe was shot at the first falling on, yet it pleased the Lord soe to encourage our party, as that they totally routed the enemy and killed the two officers that commanded them. The Commissary-Generall with his party about Athlone have lately taken in the Callogh and hath garrysoned Raclyne. Ballyleagh is likewise delivered unto him whiche commands the only passe for horse betweene Athlone and James Towne, where hee hath

greate hopes of having delivered unto us a vessle of sixteene gunnes, AP IV
belonging to Middleborough, loaden with wheate and ry, attempting
to get into Galloway, were chased by Capt. Clearke and Capt. Wallis,
and bulged on a rocke by the Isles of Aran, and all the corne lyeth
under watter unserviceable. Another vessle likewise loaden with
wheat and other commoditys attempting to get into Galloway was
taken by Capt. Clearke, and in her six Galloway marchants. I hope
such coarse will be taken that Galloway shall be blocked up on the
further side by the latter end of Aprill or the begining of May. I have
too long detained your Lordshipp, and therefore craveing your pardon
for the same and for this scribled paper, I begg leave to subscribe
myselfe.

> ' Your Excellency's
> ' Most faythfull and humble Servant,
> ' EDM. LUDLOWE [1].

' *From* DUBLIN.
' *this 2d of March,* '51.

' Our party at Dingle in Kerry have routed three companys of the
enemys and taken all their armes.'

[Address, partly cut off :—]
> ' These to his Excellency the Lord [Deputy ?].'

XVII.

*[A Declaration by the Commissioners of the Parliament of the
Commonwealth of England for the affairs of Ireland.]*

' The said Commissioners, having on the eleventh of this instant
March, received a letter or paper directed unto them, bearing date the
20 of Feb. 1651, requesting on the behalf of the Provinces of Ireland,
safe conducts unto each Province with blanks : to meet, elect, and
authorize members of each Province, to meet in some convenient
place for offering proposals to such as are or shall be authorized by
the Parliament of the Commonwealth of England for the settlement
of this Nation. Which said paper or letter is subscribed by one
Gerald Fitz Gerald, under pretence of an authority, which the said
Commissioners cannot in duty and with honour to the Parliament
acknowledge : yet for the satisfaction of those that may seem to be
concerned therin, they doe declare :

' 1. That the Settlement of this Nation doth of right belong to the
Parliament of the Commonwealth of England onely, the consideration
whereof is at present before them.

' 2. That in the Settlement thereof, the Parliament will make

---

[1] [With small Seal, and Arms.] Tanner MSS. lv. f. 155.

App. IV. distinction between such persons as have lived peaceably according to their duties, or being mislead, have since submitted to their authority and protection, and those who have acted or abetted the murthers and massacres of the Protestants, and those that adhered to them during the first year of the Rebellion, and likewise such persons as now being in armes and opposition to the said authority, shall not timely submit thereunto. And therefore the said Commissioners cannot in justice give way to any act, so much as to the prejudice of the people of this Nation, as may involve those that are peaceably minded with them who continue in hostility.

' 3. That to grant safe conduct and blank passes unto such as are in actual hostility against the Parliament, to meet together from all the Provinces to communicate counsels, is an act to which the said Commissioners cannot in prudence consent.

' 4. That for such persons as are now in actual hostility against the Parliament, and are willing to lay down armes, and submit to the authority thereof, upon timely application made to the Parliament's ministers here, on behalf of particular persons or places, such moderate termes will be consented unto as men in their condition can in reason expect.

MILES CORBET. JO. JONES. JO. WEAVER [1].

' *Dated at* DUBLIN,
' *the* 12 *of March,* 1651.'

XVIII.

[*The Commissioners of Parliament's answer to the foregoing Proposals.*]

' IRELAND.

' BY THE COMMISSIONERS OF THE PARLIAMENT OF THE COMMONWEALTH OF ENGLAND FOR THE AFFAIRS OF IRELAND.

' Upon consideration had, of the paper this day produced by Sir Richard Barnwall, and Col. Bagenall, the said Commissioners do return this ensuing answer.

' First, as to the making known the power of the said Commissioners as is desired, they do not hold the same fitting, or reasonable : but such of this Nation, whose hearts God shall incline to a timely and free submission to the power of the Parliament, those persons shall effectually know the authority of the said Commissioners to grant such things as shall bee rationally desired, and doe trust the Lord will enable the Parliament and their ministers here, to make such others, whose hearts shall be still hardned to their further destruction, sensible of the power God hath put into their hands.

[1] ' Severall Proceedings in Parliament,' April 1-8, 1652, p. 2045.

'And as to the granting passes to any persons to goe to the Parliament to negotiate for the settlement of the whole Nation, the said
Commissioners do not think it fitting, it not standing with the honor
and justice of the Parliament, to treat about the settlement of the
Nation, with such as contrary to their duty, are in hostility against
them.

'As to the residue of the said matter contained in the said paper, the
said Commissioners have given answer thereunto in a former paper of
the 11 instant : to which they refer themselves.

'EDM. LUDLOW.   MILES CORBET.

JOHN JONES.   JOHN WEAVER [1].

'*Dated at* DUBLIN,
   '15 *March*, 1651.'

XIX.

[*The Lieut.-General's answer to a letter signed Richard Blake.*]

'[SIR],

'In yours of the 9th instant which came to my hand the 17th (signed
by command of the great Councell at Galway assembled as you are
pleased to stile them, whose authority I may not acknowledge) you re-
iterate in effect the former application from the Earl of Clanrickard for the
settlement of this Nation, differing onely in this, That whereas he would
have capitulated in that affair on the place, you propose for licence to
be given unto Commissioners to repair unto the Parliament of England
about the same, which hath been occasioned through this mistake (as
I conceive) you apprehending that denyall to proceed merely from the
want of power in the ministers of the Parliament here, whereas
indeed the chief ground thereof was the unreasonableness of the proposition itself : which was in my judgement in effect this : That such
who are guilty of a bloody & cruell massacre, (at least engaged in the
withholding of them from justice who are so, whom the righteous hand
of God hath prosecuted from field to field, from city to city even to
the gates of Galway) should be admitted to capitulate about the settlement of this Nation with the Parliament of England (their lawful
magistrate) whom God hath not only permitted to be raised to their
present height, as you term it, but by his own outstretched arm and
glorious presence hath enabled to become a terror to evildoers, and
an encouragement to them that do well. And this capitulation to be
before they have even owned their guilt or delivered up those Achans
to justice for whose iniquity the land mourns. Indeed if once the
Lord would truly humble you under his omnipotent hand for your
raising & fomenting this unnatural quarrel between two nations of
late linked in love, allied in blood, and not different in laws (as your-

---

[1] 'Severall Proceedings in Parliament,' April 1-8, 1652, p 2048.

APP. IV. selves confess) & would incline you timely & readily to submit to
their authority (as the greatest part of the Nation have already done)
I should then hope that deliverance were drawing nigh at least to a
remnant of those amongst you who yet continue in disobedience : and
that such of you might be capable of the fruits of that settlement which
(at this time) the Parliament of England is intent upon. But while
you insist upon the justice of your cause, and persevere in your hostility,
its not the advantage we may partake of by a settlement, nor the uncertainty of a tedious war, proved by experience of former ages or
backt by a number of people in arms capable of foreign succours, nor
fear of having this country rendered waste and useless unto us that ought
to deter us from doing our duty, or unite us to this sinful or unworthy
compliance with you. As touching the cessation you propose for avoiding
the further effusion of Christian blood, I could wish that this tenderness
had in the beginning possessed your spirits, but how such a cessation
can be satisfactory to the Parliament of England appears not to me,
seeing they have been at so vaste a charge in their preparations for
the putting speedy issue to this war, which by the Lord's assistance
shall be heartily prosecuted by

'Your Servant
'EDMUND LUDLOW [1].

'DUBLIN,
'*this 19th March*, 1651.'

XX.

[*The Irish Commissioners to the Speaker.*]

'RIGHT HONOURABLE,
'The diligence and activity of your officers and souldiers this last
winter hath bene such, that the enemy hath thereby bene much
streigthened in all partes of this nation, and reduced to a lowe condition, att present many of them have bene putt to the sword, and they
are generally disenabled from being so destructive to your quarters as
formerly. Of late many applications have bene made by the Irish to
severall of your officers, who have seemed willing to submitt and come
under protection, but some have come to such tearmes as they have
been admitted. Amongst whom Colonell John Fitz Patrick (the
most considerable of their party) who this last year hath bene a very
active enemy, and many of your parties that should have bene elsewhere employed for your service were often constrained to attend
his motions : Fitz Patrick hath agreed to terms of submission for him-

---

[1] Irish Records, Commonwealth
Series, $\frac{A}{90}$ 50, pp. 24, 5. Printed in
a tract entitled 'A great and bloody
fight in Ireland,' 4to. 1652. British
Museum E 659 (17).

selfe and his party, being the most considerable party of the enemy in Ireland. There hath also been applications made from Clanrickard for a national treaty, and from another party of the Irish at Garench to the like purpose, but of all these and the answeares thereto, we have given particular accompt to the Councell of State, who (we doubt not) will acquaint the Parliament with soe much thereof as they shall find matteriall, and worthy theire knowledge.

'Upon advice with the officers of your army at Kilkenny in December last it was ordered, that a considerable party of horse and foot under the commaund of Commissary-Gen. Reynolds should be sent to Athlone, which place lies in the center of the nation, and the party is accordingly drawne thither, and the Commissary-Generall hath already made good use of them to your service, having reduced Ballyleage and two other garrisons in the Callogh, and thereby gayned a very considerable pass over the Shannon, and a firme hold and footing in the County of Longford (which country was before that wholly possest by the enemy) a good quantity of corne and forrage for his forces was found there, which he stood in great need of. And for a further supply of the wants of that party (they being in a wasted countrey, where reliefe cannot come to them by sea) we have sent to Athlone from Dublin and Trim about fower months provisions of wheate, bisket, and cheese. Some of the late actions of your servants here, you will find by the inclosed. We shall add noe further at present, but that we are,

<blockquote>
'Your most humble servants,
'MILES CORBETT.   EDM. LUDLOWE.
JO. JONES.   JOHN WEAVER [1].
</blockquote>

'DUBLIN,
'23rd *March*, 1651.'

XXI.

[*The Commissioners of the Parliament in Ireland to Mr. Winter's Church in England.*]

'CHRISTIAN FRIENDS,

'The good hand of God having brought Mr. Winter (your sometime pastor) into this land, where he hath received a great seal of his ministry (besides the gathering into Church fellowship a body of visible saints) and though his return to you this summer (at least for a season for your refreshment in spirit) may be expected by you, as we under-

---

[1] Tanner MSS. lv. 174. Read in Parliament, April 6, 1650. The letter to the Council of State, which is dated March 22, adds nothing material to the facts stated in this letter. The documents enclosed included Ludlow's letter of March 19 to Sir Richard Blake, and the articles with Col. Fitzpatrick.

stand by him it is, and his desire as great of seeing your faces and beholding your order, yet the great work that lies upon his shoulders in this populous city where able ministers are very scarce, and the great importunities of the flock (so lately gathered) that he will not yet leave them—hath caused us earnestly to desire his continuance in this place until the next year, when (through God's leave and good pleasure) he may make a journey to you. In the meantime, as we hope your due consideration of the great services the Lord hath for his labourers (who are but few) to do in his vineyard here will in some measure quiet your minds, so we believe you doubt not but Mr. Winter hath you often in remembrance before the Throne of Grace, that the Lord will supply all your wants through his Son and instruct you by his spirit in all wisdom and understanding : which also is the prayer of your assured, loving, and Christian friends in the Lord Jesus,

'EDMUND LUDLOW. MILES CORBET.

JOHN JONES. JOHN WEAVER [1].

' 13 *April*, 1652.'

XXII.

[The Officers of the Irish Army to the Parliament.]

' MR. SPEAKER,

' Upon the 17th of Aprill last, many of your servants came unto Kilkenny, and had a meeting with sundry of the Generall and Feild Officers, whereof some of them are now gone to their severall charges. The first two or three dayes wee were entertained as with accompts of treaties from many parties of the enemie, soe with the dayly sad newes of severall small parties of yours, which more seriously affected us all with what hath bene often (but too slightly) upon our harts, (vizt.) the observance of our general aptnesse to lenity towards and composure with this enemy, and the severall visitations upon us which ordinaryly have bene the consequence thereof, which (with the sence wee have of the bloudguiltenesse of this people in a time of peace) doth (through dread of the Lord only wee trust) occasion much remorse for particular weaknesses past in most mindes here concerning some treaties, which are liable to be attended with sparing whome he is pursuing with his great displeasure ; and whether our patient attending rather his farther severity upon them (though that may occasion your farther great care and charge, and perhaps the greater hardshipp of your poore servants here,) be not most safe, and adviseable. And whilst wee were in debate hereof and of your dealing with those who yet continue in rebellion, an abstract of some particular murthers was

---

[1] From the Irish Records, Commonwealth Series, $\frac{A}{90}$ 50, p. 56. Modernised by the transcriber.

produced by the stout Major Generall (who hath the originall examinations of them more at large) which indeed much informed not only ourselves and others of your officers, which came over in this late expedition, but also others who have bene here from the beginning of the warr professed they had never formerly such full and particular knowledge and sence thereof, and indeed soe deeply were all affected with the barbarous wickednesse of the actors in these cruell murders and massacres (being soe publicly in most places committed) that wee are much afraid our behaviour towards this people may never sufficiently avenge the same. And fearing least others who are at greater distance might be moved to the lenity which wee have found noe small temptation in ourselves, and wee not knowing but that the Parliament might be shortly in pursuance of a speedy settlement of this Nation, and thereby some tender concessions might be concluded through your being unacquainted with these abominations, wee have caused this enclosed abstract to be transcribed and made fitt for your view. And considering that soe many murthers have bene committed that few of the former English were left undestroyed (especially men who had any particular knowledge of the massacre, and of those the greatest part are since deceased,) soe that few of the rebells can be particularly discriminated by any evidence now to be produced, as the usuall course of justice doth require, yet those barbarous, cruell murthers having bene so generally joined in and since justified by the whole nation, wee humbly offer to your most serious consideration, whether (as in duty towards God the great avenger of such villanies, who hath from the beginning of this warr to this present allwayes in your appeall by warr against them appeared so signally) some of them being now allready in your power, and there being some good hopes of reducing many more of them, some rules should not be by you held forth, either by the present dispatch of the qualifications and exceptions formerly sent you, or such other as your wisdom shall judge fitting to prescribe unto your servants here. And your commands therein, and in all other wayes of truth and justice, shall be duly observed by

'Your most humble servants,

' EDM. LUDLOWE.	CHA. COOTE.	DAN. REDMAN.
HAR. WALKER.	D. AXTELL.	WILL. ALLEN.
MILES CORBETT.	HIE. SANKEY.	J. VERNON.
JO. JONES.	HEN. PRITTIE.	HEN. OWEN [?].
S. REYNOLDS.	RI. LAURENCE.	WILL. THROCKMORTON.
D. ABBOTT.	HEN. JONES.	TRIS. BERESFORD[1].
J. HEWSON.		

' KILKENNY,
    ' *5th May*, 1652.'

[1] Tanner MSS. liii. 20.   Read in Parliament, May 18.

XXIII.

[From the Irish Commissioners to the Speaker.]

' MR. SPEAKER,

' It is now full three weekes since our coming from Dublin, and hitherto our abode hath bene in this place, where wee have mett with most of your generall and feild officers (saving those in Ulster, and those remote parts,) your affaires there (upon Col. Venables his coming to us) being in some good measure settled and ordered at our being at Dublin.

' And as (by your great care) there hath bene good plenty of provisions timely made and provided, for the carrying on of your service here this summer (for which the hungry and poore naked souldiers have good cause for you to bless God) soe wee have, by the general advice of your officers, disposed of the same, as may best conduce to that end. And by the same advice and directions, and to that great end your forces are ordered and disposed of for this summer's service, in the several provinces and parts of this nation, and therein care hath bene taken for the securing your garrisons in all parts ; and there are in the several provinces moving parties ready to attend all motions of the enemy ; and in Wicklowe and many other places (where the enemy doth lie in boggs, mountains, and other fastnesses) there are new garrisons planted to prevent, as much as may be, their incursions into your quarters, and to fall in upon the enemy as opportunity shalbe offered ; and besides, there is two considerable bodies both of horse and foot, one to attend the motions of Muskerry and his party, about Kerry (which is yet wholly in the enemies power) where are many ports and harbours fit to receive relief from forreigne parts, and another about Athey in Leinster, to be ready to follow the motions of the enemy from the bogs and fastnesses in those parts, where alsoe the enemy is very considerable, and both these parties are to have communion with the other forces in those parts adjacent, as occasion shall be offered.

' Wee have had late intelligence from good hands that Clanriccard, and the enemy from Connaught, having slighted and burnt all or most of their garrisons in those parts, are gone or going towards Ulster, to joyne with Sir Phelim O'Neill, Col. Farrell, and the enemy in Cavan and other parts of Ulster, and thereupon orders are gone to three troops to joyne with Col. Venables. And the party under Sir Charles Coot, and the Commissary Generall's party about Athlone, are to follow the enemy if their motion be that way, and for the execution of those resolutions, some of the officers are already gone from us, the present exigency of affaires calling for the same.

' And before your forces could be in the feild, the horse being now weak with much duty this winter, and grasse not yet to be had in

most parts, the enemy have appeared in some places, and have driven
away cattle and other prey from some of your quarters, and have
made suddaine incursions by small parties, and have surprised the
horse of two troopes of dragoones ; and hearing of our parties drawing
towards them, they did about the end of the last week move towards
Wexford, whereupon two troopes of horse were sent to the relief of
your forces there, and by their timely coming they mett with the
enemy who had preyed the quarters to the walls of Wexford, and
being in their return with their prey, of at least 500 cowes, our party
under command of Lieut.-Coll. Throgmorton mett with them, your
forces being 140 horse, and 400 foote, and the enemy had, as the
prisoners relate, and were soe estimated, about 250 horse, and about
500 foote. And in this, your poore foote (not having pikes whereof
there is a general want) were hereby put hardly to it. And in
the first encounter your horse made some small retreat, but (through
the good hand of the Lord, who still appeares for you, and against
your enemies) after a sharp and short dispute were broken, and
200 killed in that place and on the pursuit, as wee can learn by
best intelligence, and some officers of the enemy both killed and taken
prisoners. Of our party were 21 lost, and 100 wounded, but noe officer
lost, and but few wounded.

'As to Fitz Patrick (who was the first that came in and submitted)
all the Irish party are highly incensed against him, and, to render him
odious have divulged this enclosed declaration against him, and the
clergie have excommunicated him, and all that joyne with him, and
some of his party have bene cut off by the enemy, who did also cut off
the ears of some whome they tooke prisoners : and Fitz Patrick hath
mett also with some of the enemy.

'But that that much distracts your affaires concerning these persons
that are by engagement to bee transported, is, that they must lie in our
quarters till shipping bee provided for them ; but whiles wee were in
some streights about this, there is one White that hath contracted with
Fitz-Patrick for two thousand men, and we hope one thousand of them
wilbe shipped next week, and by this meanes you will have a good
riddance of those troublesome guests, there being visibly ready to be
transported (had we but shipping ready) of Fitz-Patrick's party 2000 ;
of Odwire's party about 1000 who are come in, and armes allready
brought in to us ; of Murtagh O'Bryan's party in Clare 2000 (whereof
1200 are allready come in, and layd downe their armes) ; and of those
in the North that are come in, and mentioned in Coll. Venables'
letter enclosed there may bee 2000 more, besides many others that
of late have submitted, and made agreement with Commissary-
General Reynolds.

'There have of late bene many applications made from severall
cheif officers of the enemies party, to treat since the agreement with

Fitz Patrick, and that business is now ready for a conclusion ; and to that end, the Commissary-Generall, Coll. Hewson, Coll. Lawrence, Coll. Axtell, Adjutant-Generall Allen, with some others, are gone with instructions, agreed on at a councill of your officers by an unanimous consent ; the effect whereof are the conditions Colonell Venables was authorized to give to those in Ulster ; and the effect and matter of their instructions are mentioned in the Articles agreed on in Ulster, which are inclosed, and that agreement hath since been approved of by us, by advice at a general councill of officers.

'The time for this Treaty is to expire next Saturday, by five of the clock in the afternoone.

'At this Treaty are present, Dungan, Scurlogge, the Earl of West-meath, one from the Lord Muskerry, and indeed the heads of the most of those that are now in armes against you in all parts, save Ulster ; the issue of this you shall hear by the next.

'As to the business of Gallway, Sir Charles Coot was in possession of the place before our letter came to him, mentioned in our last to you, since that he hath sent two of his officers with an explanation of his meaning in the articles of Gallway, and since they of Gallway have yeilded in some things to the exceptions wee made, and the main exception yet remaining unsatisfied is about their houses and real estates in Gallway. But as to that, Sir Charles Coot is in some hopes they will be brought in time to yeild unto it, and at our going thither (wee hope) wee shalbe able to give you fuller accompt thereof.

'At the present, by advice of the councell of officers here, there is a regiment of ten companies of foote under Col. Stubbers sent into Gallway.

'We shall only add that Sir Charles Coot is very sensible of his yeilding to those articles of Gallway as they are, but hee assures us, his zeal to have your work and great charge put to a short issue, was the occasion of those concessions ; and if he had not taken the opportunity then offered, he conceived there was great probability, that more force would be brought into the towne, so as it might have kept all your forces this summer in those parts to attend that service.

'As to your forces wee are in a miserable and sad streight for want of pay for the poor souldiery, and yet such patience is amongst them that we hear no complaint from any of them or their officers, but they are all ready to obey all commands and orders, and are now marching into the feild (though we can have noe money from the treasury.) Wee shall only add further that we are,

'Your most humble servants,

'MILES CORBETT. JO. JONES. EDM. LUDLOWE [1].

'KILKENNY,

'*6th May*, 1652.'

[1] Tanner MSS. liii. 22. Read May 18, 1652.

XXIV.

[The Commissioners to the Council of State.]

'MAY IT PLEASE YOUR LORDSHIPS,

'Since our coming to this town, being the 17th of Aprill last, our time hath bene taken up in receiving an account from your officers of the condition of your affaires and strength of the enemy in all parts of this land, and in advising with them how the cloathes, cloth, arms and provisions might bee issued out with most equallity and advantage to your service. And although your Lordships' care and wisdom hath bene very great in making such ample provision to supply the wants of those that serve you here, yet, when wee came upon the distribution of them, wee found two thousand suites of clothes for the foote souldiers wanting to answer the number of them upon muster, notwithstanding those clothes that were provided and made att Dublin. Wee find likewise a great want of carabines, firelockes and pykes; wee have not yett had invoyces, nor a full account of all your stores of provision of victualls in or appointed for all parts, whereby wee might issue out orders for the equall distribution of the same, and give your Lordships an account how long the said stores may serve your forces; onely this wee humbly certify your Lordships that all the quantity of cheese, whereof wee have had any advise, is exceeding short and inconsiderable to serve your forces, and that there is little hope of bread or other provision in this countrey, the inhabitants in Thomond, Upper Ormond, and in severall other parts of the land being necessitated by hunger to eat their garrans and plough-horses, and to buy and steale from one another the worst kind of horses to eate, so that little or noe provision wilbee had in Ireland for your forces before the beginninge of October next. But wee presume that those that serve you at the Committee for your affaires here have all before them, and can advise what is fitt to be ordered touching future supplies. Wee send your Lordships herewith a coppie of Articles agreed upon by Col. Venables with two of the Ulster regiments of the enemy, which wee humbly desire may be reported to the Parliament for their approbation. We find that the conditions made by Commissary-Gen. Reinolds with Col. Fitz-Patricke hath taken very good effect in breaking the union and combination that was betweene the rebells not to divide or to seeke termes apart, for which the said Col. Fitz-Patricke was excommunicated by their priests, and declared against by their Councell held at Garrench; and since their submission many of Fitz-Patricke's men have bene killed by Col. Grace his forces, so that of Fitz-Patrick's, O'Dwyre's, and Murtagh O'Brian's men, and of other forces in Connaught who lately submitted to Commissary-Gen. Reinolds, there are, as is conceived by your officers, noe less than sixe thousand men that have already submitted, most of whom are willing to goe to serve the King of Spayne; and in order to their transportation and thereby ridding this country of them, wee have given power to some merchants here to presse shipping, upon good security to be given for insurance of the ships, freight and demurradge, according to the usuall course and custom of merchants, provided the forces to be transported be such as lay downe armes and are not guilty of the murthers, and in number not exceeding ten thousand men. Wee humbly desire your Lordships' approbation of this particular, it being an extraordinary act, and of very great advantage to your service in the judgment of all that serve you here. The Earl of Westmeath, Lord Slayn, Sir Walter Dungan, and divers other officers on the behalf of the enemy in arms in Leinster; the Lord Muskerry, on the behalf of the forces under his command in Kerry and Carbury, has made applications, and is now in treaty with some of your officers (commissioned to that purpose) for termes for the said forces to submitt and lay downe armes. The result of which meeting, if it comes to anything, wee shall communicate to your Lordships as soone as it comes to our hands. Since our coming to this place, some losse happened to your forces and affairs here; parte of Capt. Norwood's troope-horses, and all Capt. Pagnam's troope of dragoones on the borders of Wicklow were surprised at grasse, and Capt. Crookhorne's troope of dragoones were by playne force taken; the men being forced to forsake their horses defended themselves, and killed some of the enemy attempting to force the place. Col. Grace, out of the fastness of Glanmalyer, fell into Kildare, burnt the towne, preyed the countrey thereabouts, and putt some of the inhabitants to the sword. These successes heightened the enemy, insomuch that Sir Walter Dungan with two hundred and fifty horse and five hundred foote marched into the baronyes next adjoyning to Wexford, and tooke a prey of above 500 cowes; but some of your horse being appointed to march into that countrey to joyne with Lieut.-Colonell Throgmorton and his forces belonging to Wexford, on the last Lord's day in the afternoone joyned, being betweene the enemy and the quarters to which they were to march, and within an houre after their conjunction (being then in the whole 150 horse and 400 foote) they engaged the enemy, who had taken an advantage of ground, and stood in battalia to receive them; in which ingagement (after a very sharp dispute, your horse at first being putt to retreate, and the Irish foote comming to push of pyke with your foote who had noe pykes, but were fayne to clubb with their musketts) the Lord was pleased to appeare for his poore servants, and at the instant of time when all was given for lost, God turned the battaile, and gave your men the execution of the enemy for fyve miles and untill the night prevented further pursuite; there was slayne of the enemy upon the place above two hundred, amongst which the Lord

Gallmoy's eldest sonne was slayne, and divers other considerable persons ; there were likewise Major Art Cavenagh, two captaines, three lieutenants, two ensignes, two quarter-masters, and twenty non-commissioned officers and private troopers taken prisoners, and above one hundred good horses taken, and the prey restored : there were of your men 21 slain, and about one hundred wounded (most of them) by the enemies pykes. This was indeed a mercy wrought by the imediate hand of a God, our enemies themselves being witnesses and confessing the same. The Lord grant that by these manifestations of his love our spiritts may be drawne up, and our hearts sett on worke to praise his name. All the forces that are to take the feild this summer are ordered to march to their severall stations, and some of them already on their march, and the rest wilbee in the feild within five or six days. The late coming of the provisions, and want of money in the treasury to enable your forces to advance, putts us into great straights. Wee shall add no further at present but that wee are,

'Your Lordships' humble servants,

' MILES CORBETT. JO. JONES. EDM. LUDLOWE [1].

' KILKENNY,
   ' 6 *May*, 1652.'

XXV.

[The Commissioners to the President of the Council of State.]

' RIGHT HONOURABLE,

' Wee humbly present to your Lordships, with some explanations made by Commissioners of the Articles of Galway, and the concessions of the Galway men to those explanations. The maine Articles (concerning their residence in the towne, and the enjoyment of their houses and estates) they as yet adhere unto, which will make the place very chargable unto you to keepe, untill the Parliament's pleasure, or your advise be knowne therein. Sir Charles Coote seemes to be confident that the Galway men will declare, that if the Parliament order that noe Irish and papists bee admitted to reside in any garrison in Ireland, that then they conceive themselves bound to observe such a law, and that they shall not insist upon their Articles to free themselves from such a generall law.

' Wee humbly desire a signification of your pleasure in this particular.

' The townsmen by their Articles are to pay £5000 as a composition or their personall estate, and wee have great neede of the money, but, if we should receive it before we know your pleasure, wee are afraid wee shall thereby bee constrained to confirme the Articles. And therefore wee are very tender of doeing any Act that may amount to a con-

---

[1] Tanner MSS. liii. 24.

APP. IV. firmation, untill wee receive your Lordships' advise, (and yet this great summe and our great necessities are strong temptations unto us). In expectation whereof wee rest,

'Your most humble servants,

'MILES CORBETT. JO. JONES. EDM. LUDLOWE [1].

'KILKENNY,

'*6th May*, 1652.'

XXVI.

[From the Irish Commissioners to the Speaker.]

'[MR. SPEAKER],

'We mentioned in our last a treaty that was then begun betweene the Earl of Westmeath and others, the principall officers of the enemies party, with your servants here, which after many disputes and difficulties is now brought to an issue, and a coppie of the Articles and declarations then passed wee send here inclosed, which wee doe humbly present to your view and judgment; and whatever issue may be hereof wee can assure you the intentions and endeavours of all your servants acting therein was to doe nothing that in their judgments and consciences might be displeasing to that God who hath wrought so many and so great deliverances for you and them, or that might prejudice the English interest. Had wee had particular directions or qualifications from you nothing should have been done otherwise then as you had prescribed. But God having put this opportunity into our hands wee held it our duty to make use thereof, considering the vastness of the charge in maintaining your forces; and yet the forces here allmost all taken up in preserving garrisons and forts, and the enemy being driven out of all forts, hath nothing to doe but to be in the feild when they pleased, and then as they saw advantage to retire to their boggs and fastnesses, and in the meantime to commit stealths and plunderings to the walls and gates of your garrisons; and such is their number that at this present the Lord Muskerry, that commands the enemy in Munster, is 600 Horse and 3000 Foote, and some of his party is now before Dingle, which is the only hold you have in Kerry, and Clanriccard with the Connaught and Ulster forces are very considerable in the parts betweene Connaught and Ulster, which would require more forces than wee could draw out to make considerable bodies against them, thereby to prevent the desolation and ruin they would make in your quarters, besides those forces of the enemy in Leinster that have this year surprised many of your horse, and driven away many catle in severall parts of Leinster. And withall we do not know how the enemy may receive encouragement and hopes of help if there should

[1] Tanner MSS. liii. 27.

be any peace in forraigne parts. Wee shall only add, that considering the treachery, wickedness and malice of the generality of this people, that your servants here must not lessen their vigilancy over them; and if their armes be layd downe, as is hoped, and undertaken for, and the principall heads of that party with the souldiers under their command doe goe beyond seas, which is their purpose and desire, and which wee shall endeavour to further, wee doe hope this will render this countrey, in time, all into your possession, to be settled and governed as God shall direct and enable you. And as wee see the execution of this treaty wee shall from time to time give you further accompt thereof, and doe desire that your care in sending supplyes to enable your servants here to the remainder of the work yet here to be done, be not yet lessened but continued, which by the blessing of God may crowne all your former labours. Wee shall only add that wee are

'Your most humble servants.

'EDM. LUDLOWE.   MILES CORBETT.   JO. JONES[1].

'KILKENNY.

'13 *May,* 1652.

'Wee shall send further accompt hereof, as we shall see the execution of this treaty to fall out, by some person privy to all these transactions to give you a just accompt of all particular passages.'

XXVII.

[*The Commissioners to the Speaker.*]

'MR. SPEAKER,

'By our last, of the 13th of May from Kilkenny, sent by Captain Vernon, wee gave you account of the treaty then newly concluded on with the Earle of Westmeath, and the Leinster officers of the enemies party.

'Since that we understanding that the Lord of Muskerry and his party in Kerry, that are very considerable, did not accept thereof, but did expect some better termes, the Major-Generall and the Lord Broghill drew to Drumagh, the only considerable castle the enemy held in the county of Corke, and was indeed a strong and a secure hold for them, but by the blessing and helpe of the Lord, that was rendered to you, of which the Lieutenant-Generall gave you former account from Youghall; and finding that party of yours that reduced that place not to be sufficient for reducing Ross, where the strength of the enemy lay, upon debate and conference with Sir Hardress Waller and divers of your officers at Corke, it was resolved to draw out what

[1] Tanner MSS. liii. 31.   Read May 25.

forces could best be spared from these partes to march into Kerry; and having gotten what supplies were necessary, and could be had, they marched hence to Mallow, and did expect to be at Ross in Kerry on Sunday the 4th instant.

'Since their departure from us, wee doe hear there was some distraction amongst the enemy at Rosse, so as the cleargie party, and such as adhered to that interest, drew out of Rosse, but my Lord of Muskerry, and such as stood to him, doe keepe in Rosse; what may be the issue is not knowne.

'The greatest body of the enemy is gathered together about Ballyshannon in Ulster, under Clanrickard. And by letters of the 30th of May, from Commissary Generall Reinolds from Athlone, and by others, we do understand that the enemy have besieged Ballyshannon, a house of the Lord Folliot's, and with two guns have made batteries against it, and having two or three times beene repulsed, at last have gained it, and burnt it, before Sir Charles Coote could come to relieve it. And they have also taken the Castle of Donegale, and all the enemyes forces of Ulster, and Connaught are there conjoyned. But Sir Charles Coote with his owne party, and part of Commissary-General Reinolds' party, are in pursuite of them on one side, and Colonel Venables and his party on the other side; and Commissary-General Reinolds with one 100 horse from Col. Sankey is also marched up, and orders sent to Col. Hewson to draw downe that way also. Soe it is hoped (through the helpe of our Lord) they shalbe enabled to find out that enemy, and to engage with him. What horse and foote of the Leinster enemy doe come in, wee cannot give any account as yet, having not received ourselves any accompt of the same; only Grace his party which did infest your quarters in Leinster, most of his horse are come in, and submitted, and himselfe with twelve horse, and about seventy that marched before, are gone to Clanrickard, and his foote being in all about 1000 are at present dispersed, but doe lie scattered in the woodes, and bogges, and your forces in those parts do dayly hunt and attend them. This is the present posture of your forces here, and in all partes their hands are full; and wee doe hope you will not bee unmindful to continue your care in providing for them; the plentiful, and good provisions you have formerly ordered to be sent hither, are for the most parte all come hither, which is a great comfort to the poore souldiery; and wee doe wish wee had more of the intended recruites, such of them as are come already being very able, and fitt for your service, and were the residue that are appointed, to come over before the summer be too far spent, it would much advance your affairs as now they stand.

'We heare every day of sadd losses by the spoyles and piracies don by the French, and other piratts at sea, and we cannot hear of any of the Parliament's shipps between Kingsale and Derry, save only Capt.

Sherwin who is commanded hence for Scotland, and Capt. Peirs who APP. IV hath been out 18 monethes, and not very fitt for service, as he sayeth, who is gone to convoy some vessels with provisions to Limericke as wee heare; which is all wee shall trouble you with at present, save to assure you wee are

'Your most humble servants,

'MILES CORBETT.   JO. JONES[1].

'CORK,
'5th June, 1652.'

XXVIII.

[Edmund Ludlow to the Commissioners of Parliament.]

'TRULY HONOURABLE,

' I have received your plentifull supply as to use and comfort, both the officers and souldiers are very sencible of your kindnes to them, and care of them[2]. The Lord hath at length enclined the enemy to a submission upon termes not much differing with those with Leinster, onely wee have left out the clause for mediation with the Parliament toutching their reall estates. Rosse is to be delivered on Saterday next at noone: I signed the articles even now. The Lord of Mus-kerries sonne and his unckle, Sir Daniel Brien, I expect to be sent imediately to me as hostages; his forces abroad are to lay downe armes on the 5th of July; those in Kerry at Killarney; those towards Corke at Macroome; those towards Limerick at Killmallocke. As soon as I can see things settled here, that soe I may know what force can be spared hence for the Northerne service, I shall march with them up to you, which I hope to doe some time next weeke. The Lord direct and protect you, and give us thankfull hearts under these his gracious dispensacions. Deare friends,

'Your most affectionate and
'humble Servant,
'EDMUND LUDLOW.

'*From the Campe before* ROSSE,
'*this* 23 *of June,* 1652.'

[Endorsed :—]

'A true coppy of the Leiftenant-Generall's letter to theCommissioners of Parliament. Dated 23 Junii 1652.

'JO. HUGHES[3].'

---

[1] Tanner MSS. liii. f. 53. Printed in 'Severall Proceedings in Parliament,' p. 2230. Read in the House, June 15.

[2] 'We have sent you and the officers a tun of French wine and 4 rolls of tobacco to the soldiers,' says a letter from the Commisioners to Ludlow.

[3] Read 6 Julii 1652. Tanner MSS. liii. 67.

XXIX.

[Edmund Ludlow to William Lenthall, Speaker.]

' MR. SPEAKER,

'That those plentifull provisions which God hath put in your hearts and hands to supply us withall, for the carrieing on of your righteous undertaking this summer, might not bee wholy lost in the absence of the Lord Deputy, the enemy in Kerry and that in the north being looked upon as most considerable, at a generall Councell held at Kilkenny, it was resolved that your field force should bee applied those wayes; yet not soe as to leave the Middland parts unprovided for, (not knowing what the effect would bee, of the agreement made with the Earle of Westmeath, Sir Walter Dungan and others, of which Sir Walter Dungan hath lately sent mee this accompt inclosed) and therefore there was left with the Lord Broghill, Coll. Sankey, Col. Ingolsby, Col. Axtell, Lieut. Col. Throgmorton and Col. Hewson in their severall precincts, a competent force, both of horse and foote, through God's assistance to encounter with the enemy they had to deale withall. I doubt not in the Lord's owne tyme, but Sir Charles Coote, Commissary-Generall Reinholds and Col. Venables will give you a good accompt of the Earle of Clanricard's forces and those of Ulster, who are joyned and have beene somewhat active, but not at all to their advantage. The Major Generall and I have beene before this place neare three weekes past, the first of which was spent in a treaty with the enemy, which broake of, they insisting upon an article, for the free exercize of their religion, and for assurance of some part of their reall estates, which was totally rejected. The place beeing hardly accessible by land, wee then applied our endeavours for the procuring of boats for the landing our men in their island, wherin God hath beene pleased soe farr to succeede us, that in one weeke's tyme wee had half a dozen boates swimmeing in their Lough, and had, through the great care and industry of the Commissioners of the Parliament, from the county of Corke workmen and materialls ready for the making of boats within tenn daies to land a thousand men. But by this tyme the Lord had inclined the enemy to sollicit for condicions againe, which considering the hazard of an attempt, they haveing a thousand fighting men in the island, and the great fastnesses of this countrey possessed by a numerous and desperate enemy, haveing convenient harbours for succours from abroad, and hopeing hereby to put a period to the warr in these parts, and soe to lessen your chardge and sett at liberty your force here for some other service, wee consented unto, and after two dayes' debate agreed upon the articles heere inclosed ; wherein if wee have either fallen short of your expectacion, or exceeded your intentions in any of our concessions, wee humbly crave your pardon, and that you will beleeve wee aymed in them at your service, Arr. IV more than our owne ease, or advantage, other than the dischardge of our duty is soe. Wherin that the Lord will alwayes direct us, is the hearty prayer of

'Mr. Speaker,

'Your faithfull and most humble servant,

'EDMUND LUDLOWE.

'*From the Campe before* ROSSE,
'*the 24th of June*, 1652.

'The Lord of Muskery's sonne and Lieut. Col. Knocher O'Callaghan are hostages with mee for the performance of these Articles. God willing I shall hasten northwards with all the force that can bee spared hence, least they should stand in need of them [1].'

XXX.

[*The Commissioners to the Speaker.*]

'MR. SPEAKER,

'Since the late agreement at Kilkenny, the Lord of Muskerry in the south and the Lord Clanriccard in the north have not only declared themselves not to accept of that capitulation, but have gathered together considerable bodies of the Irish in both places.

'As to Clanriccard, since the reducing of Balleshannon Sir Charles Coote with his owne and part of Commissary-Generall Reignolds' party, have reduced Sleigo; and since that the Commissary-Generall is come to him, and as wee hear from the Commissary-Generall of the 18th instant from the camp before Ballemote are now before that castle, being the castle of the Lord Taaffe in the county of Leitrim. Coll. Venables with his party are at Belturbet in Cavan, a place very considerable to be made a garrison, in order to the reducing of the county of Cavan, and those fastnesses thereabouts, and wee doe believe part of the Leinster forces are with Venables or near to him, and Clanriccard doth lye in fastnesses between Ballimote and Belturbet, with 4000 horse and foot, but hath refused to engage with either party of ours, but hath sent for a treaty, and hath sent to the Lieut.-General and to us to appoint Commissioners, and hath sent articles to the Commissary-Generall. Our answer thereto we send enclosed, and have advised the Commissary-General to that purpose. And Grace, another of the Irish Rebells, hath gathered a body of the Irish, that formerly were of the Leinster rebells; and being beaten from his fastnesses in Leinster by Coll. Axtel, and Coll. Sankey, got over the Shannon,

[1] Original, signed by Ludlow; small seal with arms. Tanner MSS. liii. 75.

and have burnt the town of Portumney, and threatened the castle of Portumney; but Coll. Ingolsby from Limerick going to assist our freinds there, heard that Grace had joined with Burke, and were about Lough Reagh, and were about 3000 horse and foote, and so Coll. Ingolsby fell on the enemy, and as wee heard from Major Smith, from Limerick, the 22nd instant, that certaine intelligence was come to him that Ingolsby had totally routed the enemy's horse, and the foote being gott into a bogg he had encompassed the same with his horse and dragoones, and was in that posture when the messenger came from him to Limerick. As to the enemy with the Lord Muskerry in Kerry, the Lieutenant-General and the Major-General with what party could be spared from other parts are marched to Rosse, the cheif hold of the enemy there, and having left two troopes of horse, one of dragoones, and 400 foote in a fort before Ross, the Lieut.-Gen. with the body of his brigade did the 13th instant meet with a party of the enemy, and had routed them, and tooke some 50 horse, and some prey, and an abbey called Killara, where they found some 4 barrels of powder, and in those parts they have bene till the boats and other necessaries sent them from Kinsale came to them; and on the 19th instant wee received letters from them that that day they marched up with the party to the fort near Rosse Castle, and thither they have sent the boates and provisions, but on the 18th instant Muskerry sent for a new treaty, but the Lieut.-Gen. hath limited it to conclude on the 21st instant, at six in the night, and in the meantime are preparing their boates for service. But this last Saboth being 20th instant, a party of Muskerries forces having joyned with other the rebels' party that lie in the boggs and mountaines of Cork, did come into this county to drive the catle about Macroome to carry them into their quarters, but the Lord Broghill (who is left behind to secure the quarters) after a march of twenty miles, fell on the enemy who were more than double in number to the Lord Broghill's party, but the enemy would not engage, soe as the Lord Broghill's party fell on the reere of the enemies body, and tooke about 80 horse : killed about 50: took Lieut.-Col. Supple that commanded the rear guard of the enemy, and gott two colours and some good quantity of armes, and regained 200 catle the enemy were carrying away, and the rest of the enemy by the favour of a mist, and our party being much spent with a long march before the skirmish, and the impassableness of those parts could not follow them above a mile or two. Col. Clark's regiment is safely arrived at Waterford, which doth come very season-ably to strengthen your forces in these parts.

'These wonderworkings of our God wee hope will appear glorious in your eyes, and wee hope will cleerly evidence unto you the diligence, and fidelity of your poore servants here, who in order to your service are dispatched into all parts of the land, and yet their small scattered parties (through the goodness and help of the Lord) have put to

flight the armies and great bodies of the enemy. Wee shall only add
that wee are

'Your most humble servants.

'CORK,
'24th June, 1652.

'Since the writing hereof, we have received letters from the Lieut.-
Generall of the 23rd instant, from the camp before Rosse, concerning
the rendering of Rosse, and submission of that enemy, a coppy of that
letter we send also enclosed.

'MILES CORBETT. JO. JONES [1].'

XXXI.

[*The Commissioners to the Speaker.*]

'MR. SPEAKER,

'Our last frome Cork gave you an accompt of the then present
condition of your affairs. Since then the Lord of Muskerry after the
Treaty concluded at Rosse, hath been industrious to make the submission of his party as considerable as he could, soe as in severall
places there have of his party 3000 foot, and 700 horsemen mounted,
and 300 unmounted, brought in their horse and armes; and the Lord
Muskerry himself doth (as he saith) intend presently to goe for Spaine,
and carry with him 1000 men and himselfe to returne againe, if he can
obtaine any considerable command upon the carrying over of the
residue of his party, for whome he is there to make his conditions.
There is now in the fastnesses of Kerry one Murtogh O'Brian who is on
the head of such of the Irish rebells as have not submitted, and come
in with the Lord Muskerry: and Sir Hardress Waller with a considerable party is left in Kerry to clear that county, and to make such
garrisons therein, as may enable the party there to prevent the
gathering together of the enemy, or others that may come to them.

'The Earle of Clanriccard and the body of the rebells that were in a
conjunction with him, being beaten from their garrisons and castles by
a considerable party under Sir Charles Coote and Commis.-Gen.
Reignolds on the one side, and Coll. Venables with some part of the
Leinster forces sent from Coll. Hewson on the other side, and by
planting of garrisons at Belturbet, in Cavan, and securing severall
passes, have bene soe attended on all hands, that they could not
continue any longer together in a body, and the Earl of Clanriccard,
for himself, and the severall officers of the Connaught forces for themselves, and the party under their command, have also come in and
submitted; and on the last of this instant are to bring in their Horse
and armes, and have desired leave to transport 5000, so as all

[1] Tanner MSS. liii. f. 73. Read July 6.

Connaught (if they perform their conditions) will be clear of any enemy that we can hear of : and those rebells that are left in Ulster are attended by Commissary General Reignolds in Longford, and by Coll. Venables in Cavan and those parts, soe as it is hoped they wilbe reduced to such a condition, as they shall be disenabled at least to infest your quarters, some part or other of your forces continually falling upon them, as they doe move out of their fastnesses. Since the rendition of Rosse in Kerry, a considerable part of your forces under the conduct of Lieut.-Generall Ludlowe had some resolutions to march into the North, to make that body of your forces there more con- siderable ; but upon the submission of the Connaught enemy, and that there is sufficient force there to attend the remainder of the Ulster rebells at present, it is now held most adviseable that the Lieut.- Generall doe forthwith march into Wicklow and Wexford, and to beat those woods and mountaines, and to find out the enemy, and to plant some garrisons in those fastnesses, and then to move further as shalbe most conducing to your service.

' There hath bene a late meeting of very many of the officers at Clonmell, of which they gave us notice at Corke, and desired our coming thither to them, and wee were present with them in all their debates and consultations, the result whereof was put into writing, and sent by Col. Hewson, and Adjutant-General Allen, and wee did observe in every one then met a general desire to testifie their dutie, and thankfulness for the great care of the Parliament in the plentifull provisions made for them hitherto, and that nothing should be by them presented that might any way seem to be contrary to any resolutions of the Parliament concerning them, but in all things are most willing to be ordered by you, as God shall please to guide and lead you. Wee shall conclude with our humble desires that your pleasure may be knowne what you will hold out towards the settlement of the nation, and what the Irish may expect from you, and that such as fall from you (which they are very apt to do) may be by force reduced, and that such Commander in Cheif and others whome you shall please to send over may be timely sent, whereby (and by the help and blessing of God) you may see the fruit of the vast expense both of blood and treasure that you have bene at to the reducing of this nation.

' Wee are this day to march to Kilkenny, and thence to Dublin, from whence wee hope to give you further account as occasion shall be offered, and at present shall only subscribe ourselves,

' Your most humble servants,

'MILES CORBETT. JO. JONES [1].

' WATERFORD,
' 22nd *July*, 1652.'

---

[1] Tanner MSS. liii. 98.   Read August 3.

XXXII.

[*The Commissioners to the Speaker.*]

'MR SPEAKER,

' Our last of the 22nd July from Waterford did present unto you the posture your affairs then stood in, and since then there is not anything come to our knowledge worthy of your trouble. Your forces lying all dispersed in the several parts of this nation watching all motions of such of the enemy as do still hold out, and have not submitted, the most considerable whereof are in Ulster where they have of late seemed willing to submit, and have treated with some of your servants to that end, and after some time spent therein did come to a conclusion, and the commanders of the enemy's part seemed satisfied with the conditions, only they desired time to shew it to the chief of their officers; and after they had considered thereof did send back this enclosed paper; which, as we are informed, did proceed from the apprehension of the danger they were in by the murders and massacre in the beginning of the rebellion, whereof the chief of them were the most eminent actors, and yet during the treaty pretended their innocency therein, and that they would stand to a trial to clear themselves from that suspicion. They are heightened to that resolution by a friar lately come amongst them out of England (one Abbot Croyly) that pretends to give them great assurance of succours and relief from the Duke of Lorraine. Upon this (and in consideration of the enemy's present posture) your servants in those parts have resolved to make several garrisons in the bowels of their fastnesses, and to secure all passes into and from the same, and to lay waste those fastnesses and countries wherein the enemy have relief, and security from your forces. In other parts of the nation your servants are no less diligent in watching over the enemy (that doth yet stand out) near their quarters, so as there is much more security in Munster, Leinster and Connaught, than ever yet was enjoyed by your friends since the Rebellion broke out, and by the blessing of God we may hope it will continue and increase daily, being assured that your forces here will have the continuance of your care in making timely provision for them, until there be a thorough settlement of this nation upon certain grounds, which in convenient time we hope will be effected.

' And seeing it hath pleased God to reduce this nation in so good a measure to your obedience, we hold it necessary that all such as are in the power of your ministers here, and are guilty of any murders, ought to be brought to trial for the same, some being already in prison for those offences, and others are daily discovered to us that are guilty of those cruel murders. But we cannot bring them to a trial for the

APP. IV. said offences, for that in some counties where those cruelties were committed there are no inhabitants at all, the counties lying waste, and there cannot be juries in any county but such as are Papists and Irish, and such [as] have had a hand in the Rebellion, and no ways to be trusted therein ; and therefore we do humbly desire the pleasure of the Parliament to be signified what course is to be taken for the trial of such offenders, and if you please to authorise any present commission, to erect one or more Courts of Justice, and that those Commissioners, or any 12 or more of them, have power to enquire of and to hear and determine all murders done or committed in Ireland from the 20th of October 1641 to the 20th of October 1642, or that were done or committed since the 20th of October 1642 by or upon any person not being in arms : you have many servants here of known fidelity and integrity that will cheerfully obey your commands therein ; and till your pleasure be known in that or some other way we do not know how to proceed in this great case wherein the honour of God and your justice is so highly concerned [1].

'At our return from Munster to Dublin we found the sickness to break out there, and finding by our being there a great resort to that city, not only from all your garrisons, but from all parts of the nation, whereby the plague might be increased there (and your army and garrisons endangered thereby) we have removed ourselves to this place, until we shall see what the Lord shall please to do therein,

'Your [most humble servants,]

'EDMUND LUDLOW. MILES CORBET. JOHN JONES [2].

'DROGHEDA,

'*11th August*, 1652.'

XXXIII.

[*The Commissioners to the Speaker.*]

'MR. SPEAKER,

'Since our coming to this place very many of the officers of your army have given us a meeting and after some consultations in order to

---

[1] In a letter to Dr. Henry Jones, dated Aug. 5, the Commissioners had ordered him to collect evidence concerning murders and similar outrages to be laid before the proposed Court. Writing to the Council of State on Aug. 11, the Commissioners say that it is 'much upon the spirits of some' that the great outbreak of the plague was a token of God's displeasure 'because the murders and massacres which have provoked the Lord to pour out the vials of his wrath upon this nation have not been effectually enquired after and prosecuted, and thereby his justice vindicated.'

[2] Irish Records, Commonwealth Series, $\frac{A}{90}$ 50, p. 211. Modernised by the transcriber.

carry on your affaires here, the greatest part of them are gone to attend their severall charges.

'There are already gone out of this Nation of such of the Irish as have been in armes about 7000 of the parties of Odwyre, Fitzpatrick, Muskerry and Martogh O'Bryan, and Fitz Gerald. And at this present there are preparations for the carrying over many others by Sir Walter Dungan, the Lord Westmeath, and severall other officers of the Irish party.

'This day we have received intelligence of 400 of the Conough party (that hitherto have been out in rebellion) are come in, and last week did lay down their arms—but in Erra Conought (which is part of the County of Galloway, and next to Ennisbuffin) there are some that formerly submitted have run out again.

'Sir Charles Coot is gone from us to Conought, to have an eye upon them, the most considerable enemy that is still out: Sir Phelim O'Neyle and most of the officers of the Ulster party (being guilty of blood and of the first rebellion) doe head them and hold them together, and though a considerable part of them did condescend to some Articles, yet it is doubtfull of their continuance.

'But Col. Venables of the one part, and Commissary Gen. Reynolds on the other are to attend them, and (by the help of the Lord) we hope will give an account of them.

'Upon consideration that our gaols in this place and some parts of Munster were full of the murtherers, etc. we have granted a commission to severall persons of integrity and trust, that have this day begun to sit, and to execute their commission. We remain,

'Your most humble servants,

'CHARLES FLEETWOOD. EDM. LUDLOW. MILES CORBET[1].

'KILKENNY,
'14 *October*, 1652.'

XXXIV.

[*The Commissioners to the Speaker.*]

'MR. SPEAKER,
'Our last from Kilkenny gave you an account of your affairs here, and though the late laying down of arms by most of the enemy and the transportation of a very considerable part of them since, have put your affairs into a hopeful condition of settlement in some good measure, yet such is the desperate condition of those persons [who are] guilty of blood, and were the principal contrivers and actors of the Rebellion in the beginning thereof, that they leave no means unattempted to disturb your affairs; and such is the inaccessibleness of the places

[1] From 'Severall Proceedings in Parliament,' 1652, p. 2525.

App. IV. and fastnesses they are got into that there is no great action [?] likely to be done upon them this winter season, unless they be forced through famine to quit these places, which is the present endeavour of those forces that are appointed to attend their motions. Since our coming to this place we have taken into consideration the reducing of such part of your army as may stand with the safety of your affairs here, wherein we have found great readiness and assistance from your officers and servants that do command in your army; but do find that there cannot be much done therein to any present considerable advantage to lessen the charge you now are at, until your pleasure be known, and the act passed for satisfying the Adventurers and the arrears due to the soldiers (especially such as are to be reduced). Upon consideration had of the miserable waste condition of this country, and the many straits and difficulties the poor soldiers are put into through the insolvency of such counties and places appointed for their pay, which do lie waste and without inhabitant, we cannot but present the same unto you, and do most humbly desire the continuance of your former supply unto your Army and forces; and we do hope through the blessing of God and the faithful endeavours of your servants you will have a good account of the remaining work to be done here. The posture of your affairs at the present do not afford any action of any moment done of late worthy of your knowledge. We shall only take leave to subscribe etc.[1]

'DUBLIN,
'3 *Dec.*, 1652.'

XXXV.

[The Commissioners to the President of the Council of State.]

'RIGHT HONOURABLE,

'Since our last we have received intelligence of a sudden surprisal that hath been made by the enemy upon a garrison of yours in the Isle of Arran, lying in the mouth of the Bay of Galway and near the two fastnesses of Ericonnaught and Ennisbuffin, from whence the enemy landing (as we are informed) 600 men, and with the assistance of the inhabitants of that island, they have possessed themselves of it. In the attempt of which also the enemy had advantage from the weakness of the works which were not altogether finished, but principally by reason of the want of shipping and vessels in that harbour, either to relieve that garrison, or to make an assault upon the enemy at their landing; the ships appointed to attend that place, and which had directions not to depart that harbour until the works were finished,

---

[1] Irish Records, Commonwealth Series, $\frac{A}{90}$ 50, p. 357.

contrary to their order leaving it, and putting out to sea, in whose App. IV
absence this attempt was made by the enemy. Upon consideration
of which place and of the importance of it to your interest here, and
how difficult it may be to reduce the same hereafter, when the enemy
by the assistance of those from Ennisbuffin and elsewhere shall have
finished the fortifications that are already begun, by advice of a
Council of Officers here, orders are given for the drawing forth a commanded party of 1500 men, and for the fitting all other provisions and
necessaries for the reducing of it ; which because it is not to be effected
without a sufficient number of shipping, as well to land our men and
provisions and to secure the harbours, as to prevent any new approach
of the enemy, it was further judged necessary immediately to despatch
away a letter to Kinsale for the going about of three or four good ships
from thence to Galway, with such a quantity of victuals and provisions
from Kinsale as might enable them for some time to attend that
service, there being no provision of that kind to be had at Galway and
those parts [1].'

' DUBLIN,
' 20th December, 1652.'

XXXVI.

[*The Commissioners to the Speaker.*]

' MR. SPEAKER,
' By our last we gave you an account in general of the posture of
your forces in order to attend the motion of the enemy, who, though
they be for the most part in a very great measure reduced, yet many
of them do this winter lie in islands, bogs and fastnesses, and are
ready and watchful to take all advantage ; but in several parts your

[1] Irish Records, Commonwealth Series, $\frac{A}{90}$ 50, 373. The surprise of Arran caused so much excitement that the commissioners thought fit to send a letter to the commanders of the precincts ordering a day of fasting and humiliation for Dec. 30. ' Christian friends,' begins their letter, ' those unto whom the Lord hath in any measure (thro' grace) made known his free eternal unchange-able love, cannot but be sensible how he hath of late manifested some displeasure against us, by continuing the pestilence in very many of our quarters and garrisons, and stirring a vanquished and dispersed enemy to an unusual resolution of attempt-ing the surprisal of the fort and Isle of Arran, and therein to prevail not by strength but by reason of a strange spirit of despondency which possessed him that commanded that place, far unsuitable to his accustomed temper in the judgment of those that knew him.' Letter dated Dec. 23, 1652 ; Irish Records, $\frac{A}{90}$ 50, p. 378.

officers and soldiers have met with small parties of them, and have done some considerable execution against them. But the enemy in the Isles of Arran and Ennisbuffin being likely to grow more considerable, and if let alone this winter might not only give encouragement to any design of a foreign enemy, but also relieve with arms and ammunition the rest of that party now in bogs and fastnesses, and give intelligence and countenance to the enemy now in the bogs and islands, giving out with confidence their great hopes of relief and succour from them and from foreign princes and states, especially from Lorraine, whereupon by advice at a Council of War it was held necessary to send a commanded party forthwith from the garrisons and places where they might be best spared in order to reduce those Islands this winter season ; and in pursuance thereof Commissary-General Reynolds was despatched to command that party ; and those few ships that are now left in these seas are ordered to attend about those islands, and to ship the forces and provisions, and give other assistance as occasion shall be offered. By our last from Commissary-General Reynolds of the 11th instant from aboard the Sun in Galway Bay he signified that the guns and provisions were shipped, and the wind fair, and that they were ready for sail to their intended design, and that the soldiers with him (notwithstanding their long and hard march) were very cheerful and hearty in this service.

' The two great businesses which now lie before us are how to lessen your charge and how to plant the country, but neither of these can be done to any effect till we do hear your pleasure about the Bill before you for giving satisfaction to the Adventurers and also to satisfy the arrears of the soldiers. Since the late treaties with the enemy we do hold it our duty to take the most effectual course we could to bring such as had a hand in the murders and to bring them to a due trial, and to that end appointed a Court of Justice to sit at Kilkenny, Clonmell, and Cork ; in those places there have been 52 persons (many of them very considerable persons and heads of the septs) condemned for the massacres done by them in the beginning of the Rebellion ; and now the High Court doth sit at Dublin, where there is yet only preparation for their future proceedings ; and there hath gone out of this nation since June last above 12000 officers and soldiers of the Irish party, all of them stout and able fighting men, and more are willing and ready to go had we means to effect the same [1].

' DUBLIN,
' 15*th January*, 165¾.'

---

[1] Irish Records, Commonwealth Series, $\frac{A}{90}$ 50, 400.

XXXVII.

[*The Commissioners to the Council of State.*]

' RIGHT HONOURABLE,

'We have not much to trouble your Lordships with at present, but hope (if the Lord please to bless the endeavours of your servants, that a good account will be given your Lordships of the Isle of Arran. 1300 foot and other accommodations were shipped about 6 days since in the Bay of Galway for the reduction of Arran, and 600 foot more are marching by land to Ericonnaught, to be carried thence to Arran to strengthen that party if need be. They are victualled for a month, and more provisions are going up to them, in order to their going up to Buffin if the Lord give them success in this attempt upon Arran. There are gone from Ireland to the service of the King of Spain since April last about 13000, and most of those who have been in arms against you would be persuaded to follow, if any persons of ability and credit were employed to give them conditions and carry them away. Colonel Plunkett having contracted for the carrying over of many, and having sent some away, others on shipboard, and many upon their march to the waterside, died last week (some conceive of grief because he had neither money nor credit to make good his contract) which will occasion the disbanding of many desperate rogues, who know not how to live but by robbing and stealing out of bogs and fastnesses. We have upon long and serious consideration judged it very necessary in order to your service to publish the enclosed Declaration, as one effectual means to settle your interest; if there be any inconvenience in the thing we do not see, we humbly desire we may have notice of it. The High Court of Justice goes on in making inquisition after, and in diligent prosecution of murder. There were 16 condemned at Kilkenny ; 6 at Clonmell, and 32 at Cork, most of them very considerable men. And at this time the Court sits at Dublin, and another erected at Galway to try the Lord Mayo, who was by his articles to be tried there. The Lord hath pleased to own his cause very much in bringing out evidence very strangely and unexpectedly against some of the persons who were condemned [1].

' DUBLIN,
' 15 *January*, 1652.'

XXXVIII.

[*The Commissioners to the Council of State.*]

' MY LORDS,

'By our last of the 4th of February we did acquaint your Lordships of the taking of Sir Phelim O'Neill, now condemned of

[1] Irish Records, Commonwealth Series, $\frac{A}{90}$ 50, 397.

APP. IV. treason by the High Court of Justice at Dublin. At whose trial there being divers witnesses produced who affirmed in Court upon oath, that he had oft told them he had a commission from the late King for what he acted in that Rebellion, he persisting notwithstanding in denial of it, this copy was presented in Court, and read before him, which coming attested by a person of honest repute we thought it our duty to transmit the copy thereof to you; and further to acquaint you that it hath pleased the Lord also so much to bless the undertaking of your servants that Ennisbuffin is likewise surrendered to the Commissary-General upon articles, the copy whereof we here inclose to you. Whereby, as by many other great and seasonable mercies, the Lord hath much disappointed your enemies abroad, who (as we are informed by the enemy here) had designed 12 sail of frigates out of France to rendezvous at that place by the latter end of the next April, to make that their shelter for the more convenient committing of their robberies. It hath also pleased the Lord to assist another party of our forces under Col. Barrow against a party of the rebels, who in hope of safety and for the better annoyance of the country had betook themselves in certain islands and bogs, and to deliver into your hands Trinity Island lying in the County of Cavan, which was a considerable fastness of the Enemy's and able to receive about 1500 men in it. Notwithstanding all which testimonies which the Lord hath been pleased to bear against your enemies, yet such is the desperate condition of many of them that, partly under the sense of guilt and fear of being brought to condign punishment for the murders they have committed (as we have before intimated to your Lordships), partly through their extreme necessity (seeing themselves deprived of all hopes of their estates, and of all expectation also now of being transported into Spain by reason of the discouragements that are put upon them by some that are lately come over), we frequently have intelligence of divers running out and committing robberies upon the country; and more lately in the counties of Cork and Kerry, where about 1200 foot and 60 horse are got together and have possessed themselves of Whidde Island in the Bay of Bantry; having lately intercepted a small party of yours and killed a Capt. with 34 of his men, doing much mischief by frequent incursions into our quarters.

'Having intelligence that the Spanish Ambassador desires license for Major General O'Neill to transport hence 500 men, that to this purpose he hath already moved your Lordships, that likewise 4000 are desired by Colonel O'Dwire, we did the rather conceive it our duty to represent to you the probable security it may prove to the country, and conveniency for your affairs here, to give encouragement for the shipping away as many as is possible of those who have acted in arms as soldiers against you.

'We shall humbly crave leave to mind you of what by the last post

we in the behalf of the merchants and some former undertakers APP. IV.
presumed to move to you, that a regard may be had in such way as
to your Lordships' judgments shall be thought fit, for the true and
punctual performance with the merchants and undertakers in Spain,
and by the Spanish ambassador in England, after they have according
to their contract delivered these men there, without which we fear
there will be found none to undertake the carrying away more men.

'Upon consideration still of the miserable condition of this country
and the many straits and wants of your poor soldiers, through the
insolvency of such counties and places appointed for their pay, which
we are constrained daily to lay more and more waste to prevent all
relief and subsistence to the enemy, we did in the beginning of
December last solicit your Lordships and the Parliament for the
continuance of the supplies of money for the forces here; which, though
we were unwilling to press your Lordships too often about, upon our
knowledge of the great change and the importance of those affairs you
were engaged in, yet now the necessities of the soldiers here further
calling upon us, we must again be earnest with your Lordships for a
mindfulness of us, and for hastening some part of their monthly supplies
to us . . . [a passage concerning the founding a mint in Ireland is here
omitted [1].]

'DUBLIN,
'4th March, 1652.'

XXXIX.

*[By the Commissioners of the Commonwealth of England for
the affairs of Ireland.]*

'The Declaration of his Excellency the Lord Generall, and his councel
of officers coming to our knowledg, we hold it our duty to publish
the same unto all who are intrusted with the managing of publick
affairs in the country, and to mind them that it is now their duty
more than ordinary, notwithstanding the present alteration, to act
carefully and industriously in their several charges, and diligently to
discharge their respective trusts, that the common enemy may not
have advantage from hence to work disturbance against the publick
peace and welfare; and that such as are in the service of the Commonwealth in this land, must expect to be called to a strict account for
their neglect therein. And in regard the present posture of affairs is
such as extraordinarily concerns the interest and welfare of all good
people; we hold it our duty earnestly to exhort them into a special
fervent wrestling with the Lord by humble prayer and supplication,
for wisdom and strength unto those his servants, on whom the burthen

[1] Irish Records, Commonwealth Series, $\frac{A}{90}$ 50, 443.

APP. IV. and care of preserving the Commonwealth in peace, and settling the same in righteousness, doth principally lie. For which end we do appoint Wednesday the fourth of May next, and that day sennight being the eleventh of May, to be set apart for solemn seeking the Grace of the Lord by all his people in Ireland on that behalf.

'CHARLES FLEETWOOD.　　MILES CORBET.

EDM. LUDLOW.　　JO. JONES[1].

　'*Dated at* DUBLIN,
　　'*April* 29, 1653.'

XL.

[*The Commissioners to the Speaker.*]

'MR. SPEAKER,

　'Whereas through the blessing of God and the endeavours of your forces here the power of the enemy is in a good measure suppressed, and very many of the eminent actors in the murders and massacres cut off by the sword of justice and of war, and about 20000 lately transported, and about 7000 now transporting into foreign nations; and consideration being had thereof and of the great destructions in all parts of the nation, so as many counties are without inhabitants and the whole country miserably wasted and destroyed, we conceived it our duty to lessen the charge of the Commonwealth by disbanding so many of your forces as might be spared (regard being had to the security of your interest here), and having formerly given notice thereof to the Parliament and Council of State with our humble desire for passing the Bill for giving satisfaction to the soldiers for their arrears, wherein (as we are informed) some good progress was made, but by reason of the great affairs lately happening there could be no sudden despatch of that Bill; but finding necessities to press upon us here daily, we have consulted with very many of the officers and commanders of your Army called forth from all parts of the nation to the headquarters to that purpose, and advised with them both of the number that could with safety to the whole be well spared, and of the best way and means to give such as should be disbanded satisfaction for their arrears. The result whereof will appear by the inclosed papers and resolutions. And finding a general consent and approbation of these proposals amongst the officers, and there appearing no better way to us to give any reasonable satisfaction of the arrears, we intended so far to approve of them as to proceed to the disbanding of the number of forces therein propounded, and to assign them satisfaction in lands for their arrears, and to set out the same by the nearest estimate that could be made to be enjoyed by them (de bene

---

[1] Mercurius Politicus, p. 2426.

esse) upon the terms proposed, until the supreme authority of the Commonwealth were convened, and did signify their further pleasure for the confirmation or alterations of the same and more exact survey taken of the lands. And having begun to put the disbanding and way for satisfaction of arrears into a way of execution, and many of the officers being returned to their several charges, we lately received a commission under the Great Seal of England with instructions thereunto annexed for setting out lands in satisfaction of soldiers' arrears (which to the utmost of our powers shall be studiously observed by us).

' But by reason the former proposals and resolutions (as is before set forth) are in some things inconsistent with some of the instructions annexed to the Commission, we do find ourselves in some straits and difficulty, and do humbly propose the same unto you.

' First, We find the present instructions sent unto us do give us power to satisfy arrears only as incurred since June 1649, and most of the forces which for many reasons appearing unto us seemed most fit to be first disbanded, were such as have been of longest continuance in your service, and have most considerable arrears due to them before June 1649. Neither is there power for satisfying any others for their service done in England. Besides the power now sent us limits us to five Counties answer not the proposition [?] made by the Council of Officers in that particular.

' Second, We find the baronies in the County of Cork, and the barony in the County of Louth propounded for the places in which some of the soldiers now to be disbanded were to have their lands in satisfaction of their arrears, to be by the said Instructions reserved for other uses. But we conceive it of advantage to the Commonwealth that the soldiers now to be disbanded should be settled in those quarters where they have served and are best acquainted, and that it will be a succour and encouragement to such English as come over to plant upon any account, to have those that served in arms to plant amongst them. And whereas the power to state the accounts of the soldiery in Ireland by the late Act reacheth but to August last, it is humbly proposed that power be given to state all arrears till August and now next ensuing.

' Third, By the Instructions sent us provision is made for such as have right to forfeited lands to make their claim within 20 days after publication, but there is no direction given to bar those claims that are not made.

' CHARLES FLEETWOOD.   MILES CORBET.
EDMUND LUDLOW.   JOHN JONES.

' DUBLIN,
' 22 July, 1653.

' The inclosed paper from the Commissioners for stating the Accounts of the Soldiers states the defects in the Act lately passed

App. IV. for that service, which we desire may be supplied. Sent inclosed the proposals of the Officers for disbanding, and touching places for answering the arrears [1].'

XLI.

[*To Mr. Owen, Mr. Lockier, and Mr. Jenkin Lloyd.*]

'DEAR FRIENDS,

'We need not tell you of the great want of fit and able ministers for preaching the gospel in this country. From our deep sense of it we formerly invited several to that work, but (to our saddening) find but a slow compliance. We do understand the inclination of some others for coming over, but most of them are strangers to us, so that we have inclosed these several letters directed to them, desiring that you would inform yourselves of them and their abilities, and as you shall find them qualified for the work to cause these letters to be sealed and sent unto them, with such further inducements of your own as you shall conceive fit. . . .

'CHARLES FLEETWOOD.   EDMUND LUDLOW.

JOHN JONES.   MILES CORBET [2].

'31 *Aug.*, 1653.'

XLII.

[*The Commissioners for the government of Ireland to the Commanders-in-chief of the respective precincts, to be communicated to the rest of our Christian friends there.*]

'DEAR FRIENDS,

'It hath pleased the Lord through his unsearchable wisdom to exercise his poor servants in these later days with various difficulties and of divers kinds, we trust all for the increase and trial of our faith, and to preserve us from those pollutions which in a continual outward settlement we are too subject unto. And besides that he hath a purpose to accomplish his many glorious promises for increasing Righteousness even unto the reign of him whose right it is. For which we hope with rejoicing [?]. Yet have we indeed much cause to mourn and be afflicted for the great cause he hath to overturn, overturn as the Prophet speaketh, through unbelief and manifest unfitness of

[1] [The proposals of the officers, drawn up at a General Council held at Dublin Castle June 9, 1653, are printed in Mercurius Politicus, p. 2557. Another letter of the same tenor as the one given above, but going into greater detail and dated Dec. 16, 1653, is also amongst the Irish state papers.]

[2] Irish Records, Commonwealth Series, $\frac{A}{90}$ 50, p. 530.

this age to bear his name and be his servants, who are not only subject to fall short and faint in the work of moral reformation, but even ready to obstruct the spiritual government the Lord (on whose shoulders alone it is) would by his word establish over his people ; in which we have had cause to confess it is unsafe to interpose the best human skill, and that while we are most subject to assume above what is meet, even in things above our measure, there should scarcely be found any fit amongst us for any competent season to manage well the work of magistracy and the civil government of these nations, to the breaking every yoke and settling them in righteousness after the expense of so much blood and treasure to obtain it. In which though the Lord alone hath wonderfully led and preserved us, and yet being but come to the sight of our peace and liberty how apt are our hearts to forget him and his wonders, now promising ourselves that peace and prosperity by our own wisdom, which his only can get, obtain, and maintain for us. The sudden dissolution of the Parliament, whereof (we believe) you have heard, from whom (as from Instruments heretofore) we were too subject to expect above what was meet, seems still to reprove that sin of looking for salvation from the hills ; and the too little sense we have of the work of those in authority (as it makes us neglect them in our prayers, whereof they have great need), so justly (in this miscarriage) we miss of the good expected from them, which if we should slightly [? lightly] obtain would but render us still ready to sacrifice unto them and to be insensible of the mercy from the Lord, who therefore disappointeth us and staineth every instrument that he might be sought unto by all, and have the praise of and from all, which are due unto him solely, who will yet remember his poor people who truly return to him, and seek him in their low estate, for his mercy endureth for ever. Now therefore we earnestly exhort you to stir up all who fear him amongst you to lay to heart the present condition of the public affairs again exposed to the renewed endeavours of our manifold adversaries, unless the wonted faithfulness of our glorious father still preserve us. And truly had not God been on our side, well might we say ere this we had been swallowed up quick, when his poor people's enemies in England, Scotland, this country, Holland, with the help of other nations came up against us, and many a time contrived our ruin. Who knows but that he will further exercise our faith by the present shakings yet once more to make his own arm bare on our own behalf, for some fresh signal favour, whereof we have had such free and plentiful experience. It may be by the heightening of his adversaries for their falling down headlong he will yet more visibly save his people, and perhaps he will yet more thoroughly purge his floor, and make manifest such mercenary ones, who in the low estate of his work and servants are ready to forsake them ; wherein we have seen his wonderful wisdom. It may be he will more reconcile his people who in their prosperity are too ready to divide, or refine us by fire from unthankfulness, fleshly confidence, false rests, divisions, and such like provocations. Sure we are some advantage even by all our changes is intended to all that truly fear and trust in him, whom we earnestly entreat may lay to heart in our unsettlement what provocations are found amongst us, and in sincerity humbly seek his face together, which we intend through the Lord's assistance here in a special manner upon Thursday, which will be the 12th of January instant. And do heartily wish we may in faith meet together at the Throne of Grace by effectual fervent prayer, and that the further signs of his presence with us may be the unfeigned mourning over and turning from every evil way, to the healing of our backsliding and the settlement of these poor nations, especially the minds of his people to their being more thankful for and rejoicing in the appearance of truth and peace. The God of truth and peace guide and strengthen us to seek his face in faith, and to a patient waiting for and resting in the various dispensations of his blessed providence, in whom we are etc.,

> ' CHARLES FLEETWOOD. EDMUND LUDLOW.
> MILES CORBET. JOHN JONES [1].
> ' DUBLIN,
> ' 2nd January, 1653.'

XLIII.

[*The Proclamation of Cromwell in Ireland.*]

[On Jan. 30, 1654, the Commissioners republished the Proclamation of the English Council declaring Cromwell Lord Protector, dated Whitehall, 16 Dec. 1653. To this they added the following Declaration of their own.]

'IRELAND.

' BY THE COMMISSIONERS OF THE COMMONWEALTH OF ENGLAND FOR THE AFFAIRS OF IRELAND.

' The Proclamation above mentioned lately coming to our knowledge, we held it our duty for prevention of publick disturbances and interruptions in the administration of justice to publish the same: To the end that all Sheriffs, Mayors, Bayliffs, and other publick Officers and Ministers in this Nation, whom the same doth concern, may take notice thereof; Requiring all Officers and Souldiers of the Army, and all Sheriffs, Judges, Justices of the Peace, commissioners for Administration of Justice, and all others who are entrusted with the management of any publick Affairs, to be vigilant in their re-

---

[1] Irish Records, Commonwealth Series, $\frac{A}{90}$ 50, f. 593. [An earlier declaration of a similar kind was published on Nov. 9, 1653.]

spective charges and trusts, that the publique service may be carried on, and that the common enemy, upon this change of Government, may not take advantage to contrive or act new disturbances against the publick Peace. Dated at Dublin the thirteenth day of January 1653.

' Signed by order and command of the said Commissioners,

'JO. HUGHES. Sec¹.

' *Dated at* DUBLIN,
' *the thirtieth day of January,* 1653.'

XLIV.

[*From the President of the Council of State to the Commissioners for Ireland.*]

' GENTLEMEN,

' It hath been represented to his Highness and his council that you have caused the Proclamation of the 15th of December last for declaring his Highness the Lord Protector of the Commonwealth of England, Scotland, and Ireland to be published in Ireland, which is accepted by his Highness and Council as a singular testimony of your care and affection to the public justice and peace of the nation, and for which they hereby return their thanks, hoping that all the parts of the Commonwealth will receive such an eminent advantage by this change of government as shall engage the hearts of all honest men to acknowledge and bless the wisdom and goodness of that providence that hath so disposed it. Signed in the name and by the order of his Highness and the Council.

' HENRY LAWRENCE, President².

' WHITEHALL,
' *the 21st February,* 1653.'

XLV.

[*From the Council Board to the Loughrea Commissioners.*]

' WALTER CHEEVERS OF MONCKTOWNE.

' By Order of this Board of 10th of July last (made on the petition of Walter Cheevers, late of Muncktowne) you were (for the reasons therein expressed) required to take care that in the setting out of lands decreed unto him by the late Court at Athlone they should be such lands with a convenient house thereon as might enable him and his family to subsist and render his being comfortable, the which they doubt not will reasonably receive your care and due observance : Nevertheless upon reading another petition of the said Mr. Cheevers setting forth that pursuant to the said order you have only set him out

¹ Mercurius Politicus, Feb. 23—March 2, 1653.

² Irish Records, $\frac{A}{28}$ 26, p. 29.

IV. 600 Acres of Land or thereabouts and some conveniency of a house, which doth not answer either the favour intended him by the aforesaid Order or his expectations, having parted with a faire house and left a considerable estate in this County : The Council have commanded me to remind you of the said Order, and that you do forthwith sett out unto the aforesaid Mr. Cheevers so many acres more within the Line, and contiguous or as near as may be to the other already set out, as shall in the whole make up 1200 Acres with a good house thereupon for his convenience and comfortable subsistence, pursuant and as part of what falls due unto him by the aforesaid Decree of the Court.

'THOMAS HERBERT, Clerk of the Council[1].

'*Dated at the Council Chamber in* DUBLIN,
'*the 27th of August,* 1656.'

[To the Commissioners for Setting out Lands at Loughrea.]

XLVI.

'CHARLES REX.

'WALTER CHEEVERS OF MOUNCKTOWNE.

'Whereas upon a petition lately presented unto us in the name of Walter Cheevers of Mounctown, which by our report of the 4th day of October are referred to the consideration of our Right Trustie and right entirely beloved Counsellor James Marquess of Ormonde Steward of our Household and our Right trustie and well beloved Counsellor Sir Maurice Eustace our Chancellor of Ireland, Wee have been informed by their report returned unto us, not only of their particular knowledge of the said Cheevers to be a person very innocent of the Rebellion of Ireland, and very faithful to our Royal Father of Blessed Memory and our interest there, but they saw no cause or reason why he should be evicted as he hath long been from the possession of his Estate, more than that Colonel Edmund Ludlowe obtained a grant thereof from Oliver Cromwell, And therefore having presented it as just and honourable for us to grant our Order for Settling him in his Estate as is desired Saving our right to the said Lands, if any shall hereafter appear, Wee have thought good to declare it to be our will and pleasure that the said Mr. Cheevers be restored to such and so much of his Estate as is not in the possession of Adventurers or Souldiers, with a Salve for what is our right.

'Given at White Hall 22nd November 1660, in the 12th year of our Reign.

'By his Majesties command,
'EDWARD NICHOLAS[2].'

[1] Irish Records, Commonwealth Series, vol. 28, p. 179.

[2] King's Letters, Public Record Office, Dublin.

APPENDIX V.

———•———

The Copy of a Letter sent out of Wiltshire to a Gentleman in London; *wherein is laid open the dangerous Designes of the Clergy, in reference to the approaching Parliament. By a true Friend to the Publique Interest, and to all Peaceable Men.* (London: Printed for *Livewell Chapman*, at the *Crowne* in *Popes-head* Alley. 1654.)

'WORTHY SIR ;

'You will expect that I should give you a true accompt of passages relating to the choosing of Members to sit in Parliament for this County of Wilts. The truth is, the matter was most confusedly and unworthily carried without any order or discretion. As for the Clergie they exceedingly bestirred themselves, making their party as strong as ever they could, that so they might promote and carry on their Scottish interest.

'The Ringleaders of this faction were Dr. Chambers, Mr. Byfield, Strickland, these with the rest of their brethren of the Association and 'tis more then probable that the same designe is carried on by the Clergy in other Counties) gathered together a great number of people, & taught them their lesson before hand to cry up only those ten men named in their List, and to brand others, as namely Lieut. Gen. Ludlow, Col. Eyre, &c. (who were nominated by approved faithfull men in the County) with the names of Anabaptists, Levellers, to render them odious to the generality of the injudicious people, by these false and malitious imputations. Thus honest publique spirited men are most unworthily dealt withall, and trampled upon by a timeserving generation.

'Sir, I am very confident that some hundreds gave their voyces who were either Cavileers, or else of inconsiderable estates, not worth 100.l. and therefore uncapable of choosing, by the modell of the established government.

'It was agreed on at length, that the several lists should be called one by one, and so put to the Yea's and Noe's, without naming any other in competition with the former. But this order was violated by

V. the Clergies party, by which means through the instigation of this Scottish faction, Lieut. Gen. Ludlow was put by, to the great disparagement of this Country, where he hath been more serviceable to the true interests of the state, then all the men that are chosen, put them all together, and the parsons too : they were so far from giving their voyces for this faithful valiant self denying man, that the leading man among them, & their chief counsellour, whom I shall forbear to name, refused to appeare for the Lieut. Gen. intimating that he was not fit to sit in the next Parliament.

'Ye are so considerate Sir, I doubt it not, as to observe that there is a designe generally carried on by the Clergie of this Nation, to bring us againe into Egyptian bondage, to keep up and maintain the oppression of tithes, and to set up themselves and their classicall Diana by civil sanction ; in order whereunto they have endeavoured to procure a considerable number of Members that may vote in the next Parliament for an Assembly or Convention of ministers, to make cannons for inthralling the consciences of good men, where Adoniram may be one of the Scribes, who indeed was an exceeding busie man, and acted like a Pharisee at the election, his carriage not becoming a minister of Christ. But why should we wonder at him and others, their busie intermedling, and more then ordinary diligence and activity? alas poor men, they are afraid they shall loose their fat parsonages, worth 3 or 400.l. per ann. a peece. These politique state parsons, neglected the preaching of their lecture at Sarum, that they might bawle and cry with open mouth, No Ludlow, No Ludlow, till they were even hoarse again ; they chose rather to spend their breath in decrying honest men, then in preaching the Gospel of the Lord Jesus. Nor is it sufficient for these men that they have present encouragement, equall with or above other men more deserving, unles they may also impose upon, & domineer over their brethren they will not be contented. I doe plainly see they will rather joyn with the vilest men, then with such as crosse their carnall interest, and dissent from them, though never so godly.

'What shall I say of the impudency of these men? one Stone a factor for them, and vassall to them, went up and down at the election like a madd man, crying out, Now friends appear for the Church of God, or never ; poore man, can he put no difference between appearing for the lusts of men, and the Church of Christ? between the classical usurpation of the self seeking parsons, and the truth and Gospel of Christ?

'Sir, by this dayes work ye may judge of the issue and fruit of the Ministers Association in this County, which may rather be called a subtill combination, then a Christian spirituall communion as they manage it; you will hear of the like proceedings in other Counties, especially where this Association is carried on, the same being

devised as a shelter upon a politique accompt, against an approaching
storme.

' The Lord direct his Highnesse in this juncture of affaires, and make
him truly sensible of the dangerous plots of these men that would thus
rigidly impose upon their brethren.

' There will be I am confident a necessity of taking a strict review of
these elections, having been carried on in such a turbulent confused
manner, by the violent motions of the corrupt Clergy all joyning
together to uphold their Diana.

' But as it was with the Prelates, in entring their Protestation in the
former Parliament, they prepared a rodd to whipp themselves with,
and digged a pit wherein they themselves did fall : so will these men
doe, that which they have designed for upholding their corrupt interest,
will be the ruine thereof. His Highnesse and his Army cannot but
call to mind the late broyles both in this Nation, and Scotland, caused
by this sort of men, who will not cease plotting and combining
till they imbroyle the Nations againe in blood, if the Lord in mercy
prevent not.

' Sir, I had the sight of a letter writ by one Burgess a parson of the
confederacy, sent to one of his brethren in this County ; his words are
as followeth. " Sir, I hope you will be active to ingage all that ever
you can to appear with us for such men as will be valiant for the truth,
and be ready to meet Dr. Chambers, Mr. Byfield, Strickland, Ince, etc.
And that we may not be divided, there shall then be a list of the ten
to be chosen, given to every one that appeareth for the best interest.
Let us not be accessary to our owne ruine, and give occasion to the
succeeding generation to curse us, by not putting forth our interest to
the utmost, for choosing right men. If we remember the last men
that met at Westminster what they were voting for, and withall how
the monster of their malice was even brought to the birth, it will make
us active for a better choyce."

' Besides what this parson writ in his letter, he told the party before
one Mr. Dyer, that there was a commission coming out for ejecting
ministers, and that he would be in danger of being outed his living,
that should not appear with the ministers at the election.

' Thus you see Sir, they make lies their refuge, and have recourse
to carnall weapons, the instruments of a foolish shepheard, as his
Highnesse expresseth it in one of his letters to the Clergy of
Scotland.

' Well, though these rigid foolish men will not see the hand of God
which is gone out against them, but goe on in their vain wayes of
opposition, notwithstanding they have been so often disappointed, yet
the work of the Lord shall prosper, and God will ere long separate his
faithfull ministers and servants, from this corrupt selfe seeking generation of men, who will not cease from busie intermeddling in state

APP. V.   matters and raising factions, till the maintenance for the Ministry be brought into one treasury, and equally divided. In Holland (you know) where the Magistrate takes a stricter course, the ministers dare not busie themselves thus in state affaires. God forgive these men, for they cause the Ministry of Christ to be evil spoken of, and to stink in the nostrills of people, who doe but deride them as a company of vain busibodys.

'Sir, It cannot but grieve and afflict the spirits of honest men, to see a company of time-serving Cavaliers, and corrupt parsons carry on things as they do, without controll ; and in the mean while such men as are most faithfull to the publique interest, for which so much blood hath been spilt, and treasure spent, such as have been valiant in the field, and ventured their lives in the high places for the liberties of the people, such as have all along in the greatest revolutions and dangers (when this generation of men durst not show their faces unles it was at Oxon, where some of them sate and acted) appeared in their purses and persons for the true interest of the Nation, such as have poured out floods of tears and prayers for the cause of Christ, that these honest men should be thus slighted, undermined, scorned, discountenanced, and a company of unworthy time-serving men preferred and advanced, such as never did the State any faithful service, such as doe unworthily & vain-gloriously in their own persons, hunt after worldly honour, and popular applause, and doe even hate and abhor the poor despised Saints. Certainly though good men should be silent & sit still, yet the Lord himself will shortly avenge the cause of his people, & bring deliverance in a way which we think not of, which wil make the ears of some to tingle, and their hearts to ake ; we have yet the Christian weapons of faith, hope, patience, prayers and tears remaining with us, which will in due time prevaile against this corrupt party, and the lesse there is of man the more will God be seen. Let us sit still and see the Salvation of the Lord.

'*July* 13, 1654.'

END OF VOL. I.

Lightning Source UK Ltd.
Milton Keynes UK
UKOW06f0707060717
304790UK00011B/727/P